FINANCIAL
MATHEMATICS
HANDBOOK

FINANCIAL MATHEMATICS HANDBOOK

Robert Muksian, Ph.D.

PRENTICE-HALL, INC.   Englewood Cliffs, New Jersey

Prentice-Hall International, Inc., *London*
Prentice-Hall of Australia, Pty, Ltd., *Sydney*
Prentice-Hall Canada, Inc., *Toronto*
Prentice-Hall of India Private, Ltd., *New Delhi*
Prentice-Hall of Japan, Inc., *Tokyo*
Prentice-Hall of Southeast Asia Pte, Ltd., *Singapore*
Whitehall Books, Ltd., Wellington, *New Zealand*
Editora Prentice-Hall do Brasil Ltda., *Rio de Janeiro*

Library of Congress Cataloging in Publication Data

Muksian, Robert
  Financial mathematics handbook.

  Includes index.
  1. Business mathematics. I. Title.
HF5691.M84   1984   658.1'5'0151   83-13963
ISBN 0-13-316406-3

Printed in the United States of America

The Author

Robert Muksian, Ph.D., is Professor of Mathematics and Chairman of the Mathematics Department at Bryant College, Smithfield, Rhode Island. A specialist in the application of mathematics to financial concepts, Dr. Muksian serves as a consultant to pension actuaries and conducts research in the forecasting of cyclical economic events.

Dr. Muksian has previously taught at the United States Naval Academy and the University of Rhode Island. He is a member of the Board of Trustees of Cranston General Hospital in Cranston, Rhode Island, and has served as Treasurer of the Corporation and Chairman of the Finance Committee. In addition, he has been a member of the Board of Trustees of the University of New England in Biddeford, Maine.

Dr. Muksian received B.S., M.S. and Ph.D. degrees in mechanical engineering from the University of Rhode Island. He has published in the *Journal of Biomechanics*.

To
Barbara—my wife
Karen and Robin—my daughters

Acknowledgement

The efforts of many people made this Handbook
a reality. To the staff at Prentice-Hall, to
those who listened to my ideas, read my work,
and made appropriate comments, and to the typist
who "bore with me"—you all know who you are—
thank you very much.

R.M., 1984

What This Book Will Do For You

This handbook can free you from relying on other people, waiting for their convenience, and paying for the quantitative information you may need in order to make financial decisions. Some of the mathematical concepts which are necessary for financial decision-making are complex, and some of the associated calculations are normally time-consuming. However, with this handbook and a hand-held calculator, complex financial formulas are easy to use and results can be quickly determined by you.

Each formula represents a fundamental concept or the algebraic solution for a particular element of the fundamental concept. That is, the algebra has been performed. You need only "plug in the numbers."

Each formula is followed by an example of its use with a detailed numerical solution. Where repetitive calculations are necessary and obtaining solutions can be time-consuming, computer programs for use on personal (or other) computers are included.

THE ORGANIZATION OF THIS HANDBOOK

This handbook is organized into 17 chapters.

There follow 6 chapters dealing with the MATHEMATICS OF FINANCE; 5 chapters dealing with FINANCIAL DECISION-MAKING; 3 chapters dealing with FEDERAL TAXES, DEPRECIATION (both pre- and post-1981), and some of the common ACCOUNTING RATIOS which are used in financial reporting; 2 chapters on MARKETING; and a chapter on STATISTICS. Chapters 9 and 13 include SPECIAL PURPOSE TABLES, and there is an APPENDIX which includes 10 GENERAL PURPOSE TABLES which can be used for situations involving simple or compound interest—including continuous compounding that is modified for a BANK YEAR of 360 days.

THIS HANDBOOK AS YOUR DESK REFERENCE

Within the 17 chapters and Appendix of this handbook are formulas and tables which can help you in virtually every aspect of financial planning and analysis. How can this handbook be useful to you?

* Chapter 1 is the beginning of the mathematics of finance. It shows you how to calculate the GROWTH of MONEY for SEQUENTIAL and SIMULTANEOUS SHORT-TERM investments utilizing the concepts of SIMPLE INTEREST and SIMPLE DISCOUNT. It then shows you how to calculate AVERAGE RATES OF RETURN, the EQUIVALENT simple interest rate for a given simple discount rate and vice-versa.

* For LONG-TERM investments, with both DISCRETE and CONTINUOUS COMPOUNDING of INTEREST, this handbook shows you how to predict the GROWTH of money at both FIXED and VARYING interest rates, for SEQUENTIAL and SIMUL-

TANEOUS NON-PERIODIC investments, and the AVERAGE RATES of RETURN. It also shows you how the use of logarithms can give you the EXACT TIME which is required to achieve a specified FUTURE AMOUNT, how to APPROXIMATE that time by using tables, the EFFECTIVE ANNUAL INTEREST RATE, and the RATE OF RETURN of an investment for a given time and a given future amount. See Chapter 2.

    * This handbook shows you how to perform the calculations for all categories of ANNUITIES utilizing both DISCRETE and CONTINUOUS COMPOUNDING of INTEREST. It includes the calculations for LEVEL PERIODIC PAYMENTS, for IN-CREASING PERIODIC PAYMENTS, and for a COMBINATION of INCREASING and LEVEL PERIODIC PAYMENTS with applications to SINKING-FUNDS, TRUST FUNDS, and AMORTIZATIONS of PENSION TRUSTS or DEBTS. When the periodic payment dates and interest conversion dates coincide, the annuities are classified as SIMPLE. See Chapter 3 if PAYMENTS are made at the ENDS of PERIODS. See Chapter 4 if PAY-MENTS are made at the BEGINNINGS of PERIODS. See Chapter 5 if the beginning of payments is DEFERRED. When payment dates and interest conversion dates do not coincide, the annuities are classified as COMPLEX (GENERAL). See Chapter 6. Chapter 6 also includes COMPUTER PROGRAMS for the COMBINATION OF INCREASING and LEVEL PAYMENTS which are applicable to both SIMPLE and COMPLEX annuities.

    * In order to help you make DECISIONS for CAPITAL INVESTMENTS, this handbook shows you how to calculate the PRESENT VALUE of an estimated CASH FLOW and the RATE of RETURN that a cash flow represents. It includes a COMPUTER PRO-GRAM for the RATE of RETURN calculations. This handbook also shows you how to calculate a CAPITALIZED COST for both LEVEL and INFLATION affected (INCREASING) REPLACEMENT COSTS. See Chapter 7.

    * It also shows you how to calculate the price of a BOND and the APPROXIMATE YIELD-TO-MATURITY. It includes a COMPUTER PROGRAM for the EXACT YIELD-TO-MATURITY. This handbook also shows you how to construct tables for the AMORTI-ZATION of a PREMIUM, the ACCUMULATION of a DISCOUNT, and the determination of a COUPON RATE. See Chapter 8.

    * This handbook shows you how to predict a FINAL PAYMENT or to calculate the EQUAL PAYMENT for the LIQUIDATION of a SHORT-TERM DEBT by using the UNITED STATES RULE, the MERCHANTS' RULE, and ADD-ON INTEREST. TABLES are included to SIMPLIFY the determination of the equal payments for the United States and Merchants' Rules. The handbook also shows you how to calculate a REFUND for early liquidation of a debt when the RULE of 78 is applied, and it shows you the calculations for the CONSOLIDATION of DEBTS. See Chapter 9.

    * This handbook shows you how to calculate the PAYBACK period for REVENUE and COST equations which are straight-lines. It then extends the concept of the PAYBACK period to include the TIME-VALUE of MONEY allowing a payback to be determined by REVENUE or COST SAVINGS for a specified rate of return (CAPITAL RECOVERY with RETURN). See Chapter 10.

    * Also included in this handbook are formulas for ELEMENTARY INVENTORY MODELS which show you how to calculate MINIMUM COST PURCHASE QUANTITIES and MINIMUM COST PRODUCTION QUANTITIES. It also includes a MANUFACTURE or PURCHASE DECISION. See Chapter 11.

    * This handbook shows you how to easily DERIVE formulas for calculating cor-porate TAXES, and it shows you how to calculate an EFFECTIVE TAX RATE over a range of taxable income. See Chapter 12.

    * This handbook shows you how to calculate the DEPRECIATION, BOOK VALUE, and ACCUMULATED DEPRECIATION, for any given year during the useful life of an

asset, by any of the pre-1981 methods. It shows you how to PRE-DETERMINE the year when the accumulated depreciation will be a specified FRACTION of the DEPRECIABLE COST, and it shows you how to calculate the year when you should CONVERT FROM ACCELERATED DECLINING BALANCE TO STRAIGHT-LINE DEPRECIATION when the residual (salvage) value of the asset may be considered to be negligible. For non-negligible residual values, a TABLE is included for that determination. This handbook also includes the ACCELERATED COST RECOVERY SYSTEM of depreciation for assets purchased subsequent to 1980. See Chapter 13.

* Some common ACCOUNTING RATIOS and the information that can be gleaned from them are included in this handbook. See Chapter 14.

* This handbook shows you how to calculate a SELLING PRICE when a SERIES of TRADE DISCOUNTS apply, and it shows you how to calculate a BALANCE DUE after a PARTIAL PAYMENT when a CASH DISCOUNT applies. See Chapter 15.

* Also, this handbook shows you how to calculate SELLING PRICE (and PROFIT) when MARKUP is based on COST or is based on SELLING PRICE. It also shows you how to calculate a SELLING PRICE that will return a desired GROSS PROFIT when LOSSES in merchandise occur. This handbook enables the calculation of the EQUIVALENCE between MARKUP RATES which are based on COST and SELLING PRICE. See Chapter 16.

* Can you escape STATISTICS? You are shown how to calculate the AVERAGE of DISCRETE data and GROUPED data. Most IMPORTANT, this handbook shows you how to determine if the average is truly representative of the data. Remember, if you place your left hand in boiling water and your right hand in ice water, *on the AVERAGE you will be comfortable.* See Chapter 17.

* An APPENDIX comprised of 10 TABLES is included in the handbook.

Table A-1 is a table of JULIAN dates where each day of the year is assigned a number. It can be used to quickly determine the number of days between two dates. Its use is explained in Chapter 1.

Table A-2 is a COMPOUND INTEREST table and supplies values for the FUTURE AMOUNT of $1, PRESENT VALUE of $1, FUTURE AMOUNT of $1 per period, PRESENT VALUE of $1 per period, periodic SINKING FUND payment for a future amount of $1, and the AMORTIZATION of a debt of $1. The values in the table are carried to 8 decimal places, and the range of interest rates is $\frac{5}{12}$% to 2% by $\frac{1}{12}$% increments and from $2\frac{1}{2}$% to 34% by $\frac{1}{2}$% increments. The associated number of periods range from 240 at $\frac{5}{12}$% to 25 at 34%.

Table A-3 is a COMPOUND INTEREST table for the FUTURE AMOUNT and PRESENT VALUE OF ANNUITIES of $1 per period for FRACTIONAL periods in COMPLEX ANNUITIES. The range of interest rate is $\frac{5}{12}$% to 34% as in Table A-2.

Table A-4 is a COMPOUND INTEREST table for the FUTURE AMOUNT and PRESENT VALUE of $1 for FRACTIONAL periods in COMPLEX ANNUITIES. The range of interest rates is $\frac{5}{12}$% to 34% as in Table A-2.

Tables A-2, A-3, and A-4 will enable you to quickly and easily perform the calculations in relatively complex formulas with DISCRETE compounding using a basic calculator only. Tables A-5 and A-6 supply values for the Future Amount and Present Value of $1, respectively, for CONTINUOUS COMPOUNDING with the necessary compensation for the BANK YEAR. Tables A-7 and A-8 are the same as Tables A-5 and A-6, respectively, but WITHOUT the bank year compensation.

Tables A-9 and A-10 are common logarithms and natural logarithms respectively.

HOW YOU CAN USE THIS HANDBOOK

The preceding commentary told you how this book is organized and the topics which are included. Now, as some possible uses of the handbook, consider the following.

* You must make periodic payments to a sinking fund. You would like to "toy" with the idea of a uniformly increasing periodic payment to the fund rather than a level periodic payment. What should be the initial payment? With this approach, if the uniformly increasing payment rate is the inflation rate, the fund would be paid in real dollars. You have a client who would like to project the future amount of his pension account, or you would like to project that future amount for yourself. Using a "realistic" assumption on future interest rates, you can have the answer in seconds. Suppose you or your client would like to reduce a debt by amortization of principal and interest but with uniformly increasing periodic payments rather than a level payment reduction of the debt. Using a "realistic" assumption on future interest rates, you can have the amount of the initial payment in "very short order." The same concept can be used in the reduction of an individual retirement fund. If the payment of a penalty for early distribution of funds can be offset by a favorable tax situation, the initial withdrawal for a uniformly increasing withdrawal rate, can be determined rather quickly. Depending on the timing and frequency of the payments, Chapters 3 through 6 can be used for fast answers with easy calculations.

* You are presented with several alternative proposals for the investment of capital, and you must make a decision and justify it. Chapter 7 shows you several methods by which a correct decision can be made. Also, for a given cash flow at a current rate of return, Chapter 7 shows how to calculate the selling price of an appreciating asset in order to achieve a specified rate of return.

* Payback for a capital investment is conventionally determined by dividing the fixed cost of the asset by the marginal profit, but if the associated costs are not accurate, the marginal profit will not be readily discernible. Therefore, you might like to determine the payback period based on revenue from the asset, or you might like to know the payback period of a cost savings asset and include the opportunity cost of investing the capital elsewhere at your internal rate of return. Chapter 10 shows you how this can be done.

* One of your assistants tells you that the profit from an investment has averaged $1,000,000 per month for the last 10 months. Now, as an extreme example, you could have had a one-million-dollar profit in the first month, zero profit per month for the next 8 months, and nine million dollars profit in the 10th month. This sequence would give an average profit of one million dollars per month. Your assistant would not be "telling a lie" but that average would not be representative of the true profit flow. Chapter 17 shows you how to determine if an "average" is representative of the data.

TECHNICAL CONCEPTS FOR EASY READING

This handbook of mathematical formulas is written for individuals who must use mathematical concepts in their work but are not, necessarily, mathematically oriented. The basic approach is to "do the algebra for you." All that is required for your use is to substitute numbers for letters. For example, interest is defined as principal times rate times time. Rather than a single formula, $I = PRT$, additional formulas such as $R = I/PT$, $T = I/PR$, and $P = I/RT$, which are algebraic manipulations of the definition, will be presented in order for you to use the formula which is most appropriate for your immediate problem.

Because this handbook is not intended to be a "mathematics" handbook, some liberties have been taken at the expense of mathematical vigor. These liberties include the following:

* The definition of the summation of a string of variables is normally (and formally) presented in the form

$$\sum_{j=1}^{N} E_j = E_1 + E_2 + E_3 + \ldots + E_N$$

however, the definition in this handbook is

$$\sum E_j = E_1 + E_2 + E_3 + \ldots + E_N$$

because the "non-mathematical" concept that is intended is to "add the E's."

* The definition of the product of a string of variables is normally (and formally) presented in the form

$$\prod_{j=1}^{N} E_j = (E_1)(E_2)(E_3)\ldots(E_N)$$

however, the definition in this handbook is

$$\prod E_j = (E_1)(E_2)(E_3)\ldots(E_N)$$

because the "non-mathematical" concept that is intended is to "multiply the E's."

* The representation of numbers should indicate that numbers are exact or rounded. The liberty that has been taken in this handbook is to indicate all numbers as if they are exact to the indicated number of decimal places. For example, the effective annual interest rate of 12% compounded continuously is displayed as 12.93776 (%) on my calculator. This display is, in fact, a truncated value, and therefore, an approximation. In practice, this number would be stated as if it were exactly 12.94% or 12.938%, and that practice has been followed in the solution of examples.

* Different authors use different conventions when representing the notation for logarithms. The notation in this handbook follows that used on hand-held calculators; log for base 10 logarithms and ln for natural logarithms.

* Because the "mathematics competencies" of the individuals who will use this handbook will be varied, the following sequence has been used. In Chapter 2, formulas for discrete compounding of interest are presented in one section, and formulas for continuous compounding of interest are presented in a separate section. Chapter 3 presents formulas for discrete and continuous compounding of interest in an immediate sequence at the beginning of each topic. As the "mathematics competency" increases from Chapter 2 to Chapter 3, the simultaneous presentation of the formulas should not present a difficulty to the user. Because all formulas that deal with compound interest involve interest rates, and because the difference between discrete and continuous compounding of interest formulas is simply notation of the interest rate, a unified interest rate notation is introduced in Chapter 4 and continued throughout all annuity formulas in subsequent chapters. This unified symbol notation enables the use of a single formula for discrete and continuous compounding, and as the "mathematics competency" of the user increases from Chapter 2 to Chapter 3 to Chapter 4 and beyond, the unified symbol should not present a difficulty.

* In order to represent certain elements of annuities, different authors use different (but somewhat conventional) notations. For example, the "Future Amount of \$1 Per Period" is symbolized as $S_{\overline{n}|}$, $s_{\overline{n}|i}$, or $S(i, n)$ which is a mathematical notation for a functional relationship. A somewhat different notation is used in *Economic Decision Analysis* by Fabrycky and Thuesen and published by Prentice-Hall, Inc. A slightly modified version of Fabrycky and Thuesen is used in this handbook. The letter "S" is used to represent the future amount, the letter "p" is used to represent the periodic payment, and the letters "i" and "n" are used to represent the periodic interest rate and number of periods, respectively. In this handbook, the "Future Amount of \$1 Per Period" is represented by the notation $(S/p, i, n)$ which is read as S *given* p, i, n. The rationale for its use is that the S/p is a ratio which must be multiplied by "p" in order to obtain "S" under the conditions of "i" and "n." Similarly, if "V" represents the "Present Value of \$1 Per Period," the notation would be $(V/p, i, n)$. Conversely, in order to determine the respective periodic payments, the notations become $(p/S, i, n)$ and $(p/V, i, n)$. The advantage of this notation is that all the elements of annuity formulas are embodied in the notation, and for non-mathematically inclined individuals, the notation tends to be a guide toward which formula (or table) to use.

CONTENTS

LIST OF TABLES

FINANCIAL
MATHEMATICS
HANDBOOK

The Use of Simple Interest and Simple Discount Formulas for Fast Answers To Short-Term Investments

Short-term may be defined as the length of time during which interest is not compounded. Therefore, without compounding, the growth of money is based on the principles of simple interest. This chapter shows the use of formulas which are appropriate for such investments. Within the text are one or more examples which indicate the use of each formula. These examples include:

1. The use of a Julian calendar in order to determine the number of days between calendar dates. Page 2.
2. Determining the average interest rate for a series of sequential investments when the interest is withdrawn at each maturity date. Page 5
3. Determining the average interest rate for a series of sequential investments when the principal is increased or decreased at each maturity date. Page 5
4. Determining the average interest rate to the first maturity date when different amounts are invested simultaneously at different rates for different terms. Page 6
5. Determining the future amount when an investment and interest are "rolled over" several times at different interest rates. Page 8
6. Determining the average interest rate when an investment is "rolled over" several times at different interest rates. Page 8
7. Determining the average interest rate to the first maturity date when several investments are made at different interest rates before that maturity date. Page 9
8. Determining the proceeds from a note on a discounted basis. Page 11
9. Determining a loan amount, on a discounted basis, for specified proceeds. Page 12
10. Determining the proceeds, on a discounted basis, from the purchase or sale of an interest-bearing note. Page 12
11. Determining the simple interest rate given a discount rate and conversely. Page 13

If you perform the calculations in the examples, your results may differ from the indicated results, depending upon the number of decimal places you carry at each step of the solutions.

1.1   SIMPLE INTEREST

The nomenclature for simple interest is as follows:

P—Principal for the interest period
I—Interest
i—Annual interest rate (Rate of Return)
t—Time expressed as years
n—Exact number of days between dates
N—Number of investments

Definition of Simple Interest

$$I = Pit \qquad (1.1\text{-}1)$$

Ordinary Simple Interest

Ordinary simple interest is based on a 360-day year, and the time associated with ordinary simple interest is called *ordinary time*. Then, in ordinary simple interest calculations, t is expressed as n/360, and Eq. (1.1-1) becomes

$$I = Pi(n/360) \qquad (1.1\text{-}2)$$

Example 1.   The ordinary interest on a $15,000 note at 13%, due in 245 days, is determined from Eq. (1.1-2) as

$$I = (15000)\,(0.13)\,(245/360) \quad \text{or} \quad \$1,327.08.$$

Exact Simple Interest

Exact simple interest is based on a 365-day year, and the time associated with exact simple interest is called *exact time*. For exact interest calculations, t is expressed as n/365, and Eq. (1.1-1) becomes

$$I = Pi(n/365) \qquad (1.1\text{-}3)$$

Example 2.   The exact interest on a $15,000 note at 13%, due in 245 days, is determined from Eq. (1.1-3) as

$$I = (15000)\,(0.13)\,(245/365) \quad \text{or} \quad \$1,308.90$$

The Julian Calendar

As an alternative to "counting" the number of days in the intervening months between dates, a calendar of Julian dates may be used. Table A-1 (page 268) in the Appendix is such a calendar, and

$$n = \text{Day 2} - \text{Day 1} \qquad (1.1\text{-}4)$$

Example 3. Using a calendar of Julian dates, the exact number of days between March 2 and November 1 is determined as follows. A portion of Table A-1 is shown below.

Day of Month	Mar.	Nov.
1	60	305
2	61	306

Since March 2 is day 61 and November 1 is day 305,

$$n = 305 - 61 = 244 \text{ days.}$$

When two calendar years are involved, the exact number of days between two dates may be determined from a Julian calendar as

$$n = 365 - \text{Day 1} + \text{Day 2} \tag{1.1-5}$$

Example 4. The exact number of days between October 8, 19X1 and May 17, 19X2 may be determined as follows from Table A-1.

$$\text{Day 1 is October 8} = 281$$
$$\text{Day 2 is May 17} = 137$$

Then,

$$n = 365 - 281 + 137 = 221 \text{ days}$$

In order to determine the due date given an execution date and the number of days, Eq. (1.1-4) may be rearranged to

$$\text{Day 2} = \text{Day 1} + n \tag{1.1-6}$$

Example 5. The due date for a 240-day note dated September 12 may be determined from Table A-1 and Eq. (1.1-6) as

$$\text{Day 2} = 255 + 240 = 495$$
$$= 495 - 365 = 130$$
$$= \text{May 10 of the next year.}$$

Annual Interest Rate

Annual interest rate may be determined from Eq. (1.1-1) as

$$i = \frac{I}{Pt} \ (\times \ 100 \text{ for } \%) \tag{1.1-7}$$

where t is the exact number of years or days. For durations which are not integer numbers of years, Eq. (1.1-3) may be rearranged to

$$i = \frac{365 \ I}{Pn} \ (\times \ 100 \text{ for } \%) \tag{1.1-8}$$

Example 6. If the interest on 240-day Treasury Bills, purchased for $18,566.67, is $1,433.33, the annual interest rate may be determined from Eq. (1.1-8)

$$i = \frac{(365)\,(1433.33)}{(18566.67)\,(240)} \times 100 = 11.74\%$$

Example 7. On February 12, you purchase 100 shares of common stock at 14-1/2 with a broker's commission of $40. The corporation declares dividends per share of common stock of $0.25 on March 31, $0.50 on June 30, $0.75 on September 30, and $0.75 on December 31. Your rate of return for that calendar year would be determined as follows.

Dividends:

March 31:	0.25 × 100 = $25
June 30:	0.50 × 100 = 50
Sept. 30:	0.75 × 100 = 75
Dec. 31:	0.75 × 100 = 75

Total Dividends = $225 = I
Investment = 14-1/2 × 100 + 40 = $1490 = P
Time: 2/12 to 12/31 = 365 − 43 = 322 days = n

From Eq. (1.1-8)

$$i = \frac{(365)\,(225)}{(1490)\,(322)} \times 100 = 17.12\%$$

Time

Equation (1.1-1) may be rearranged to determine the time required to earn a specified interest at a specified rate.

$$t = \frac{I}{Pi} \tag{1.1-9}$$

The required number of days is determined by

$$n = 365\,t \tag{1.1-10}$$

Example 8. A $100,000 investment on June 8, at 18%, will earn $10,000 interest in the time determined by Eq. (1.1-9).

$$t = \frac{10000}{(100000)\,(0.18)} = 0.5556 \text{ years}$$

From Eq. (1.1-10)

$$n = (365)\,(0.5556) = 203 \text{ days.}$$

Using Table A-1, June 8 is day 159. From Eq. (1.1-6)

$$\text{Day 2} = 159 + 203 = 362$$
$$= \text{December 28}$$

Average Interest Rate—Sequential Investments

The symbol, Σ, is read as "summation of" and is defined by

$$\sum E_j = E_1 + E_2 + E_3 + \ldots + E_N \tag{1.1-11}$$

where E may be any algebraic expression. The average rate of return is defined by the symbol i_A.

I. *Constant Principal—Varying Rates and Times*

A. Time measured in years.

$$i_A = \frac{\sum i_j t_j}{\sum t_j} \;(\times 100 \text{ for } \%) \tag{1.1-12}$$

B. Time measured in days.

$$i_A = \frac{\sum i_j n_j}{\sum n_j} \;(\times 100 \text{ for } \%) \tag{1.1-13}$$

Example 9. \$100,000 was invested in a money market fund for a period of 90 days. The yields were 14% for 30 days, 16% for 45 days, and 17% for 15 days. At each maturity date, the interest was withdrawn. Since the investment principal remained constant, the average rate of return is determined from Eq. (1.1-13) with N = 3.

$$i_A = \frac{(0.14)\,(30) + (0.16)\,(45) + (0.17)\,(15)}{30 + 45 + 15} \times 100 = 15.5\%$$

II. *Varying Principal, Rates, and Times*

A. Time measured in years.

$$i_A = \frac{N \sum P_j i_j t_j}{\left[\sum P_j\right]\left[\sum t_j\right]} \;(\times 100 \text{ for } \%) \tag{1.1-14}$$

B. Time measured in days.

$$i_A = \frac{N \sum P_j i_j n_j}{\left[\sum P_j\right]\left[\sum n_j\right]} \;(\times 100 \text{ for } \%) \tag{1.1-15}$$

Example 10. Over a period of 90 days the following investment activity occurred in a money market fund.

At day 1, \$100,000 at 14% for 30 days
At day 30, 120,000 at 16% for 45 days
At day 75, 140,000 at 17% for 15 days

The average rate of return is determined from Eq. (1.1-15) because the principal varied during the term of the investments. Since there were 3 investment terms during the 90-day period, N = 3.

$$P_1 i_1 n_1 = (100000)(0.14)(30) = 420{,}000$$
$$P_2 i_2 n_2 = (120000)(0.16)(45) = 864{,}000$$
$$P_3 i_3 n_3 = (140000)(0.17)(15) = 357{,}000$$

Summation of $P_j i_j n_j = 1{,}641{,}000$
Summation of $P_j = 100000 + 120000 + 140000 = 360{,}000$
Summation of $n_j = 30 + 45 + 15 = 90$

Substituting the summations into Eq. (1.1-15) gives the average interest rate.

$$i_A = \frac{3(1641000)}{(360000)(90)} \times 100 = 15.194\%$$

An alternative to Eq. (1.1-15), when the interest for each period is known, is to use Eq. (1.1-16).

$$i_A = \frac{365\, N\, \sum I_j}{\left[\sum P_j\right]\left[\sum n_j\right]} \quad (\times 100 \text{ for } \%) \qquad (1.1\text{-}16)$$

For ordinary interest, 365 is replaced by 360 in Eq. (1.1-16).

Example 11.   From the information of Example 10,

$$I_1 = (100000)(0.14)(30/365) = 1{,}150.68$$
$$I_2 = (120000)(0.16)(45/365) = 2{,}367.12$$
$$I_3 = (140000)(0.17)(15/365) = 978.08$$

Summation of $I_j = 4{,}495.88$
Summation of $P_j = 100000 + 120000 + 140000 = 360{,}000$
Summation of $n_j = 30 + 45 + 15 = 90$

Substituting the summations into Eq. (1.1-16) gives the average interest rate.

$$i_A = \frac{(365)(3)(4495.88)}{(360000)(90)} \times 100 = 15.194\%$$

Average Interest Rate—Multiple, Simultaneous Investments

When multiple investments, with different maturity dates, are made at the same time, the average interest rate to the earliest maturity date may be determined by

$$i_A = \frac{\sum P_j i_j}{\sum P_j} \quad (\times 100 \text{ for } \%) \qquad (1.1\text{-}17)$$

Example 12.   On one day, \$100,000 is invested at 19% for 30 days, \$150,000 is invested at 16% for 90 days, and \$200,000 is invested at 14% for 180 days. The average interest rate for the first 30 days may be determined from Eq. (1.1-17).

$$P_1 i_1 = (100000)(0.19) = 19{,}000$$
$$P_2 i_2 = (150000)(0.16) = 24{,}000$$
$$P_3 i_3 = (200000)(0.14) = 28{,}000$$

Summation of $P_j i_j$ = 71,000
Summation of P_j = 450,000

Substituting the summations into Eq. (1.1-17) gives the average interest rate for the first 30 days.

$$i_A = \frac{71000}{450000} \times 100 = 15.778\%$$

1.2 FUTURE AMOUNT

The nomenclature for the future amount at simple interest is as follows:

P—Principal for the interest period
I—Interest
i—Annual interest rate (Rate of Return)
t—Time expressed as years
n—Exact number of days
S—Future amount of P
N—Number of investments

Definition of Future Amount

$$S = P + I \qquad (1.2\text{-}1)$$

If the future amount of P is desired without the determination of interest, Eq. (1.2-1) in conjunction with Eq. (1.1-1) becomes

$$S = P(1 + it) \qquad (1.2\text{-}2)$$

Future Amount at Ordinary Interest

$$S = P(1 + in/360) \qquad (1.2\text{-}3)$$

Example 1. The future amount of $15,000 at 13% ordinary interest for 245 days is determined from Eq. (1.2-3).

$$S = (15000) [1 + (0.13) (245/360)] = \$16,327.08$$

The accrued interest is the difference between S and P and is $1,327.08 (see Example 1, page 2).

Future Amount at Exact Interest

$$S = P(1 + in/365) \qquad (1.2\text{-}4)$$

Example 2. The future amount of $15,000 at 13% exact interest for 245 days is determined from Eq. (1.2-4).

$$S = (15000) [1 + (0.13) (245/365)] = \$16,308.90$$

The accrued interest is the difference between S and P and is $1,308.90 (see Example 2, page 2).

Future Amount—Pseudo-Compound Interest

If the future amount of a single principal is reinvested at different (or same) interest rates and lengths of time, the process is a pseudo-compounding of interest in that a single interest rate is not being compounded at a constant frequency. The symbol $\prod$ is read as "the product of" and is defined by

$$\prod E_j = (E_1)(E_2)(E_3) \ldots (E_N) \tag{1.2-5}$$

The future amount at pseudo-compound interest at the end of N periods of time is defined by

$$S = P \prod (1 + i_j t_j) \tag{1.2-6}$$

and for a series of short-term (days) reinvestments

$$S = P \prod (1 + i_j n_j / 365) \tag{1.2-7}$$

For ordinary interest, 365 is replaced by 360 in Eq. (1.2-7).

> **Example 3.** The future amount of \$100,000 invested at 14% for 30 days; the accumulated amount reinvested at 16% for 45 days; and the second accumulated amount reinvested at 17% for 15 days are determined from Eq. (1.2-7) with $N = 3$.
>
> $$\begin{aligned} S &= (100000)[1 + (0.14)(30/365)][1 + (0.16)(45/365)][1 + (0.17)(15/365)] \\ &= (100000)(1.0115068)(1.019726)(1.0069863) \\ &= \$103,866.59 \end{aligned}$$
>
> The average rate of return for the 90-day period of this example may be determined from Eq. (1.1-8). The interest for the period is \$3,866.59. Then,
>
> $$i_A = \frac{(365)(3866.59)}{(100000)(90)} \times 100 = 15.68\%$$

Average Interest Rate—Pseudo-Compound Interest

The average interest rate with pseudo-compound interest may be determined directly (without calculating the future amount as in Example 3).

$$i_A = \frac{365 \left\{ \left[\prod(1 + i_j n_j / 365) \right] - 1 \right\}}{\sum n_j} \quad (\times 100 \text{ for } \%). \tag{1.2-8}$$

For ordinary interest, 365 is replaced by 360 in Eq. (1.2-8).

> **Example 4.** The average interest rate for Example 3 using Eq. (1.2-8), with $N = 3$, is
>
> $$i_A = \frac{365\{[1 + (0.14)(30/365)][1 + (0.16)(45/365)][1 + (0.17)(15/365)] - 1\}}{30 + 45 + 15}$$
>
> $$= \frac{365}{90}[(1.0115068)(1.019726)(1.0069863) - 1] \times 100 = 15.68\%$$

1.3   PRESENT VALUE

The nomenclature for the present value at simple interest is as follows:

P—Principal for the interest period
I—Interest
i—Annual interest rate (Rate of Return)
t—Time expressed as years
n—Exact number of days
V—Present value (present worth)
S—Future amount of P or V
N—Number of investments

Definition of Present Value

The amount of money required at time 0 that will grow to S at time t.

$$V = \frac{S}{1 + it} \qquad (1.3\text{-}1)$$

Present Value at Ordinary Interest

$$V = \frac{S}{1 + in/360} \qquad (1.3\text{-}2)$$

Example 1. In order to have $10,000 in 135 days, the amount of money that must be invested at 18% ordinary interest is determined from Eq. (1.3-2).

$$V = \frac{10000}{1 + (0.18)(135/360)} = \$9.367.68 \qquad (1.3\text{-}3)$$

Present Value at Exact Interest

$$V = \frac{S}{1 + in/365} \qquad (1.3\text{-}4)$$

Example 2. In order to have $10,000 in 135 days, the amount of money that must be invested at 18% exact interest is determined from Eq. (1.3-4).

$$V = \frac{10000}{1 + (0.18)(135/365)} = \$9,375.80$$

Average Interest Rate—Overlapping Investments

For a series of short-term investments in which the "last" investment is made before the "first" investment instrument matures, the average interest rate from the date of the first investment to the maturity date of the first investment instrument can be determined by

$$i_A = \frac{365}{n_1} \left\{ \frac{\sum S_j}{\sum V_j} - 1 \right\} (\times 100 \text{ for } \%) \qquad (1.3\text{-}5)$$

where

$$S_j = P_j(1 + i_j n_j/365)$$

$$V_j = \frac{S_j}{1 + i_j n_1/365} \tag{1.3-6}$$

For ordinary interest, 365 is replaced by 360 in Eqs. (1.3-5) and (1.3-6).

Example 3. On March 12, $100,000 is invested at 16% exact interest for 90 days. On March 27, $125,000, is invested at 17.5% exact interest for 180 days. On April 30, $250,000 is invested at 19% exact interest for 60 days. This sequence of investments is shown in Figure 1-1.

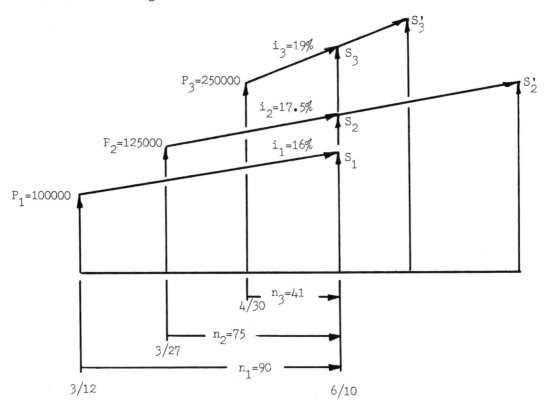

Figure 1-1.

The values of n_2 and n_3 may be determined by using Table A-1 (or counting the days) between the respective investment dates and the maturity date of the first instrument. From Eqs. (1.3-6)

$$S_1 = (100000)\,[1 + (0.16)\,(90/365)] = 103{,}945.21$$

$$S_2 = (125000)\,[1 + (0.175)\,(75/365)] = 129{,}494.86$$

$$S_3 = (250000)\,[1 + (0.19)\,(41/365)] = 255{,}335.62$$

Summation of S_j = $488,755.69

$$V_1 = 100,000$$

$$V_2 = \frac{129494.86}{1 + (0.175)(90/365)} = 124,138.21$$

$$V_3 = \frac{255335.62}{1 + (0.19)(90/365)} = 243,908.67$$

Summation of V_j = \$468,046.88

Substituting the two summations into Eq. (1.3-5) gives

$$i_A = \frac{365}{90}\left[\frac{488775.69}{468046.88} - 1\right] \times 100 = 17.96\%$$

Referring to Figure 1-1, when the instrument for P_1 matures on 6/10, if S_1 is re-invested (the interest could be withdrawn and P_1 reinvested), then Eqs. (1.3-5) and (1.3-6) could be repeated where P_2 would become P_1, P_3 would become P_2, and S_1 would become P_3. Then, the average interest rate could be determined to the next earliest maturity date.

1.4   SIMPLE DISCOUNT

The nomenclature for discounts is as follows:

S—Future amount
V—Principal investment (Present Value)
P—Proceeds after discount
D—Discount
I—Interest
i—Simple interest rate
d—Simple discount rate
n—Number of days to maturity for interest-bearing note
m—Number of days for discount
t—Years

Definition of Discount

$$D = Sdt \tag{1.4-1}$$

Ordinary discount is based on a 360-day year and is defined by

$$D = Sdm/360 \tag{1.4-2}$$

Exact discount is based on a 365-day year and is defined by

$$D = Sdm/365 \tag{1.4-3}$$

Proceeds of Discounted Notes

Basically, the proceeds from a discounted note is defined by

$$P = S(1 - dt) \tag{1.4-4}$$

I. For ordinary discount

$$P = S(1 - dm/360) \tag{1.4-5}$$

II. For exact discount

$$P = S(1 - dm/365) \qquad (1.4-6)$$

Example 1.   The proceeds from a $10,000 note discounted at 18% exact for 20 days is determined from Eq. (1.4-6).

$$P = (10000) [1 - (0.18) (20/365)] = \$9,901.37$$

Loan Required for Specified Proceeds

When a needed amount of funds (proceeds) is known and is to be borrowed on a discounted basis, the amount of the loan is determined by

$$S = \frac{P}{1 - dt} \qquad (1.4-7)$$

where t is replaced by m/360 for ordinary discount and by m/365 for exact discount.

Example 2.   In order to realize proceeds of $10,000 from a 90-day note discounted at 18% ordinary, the amount to be repaid can be determined from Eq. (1.4-7) with $t = m/360$.

$$S = \frac{10000}{1 - (0.18) (90/360)} = \$10,471.20$$

The simple exact interest rate on such a loan can be determined from Eq. (1.1-8) where $I = S - P$. For this example

$$i = \frac{365 (10471.20 - 10000)}{(10000) (90)} \times 100 = 19.11\%$$

A formula for the relationship between discount rate and interest rate is given in Section 1.5.

Non-Interest-Bearing Notes

The proceeds from a non-interest-bearing note, which is discounted prior to the maturity date of the note, can be determined from Eqs. (1.4-5) or (1.4-6).

Example 3.   A note for $5,000 is due on June 5. A bank is willing to purchase the note on April 17 at a 20% ordinary discount rate. The proceeds from the sale of the note can be determined from Eq. (1.4-5). The number of days between April 17 and June 5 may be determined from Table A-1 as Day 156 - Day 107 = 49 days. Using Eq. (1.4-5) gives

$$P = (5000) [1 - (0.20) (49/360)] = \$4,863.89$$

Interest-Bearing Notes

When a note indicates the principal and interest rate of a loan, the maturity value (future amount) of the note must be determined prior to discounting the note. For interest-bearing notes, the proceeds from discounting the note can be determined from

$$P = V(1 + it_1) (1 - dt_2) \qquad (1.4-8)$$

where t_1 is the time to maturity from the inception of the note, and t_2 is the time to maturity from the date of discount. The time t_1 is defined by n/360 or n/365, and the time t_2 is defined by m/360 or m/365 both depending upon the use of ordinary or exact interest.

Example 3. You hold a note for $5,000 plus 15% exact simple interest, dated June 5 and due on December 2. If a bank is willing to buy the note from you, on October 8, at an ordinary discount rate of 18%, your proceeds from that sale can be determined from Eq. (1.4-8). Using Table A-1, the term of the note to maturity is

$$n = \text{Day } 336 - \text{Day } 156 = 180$$

The term of the discount is

$$m = \text{Day } 336 - \text{Day } 281 = 55$$

Then,

$$P = (5000) \, [1 + (0.15) \, (180/365)] \, [1 - (0.18) \, (55/360)]$$

$$= (5000) \, (1.0739726) \, (0.9725) = \$5,222.19$$

1.5 DISCOUNT AND INTEREST RATE CONVERSIONS

The nomenclature for conversions of discount rate to interest rate, and conversely, is

   i—Exact simple interest rate
   d—Discount rate
  t_E—Exact time in years
  t_O—Ordinary time in years
  m—Number of days of discount

Definitions

In order to determine the simple interest rate comparable to a given discount rate,

$$i = \frac{t}{t_E} \left[\frac{d}{1 - dt} \right] \quad (\times 100 \text{ for } \%) \tag{1.5-1}$$

and in order to determine the discount rate comparable to a given simple interest rate,

$$d = \frac{t_E}{t} \left[\frac{i}{1 + it_E} \right] \quad (\times 100 \text{ for } \%) \tag{1.5-2}$$

Ordinary Discount

For ordinary discount, $t = m/360$ and $t_E = m/365$. Eqs. (1.5-1) and (1.5-2) become, respectively,

$$i = \frac{365}{360} \left[\frac{d}{1 - dm/360} \right] \quad (\times 100 \text{ for } \%) \tag{1.5-3}$$

and

$$d = \frac{360}{365} \left[\frac{i}{1 + im/365} \right] \text{ (} \times \text{ 100 for \%)} \tag{1.5-4}$$

Example 1.   Treasury Bills with an accrued interest period of 240 days are purchased at a 10.75% discount. The comparable simple interest rate for the interest period can be determined from Eq. (1.5-3).

$$i = \frac{365}{360} \left[\frac{0.1075}{1 - (0.1075)(240/360)} \right] \times 100$$

$$= \frac{365}{360} \left[\frac{0.1075}{0.9283333} \right] \times 100 = 11.741\%$$

Example 2.   In order to earn 13% simple interest, the purchase of an ordinary discounted note for 240 days should not be at a discount rate less than the rate computed by Eq. (1.5-4).

$$d = \frac{360}{365} \left[\frac{0.13}{1 + (0.13)(240/365)} \right] \times 100$$

$$= \frac{360}{365} \left[\frac{0.13}{1.0854795} \right] \times 100 = 11.812\%$$

Exact Discount

For exact discount, both t and t_E equal m/365 and Eq. (1.5-1) and (1.5-2) become respectively,

$$i = \frac{d}{1 - dm/365} \text{ (} \times \text{ 100 for \%)} \tag{1.5-5}$$

and

$$d = \frac{i}{1 + im/365} \text{ (} \times \text{ 100 for \%)} \tag{1.5-6}$$

Example 3.   A bank loan at 18% exact discount for 90 days has a simple interest rate as determined by Eq. (1.5-5).

$$i = \frac{0.18}{1 - (0.18)(90/365)} \times 100 = 18.836\%$$

Example 4.   A bank specifies that discounted loans must earn 20% exact simple interest. The bank would, then, charge an exact discount rate on a 180-day loan as determined by Eq. (1.5-6).

$$d = \frac{0.20}{1 + (0.20)(180/365)} \times 100 = 18.204\%$$

CHAPTER **2**

How to Use Compound Interest Formulas
and Tables for Fast Answers
To Long-Term Investments

Long-term may be defined as a duration of time wherein the growths (interest) of investments are periodically compounded. Two types of compounding are available— discrete and continuous. In discrete compounding, interest is compounded a finite number of times per year, and in continuous compounding, interest is compounded an infinite number of times per year. This chapter shows the use of formulas for both types of compounding. Within the text are one or more examples which indicate the use of each formula. These examples include:

1. Determining the future amount at compound interest of a single investment at a constant interest rate. Pages 17, 24
2. Determining the effective annual interest rate (APR) for a specified compounding frequency. Pages 19, 25
3. Determining the time required for an investment to grow to a specified amount in the future. Pages 19, 25
4. Determining the periodic (and annual) interest rate necessary for a specified investment to grow to a specified amount in a specified time. Pages 20, 26
5. Determining the geometric mean interest rate (which is the true average interest rate) when interest rates vary over the term of the investment of a single principal. Pages 22, 27
6. Determining the future amount when interest rates vary over the term of the investment of a single principal. Pages 22, 26
7. Determining the weighted average interest rate which is a reasonably close approximation to the geometric mean interest rate. Pages 23, 27
8. Determining the average interest rates to the maturity date of the first investment when several investments are made simultaneously at different interest rates and different maturity dates. Page 27
9. Determining the present value of a specified future amount. Pages 29, 35

10. Determining the average interest rate to the maturity date of the first investment when several investments are made at different interest rates before
that maturity date. Pages 29, 31, 35, 37

11. Determining the required interest rate of a latest investment, to the maturity
date of a first investment, in order that the average interest rate of all investments to the maturity date of a first investment does not fall below a specified interest rate. Pages 33, 37

If you perform the calculations in the examples, your results may differ from the indicated results, depending upon the number of decimal places you carry at each step of the
solutions.

2.1 COMPOUNDING FREQUENCY AND PERIODIC INTEREST RATE

The nomenclature for compounding frequency and periodic interest rate is as follows:

f—The compounding frequency which is the number of times each year that interest
is computed and added to a principal.
R—The nominal annual interest rate.
i—The periodic interest rate—a simple interest rate during a compounding period.

Compounding Frequency

Compounding frequency is based on the conventional interest conversion periods as
indicated in the following tabulation.

Interest Conversion	$\underline{f}$
Annually	1
Semi-annually	2
Quarterly	4
Monthly	12
Daily	365
Continuously	Infinite

Periodic Interest Rate

The definition of the periodic interest rate is

$$i = \frac{R}{f} \tag{2.1-1}$$

Example 1. Refresh your memory! What is the periodic interest rate for 12%
compounded:

    a) annually?
    b) semi-annually?
    c) quarterly?
    d) monthly?
    e) daily?

From Eq. (2.1-1):
For a); $i = 12\%/1 = 12\% = .12$ for the calculator.
For b); $i = 12\%/2 = 6\% = .06$ for the calculator.
For c); $i = 12\%/4 = 3\% = .03$ for the calculator.
For d); $i = 12\%/12 = 1\% = .01$ for the calculator.
For e); $i = 12\%/365 = .0328767\% = 0.000328767$ for the calculator.

When interest is calculated on the basis of continuous compounding Eq. (2.1-1) indicates R is to be divided by infinity which implies $i = 0$. Yet, if $i = 0$, there would be no growth of interest-earning money—a contradictory dilemma which will be discussed in Section 2.2.

2.2   FUTURE AMOUNT

The nomenclature, in addition to that of Section 2.1, for the future amount at compound interest is as follows:

e—Base of the natural logarithms.
k—Conversion of ordinary year to exact year = 365/360.
n—Number of compounding periods during term of investment.
P—Principal amount of an investment.
R—Nominal annual interest rate.
R_A—Average annual interest rate.
R_e—Effective annual interest rate (APR).
R_M—Geometric mean annual interest rate.
R_R—Real annual interest rate.
r—Annual inflation rate.
S_n—Future amount after n periods.
S_t—Future amount after t years.
S_T—Future amount in "today's" dollars.
t—Number of years of compound interest.
t'—Number of years during which i remains constant.
$\Sigma\ E_j$—Summation of E's = $E_1 + E_2 + \ldots + E_N$.
$\Pi\ E_j$—Product of E's = $(E_1)(E_2)\ldots(E_N)$.

A.   Discrete Compounding

For discrete compounding, n is defined by

$$n = ft \tag{2.2-1}$$

and the future amount is defined by

$$S_n = P(1 + i)^n \tag{2.2-2}$$

Compound Interest Tables

Compound interest tables tabulate all values for a principal of $1.00. Therefore, when such tables are to be used, only the values of i and n are necessary. Table A-2 in the Appendix is a table for compound interest for values of i from 5/12% to 34%.

Example 1. You open a trustee term account with \$5,000 for a new-born child. Making an assumption that the account will earn 12% interest compounded monthly, you would like to know how much the account will show after 18 years. From Eq. (2.1-1),

$$i = 12\%/12 = 1\% \text{ per period}$$

From Eq. (2.2-1)

$$n = (12)\,(18) = 216 \text{ periods}$$

The future amount of the \$5,000 is determined from Eq. (2.2-2),

$$S_n = 5000\,(1 + 1\%)^{216}$$

a) Turning to Table A-2 for 1%, under the first column and opposite 216, read 8.5786063. Then the future amount is

$$S_n = (5000)\,(8.5786063) = \$42,893.03$$

b) Using the calculator:

> Enter 12; Depress %
> Depress $\div$; Enter 12; Depress =
> Display shows 0.01
> Depress +; Enter 1; Depress =
> Display shows 1.01
> Depress y^x; Enter 216; Depress =
> Display shows 8.5786061
> Depress $\times$; Enter 5000; Depress =
> Display shows 42893.03

Note that the first 4 lines of this sequence can be eliminated by determining i mentally and entering 1.01 directly.

Number of Periods Exceeding Table Limit

When Table A-2 is to be used for the determination of S in Eq. (2.2-2), situations may arise when the number of periods exceeds the limit in the table. For example, 12% compounded monthly for 25 years results in 1% per period for 300 periods. In Table A-2, the number of periods is limited to 240. The laws of exponents from algebra allow the expression $(1 + i)^n$ to be rearranged to

$$(1 + i)^n = (1 + i)^{n_1}\,(1 + i)^{n_2}\,(1 + i)^{n_3}\,\ldots$$

where

$$n = n_1 + n_2 + n_3 + \ldots$$

Then, ANY combination of sub-periods which total n may be used. As illustrations,

$$300 = 240 + 60$$
$$= 100 + 100 + 100$$
$$= 150 + 150$$

Example 2. For 1% per period and 300 periods,

$$(1 + 1\%)^{300} = (1 + 1\%)^{240}(1 + 1\%)^{60}$$

and from Table A-2, under future amount,

$$(1 + 1\%)^{300} = (10.89255365)(1.81669670)$$
$$= 19.788467$$

If the number of periods, n, is even, a more direct approach is available. Divide n by 2 and square the value from Table A-2.

Example 3.   For 1% per period and 300 periods

$$(1 + 1\%)^{300} = [(1 + 1\%)^{150}]^2$$

and from Table A-2, under Future Amount

$$(1 + 1\%)^{300} = (4.44842290)^2$$
$$= 19.788467$$

The method of Example 3 is more direct than the method of Example 2 because only one value is needed from the table; however, it is applicable only when n is an even number of periods.

Effective Annual Interest Rate

Given a nominal annual rate and a compounding frequency, the effective annual interest rate, R_e, can be determined by

$$R_e = [(1 + i)^f - 1] \; (\times \text{ 100 for \%}) \qquad (2.2\text{-}3)$$

Example 4.   The effective annual interest rate of 18% compounded monthly can be determined from Table A-2 opposite n = f or by the calculator. For both approaches, Eq. (2.1-1) is used for determining the value of i.

$$i = 18\%/12 = 1 \; 1/2\% = 0.015$$

a)   Turning to Table A-2 for 1 1/2%, under the first column, and opposite 12, read 1.19561817. From Eq. (2.2-3)

$$R_e = 1.19561817 - 1 = 0.19561817$$
$$= 19.561817\% = 19.562\%$$

Note that when seeking the effective annual interest rate for a given nominal rate and a compounding frequency, the decimal part of the future amount, opposite f, is the appropriate value.

b)   Using a calculator:

Enter 1.015; depress y^x
Enter 12; depress =
Display shows 1.1956182
Read the decimal part of the display

Time Required to Achieve a Specified Future Amount

Using the laws of logarithms, Eq. (2.2-2) can be solved for n.

$$n = \frac{\log (S_n/P)}{\log (1 + i)} \qquad (2.2\text{-}4)$$

and Eq. (2.2-1) can be rearranged to

$$t = \frac{n}{f} \qquad (2.2\text{-}5)$$

Example 5. You bought "blue chip" common stock last year, as a long-term investment, at $60 per share. A recent report points out that the market price of that stock has increased an average of 8% per year over the past 10 years. If this historical growth rate continues, the price of the stock will double in the length of time determined by Eqs. (2.2-4) and (2.2-5). For doubling, S = 2(60) = 120. Since the growth rate is, in effect, 8% compounded annually, i = 8%/1 = 0.08. Then, from Eq. (2.2-4) and either Table 2-1 or Table 2-2 or the calculator with log x or ln x,

$$n = \frac{\log (120/60)}{\log (1 + 8\%)} = \frac{\log (120/60)}{\log (1.08)}$$

$$= \frac{0.30103}{0.0334238} = 9.0064683$$

$$= 9 \text{ periods}$$

From Eq. (2.2-5), since f = 1 (annual compounding),

$$t = 9/1 = 9 \text{ years from the purchase date.}$$

In order to use Table A-2 for determining the time required to achieve a specified future amount, for a given i, search the first column (Future Amount) until the value which is closest to S/P is observed. Read the number of periods opposite this approximate value of S/P. Then use Eq. (2.2-5) to convert number of periods to numbers of years. For Example 5, the value of 1.99900463 is found opposite 9 in the 8% table of Table A-2.

Interest Rate—Given Time and Future Amount

When the principal, future amount, and time are known values, Eq. (2.2-2) yields the value for i (or R if n represents a number of years).

$$i = [\sqrt[n]{S_n/P} - 1] \; (\times 100 \text{ for } \%) \qquad (2.2\text{-}6)$$

In order to solve Eq. (2.2-6) either logarithms or a calculator with a $\sqrt[x]{y}$ function may be used to determine the value of $\sqrt[n]{(S/P)}$. A third alternative is to search Table A-2 with the value of S/P. Under the Future Amount column, look opposite n for each interest rate until the value of S/P (or very close to it) is seen. That interest rate, then, is the approximate periodic rate.

Example 6. Suppose that 10 years ago you established trusts for your children by assigning $5,000 worth of common stock to each of them. At the present time you anticipate a significant decline of the value of each of these trusts and decide to convert the trusts to cash. Each trust realizes a net proceeds of $15,000. You would like to know what the rate of return has been for the 10 years.

a) Solution by calculator using Eq. (2.2-6).

> Enter 15000; Depress ÷
> Enter 5000; Depress =
> Depress $\sqrt[x]{y}$; Enter 10; Depress =
> Display shows 1.1161232

The decimal part of the display is R and equals 0.1161232. The value of the trust grew at a rate of 11.612% compounded annually.

b) Solution by common logarithms using Eq. (2.2-6). From the laws of logarithms and $\sqrt[x]{y} = y^{1/x}$

$$\log\left[\frac{15000}{5000}\right]^{1/10} = \frac{1}{10}\log 3$$

From Table A-9, log 3 = 0.477121 and

$$\log\left[\frac{15000}{5000}\right]^{1/10} = \frac{1}{10}(0.477121) = 0.0477121$$

The value, 0.0477121, is found in Table A-9 between N = 1.11 and N = 1.12. As a reasonable approximation, we could say N = 1.115 (midway between the two). Then

$$\left[\frac{15000}{5000}\right]^{1/10} = 1.115$$

Reading the decimal part as R, the value of the trust grew approximately 11.5% compounded annually.

c) Solution by natural logarithms using Eq. (2.2-6). As in b) above

$$\ln\left[\frac{15000}{5000}\right]^{1/10} = \frac{1}{10}\ln 3$$

From Table A-10, ln 3 = 1.098612 and

$$\ln\left[\frac{15000}{5000}\right]^{1/10} = 0.1098612$$

The value, 0.1098612, is found in Table A-10 between N = 1.11 and N = 1.12. The resulting rate is the same as in b) above.

d) Solution by searching the compound interest table. Using Eq. (2.2-2) in the form

$$(1 + i)^n = \frac{S}{P}$$

Since n = 10 years

$$(1 + R)^{10} = \frac{15000}{5000} = 3$$

Searching the Future Amount column of Table A-2 opposite n = 10 yields a value of 2.96994683 at 11 1/2%. This value is sufficiently close to 3 to conclude an approximate 11 1/2% annually compounded growth rate for the securities.

In methods b), c), and d) of Example 6, values closer to the true value of i could be obtained by interpolation of the tables.

The Geometric Mean Interest Rate

When annual interest rates which are compounded periodically change during the term of investment, the geometric mean interest rate is an interest rate compounded annually which gives the same future amount of \$1.

$$R_M = \left[\sqrt[t]{\prod (1 + i_j)^{f_j t_j'}} - 1 \right] \ (\times 100 \text{ for } \%) \tag{2.2-7}$$

where R_M = the geometric mean interest rate
$\quad$ f = the compounding frequency which determines i
$\quad$ t_j' = the number of years during which i remains constant
$\Sigma \ t_j' = t$

Example 7. If a history of interest (growth) rates over a 10 year period is as follows,

$$R_1 = 7\% \text{ compounded annually for 2 years}$$
$$R_2 = 8\% \text{ compounded quarterly for 5 years}$$
$$R_3 = 9\% \text{ compounded monthly for 3 years}$$

the geometric mean interest (growth) rate is determined as follows:

$i_1 = 7\%$	$f_1 = 1$	$t_1' = 2$	$f_1 t_1' = 2$
$i_2 = 8\%/4 = 2\%$	$f_2 = 4$	$t_2' = 5$	$f_2 t_2' = 20$
$i_3 = 9\%/12 = 3/4\%$	$f_3 = 12$	$t_3' = 3$	$f_3 t_3' = 36$

For use in Eq. (2.2-7)

$$\prod (1 + i_j)^{f_j t_j'} = (1 + 7\%)^2 (1 + 2\%)^{20} (1 + 3/4\%)^{36}$$
$$= (1.07)^2 (1.02)^{20} (1.0075)^{36}$$

From Table A-2 or the y^x function on the calculator

$$\prod (1 + i_j)^{f_j t_j'} = (1.1449)(1.4859474)(1.3086454)$$
$$= 2.2263476$$

From Eq. (2.2-7)

$$R_M = [\sqrt[10]{2.2263476} - 1] \times 100$$
$$= (1.0833263 - 1) \times 100$$
$$= 8.33263\% \text{ compounded annually}$$

Future Amount—Varying Interest Rates

When a single principal is invested at compound interest for a period of time and the interest rate changes during the period, the future amount of that principal can be determined by

$$S_t = P \prod (1 + i_j)^{f_j t_j'} \tag{2.2-8}$$

Example 8. Suppose you had \$100,000 vested in a pension fund at age 55 when you terminated employment with that particular company. Further suppose that you are now 62 and the annuity from that pension fund will begin in 3 years. In order to plan for your retirement, you would like to determine the value of that \$100,000 fund 3 years hence. Researching the history of the growth of the fund for the previous 7 years, you determine that the fund grew at a rate of 8% per year for the first two years, 9% per year for the next 3 years, and 10% per year for the next 2 years. Communications with the trustees of the fund indicate a 12% per year growth of the fund for the next 3 years. The future amount of the original vested amount can be determined by Eqs. (2.2-7) and (2.2-8). Since the growth rates are annual, the interests are being compounded annually. Thus,

$$
\begin{array}{llll}
i_1 = 8\% & f_1 = 1 & t_1' = 2 & f_1 t_1' = 2 \\
i_2 = 9\% & f_2 = 1 & t_2' = 3 & f_2 t_2' = 3 \\
i_3 = 10\% & f_3 = 1 & t_3' = 2 & f_3 t_3' = 2 \\
i_4 = 12\% & f_4 = 1 & t_4' = 3 & f_4 t_4' = 3
\end{array}
$$

For use in Eqs. (2.2-7) and (2.2-8)

$$\prod(1 + i_j)^{f_j t_j'} = (1 + 8\%)^2 (1 + 9\%)^3 (1 + 10\%)^2 (1 + 12\%)^3$$

$$= (1.08)^2 (1.09)^3 (1.10)^2 (1.12)^3$$

From Table A-2 or the y^x function on the calculator

$$\prod(1 + i_j)^{f_j t_j'} = (1.1664)(1.295029)(1.21)(1.404928)$$

$$= 2.567831$$

From Eq. (2.2-7), the geometric mean growth rate is

$$R_M = [\sqrt[10]{2.567831} - 1] \times 100$$

$$= (1.0988961 - 1) \times 100$$

$$= 9.88961\% \text{ compounded annually}$$

From Eq. (2.2-8), the future amount is

$$S_t = 100000 (2.567831)$$

$$= \$256,783.10$$

Note: Because $(1 + R_M)^t = \Pi (1 + i_j)^{f_j t_j'}$

$$S_t = P(1 + R_M)^t \tag{2.2-9}$$

The Weighted Average Interest Rate

A reasonably close approximation to the geometric mean interest rate is the weighted average interest rate where each periodic interest rate is weighted by the number of periods.

$$R_A = \frac{\sum i_j f_j t_j'}{t} \% \tag{2.2-10}$$

where i is used in % magnitude.

Example 9. The average interest rate for the data of Example 8 would be determined by Eq. (2.2-10) to be

$$R_A = \frac{8(2) + 9(3) + 10(2) + 12(3)}{2 + 3 + 2 + 3}$$

$$= \frac{99}{10} = 9.9\% \text{ compounded annually.}$$

The future amount in Example 8 would be, then, determined by Eq. (2.2-9) as

$$S_t = 100000 \, (1.099)^{10}$$

$$= 100000 \, (2.5702592)$$

$$= \$257,025.92$$

B.   Continuous Compounding

The future amount at compound interest is defined as

$$S_n = P(1 + i)^n$$

where i = R/f and n = ft (see Eqs. 2.1-1, 2.2-1, and 2.2-2). Substituting the values of i and n into the definition

$$S_t = P(1 + R/f)^{ft}$$

Multiplying and dividing ft by R gives

$$S_t = P[(1 + R/f)^{f/R}]^{Rt}$$

For continuous compounding, as mentioned in Section 2.1, f becomes infinite, and from the theory of limits in mathematics, as f approaches infinity, the expression within the brackets approaches the value of the base of the natural logarithms. The value of this base is a non-terminating, non-repeating decimal, and to 7 decimal places it is 2.7182818. Conventionally, the base of the natural logarithms is given the symbol e.

For continuous compounding of interest, the future amount can be determined by

$$S_t = Pe^{Rt} \tag{2.2-11}$$

With the product Rt defined as x, the value of e^{Rt} may be obtained by calculator or in Table A-7. In order to distinguish between ordinary time and exact time, t may be multiplied by the ratio 365/360 for exact time. Then Eq. (2.2-11) becomes

$$S_t = Pe^{kRt} \tag{2.2-12}$$

where k = 365/360, and values of e^{kRt} can be obtained in Table A-5.

> **Example 10.**   Recall the trustee account of Example 1 of this section where $5,000 is invested for 18 years. At 12% compounded continuously,
>
> $$S_t = 5000 \, e^{(365/360)(0.12)(18)}$$
>
> $$= 5000 \, e^{2.19}$$
>
> Using Table A-5 with x = 2.19 or the calculator $e^{2.19}$ = 8.935213 and the future amount of the $5000 is
>
> $$S_t = 5000 \, (8.935213) = \$44,676.07$$

Comparing the future amounts indicated by Example 1 and this example shows a difference of $1,783.04 in favor of continuous compounding.

Values of kRt Exceeding the Table

Table A-5 shows values of e^{kRt} from 0.000 to 9.99. In financial transactions values of kRt exceeding the table will be encountered rarely. The combination of interest rate and time must be such that the product Rt must be at least 9.86 in order for kRt to exceed 9.99. However, should an occasion warrant a value of Rt of at least 9.86, the law of exponents as applied to discrete compounding may be used (see Section 2.1A). The value of kRt is segmented into values which are listed in the table.

Example 11. Suppose $10 is invested at 25% compounded continuously for 40 years. From Eq. (2.2-12)

$$S_t = 10 \, e^{(365/360)(0.25)(40)}$$

$$= 10 \, e^{10.139}$$

10.139 exceeds the values in Table A-5, but 10.139 can be segmented in any manner so that the sum of the segments equals 10.139. One combination is 5, 5 and 0.139 both of which are tabulated in Table A-5. Then,

$$S_t = 10 \, e^5 e^5 e^{0.139}$$

$$= 10(148.413159)(148.413159)(1.1491241)$$

$$= \$253,111.42$$

With the calculator, $e^{10.139}$ can be obtained directly.

Effective Annual Interest Rate

Given a nominal interest compounded continuously, the effective annual interest rate may be determined by

$$R_e = [e^{kR} - 1] \, (\times 100 \text{ for } \%) \tag{2.2-13}$$

which is the decimal part of e^{kR}.

Example 12. The effective annual interest rate of 18% compounded continuously can be determined from Eq. (2.2-13) as

$$R_e = [e^{(365/360)(0.18)} - 1] \times 100$$

$$= (e^{0.1825} - 1) \times 100$$

$$= (1.2002142 - 1) \times 100$$

$$= 20.021\%$$

If Table A-5 is used, it must be interpolated between 0.182 and 0.183.

Time Required to Achieve a Specified Future Amount

Using the laws of logarithms, Eq. (2.2-12) may be solved for t.

$$t = \frac{\ln (S_t/P)}{kR} \tag{2.2-14}$$

Example 13. $1,500 is deposited in an Individual Retirement Account. Assuming that the account earns interest at 12% compounded continuously, how many years are required in order for the account to grow to 5,000? Using Eq. (2.2-14)

$$t = \frac{\ln (5000/1500)}{(365/360)\,(0.12)}$$

$$= \frac{\ln (3.3333333)}{0.1216667} = \frac{1.2039728}{0.1216667}$$

$$= 9.8956642$$

$$= 9 \text{ years and } 327 \text{ days}$$

Interest Rate—Given Time and Future Amount

In order to determine the required interest rate for a given future amount and time period, Eq. (2.2-14) can be rearranged to determine R.

$$R = \frac{\ln (S_t/P)}{kt} \; (\times \, 100 \text{ for } \%) \qquad (2.2\text{-}15)$$

Example 14. What interest rate, compounded continuously, is required in order to double a principal in 10 years? In order that a principal is doubled, $S_n = 2P$. Using Eq. (2.2-15)

$$R = \frac{\ln (2P/P)}{kt} = \frac{\ln 2}{(365/360)\,(10)}$$

$$= \frac{0.6931472}{10.138889} = 0.0683652$$

$$= 6.837\%$$

Future Amount—Varying Interest Rates

When a single principal is invested at continuously compounded interest for a period of time and the interest rate changes during that period, the future amount of that principal can be determined by

$$S_t = Pe^{k \, \Sigma \, R_j t_j} \qquad (2.2\text{-}16)$$

Example 15. An individual had placed \$1,500 in an Individual Retirement account 5 years ago at 12% compounded continuously. The account has matured and is "rolled over" at 13% compounded continuously for 5 additional years. The future amount of that account can be determined from Eq. (2.2-16). Since this example contains 2 time periods,

$$\sum R_j t_j = R_1 t_1 + R_2 t_2 = (0.12)\,(5) + (0.13)\,(5) = 1.25$$

Then,

$$S_t = 1500 \, e^{(365/360)\,(1.25)}$$

$$= 1500 \, e^{1.2673611}$$

$$= 1500 \,(3.5514683)$$

$$= \$5,327.20$$

If Table A-5 is used, it must be interpolated between 1.26 and 1.27.

The Geometric Mean and Average Interest Rates

For continuously compounded interest, the geometric mean and average interest rates are the same and can be determined by

$$R_M = \frac{\sum R_j t_j}{t} \% \tag{2.2-17}$$

Example 16. The average interest rate at continuous compounding for 12% for 5 years followed by 13% for 5 years is

$$R_M = \frac{(12)(5) + (13)(5)}{5 + 5}$$

$$= 12.5\%$$

Using 0.125 and 10 years in Eq. (2.2-12) will confirm the result of Example 15.

C. Average Interest Rate—Multiple, Simultaneous Investments

When multiple investments, with different interest rates, are made at the same time, the average interest rate to a future point in time can be determined as follows:

For *discrete* compounding:

$$R_A = \left[\sqrt[t_1]{\frac{\sum P_j (1 + i_j)^{n_1}}{\sum P_j}} - 1 \right] (\times 100 \text{ for } \%) \tag{2.2-18}$$

For *continuous* compounding

$$R_A = \frac{1}{kt_1} \ln \left[\frac{\sum P_j e^{kR_j t_1}}{\sum P_j} \right] (\times 100 \text{ for } \%) \tag{2.2-19}$$

Example 20. Suppose you made the following investments on the same day. $100,000 at 12% for 2.5 years, $150,000 at 14% for 3 years and $200,000 at 16% for 4 years. What would be your average rate of return over the first 2.5 years at a) monthly compounding and b) continuous compounding of interest?

  a)   For monthly compounding, $t_1 = 2.5$ years, $n_1 = 12(2.5) = 30$ periods. For Eq. (2.2-18)

$$P_1 (1 + i_1)^{n_1} = 100000 (1 + 12\%/12)^{30} = (100000)(1.347849) = \$134,784.89$$

$$P_2 (1 + i_2)^{n_1} = 150000 (1 + 14\%/12)^{30} = (150000)(1.4161955) = 212,429.33$$

$$P_3 (1 + i_3)^{n_1} = 200000 (1 + 16\%/12)^{30} = (200000)(1.4878867) = 297,577.34$$

Summation of $P_j (1 + i_j)^{n_1} = \$644,791.56$
Summation of $P_j = \$450,000$

From Eq. (2.2-18)

$$R_A = \left[\sqrt[2.5]{\frac{644791.56}{450000}} - 1 \right] \times 100$$

$$= (1.1547361 - 1) \times 100$$

$$= 15.47361\%$$

$$= 15.474\% \text{ compounded annually}$$

Note: The $\sqrt[x]{y}$ function on the hand-held calculator enables the easy extraction of the decimal root of the radicand.

  b)   For continuous compounding, $t_1 = 2.5$ years. For Eq. (2.2-19)

$$P_1 e^{kR_1 t_1} = 100000\, e^{(365/360)(0.12)(2.5)} = (100000)(1.355495) = \$135,549.50$$

$$P_2 e^{kR_2 t_1} = 150000\, e^{(365/360)(0.14)(2.5)} = (150000)(1.4259826) = 213,879.39$$

$$P_3 e^{kR_3 t_1} = 200000\, e^{(365/360)(0.16)(2.5)} = (200000)(1.5001357) = 300,027.14$$

Summation of $P e^{kR_j t_1} = \$649,474.03$
Summation of $P_j = \$450,000$

From Eq. (2.2-19)

$$R_A = \left\{ \frac{1}{(365/360)(2.5)} \ln \left[\frac{649474.03}{450000} \right] \right\} \times 100$$

$$= (0.3945205)(0.3669153) \times 100$$

$$= 14.47556$$

$$= 14.476\% \text{ compounded continuously}$$

From Eq. (2.2-13)

$$R_A = [e^{(365/360)(0.1447556)} - 1] \times 100$$

$$R_A = (1.158083 - 1) \times 100$$

$$= 15.8083\% \text{ compounded annually}$$

2.3   PRESENT VALUE

The nomenclature, in addition to that of Section 2.1 and 2.2, for present value analyses is

  V—The present value of a future amount
  V′—The present value of a future amount at a point in time when the latest of a sequence of overlapping investments is introduced.
  i_N—The interest rate which is required of the latest investment of a sequence of overlapping investments in order that the combined investments, at the point in time when the latest investment is introduced, earn a specified average interest rate. For discrete compounding of interest.
  R_N—The same as i_N but for continuously compounded interest
  N—When used as a subscript, refers to the latest (N-th) investment of a sequence of overlapping investments

A. Discrete Compounding of Interest

The present value, of a future amount, at a point in time prior to the maturity of an investment which is earning discretely compounded interest, can be determined as follows.

$$V_n = S_n(1 + i)^{-n} \qquad (2.3\text{-}1)$$

where V_n is the present value on an interest conversion date. The expression $(1 + i)^{-n}$ is the present value of $1 and can be found in the second column of Table A-2. In order to determine the value of $(1 + i)^{-n}$ using the y^x function on the hand-held calculator,

        Enter $(1 + i)$; Depress y^x
        Enter n; Depress $+/-$
        Depress $=$.

Example 1.   You are a proud grandparent of a new-born child, and you wish to provide for the college education of that child by establishing a trust. You estimate that the four-year college cost will be $80,000 in 18 years, and you are reasonably certain that the trust will earn a minimum of 12% interest compounded monthly. The amount you must commit to the trust now can be determined by Eq. (2.3-1). For 12% compounded monthly, $i = 1\%$, and for $t = 18$, $n = ft = (12)(18) = 216$ periods. Then

$$V_n = 80000(1 + 1\%)^{-216}$$

$$= 80000(0.1165691)$$

$$= \$9,325.53$$

Average Interest (Growth) Rate—Overlapping Investments

For a series of long-term investments so that the "last" investment is made before the "first" investment instrument matures, the average interest (growth) rate of such overlapping investments can be determined as follows:

    I.   *From the Beginning of the Investment Sequence*

The average interest (growth) rate from a "first" investment to a point in time after a "last" investment can be determined by

$$R_A = \left[\sqrt[t_1]{\frac{\sum S_j}{\sum V_j}} - 1 \right] (\times\ 100\ \text{for}\ \%) \qquad (2.3\text{-}2)$$

where

$$\left. \begin{array}{l} S_j = P_j(1 + i_j)^{t_j} \\ V_j = S_j(1 + i_j)^{-t_1} \end{array} \right\} \qquad (2.3\text{-}3)$$

Each V is the present value of the corresponding S at the beginning of the investment sequence.

Example 2.   Suppose your corporation invests $100,000 for an asset that has a 10-year useful life, and its value is expected to increase by 15% compounded annually. One year later, an asset with a useful life of 25 years is purchased for $150,000, and its value is expected to increase by 10% compounded annually. One additional year later, an asset with a useful life of 15 years is purchased for $125,000, and its value is expected to increase by 12% compounded annually. It is desired to know the average

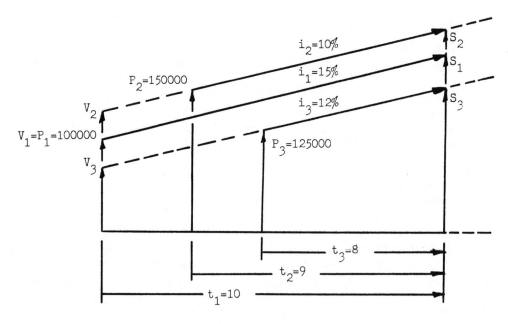

Figure 2-1.

growth rate over the life of the first asset. These transactions are depicted in Figure 2-1.

From the given information: $t_1 = 10$, $t_2 = 9$, and $t_3 = 8$. From Eqs. (2.3-3)

$S_1 = 100000(1 + 15\%)^{10} = 100000(4.0455578) = \$404,555.78$

$S_2 = 150000(1 + 10\%)^9 = 150000(2.3579477) = 353,692.15$

$S_3 = 125000(1 + 12\%)^8 = 125000(2.4759632) = 309,495.40$

Summation of S_j = \$1,067,743.33

$V_1 = \$100,000$

$V_2 = 353,692.15(1 + 10\%)^{-10} = 353,692.15(0.3855433) = 136,363.63$

$V_3 = 309,495.40(1 + 12\%)^{-10} = 309,495.40(0.3219732) = 99,649.24$

Summation of V_j = \$336,012.87

From Eq. (2.3-2), the average expected growth rate for the first 10 years is

$$R_A = [\sqrt[10]{1067743.33/336012.87} - 1] \times 100$$

$$= (1.122564 - 1) \times 100$$

$$= 12.2564\% \text{ compounded annually}$$

Thus, the three investments, at different times and growth rates, are equivalent to a single investment of \$336,012.87 at 12.2564% compounded annually for 10 years.

II. *From the Latest Investment of the Sequence*

The average interest (growth) rate from the point in time when an investment is introduced to a sequence of overlapping investments to a future point in time can be determined by

$$R_A = \left[\sqrt[t_N]{\frac{\sum S_j}{\sum V_j'}} - 1 \right] \text{ (× 100 for %)} \tag{2.3-4}$$

where

$$\left. \begin{array}{l} S_j = P_j (1 + i_j)^{t_j} \\ V_j' = S_j (1 + i_j)^{-t_N} \end{array} \right\} \tag{2.3-5}$$

Each V' is the present value of the corresponding S at the point in time when an investment is introduced.

Example 3.   For the investment sequence of Example 2, determine the average growth rate, through the remaining life of the first asset, as each asset is introduced to the sequence.   When the sequence begins with the $100,000 investment at 15% compounded annually, the average growth rate is 15% compounded annually.

    1.   Introduction of P_2 ($150,000 at 10% compounded annually).   Refer to Figure 2-2.

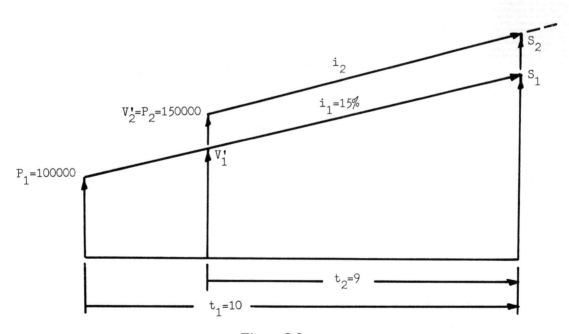

Figure 2-2.
R_A given i_2 (Example 3).
Required i_2 given R_A (Example 4).

From Eqs. (2.3-5)

$$S_1 = 100000(1 + 15\%)^{10} = 100000(4.0455578) = \$404,555.78$$

$$S_2 = 150000(1 + 10\%)^9 = 150000(2.3579477) = 353,692.15$$

Summation of S_j = \$758,247.93

The present values at the time P_2 is introduced into the sequence are:

$$V_1' = 404555.78(1 + 15\%)^{-9} = 404555.78(0.2842624) = \$115,000$$

$$V_N' = P_2 = 150000$$

Summation of V_j' = \$265,000

From Eq. (2.3-4)

$$R_A = [\sqrt[9]{758247.93/265000} - 1] \times 100$$

$$= (1.1239047 - 1) \times 100$$

$$= 12.39047\% \text{ compounded annually}$$

Thus, the introduction of a \$150,000 asset growing at 10% compounded annually reduces the average growth rate, for the remaining 9 years of the useful life of the first asset, from 15% to 12.39%.

2.   Introduction of P_3 (\$125,000 at 12% compounded annually). Refer to Fig. 2-3.

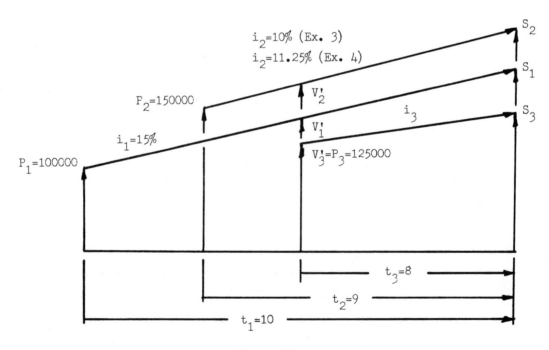

Figure 2-3.
R_A given i_3 (Example 3).
Required i_3 given R_A (Example 4).

S_1 and S_2 have been, previously, determined in 1 above as

$$S_1 = \$404,555.78$$

$$S_2 = 353,692.15$$

From Eqs. (2.3-5)

$$S_3 = 125000(1 + 12\%)^8 = 125000(2.4759632) = \$309,495.40$$

Summation of $S_j = \$1,067,743.33$

The present values at the time P_3 is introduced into the sequence are:

$$V_1' = 404555.78(1 + 15\%)^{-8} = 404555.78(0.3269018) = \$132,250$$

$$V_2' = 353692.15(1 + 10\%)^{-8} = 353692.15(0.4665074) = 165,000$$

$$V_N' = P_3 = 125000$$

Summation of $V_j' = \$422,250$

From Eq. (2.3-4)

$$R_A = [\sqrt[8]{1067743.33/422250} - 1] \times 100$$

$$= (1.1229545 - 1) \times 100$$

$$= 12.29545\% \text{ compounded annually}$$

Thus, the introduction of a third asset of \$125,000, growing at 12% compounded annually, reduces the average growth rate from 12.39% to 12.295% compounded annually for the remaining 8 years of the useful life of the first asset.

Note that in Example 2, the sequence is viewed from the perspective that the present value of the three investments (\$336,012.87) was invested at the beginning of year 1. Having a longer time for growth, the average growth rate of that present value could be smaller than the average growth rates of Example 3 where greater present values have shorter periods of time to grow to the combined future amount.

III.   *Required Interest (Growth) Rate for Specified Average Rate*

Given a sequence of overlapping investments, wherein the average interest (growth) rate from the time an investment is introduced to a future point in time cannot fall below a specified amount, the required interest (growth) rate of the latest investment can be determined by

$$i_N = \left[\sqrt[t_N]{\frac{\left(\sum V_j'\right)(1 + R_A)^{t_N} - \sum S_j}{P_N}} - 1 \right] (\times 100 \text{ for } \%) \qquad (2.3-6)$$

where $\sum V_j'$ is over the N investments, and $\sum S_j$ is over the $(N - 1)$ previous investments. Each V' and S is determined by Eqs. (2.3-5)

Example 4.   If the corporation of Example 2 required that the average growth rate, after the introduction of a new asset, must not fall below 13%, what must be the expected growth rates of P_2 and P_3, respectively, in order that the average growth rate for the remainder of the useful life of the first asset be 13%?

1. For the introduction of P_2, N = 2. Refer to Fig. 2-2. From Eqs. (2.3-5)

    Summation of $S_j = S_1 = 100000(1 + 15\%)^{10} = 404{,}555.78$

    Summation of $V'_j = V'_1 + P_2$

    $V'_1 = 404555.78(1 + 15\%)^{-9} = 115{,}000$

    $P_2 = 150000$

    Summation of $V'_j = 265{,}000$

From Eq. (2.3-6)

$$i_2 = \left[\sqrt[9]{\frac{(265000)(1 + 13\%)^9 - 404555.78}{150000}} - 1 \right] \times 100$$

$$= (1.1124879 - 1) \times 100$$

$$= 11.24879$$

$$= 11.25\% \text{ compounded annually}$$

Thus, P_2 must have a growth rate of 11.25% compounded annually in order that the two investments have an average growth rate of 13% for the remaining 9 years of the useful life of the first asset.

2. For the introduction of P_3, N = 3. Refer to Fig. 2-3. Assuming that the value of the second asset will grow at 11.25% compounded annually, when P_3 is introduced one year later: From Eqs. (2.3-5)

    Summation of $S = S_1 + S_2$

    $S_1 = 100000(1 + 15\%)^{10} = \$404{,}555.78$

    $S_2 = 150000(1 + 11.25\%)^9 = 391{,}553.79$

    Summation of $S_j = \$796{,}109.57$

    Summation of $V'_j = V'_1 + V'_2 + P_3$

    $V'_1 = 404555.78(1 + 15\%)^{-8} = \$132{,}250$

    $V'_2 = 391553.79(1 + 11.25\%)^{-8} = 166{,}875$

    $V'_3 = P_3 = 125{,}000$

    Summation of $V'_j = \$424{,}125$

From Eq. (2.3-6)

$$i_3 = \left[\sqrt[8]{\frac{(424125)(1 + 13\%)^8 - 796109.57}{125000}} - 1 \right] \times 100$$

$$= (1.1296159 - 1) \times 100$$

$$= 12.96159$$

$$= 12.962\% \text{ compounded annually}$$

Thus, P_3 must have a growth rate of 12.962% compounded annually in order that the three investments will have an average growth rate of

13% compounded annually for the remaining 8 years of the useful life of the first asset.

B.   Continuous Compounding of Interest

The present value, of a future amount, at a point in time prior to the maturity of an investment which is earning continuously compounded interest, can be determined as follows.

$$V_t = S_t \, e^{-kRt} \tag{2.3-7}$$

where V_t is the present value of an interest conversion date. The values of e^{-kRt} can be found in Table A-6 or can be determined by the hand-held calculator by negating the value of (kRt) with the $+/-$ key and then using the e^x function. If $k = 365/360$,

Enter 365	Depress $\div$
Enter 360	Depress $\times$
Enter R	Depress $\times$
Enter t	Depress $=$
Depress $+/-$	Depress e^x (INV, ln on TI-50)

Example 5.   If the trust of Example 1 could earn 12% compounded continuously, the amount that must be committed now in order that the account would grow to $80,000 in 18 years can be determined by Eq. (2.3-7)

$$V_t = 80000 \, e^{-(365/360)(0.12)(18)}$$

$$= 80000(0.1119167)$$

$$= \$8,953.34$$

Average Interest Rate—Overlapping Investments

I.   *From the Beginning of an Investment Sequence*

The average interest rate from a "first" investment to a point in time after a "last" investment can be determined by

$$R_A = \frac{1}{kt_1} \ln \left[\frac{\sum S_j}{\sum V_j} \right] \quad (\times \, 100 \text{ for } \%) \tag{2.3-8}$$

where

$$\left.\begin{array}{l} S_j = P \, e^{kR_j t_j} \\ V_j = S_j \, e^{-kR_j t_1} \end{array}\right\} \tag{2.3-9}$$

Each V is the present value, of the corresponding S, at the beginning of the investment sequence.

Example 6.   Two years ago you decided to make a series of long-term investments in savings certificates. At that time you deposited $7,500 in an account that was paying 12% compounded continuously and guaranteed for 8 years. Today you deposited $7,500 in a similar account which is guaranteed for 8 years and is paying 14% compounded continuously. You desire to know what will be the average interest rate over the first 8-year period. This situation is depicted in Figure 2.4.

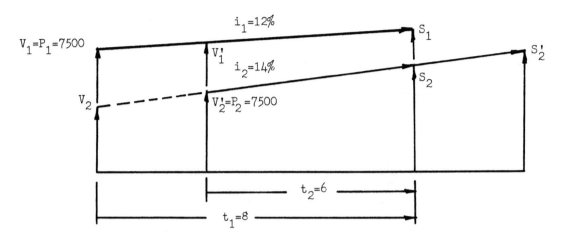

Figure 2-4

From Eqs. (2.3-9)

$$S_1 = 7500\ e^{(365/360)(0.12)(8)} = 7500(2.6467523) = \$19,850.64$$

$$S_2 = 7500\ e^{(365/360)(0.14)(6)} = 7500(2.3435495) = \ \ 17,576.62$$

Summation of S_j = $37,427.26

$$V_1 = P_1 = \$7,500$$

$$V_2 = 17576.62\ e^{-(365/360)(0.14)(8)} = 17576.62(0.3212436) = 5,646.38$$

Summation of V_j = $13,146.38

From Eq. (2.3-8)

$$R_A = \frac{1}{(365/360)(8)}\ \ln\left[\frac{37427.36}{13146.38}\right] \times 100$$

$$= (0.1232877)(1.0462556) \times 100$$

$$= 12.899\%\ \text{compounded continuously}$$

Thus, these two deposits, two years apart and at different interest rates, are equivalent to a deposit of $13,146.38 at 12.899% compounded continuously for 8 years.

II. *From the Latest Investment of the Sequence*

The average interest rate from the point in time when an investment is introduced to a sequence of overlapping investments to a future point in time can be determined by

$$R_A = \frac{1}{kt_N}\ \ln\left[\frac{\sum S_j}{\sum V_j'}\right]\ (\times\ 100\ \text{for}\ \%) \tag{2.3-10}$$

where

$$\left.\begin{array}{l} S_j = P\ e^{kR_j t_j} \\ V_j' = S\ e^{-kR_j t_N} \end{array}\right\} \tag{2.3-11}$$

Each V' is the present value of the corresponding S at the point in time when the latest investment is introduced.

Example 7. Referring to Figure 2-4, the average interest rate during the 6 remaining years of the first investment of Example 6 is determined by Eqs. (2.3-10) and (2.3-11). From Eqs. (2.3-11)

$$S_1 = 7500 \ e^{(365/360)(0.12)(8)} = 7500(2.6467523) = \$19,850.64$$

$$S_2 = 7500 \ e^{(365/360)(0.14)(6)} = 7500(2.3435495) = \ \ 17,576.62$$

Summation of S_j = \$37,427.26

$$V_1' = 19850.64 \ e^{-(365/360)(0.12)(6)} = 19850.64(0.481909) = \$9,566.20$$

$$V_N' = P_2 = 7500$$

Summation of V_j = \$17,066.20

From Eq. (2.3-10)

$$R_A = \frac{1}{(365/360)(6)} \ \ln\left[\frac{37427.26}{17066.20}\right] \times 100$$

$$= (0.1643836)(0.7852994) \times 100$$

$$= 12.909\% \text{ compounded continuously}$$

Thus, the introduction of the second investment, two years after the first investment, gives an average interest rate, for the two investments, of 12.909% for the remaining 6 years of the maturity of the first investment.

III. *Required Interest Rate for Specified Average Rate*

Given a sequence of overlapping investments, wherein the average interest rate from the time an investment is introduced to a future point in time cannot fall below a specified amount, the required interest rate can be determined by

$$R_N = \frac{1}{kt_N} \ \ln\left[\frac{(\sum V_j') \ e^{kR_At_N} - \sum S_j}{P_N}\right] \ (\times 100 \text{ for } \%) \qquad (2.3\text{-}12)$$

where $\sum V_j'$ is over the N investments, and $\sum S_j$ is over the (N – 1) previous investments. Each V' and S is determined by Eqs. (2.3-11).

Example 8. For Example 6, if an average interest rate of 13% compounded continuously is desired for the 6 remaining years of the first investment, the required interest rate for the second investment can be determined by Eqs. (2.3-11) and (2.3-12). Since N = 2, the summation of S is the future amount of the first investment only. From Eqs. (2.3-11).

$$S_1 = 7500 \ e^{(365/360)(0.12)(8)} = 7500(2.6467523) = \$19,850.64$$

Summation of S_j = S_1 = \$19,850.64

Summation of V_j' = $V_1' + P_2$

$$V_1' = 19850.64 \ e^{-(365/360)(0.12)(6)} = 19850.64(0.481909) = \$9,566.20$$

$$V_N' = P_2 = \$7,500$$

Summation of $V_j' = \$17,066.20$

From Eq. (2.3-12)

$$R_2 = \frac{1}{(365/360)\,(6)} \ln \left[\frac{17066.20\ e^{(365/360)\,(0.13)\,(6)} - 19850.64}{7500} \right] \times 100$$

$$= (0.1643836) \ln \left[\frac{(17066.20)\,(2.2052334) - 19850.64}{7500} \right] \times 100$$

$$= (0.1643836)\,(0.8634138) \times 100$$

$$= 14.193\% \text{ compounded continuously}$$

Thus, in Example 6, if the $7,500, which is invested two years after the first $7,500, can earn 14.194% compounded continuously, the two investments will earn slightly more than 13% compounded continuously for the 6 remaining years of the maturity life of the first investment.

CHAPTER 3

Formulas and Tables for Annuities When Payments Occur at the Ends of Interest Conversion Periods

An annuity is defined as an amount payable at regular periods. When the periodic payments are made as a long-term investment stream into an account that is growing, the future amount of that account after n interest conversions can be determined by adding the future amounts of the n individual investments as determined by Eq. (2.2-2) or (2.2-12). For discrete compounding of interest

$$S_n = \sum P_j (1 + i_j)^{n_j}$$

and for continuous compounding of interest

$$S_t = \sum P_j \, e^{k R_j t_j}$$

The present value, of a long-term investment, which is to be reduced by periodic payments from the account is the sum of the present values of the n payments as determined by Eq. (2.3-1) or (2.3-7). For discrete compounding of interest

$$V_n = \sum S_j (1 + i_j)^{-n_j}$$

and for continuous compounding of interest

$$V_t = \sum S_j \, e^{-k R_j t_j}$$

where the S_j are the future periodic payments to be made from the account which started at V_t.

If any of the parameters in the formulas above are variable, the summation processes must be performed manually (probably by calculator or computer). With variable payments or irregular intervals, the formulas above fail as financial planning devices. However, with either level payments or payments which increase or decrease at uniform rates and with equally spaced payments coinciding with interest conversion dates, the summation processes reduce to relatively simple formulas which can be extremely helpful as financial planning devices. This chapter provides such formulas.

Within the text are one or more examples which indicate the use of each formula. The examples address a specific type of monetary problem, but the concepts which are treated are general. The examples include:

1. Determining the amount of money that will be available at the end of a series of level or uniformly increasing payments, such as for Individual Retirement Accounts, Keogh Plans, or pension contributions in general, for level and changing interest rates. Pages 41, 43, 49

39

2. Determining the number of payments that will be required in order to achieve a specified future amount for level and changing interest rates. Pages 42, 45

3. Determining the required level periodic payment to a sinking fund for level and changing interest rates and determining the initial payment, to a sinking fund, for payments which are to increase at a constant rate, such as for trust funds and bond redemption. A procedure for a combination of level and increasing payments is also shown. Pages 46, 47, 50, 53

4. Determining the effect of payments which increase at a constant rate, such as the magnitude at a given payment number and the total of such payments. Pages 52, 54

5. Determining the amount of money required (the present value) one interest conversion period prior to receiving or disbursing a specified level periodic payment or a specified initial payment, for payments which are to increase at a constant rate, such as for liquidation of a pension account or trust with a specified number of payments. Pages 55, 62

6. Determining the level periodic payment and the initial payment, for payments which are to increase at a constant rate, for the amortization of a debt, such as a mortgage, or the liquidation of a personal account given the present value. If the interest rate changes at a given present value, a new periodic payment can be determined for the remaining term. Pages 64, 65

7. Determining the present value of a level payment amortization after a given payment number and determining the new term of an amortization where the interest rate changes but the payment level remains constant. Pages 57, 58, 60

8. Determining the payment number when the present value of an amortization is some specified fraction of the original amount, such as the reduction of an account to a level which can be used to fund an estate trust free of estate taxes. Page 59

If you perform the calculations in the examples, your results may differ from the indicated results, depending upon the number of decimal places you carry at each step of the solutions. For example, if 12% compounded continuously is rounded to 0.1294 (12.94% effective annual rate) the results will be different than if it is used in calculations as 0.1293776 (the limit on the TI-50).

3.1   FUTURE AMOUNT AND SINKING FUND PAYMENTS

This section provides formulas for determining the future amount of a series of *equal* periodic payments and the future amount of a series of *periodic payments which increase (decrease) periodically at a constant rate.* This section also provides formulas for the determination of the *equal* periodic payments necessary to achieve a specified future amount and the *initial payment for a series of payments which increase (decrease) at a constant rate.* Also, a procedure for a combination of a series of uniformly increasing (decreasing) periodic payments in conjunction with a series of equal periodic payments is provided.

Simple ordinary annuities are defined as annuities where the payment dates coincide with interest conversion dates (simple) and payments occur at the end of periods (ordinary). This type of annuity is also called an *immediate annuity* in actuarial problems.

The nomenclature for simple ordinary annuities is as follows:

e—Base of the natural logarithms.

f—The compounding frequency which is the number of times each year that interest is computed and added to principal.

g—The periodic rate by which a periodic payment is increased (decreased). g is positive for increasing rates and negative for decreasing rates.

G—The annual rate by which an annual payment is increased (decreased). G is positive for increasing rates and negative for decreasing rates.

i—The periodic interest rate—a simple interest rate during a compounding period.

k—Conversion of ordinary year to exact year = 365/360.

n—Total number of payments or interest conversions.

N—Number of payments (interest conversions) remaining in the annuity.

p—Equal periodic payment.

p_o—Initial payment of a uniformly increasing (decreasing) series of payments.

p_m—The m-th payment of a uniformly increasing (decreasing) series of payments.

R—Nominal annual interest rate.

R_e—Effective annual interest rate.

S_n—The future amount of an annuity after n payments.

S_t—The future amount of an annuity after t years (primarily used when interest is compounded continuously).

S_o—The basis amount when there is a change in the level of equal payments and/or the interest rate.

t—Time expressed as a number of years.

T—Total of payments.

Given a nominal annual interest rate compounded at discrete intervals, the periodic interest rate and total number of periods are, respectively, $i = R/f$ and $n = ft$ (see Eqs. (2.1-1) and (2.2-1)).

Given a nominal annual interest rate compounded continuously, the effective annual rate is $R_e = e^{kR} - 1$ (see Eq. (2.2-13)).

Future Amount—Level Payments and Interest Rate

I. *Discrete Compounding of Interest*

If level payments are made at the end of equally spaced periods and if interest conversion occurs at the same time as the payments, the future amount of those payments can be determined by

$$S_n = p \left[\frac{(1 + i)^n - 1}{i} \right] \tag{3.1-1}$$

The expression within the brackets of Eq. (3.1-1) is the future amount of a simple ordinary annuity of $1 per period and may be denoted by symbolic terms for simplicity. Two such denotations are $s_{\overline{n}|i}$ which is read as s sub n angle i and $(S/p,i,n)$ which is read as *S given p, i, and n*. Since the notation $(S/p,i,n)$ includes all the elements of Eq. (3.1-1) it will be used when the value can be determined from Table A-2. Thus,

$$S_n = p(S/p,i,n) \tag{3.1-2}$$

II. *Continuous Compounding of Interest*

If level payments are made at the end of each year and if interest is compounded continuously and added to the principal at the same time as the payment, the future amount of those level payments can be determined by

$$S_t = p\left[\frac{(1 + R_e)^t - 1}{R_e}\right] \tag{3.1-3}$$

Example 1.   You are advising a client to make annual deposits of $1,500 into an Individual Retirement Account.   You inform your client that the interest rates in the future probably will not be less than 12%. For informational purposes, you would like to inform the client what the future amount will be if 25 annual payments are made. Assuming that the annual interest rate does not fall below 12%, the minimum future amount can be determined by Eq. (3.1-1), Table A-2 in conjunction with Eq. (3.1-2) or Eq. (3.1-3) depending upon the type of compounding in effect.

Discrete Compounding. Since deposits are to be made annually, it is assumed that the interest is compounded annually.   Therefore, $i = R/f = 12\%/1 = 12\%$, and $n = ft = (1)(25) = 25$.

   a)   Equation (3.1-2) and Table A-2. The third column of Table A-2 is labeled "Amount of Annuity" and gives the future amount of $1 per period. In the 12% table, opposite 25 periods, read the value 133.33387006. This is the value of $(S/p,i,n)$. Then

$$S_n = (1500)(133.3338701) = \$200,000.81$$

   b)   Equation (3.1-1) and the y^x function on the calculator.

Enter 1.12	Depress y^x	
Enter 25	Depress =	
Display shows 17.000064		$= (1 + i)^n$
Depress –	Enter 1 Depress =	
Display shows 16.000064		$= (1 + i)^n - 1$
Depress ÷	Enter 0.12 Depress =	
Display shows 133.33387		$= ((1 + i)^n - 1)/i$
Depress ×	Enter 1500 Depress =	
Display shows 200000.81		

Continuous Compounding. For Eq. (3.1-3), $R_e = e^{(365/360)(0.12)} - 1 = 0.1294$. Then,

$$S_n = (1500)\left[\frac{(1.1294)^{25} - 1}{0.1294}\right] = \$231,265.56$$

Thus, you can inform your client that if the future interest rates remain near (but above) 12%, the 25 annual deposits of $1,500 will grow to over $200,000 or over $231,000 depending upon the manner of compounding interest.

Number of Level Payments—Specified Future Amount

I. *Discrete Compounding of Interest*

The number of level payments needed in order to achieve a specified future amount can be determined by applying the laws of logarithms to Eq. (3.1-1).

$$n = \frac{\log[(S_n i/p) + 1]}{\log(1 + i)} \tag{3.1-4}$$

and Eq. (3.1-2) can be rearranged to

$$(S/p,i,n) = S_n/p \tag{3.1-5}$$

II. *Continuous Compounding of Interest*

Replacing i by R_e and n by t, Eq. (3.1-4) becomes

$$t = \frac{\log\,[(S_t R_e/p) + 1}{\log\,(1 + R_e)} \tag{3.1-6}$$

Example 2. Your client in Example 1 desires to have a "nest egg" of at least $300,000 in the IRA when he retires at age 65. If he is now 35 years of age and if it is reasonable to assume that a $1,500-per-year deposit is assured, will the goal of $300,000 be attainable? Assuming interest rates remain near (but above) 12% Eq. (3.1-4), (3.1-5) or (3.1-6) can be used to answer the question.

Discrete Compounding. Since deposits are to be made annually, it is assumed that the interest is compounded annually. Therefore, i = R/f = 12%/1 = 12%.

a) Equation (3.1-4).

$$n = \frac{\log\,\{[(300000)\,(0.12)/(1500)] + 1\}}{\log\,1.12}$$

$$= \frac{\log\,25}{\log\,1.12} = 28.4 \text{ periods}$$

Since each period is one year, it will require 29 years to achieve the goal, and since your client is 35 years of age, the goal is attainable.

b) Equation (3.1-5) and Table A-2. From Eq. (3.1-5)

$$(S/p,i,n) = \frac{300000}{1500} = 200$$

Then, searching the third column in the 12% table of Table A-2 the value of 200 occurs between 190.69888739 and 214.58275388 which occur at 28 and 29 periods, respectively. Thus, 200 occurs between 28 and 29 periods (years).

Continuous Compounding. In Example 1, it was shown that $R_e = 0.1294$. From Eq. (3.1-6)

$$t = \frac{\log\,\{[(300000)\,(0.1294)/(1500)] + 1\}}{\log\,1.1294}$$

$$= \frac{\log\,26.88}{\log\,1.1294} = 27.05 \text{ years}$$

Due to continuous compounding of interest, the $300,000 goal would be achieved in a shorter period of time.

Future Amount—Change in Payment Level and/or Interest Rate

The future amount of an annuity, with level payments, wherein the level of payments and/or the interest rate changes at a point of time into the annuity can be determined by:

I. *Discrete Compounding of Interest*

$$S_n = S_o(1 + i)^N + p_N\left[\frac{(1 + i)^N - 1}{i}\right]$$ (3.1-7)

$$S_n = S_o(1 + i)^N + p_N(S/p, i, N)$$ (3.1-8)

II. *Continuous Compounding of Interest*

$$S_t = S_o(1 + R_e)^N + p_N\left[\frac{(1 + R_e)^N - 1}{R_e}\right]$$ (3.1-9)

S_o is the future amount of the payments prior to the change in level of the payments and/or interest rate, and N is the number of future payments after a change.

Example 3. The accumulated benefits in a pension fund of an individual total $13,000. Contributions had been made at a level of $100 per month, and the fund had been invested at an interest rate of 7% compounded monthly. The future amount of the fund at the end of the next 15 years can be determined by Eq. (3.1-7) or (3.1-8) for the following changes.

Discrete Compounding.
   a)   Payment level increases to $150 per month. Interest rate remains constant. $i = R/f = 7\%/12$ and $N = ft = (12)(15) = 180$, Eq. (3.1-7) gives the future amount as

$$S_n = (13000)(1 + 7\%/12)^{180} + 150\left[\frac{(1 + 7\%/12)^{180} - 1}{7\%/12}\right]$$

Using the calculator or Table A-2

$$S_n = (13000)(2.8489467) + (150)(316.9622967)$$

$$= \$84,580.65$$

   b)   Interest rate increases to 8% compounded monthly. Payment level remains constant. $i = R/f = 8\%/12 = 2\%/3$ and $N = 180$, Eq. (3.1-7) gives the future amount as

$$S_n = (13000)(1 + 2\%/3)^{180} + 100\left[\frac{(1 + 2\%/3)^{180} - 1}{2\%/3}\right]$$

Using the calculator or Table A-2

$$S_n = (13000)(3.3069215) + 100(346.0382216)$$

$$= \$77,593.80$$

   c)   Payment level increases to $150 per month and interest rate increases to 8% compounded monthly. Eq. (3.1-7) gives the future amount as

$$S_n = (13000)(1 + 2\%/3)^{180} + 150\left[\frac{(1 + 2\%/3)^{180} - 1}{2\%/3}\right]$$

$$= (13000)(3.3069215) + 150(346.0382216)$$

$$= \$94,895.71$$

Continuous Compounding. When continuous compounding of interest is in effect, the statement of this example becomes a complex annuity because interest conversion and payment dates do not coincide. Complex annuities are discussed in Chapter 6. However, if a deposit of $1,800 per year is made into an account earning interest at 8% compounded continuously for 15 years starting with a $13,000 base,

$$R_e = e^{(365/360)(0.08)} - 1 = 0.0845$$

and from Eq. (3.1-9)

$$S_t = (13000)(1.0845)^{15} + (1800)\left[\frac{(1.0845)^{15} - 1}{0.0845}\right]$$

$$= (13000)(3.376318) + (1800)(28.122107)$$

$$= \$94,511.93$$

Number of Level Payments After a Change—Specified Future Amount

If a change occurs in the payment level and/or interest rate, the number of payments at a new level and/or interest rate can be determined by applying the laws of logarithms to Eqs. (3.1-7) and (3.1-9).

I. *Discrete Compounding of Interest*

$$N = \frac{\log\left[\dfrac{S_n i + p_N}{S_o i + p_N}\right]}{\log(1 + i)} \tag{3.1-10}$$

II. *Continuous Compounding of Interest*

$$t_N = \frac{\log\left[\dfrac{S_t R_e + p_N}{S_o R_e + p_N}\right]}{\log(1 + R_e)} \tag{3.1-11}$$

Example 4. An individual has an account with an accumulation of $13,000. Annual deposits of $1,800 are to be made, and it is desired to have a total accumulation of at least $150,000. It is assumed that the account will earn interest at 10% throughout the term of deposits. The number of future payments is desired.

Discrete Compounding. Since annual deposits are to be made, it is assumed that annual compounding is in effect. Therefore, $i = R/f = 10\%/1 = 10\%$. From Eq. (3.1-10)

$$N = \frac{\log\left[\dfrac{(150000)(0.10) + 1800}{(13000)(0.10) + 1800}\right]}{\log 1.10}$$

$$= \frac{\log 5.4193548}{\log 1.10} = 17.7 \text{ payments}$$

Therefore, it will require 18 annual deposits to achieve at least $150,000.

Continuous Compounding. For 10% compounded continuously

$$R_e = e^{(365/360)(0.10)} - 1 = 0.1067$$

From Eq. (3.1-11)

$$t_N = \frac{\log \left[\dfrac{(150000)(0.1067) + 1800}{(13000)(0.1067) + 1800} \right]}{\log 1.1067}$$

$$= \frac{\log 5.5865834}{\log 1.1067} = 16.96 \text{ payments}$$

Therefore, it will require 17 annual deposits to achieve at least $150,000.

Sinking Fund—Level Payments and Interest Rate

When it is desired to know the necessary level payment in order to achieve a specified future amount in a specified period of time, Eq. (3.1-1) and Eq. (3.1-3) can be rearranged as follows:

I. *Discrete Compounding of Interest*

$$p = S_n \left[\frac{i}{(1 + i)^n - 1} \right] \tag{3.1-12}$$

$$p = S_n(p/S,i,n) \tag{3.1-13}$$

$(p/S,i,n)$ is the necessary level payment in order to achieve a future amount of $1 in a specified period of time. Values of $(p/S,i,n)$ are tabulated in Table A-2 under the column labeled "Sinking Fund." For those interest rates which are not included in Table A-2, Eq. (3.1-12) must be used.

II. *Continuous Compounding of Interest*

$$p = S_t \left[\frac{R_e}{(1 + R_e)^t - 1} \right] \tag{3.1-14}$$

Example 5. Your corporation sells $1,000,000 of 20-year bonds at face value and establishes a sinking fund for the redemption of the bonds. You estimate that payments into the fund will earn at least 20% compounded annually over the 20-year period. The necessary annual payment into the fund can be determined by Eq. (3.1-12) or (3.1-13). $i = R/f = 20\%/1 = 20\%$ and $n = ft = (1)(20) = 20$, using the calculator or Table A-2 gives

$$p = (1000000)(0.0053565)$$

$$= \$5,356.50 \text{ per year}$$

Example 6. You establish trusts for the college education of your children. You would like an accumulation of at least $150,000 in 18 years. Assuming that the accounts will not earn less than 10% interest compounded continuously, the total annual payments can be determined by Eq. (3.1-14).

$$R_e = e^{(365/360)(0.10)} - 1 = 0.1067$$

$$p = (150000) \left[\frac{0.1067}{(1.1067)^{18} - 1} \right] = \$3,076.65 \text{ per year}$$

New Level Payments—Change in Sinking Fund and/or Interest Rate

After a series of payments have been made into a sinking fund, if the specified future amount of that fund and/or the interest rate at which the fund is invested changes, the new level payment can be determined by rearranging Eqs. (3.1-7), (3.1-8), and (3.1-9) to:

    I.   *Discrete Compounding of Interest*

$$p_N = [S_n - S_o(1 + i)^N] \left[\frac{i}{(1 + i)^N - 1} \right] \tag{3.1-15}$$

$$p_N = [S_n - S_o(1 + i)^N] \ (p/S,i,N) \tag{3.1-16}$$

    II.   *Continuous Compounding of Interest*

$$p_N = [S_t - S_o(1 + R_e)^{t_N}] \left[\frac{R_e}{(1 + R_e)^{t_N} - 1} \right] \tag{3.1.17}$$

where S_o is the accumulated amount in the fund when a change occurs, and N is the remaining number of payments.

> **Example 7.** Suppose that 5 years have elapsed since the \$1,000,000 of bonds of Example 5 were issued, and that the growth rate of the sinking fund has been 20% compounded annually. You now estimate that the sinking fund investments can earn 22% compounded annually. The new level payment can be determined as follows. Your financial records should indicate that $S_o = \$39,860.93$. (From Example 5, p = \$5,356.50 and $S_o = (5356.50) \ (S/p,20\%,5) = (5356.50) \ (7.4416)$). Since the bonds were issued for 20 years, and 5 years have elapsed, N = 15. i = R/f = 22%/1 = 22%. From Eq. (3.1-15) or (3.1-16) and Table A-2
>
> $$p_N = [1000000 - (39860.93) \ (1 + 22\%)^{15}] \ (p/S,22\%,15)$$
>
> $$= [1000000 - (39860.93) \ (19.742287)] \ (0.01173816)$$
>
> $$= \$2,500.85 \text{ per year}$$

Thus, if the sinking fund earns interest at a rate of 22% for the remaining 15 years of the bond life, the annual payments can be reduced to \$2,500.85 per year from the \$5,356.50 per year during the 5 years the fund was earning 20%. Should a subsequent change of interest rate occur or should the specified future amount be altered, a new S_o, i, and N would be applied in Eq. (3.1-15) or (3.1-16) and a subsequent level determined. If the interest rates for this fund occur as indicated, the future of the fund from the first year would tabulate as follows.*

Year	Payment	Interest Rate	Accumulation
1	$5,356.50	20%	$ 5,356.50
2	5,356.50	20%	11,784.30
3	5,356.50	20%	19,497.66
4	5,356.50	20%	28,753.69
5	5,356.50	20%	39,860.93
6	2,500.85	22%	51,131.19
7	2,500.85	22%	64,880.90
8	2,500.85	22%	81,655.54
9	2,500.85	22%	102,120.61
10	2,500.85	22%	127,088.00
11	2,500.85	22%	157,548.20
12	2,500.85	22%	194,709.66
13	2,500.85	22%	240,046.64
14	2,500.85	22%	295,357.74
15	2,500.85	22%	362,837.30
16	2,500.85	22%	445,162.36
17	2,500.85	22%	545,598.92
18	2,500.85	22%	668,131.54
19	2,500.85	22%	817,621.33
20	2,500.85	22%	999,998.87

*The accumulation for a given year equals 1.2 or 1.22 times the accumulation of the previous year plus the payment of the given year. The $1.13 deficit of the $1,000,000 is due to rounding of the decimals to the second decimal place.

Example 8. After you have made the 10th payment into the trust accounts of Example 6, you become convinced that interest rates will not fall below 12% compounded continuously. The annual payments for the remaining 8 years can be determined by Eq. (3.1-17). After the 10th payment, your records should indicate an accumulation of $50,637.17 if the interest rate was constant at 10% compounded continuously (with p = 3076.65 from Example 6 and Eq. (3.1-3)). This is the value of S_0. The new interest rate is

$$R_e = e^{(365/360)(0.12)} - 1 = 0.1294$$

and from Eq. (3.1-17)

$$p_8 = [150000 - (50637.17)(1.1294)^8] \left[\frac{0.1294}{(1.1294)^8 - 1} \right]$$

$$= (150000 - 134045.33)(0.0785589)$$

$$= \$1,253.38 \text{ per year for the remaining 8 years.}$$

Future Amount—Payments Changing at a Constant Rate

If payments to an annuity begin at a certain level and increase at a constant rate which is coincident with the interest conversions, the future amount can be determined by:

I. *Discrete Compounding of Interest*

$$S_n = p_0 \left[\frac{(1 + i)^n - (1 + g)^n}{i - g} \right] \qquad (3.1\text{-}18)$$

where g is a payment growth rate per period. If the annual payment growth rate is G%,

$$g = \frac{G}{f} \qquad (3.1\text{-}19)$$

and if g = i (G = R), Eq. (3.1.18) reduces to

$$S_n = np_0(1 + g)^{n-1} \qquad (3.1\text{-}20)$$

II. *Continuous Compounding of Interest*

$$S_t = p_0 \left[\frac{(1 + R_e)^t - (1 + G)^t}{R_e - G} \right] \qquad (3.1\text{-}21)$$

and if G = R_e

$$S_t = tp_0(1 + G)^{t-1} \qquad (3.1\text{-}22)$$

Example 9. You hire a 45-year-old individual at $30,000 per year. Your company pension plan requires you to pay the plan 5% of the employee's salary. Historically, your company has given salary increases of at least 6%, and it is assumed that future increases will be no less than 6%. Assuming that the pension fund can be invested at an interest rate of at least 10%, the least amount in the pension account of this employee at age 65 can be determined by Eq. (3.1-18) or (3.1-21).

Discrete Compounding. Assuming that annual payments are made into the pension fund and that interest is compounded annually:

$$p_0 = (30000)(0.05) = \$1,500$$

$$i = R/f = 10\%/1 = 10\% = 0.10$$

$$g = G/f = 6\%/1 = 6\% = 0.06$$

$$n = ft = (1)(20) = 20$$

From Eq. (3.1-18)

$$S_n = (1500) \left[\frac{(1 + 10\%)^{20} - (1 + 6\%)^{20}}{0.10 - 0.06} \right]$$

Using the calculator or Table A-2

$$S_n = (1500) \left[\frac{(6.7274999) - (3.2071355)}{0.04} \right]$$

$$= \$132,013.67$$

Continuous Compounding. Assuming that annual payments are made into the pension fund and that interest is compounded continuously:

$$p_o = (30000)(0.05) = \$1,500$$

$$R_e = e^{(365/360)(0.10)} - 1 = 0.1067$$

$$G = 0.06$$

$$t = 20$$

From Eq. (3.1-21)

$$S_t = (1500)\left[\frac{(1.1067)^{20} - (1.06)^{20}}{0.1067 - 0.06}\right]$$

$$= (1500)\left[\frac{7.5962317 - 3.2071355}{0.0467}\right]$$

$$= \$140,977.39$$

Example 10. Suppose that the interest rate of the pension fund of Example 9 is 6% compounded annually—the same as the salary increase rate. The future amount under this condition can be determined by Eq. (3.1-20). Using the calculator or Table A-2

$$S_n = (20)(1500)(1 + 6\%)^{19}$$

$$= (20)(1500)(3.0255995)$$

$$= \$90,767.99$$

Sinking Fund–Initial Payment for Payments Changing at Constant Rate

Rearrangement of Eqs. (3.1-18), (3.1-20), (3.1-21), and (3.1-22) to solve for p_o enables the determination of the initial payment into an annuity, where the periodic payments can be increased at a constant rate, in order to achieve a specified future amount.

I. *Discrete Compounding of Interest*

$$p_o = S_n\left[\frac{i - g}{(1 + i)^n - (1 + g)^n}\right] \tag{3.1-23}$$

and if $g = i$

$$p_o = \frac{S_n}{n(1 + g)^{n-1}} \tag{3.1-24}$$

II. *Continuous Compounding of Interest*

$$p_o = S_t\left[\frac{R_e - G}{(1 + R_e)^t - (1 + G)^t}\right] \tag{3.1-25}$$

and if $G = R_e$

$$p_o = \frac{S_t}{t(1 + G)^{t-1}} \tag{3.1-26}$$

Example 11. Recall the sinking fund of Example 5 for $1,000,000 of 20-year bonds. Suppose it is expected that the revenue from the utilization of the million dollars will increase with time, and greater contributions toward liquidation of the bonds can be made in the latter years. If the sinking fund can be expected to earn interest at 20% compounded annually and it is decided to increase annual payments to the fund by 10% per year, the initial payment can be determined by Eq. (3.1-23).

$$i = R/f = 20\%/1 = 20\% = 0.2$$

$$g = G/f = 10\%/1 = 10\% = 0.1$$

$$n = ft = (1)(20) = 20$$

$$p_o = (1000000)\left[\frac{0.2 - 0.1}{(1 + 20\%)^{20} - (1 + 10\%)^{20}}\right]$$

Using the calculator or Table A-2

$$p_o = (1000000)\left[\frac{0.1}{38.3376 - 6.7275}\right]$$

$$= \$3,163.55$$

Example 12. If the payments of Example 11 are increased 20% per year, the initial payment can be determined by Eq. (3.1-16)

$$p_o = \frac{1000000}{(20)(1 + 20\%)^{19}}$$

Using the calculator or Table A-2

$$p_o = \frac{1000000}{(20)(31.948)}$$

$$= \$1,565.04$$

Example 13. Refer to the trust fund of Example 6. Suppose you decide that you would like to begin payments at a relatively low level and increase the payments by 5% per year. In order to accumulate $150,000 in 18 years at 10% compounded continuously, the initial payment can be determined by Eq. (3.1-25)

$$R_e = e^{(365/360)(0.10)} - 1 = 0.1067$$

$$G = 0.05$$

From Eq. (3.1-25)

$$p_o = (150000)\left[\frac{0.1067 - 0.05}{(1.1067)^{18} - (1.05)^{18}}\right]$$

$$= (150000)\left[\frac{0.0567}{6.2020945 - 2.4066192}\right]$$

$$= \$2,240.83$$

Example 14.   If you decide that you will increase the annual payments in Example 13 by the same rate as the interest rate, Eq. (3.1-26) can be used to determine the initial payment.

$$p_o = \frac{150000}{(18)\,(1.1067)^{17}}$$

$$= \frac{150000}{(18)\,(5.6041335)}$$

$$= \$1,487.00$$

Changing Payments—Payment Level at a Given Payment Number

Before initiating a payment series where the payments begin at a relatively low level and periodically increase at a constant rate, it might be advisable to ascertain the payment level over the later years. For payments which increase at a constant rate, the payment level for a given payment number, m, can be determined by

$$p_m = p_o(1 + g)^{m-1} \qquad (3.1-27)$$

Example 15.   For Example 11, the payment for the 20th year will be

$$p_N = (3163.55)\,(1 + 10\%)^{19}$$

Using the calculator or Table A-2

$$p_N = (3163.55)\,(6.115909)$$

$$= \$19,347.98$$

For Example 12, the payment for the 20th year will be

$$p_N = (1565.04)\,(1 + 20\%)^{19}$$

Using the calculator or Table A-2

$$p_N = (1565.04)\,(31.948)$$

$$= \$50,000$$

For either of these alternatives, the payment level for the last year may be prohibitive, and the level payments of Example 5 ($5,356.50) may be chosen.

Payment Number—Payment Reaching a Specified Level

Given a payment series wherein it is desired to determine the payment number when the payment will reach a specified level, the laws of logarithms applied to Eq. (3.1-27) gives the payment number as

$$m = 1 + \frac{\log\,(p_m/p_o)}{\log\,(1 + g)} \qquad (3.1-28)$$

Example 16.   In Example 11 it is shown that a sinking fund for $1,000,000 could be started with a payment of $3,163.55 if the annual payment is increased by 10% per year and the fund earned interest at 20% compounded annually. In Example 15 it is shown that, for the conditions of Example 11, the 20th (and last) payment would be

$19,347.98. Suppose you would like to know when the payment level will reach $10,000. From Eq. (3.1-28)

$$m = 1 + \frac{\log(10000/3163.55)}{\log(1 + 10\%)}$$

$$= 1 + \frac{0.4998253}{0.0413927}$$

$$= 1 + 12.07$$

$$= 13 \text{ periods}$$

Thus, the payment for year 13 will be slightly less than $10,000 because of rounding 12.07 to 12. For the condition of Example 12 g = 20%, the number of payments necessary to reach a $10,000 payment is

$$m = 1 + \frac{\log(10000/1565.04)}{\log(1 + 20\%)}$$

$$= 1 + \frac{0.8054746}{0.0791812}$$

$$= 1 + 10.17$$

$$= 11 \text{ periods (years)}$$

Sinking Fund—Combination of Increasing and Level Payments

If it is advantageous, for a sinking fund, to begin periodic payments at a relatively low level, increase the level of payment at a constant rate until a specified amount is reached, and continue payments at a constant level, the following procedure may be used.

1. Determine the initial payment, p_o, from Eq. (3.1-23), (3.1-24), (3.1-25), or (3.1-26) as appropriate.
2. Determine the number, m, for the specified payment amount, p_m, from Eq. (3.1-28).
3. With $N = n - m$, Eqs. (3.1-7), (3.1-8), and (3.1-9) enable the determination of S_o at payment number m, after which the payment level becomes constant at p_N.
4. Solve Eq. (3.1-23), (3.1-24), (3.1-25), or (3.1-26) for p_o where S_n or S_t is replaced by S_o from step 3 and n is replaced by m.
5. If p_o from step 4 does not equal p_o from step 1, replace p_o in step 2 by that of step 4 and repeat steps 2, 3, and 4. Continue replacing p_o in step 2 by that of step 4 and repeating steps, 2, 3, and 4 until the value of m repeats. The preceding computation of p_o will be the starting level of payments.

Because a large number of iterations may be required, computer programs which perform the iterations are included in Chapter 6 as Program 6-1 for discrete compounding and Program 6-2 for continuous compounding (see pages 132–135).

Example 17. A 20-year sinking fund for $1,000,000 is established with the fund expected to earn interest at 20% compounded annually. It is desired to increase annual payments by 10% per year until a payment of $10,000 is reached after which the fund will be completed with level payments.

The computer solution for Example 17 is shown below.

```
THE MAXIMUM PAYMENT FOR THE LAST N YEARS IS        10000
THE GROWTH RATE FOR THE FIRST M YEARS IS           10  %
THE NOMINAL ANNUAL INTEREST RATE IS                20  %
THE COMPOUNDING FREQUENCY IS                       1
THE NUMBER OF PAYMENTS PER YEAR IS                 1
THE NUMBER OF YEARS TO ACHIEVE S IS                20
THE DESIRED FUTURE AMOUNT (S) IS                   1000000

FOR DISCRETE COMPOUNDING OF INTEREST

THE NUMBER OF ITERATIONS IS                        3
THE INITIAL ANNUAL AMOUNT IS $                     3359
THE GROWTH OF PO AT   10   % PER YEAR CEASES AT     12
THE VALUE IN THE ACCOUNT THEN IS $                 194080
THE NUMBER OF YEARS AT $   10000   PER YEAR IS      8
THE FUTURE AMOUNT AT THE END OF   20   YEARS IS $   999498
```

Total of Payments

The total of the payments contributed to an annuity can be determined as follows:

a)   Level Payments

$$T = np \tag{3.1-29}$$

Thus, the total of payments for the Individual Retirement Account of Example 1 is

$$T = (25)(1500) = \$37,500$$

and the total of payments for the bond sinking fund of Example 5 is

$$T = (20)(5356.50) = \$107,130$$

b)   Payments Increasing at a Uniform Rate

$$T = p_o \left[\frac{(1+g)^n - 1}{g} \right] \tag{3.1.30}$$

Thus, the total of payments in the employee's pension fund of Example 9 is

$$T = (1500) \left[\frac{(1+6\%)^{20} - 1}{6\%} \right]$$

$$= (1500)(S/p, 6\%, 20)$$

$$= (1500)(36.7855912) = \$55,178.39$$

and the total of payments for the bond sinking fund of Example 11 is

$$T = (3163.55) \left[\frac{(1+10\%)^{20} - 1}{10\%} \right]$$

$$= (3163.55)(S/p, 10\%, 20)$$

$$= (3163.55)(57.2749995) = \$181,192.32$$

c)   Combination of Increasing and Level Payments

$$T = p_o \left[\frac{(1 + g)^m - 1}{g} \right] + Np_N \tag{3.1-31}$$

Thus, the total contribution for the bond sinking fund of Example 17 is

$$T = (3359) \left[\frac{(1 + 10\%)^{12} - 1}{10\%} \right] + (8)(10000.00)$$

$$= (3359)(S/p,10\%,12) + 80000.00$$

$$= (3359)(21.384284) + 80000.00$$

$$= \$151,829.81$$

Note: A comparison of the total of payments for the bond sinking fund for Example 5 (a above) of \$107,130, for the bond sinking fund for Example 11 (b above) of \$181,192.32, and for the bond sinking fund for Example 17 (c above) of \$151,829.81 shows that level payments result in the lowest total of payments, and level payments should always be used unless mandated otherwise by policy or the economics of cash flow.

3.2   PRESENT VALUE AND AMORTIZATION

This section provides formulas for determining the amount of money needed one period before the beginning of a series of specified *equal* periodic payments or withdrawals and the amount of money needed one period before the beginning of a series of *periodic payments which increase (decrease) periodically at a constant rate.* This section also provides formulas for amortizing a present value by equal or uniformly increasing (decreasing) periodic payments.

The nomenclature, in addition to that of Section 3.1 is as follows

F—A specified fraction of the original present value of an annuity
V—Present value
V_n—Present value for a full term of n payments
V_m—Present value after m payments
V_N—Present value of N remaining payments
V_t—Present value for a full term of t years
N′—New Term after a change of interest rate and/or payment

Given a nominal annual interest rate compounded at discrete intervals, the periodic interest rate and total number of periods are, respectively, $i = R/f$ and $n = ft$ (see Eq. (2.1-1) and (2.2-1)). For continuous compounding $R_e = e^{kR} - 1$ (see Eq. (2.2-13)).

Present Value—Level Payments and Interest Rate

I.   *Discrete Compounding of Interest*

If level payments are made (or received) at the end of equally spaced periods and if interest conversion occurs at the same time as the payments, the present value of those payments can be determined by

$$V_n = p \left[\frac{1 - (1 + i)^{-n}}{i} \right] \tag{3.2-1}$$

The expression within the brackets of Eq. (3.2-1) is the present value of an annuity of $1 per period and may be denoted by symbolic terms for simplicity. Two such terms are $a_{\overline{n}|i}$ which is read as a sub n angle i and $(V/p,i,n)$ which is read as *V given p, i, and n.* Since the notation $(V/p,i,n)$ contains all the elements of Eq. (3.2-1) it will be used when the value can be determined from Table A-2. Thus,

$$V_n = p(V/p,i,n) \tag{3.2-2}$$

II.   *Continuous Compounding of Interest*

If payments occur annually and interest is compounded continuously, the present value of those payments can be determined by

$$V_t = p\left[\frac{1 - (1 + R_e)^{-t}}{R_e}\right] \tag{3.2-3}$$

Example 1.   During the first 15 years of retirement you would like to withdraw $1,000 per month from your IRA. If your account is earning 12% compounded monthly, the total amount that is required one month before the first withdrawal can be determined by Eqs. (3.2-1) or by using Table A-2 and Eq. (3.2-2). Since $R = 12\%$ compounded monthly, $i = R/f = 12\%/12 = 1\%$, and $n = ft = (12)(15) = 180$.

Discrete Compounding.
a)   The fifth column of Table A-2 is labeled, "Present Value of Annuity" and is the present value of $1 per period. Opposite 180 periods, under 1%, read the value of $(V/p,i,n)$ as 83.321664. From Eq. (3.2-2)

$$V_n = (1000)(83.321664)$$

$$= \$83,321.66$$

b)   Using the y^x function on the calculator and Eq. (3.2-1)

Enter 1.01	Depress y^x
Enter 180	Depress +/−
Display shows −180	
Depress =	Display shows 0.1667834 $= (1 + 1\%)^{-180}$
Depress −	Enter 1
Depress =	Depress +/−
Display shows	0.83332166 $= 1 - (1 + 1\%)^{-180}$
Depress ÷	Enter 0.01
Depress =	Display shows 83.321664
Depress ×	Enter 1000
Display shows 83321.66	

Thus, if a tax-sheltered account of $83,321.66 is earning interest at 12% compounded monthly, that account may be reduced at the rate of $1,000 per month for 180 months, and such an account will purchase a total of $180,000.

Continuous Compounding.
If withdrawal from this IRA were to occur each year, starting one year from now, at a level of $12,000 per year and if the interest rate is no less than 12% compounded continuously for the subsequent 15 years, the amount that is required one year before the first withdrawal can be determined as follows.

$$R_e = e^{(365/360)(0.12)} - 1 = 0.1294$$

From Eq. (3.2-3)

$$V_t = (12000) \left[\frac{1 - (1.1294)^{-15}}{0.1294} \right]$$

$$= (12000)(6.4824602)$$

$$= \$77,789.52$$

Number of Level Payments—Given a Present Value

The number of level payments available, given the present value of those payments, can be determined by applying the laws of logarithms to Eqs. (3.2-1) and (3.2-3)

I. *Discrete Compounding of Interest*

$$n = - \frac{\log (1 - V_n i/p)}{\log (1 + i)} \tag{3.2-4}$$

II. *Continuous Compounding of Interest*

$$t = - \frac{\log (1 - V_t R_e /p)}{\log (1 + R_e)} \tag{3.2-5}$$

Example 2.   Refer to the IRA of Example 1 in Section 3.1 wherein an accumulation of $200,000 is available. If that account earns no less than 12% and you decide to withdraw $30,000 annually during retirement, the number of years of the annuity can be determined by Eq. (3.2-4) or (3.2-5).

Discrete Compounding.   Since the withdrawals are to be $30,000 annually, it is assumed that the interest rate is 12% compounded annually. Then, $i = R/f = 12\%/1 = 12\%$. From Eq. (3.2-4)

$$n = - \frac{\log [1 - (200000)(0.12)/(30000)]}{\log (1 + 0.12)}$$

$$= - \frac{\log 0.2}{\log 1.12} = 14.2 \text{ periods (years)}$$

For an approximation of n, Eq. (3.2-2) can be rearranged to

$$(V/p,i,n) = \frac{V_n}{p} \tag{3.2-4a}$$

and Table A-2 can be used to determine the approximation of n.

$$(V/p,i,n) = \frac{200000}{30000} = 6.666667$$

In the 12% table of Table A-2, the value 6.666667, under the "Present Value of Annuity" occurs between $n = 14$, $(V/p,i,n) = 6.62816825$, and $n = 15$, $(V/p,i,n) = 6.81086449$.

Continuous Compounding. If the interest is compounded continuously,

$$R_e = e^{(365/360)\,(0.12)} - 1 = 0.1294$$

From Eq. (3.2-5)

$$t = -\frac{\log\,[1 - (200000)\,(0.1294)/(30000)]}{\log 1.1294}$$

$$= -\frac{\log 0.1373333}{\log 1.1294} = 16.3 \text{ years}$$

Present Value After m Level Payments

Given an annuity of level payments and a constant interest rate, the amount remaining in the account of the annuity can be determined by finding the present value of the remaining payments. In an annuity of n equal payments, the number of remaining payments after m payments are made (received) is

$$N = n - m \tag{3.2-6}$$

and Eq. (3.2-1), (3.2-2), or (3.2-3) may be used with N replacing n or t.

Example 3.   Suppose you were to die 10 years after the annuities of a) Example 1 and b) Example 2 begin. The amount remaining in each account can be determined by Eq. (3.2-6) in conjunction with Eq. (3.2-1), (3.2-2) or (3.2-3)

Discrete Compounding.
a)   For Example 1. After 10 years, the number of payments received will have been $(12)\,(10) = 120$. Then, $N = 180 - 120 = 60$. Using Table A-2 and Eq. (3.2-2) with $i = 1\%$ (12% compounded monthly)

$$V_N = (1000)\,(44.955038)$$

$$= \$44,955.04$$

b)   For Example 2. After 10 years, the number of payments received will have been $(1)\,(10) = 10$. Then, the number of payments remaining is $N = 14.2 - 10 = 4.2$. With $i = 12\%$ (12% compounded annually). From Eq. (3.2-1)

$$V_N = (30000)\left[\frac{1 - (1.12)^{-4.2}}{0.12}\right]$$

$$= (30000)\,(3.1560366)$$

$$= \$94,681.10$$

Continuous Compounding.
a)   For Example 1. Assuming withdrawals of $12,000 per year and an interest rate of 12% compounded continuously, Eq. (3.2-6) gives

$$N = 15 - 10 = 5 \text{ years remaining.}$$

With $R_e = 0.1294$ (12% compounded continuously) Eq. (3.2-3) gives

$$V_N = (12000) \left[\frac{1 - (1.1294)^{-5}}{0.1294} \right]$$

$$= (12000) (3.5223865)$$

$$= \$42,268.64$$

b)   For Example 2. The term for withdrawing \$30,000 per year with an interest rate of 12% compounded continuously is 16.3 years. From Eq. (3.2-6)

$$N = 16.3 - 10 = 6.3$$

From Eq. (3.2-3)

$$V_N = (30000) \left[\frac{1 - (1.1294)^{-6.3}}{0.1294} \right]$$

$$= (30000) (4.1377253)$$

$$= \$124,131.76$$

Payment Number, m, When V_N Equals a Specified Fraction of V_n

If it is desired to know the payment number when the present value of an amortization is a specified fraction, F, of the original amount:

     I.   *Discrete Compounding of Interest*

$$m = n + \frac{\log (1 - FV_n i/p)}{\log (1 + i)} \tag{3.2-7}$$

     II.   *Continuous Compounding of Interest*

$$m = t + \frac{\log (1 - FV_t R_e /p)}{\log (1 + R_e)} \tag{3.2-8}$$

Example 4.   An annuity is to begin in one month. The account is tax-sheltered at \$130,000. and is earning interest at 9%. If monthly payments are to be \$1,500 and if it is desired to know when the balance will be 40% of the original amount, the payment number can be determined as follows.

Discrete Compounding. Since monthly payments are indicated, it is assumed that the interest rate is 9% compounded monthly. Then $i = R/f = 9\%/12 = 3\%/4 = 0.0075$. The total number of payments can be determined by Eq. (3.2-4) as

$$n = - \frac{\log [1 - (130000) (0.0075)/(1500)]}{\log 1.0075}$$

$$= 140.5 \text{ months}$$

The number of months required, in order that the balance is 40% of the original amount, can be determined by Eq. (3.2-7) with $F = 0.4$

$$m = 140.5 + \frac{\log [1 - (0.4) (130000) (0.0075)/(1500)]}{\log 1.0075}$$

$$= 140.5 + \frac{\log 0.74}{\log 1.0075}$$

$$= 140.5 + \frac{-0.1307683}{0.0032451}$$

$$= 140.5 - 40.3$$

$$= 100 \text{ months} = 8 \text{ years and 4 months}$$

Therefore, after 100 payments, the present value of the annuity will be slightly greater than 40% of $130,000 ($52,000) if the interest rate remains constant at 9% compounded monthly.

Continuous Compounding. Assuming annual payments of $18,000, (12) (1500 per month) and an interest rate of 9% compounded continuously, the term of the annuity can be determined by Eq. (3.2-5) with

$$R_e = e^{(365/360) (0.09)} - 1 = 0.0955$$

$$t = -\frac{\log [1 - (130000) (0.0955)/(18000)]}{\log 1.0955}$$

$$= 12.83 \text{ years}$$

The number of years required, in order that the balance is 40% of the original amount, can be determined by Eq. (3.2-8) with $F = 0.4$.

$$m = 12.83 + \frac{\log [1 - (0.4) (130000) (0.0955)/(18000)]}{\log 1.0955}$$

$$= 12.83 + \frac{\log 0.724111}{\log 1.0955}$$

$$= 12.83 + \frac{-0.1401948}{0.0396124}$$

$$= 12.83 - 3.6$$

$$= 9.23$$

Therefore, after 9 years, the balance will be slightly greater than 40% of $130,000 ($52,000) if the interest rate remains constant at 9% compounded continuously.

Change in the Term Due to Change in Interest Rate and/or Payment

Given an annuity of periodic equal payments which are based on a specified term and interest rate, if the interest rate changes after m payments, the new term for the same periodic payments can be determined as follows:

I. *Discrete Compounding of Interest*

$$N' = -\frac{\log (1 - V_N i/p)}{\log (1 + i)} \tag{3.2-9}$$

II. *Continuous Compounding of Interest*

$$N' = -\frac{\log (1 - V_N R_e/p)}{\log (1 + R_e)} \tag{3.2-10}$$

V_N is determined by Eq. (3.2-1), (3.2-2), (3.2-3) in conjunction with Eq. (3.2-6)

Example 5. The monthly payment for a \$50,000 mortgage at 12% for 20 years (240 payments) is \$550.54 per month. After 5 years (the 60th payment) the interest rate is increased to 14%. In order to maintain the same monthly payments, the term would be increased as determined by Eq. (3.2-9). From Eq. (3.2-6), after the 60th payment at 12% interest, the number of payments remaining of the original term is

$$N = 240 - 60 = 180$$

From Eq. (3.2-1) or Table A-2 under 1% and opposite 180, the present value of the mortgage is

$$V_N = (550.54) (83.321664)$$

$$= \$45,871.91$$

From Eq. (3.2-9) with i = 14%/12 = 1 1/6% = 0.0116667

$$N = -\frac{\log [1 - (45871.91) (0.0116667)/(550.54)]}{\log 1.0116667}$$

$$= -\frac{\log 0.0279111}{\log 1.0116667}$$

$$= 308.5 \text{ payments after the change}$$

Thus, the term of the mortgage would be extended by 128.5 (308.5 – 180) payments or 128.5/12 = 10 years and 9 months unless a future reduction of the interest rate occurs.

Example 6. In the tax-sheltered annuity of Example 4, it is shown that \$130,000 will be liquidated in 12.83 years if the interest rate remains constant at 9% compounded continuously, and annual withdrawals are \$18,000. Suppose that after the 5th year, the interest rate is increased to 11% compounded continuously. The new term of \$18,000 per year withdrawals can be determined as follows. After the 5th withdrawal, the balance in the account would be (as determined by Eq. (3.2-3) in conjunction with Eq. (3.2-6)) \$96,202.40

$$R_e = e^{(365/360)(0.09)} - 1 = 0.0955$$

$$N = 12.83 - 5 = 7.83$$

From Eq. (3.2-3)

$$V_N = (18000) \left[\frac{1 - (1.0955)^{-7.83}}{0.0955}\right] = \$96,202.40$$

After the change in the interest rate to 11%

$$R_e = e^{(365/360)(0.11)} - 1 = 0.118$$

From Eq. (3.2-10)

$$N' = -\frac{\log\,[1 - (96202.4)\,(0.118)/(18000)]}{\log\,1.118}$$

$$= -\frac{\log\,0.3693398}{\log\,1.118}$$

$$= 8.93\ \text{years}$$

Thus, the increase in the interest rate will add one additional year to the withdrawals of $18,000.

Present Value—Payments Changing at a Constant Rate

If the periodic payments of an annuity increase at a constant rate with the increase in payment occurring at the interest conversion date, the present value of that annuity can be determined as follows:

I. *Discrete Compounding of Interest*

$$V_n = p_o \left\{ \frac{1 - \left[\dfrac{1+g}{1+i}\right]^n}{i - g} \right\} \tag{3.2-11}$$

and if $g = i$

$$V_n = \frac{np_o}{(1+i)} \tag{3.2-12}$$

II. *Continuous Compounding of Interest*

$$V_t = p_o \left\{ \frac{1 - \left[\dfrac{1+G}{1+R_e}\right]^t}{R_e - G} \right\} \tag{3.2-13}$$

and if $G = R_e$

$$V_t = \frac{tp_o}{1 + R_e} \tag{3.2-14}$$

Example 7. During the first 15 years of your retirement you would like to withdraw annually increased amounts from your IRA starting with $12,000 and increasing the annual withdrawal by 6% per year to help offset the effects of inflation. If the account is earning interest at 12%, the total amount that is required one year before the first withdrawal can be determined as follows:

Discrete Compounding. Since withdrawals are annual, it is assumed that the interest rate is 12% compounded annually. Then, $i = R/f = 12\%/1 = 12\%$. For annual increases, $g = G/1 = 6\%/1 = 6\%$, and $n = ft = (1)\,(15) = 15$. From Eq. (3.2-11),

$$V_n = (12000) \left\{ \frac{1 - \left[\frac{1.06}{1.12} \right]^{15}}{0.12 - 0.06} \right\}$$

$$= (12000) \left[\frac{1 - 0.4378422}{0.06} \right]$$

$$= \$112,431.55$$

Comparing this present value with that of Example 1 shows that the present value of this annuity must be $29,110 greater than that of Example 1. However, the total amount that would be received by the 180 level payments of Example 1 is $180,000, and the total amount that would be received by this uniformly increasing annuity is determined by Eq. (3.1-30) as

$$T = (12000) \left[\frac{(1 + 6\%)^{15} - 1}{6\%} \right]$$

Using the calculator or Table A-2

$$T = (12000) \ (23.2759699)$$

$$= \$279,311.64$$

Thus, the additional $29,110 "up front" purchases an additional $99,312 (279312 – 180000) over the term of the annuity. The amount of the annuity in any year can be determined by Eq. (3.1-27). For the 15th year, this amount would be

$$P_{15} = (12000) \ (1 + 6\%)^{14}$$

Using the calculator or Table A-2

$$P_{15} = (12000) \ (2.260904) = \$27,130.85$$

If the interest rate remains constant at 12% compounded annually, the depletion of the IRA would tabulate as follows.*

Year	Withdrawal	Balance	Year	Withdrawal	Balance
0		$112,431.55	8	$18,043.56	$101,953.38
1	$12,000.00	113,923.34	9	19,126.18	95,061.60
2	12,720.00	114,874.14	10	20,273.75	86,195.24
3	13,483.20	115,175.84	11	21,490.17	75,048.50
4	14,292.19	114,704.75	12	22,779.58	61,274.74
5	15,149.72	113,319.60	13	24,146.36	44,481.35
6	16,058.71	110,859.24	14	25,595.14	24,223.98
7	17,022.23	107,140.12	15	27,130.85	0

*The balance for a given year = (1 + i) times the balance of the previous year less the withdrawal.

In the event that it is desired that the annual increase of the withdrawal of this example be equal to the interest rate of 12%, the total amount required one year before the annuity begins can be determined by Eq. (3.2-12).

$$V_n = \frac{(15)(12000)}{1.12} = \$160,714.29$$

The total amount of the payments in this case would be

$$T = (12000)\left[\frac{(1 + 12\%)^{15} - 1}{12\%}\right]$$

$$= (12000)(37.2797147)$$

$$= \$447,356.58$$

Continuous Compounding. For continuous compounding of interest,

$$R_e = e^{(365/360)(0.12)} - 1 = 0.1294$$

$$G = 6\% = 0.06$$

From Eq. (3.2-13)

$$V_t = (12000)\left\{\frac{1 - \left[\frac{1.06}{1.1294}\right]^{15}}{0.1294 - 0.06}\right\}$$

$$= (12000)\left[\frac{1 - 0.3862524}{0.0694}\right]$$

$$= \$106,123.50$$

Thus, if the account earns 12% compounded continuously, an annuity starting at \$12,000 and increasing 6% per year can be sustained for 15 years.

Amortization—Level Payments and Interest Rate

I. *Discrete Compounding of Interest*

Given that an account is to be amortized by a series of equally spaced level payments over a fixed term, the periodic, level payment can be determined by rearranging Eq. (3.2-1)

$$p = V_n\left[\frac{i}{1 - (1 + i)^{-n}}\right] \tag{3.2-15}$$

The expression within the brackets is the periodic payment that will amortize an account of \$1 and can be denoted as $1/a_{\overline{n}|i}$ or $(p/V,i,n)$. Values of $(p/V,i,n)$ can be found in Table A-2 under the column headed, "Amortization." Thus, when Table A-2 is to be used,

$$p = V_n(p/V,i,n) \tag{3.2-16}$$

II. *Continuous Compounding of Interest*

If an account, which is to be amortized over a fixed term is earning continuously compounded interest, the annual payment can be determined by

$$p = V_t \left[\frac{R_e}{1 - (1 + R_e)^{-t}} \right] \qquad (3.2\text{-}17)$$

Example 8. A \$50,000 loan is to be liquidated by a series of level monthly payments over a period of 20 years. If the interest rate remains constant at 12% compounded monthly, the monthly payment can be determined as follows. Since R = 12% compounded monthly, $i = R/f = 12\%/12 = 1\%$ and $n = ft = (12)(20) = 240$.

a) Using Table A-2. In the table for 1%, under the "Amortization" column, and opposite n = 240, read the value of $(p/V,i,n)$. Then

$$p = (50000)(0.01101086)$$

$$= \$550.54 \text{ per month}$$

b) Using Eq. (3.2-15). In order to avoid the use of parentheses, the denominator of the expression is determined first. This value is divided by the numerator, i, and the reciprocal is determined

Enter 1.01	Depress y^x
Enter 240	Depress +/−
Display shows −240	
Depress =	Display shows $0.0918058 = (1 + i)^{-n}$
Depress −	Enter 1
Depress =	Display shows $-0.9081942 = -(1 - (1 + i)^{-n})$
Depress +/−	Depress ÷
Enter 0.01	Depress =
Display shows 90.819416	$\qquad = (1 - (1 + i)^{-n})/i$
Depress 1/x	Display shows $0.0110109 = i/(1 - (1 + i)^{-n})$
Depress ×	Enter 50000
Depress =	Display shows 550.54307

Example 9. One year before you retire, your IRA contains \$150,000 and earns interest at 12% compounded continuously. Annual withdrawals for 15 years can be determined by Eq. (3.2-17).

$$R_e = e^{(365/360)(0.12)} - 1 = 0.1294$$

$$p = (150000) \left[\frac{0.1294}{1 - (1.1294)^{-15}} \right]$$

$$= (150000)(0.1542624)$$

$$= \$23,139.36 \text{ per year for 15 years.}$$

Amortization—Total Interest over Term

If an account is depleted by level payments at a constant interest rate over the entire term of the amortization, the total interest can be determined by

$$I = np - V_n \qquad (3.2\text{-}18)$$

Example 10. The total interest on the mortgage of Example 8, as determined by Eq. (3.2-18), is

$$I = (240) (550.54) - 50000$$

$$= \$82,129.60$$

and the total interest on the annuity of Example 9 is

$$I = (15) (23139.36) - 150000$$

$$= \$197,090.40$$

Amortization—Initial Payment for Payments Changing at a Constant Rate

I. *Discrete Compounding of Interest*

Given that an account is to be amortized over a fixed term at a constant interest rate: If the periodic payments of an annuity increase at a constant rate with the increase occurring at the interest conversion date, the initial payment of such an annuity can be determined by rearranging Eqs. (3.2-11) and (3.2-12).

$$p_0 = V_n \left\{ \frac{i - g}{1 - \left[\dfrac{1 + g}{1 + i} \right]^n} \right\} \tag{3.2-19}$$

and if $g = i$

$$p_0 = \frac{V_n(1 + i)}{n} \tag{3.2-20}$$

II. *Continuous Compounding of Interest*

If periodic payments are annual, and they are increased G% annually, the initial payment for continuously compounded interest can be determined by rearranging Eqs. (3.2-13) and (3.2-14).

$$p_0 = V_t \left\{ \frac{R_e - G}{1 - \left[\dfrac{1 + G}{1 + R_e} \right]^t} \right\} \tag{3.2-21}$$

and if $G = R_e$

$$p_0 = \frac{V_t(1 + R_e)}{t} \tag{3.2-22}$$

Example 11. You own an IRA of $150,000 at age 59 and plan to make 15 annual withdrawals beginning at age 60. In order to compensate, to some extent, for the effects of inflation, you plan to increase the annual withdrawal by 5% each year. Assuming the account will not earn less than 12%, the initial withdrawal can be determined as follows.

Discrete Compounding. For annual compounding, $i = R/f = 12\%/1 = 12\%$; for annual increases, $g = G/1 = 5\%/1 = 5\%$; and $n = ft = (1) (15) = 15$. From Eq. (3.2-19)

$$p_0 = (150000) \left\{ \frac{0.12 - 0.05}{1 - \left[\frac{1.05}{1.12}\right]^{15}} \right\}$$

$$= (150000) \left[\frac{0.07}{0.620188} \right]$$

$$= \$16{,}930.36$$

A tabulation of this annuity is as follows.

Payment No.	Age	Withdrawal	Balance
0	59		$150,000.00
1	60	$16,930.36	151,069.64
2	61	17,776.88	151,421.12
3	62	18,665.72	150,925.93
4	63	19,599.01	149,438.03
5	64	20,578.96	146,791.64
6	65	21,607.91	142,798.72
7	66	22,688.30	137,246.27
8	67	23,822.72	129,893.10
9	68	25,013.85	120,466.42
10	69	26,264.55	108,657.84
11	70	27,577.77	94,119.02
12	71	28,956.66	76,456.64
13	72	30,404.49	55,226.95
14	73	31,924.72	29,929.46
15	74	33,520.96	0

The total amount of the withdrawals can be determined by adding the withdrawals or by Eq. (3.1-30).

$$T = (16930.36) \left[\frac{(1 + 5\%)^{15} - 1}{5\%} \right] = \$365{,}332.85$$

Had you decided to annually withdraw equal amounts, the level withdrawals could have been determined by Eq. (3.2-16) as

$$p = (150000) \, (p/V, i, n)$$

$$= (150000) \, (0.14682424)$$

$$= \$22{,}023.63$$

The total amount of these level withdrawals would be np or

$$T = (15) \, (22023.63)$$

$$= \$330{,}354.45$$

Therefore, if up to approximately $5,000 per year is not needed during the "early years of retirement," and if you can reasonably expect to survive to age 74, the uniformly increasing withdrawals result in approximately $35,000 of additional income from the $150,000 account.

The number of withdrawals that are required in order that the amount of the withdrawal would be equal to the amount of level withdrawals can be determined by Eq. (3.1-28)

$$m = 1 + \frac{\log (22023.63/16930.36)}{\log (1.05)}$$

$$= 1 + 5.39 = 6.39$$

Therefore, the withdrawal for the 7th year, and each year thereafter, will be larger than $22,023 (see the withdrawal for age 66 in the tabulation above).

If the interest rate changes during the term of the annuity, Eq. (3.2-19) can be re-solved for a "new" p_o using the balance as the present value for the remaining number of years.

Continuous Compounding.   If this IRA is earning interest at 12% compounded continuously, Eq. (3.2-21) would be used to determine the initial withdrawal.

$$R_e = e^{(365/360)(0.12)} - 1 = 0.1294$$

$$p_o = (150000) \left\{ \frac{0.1294 - 0.05}{1 - \left[\dfrac{1.05}{1.1294} \right]^{15}} \right\}$$

$$= (150000)(0.1194093)$$

$$= \$17,911.39$$

The total amount of the withdrawals can be determined by Eq. (3.1-30) as

$$T = (17911.39) \left[\frac{(1.05)^{15} - 1}{0.05} \right] = \$386,502.07$$

CHAPTER 4

Formulas and Tables for Annuities
When Payments Occur at the Beginnings
of Interest Conversion Periods

The formulas in Chapter 3 provide answers to financial planning problems if the analyses are based on a concept that the first and all subsequent payments will occur at the ends of interest conversion periods. However, in many financial planning situations the "answers" are needed for payments which begin "today" with all subsequent payments being made at the beginnings of interest conversion periods. The summation processes for future amounts and present values at both discrete and continuous compounding of interest are the same as discussed at the beginning of Chapter 3 (page 39). With either level payments or payments which increase or decrease at uniform rates and with equally spaced payments coinciding with interest conversion dates, those summation processes reduce to relatively simple formulas which can be extremely helpful as financial planning devices. This chapter provides such formulas.

In order to be able to provide a single formula for both discrete and continuous compounding of interest, the symbol notation for interest rates is unified in this chapter (see the Technical Concepts for Easy Reading (page x) for the rationale which leads to this unification). The single notation, i^*, is used as a general interest rate. For discrete compounding

$$i^* = i = R/f$$

and for continuous compounding,

$$i^* = R_e = e^{kR} - 1$$

Within the text are one or more examples which indicate the use of each formula. The examples address a specific type of monetary problem, but the concepts which are treated are general. The examples include:

1. Determining the amount of money that will be available one interest conversion period after the last payment of a series of level or uniformly increasing payments which begin "today," such as for Individual Retirement Accounts, Keogh Plans, or pension contributions in general, for level and changing interest rates. Pages 72, 74, 78

69

2. Determining the number of payments, beginning "today," that will be required in order to achieve a specified future amount, one interest conversion period after last payment, for level and changing interest rates. Pages 73, 75

3. Determining the required level periodic payment, beginning "today," to a sinking fund for level and changing interest rates and determining the initial payment, to a sinking fund "today," for payments which are to increase at a constant rate, such as for trust funds and bond redemption. A procedure for a combination of level and increasing payments is also shown. Pages 76, 79, 82

4. Determining the effect of payments which increase at a constant rate, such as the magnitude at a given payment number and the total of such payments. Pages 80, 81

5. Determining the amount of money required (the present value) "today" in order to receive or disburse, beginning "today," a specified level periodic payment or a specified initial payment, for payments which are to increase at a constant rate, such as for the liquidation of a pension account or trust with a specified number of payments. Pages 84, 89

6. Determining the level periodic payment, beginning "today," and the initial payment "today," for payments which are to increase at a constant rate, for the amortization of a debt, such as a mortgage, or the liquidation of a personal account given the present value. If the interest rate changes at a given present value, a new periodic payment, beginning "today" can be determined for the remaining term. Pages 91, 92

7. Determining the present value of an amortization of level payments on the date a given payment number is due and determining the new term of an amortization where the interest rate changes but the payment level remains constant. Pages 85, 86, 88

8. Determining the payment number when the present value of an amortization is some specified fraction of the original amount, such as for the reduction of an account to a level which can be used to fund an estate trust free of estate taxes. Page 87

If you perform the calculations in the examples, your results may differ from the indicated results, depending upon the number of decimal places you carry at each step of the solutions. For example, if 12% compounded continuously is rounded to 0.1294 (12.94% effective annual rate) the results will be different than if it is used in calculations as 0.1293776 (the limit on the TI-50).

4.1   FUTURE AMOUNT AND SINKING FUND PAYMENTS

This section provides formulas for determining the future amount of a series of *equal* periodic payments and the future amount of a series of *periodic payments which increase (decrease) periodically at a constant rate.* This section also provides formulas for the determination of the *equal* periodic payments necessary to achieve a specified future amount and the *initial payment for a series of payments which increase (decrease) at a constant rate.* Also, a procedure for a combination of a series of uniformly increasing (decreasing) periodic payments in conjunction with a series of equal periodic payments is provided.

Simple annuities due are defined as annuities where the payment dates coincide with interest conversion dates (simple), the payments occur at the beginning of periods, and the annuity terminates one period after the last payment. It should be noted that n payments are made over n – 1 periods, and that the number of years between two points in time can be determined by

$$t = t_n - t_m + 1 \tag{4.1-1}$$

where t_n represents the end of year n, and t_m represents the beginning of year m.

The nomenclature for simple annuities due is as follows:

e—Base of the natural logarithms.

f—The compounding frequency, which is the number of times each year that interest is computed and added to principal.

g—The periodic rate by which a periodic payment is increased (decreased).

G—The annual rate by which an annual payment is increased (decreased).

i—The periodic interest rate—a simple interest rate during a compounding period.

g^*—A general periodic rate by which a periodic payment is increased (decreased). It is used in order to enable the use of a single equation to represent discrete and continuous compounding of interest.

i^*—A general periodic interest rate. It is used in order to enable the use of a single equation to represent discrete and continuous compounding of interest.

k—Conversion of ordinary year to exact year = 365/360.

n—Total number of payments or interest conversions.

N—Number of payments (interest conversions) remaining in the annuity.

p—Equal periodic payment.

p_o—Initial payment of a uniformly increasing (decreasing) series of payments.

p_m—The m-th payment of a uniformly increasing (decreasing) series of payments.

R—Nominal annual interest rate.

R_e—Effective annual interest rate.

S_n—The future amount of an annuity after n payments.

S_d—The future amount of an annuity due.

S_o—The basis amount when there is a change in the level of equal payments and/or the interest rate.

t—Time expressed as a number of years.

T—Total of payments.

Given a nominal annual interest rate, R:

    I.   *If the interest is compounded discretely;*

$$i^* = i = R/f \tag{4.1-2}$$

$$n = ft \tag{4.1-3}$$

    II.   *If the interest is compounded continuously;*

$$i^* = R_e = e^{kR} - 1 \tag{4.1-4}$$

In general,

$$S_d = (1 + i^*) S_n \tag{4.1-5}$$

where S_n is the future amount of a simple ordinary annuity. For comparison purposes, all examples in this section relate to the corresponding examples of Section 3.1 unless otherwise noted.

Future Amount—Level Payments and Interest Rate

If level payments are made at the beginning of equally spaced periods, and if interest conversion occurs at the same time as the payments, the future amount of those payments, one period after the last payment, can be determined by

$$S_d = p(1 + i^*) \left[\frac{(1 + i^*)^n - 1}{i^*} \right] \qquad (4.1\text{-}6)$$

For the use of Table A-2, Eq. (4.1-6) becomes

$$S_d = p(1 + i) (S/p,i,n) \qquad (4.1\text{-}7)$$

Example 1. Your are advising a client to make annual deposits of $1,500 into an Individual Retirement Account beginning "today." You inform your client that the interest rate in the future probably will not be less than 12%. For informational purposes, you would like to inform the client what the future amount will be if 25 annual payments are made and the total is allowed to earn interest for one additional year. Assuming that the annual interest rate does not fall below 12%, the minimum future amount, one year after the last deposit can be determined by Eq. (4.1-6) or Eq. (4.1-7) in conjunction with Table A-2.

Discrete Compounding. Since deposits are to be made annually, it is assumed that the interest is compounded annually. Then, $i^* = i = R/f = 12\%/1 = 12\%$, and $n = ft = (1)(25) = 25$.

a)   Equation (4.1-6) and the y^x function on the calculator

$$S_d = (1500)(1.12) \left[\frac{(1.12)^{25} - 1}{0.12} \right] = \$224,000.90$$

Enter 1.12	Depress y^x
Enter 25	Depress =
Display shows 17.000064	
Depress –	Enter 1 Depress =
Display shows 16.000064	
Depress ÷	Enter 0.12 Depress =
Display shows 133.33387	
Depress ×	Enter 1.12
Depress ×	Display shows 149.33393
Enter 1500	Depress =
Display shows 224000.9	

b)   Equation (4.1-7) and Table A-2. In the 12% table, opposite 25 periods, in the column labeled "Amount of Annuity," read 133.3338701. From Eq. (4.1-7)

$$S_d = (1500)(1.12)(133.3338701) = \$224,000.90$$

Continuous Compounding. In order to use Eq. (4.1-6) for continuously compounded interest,

$$i^* = R_e = e^{kR} - 1 = e^{(365/360)(0.12)} - 1 = 0.1294$$

Then,

$$S_d = (1500)(1.1294)\left[\frac{(1.1294)^{25} - 1}{0.1294}\right] = \$261,191.33$$

Thus, you can inform your client that if a deposit of $1,500 is made today and annually, the total amount in the account 25 years from today will be at least $224,000 or $261,191, depending upon the method of compounding interest, if interest rates remain at 12% or greater.

Number of Level Payments—Specified Future Amount

The number of level payments needed in order to achieve a specified future amount can be determined by applying the laws of logarithms to Eq. (4.1-6).

$$n = \frac{\log\{[S_d i^*/p(1 + i^*)] + 1\}}{\log(1 + i^*)} \tag{4.1-8}$$

and Eq. (4.1-7) can be rearranged to

$$(S/p,i,n) = \frac{S_d}{p(1 + i)} \tag{4.1-9}$$

Example 2. Your client in Example 1 desires to have a "nest egg" of at least $300,000 in the IRA when he retires at age 65. If he is now 35 years of age and if it is reasonable to assume that a $1,500 per year deposit, beginning "today," is assured, will the goal of $300,000 be attainable?

Discrete Compounding. Since deposits are to be made annually, it is assumed that the interest is compounded annually. Then, $i^* = i = R/f = 12\%/1 = 12\%$.

a) Equation (4.1-8)

$$n = \frac{\log\{[(300000)(0.12)/(1500)(1.12)] + 1\}}{\log 1.12}$$

$$= \frac{\log 22.428571}{\log 1.12} = 27.45 \text{ payments}$$

Since each period is one year, it will require 28 annual payments followed by one year of growth for a total of 28 years. The client will then be 63 years of age, and the goal is attainable.

b) Equation (4.1-9) and Table A-2.

$$(S/p,i,n) = \frac{300000}{(1500)(1.12)} = 178.57143$$

Searching the "Amount of Annuity" column in the 12% table of Table A-2, 178.57143 is between the values 169.374006 and 190.69888739 which occur at 27 and 28 periods, respectively.

Continuous Compounding. In order to use Eq. (4.1-8) for continuously compounded interest,

$$i^* = R_e = e^{(365/360)(0.12)} - 1 = 0.1294$$

Then,

$$n = \frac{\log\{[(300000)(0.1294)/(1500)(1.1294)] + 1\}}{\log 1.1294}$$

$$= \frac{\log 23.914822}{\log 1.1294} = 25.736 \text{ payments}$$

Due to continuous compounding, the goal of \$300,000 would be achieved in a shorter period of time.

Future Amount—Change in Payment Level and/or Interest Rate

The future amount of an annuity due, with level payments, wherein the level of payments and/or interest rate changes at a point of time into the annuity, can be determined by

$$S_d = S_o(1 + i^*)^N + p_N(1 + i^*)\left[\frac{(1 + i^*)^N - 1}{i^*}\right] \tag{4.1-10}$$

For use of Table A-2

$$S_d = S_o(1 + i)^N + p_N(1 + i)(S/p,i,n) \tag{4.1-11}$$

S_o is the future amount of the payments at the point in time when the first payment at the change of payment and/or interest rate is due.

Example 3.   The accumulated benefits in a pension fund of an individual total \$13,000. Contributions had been made at a level of \$100 per month, and the fund had been invested at an interest rate of 7% compounded monthly. The future amount at the end of the next 15 years can be determined by Eq. (4.1-10) or (4.1-11) if the interest rate increases to 8% compounded monthly and the payment increases to \$150 per month (this relates to Example 3c of Section 3.1). Assume that the new interest rate and new payment level begin "today."

Discrete Compounding.   For monthly compounding, $i^* = i = R/f = 8\%/12 = 2/3\%$. Since the future amount at the end of the next 15 years is desired, from Eq. (4.1-1),

$$n = (12)(15 - 1 + 1) = 180$$

$$S_d = (13000)(1 + 2/3\%)^{180} + (150)(1 + 2/3\%)\left[\frac{(1 + 2/3\%)^{180} - 1}{2/3\%}\right]$$

Using the y^x function on the calculator and Eq. (4.1-10) or Table A-2 and Eq. (4.1-11)

$$S_d = (13000)(3.3069217) + (150)(1.0066667)(346.0382216)$$

$$= \$95,241.76$$

Continuous Compounding.   When continuous compounding of interest is in effect, the statement of this example becomes a complex annuity. Complex annuities are discussed in Chapter 6. However, if a deposit of \$1,800 per year is made, beginning "today" when the basis of the annuity is \$13,000, and the account is earning 8% compounded continuously, the number of periods to the end of year 15 is

$$n = 15 - 1 + 1 = 15$$

$$i^* = R_e = e^{(365/360)(0.08)} - 1 = 0.0845$$

and

$$S_d = (13000)(1.0845)^{15} + (1800)(1.0845)\left[\frac{(1.0845)^{15} - 1}{0.0845}\right]$$

$$= (13000)(3.376318) + (1800)(1.0845)(28.122107)$$

$$= \$98,789.30$$

Number of Level Payments After a Change—Specified Future Amount

If a change occurs in the payment level and/or interest rate, the number of payments, beginning on the date when the change occurs, at a new level payment and/or interest rate, can be determined by applying the laws of logarithms to Eq. (4.1-10).

$$N = \frac{\log\left[\dfrac{S_d i^* + p_N(1 + i^*)}{S_o i^* + p_N(1 + i^*)}\right]}{\log(1 + i^*)} \tag{4.1-12}$$

Example 4. An individual has an account with an accumulation of \$13,000. Annual deposits of \$1,800 are to be made, and it is desired to have a total accumulation of at least \$150,000. It is assumed that the account will earn interest at 10% throughout the term of deposits. If the \$13,000 is as of "today," and the first deposit is to be made "today," the number of future payments is desired.

Discrete Compounding. Since annual deposits are to be made, it is assumed that annual compounding is in effect. Then, $i^* = i = R/f = 10\%/1 = 10\%$. From Eq. (4.1-12)

$$N = \frac{\log\left[\dfrac{(150000)(0.10) + (1800)(1.1)}{(13000)(0.10) + (1800)(1.1)}\right]}{\log 1.10}$$

$$= \frac{\log 5.1768293}{\log 1.1} = 17.25 \text{ payments}$$

Therefore, it will require 17 payments, beginning "today," plus 1/4 of a payment (\$450) at the beginning of year 18 in order to have approximately \$150,000 at the end of 3 months of year 18.

Continuous Compounding. For 10% compounded continuously,

$$i^* = R_e = e^{(365/360)(0.10)} - 1 = 0.1067$$

$$N = \frac{\log\left[\dfrac{(150000)(0.1067) + (1800)(1.1067)}{(13000)(0.1067) + (1800)(1.1067)}\right]}{\log 1.1067}$$

$$= \frac{\log 5.3258976}{\log 1.1067} = 16.5 \text{ payments}$$

Due to continuous compounding, 16 annual payments, beginning "today" plus 1/2 of a payment ($900) at the beginning of year 17 in order to have approximately $150,000 at the end of 6 months of year 17, are necessary.

Sinking Fund—Level Payments and Interest Rate

When it is desired to achieve a specified future amount in a specified period of time, the necessary level payment, beginning "today" and terminating one period before the expiration of the time requirement, can be determined by rearranging Eqs. (4.1-6) and (4.1-7) to

$$p = \frac{S_d}{(1 + i^*)} \left[\frac{i^*}{(1 + i^*)^n - 1} \right] \tag{4.1-13}$$

For use of Table A-2

$$p = \frac{S_d(p/S,i,n)}{(1 + i)} \tag{4.1-14}$$

Example 5. Your corporation sells $1,000,000 of 20-year bonds at face value and establishes a sinking fund for the redemption of the bonds. You estimate that the payments into the fund will earn interest at 20% compounded annually over the 20-year period. If the first payment is made "today" and the last payment is to be made one year before the maturity date of the bonds, the amount of the annual payment can be determined by Eq. (4.1-13) or Eq. (4.1-14) and Table A-2. Since the interest is compounded annually, $i^* = i = R/f = 20\%/1 = 20\%$ and $n = 20 - 1 + 1 = 20$.

$$p = \frac{1000000}{1.20} (0.0053565) = \$4,463.75 \text{ per year.}$$

Example 6. You establish trusts for the college education of your children. You would like an accumulation of at least $150,000 in 18 years. Depositing the first payment into the trust "today," and making the final deposit at the beginning of the 18th year, if the trusts earn interest at no less than 10% compounded continuously, the total annual payments can be determined by Eq. (4.1-13). For continuously compounded interest, and $n = 18 - 1 + 1 = 18$,

$$i^* = R_e = e^{(365/360)(0.10)} - 1 = 0.1067$$

$$p = \frac{(150000)}{(1.1067)} \left[\frac{0.1067}{(1.1067)^{18} - 1} \right] = \$2,780.02 \text{ per year}$$

New Level Payments—Change in Sinking Fund and/or Interest Rate

After a series of payments have been made into a sinking fund, if the specified future amount of that fund and/or the interest rate at which the fund is invested changes, the new level payments can be determined by rearranging Eqs. (4.1-10) and (4.1-11) to

$$p_N = \left[\frac{S_d - S_o(1 + i^*)^N}{(1 + i^*)} \right] \left[\frac{i^*}{(1 + i^*)^N - 1} \right] \tag{4.1-15}$$

For use of Table A-2

$$p_N = \left[\frac{S_d - S_o(1 + i)^N}{(1 + i)} \right] (p/S,i,N) \qquad (4.1\text{-}16)$$

Example 7.   Suppose that 5 years have elapsed since the $1,000,000 of bonds of Example 5 were issued, and that the growth rate of the sinking fund has been 20% compounded annually. You now estimate that the fund investments can earn 22% compounded annually. The new level payments can be determined as follows. Since 5 years have elapsed, you are at the beginning of year 6. Your records should indicate an accumulation of $39,860.93. (This follows from the use of Eq. (4.1-6) or (4.1-7) with p = 4463.75 from Example 5, and since the new interest rate is beginning with year 6, the number of payments at the old rate is 5). From the beginning of year 6 to the end of year 20, there are 20 - 6 + 1 = 15 payments as determined by Eq. (4.1-1). From Eq. (4.1-15) or (4.1-16) with i* = 22%

$$p_N = \left[\frac{1000000 - (39860.93)(1 + 22\%)^{15}}{1.22} \right] (p/S,22\%,15)$$

$$= \left[\frac{1000000 - (39860.93)(19.742287)}{1.22} \right] (0.01173816)$$

$$= \$2,049.88$$

If the sinking fund earns 20% from the beginning of year 1 to the end of year 5 (5 years) and 22% from the beginning of year 6 to the end of year 20 (15 years), 5 payments of $4,463.75 and 15 payments of $2,049.88 will accrue to $1,000,000. By making a payment of $4,463.75 on the bond issue date, significant differences in annual payments occur when compared to a one year delay in making the first payment (see Examples 5 and 7 of Section 3.1). The tabulation of payments and fund balance is shown below.

Beginning of Year	Payment	Interest Rate	Accumulation
1	$4,463.75	20%	$ 4,463.75
2	4,463.75	20%	9,820.25
3	4,463.75	20%	16,248.05
4	4,463.75	20%	23,961.41
5	4,463.75	20%	33,217.44
End of 5 = S_o		20%	39,860.93
6	2,049.88		41,910.81
7	2,049.88	22%	53,181.07
8	2,049.88	22%	66,930.78
9	2,049.88	22%	83,705.44
10	2,049.88	22%	104,170.51
11	2,049.88	22%	129,137.90
12	2,049.88	22%	159,598.12
13	2,049.88	22%	196,759.40
14	2,049.88	22%	242,096.58
15	2,049.88	22%	297,407.71

Beginning of Year	Payment	Interest Rate	Accumulation
16	$2,049.88	22%	$364,887.28
17	2,049.88	22%	447,212.36
18	2,049.88	22%	547,648.96
19	2,049.88	22%	670,181.62
20	2,049.88	22%	819,671.45
End of 20 = S_d		22%	999,999.17

The Accumulation for a given year is $(1 + i)$ times the Accumulation of the previous year plus the payment for the given year. The 83-cent discrepancy at the end of year 20 is due to rounding of decimals to the second decimal place.

Example 8. On the date you are going to make the 11th payment into the trust accounts of Example 6, the interest rate has been increased from 10% to 12% compounded continuously. In order for the trusts to accumulate to $150,000 by the end of the 18th year, the 11th and remaining payments can be determined as follows. The end of the 18th year indicates that the last payment is to be made at the beginning of the 18th year. From Eq. (4.1-1), $n = 18 - 11 + 1 = 8$ payments remain. For 12% compounded continuously,

$$i^* = R_e = e^{(365/360)(0.12)} - 1 = 0.1294$$

Your records should indicate that at the beginning of the 11th year the accounts have accumulated $50,637.14. (This follows from Eq. (4.1-6) with $i^* = 0.1067$, $p = 2780.02$ (from Example 6), and $n = 10$.) From Eq. (4.1-15),

$$p_N = \left[\frac{150000 - (50637.14)(1.1294)^8}{1.1294} \right] \left[\frac{0.1294}{(1.1294)^8 - 1} \right]$$

$$= \$1,109.78 \text{ per year for the remaining 8 years.}$$

Future Amount—Payments Changing at a Constant Rate

If payments to an annuity begin "today" at a certain level and increase at a constant rate which is coincident with the interest conversions, the future amount can be determined by

$$S_d = p_o(1 + i^*) \left[\frac{(1 + i^*)^n - (1 + g^*)^n}{i^* - g^*} \right] \tag{4.1-17}$$

and if $g^* = i^*$

$$S_d = np_o(1 + i^*)^n \tag{4.1-18}$$

Example 9. Recall Example 1 of this section wherein you advise your client to make $1,500 annual deposits for 25 years. Suppose that client can afford only $1,000 this year but expects future earnings to be such that the annual deposit could be increased 5% per year. Assuming the interest rate remains at or above 12%, the least amount that will be available after 25 payments, if payments begin "today," can be determined by Eq. (4.1-17).

Discrete Compounding. $i^* = i = R/f = 12\%/1 = 12\%$. $g^* = G/f = 5\%/1 = 5\%$. Then

$$S_d = (1000)(1 + 12\%) \left[\frac{(1 + 12\%)^{25} - (1 + 5\%)^{25}}{0.12 - 0.05} \right]$$

$$= (1000)(1.12) \left[\frac{17.00006441 - 3.38635494}{0.07} \right]$$

$$= \$217,819.35$$

Continuous Compounding. $g^* = 5\%$. $i^* = R_e = e^{(365/360)(0.12)} - 1 = 0.1294$

$$S_d = (1000)(1.1294) \left[\frac{(1.1294)^{25} - (1.05)^{25}}{0.1294 - 0.05} \right]$$

$$= (1000)(1.1294) \left[\frac{20.950509 - 3.38635494}{0.0794} \right]$$

$$= \$249,835.71$$

Example 10. Suppose your client in Example 9 is able to start payments with $1,000 and in the future is able to increase the annual payments by the same rate as the interest rate, 12%. After 25 such annual payments, the future amount, one year after the 25th payment can be determined by Eq. (4.1-18).

Discrete Compounding. $i^* = i = R/f = 12\%/1 = 12\%$ and $g^* = 12\%$.

$$S_d = (25)(1000)(1.12)^{25} = \$425,001.61$$

Continuous Compounding. $i^* = R_e = e^{(365/360)(0.12)} - 1 = 0.1294$ and $g^* = 0.1294$.

$$S_d = (25)(1000)(1.1294)^{25} = \$523,762.73$$

Sinking Fund—Initial Payment for Payments Changing at Constant Rate

Rearrangement of Eqs. (4.1-17) and (4.1-18) to solve for p_o enables the determination of the initial payment into an annuity, where the periodic payments can be increased at a constant rate in order to achieve a specified future amount.

$$p_o = \frac{S_d}{(1 + i^*)} \left[\frac{i^* - g^*}{(1 + i^*)^n - (1 + g^*)^n} \right] \tag{4.1-19}$$

and for $g^* = i^*$

$$p_o = \frac{S_d}{n(1 + i^*)^n} \tag{4.1-20}$$

Example 11. Recall the sinking fund of Example 5 of this section for $1,000,000 of 20-year bonds. Suppose it is expected that the revenue from the utilization of the million dollars will increase with time and greater contributions toward redemption of the bonds can be made during the latter years. If the sinking fund can be expected to earn 20% compounded annually and it is decided to increase annual payments by 10% per year, the initial contribution, on the date that the million dollars is received, can be determined by Eq. (4.1-19). For annual compounding, $i^* = i = R/f = 20\%/1 = 20\%$ and $g^* = g = G/f = 10\%/1 = 10\%$.

$$p_o = \frac{1000000}{1.20}\left[\frac{0.20 - 0.10}{(1 + 20\%)^{20} - (1 + 10\%)^{20}}\right]$$

$$= \frac{1000000}{1.20}\left[\frac{0.1}{38.3376 - 6.7275}\right]$$

$$= \$2,636.29$$

Example 12. If the payments of Example 11 are increased by 20% per year, the initial payment can be determined by Eq. (4.1-20) for $g^* = 0.20$,

$$p_o = \frac{1000000}{(20)(1.20)^{20}} = \frac{1000000}{(20)(38.3376)} = \$1,304.20$$

Example 13. Refer to the trust fund of Example 6 of this section. You decide that you would like to begin payments at a relatively low level and increase payments by 5% per year. In order to accumulate \$150,000 at the end of 18 years at 10% compounded continuously, the initial payment can be determined by Eq. (4.1-20).

$$R_e = e^{(365/360)(0.10)} - 1 = 0.1067$$

$$g^* = g = G/f = 5\%/1 = 5\%$$

$$p_o = \frac{150000}{1.1067}\left[\frac{0.1067 - 0.05}{(1.1067)^{18} - (1.05)^{18}}\right]$$

$$= \frac{150000}{1.1067}\left[\frac{0.0567}{6.2020945 - 2.4066192}\right]$$

$$= \$2,024.78$$

Example 14. If you decide that you will increase the annual payments in Example 13 at the same rate as the interest rate, Eq. (4.1-20) can be used to determine the initial payment.

$$p_o = \frac{150000}{(18)(1.1067)^{18}} = \$1,343.63$$

Increasing Payments—Payment Level at a Given Payment Number

Before initiating a payment series where the payments begin at a relatively low level and periodically increase at a constant rate, it might be advisable to ascertain the payment level over the latter years. For payments which increase at a constant rate, the payment level for a given payment number, m, can be determined by Eq. (3.1-27) which is repeated here for convenience.

$$p_m = p_o(1 + g^*)^{m-1} \qquad (4.1-21)$$

Example 15.   For Example 11, the 20th payment will be

$$p_{20} = (2636.29)(1 + 10\%)^{19} = \$16,123.31$$

For Example 12, the 20th payment will be

$$p_{20} = (1304.20)(1 + 20\%)^{19} = \$41,666.58$$

For Example 13, the 18th payment will be

$$p_{18} = (2024.78)(1.05)^{17} = \$4,640.83$$

For Example 14, the 18th payment will be

$$p_{18} = (1343.63)(1.1067)^{17} = \$7,529.88$$

Payment Number—Payment Reaching a Specified Level

Given a payment series wherein it is desired to determine the payment number when the payment will reach a specified level, the laws of logarithms applied to Eq. (4.1-27) gives the payment number as

$$m = 1 + \frac{\log (p_m/p_o)}{\log (1 + g^*)} \tag{4.1-22}$$

Example 16.   In Example 11 it is shown that a sinking fund for $1,000,000 could be started with a payment of $2,636.29 if the annual payment is increased by 10% and the fund earned interest at 20% compounded annually. In Example 15 it is shown that, for the conditions of Example 11, the 20th payment would be $16,123.31. You would like to know when the payment level will reach $10,000. From Eq. (4.1-22)

$$m = 1 + \frac{\log (10000/2636.29)}{\log (1 + 10\%)}$$

$$= 1 + \frac{0.5790068}{0.0413927}$$

$$= 1 + 13.99 = 14.99$$

$$= 15\text{th payment}$$

For the condition of Example 12, $g^* = 20\%$ and $p_o = \$1,304.20$. The number of payments necessary to reach the $10,000 level is

$$m = 1 + \frac{\log (10000/1304.20)}{\log (1 + 20\%)}$$

$$= 1 + \frac{0.8846558}{0.0791812}$$

$$= 1 + 11.17 = 12.17$$

When the 12th payment is made, that payment will be slightly less than $10,000 (from Eq. (4.1-21) it will be $9,690.32).

Sinking Fund—Combination of Increasing and Level Payments

If it is advantageous, for a sinking fund, to begin periodic payments at a relatively low level, increase the level of payment at a constant rate until a specified amount is reached, and continue payments at a constant level, the following procedure may be used.

1.   Determine p_o from Eq. (4.1-19) or (4.1-20) as appropriate.

2.   With the value of p_o from step 1, solve Eq. (4.1-21) for m using the specified constant payment level for p_m. Truncate this value of m to the next lower whole number.

3.   With $N = n - m$, Eqs. (4.1-10) and (4.1-11) enable the determination of S_o at the payment number m, after which the payment level becomes constant at p_N.

4.   Solve Eq. (4.1-19) or (4.1-20) for p_o where S_d is replaced by S_o from step 3 and n is replaced by m.

5.   If p_o from step 4 does not equal p_o from step 1, replace the p_o in step 2 by that of step 4 and repeat steps 2, 3, and 4. Continue replacing p_o in step 2 by that of step 4 and repeating steps 2, 3, and 4 until the value of m repeats. The preceding computation of p_o will be the starting level of payments.

Because a large number of iterations may be required, computer programs which perform the iterations are included in Chapter 6 as Program 6-3 for discrete compounding and Program 6-4 for continuous compounding (see pages 148–150).

> **Example 17.** A 20-year sinking fund for $1,000,000 is established with the fund expected to earn interest at 20% compounded annually. It is desired to increase annual payments by 10% per year until a required payment of approximately $10,000 is reached, after which the fund will be completed with level payments of approximately $10,000 per year. The initial payment, to be made on the date the bond revenue is received, is desired.
>
> The computer solutions for Example 17 are shown below.

```
THE MAXIMUM PAYMENT FOR THE LAST N YEARS IS          10000
THE GROWTH RATE FOR THE FIRST M YEARS IS             10  %
THE NOMINAL ANNUAL INTEREST RATE IS                  20  %
THE COMPOUNDING FREQUENCY IS                         1
THE NUMBER OF PAYMENTS PER YEAR IS                   1
THE NUMBER OF YEARS TO ACHIEVE S IS                  20
THE DESIRED FUTURE AMOUNT (S) IS                     1000000

FOR DISCRETE COMPOUNDING OF INTEREST

THE NUMBER OF ITERATIONS IS                          3
THE INITIAL ANNUAL AMOUNT IS $                       2718
THE GROWTH OF PO AT   10   % PER YEAR CEASES AT       15
THE VALUE IN THE ACCOUNT THEN IS $                   366235
THE NUMBER OF YEARS AT $  10000   PER YEAR IS         5
THE FUTURE AMOUNT AT THE END OF   20   YEARS IS $     1000608
```

Total of Payments

The total of payments contributed to an annuity can be determined as follows:

a)   Level Payments

$$T = np \qquad\qquad (4.1\text{-}23)$$

Thus, the total of payments for the Individual Retirement Account of Example 1 is

$$T = (25)(1500) = \$37,500$$

and the total of payments for the bond sinking fund of Example 5 is

$$T = (20)(4463.75) = \$89,275$$

Note the difference between this total and the total when the first payment is made at the end of the first year (\$107,130 as shown in Section 3.1). By making the first payment at the beginning of the first year there is a savings of $107130 - 89275$ or \$17,855.

b) Payments Increasing at a Uniform Rate

$$T = p_0 \left[\frac{(1 + g^*)^n - 1}{g^*} \right] \tag{4.1-24}$$

Thus, the total of payments into the bond sinking fund of Example 11 is

$$T = (2636.29) \left[\frac{(1 + 10\%)^{20} - 1}{0.1} \right] = \$150,993.51$$

c) Combination of Increasing and Level Payments.

$$T = p_0 \left[\frac{(1 + g^*)^m - 1}{g^*} \right] + Np_N \tag{4.1-25}$$

Thus, the total of payments into the bond sinking fund of Example 17 is

$$T = (2718) \left[\frac{(1 + 10\%)^{15} - 1}{0.1} \right] + (5)(10000) = \$136,357.61$$

Note: The totals of payments of b and c above are \$30,199 and \$15,472, less, respectively, than the corresponding totals of the ordinary annuity of Section 3.1 (page 40). The use of level payments generates the lowest total of payments and should be used unless cash flow or other economic considerations prevail.

4.2   PRESENT VALUE AND AMORTIZATION

For simple ordinary annuities, Section 3.2, the present value is the amount of money needed one period prior to the first payment. For annuities due, the present value is the amount of money needed on the day of the first payment. This section provides formulas for simple annuities due wherein payments begin "today" and are made at the beginning of equally spaced, subsequent intervals. These annuities due are considered to be simple in that interest conversion dates coincide with payment dates. Both *equal* and *uniformly increasing* periodic payments are discussed.

The nomenclature, in addition to that of Section 4.1 is as follows:

F—A specified fraction of the original present value of an annuity.
V—Present value.
V_d—Present value for a full term of n payments.
V_m—Present value after m payments.
V_N—Present value of N remaining payments.
N'—New term after a change of interest rate and/or payment.

Given a nominal annual interest rate, R:

I. *If the interest is compounded discretely,*

$$i^* = i = R/f \qquad \qquad (4.2\text{-}1)$$

$$n = f(t_n - t_m + 1) \qquad \qquad (4.2\text{-}2)$$

II. *If the interest is compounded continuously,*

$$i^* = R_e = e^{kR} - 1 \qquad \qquad (4.2\text{-}3)$$

In general,

$$V_d = (1 + i^*) V_n$$

where V_n is the present value of a simple ordinary annuity. For comparison purposes, all examples in this section relate to the corresponding examples of Section 3.2 unless otherwise noted.

Present Value—Level Payments and Interest Rate

If level payments are made (or received) at the beginning of equally spaced periods and if interest conversion occurs at the same time as the payments, the present value of those payments can be determined by

$$V_d = p(1 + i^*) \left[\frac{1 - (1 + i^*)^{-n}}{i^*} \right] \qquad \qquad (4.2\text{-}4)$$

For use of Table A-2

$$V_d = p(1 + i) (V/p,i,n) \qquad \qquad (4.2\text{-}5)$$

where $(V/p,i,n)$ is obtained from Table A-2.

> **Example 1.** During the first 15 years of retirement you would like to withdraw $1,000 per month from your IRA. If your account is earning 12% compounded monthly, the total amount that is required "today," if the first withdrawal is made today and on the same day each month thereafter, can be determined by Eq. (4.2-4) or (4.2-5).

Discrete Compounding.

a) Equation (4.2-4) and the y^x function on the calculator.

$$i^* = i = R/f = 12\%/12 = 1\% = 0.01$$

$$n = ft = (12)(15 - 1 + 1) = 180$$

$$V_d = (1000)(1.01) \left[\frac{1 - (1.01)^{-180}}{0.01} \right]$$

Enter 1.01	Depress y^x
Enter 180	Depress +/−
Display shows −180	
Depress =	Display shows 0.1667834
Depress −	Enter 1
Depress =	Depress +/−

Display shows   0.83332166
Depress ÷   Enter 0.01
Depress =   Display shows 83.321663
Depress ×   Enter 1000
Depress ×   Display shows 83321.663
Enter 1.01   Depress =
Display shows 84154.879

b)   Equation (4.2-5) and Table A-2

$$V_d = (1000)\,(1.01)\,(V/p,i,n)$$

In the 1% table of Table A-2, opposite 180, under the "Present Value of Annuity" column, read the value of $(V/p,i,n)$ as 83.321664. Then

$$V_d = (1000)\,(1.01)\,(83.321664)$$

$$= \$84{,}154.88$$

Continuous Compounding. If withdrawal from this IRA were to occur each year, starting "today," at a level of $12,000 per year, withdrawals can occur on the same day for each of the next 14 years, giving a total of 15 withdrawals. For continuous compounding at 12%,

$$i^* = R_e = e^{(365/360)\,(0.12)} - 1 = 0.1294$$

$$V_d = (12000)\,(1.1294)\left[\frac{1 - (1.1294)^{-15}}{0.1294}\right]$$

$$= (12000)\,(1.1294)\,(6.4824602)$$

$$= \$87{,}855.49$$

Number of Level Payments—Given a Present Value

The number of level payments available, given the present value of those payments, can be determined by applying the laws of logarithms to Eq. (4.2-4)

$$n = -\frac{\log\,[1 - V_d i^*/p(1 + i^*)]}{\log\,(1 + i^*)} \tag{4.2-6}$$

or for an approximation of n, Eq. (4.2-5) can be rearranged to solve for $(V/p,i,n)$.

$$(V/p,i,n) = \frac{V_d}{p(1 + i^*)} \tag{4.2-7}$$

where the value of n can be approximated under the "Present Value of Annuity" column in Table A-2 for the calculated $(V/p,i,n)$.

Example 2. Refer to the IRA of Example 1 of this section wherein an accumulation of $224,000 is available. If that account earns no less than 12% and you decide to withdraw $30,000 annually, starting "today," the number of such withdrawals can be determined by Eq. (4.2-6).

Discrete Compounding. For 12% compounded annually $i^* = i = R/f = 12\%/1 = 12\%$.

$$n = -\frac{\log[1 - (224000)(0.12)/(30000)(1.12)]}{\log(1 + 0.12)}$$

$$= -\frac{\log 0.2}{\log 1.12} = 14.2 \text{ payments}$$

For an approximation of n, Eq. (4.2-7) gives

$$(V/p,i,n) = \frac{224000}{(30000)(1.12)} = 6.6666667$$

In the 12% table of Table A-2, the value 6.6666667, under the "Present Value of Annuity," occurs between $n = 14$, $(V/p,i,n) = 6.62816825$, and $n = 15$, $(V/p,i,n) = 6.81086449$.

Continuous Compounding. For 12% compounded continuously

$$i^* = R_e = e^{(365/360)(0.12)} - 1 = 0.1294$$

$$n = -\frac{\log[1 - (224000)(0.1294)/(30000)(1.1294)]}{\log 1.1294}$$

$$= -\frac{\log 0.1445133}{\log 1.1294} = 15.9 \text{ payments}$$

Present Value After m Level Payments

Given an annuity due of level payments and a constant interest rate, the amount that will be available on the next payment date can be determined by finding the present value of the remaining payments. In an annuity of n equal payments, the number of remaining payments after m payments are made (received) is

$$N = n - m \tag{4.2-8}$$

and Eq. (4.2-4) or (4.2-5) can be used with N replacing n.

Example 3. Suppose you were to die after making 10 years of withdrawals from the accounts of a) Example 1 and b) Example 2 of this section. The amount available, in each account, on the next payment date can be determined by Eq. (4.2-8) in conjunction with Eq. (4.2-4) or (4.2-5).

Discrete Compounding.

a)   For Example 1. At the end of 10 years, the number of payments will have been $(12)(10) = 120$. Then $N = 180 - 120 = 60$. Using Table A-2 and Eq. (4.2-5) with $i = 1\%$.

$$V_N = (1000)(1.01)(44.955038) = \$45,404.59$$

b)   For Example 2. At the end of 10 years, 10 withdrawals will have been made. Then, the number of withdrawals available will be $14.2 - 10 = 4.2$. With $i = 12\%$, Eq. (4.2-4) gives

$$V_N = (30000)(1.12)\left[\frac{1-(1.12)^{-4.2}}{0.12}\right]$$

$$= (30000)(1.12)(3.1560366)$$

$$= \$106,042.83$$

Continuous Compounding.

a) For Example 1. Assuming withdrawals of $12,000 per year and an interest rate of 12% compounded continuously, $N = 15 - 10 = 5$. With $R_e = 0.1294$, Eq. (4.2-4) gives

$$V_N = (12000)(1.1294)\left[\frac{1-(1.1294)^{-5}}{0.1294}\right]$$

$$= (12000)(1.1294)(3.5223865)$$

$$= \$47,738.20$$

b) For Example 2. The term for withdrawing $30,000 per year with an interest rate of 12% compounded continuously is 15.9 years. Then $N = 15.9 - 10 = 5.9$. With $R_e = 0.1294$

$$V_N = (30000)(1.1294)\left[\frac{1-(1.1294)^{-5.9}}{0.1294}\right]$$

$$= (30000)(1.1294)(3.9586484)$$

$$= \$134,126.92$$

Payment Number, m, When V_N Equals a Specified Fraction of V_d

If it is desired to know the payment number when the present value, on the next payment date, of an amortization is a specified fraction F, of the original amount

$$m = n + \frac{\log[1 - FV_d i^*/p(1+i^*)]}{\log(1+i^*)} \tag{4.2-9}$$

Example 4. An annuity begins "today." The account is tax-sheltered at $130,000 and is earning interest at 9%. If monthly payments are to be $1,500 and it is desired to know when the balance will be 40% of the original amount, the payment number can be determined as follows.

Discrete Compounding. Since monthly payments are indicated, it is assumed that the interest rate is 9% compounded monthly. Then, $i^* = i = R/f = 9\%/12 = 3/4\% = 0.0075$. The total number of payments can be determined by Eq. (4.2-6) as

$$n = -\frac{\log[1 - (130000)(0.0075)/(1500)(1.0075)]}{\log 1.0075}$$

$$= 138.66 \text{ payments}$$

With F = 0.40, Eq. (4.2-9) gives

$$m = 138.66 + \frac{\log [1 - (0.40)(130000)(0.0075)/(1500)(1.0075)]}{\log (1.0075)}$$

$$= 138.66 + \frac{\log 0.7419355}{\log 1.0075}$$

$$= 138.66 + \frac{-0.1296338}{0.0032451}$$

$$= 138.66 - 39.95$$

$$= 98.7$$

Therefore, when the 98th payment occurs, the balance will be slightly greater than 40% of $130,000 ($52,000). Eq. (4.2-4) gives the present value of the remaining 40.66 payments as $52,793 on the day of the 99th payment.

Continuous Compounding. Assuming annual payments of $18,000, (12)(1500 per month), and an interest rate of 9% compounded continuously,

$$i^* = R_e = e^{(365/360)(0.09)} - 1 = 0.0955$$

$$n = - \frac{\log [1 - (130000)(0.0955)/(18000)(1.0955)]}{\log 1.0955}$$

$$= 10.89$$

In order for the amount available on the next payment date to be 40% of the original amount, Eq. (4.2-9) gives

$$m = 10.9 + \frac{\log [1 - (0.4)(130000)(0.0955)/(18000)(1.0955)]}{\log 1.0955}$$

$$= 10.9 + \frac{-0.1260045}{0.0396124}$$

$$= 10.89 - 3.18 = 7.71$$

Therefore, when the 8th withdrawal occurs, the balance will be slightly less than 40% of $130,000 ($52,000). Eq. (4.2-4) gives the present value of the remaining 2.9 payments as $47,990 on the day of the 9th payment.

Change in the Term Due to Change in Interest Rate and/or Payment

Given an annuity due of equal periodic payments which are based on a specified term and interest rate, if the interest rate and/or payment level change, the new term can be determined by

$$N' = - \frac{\log [1 - V_N i^*/p(1 + i^*)]}{\log (1 + i^*)} \tag{4.2-10}$$

Example 5. Suppose that the annuity due in Example 4 of this section is at the $52,793 level and interest rates are increased to 12% compounded monthly. The remaining term will be increased to the value given by Eq. (4.2-10). For monthly compounding $i^* = i = R/f = 12\%/12 = 1\%$. With payments remaining constant at $1,500,

$$N' = -\frac{\log [1 - (52793) (0.01)/(1500) (1.01)]}{\log 1.01}$$

$$= -\frac{\log 0.6515314}{\log 1.01} = 43.06 \text{ payments after the change}$$

Example 6. Suppose the annuity due in Example 4 which pays $18,000 per year with interest compounded continuously at 9% has the interest rate increased to 12% compounded continuously when the account is at $47,990. The remaining term of $18,000 per year will be increased to the value given by Eq. (4.2-10). For 12% compounded continuously,

$$i^* = R_e = e^{(365/360)(0.12)} - 1 = 0.1294$$

$$N' = -\frac{\log [1 - (47990) (0.1294)/(18000) (1.1294)]}{\log 1.1294}$$

$$= -\frac{\log 0.6945327}{\log 1.1294} = 3$$

Thus, the change in interest rate will generate 3 payments of $18,000 each rather than 2 such payments plus a fraction of $18,000 as in Example 4.

Present Value—Payments Changing at a Constant Rate

If the periodic payments of an annuity increase at a constant rate, with the increase in payment occurring at the interest conversion date, the present value of that annuity can be determined by

$$V_d = p_0(1 + i^*)\left\{\frac{1 - \left[\frac{1 + g^*}{1 + i^*}\right]^n}{i^* - g^*}\right\} \tag{4.2-11}$$

and if $g^* = i^*$

$$V_d = np_0 \tag{4.2-12}$$

Example 7. During the first 15 years of your retirement you would like to withdraw annually increased amounts from your IRA starting "today" and increasing the annual withdrawal by 6% per year. If the account is earning interest at 12%, the total amount that is required just prior to the withdrawal "today" can be determined as follows:

Discrete Compounding. Since withdrawals are annual, it is assumed that the account is earning interest at 12% compounded annually. Then, $i^* = i = R/f = 12\%/1 = 12\%$. $g^* = g = G/f = 6\%/1 = 6\%$. $n = ft = (1) (15) = 15$. From Eq. (4.2-11)

$$V_d = (12000)\,(1.12) \left\{ \frac{1 - \left[\dfrac{1.06}{1.12}\right]^{15}}{0.12 - 0.06} \right\}$$

$$= (12000)\,(1.12)\,(9.3692962)$$

$$= \$125,923.34$$

If the interest rate remains constant at 12% compounded annually, the depletion of this account would tabulate* as follows.

Beginning of Year	Withdrawal	Balance
1	$12,000.00	$113,923.34
2	12,720.00	114,874.14
3	13,483.20	115,175.84
4	14,292.19	114,704.75
5	15,149.72	113,319.60
6	16,058.71	110,859.24
7	17,022.23	107,140.12
8	18,043.56	101,953.37
9	19,126.18	95,061.60
10	20,273.75	86,195.24
11	21,490.17	75,048.50
12	22,779.58	61,274.74
13	24,146.36	44,481.34
14	25,595.14	24,223.96
15	27,130.85	0

*The balance for a given year is 1.12 times the balance of the previous year minus the withdrawal of the given year.

The total of the withdrawals can be determined by Eq. (4.1-26) as

$$T = (12000) \left[\frac{(1.06)^{15} - 1}{0.06} \right] = \$279,311.64$$

If you want the annual increase of the withdrawal of this example to be equal to the interest rate of 12%, the total amount required just prior to the first withdrawal can be determined by Eq. (4.2-12).

$$V_d = (15)\,(12000) = \$180,000$$

Continuous Compounding. For continuous compounding of interest

$$i^* = R_e = e^{(365/360)\,(0.12)} - 1 = 0.1294$$

$$g^* = G = 6\% = 0.06$$

From Eq. (4.2-11)

$$V_d = (12000)(1.1294)\left\{\frac{1 - \left[\dfrac{1.06}{1.1294}\right]^{15}}{0.1294 - 0.06}\right\}$$

$$= (12000)(1.1294)(8.8436248)$$

$$= \$119,855.88$$

Amortization—Level Payments and Interest Rate

Given that an account is to be amortized by a series of equally spaced level payments over a fixed term, the periodic, level payment starting "today" can be determined by rearranging Eq. (4.2-4) to

$$p = \frac{V_d}{(1 + i^*)}\left[\frac{i^*}{1 - (1 + i^*)^{-n}}\right] \tag{4.2-13}$$

For use of Table A-2

$$p = \frac{V_d}{(1 + i)}(p/V, i, n) \tag{4.2-14}$$

Example 8. This example relates to Example 9 of Section 3.2. Your IRA account is posted at $150,000 when you are about to make your first withdrawal. If the account earns interest at 12%, annual withdrawals for 15 years can be determined as follows:

Discrete Compounding. Since withdrawals are annual, it is assumed that the interest rate is 12% compounded annually. Then, $i^* = i = R/f = 12\%/1 = 12\%$. $n = ft = (1)(15) = 15$.

a) Equation (4.2-13) and the y^x function on the calculator. In order to avoid using parentheses, the denominator of the bracketed expression is determined first. This value is divided by the numerator, i^*, and the reciprocal is obtained.

$$p = \frac{150000}{1.12}\left[\frac{0.12}{1 - (1.12)^{-15}}\right]$$

Enter 1.12	Depress y^x
Enter 15	Depress +/−
Depress =	Display shows 0.1826963
Depress −	Enter 1
Depress =	Depress +/−
Depress ÷	Enter 0.12
Depress =	Display shows 6.8108645
Depress 1/x	Display shows 0.1468242
Depress ÷	Enter 1.12
Depress ×	Enter 150000
Display shows 19663.96	

b)   Equation (4.2-14) and Table A-2. In the 12% table of Table A-2, under the column "Amortization," read the value 0.14682424 opposite 15 periods.

$$p = \frac{150000}{1.12} (0.14682424)$$

$$= \$19,663.96 \text{ per year for 15 years.}$$

Continuous Compounding. For 12% compounded continuously

$$i* = R_e = e^{(365/360)(0.12)} - 1 = 0.1294$$

$$p = \frac{150000}{1.1294} \left[\frac{0.1294}{1 - (1.1294)^{-15}} \right]$$

$$= \frac{150000}{1.1294} (0.1542624)$$

$$= \$20,488.19 \text{ per year for 15 years.}$$

Amortization—Total Interest over Term

If an account is depleted by level payments at a constant interest rate over the entire term of an amortization, the total interest can be determined by

$$I = np - V_d \qquad (4.2\text{-}15)$$

Example 9.   The total interest on the amortization of Example 8 can be determined by Eq. (4.2-15).

Discrete Compounding.

$$I = (15)(19663.96) - 150000 = \$144,959.40$$

Continuous Compounding.

$$I = (15)(20488.19) - 150000 = \$157,322.85$$

Amortization—Initial Payment for Payments Changing at a Constant Rate

Given that an account is to be amortized over a fixed term at a constant interest rate, if the periodic payments of an annuity due increase at a constant rate with the increase occurring at the interest conversion date, the initial payment of such an annuity can be determined by rearranging Eqs. (4.2-11) and (4.2-12).

$$p_o = \frac{V_d}{(1 + i*)} \left\{ \frac{i* - g*}{1 - \left[\dfrac{1 + g*}{1 + i*} \right]^n} \right\} \qquad (4.2\text{-}16)$$

or if $g* = i*$

$$p_o = \frac{V_d}{n} \qquad (4.2\text{-}17)$$

Example 10. This example relates to Example 11 in Section 3.2. You own an IRA of $150,000 and plan to make 15 annual withdrawals beginning "today." You would like to increase the annual withdrawal by 5% per year, and if the account will earn no less than 12% interest, the initial withdrawal can be determined by Eq. (4.2-16).

Discrete Compounding. Since annual withdrawals are to be made, it is assumed that the interest rate is 12% compounded annually. Then, $i^* = i = R/f = 12\%/1 = 12\%$. $g^* = G = 6\%$. $n = ft = (1)(15) = 15$.

$$P_0 = \frac{150000}{1.12} \left\{ \frac{0.12 - 0.05}{1 - \left[\dfrac{1.05}{1.12}\right]^{15}} \right\}$$

$$= \frac{150000}{1.12}(0.1128691)$$

$$= \$15,116.39$$

A tabulation of this annuity due is shown below.

Beginning of Year	Withdrawal	Balance
1	$15,116.39	$134,883.61
2	15,872.21	135,197.43
3	16,665.82	134,755.31
4	17,499.11	133,426.83
5	18,374.07	131,063.98
6	19,292.77	127,498.89
7	20,257.41	122,541.35
8	21,270.28	115,976.03
9	22,333.79	107,559.36
10	23,450.48	97,016.00
11	24,623.01	84,034.92
12	25,854.16	68,264.94
13	27,146.87	49,309.87
14	28,504.21	26,722.84
15	29,929.42	0

The total amount of the withdrawals can be determined by adding the withdrawals or by Eq. (4.1-26)

$$T = (15116.39)\left[\frac{(1 + 5\%)^{15} - 1}{5\%}\right] = \$326,189.98$$

Had you decided to annually withdraw equal amounts, the level withdrawals could have been determined by Eq. (4.2-14) as

$$p = \frac{150000}{1.12}(0.14682424)$$

$$= \$19,663.96$$

The total amount of these level withdrawals would be np or

$$T = (15)(19663.96)$$

$$= \$294,959.40$$

Therefore, if up to approximately \$4,500 per year is not needed during the "early years of retirement," and if you can reasonably expect to survive 15 years, the uniformly increasing withdrawals will result in approximately \$31,000 of additional income.

The number of withdrawals that are required for the amount of the withdrawal to be equal to the amount of level withdrawals can be determined by Eq. (4.1-22).

$$m = 1 + \frac{\log(19663.96/15116.39)}{\log 1.05}$$

$$= 1 + 5.39 = 6.39$$

Therefore, the withdrawal for the 7th year and each year thereafter will be larger than \$19,663.96 (see the 7th year in the tabulation above).

If the interest rate changes during the term of the annuity, Eq. (4.2-16) can be re-solved for a "new" p_0 using the balance, just before the withdrawal of the "new" initial amount, as the present value.

Continuous Compounding. For 12% continuously compounded interest,

$$i^* = R_e = e^{(365/360)(0.12)} - 1 = 0.1294$$

$$p_0 = \frac{150000}{1.1294} \left\{ \frac{0.1294 - 0.05}{1 - \left[\dfrac{1.05}{1.1294} \right]^{15}} \right\}$$

$$= \frac{150000}{1.1294}(0.1194093)$$

$$= \$15,859.21$$

The total amount of the withdrawals can be determined by Eq. (4.1-24)

$$T = (15859.21)\left[\frac{(1.05)^{15} - 1}{0.05} \right] = \$342,218.97$$

CHAPTER 5

Formulas and Tables for
Deferred Annuities

If the funding or liquidation of an account is to be accomplished by periodic payments which begin at a future date, the nature of the funding or liquidation is a deferred annuity. Because the future dates are pre-determinable, the analyses may be treated as simple ordinary annuities (payments occur at the ends of interest conversion periods) when those payments begin. This chapter provides formulas which are appropriate for equally spaced payments for both discrete and continuous compounding of interest for deferred annuities.

The unification of the symbol notation for interest rates, i^*, which was introduced in Chapter 4 is continued in this chapter. For discrete compounding

$$i^* = i = R/f$$

and for continuous compounding

$$i^* = R_e = e^{kR} - 1$$

Within the text are one or more examples which indicate the use of each formula. The examples address a specific type of monetary problem, but the concepts which are treated are general. The examples include:

1. Determining the present value of an annuity of level payments or payments which are to increase at a constant rate when the first payment is deferred for a specified period, as funding a trust for college education. Pages 96, 102
2. Determining the level payments or the initial payment, for payments which are to increase at a constant rate, given a present value and a period of deferment, such as the amortization of a construction loan. Pages 98, 104
3. Determining the term of a level payment annuity or an annuity with payments which increase at a constant rate given a present value and period of deferment, such as the number of withdrawals that can be made from a Keogh account from a single deposit. Pages 99, 105
4. Determining the necessary period of deferment for a specified level or uniformly increasing payment with a specified term. Pages 101, 106

If you perform the calculations in the examples, your results may differ from the indicated results, depending upon the number of decimal places you carry at each step of the solutions. For example, if 12% compounded continuously is rounded to 0.1294 (12.94% effective annual rate) the results will be different than if it is used in calculations as 0.1293776 (the limit on the TI–50).

5.1   FUTURE AMOUNT AND SINKING FUND PAYMENTS

The formulas for the future amount and sinking fund payments for simple deferred annuities are the same as the formulas for simple ordinary annuities (Chapter 3.1). The annuity is considered to begin one period before the first payment and payments are considered as occurring at the ends of periods.

In general, the term of a deferred annuity is the number of periods from "now" to the maturity date of the annuity less the number of periods of deferment. With d being the number of periods of deferment, for discrete compounding

$$n = ft - d \tag{5.1-1}$$

and for continuous compounding

$$t_n = t - d \tag{5.1-2}$$

5.2   PRESENT VALUE AND AMORTIZATION

This section provides formulas for determining the amount of money that is needed "today" in order to fund an annuity which is to begin payments at some future point in time. Included are formulas for *equal* periodic payments and *payments which change at a constant rate.*

When the payments of a deferred annuity begin, the formulas in Section 3.2 can be used because the value of V_n will have been established. The nomenclature for simple deferred annuities is as follows:

d—Number of periods in the period of deferment.
e—Base of the natural logarithms.
f—The compounding frequency which is the number of times each year that interest is computed and added to principal.
g—The periodic rate by which a periodic payment is increased (decreased).
G—The annual rate by which an annual payment is increased (decreased).
i*—A unified interest rate.
i—The periodic interest rate—a simple interest rate during a compounding period.
k—Conversion of ordinary year to exact year = 365/360.
n—Number of payment periods.
p—Equal periodic payment.
p_o—Initial payment of a uniformly increasing (decreasing) series of payments.
R—Nominal annual interest rate.
R_e—Effective annual interest rate.
V_n—Present value one period before the first payment.
V_{d+n}—Present value of the simple deferred annuity.
t—Time expressed as a number of years.

Present Value—Level Payments

Given a specified level periodic payment to begin after a period of deferment, the present value of that annuity is

$$V_{d+n} = p(1 + i^*)^{-d} \left[\frac{1 - (1 + i^*)^{-n}}{i^*} \right] \tag{5.2-1}$$

and for the use of Table A-2

$$V_{d+n} = p(1 + i)^{-d} (V/p,i,n) \tag{5.2-2}$$

or

$$V_{d+n} = p\{[V/p,i,(d + n)] - (V/p,i,d)\} \tag{5.2-3}$$

Example 1. You would like to fund a trust "today" so that $20,000 per year for 8 years can be withdrawn to pay education costs through graduate school. The first withdrawal from the trust is to occur in 18 years. If the interest rate throughout the life of the trust is no less than 10%, the amount of the funding "today" can be determined as follows. Since the first withdrawal occurs in 18 years, the period of deferment, d, is 17 years.

Discrete Compounding. Since annual withdrawals are indicated, it is assumed that the interest is compounded annually. Then, $i^* = i = R/f = 10\%/1 = 10\% = 0.10$, and $n = ft = (1)(8) = 8$.

a) Using Eq. (5.2-1) and the y^x function on the calculator.

$$V_{d+n} = (20000) (1.10)^{-17} \left[\frac{1 - (1.10)^{-8}}{0.10} \right]$$

Enter 1.1	Depress y^x
Enter 8	Depress +/–
Display shows –8	Depress =
Display shows 0.4665074	Depress –
Enter 1	Depress =
Depress +/–	Display shows 0.5334926
Depress ÷	Enter 0.1
Depress =	Display shows 5.3349262
Depress X	Enter 1.1
Depress y^x	Enter 17
Depress +/–	Display shows –17
Depress =	Display shows 1.0554867
Depress X	Enter 20000
Depress =	Display shows 21109.734

b) Using Eq. (5.2-2) and Table A-2.

$$V_{d+n} = (20000) (1 + 10\%)^{-17} (V/p,i,n)$$

In the 10% table of Table A-2, opposite $n = 8$, read the value of $(V/p,i,n)$ as 5.3349262. Under the "Present Value" column, opposite $d = 17$, read the value of $(1 + 10\%)^{-17}$ as 0.19784467. Then,

$$V_{d+n} = (20000) (0.19784467) (5.3349262)$$

$$= \$21,109.73$$

c) Using Eq. (5.2-3) and Table A-2.

$$V_{d+n} = (20000) [(V/p,i,25) - (V/p,i,17)]$$

In the 10% table of Table A-2, opposite $d + n = 25$, read the value of $[V/p,i,(d + n)]$ as 9.07704002, and opposite $d = 17$, read the value of $(V/p,i,d)$ as 8.02155331. Then,

$$V_{d+n} = (20000) (9.07704002 - 8.02155331)$$

$$= \$21,109.73$$

Thus, if the interest rate over the 25-year period is at least 10% compounded annually, \$21,109.73 invested "today" will purchase an annuity of \$20,000 per year for 8 years beginning 18 years from "today" – a total of \$160,000 over the 25-year period.

Continuous Compounding. For 10% compounded continuously,

$$i^* = R_e = e^{(365/360)(0.10)} - 1 = 0.1067$$

From Eq. (5.2-1),

$$V_{d+n} = (20000) (1.1067)^{-17} \left[\frac{1 - (1.1067)^{-8}}{0.1067} \right]$$

$$= (20000) (0.1784397) (5.2072506)$$

$$= \$18,583.61$$

Level Payments Given a Present Value

If a known amount is invested "today" in order to provide for a deferred annuity with a specified period of deferment and a specified term, that present value will provide level payments as determined by

$$p = V_{d+n}(1 + i^*)^d \left[\frac{i^*}{1 - (1 + i^*)^{-n}} \right] \tag{5.2-4}$$

For the use of Table A-2

$$p = V_{d+n}(1 + i)^d (p/V,i,n) \tag{5.2-5}$$

or

$$p = \frac{V_{d+n}}{[V/p,i,(d + n)] - (V/p,i,d)} \tag{5.2-6}$$

Example 2.   You negotiate a loan for \$1,000,000 so that the first payment is due in 27 months with a 20-year amortization payable quarterly. If the interest rate is 15%, the deferred quarterly payment can be determined as follows. For quarterly payments $f = 4$, and $i^* = i = R/f = 15\%/4 = 3\ 3/4\%$. Since 27 months requires 9 quarters to the first payment, $d = 9 - 1 = 8$, and $n = ft = (4) (20) = 80$.

a)   Using Eq. (5.2-4) and the y^x function of the calculator.

$$p = (1000000) (1.0375)^8 \left[\frac{0.0375}{1 - (1.0375)^{-80}} \right]$$

Enter 1.0375	Depress y^x
Enter 80	Depress +/–
Depress =	Display shows 0.0525959
Depress –	Enter 1
Depress =	Depress +/–

Display shows 0.9474041   Depress ÷
Enter 0.0375   Depress =
Display shows 25.26411   Depress 1/x
Display shows 0.0395818   Depress ×
Enter 1.0375   Depress y^x
Enter 8   Depress =
Display shows 0.0531375   Depress ×
Enter 1000000   Depress =
Display shows 53137.47

b) Using Eq. (5.2-5) and Table A-2.

$$p = (1000000) (1 + 3\ 3/4\%)^8\ (p/V,i,80)$$

From Table A-2

$$p = (1000000) (1.34247078) (0.03958184)$$

$$= \$53,137.41$$

c) Using Eq. (5.2-6) and Table A-2

$$i = 3\ 3/4\%$$

$$d + n = 8 + 80 = 88$$

$$p = \frac{1000000}{(V/p,i,88) - (V/p,i,8)}$$

From Table A-2

$$p = \frac{1000000}{25.62190926 - 6.80279553}$$

$$= \$53,137.47 \text{ per quarter for 20 years, beginning in 2 years,}$$
for total receipts of \$4,250,997.60

Example 3. Suppose, in Example 1, you had \$10,000 with which to fund the trust that is deferred 18 years with a subsequent payout of 8 years. If the trust earned at least 10% interest compounded continuously, the level of the 8 payments can be determined by Eq. (5.2-4). For 10% compounded continuously,

$$i^* = R_e = e^{(365/360)(0.10)} - 1 = 0.1067$$

$$p = (10000) (1.1067)^{17} \left[\frac{0.1067}{1 - (1.1067)^{-8}} \right]$$

$$= (10000) (5.6041335) (0.1920399)$$

$$= \$10,762.17 \text{ per year for 8 years}$$
for a total payout of \$86,097.36.

Term of Annuity for a Given Deferment Period

If an amount of money available "today" is to be used as the source of a level payment annuity which is to begin after a specified period of deferment, the term of that annuity can be determined by

$$n = -\frac{\log\left[1 - \frac{V_{d+n}i^*(1 + i^*)^d}{p}\right]}{\log(1 + i^*)} \qquad (5.2\text{-}7)$$

and for an approximation using Table A-2

$$[V/p,i,(d + n)] = \frac{V_{d+n}}{p} + (V/p,i,d) \qquad (5.2\text{-}8)$$

Equation (5.2-8) enables the approximation of (d + n), and n can be determined by

$$n = (d + n) - d \qquad (5.2\text{-}9)$$

Example 4. You open a Keogh account with \$7,500 "today." With the first withdrawal to occur in 15 years, you would like to liquidate this account with \$5,000 annual withdrawals. If the interest rate does not fall below 10%, the minimum term of the annuity can be determined as follows.

Discrete Compounding. Since annual withdrawals are indicated, it is assumed that the interest rate is 10% compounded annually. Then, $i^* = i = R/f = 10\%/1 = 10\% = 0.10$. Since the first withdrawal is to occur in 15 years, the period of deferment is 14 years.

a)   Using Eq. (5.2-7)

$$n = -\frac{\log\left[1 - \frac{(7500)(0.10)(1.10)^{14}}{5000}\right]}{\log 1.10}$$

$$= -\frac{\log\left[1 - \frac{(7500)(0.10)(3.7974983)}{5000}\right]}{\log 1.10}$$

$$= -\frac{\log 0.4303753}{\log 1.10} = 8.85 \text{ years}$$

b)   Using Eqs. (5.2-8) and (5.2-9) and Table A-2. In the 10% table of Table A-2 under "Present Value of Annuity" read the value of (V/p,i,14).

$$[V/p,i,(d + n)] = \frac{7500}{5000} + 7.3666874$$

$$= 8.8666875$$

In the same column of the 10% table, read down until a value close to 8.8666875 is found. It will be seen that this value occurs between 22 and 23 periods. Thus,

$$(d + n) = 22^+ \text{ years}$$

and from Eq. (5.2-9)

$$n = 22^+ - 14 = 8^+ \text{ years.}$$

Continuous Compounding. For 10% compounded continuously,

$$i^* = R_e = e^{(365/360)\,(0.10)} - 1 = 0.1067$$

From Eq. (5.2-7)

$$n = -\frac{\log\left[1 - \dfrac{(7500)\,(0.1067)\,(1.1067)^{14}}{5000}\right]}{\log 1.1067}$$

$$= 10.69 \text{ years}$$

Note: Depending upon the method of compounding, $7,500 "today" will purchase $5,000 per year for 9 to 11 years. Thus, if $7,500 is deposited in a 10% account in each of the next 14 years and the withdrawal from each of those accounts is deferred for 14 years, the annual annuity available, beginning 15 years from "today," could be as follows:

Enters	Terminates	Years From Today	Annuity Amount
1		15	$ 5,000
2		16	10,000
3		17	15,000
4		18	20,000
5		19	25,000
6		20	30,000
7		21	35,000
8		22	40,000
9	1	23	45,000
10	2	24	45,000
11	3	25	45,000
12	4	26	45,000
13	5	27	45,000
14	6	28	45,000
	7	29	40,000
	8	30	35,000
	9	31	30,000
	10	32	25,000
	11	33	20,000
	12	34	15,000
	13	35	10,000
	14	36	5,000

No. 1 "Enters" 15 "Years From Today" and "Terminates" 23 "Years From Today," etc.

Period of Deferment—Given Level Annuity

For a given amount of money available "today" and a specified level payment and term of a deferred annuity, the required period of deferment can be determined by

$$d = \frac{\log\left\{\dfrac{p}{V_{d+n}}\left[\dfrac{1 - (1 + i^*)^{-n}}{i^*}\right]\right\}}{\log(1 + i^*)} \qquad (5.2\text{-}10)$$

Example 5. Suppose you have \$10,000 "today" which you would like to use to purchase a \$10,000 per year annuity for 5 years at some future date. If the interest rate does not fall below 12%, the minimum period of deferment can be determined by Eq. (5.2-10).

Discrete Compounding. Since an annual annuity is indicated, it is assumed that the interest rate is 10% compounded annually. Then, $i^* = i = R/f = 12\%/1 = 12\% = 0.12$.

$$d = \frac{\log\left\{\dfrac{(10000)}{(10000)}\left[\dfrac{1 - (1.12)^{-5}}{0.12}\right]\right\}}{\log 1.12}$$

$$= \frac{\log 3.6047762}{\log 1.12} = 11.31 \text{ years}$$

Since the period of deferment is 11.31 years, the first \$10,000 withdrawal can be made 12.31 years from "today."

Continuous Compounding. For 12% compounded continuously,

$$i^* = R_e = e^{(365/360)(0.12)} - 1 = 0.1294$$

$$d = \frac{\log\left\{\dfrac{(10000)}{(10000)}\left[\dfrac{1 - (1.1294)^{-5}}{0.1294}\right]\right\}}{\log 1.1294}$$

$$= 10.35 \text{ years.}$$

The first \$10,000 withdrawal can be made 11.35 years from "today."

Present Value—Payments Changing at a Constant Rate

Given that a periodic payment is to begin after a period of deferment, the present value of that annuity is

$$V_{d+n} = p_0(1 + i^*)^{-d}\left\{\frac{1 - \left[\dfrac{1 + g^*}{1 + i^*}\right]^n}{i^* - g^*}\right\} \qquad (5.2\text{-}11)$$

and if $g^* = i^*$

$$V_{d+n} = np_0(1 + i^*)^{-(d+1)} \qquad (5.2\text{-}12)$$

Example 6. You would like to find a trust "today" so that an annuity, beginning at \$20,000 and increasing 5% per year, for 8 years will be available in 18 years. If the interest rate throughout the life of the trust is no less than 10%, the amount of funding "today" can be determined as follows. Since the first payment is due in 18 years, the period of deferment, d, is 17 years.

Discrete Compounding. Since annual withdrawals are indicated, it is assumed that the interest is 10% compounded annually, and since annual increases are specified, the growth rate is 5% compounded annually. Then,

$$i^* = R/f = 10\%/1 = 10\% = 0.10$$

$$g^* = G/f = 5\%/1 = 5\% = 0.05$$

$$n = ft = (1)(8) = 8$$

From Eq. (5.2-11)

$$V_{d+n} = (20000)(1.10)^{-17} \left\{ \frac{1 - \left[\frac{1.05}{1.10}\right]^8}{0.10 - 0.05} \right\}$$

$$= (20000)(0.1978447)(6.2151226)$$

$$= \$24,592.58$$

This deferred annuity would tabulate* as follows:

Beginning of Year	Withdrawal	Amount
1		$ 24,592.58
17		124,302.46
18	$20,000.00	116,732.71
19	21,000.00	107,405.98
20	22,050.00	96,096.57
21	23,152.50	82,553.73
22	24,310.13	66,498.98
23	25,525.63	47,623.24
24	26,801.91	25,583.66
25	28,142.01	0

*Beginning with year 18, the amount equals 1.1 times the amount of the previous year minus the withdrawal of that year.

Note: Comparing this annuity with the level payments of Example 1 of this section shows that approximately $31,000 more is available for an additional $3,483 "up front." The total of payments is $190,982 against $160,000.

Had it been desired that the annual withdrawal equal the interest rate, Eq. (5.2-12) gives the present value as

$$V_{d+n} = (8)(20000)(1.10)^{-18} = \$28,777.41$$

Continuous Compounding. For 10% compounded continuously,

$$i^* = R_e = e^{(365/360)(0.10)} - 1 = 0.1067$$

From Eq. (5.2-11)

$$V_{d+n} = (20000)(1.1067)^{-17} \left\{ \frac{1 - \left[\dfrac{1.05}{1.1067} \right]^8}{0.1067 - 0.05} \right\}$$

$$= (20000)(0.1784397)(6.0571244)$$

$$= \$21,616.63$$

Initial Payment—Payments Changing at a Constant Rate

If an amount is invested "today" in order to provide for a deferred annuity with a specified period of deferment, a specified term, and payments increasing at a constant rate, the initial payment can be determined by

$$p_o = V_{d+n}(1 + i^*)^d \left\{ \frac{i^* - g^*}{1 - \left[\dfrac{1 + g^*}{1 + i^*} \right]^n} \right\} \qquad (5.2\text{-}13)$$

and if $g^* = i^*$

$$p_o = \frac{V_{d+n}(1 + i^*)^{d+1}}{n} \qquad (5.2\text{-}14)$$

Example 7. You agree to lend \$1,000,000 with the first payment due in 27 months and quarterly payments thereafter for 20 years. The terms of the loan are such that the quarterly payments will increase 2% each quarter. If the interest rate is 15%, the initial deferred payment can be determined as follows. For quarterly payments $f = 4$, and $i^* = R/f = 15\%/4 = 3\text{-}3/4\% = 0.0375$. $g^* = g = 2\% = 0.02$. Since 27 months requires 9 quarters, the period of deferment, d, is 8, and $n = ft = (4)(20) = 80$. From Eq. (5.2-13)

$$p_o = (1000000)(1.0375)^8 \left\{ \frac{0.0375 - 0.02}{1 - \left[\dfrac{1.02}{1.0375} \right]^{80}} \right\}$$

$$= (1000000)(1.3424708)(0.023535)$$

$$= \$31,595.11$$

The total receipts would be \$6,122,246.30 (see Eq. (3.1-30)).

Note: Should you negotiate such a loan? Comparing the results of this amortization with the level payments of Example 2 of this section, sacrificing approximately \$21,500 at the first payment will generate approximately \$1,870,000 of additional interest.

Example 8. Suppose, in Example 6, you had \$10,000 with which to fund the trust that is deferred 18 years with a subsequent payout of 8 years with payments increasing

5% per year. For an interest rate of 10% compounded continuously, the initial payment can be determined by Eq. (5.2-13).

$$i^* = R_e = e^{(365/360)(0.10)} - 1 = 0.1067$$

$$p_o = (10000)(1.1067)^{17}\left\{\frac{0.1067 - 0.05}{1 - \left[\dfrac{1.05}{1.1067}\right]^8}\right\}$$

$$= (10000)(5.6041335)(0.1650948)$$

$$= \$9,252.14$$

The total receipts would be $88,349.69 (see Eq. 3.1-30)).

Note: Comparing this with Example 3 of this section shows that approximately $9,000 additional is available over the 8-year payout period.

Term of Annuity for a Given Deferment Period
Payments Changing at a Constant Rate

If an amount of money is invested "today" in order to provide for a deferred annuity with a specified period of deferment, a specified initial payment, and a specified growth rate for payments, the term of such an annuity can be determined by

$$n = \frac{\log\left[1 - \dfrac{V_{d+n}(i^* - g^*)(1 + i^*)^d}{p_o}\right]}{\log\left[\dfrac{1 + g^*}{1 + i^*}\right]} \tag{5.2-15}$$

and if $g^* = i^*$

$$n = \frac{V_{d+n}(1 + i^*)^{d+1}}{p_o} \tag{5.2-16}$$

Example 9. Referring to Example 7 of this section, suppose it is agreed that the initial payment is to be $40,000. The term of that amortization can be determined as follows. From Example 7 $i^* = i = 3\ 3/4\% = 0.0375$, $g^* = g = 2\% = 0.02$, $d = 8$, and $V_{d+n} = 1,000,000$. From Eq. (5.2-15)

$$n = \frac{\log\,[1 - (1000000)(0.0375 - 0.02)(1.0375)^8/(40000)]}{\log\left[\dfrac{1.02}{1.0375}\right]}$$

$$= \frac{\log 0.4126690}{\log 0.9831325} = \frac{-0.3843981}{-0.0073879}$$

$$= 52.03 \text{ payments}$$

Since payments are quarterly, the number of years is 52.03/4 or 13 years. For these circumstances, the payor should be cautioned that the 52nd payment will be $109,816.79 (see Eq. 3.1-27)).

Example 10. Referring to Example 8 of this section, suppose you specify the initial payment from the trust to be $10,000. The term of that annuity can be determined as follows. From Example 8, $i^* = R_e = 0.1067$, $g^* = g = 5\% = 0.05$, and $d = 17$. From Eq. (5.2-15)

$$n = \frac{\log [1 - (10000) (0.1067 - 0.05) (1.1067)^{17}/(10000)]}{\log \left[\dfrac{1.05}{1.1067}\right]}$$

$$= \frac{\log 0.6822456}{\log 0.9487666} = 7.27 \text{ years}$$

Period of Deferment for a Given Annuity Payments Changing at a Constant Rate

For a given amount of money "today" and a specified initial payment, a specified growth rate of payments, and a specified term, the required period of deferment can be determined by

$$d = \frac{\log \dfrac{p_o}{V_{d+n}} \left\{ \dfrac{1 - \left[\dfrac{1 + g^*}{1 + i^*}\right]^n}{i^* - g^*} \right\}}{\log (1 + i^*)} \tag{5.2-17}$$

and if $g^* = i^*$

$$d = \frac{\log [p_o n/V_{d+n}]}{\log (1 + i^*)} - 1 \tag{5.2-18}$$

Example 11. In Example 6 of this section, the period of deferment was specified as 17 years. Suppose you needed to determine that period for the conditions of that example. From Example 6, $i^* = i = 10\% = 0.10$, $g^* = g = 5\% = 0.05$, $n = 8$, $p_o = 20000$ and $V_{d+n} = 24592.58$ for discrete compounding. From Eq. (5.2-17)

$$d = \frac{\log \dfrac{(20000)}{(24592.58)} \left\{ \dfrac{1 - \left[\dfrac{1.05}{1.10}\right]^8}{0.10 - 0.05} \right\}}{\log 1.10}$$

$$= \frac{\log 5.0544697}{\log 1.10} = 16.9999999$$

$$= 17 \text{ years}$$

CHAPTER 6

Formulas and Tables for Annuities When Payments and Interest Conversions Do Not Coincide

The more practical type of annuity is that payment dates and interest conversion dates do not coincide. This type of annuity is called a *complex annuity*, and this chapter provides appropriate formulas. The formulas allow for payments which are made at the ends of payment intervals (complex ordinary annuities), payments which are made at the beginnings of payment intervals (complex annuities due), and payments which are deferred. The formulas include discrete and continuous compounding of interest, and the unified symbol notation for interest rate, i^*, which was introduced in Chapter 4 is continued in this chapter.

Within the text are one or more examples which indicate the use of each formula. The examples address a specific type of monetary problem, but the concepts which are treated are general. The examples include:

1. Determining the number of interest conversions per payment interval and the total number of interest conversions for a specified term. Page 108
2. Determining the amount of money that will be available at the end of a series of level or uniformly increasing payments, such as for Individual Retirement Accounts, Keogh Plans, or pension contributions in general, for level and changing interest rates. Pages 110, 116, 123, 128
3. Determining the number of payments that will be required in order to achieve a specified future amount for level and changing interest rates. Pages 114, 118
4. Determining the required level periodic payment to a sinking fund for level and changing interest rates and determining the initial payments, to a sinking fund, for payments which are to increase at a constant rate, such as for trust funds and bond redemption. A procedure for a combination of level and increasing payments is shown. Computer programs for this procedure for discrete and continuous compounding are included. Pages 119, 121, 125, 130
5. Determining the amount of money required (the present value) for the disbursement by a specified level periodic payment or a specified initial payment for payments which are to increase at a constant rate, such as for liquidation of a pension account or trust with a specified number of payments. Pages 135, 142

6. Determining the level periodic payment and the initial payment, for payments which are to increase at a constant rate, for the amortization of a debt, such as a mortgage, or liquidation of a personal account given the present value. If the interest rate changes at a given present value, a new periodic payment can be determined for the remaining term. Pages 143, 145
7. Determining the present value of a level payment amortization after a given payment number, and determining the new term of an amortization where interest rate changes but payment level remains constant. Pages 137, 139, 141
8. Determining the payment number when the present value of an amortization is some specified fraction of the original amount, such as the reduction of an account to a level which can be used to fund an estate trust free of estate taxes. Page 139

The numerical accuracy of the examples may differ from the accuracy you obtain due to the number of decimal places you use from the values in the tables or from your calculations to determine periodic interest rates. For example, if 12% compounded continuously is rounded to 0.1294 (12.94% effective annual rate) the results will be different than if it is used in calculations as 0.1293776 (the limit on the TI-50).

The nomenclature for complex annuity formulas is the same as for the simple annuity formulas of Chapters 3, 4, and 5. Additionally:

c—Number of interest conversion periods per payment interval.

f'—The number of equally spaced payments per year.

i'—Psuedo-periodic interest rate for continuous compounding of interest.

p_o—Initial annual amount for payments where the annual amount changes at a constant rate.

For all formulas in this chapter, unless otherwise indicated, the following substitutions apply.

I. *Discrete Compounding of Interest*

$$c = f/f'$$

$$n = f't$$

$$i^* = i = R/f$$

II. *Continuous Compounding of Interest*

$$c = 1$$

$$(1 + i^*)^c - 1 = i^*$$

$$i' = R/f'$$

$$n = f't$$

$$i^* = e^{ki'} - 1$$

$$R_e = e^{kR} - 1$$

6.1 NUMBER OF INTEREST CONVERSIONS

An annuity is complex when the equally spaced periodic payment dates do not coincide with the interest conversion dates. Two such modes are possible.

A.   Payments occur less frequently than interest conversions.
B.   Payments occur more frequently than interest conversions.

Discrete Compounding

In order to have a direct approach for either of the two possibilities a new term is defined.

Let:

c   be the number of interest conversion periods per payment interval.
f   be the number of interest conversions per year—the frequency of compounding.
f′   be the number of equally spaced payments per year.

Then

$$c = \frac{f}{f'} \qquad (6.1\text{-}1)$$

The value of c may be greater or less than 1. If tables are to be used, and c is greater than 1, the "appropriate" value, opposite n = c, may be found in Table A-2. If c is less than 1, the "appropriate" value may be found in Table A-3 or Table A-4 opposite the value of c. These "appropriate" values are discussed below.

Example 1.   The value of c is desired for the following.

a)   Monthly compounding—semi-annual payments.
For monthly compounding, f = 12.
For semi-annual payments, f′ = 2.

$$c = \frac{12}{2} = 6 \text{ conversions/payment}$$

b)   Semi-annual compounding—annual payments.
For semi-annual compounding, f = 2.
For annual payments, f′ = 1.

$$c = \frac{2}{1} = 2 \text{ conversions/payment}$$

c)   Quarterly compounding—weekly payments.
For quarterly compounding, f = 4.
For weekly payments, f′ = 52.

$$c = \frac{4}{52} = \frac{1}{13} \text{ conversions/payment}$$

d)   Annual compounding—quarterly payments.
For annual compounding, f = 1.
For quarterly payments, f′ = 4.

$$c = \frac{1}{4} \text{ conversions/payment}$$

For simple annuities, the letter n was used to represent both interest conversion periods and payment periods. As c is defined by Eq. (6.1-1), its units are interest conversions per payment period, therefore, in order to obtain the number of interest conversions in a complex annuity, c must be multiplied by the number of payments. For complex annuities, the letter n is used to represent the number of payments. Then,

$$n = f't \qquad (6.1\text{-}2)$$

and the number of interest conversions becomes nc.

Example 2. If Example 1 referred to a 10-year annuity, the number of interest conversions could be determined as follows.

a)   From Example 1, $f = 12$, $f' = 2$, and $c = 6$. From Eq. (6.1-2)

$$n = (2)(10) = 20$$

and the number of interest conversions in 10 years would be

$$nc = (20)(6) = 120.$$

b)   From Example 1, $f = 2$, $f' = 1$, and $c = 2$. From Eq. (6.1-2)

$$n = (1)(10) = 10$$

and the number of interest conversions in 10 years would be

$$nc = (10)(2) = 20.$$

c)   From Example 1, $f = 4$, $f' = 52$, and $c = 1/13$. From Eq. (6.1-2)

$$n = (52)(10) = 520$$

and the number of interest conversions in 10 years would be

$$nc = (520)(1/13) = 40.$$

d)   From Example 1, $f = 1$, $f' = 4$, and $c = 1/4$. From Eq. (6.1-2)

$$n = (4)(10) = 40$$

and the number of interest conversions in 10 years would be

$$nc = (40)(1/4) = 10.$$

Continuous Compounding

In order that the formulas for discrete compounding of interest can be reduced to apply for continuous compounding of interest in complex annuities, c is defined by $c = 1$, and a pseudo-periodic interest rate, i', is used to determine i^*. As a definition,

$$i' = \frac{R}{f'} \qquad (6.1\text{-}3)$$

6.2   COMPLEX ORDINARY ANNUITIES

An annuity is defined in Chapter 3 as *ordinary* when payments are made at the *ends of periods*. The same definition applies for complex ordinary annuities except that payments are made at the *ends of payment intervals*.

Future Amount—Level Payments and Constant Interest Rate

The future amount of a complex ordinary annuity can be determined by

$$S_{nc} = p\left[\frac{(1 + i^*)^{nc} - 1}{(1 + i^*)^c - 1}\right] \qquad (6.2\text{-}1)$$

For the use of Tables A-2 and A-3,

$$S_{nc} = p \left[\frac{(S/p,i,nc)}{(S/p,i,c)} \right] \tag{6.2-2}$$

In general, for:

    I.   *Discrete Compounding of Interest*

$$\left. \begin{array}{l} c = f/f' \\ n = f't \\ i^* = i = R/f \end{array} \right\} \tag{6.2-3}$$

    II.   *Continuous Compounding of Interest*

$$\left. \begin{array}{l} c = 1 \\ (1 + i^*)^c - 1 = i^* \\ i' = R/f' \\ n = f't \\ i^* = e^{ki'} - 1 \end{array} \right\} \tag{6.2-4}$$

Example 1.   You are advising a client to make deposits of $1,500 into an Individual Retirement Account at the end of each year. For informational purposes you would like to inform your client what amount will be available at the end of 25 years if interest rates do not fall below 12%. Depending upon the method of compounding interest, Eq. (6.2-1) or Eq. (6.2-2), in conjunction with Table A-2 or Table A-3, can be used to determine the future amount.

Discrete Compounding.   Assuming interest is compounded quarterly, $f = 4$, and

$$i^* = i = R/f = 12\%/4 = 3\% = 0.03$$

For annual deposits, $f' = 1$, and

$$c = f/f' = 4/1 = 4$$

For $t = 25$ years

$$n = f't = (1)(25) = 25$$

and

$$nc = (25)(4) = 100$$

    a)   Using Eq. (6.2-1) and the y^x function on the calculator.

$$S_{nc} = (1500) \left[\frac{(1.03)^{100} - 1}{(1.03)^4 - 1} \right]$$

The denominator is calculated first and stored in memory.

Enter 1.03	Depress y^x
Enter 4	Depress =
Display shows 1.1255088	Depress −
Enter 1	Depress =

Display shows 0.1255088	Store in memory
Enter 1.03	Depress y^x
Enter 100	Depress =
Display shows 19.218632	Depress −
Enter 1	Depress =
Display shows 18.218632	Depress ÷
Recall memory	Depress =
Display shows 145.15819	Depress ×
Enter 1500	Depress =
Display shows 217737.29	

b) Using Eq. (6.2-2) and Tables A-2 and/or A-3. Since c and nc are greater than 1, Table A-2 is used to determine (S/p,i,c) and (S/p,i,nc). In the 3% table of Table A-2, under "Amount of Annuity," read the values of (S/p,i,4) and (S/p,i,100) as 4.183627 and 607.2877327, respectively. Then from Eq. (6.2-2),

$$S_{nc} = (1500) \left[\frac{607.2877327}{4.183627} \right]$$

$$= (1500)(145.15819)$$

$$= \$217,737.29$$

Comparing this result with the discrete compounding, annually, of Example 1 of Chapter 3.1 shows that annual payments combined with quarterly compounding results in approximately \$18,000 additional at the end of the payments.

Continuous Compounding. For continuous compounding, c = 1, and for annual payments, f' = 1. Then

$$i' = R/f' = 12\%/1 = 0.12$$

and

$$i^* = e^{ki'} - 1 = e^{(365/360)(0.12)} - 1 = 0.1294$$

For t = 25 years

$$n = f't = (1)(25) = 25$$

and nc = 25. From Eq. (6.2-1)

$$S_{nc} = (1500) \left[\frac{(1.1294)^{25} - 1}{0.1294} \right] = \$231,265.56$$

which is the same as the result of continuous compounding with annual payments in Example 1 of Chapter 3.1.

Example 2. Suppose semi-annual payments of \$750 are made into an account that will earn no less than 12% interest. The least future amount at the end of 25 years can be determined as follows.

Discrete Compounding. Assuming interest is compounded annually, f = 1 and

$$i^* = R/f = 12\%/1 = 12\% = 0.12$$

For semi-annual deposits, $f' = 2$ and

$$c = f/f' = 1/2$$

For $t = 25$ years

$$n = f't = (2)(25) = 50$$

and

$$nc = (50)(1/2) = 25$$

a)   Using Eq. (6.2-1)

$$S_{nc} = (750)\left[\frac{(1.12)^{25} - 1}{(1.12)^{1/2} - 1}\right]$$

The denominator is calculated first and stored in memory.

Enter 1	Depress $\div$
Enter 2	Depress =
Display shows 0.5	Store in memory
Enter 1.12	Depress y^x
Recall memory	Depress =
Display shows 1.0583005	Depress −
Enter 1	Depress =
Display shows 0.0583005	Store in memory
Enter 1.12	Depress y^x
Enter 25	Depress =
Display shows 17.000064	Depress −
Enter 1	Depress =
Display shows 16.000064	Depress $\div$
Recall memory	Depress =
Display shows 274.44118	Depress $\times$
Enter 750	Depress =
Display shows 205830.88	

b)   Using Eq. (6.2-2) and Table A-2 or A-3. In the 12% table of Table A-2, under "Amount of Annuity" and opposite 25, read the value of $(S/p,i,nc)$ as 133.33387006. In the 12% table of Table A-3, under "Amount of Annuity" and opposite 1/2, read the value of $(S/p,i,c)$ as 0.48583770. Then,

$$S_{nc} = (750)\left[\frac{133.33387006}{0.48583770}\right] = \$205{,}830.88$$

Continuous Compounding. For continuous compounding $c = 1$, and for semi-annual payments, $f' = 2$. Then

$$i' = R/f' = 12\%/2 = 6\% = 0.06$$

$$i^* = e^{ki'} - 1 = e^{(365/360)(0.06)} - 1 = 0.0627$$

For $t = 25$ years

$$n = f't = (2)(25) = 50$$

and nc = (50) (1) = 50. From Eq. (6.2-1)

$$S_{nc} = (750) \left[\frac{(1.0627)^{50} - 1}{0.0627} \right] = \$238,261.59$$

Number of Level Payments—Specified Future Amount

The number of level payments that is required in order to achieve a specified future amount can be determined by

$$n = \frac{1}{c} \left\{ \frac{\log \{[S_{nc}[(1 + i^*)^c - 1]/p] + 1\}}{\log (1 + i^*)} \right\} \tag{6.2-5}$$

where:

I. *Discrete Compounding of Interest*

$$c = f/f'$$

$$n = f't$$

$$i^* = i = R/f$$

II. *Continuous Compounding of Interest*

$$c = 1$$

$$[(1 + i^*)^c - 1] = i^*$$

$$i' = R/f'$$

$$n = f't$$

$$i^* = e^{ki'} - 1$$

For the use of Tables A-2 and A-3

$$(S/p,i,nc) = \frac{S_{nc}(S/p,i,c)}{p} \tag{6.2-6}$$

Since Eq. (6.2-6) enables the determination of nc from Table A-2,

$$n = \frac{(nc)}{c} \tag{6.2-7}$$

Example 3. It is desired to know the number of annual payments of $1,500 that will be necessary to achieve $300,000 if the interest rate is no less than 12%.

Discrete Compounding. Assuming monthly compounding, f = 12, and

$$i^* = i = R/f = 12\%/12 = 1\% = 0.01$$

For annual deposits, f' = 1, and

$$c = f/f' = 12/1 = 12$$

a)   Using Eq. (6.2-5).

$$n = \frac{1}{12} \left\{ \frac{\log \{[(300000)\,[(1.01)^{12} - 1]/1500] + 1\}}{\log 1.01} \right\}$$

$$= \frac{1}{12} \left[\frac{\log 26.365005}{\log 1.01} \right] = 27.40 \text{ payments}$$

Since payments are annual, n = 27.4 years to achieve $300,000.

b)   Using Eq. (6.2-6) and Tables. Since c is greater than 1, the 1% table of Table A-2 gives (S/p,i,12) as 12.68250301. Then,

$$(S/p,i,nc) = \frac{(300000)\,(12.68250301)}{1500}$$

$$= 2536.5006$$

In the 1% table of Table A-2, under the "Amount of Annuity," find the values of 2514^+ and 2540^+ opposite 328 and 329 periods, respectively. The values, 328 and 329, are values of nc. Then, since the value 2536^+ is between 2514^+ and 2540^+, the value of nc is between 328 and 329, and

$$n = (nc)/c = 328^+/12 = 27.3^+$$

Continuous Compounding. For continuous compounding, c = 1 and for annual payments, $f' = 1$.

$$i' = R/f' = 12\%/1 = 0.12$$
$$i* = e^{ki'} - 1 = e^{(365/360)\,(0.12)} - 1 = 0.1294$$

From Eq. (6.2-5)

$$n = \frac{\log \{[(300000)\,(0.1294)/1500] + 1\}}{\log 1.1294}$$

$$= 27.05$$

Example 4.   It is desired to know the number of years that will be required for $150 per month to accumulate to $100,000 if the interest rate is 7%.

Discrete Compounding. Assuming semi-annual compounding, f = 2 and

$$i* = i = R/f = 7\%/2 = 3\,1/2\% = 0.035$$

For monthly payments, $f' = 12$ and

$$c = f/f' = 2/12 = 1/6$$

a)   Using Eq. (6.2-5)

$$n = \frac{1}{1/6} \left\{ \frac{\log \{[(100000)\,[(1.035)^{1/6} - 1]/150] + 1\}}{\log 1.035} \right\}$$

(The value of $(1.035)^{1/6}$ can be determined by the calculator or Table A-4)

$$n = 6 \left[\frac{\log 4.8333595}{\log 1.035} \right]$$

$$= 274.79239 \text{ payments}$$

Since there are 12 payments per year,

$$t = n/12 = 274.79239/12 = 22.9 \text{ years}$$

b)   Using Eq. (6.2-6) and Tables. Since c is less than 1, the value of $(S/p,i,c)$ is determined from Table A-3 under 3 1/2%, opposite 1/6, as 0.16428684. Then

$$S_{nc} = \frac{(100000)(0.16428684)}{(150)}$$

$$= 109.52453$$

In the 3 1/2% table of Table A-2, under "Amount of Annuity," find the value of 109^+ between the values opposite 45 and 46 periods. Then the value of nc is 45^+ and,

$$n = (nc)/c = \frac{45^+}{1/6} = 6(45^+) = 270^+$$

and $t = 270/12 = 22.5^+$ years.

Continuous Compounding. For continuous compounding, $c = 1$. Then,

$$i' = R/f' = 7\%/12 = 0.07/12 = 0.0058333$$

and

$$i^* = e^{ki'} - 1 = e^{(365/360)(0.0058333)} - 1 = 0.0059318$$

From Eq. (6.2-5)

$$n = \frac{\log\{[(100000)(0.0059318)/150] + 1\}}{\log 1.0059318}$$

$$= \frac{\log 4.9545333}{\log 1.0059318} = 270.58 \text{ payments}$$

and $t = 270.58/12 = 22.55$ years.

Future Amount—Change in Payment Level and/or Interest Rate

The future amount of an annuity with level payments, wherein the level of payments and/or interest rate changes at a time into the annuity, can be determined by

$$S_{nc} = S_o(1 + i^*)^{Nc} + p_N \left[\frac{(1 + i^*)^{Nc} - 1}{(1 + i^*)^c - 1} \right] \tag{6.2-8}$$

where:

I.   *Discrete Compounding of Interest*

$$c = f/f'$$

$$N = f't$$

$$i^* = i = R/f$$

II.   *Continuous Compounding of Interest*

$$c = 1$$

$$[(1 + i^*)^c - 1] = i^*$$

$$i' = R/f'$$

$$N = f't$$

$$i^* = e^{ki'} - 1$$

For the use of Tables A-2 and A-3

$$S_{nc} = S_o(1 + i^*)^{Nc} + p_N \left[\frac{(S/p,i,Nc)}{(S/p,i,c)} \right] \tag{6.2-9}$$

Example 5.   The accumulated benefits in a pension fund of an individual total $13,000. Contributions had been made at a level of $100 per month, and the fund had been invested at an interest rate of 7% compounded annually. If the payment level is increased to $150 per month, the future amount at the end of the next 15 years is desired.

Discrete Compounding. For annual compounding f = 1 and

$$i^* = i = R/f = 7\%/1 = 7\% = 0.07$$

For monthly payments, f' = 12 and

$$c = f/f' = 1/12$$

For t = 15 years, N = f't = (12) (15) = 180 and

$$Nc = (180) (1/12) = 15$$

a)   Using Eq. (6.2-8).

$$S_{nc} = (13000) (1.07)^{15} + (150) \left[\frac{(1.07)^{15} - 1}{(1.07)^{1/12} - 1} \right]$$

(The value $(1.07)^{1/12}$ can be determined by the calculator or Table A-4.)

$$S_{nc} = (13000) (2.7590315) + (150) \left[\frac{1.7590315}{0.0056541} \right]$$

$$= 35867.41 + 46666.09$$

$$= \$82,533.50$$

b)   Using Eq. (6.2-9) and Tables. Since Nc = 15, the 7% table of Table A-2 is used for (S/p,i,Nc), and since c = 1/12, the 7% table of Table A-3 is used for (S/p,i,c). Then,

$$S_{nc} = (13000) (1 + 7\%)^{15} + (150) \left[\frac{(S/p,i,Nc)}{(S/p,i,c)} \right]$$

$$= (13000) (2.75903154) + (150) \left[\frac{25.1290220}{0.08077351} \right]$$

$$= 35867.41 + 46665.72$$

$$= \$82,533.13$$

Continuous Compounding. For 7% compounded continuously, $c = 1$. Then

$$i' = R/f' = 7\%/12 = 0.07/12 = 0.0058333$$

$$i^* = e^{ki'} - 1 = e^{(365/360)(0.0058333)} - 1 = 0.0059318$$

For $t = 15$ years, $N = f't = (12)(15) = 180$ and $Nc = 180$. From Eq. (6.2-8)

$$S_{nc} = (13000)(1.0059318)^{180} + (150)\left[\frac{(1.0059318)^{180} - 1}{0.0059318}\right]$$

$$= (13000)(2.8995912) + (150)(320.23858)$$

$$= 37694.69 + 48035.79$$

$$= \$85,730.48$$

Number of Level Payments After a Change—Specified Future Amount

If a change occurs in the payment level and/or interest rate, the number of payments at a new payment level and/or interest rate can be determined by

$$N = \frac{1}{c}\left\{\frac{\log\left[\dfrac{S_{nc}[(1 + i^*)^c - 1] + p_N}{S_o[(1 + i^*)^c - 1] + p_N}\right]}{\log(1 + i^*)}\right\} \tag{6.2-10}$$

where:

    I. *Discrete Compounding of Interest*

$$c = f/f',$$

$$N = f't$$

$$i^* = i = R/f$$

    II. *Continuous Compounding of Interest*

$$c = 1$$

$$[(1 + i^*)^c - 1] = i^*$$

$$i' = R/f'$$

$$N = f't$$

$$i^* = e^{ki'} - 1$$

Example 6. An individual has an account with an accumulation of \$13,000. Monthly deposits of \$150 are to be made into an account which will earn interest at no less than 10%. The number of payments and number of years required to accumulate \$150,000 can be determined by Eq. (6.2-10).

Discrete Compounding. Assuming annual compounding, $f = 1$ and

$$i^* = i = R/f = 10\%/1 = 10\% = 0.10$$

For monthly payments, $f' = 12$ and

$$c = f/f' = 1/12.$$

a) Using Eq. (6.2-10) and the y^x function on the calculator.

$$N = \frac{1}{1/12} \left\{ \frac{\log \left[\dfrac{(150000)\,[(1.1)^{1/12} - 1] + 150}{(13000)\,[(1.1)^{1/12} - 1] + 150} \right]}{\log 1.10} \right\}$$

$$= 12 \left\{ \frac{\log \left[\dfrac{1346.1209}{253.66381} \right]}{\log 1.10} \right\} = 12 \left[\frac{\log 5.3067124}{\log 1.10} \right]$$

$$= 210.13 \text{ payments} = 17.51 \text{ years}$$

b) Using Eq. (6.2-10) and Table A-4. Since $c = 1/12$ and is less than 1, the values of $(1 + i^*)^c$ can be found in Table A-4 under 10%. Thus,

$$N = \frac{1}{1/12} \left\{ \frac{\log \left[\dfrac{(150000)\,[1.00797414 - 1] + 150}{(13000)\,[1.00797414 - 1] + 150} \right]}{\log 1.10} \right\}$$

$$= 12 \left\{ \frac{\log \left[\dfrac{(150000)\,(0.00797414) + 150}{(13000)\,(0.00797414) + 150} \right]}{\log 1.10} \right\}$$

$$= 210.13 \text{ payments} = 17.51 \text{ years}$$

Continuous Compounding. For continuous compounding, $c = 1$. Then,

$$i' = R/f' = 10\%/12 = 0.10/12 = 0.0083333$$

$$i^* = e^{ki'} - 1 = e^{(365/360)(0.0083333)} - 1 = 0.0084848$$

$$N = \frac{\log \left[\dfrac{(150000)\,(0.0084848) + 150}{(13000)\,(0.0084848) + 150} \right]}{\log 1.0084848}$$

$$= \frac{\log 5.4656433}{\log 1.0084848}$$

$$= 201.03 \text{ payments} = 16.75 \text{ years.}$$

Sinking Fund—Level Payments and Interest Rate

When it is desired to know the necessary level payment in order to achieve a specified future amount in a specified period of time,

$$p = S_{nc} \left[\frac{(1 + i^*)^c - 1}{(1 + i^*)^{nc} - 1} \right] \tag{6.2-11}$$

where:

> I. *Discrete Compounding of Interest*
>
> $$c = f/f'$$
>
> $$n = f't$$
>
> $$i^* = i = R/f$$
>
> II. *Continuous Compounding of Interest*
>
> $$c = 1$$
>
> $$[(1 + i^*)^c - 1] = i^*$$
>
> $$i' = R/f'$$
>
> $$n = f't$$
>
> $$i^* = e^{ki'} - 1$$

For use of Tables A-2 and A-3

$$p = S_{nc} \left[\frac{(S/p,i,c)}{(S/p,i,nc)} \right] \tag{6.2-12}$$

Example 7. Your corporation sells \$1,000,000 of 20-year bonds at face value and establishes a sinking fund for the redemption of the bonds. You estimate that the fund will earn interest at 20% compounded annually and desire to know what quarterly payments are necessary to the sinking fund. For annual compounding, f = 1 and

$$i^* = i = R/f = 20\%/1 = 20\% = 0.20$$

For quarterly payments, f' = 4 and

$$c = f/f' = 1/4.$$

For t = 20 years,

$$n = f't = (4)(20) = 80$$

and

$$nc = (80)(1/4) = 20$$

   a) Using Eq. (6.2-11).

$$p = (1000000) \left[\frac{(1.20)^{1/4} - 1}{(1.20)^{20} - 1} \right]$$

Using the y^x function on the calculator or Tables A-2 and A-4

$$p = (1000000) \left[\frac{1.0466351 - 1}{38.3376 - 1} \right]$$

$$p = (1000000)(0.001249)$$

$$= \$1,249.01 \text{ per quarter}$$

   b) Using Eq. (6.2-12) and Tables. Since c is less than 1, Table A-3 is used to determine (S/p,i,c). From the 20% tables of Tables A-2 and A-3

$$p = (1000000) \left[\frac{0.2331757}{186.68799962} \right]$$

$$= \$1,249.01 \text{ per quarter.}$$

Example 8. You establish trusts for the education of your children. You would like an accumulation of $150,000 in 18 years. Assuming that the accounts will not earn less than 10% interest compounded continuously, the minimum quarterly payments can be determined by Eq. (6.2-11). For continuous compounding, $c = 1$. Then

$$i' = R/f' = 10\%/4 = 0.10/4 = 0.025$$

and

$$i^* = e^{ki'} - 1 = e^{(365/360)(0.025)} - 1 = 0.02567$$

$$nc = n = f't = (4)(18) = 72$$

$$p = (150000) \left[\frac{1.02567 - 1}{(1.02567)^{72} - 1} \right]$$

$$= (150000) \left[\frac{0.02567}{5.2022752} \right]$$

$$= \$740.16 \text{ per quarter.}$$

New Level Payments—Change in Sinking Fund and/or Interest Rate

After a series of payments have been made into a sinking fund, if the specified future amount of that fund and/or the interest rate at which the fund is invested changes, the new level payment can be determined by

$$p_N = [S_{nc} - S_0(1 + i^*)^{Nc}] \left[\frac{(1 + i^*)^c - 1}{(1 + i^*)^{Nc} - 1} \right] \qquad (6.2\text{-}13)$$

where:

I. *Discrete Compounding of Interest*

$$c = f/f'$$

$$N = f't$$

$$i^* = i = R/f$$

II. *Continuous Compounding of Interest*

$$c = 1$$

$$[(1 + i^*)^c - 1] = i^*$$

$$i' = R/f'$$

$$N = f't$$

$$i^* = e^{ki'} - 1$$

For the use of Tables A-2 and A-3

$$p_N = [S_{nc} - S_0(1 + i^*)^{Nc}] \left[\frac{(S/p,i,c)}{(S/p,i,Nc)} \right] \qquad (6.2\text{-}14)$$

Example 9.   Suppose that 5 years have elapsed since the $1,000,000 of bonds in Example 7 were issued, and the sinking fund account is at $40,000. You estimate that the fund can earn 22% compounded annually. If the interest rate does not change, the new quarterly payments for the remaining 15 years can be determined as follows. For annual compounding, f = 1 and

$$i^* = i = R/f = 22\%/1 = 22\% = 0.22.$$

For quarterly payments, f' = 4 and

$$c = f/f' = 1/4$$

For t = 15 years, N = f't = (4) (15) = 60 and

$$Nc = (60) (1/4) = 15.$$

a)   Using Eq. (6.2-13).

$$p_N = [1000000 - (40000) (1.22)^{15}] \left[\frac{(1.22)^{1/4} - 1}{(1.22)^{15} - 1} \right]$$

(The value $(1.22)^{1/4}$ can be determined by calculator or Table A-4)

$$p_N = [1000000 - 789691.48] \left[\frac{0.0509691}{18.742287} \right]$$

$$= \$571.93 \text{ per quarter}$$

b)   Using Eq. (6.2-14) and Tables. Since c is less than 1, (S/p,i,c) can be determined from Table A-3.

$$p_N = [1000000 - (40000) (1 + 22\%)^{15}] \left[\frac{(S/p,i,c)}{(S/p,i,Nc)} \right]$$

From Tables A-2, A-3, and A-4 in the 22% tables

$$p_N = [1000000 - (40000) (19.74228696)] \left[\frac{0.23167784}{85.19221343} \right]$$

$$= (1000000 - 789691.44) (0.0027195)$$

$$= \$571.93 \text{ per quarter}$$

Example 10.   Suppose 10 years have elapsed since you began funding the trusts of Example 8, and there is an accumulation of $51,000. You are reasonably certain that the interest rate will not fall below 12% for the remaining 8 years of the trusts. The new quarterly payments can be determined as follows. For continuous compounding c = 1 and Nc = N = f't = (4) (8) = 32. Then

$$i' = R/f' = 12\%/4 = 0.12/4 = 0.03$$

and

$$i^* = e^{ki'} - 1 = e^{(365/360)(0.03)} - 1 = 0.0309$$

From Eq. (6.2-13)

$$p_N = [150000 - (51000)(1.0309)^{32}]\left[\frac{0.0309}{(1.0309)^{32} - 1}\right]$$

$$= [150000 - 135051.51]\left[\frac{0.0309}{1.6480688}\right]$$

$$= \$280.27 \text{ per quarter}$$

Future Amount—Annual Payment Amount Changing at a Constant Rate

If payments to an annuity are to begin at a specified annual amount, p_o, with f' equal payments equally spaced during the year, and if subsequent annual amounts are increased (decreased) at a constant rate, the future amount can be determined by:

I. *Discrete Compounding of Interest*

$$S_{nc} = \frac{p_o}{f'}\left[\frac{(1 + i^*)^f - 1}{(1 + i^*)^c - 1}\right]\left[\frac{(1 + R)^t - (1 + G)^t}{R - G}\right] \qquad (6.2\text{-}15)$$

where $c = f/f'$ and $i^* = i = R/f$. The various elements of Eq. (6.2-15) can be determined by the y^x function on the hand-held calculator or Table A-2 (when the exponents are greater than 1) and Table A-4 (when the exponents are less than 1). For the use of Table A-3, Eq. (6.2-15) becomes

$$S_{nc} = \frac{p_o}{f'}\left[\frac{(S/p,i,f)}{(S/p,i,c)}\right]\left[\frac{(1 + R)^t - (1 + G)^t}{R - G}\right] \qquad (6.2\text{-}16)$$

where, $(S/p,i,f)$ can be determined from Table A-2, and $(S/p,i,c)$ can be determined from Table A-3 if c is less than 1.

If the annual growth rate of the payments is equal to the interest rate ($G = R$), Eqs. (6.2-15) and (6.2-16) become

$$S_{nc} = \frac{tp_o(1 + G)^{t-1}}{f'}\left[\frac{(1 + i^*)^f - 1}{(1 + i^*)^c - 1}\right] = \frac{tp_o(1 + G)^{t-1}}{f'}\left[\frac{(S/p,i,f)}{(S/p,i,c)}\right] \qquad (6.2\text{-}17)$$

II. *Continuous Compounding of Interest*

For continuous compounding of interest, Eq. (6.2-15) reduces to

$$S_t = \frac{p_o}{f'}\left[\frac{R_e}{i^*}\right]\left[\frac{(1 + R_e)^t - (1 + G)^t}{R_e - G}\right] \qquad (6.2\text{-}18)$$

where

$$\left.\begin{array}{l} i' = R/f' \\ i^* = e^{ki'} - 1 \\ R_e = e^{kR} - 1 \end{array}\right\} \qquad (6.2\text{-}19)$$

If $G = R_e$, Eq. (6.2-18) reduces to

$$S_t = \frac{tp_o(1 + G)^{t-1}}{f'}\left[\frac{R_e}{i^*}\right] \qquad (6.2\text{-}20)$$

Example 11.   You hire a 45-year-old individual at $30,000 per year. Your company pension plan requires you to pay the plan 5% of the employee's salary in quarterly installments. Historically, your company has given salary increases of at least 6% per year, and it is assumed that future increases will be no less than 6%. Assuming that the pension fund can be invested at a rate of at least 10%, the least amount in the pension account of the employee at age 65 can be determined as follows.

Discrete Compounding.   Assuming that the interest rate is 10% compounded annually, $f = 1$. Then

$$i^* = i = R/f = 10\%/1 = 10\% = 0.10$$

For quarterly payments, $f' = 4$ and

$$c = f/f' = 1/4$$

From age 45 to age 65 is 20 years. Then

$$n = f't = (4)(20) = 80$$

and

$$nc = (80)(1/4) = 20$$

The initial annual contribution is 5% of $30,000 or $1,500. Then

$$p_0/f' = 1500/4 = 375$$

a)   Using Eq. (6.2-15).

$$S_{nc} = (375) \left[\frac{(1 + 10\%)^1 - 1}{(1 + 10\%)^{1/4} - 1} \right] \left[\frac{(1 + 10\%)^{20} - (1 + 6\%)^{20}}{10\% - 6\%} \right]$$

The value of $(1 + 10\%)^{1/4}$ can be found in Table A-4 and the remaining values can be found in Table A-2, or all values can be determined with the calculator.

$$S_{nc} = (375) \left[\frac{0.10}{1.02411369 - 1} \right] \left[\frac{6.72749995 - 3.20713547}{0.10 - 0.06} \right]$$

$$= \$136,866.40$$

b)   Using Eq. (6.2-16).

$$S_{nc} = (375) \left[\frac{(S/p,i,1)}{(S/p,i,1/4)} \right] \left[\frac{(1 + 10\%)^{20} - (1 + 6\%)^{20}}{10\% - 6\%} \right]$$

Since c is less than 1, the value of $(S/p,i,1/4)$ can be found in Table A-3, and the remaining values can be found in Table A-2.

$$S_{nc} = (375) \left[\frac{1}{0.24113689} \right] \left[\frac{6.72749995 - 3.20713547}{0.10 - 0.06} \right]$$

$$= \$136,865.95$$

Continuous Compounding. For continuous compounding,

$$i' = R/f' = 10\%/4 = 0.10/4 = 0.025$$

$$i* = e^{(365/360)(0.025)} - 1 = 0.02567$$

$$R_e = e^{kR} - 1 = e^{(365/360)(0.10)} - 1 = 0.1067$$

From Eq. (6.2-18),

$$S_t = (375)\left[\frac{0.1067}{0.02567}\right]\left[\frac{(1.1067)^{20} - (1.06)^{20}}{0.1067 - 0.06}\right]$$

Using the y^x function on the calculator,

$$S_t = (375)(4.156603)\left[\frac{7.5962317 - 3.20713547}{0.0467}\right]$$

$$= \$146,496.77$$

Example 12.   Suppose the growth rate for the contribution of Example 11 is the same as the interest rate. The respective future amounts would be determined as follows.

Discrete Compounding. $G = R = 10\%$. From Eq. (6.2-17)

$$S_{nc} = (20)(375)(1.10)^{19}\left[\frac{1}{0.24113689}\right] = \$190,221.14$$

Continuous Compounding. $G = R_e = 10.67\%$. From Eq. (6.2-20)

$$S_t = (20)(375)(1.1067)^{19}\left[\frac{0.1067}{0.02567}\right] = \$213,977.50$$

Sinking Fund—Initial Annual Amount
Annual Amount Changing at a Constant Rate

For a specified future amount, rearrangement of Eqs. (6.2-15), (6.2-16), (6.2-17), (6.2-18) and (6.2-20) to solve for p_o enables the determination of the initial annual amount payable in f' equal payments equally spaced during the year.

I.   *Discrete Compounding of Interest*

$$p_o = f'S_{nc}\left[\frac{(1 + i*)^c - 1}{(1 + i*)^f - 1}\right]\left[\frac{R - G}{(1 + R)^t - (1 + G)^t}\right] \qquad (6.2\text{-}21)$$

where $c = f/f'$ and $i* = R/f$. The elements of Eq. (6.2-21) can be determined by using the y^x function on the calculator or Tables A-2 and A-4.

$$p_o = f'S_{nc}\left[\frac{(S/p,i,c)}{(S/p,i,f)}\right]\left[\frac{R - G}{(1 + R)^t - (1 + G)^t}\right] \qquad (6.2\text{-}22)$$

The elements of Eq. (6.2-22) can be determined by using the y^x function on the calculator or Tables A-2 and A-3.

For the case where $G = R$,

$$p_o = \frac{f'S_{nc}}{t(1 + G)^{t-1}} \left[\frac{(1 + i^*)^c - 1}{(1 + i^*)^f - 1}\right] = \frac{f'S_{nc}}{t(1 + G)^{t-1}} \left[\frac{(S/p,i,c)}{(S/p,i,f)}\right] \qquad (6.2\text{-}23)$$

II.   *Continuous Compounding of Interest*

For continuous compounding of interest, Eq. (6.2-21) reduces to

$$p_o = f'S_t \left[\frac{i^*}{R_e}\right]\left[\frac{R_e - G}{(1 + R_e)^t - (1 + G)^t}\right] \qquad (6.2\text{-}24)$$

where

$$i' = R/f'$$

$$i^* = e^{ki'} - 1$$

$$R_e = e^{kR} - 1$$

For the case where $G = R_e$, Eq. (6.2-24) reduces to

$$p_o = \frac{f'S_t}{t(1 + G)^{t-1}} \left[\frac{i^*}{R_e}\right] \qquad (6.2\text{-}25)$$

Example 13.   Recall the sinking fund of Example 7 for $1,000,000 of 20-year bonds. Suppose it is expected that the revenue from the utilization of the million dollars will increase with time, and greater contributions toward the redemption of the bonds can be made in the latter years. If the sinking fund can be expected to earn interest at 20% compounded annually, and if the payments are to be made quarterly with the annual amount increased 10% per year, the initial annual amount and quarterly payment can be determined as follows. For annual compounding, $f = 1$ and

$$i^* = i = R/f = 20\%/1 = 20\% = 0.20$$

For quarterly payments, $f' = 4$ and

$$c = f/f' = 1/4$$

$$t = 20$$

a)   Using Eq. (6.2-21).

$$p_o = (4)\,(1000000) \left[\frac{(1 + 20\%)^{1/4} - 1}{(1 + 20\%)^1 - 1}\right]\left[\frac{20\% - 10\%}{(1 + 20\%)^{20} - (1 + 10\%)^{20}}\right]$$

The value of $(1 + 20\%)^{1/4}$ can be found in Table A-4, and the remaining values can be found in Table A-2, or all values can be determined with the calculator.

$$p_o = (4000000) \left[\frac{1.04663514 - 1}{0.20}\right]\left[\frac{0.20 - 0.10}{38.33759992 - 6.72749995}\right]$$

$$= \$2,950.65$$

the first year and to be increased 10% per year. Quarterly payments during the first year would be $737.66.

b) Using Eq. (6.2-22).

$$p_o = (4)\,(1000000)\left[\frac{(S/p,i,1/4)}{(S/p,i,1)}\right]\left[\frac{0.20 - 0.10}{38.33759992 - 6.72749995}\right]$$

The value of $(S/p,i,1/4)$ can be found in Table A-3, and the value of $(S/p,i,1)$ can be found in Table A-2 as 1. Then

$$p_o = (4000000)\left[\frac{0.2331757}{1}\right]\left[\frac{0.20 - 0.10}{38.33759992 - 6.72749995}\right]$$

$$= \$2,950.65$$

Example 14. Suppose you desire to increase annual payments at the same rate as the interest rate in Example 13. $G = 20\%$. From Eq. (6.2-23)

$$p_o = \frac{(4)\,(1000000)}{(20)\,(1.2)^{19}}\left[\frac{(S/p,i,1/4)}{(S/p,i,1)}\right] = \frac{(4000000)}{(20)\,(31.948)}\left[\frac{0.2331757}{1}\right]$$

$$= \$1,459.72$$

Example 15. Recall the trusts of Example 8. Suppose you decide to begin quarterly payments at a relatively low level and increase the annual amount by 5% per year. In order to accumulate \$150,000 in 18 years at an interest rate of 10% compounded continuously, the initial annual amount (and quarterly payment) can be determined by Eq. (6.2-24). For quarterly payments, $f' = 4$ and $i' = R/f' = 10\%/4 = 0.025$.

$$i^* = e^{(365/360)\,(0.025)} - 1 = 0.02567$$

$$R_e = e^{(365/360)\,(0.10)} - 1 = 0.1067$$

$$p_o = (4)\,(150000)\left[\frac{0.02567}{0.1067}\right]\left[\frac{0.1067 - 0.05}{(1.1067)^{18} - (1.05)^{18}}\right]$$

$$= (600000)\,(0.2405811)\left[\frac{0.0567}{6.2020945 - 2.4066192}\right]$$

$$= \$2,156.40$$

the first year and to be increased by 5% per year. Quarterly payments during the first year amount to \$539.10.

Example 16. Suppose you decide that you will increase the annual amount by the effective annual interest in Example 15. $G = 10.67\%$. The initial annual payment can be determined by Eq. (6.2-25) as

$$p_o = \frac{(4)\,(150000)}{(18)\,(1.1067)^{17}}\left[\frac{0.02567}{0.1067}\right]$$

$$= \$1,430.97$$

Changing Annual Amount—Payment Level at a Given Year

See Eq. (3.1-27) with m defined as the given year.

Year—Annual Amount Reaching a Specified Level

See Eq. (3.1-28) with m defined as the year to be determined.

Future Amount—Low Yield Converted to High Yield

If equal deposits are made at equal intervals into a low yield, R_1%, account during a year and the annual future amount of those deposits is converted annually to a high yield, R%, instrument, the future amount after t years can be determined by

$$\text{I.} \quad \textit{Discrete Compounding of Interest}$$

$$S_{nc} = p \left[\frac{(1 + i_1^*)^f - 1}{(1 + i_1^*)^c - 1} \right] \left[\frac{(1 + R)^t - 1}{R} \right] \tag{6.2-26}$$

where

$$\left. \begin{array}{l} c = f/f' \\ i_1^* = i_1 = R_1/f \end{array} \right\} \tag{6.2-27}$$

For the use of Tables A-2 and A-3

$$S_{nc} = p \left[\frac{(S/p, i, f)}{(S/p, i, c)} \right] (S/p, R, t) \tag{6.2-28}$$

$$\text{II.} \quad \textit{Continuous Compounding of Interest}$$

For continuous compounding, Eq. (6.2-26) reduces to

$$S_t = p \left[\frac{R_{1e}}{i_1^*} \right] \left[\frac{(1 + R_e)^t - 1}{R_e} \right] \tag{6.2-29}$$

where

$$\left. \begin{array}{l} i_1' = R_1/f' \\ i_1^* = e^{k i_1'} - 1 \\ R_{1e} = e^{k R_1} - 1 \\ R_e = e^{k R} - 1 \end{array} \right\} \tag{6.2-30}$$

Example 17. Suppose your client in Example 1 is planning to deposit \$125 per month in a 5 1/4% savings account and, annually, to convert the whole account into a 12% Term Account. The amount that will be available to your client at the end of 25 years can be determined as follows.

Discrete Compounding. Assuming that the 5 1/4% savings account is compounded monthly, f = 12, and it is assumed that the high yield account is 12% compounded annually. Then,

$$i_1^* = i_1 = R_1/f = 5\ 1/4\%/12 = 21/48\% = 7/16\% = 0.004375$$

For monthly payments, $f' = 12$, and

$$c = f/f' = 12/12 = 1$$

$$t = 25$$

a)   Using Eq. (6.2-26).

$$S_{nc} = (125) \left[\frac{(1.004375)^{12} - 1}{0.004375} \right] \left[\frac{(1.12)^{25} - 1}{0.12} \right]$$

$$= (125) \left[\frac{1.0537819 - 1}{0.004375} \right] \left[\frac{17.000064 - 1}{0.12} \right]$$

$$= \$204,884.25$$

b)   Using Eq. (6.2-28) and Tables. Since they do not include an interest rate of 5 1/4/12%, the tables must be interpolated between 5/12% and 6/12% (1/2%). For 5 1/4/12%, the interpolated values will be

The value of 5/12% + 1/4 (the difference between 1/2% and 5/12%).

For $(S/p,i,f) = (S/p,i,12)$, in Table A-2 between 5/12% and 1/2%,

$$(S/p,i,12) = 12.27885549 + (1/4) (12.33556237 - 12.27885549)$$

$$= 12.293307$$

For $(S/p,i,c) = (S/p,i,1)$, in Table A-2,

$$(S/p,i,1) = 1.$$

For $(S/p,R,t) = (S/p,R,25)$, in Table A-2 under 12%

$$(S/p,R,25) = 133.33387006$$

Then, from Eq. (6.2-28)

$$S_{nc} = (125) \left[\frac{12.293307}{1} \right] (133.33387006)$$

$$= \$204,889.27$$

The difference between the interpolated result of b) above ($204,889.27) and the directly calculated result of a) above ($204,884.25) is $5.02 which is negligible. *Remember that interpolation is an approximation.*

Continuous Compounding. For use in Eq. (6.2-29),

$$i_1' = R_1/f' = 5\ 1/4\%/12 = 0.0525/12 = 0.004375$$

$$i_1^* = e^{ki_1'} - 1 = e^{(365/360)(0.004375)} - 1 = 0.00445$$

$$R_{1e} = e^{kR_1} - 1 = e^{(365/360)(0.0525)} - 1 = 0.0547$$

$$R_e = e^{kR} - 1 = e^{(365/360)(0.12)} - 1 = 0.1294$$

Then,

$$S_t = (125) \left[\frac{0.0547}{0.00445} \right] \left[\frac{(1.1294)^{25} - 1}{0.1294} \right]$$

$$= \$236,895.63$$

Sinking Fund—Combination of Increasing and Level Payments

If it is advantageous, for a sinking fund, to begin annual payments at a relatively low level; increase the level of the annual amount at a constant rate until a specified amount is reached or approximated; and continue the annual amount at the specified constant level, and if these annual amounts are to be paid in f' equal amounts at f' equal intervals during the year, the following procedure may be used.

1.   Determine an initial annual amount, p_o, which if increased at a constant annual rate would result in the specified future amount of the sinking fund. For discrete compounding, Eq. (6.2-21), (6.2-22), or (6.2-23) can be used as appropriate.

$$p_o = f'S_{nc} \left[\frac{(1 + i^*)^c - 1}{(1 + i^*)^f - 1} \right] \left[\frac{R - G}{(1 + R)^t - (1 + G)^t} \right]$$

where

$$c = f/f' \quad \text{and} \quad i^* = i = R/f$$

$$p_o = f'S_{nc} \left[\frac{(S/p,i,c)}{(S/p,i,f)} \right] \left[\frac{R - G}{(1 + R)^t - (1 + G)^t} \right]$$

and if $G = R$

$$p_o = \frac{f'S_{nc}}{t(1 + G)^{t-1}} \left[\frac{(1 + i^*)^c - 1}{(1 + i^*)^f - 1} \right] = \frac{f'S_{nc}}{t(1 + G)^{t-1}} \left[\frac{(S/p,i,c)}{(S/p,i,f)} \right]$$

For continuous compounding, Eq. (6.2-24) or (6.2-25) can be used as appropriate. For

$$i' = R/f'$$

$$i^* = e^{ki'} - 1$$

$$R_e = e^{kR} - 1$$

$$p_o = f'S_t \left[\frac{i^*}{R_e} \right] \left[\frac{R_e - G}{(1 + R_e)^t - (1 + G)^t} \right]$$

and if $G = R_e$

$$p_o = \frac{f'S_t}{t(1 + G)^{t-1}} \left[\frac{i^*}{R_e} \right]$$

2.   Determine the year, m, for the specified constant annual amount, p_N, from Eq. (3.1-28).

$$m = 1 + \frac{\log (p_N/p_o)}{\log (1 + G)}$$

Normally, m will *not* be a whole number. If a calculator with a y^x function is being used, the decimal value of m may be retained until all calculations are completed, and the final value of m can be rounded to the nearest whole number. Alternatively, or if tables are being used, m may be rounded to the nearest whole number immediately.

3. Determine, S_o, the necessary accumulation at the end of year m in order to have S_{nc} at the end of year t. In order to determine S_o, let $t_N = t - m$, $N = f't_N$, and $Nc = f't_N c$. Rearranging Eq. (6.2-8) or (6.2-9) gives

$$S_o = \frac{S_{nc}}{(1 + i^*)^{Nc}} - \left[\frac{(p_N/f')}{(1 + i^*)^{Nc}}\right]\left[\frac{(1 + i^*)^{Nc} - 1}{(1 + i^*)^c - 1}\right] \qquad (6.2\text{-}31)$$

where:

I. *Discrete Compounding of Interest*

$$c = f/f'$$

$$n = f't$$

$$i^* = i = R/f$$

II. *Continuous Compounding of Interest*

$$c = 1$$

$$[(1 + i^*)^c - 1] = i^*$$

$$i' = R/f'$$

$$n = f't$$

$$i^* = e^{ki'} - 1$$

For use of Table A-3

$$S_o = \frac{S_{nc}}{(1 + i^*)^{Nc}} - \left[\frac{(p_N/f')}{(1 + i^*)^{Nc}}\right]\left[\frac{(S/p,i,Nc)}{(S/p,i,c)}\right] \qquad (6.2\text{-}32)$$

4. In the appropriate equation of Step 1, replace S_{nc} or S_t by S_o from Step 3, replace t by m and re-solve for p_o in Step 1.

5. If the value of p_o from Step 4 does not equal the value of p_o from Step 1 within an acceptable difference, replace p_o in Step 2 by the value of p_o from Step 4 and repeat Steps 2, 3, 4, and 5 until either p_o or m repeat.

When p_o or m repeat, the last value of p_o will be the starting annual amount. If values of m have been rounded to the nearest whole number, an average of the two values of p_o which resulted in the same value of m may be used as the starting value of p_o.

Computer Programs. Because the number of iterations for convergence to the final value of p_o can be large (especially if the value of m is not rounded to the nearest whole number), and because of the availability of personal computers, the following two programs, in the BASIC language, are "no frills" programs that perform the iterations until successive values of p_o are within \$1, and then m is rounded to the nearest whole number.

The necessary data are:

1. The desired future amount—S.
2. The desired level payment—p.
3. The nominal annual interest rate—R.
4. The nominal annual growth rate—G.
5. The term of the annuity (sinking fund)—t.
6. The compounding frequency—f.
7. The payment frequency—f'.

These values are "read" in statement 0030, and the corresponding values are listed in statement 0040 in the sequence:

$$S, p, R, G, t, f, f'$$

when interest is compounded discretely and in the sequence:

$$S, p, R, G, t, f'$$

when interest is compounded continuously.

The statement PRINT CHR\$(12) appears twice in each of the following programs—statements 0090 and 0510 and statements 0090 and 0530 respectively. This statement is used to advance the paper to the top of the next page. It has no other use in the program.

The symbol, $\wedge$, in statement 0230 and elsewhere is analogous to the upward directed arrow in BASIC.

These programs can be used for the combination of increasing and level payment annuities which are discussed in Chapter 3. In order to be used for that simple ordinary annuity, the value of f' is made equal to 1.

Example 18. A self-employed individual would like to have a tax-sheltered account with approximately $1,000,000 at the end of 25 years. This individual plans to increase annual contributions by 8% per year until a level of approximately $7,500 is reached and then maintain annual amounts at $7,500. If the annual contributions are to be made in semiannual, equal amounts into an account that will earn no less than 12% interest, the *initial* annual (and semiannual) amount can be determined by:

Discrete Compounding. Program 6-1.

```
THE MAXIMUM PAYMENT FOR THE LAST N YEARS IS          7500
THE GROWTH RATE FOR THE FIRST M YEARS IS             8  %
THE NOMINAL ANNUAL INTEREST RATE IS                  12   %
THE COMPOUNDING FREQUENCY IS                         1
THE NUMBER OF PAYMENTS PER YEAR IS                   2
THE NUMBER OF YEARS TO ACHIEVE S IS                  25
THE DESIRED FUTURE AMOUNT (S) IS                     1000000

FOR DISCRETE COMPOUNDING OF INTEREST

THE NUMBER OF ITERATIONS IS                          6
THE INITIAL ANNUAL AMOUNT IS $                       6311
THE GROWTH OF PO AT  8  % PER YEAR CEASES AT         3
THE VALUE IN THE ACCOUNT THEN IS $                   23580
THE NUMBER OF YEARS AT $  7500  PER YEAR IS          22
THE FUTURE AMOUNT AT THE END OF  25  YEARS IS $      999321
```

```
0010 REM PROGRAM 6-1
0020 REM DISCRETE COMPOUNDING OF INTEREST
0030 READ S, P, R, G, T, F, F1
0040 DATA 1000000, 7500, 12, 8, 25, 1, 2
0050 LET R=R/100
0060 LET I=R/F
0070 LET G=G/100
```

Program 6-1 (Continued)

```
0080 LET C=F/F1
0090 PRINT CHR$(12)
0100 PRINT
0110 PRINT "THE MAXIMUM PAYMENT FOR THE LAST N YEARS IS ",P
0120 PRINT "THE GROWTH RATE FOR THE FIRST M YEARS IS     ",(100*G);
0130 PRINT " %"
0140 PRINT "THE NOMINAL ANNUAL INTEREST RATE IS          ",(100*R);
0150 PRINT " %"
0160 PRINT "THE COMPOUNDING FREQUENCY IS                 ",F
0170 PRINT "THE NUMBER OF PAYMENTS PER YEAR IS           ",F1
0180 PRINT "THE NUMBER OF YEARS TO ACHIEVE S IS          ",T
0190 PRINT "THE DESIRED FUTURE AMOUNT (S) IS             ",S
0200 PRINT
0210 PRINT "FOR DISCRETE COMPOUNDING OF INTEREST"
0220 LET J=1
0230 LET PO=F1*S*(((1+I)^C-1)/((1+I)^F-1))*(R-G)/((1+R)^T-(1+G)^T)
0240 LET M=1+LOG(P/PO)/LOG(1+G)
0250 LET T1=T-M
0260 LET N=F1*T1
0270 LET E=N*C
0280 LET SO=S/(1+I)^E-(P/F1)/(1+I)^E*((1+I)^E-1)/((1+I)^C-1)
0290 LET QO=F1*SO*(((1+I)^C-1)/((1+I)^F-1))*((R-G)/((1+R)^M-(1+G)^M))
0300 LET Q1=PO-QO
0310 IF J=1000 THEN GOTO 0360
0320 IF ABS(Q1)<=1 THEN GOTO 0360
0330 LET PO=QO
0340 LET J=J+1
0350 GOTO 0240
0360 PRINT
0370 LET L=INT(T1+.5)
0380 LET K=INT(M+.5)
0390 LET E=INT(E+.5)
0400 LET SO=(PO/F1)*((1+I)^F-1)/((1+I)^C-1)*((1+R)^K-(1+G)^K)/(R-G)
0410 LET S1=SO*(1+I)^L+(P/F1)*((1+I)^E-1)/((1+I)^C-1)
0420 PRINT "THE NUMBER OF ITERATIONS IS ",,J
0430 PRINT "THE INITIAL ANNUAL AMOUNT IS $ ",,INT(PO+.5)
0440 PRINT "THE GROWTH OF PO AT ";(100*G);
0450 PRINT " % PER YEAR CEASES AT ",INT(M+.5)
0460 PRINT "THE VALUE IN THE ACCOUNT THEN IS $ ",,INT(SO+.5)
0470 PRINT "THE NUMBER OF YEARS AT $ ";P;
0480 PRINT " PER YEAR IS ",INT(T1+.5)
0490 PRINT "THE FUTURE AMOUNT AT THE END OF ";T;
0500 PRINT " YEARS IS $",INT(S1+.5)
0510 PRINT CHR$(12)
0520 STOP
0530 END
```

Continuous Compounding. Program 6-2.

THE MAXIMUM PAYMENT FOR THE LAST N YEARS IS	7500
THE GROWTH RATE FOR THE FIRST M YEARS IS	8 %
THE NOMINAL ANNUAL INTEREST RATE IS	12 %
THE NUMBER OF PAYMENTS PER YEAR IS	2
THE NUMBER OF YEARS TO ACHIEVE S IS	25
THE DESIRED FUTURE AMOUNT (S) IS	1000000

FOR CONTINUOUS COMPOUNDING OF INTEREST

THE NUMBER OF ITERATIONS IS	4
THE INITIAL ANNUAL AMOUNT IS $	4467
THE GROWTH OF PO AT 8 % PER YEAR CEASES AT	8
THE VALUE IN THE ACCOUNT THEN IS $	74253
THE NUMBER OF YEARS AT $ 7500 PER YEAR IS	17
THE FUTURE AMOUNT AT THE END OF 25 YEARS IS $	1000692

```
0010 REM PROGRAM 6-2
0020 REM CONTINUOUS COMPOUNDING OF INTEREST
0030 READ S,P,R,G,T,F1
0040 DATA 1000000,7500,12,8,25,2
0050 LET R=R/100
0060 LET I=R/F1
0070 LET G=G/100
0080 LET C=1
0090 PRINT CHR$(12)
0100 PRINT
0110 PRINT "THE MAXIMUM PAYMENT FOR THE LAST N YEARS IS ",P
0120 PRINT "THE GROWTH RATE FOR THE FIRST M YEARS IS     ",(100*G);
0130 PRINT " %"
0140 PRINT "THE NOMINAL ANNUAL INTEREST RATE IS          ",(100*R);
0150 PRINT " %"
0160 PRINT "THE NUMBER OF PAYMENTS PER YEAR IS           ",F1
0170 PRINT "THE NUMBER OF YEARS TO ACHIEVE S IS          ",T
0180 PRINT "THE DESIRED FUTURE AMOUNT (S) IS             ",S
0190 LET K=365/360
0200 LET R=EXP(K*R)-1
0210 LET I=EXP(K*I)-1
0220 PRINT
0230 PRINT "FOR CONTINUOUS COMPOUNDING OF INTEREST"
0240 LET J=1
0250 LET PO=F1*S*(I/R)*(R-G)/((1+R)^T-(1+G)^T)
0260 LET M=1+LOG(P/PO)/LOG(1+G)
0270 LET T1=T-M
0280 LET N=F1*T1
0290 LET E=N*C
0300 LET SO=S/(1+I)^E-(P/F1)/(1+I)^E*((1+I)^E-1)/I
0310 LET QO=F1*SO*(I/R)*(R-G)/((1+R)^M-(1+G)^M)
0320 LET Q1=PO-QO
0330 IF J=1000 THEN GOTO 0380
0340 IF ABS(Q1)<=1 THEN GOTO 0380
```

Program 6-2 (Continued)

```
0350 LET PO=QO
0360 LET J=J+1
0370 GOTO 0260
0380 PRINT
0390 LET L=INT(T1+.5)
0400 LET T2=INT(M+.5)
0410 LET E=INT(E+.5)
0420 LET SO=PO/F1*(R/I)*((1+R)^T2-(1+G)^T2)/(R-G)
0430 LET S1=SO*(1+R)^L+(P/F1)*(R/I)*((1+R)^L-1)/R
0440 PRINT "THE NUMBER OF ITERATIONS IS ",,J
0450 PRINT "THE INITIAL ANNUAL AMOUNT IS $ ",,INT(PO+.5)
0460 PRINT "THE GROWTH OF PO AT ";(100*G);
0470 PRINT " % PER YEAR CEASES AT ",INT(M+.5)
0480 PRINT "THE VALUE IN THE ACCOUNT THEN IS $ ",,INT(SO+.5)
0490 PRINT "THE NUMBER OF YEARS AT $ ";P;
0500 PRINT " PER YEAR IS ",INT(T1+.5)
0510 PRINT "THE FUTURE AMOUNT AT THE END OF ";T;
0520 PRINT " YEARS IS $",INT(S1+.5)
0530 PRINT CHR$(12)
0540 STOP
0550 END
```

Total of Payments

See Eqs. (3.1-32), (3.1-33), and (3.1-34) with m defined as the number of years.

Present Value—Level Payments and Interest Rate

The present value of a complex ordinary annuity can be determined by

$$V_{nc} = p \left[\frac{1 - (1 + i^*)^{-nc}}{(1 + i^*)^c - 1} \right]$$

(6.2-33)

where:

I.   *Discrete Compounding of Interest*

$$c = f/f'$$

$$n = f't$$

$$i^* = i = R/f$$

II.   *Continuous Compounding of Interest*

$$c = 1$$

$$[(1 + i^*)^c - 1] = i^*$$

$$i' = R/f'$$

$$n = f't$$

$$i^* = e^{ki'} - 1$$

For use of Tables A-2 and A-3

$$V_{nc} = p \left[\frac{(V/p,i,nc)}{(S/p,i,c)} \right] \tag{6.2-34}$$

Example 19. During the first 15 years of retirement you would like to withdraw $1,000 per month from your IRA. If the account is earning interest at 12%, the amount necessary one month before the first withdrawal can be determined by Eq. (6.2-33) or (6.2-34).

Discrete Compounding. Assuming an annual compounding frequency f = 1, and

$$i^* = i = R/f = 12\%/1 = 12\% = 0.12$$

For monthly withdrawals, f' = 12 and

$$c = f/f' = 1/12$$

For t = 15 years

$$n = f't = (12)(15) = 180$$

and

$$nc = (180)(1/12) = 15$$

a) Using Eq. (6.2-33)

$$V_{nc} = (1000) \left[\frac{1 - (1.12)^{-15}}{(1.12)^{1/12} - 1} \right]$$

The denominator is determined first.

Enter 1	Depress ÷
Enter 12	Depress =
Display shows 0.0833333	Store in memory
Enter 1.12	Depress y^x
Recall memory	Depress =
Display shows 1.0094888	Depress –
Enter 1	Depress =
Display shows 0.0094888	Store in memory
Enter 1.12	Depress y^x
Enter 15	Depress +/–
Display shows –15	Depress =
Display shows 0.1826963	Depress –
Enter 1	Depress =
Display shows –0.8173037	Depress +/–
Display shows 0.8173037	Depress ÷
Recall memory	Depress =
Display shows 86.133596	Depress X
Enter 1000	Depress =
Display shows 86133.596	

b) Using Eq. (6.2-34) and Tables A-2 and A-3.

$$V_{nc} = (1000) \left[\frac{(V/p,i,15)}{(S/p,i,1/12)} \right]$$

In the 12% table of Table A-2 under "Present Value of Annuity" find the value of $(V/p,i,15)$ as 6.81086449, and in Table A-3 find the value of $(S/p,i,1/12)$ as 0.07907327. Then

$$V_{nc} = (1000) \left[\frac{6.81086449}{0.07907327} \right] = \$86,133.66$$

Continuous Compounding. For 12% compounded continuously, c = 1. For monthly withdrawals, $f' = 12$. Then,

$$i' = R/f' = 12\%/12 = 0.12/12 = 0.01$$

$$i^* = e^{ki'} - 1 = e^{(365/360)(0.01)} - 1 = 0.0102$$

For t = 15 years,

$$n = f't = (12)(15) = 180$$

and nc = 180. From Eq. (6.2-33)

$$V_{nc} = (1000) \left[\frac{1 - (1.0102)^{-180}}{0.0102} \right] = \$82,260.40$$

Number of Level Payments—Given a Present Value

The number of level payments available in a complex ordinary annuity given the present value of those payments can be determined by

$$n = -\frac{1}{c} \left\{ \frac{\log \left[1 - V_{nc}[(1 + i^*)^c - 1]/p \right]}{\log(1 + i^*)} \right\} \qquad (6.2-35)$$

where:

    I. *Discrete Compounding of Interest*

$$c = f/f'$$

$$n = f't$$

$$i^* = i = R/f$$

    II. *Continuous Compounding of Interest*

$$c = 1$$

$$[(1 + i^*)^c - 1] = i^*$$

$$i' = R/f'$$

$$n = f't$$

$$i^* = e^{ki'} - 1$$

For use of Tables A-2 and A-3

$$(V/p,i,nc) = \frac{V_{nc}(S/p,i,c)}{p} \qquad (6.2-36)$$

Eq. (6.2-36) enables the determination of nc from Table A-2, and from Eq. (6.2-7)

$$n = \frac{(nc)}{c}$$

Example 20.   An accumulation of $200,000 is available in an account that earns interest at a rate which is no less than 12%. If $2,500 per month is desired beginning in one month, the total number of monthly withdrawals can be determined as follows.

Discrete Compounding. Assuming an annual compounding frequency, $f = 1$, and

$$i^* = i = R/f = 12\%/1 = 12\% = 0.12$$

For monthly withdrawals, $f' = 12$ and

$$c = f/f' = 1/12$$

a)   Using Eq. (6.2-35)

$$n = -\frac{1}{1/12}\left\{\frac{\log\left[1 - (200000)\left[(1.12)^{1/12} - 1\right]/2500\right]}{\log 1.12}\right\}$$

$$= (-12)\left[\frac{\log\left(1 - 0.7591033\right)}{\log 1.12}\right]$$

$$= (-12)\left[\frac{\log 0.2408967}{\log 1.12}\right]$$

$$= (-12)\left[\frac{-0.6181692}{0.049218}\right]$$

$$= (-12)\,(-12.559814) = 150.72 \text{ months}$$

b)   Using Eq. (6.2-36). The value of $(S/p,i,1/12)$ can be determined from Table A-3 as 0.07907327. Then

$$(V/p,i,nc) = \frac{(200000)\,(0.07907327)}{2500} = 6.325864$$

In the 12% table of Table A-2, under "Present Value of Annuity" note that the value 6.325864 occurs between 12 and 13 periods. For a quick interpolation, rounding all values to the first decimal place gives

$$(V/p,i,nc) = 6.2 \text{ for } (nc) = 12$$

$$(V/p,i,nc) = 6.4 \text{ for } (nc) = 13$$

Then, the value 6.325864 rounded to 6.3 is midway between 6.2 and 6.4. Therefore, (nc) is midway between 12 and 13, and for $(nc) = 12.5$, $n = (nc)/c$ or

$$n = \frac{12.5}{1/12} = (12.5)\,(12) = 150 \text{ months}$$

Continuous Compounding. For continuous compounding, $c = 1$. For monthly withdrawals, $f' = 12$. Then,

$$i' = R/f' = 12\%/12 = 0.12/12 = 0.01$$

$$i^* = e^{ki'} - 1 = e^{(365/360)(0.01)} - 1 = 0.0102$$

From Eq. (6.2-35)

$$n = -\left[\frac{\log\left[1 - (200000)(0.0102)/2500\right]}{\log 1.0102}\right]$$

$$= -\left[\frac{-0.7351822}{0.0044074}\right] = 166.81 \text{ months}$$

Present Value After m Level Payments

Given an annuity of level payments and a constant interest rate, the amount remaining in the account of the annuity can be determined by finding the present value of the remaining payments. In an annuity of n equal payments, the number of remaining payments after m payments are made (received) is

$$N = n - m \qquad\qquad (6.2\text{-}37)$$

and Eqs. (6.2-33) and (6.3-34) may be used by replacing n by N.

> **Example 21.** For estate planning purposes, you would like to know what balance would remain in the account of Example 19, should you die at the end of 10 years, if the interest rate does not go below 12%. For 10 years of monthly payments, $m = 120$, and since $n = 180$, $N = 60$.
>
> *Discrete Compounding.* Assuming annual compounding, $f = 1$, and
>
> $$i^* = i = R/f = 12\%/1 = 12\% = 0.12$$
>
> For monthly payments, $f' = 12$ and
>
> $$c = f/f' = 1/12$$
>
> Since $N = 60$, $Nc = (60)(1/12) = 5$. From Eq. (6.2-34)
>
> $$V_{Nc} = (1000)\left[\frac{3.6047762}{0.07907327}\right] = \$45,587.84$$
>
> *Continuous Compounding.* For continuous compounding, $c = 1$. For monthly withdrawals, $f' = 12$. Then
>
> $$i' = R/f' = 12\%/12 = 0.12/12 = 0.01$$
> $$i^* = e^{ki'} - 1 = e^{(365/360)(0.01)} - 1 = 0.0102$$
>
> For $N = 60$, $Nc = 60$. Then, from Eq. (6.2-33)
>
> $$V_{Nc} = (1000)\left[\frac{1 - (1.0102)^{-60}}{0.0102}\right] = \$44,710.89$$

Payment Number, m, When V_{Nc} Equals a Specified Fraction, F, of V_{nc}

If it is desired to know the payment number when the present value of an amortization is a specified fraction, F, of the original amount, that payment number, m, can be determined by

$$m = n + \frac{1}{c}\left\{\frac{\log\left[1 - FV_{nc}[(1 + i^*)^c - 1]/p\right]}{\log(1 + i^*)}\right\} \qquad\qquad (6.2\text{-}38)$$

where:

I.   *Discrete Compounding of Interest*

$$c = f/f'$$

$$n = f't$$

$$i^* = i = R/f$$

II.   *Continuous Compounding of Interest*

$$c = 1$$

$$[(1 + i^*)^c - 1] = i^*$$

$$i' = R/f'$$

$$n = f't$$

$$i^* = e^{ki'} - 1$$

Example 22.   An annuity is to begin in one month. The account is tax-sheltered at $130,000 and is earning interest at 9%. If monthly payments are to be $1,500 and if it is desired to know when the balance will be 40% of the original amount, the payment number can be determined as follows.

Discrete Compounding.   Assuming annual compounding, $f = 1$ and

$$i^* = i = R/f = 9\%/1 = 9\% = 0.09$$

For monthly payments, $f' = 12$ and

$$c = f/f' = 1/12.$$

The total number of payments of $1,500 per month can be determined from Eq. (6.2-35) as

$$n = -\frac{1}{1/12} \left\{ \frac{\log [1 - (130000) [(1.09)^{1/12} - 1]/1500]}{\log 1.09} \right\}$$

The value of $(1.09)^{1/12}$ can be determined by the calculator or Table A-4.

$$n = -12 \left[\frac{\log [1 - (130000) (1.00720732 - 1)/1500]}{\log 1.09} \right]$$

$$= 136.44 \text{ months}$$

In order to reach 40% of $130,000, Eq. (6.2-38) gives

$$m = 136.44 + \frac{1}{1/12} \left\{ \frac{\log [1 - (0.4) (130000) [(1.09)^{1/12} - 1]/1500]}{\log 1.09} \right\}$$

$$= 136.44 + 12 \left\{ \frac{\log [1 - (0.40) (130000) (1.00720732 - 1)/1500]}{\log 1.09} \right\}$$

$$= 136.44 + 12 \left[\frac{-0.1248537}{0.0374265} \right]$$

$$= 136.44 - 40.03$$

$$= 96.41 \text{ months}$$

Therefore, the balance of the account will be at 40% of $130,000 between the 96th and 97th payment.

Continuous Compounding. For continuous compounding, c = 1. For monthly withdrawals, $f' = 12$. Then,

$$i' = R/f' = 9\%/12 = 0.09/12 = 0.0075$$

$$i^* = e^{ki'} - 1 = e^{(365/360)(0.0075)} - 1 = 0.0076$$

The total number of $1,500 withdrawals can be determined by Eq. (6.2-35) as

$$n = -\frac{\log\,[1 - (130000)\,(0.0076)/1500]}{\log 1.0076} = 141.97 \text{ months}$$

In order to reach 40% of $130,000, Eq. (6.2-38) gives

$$m = 141.97 + \frac{\log\,[1 - (0.40)\,(130000)\,(0.0076)/1500]}{\log 1.0076}$$

$$= 141.97 - 40.39 = 101.58 \text{ months}$$

Change in Term Due to Change in Interest Rate and/or Payment

Given a complex annuity of periodic equal payments which are based on a specified term and interest rate, if the interest rate changes after m payments, the new term for the same periodic payments can be determined by Eq. (6.2-35) or (6.2-36) with V_{nc} replaced by V_{Nc} (the present value at the time of the change in rate or payment and one period prior to the first payment after the change).

Example 23. Suppose that in Example 22 the interest rate changed from 9% to 12% when the account reached $52,000. The new term of $1,500 per month payments could be determined by Eq. (6.2-35) or (6.2-36) with $V_{Nc} = 52000$.

Discrete Compounding. Assuming annual compounding, f = 1 and

$$i^* = i = R/f = 12\%/1 = 12\% = 0.12$$

For monthly payments, $f' = 12$ and

$$c = f/f' = 1/12$$

Using Eq. (6.2-36), the value of $(S/p,i,1/12)$ can be determined from Table A-3 as 0.07907327. Then

$$(V/p,i,nc) = \frac{(52000)\,(0.07907327)}{1500} = 2.7412043$$

From Table A-2, the number of periods for $(V/p,i,nc) = 2.7412043$ is approximately 3.5. Then, from Eq. (6.2-7), the new term is approximately

$$n = \frac{(nc)}{c} = \frac{3.5}{1/12} = (12)\,(3.5) = 42 \text{ months}$$

Note that in Example 22 the total number of payments is 136[+] and that $52,000 (40% of 130000) is reached after 96[+] payments. Then, 40 payments remain. When the interest rate is increased by 3% as in this example, the number of $1,500 payments is increased by 2.

Continuous Compounding. For continuous compounding, c = 1. For monthly payments, f' = 12. Then

$$i' = R/f' = 12\%/12 = 0.12/12 = 0.01$$

$$i^* = e^{ki'} - 1 = e^{(365/360)(0.01)} - 1 = 0.0102$$

From Eq. (6.2-35)

$$n = -\frac{\log[1 - (52000)(0.0102)/1500]}{\log 1.0102} = 43 \text{ months}$$

A comparison with Example 22 shows an increase of 3 in the number of $1,500 payments if the interest rate is increased by 3% when the account is at $52,000.

Present Value—Annual Amount Changing at a Constant Rate

If payments of an annuity are to begin at a specified annual amount, p_o, with f' equal payments equally spaced during the year, and if subsequent annual amounts are to be increased (decreased) at a constant rate, the present value can be determined as follows.

I.   *Discrete Compounding of Interest*

$$V_{nc} = \frac{p_o}{f'}\left[\frac{(1 + i^*)^f - 1}{(1 + i^*)^c - 1}\right]\left\{\frac{1 - \left[\dfrac{1 + G}{1 + R}\right]^t}{R - G}\right\} \tag{6.2-39}$$

where c = f/f' and $i^* = i = R/f$. The values of $(1 + i^*)^f$ and $(1 + i^*)^c$ can be determined by Table A-2 or A-4, but since the ratio $(1 + G)/(1 + R)$ would not normally be an element of either of those tables, Eq. (6.2-39) would be a calculator-oriented formula. If G = R, Eq. (6.2-39) reduces to

$$V_{nc} = \frac{tp_o}{f'(1 + G)}\left[\frac{(1 + i^*)^f - 1}{(1 + i^*)^c - 1}\right] = \frac{tp_o}{f'(1 + G)}\left[\frac{(S/p,i,f)}{(S/p,i,c)}\right] \tag{6.2-40}$$

II.   *Continuous Compounding of Interest*

$$V_t = \frac{p_o}{f'}\left[\frac{R_e}{i^*}\right]\left\{\frac{1 - \left[\dfrac{1 + G}{1 + R_e}\right]^t}{R_e - G}\right\} \tag{6.2-41}$$

where

$$i' = R/f'$$

$$i^* = e^{ki'} - 1$$

$$R_e = e^{kR} - 1$$

For $G = R_e$,

$$V_t = \frac{tp_o}{f'(1 + G)}\left[\frac{R_e}{i^*}\right] \tag{6.2-42}$$

Example 24. During the first 15 years of your retirement you would like to withdraw annually increased amounts from your IRA starting with \$12,000 and increasing the annual amount by 6% per year to help offset the effects of inflation. You wish to receive the annual amount in equal monthly payments. If the account will earn no less than 12% interest, the present value, one month before the first payment, can be determined as follows.

Discrete Compounding. Assuming annual compounding, $f = 1$ and

$$i^* = i = R/f = 12\%/1 = 12\% = 0.12$$

$$G = 6\% = 0.06$$

For monthly payments, $f' = 12$ and

$$c = f/f' = 1/12$$

For $t = 15$ years

$$n = f't = (12)(15) = 180$$

and

$$nc = (180)(1/12) = 15.$$

From Eq. (6.2-39)

$$V_{nc} = \frac{12000}{12} \left[\frac{(1.12)^1 - 1}{(1.12)^{1/12} - 1} \right] \left\{ \frac{1 - \left[\dfrac{1.06}{1.12}\right]^{15}}{0.12 - 0.06} \right\}$$

$$= (1000)(12.6465)(9.3692962)$$

$$= \$118,488.80$$

Continuous Compounding. For continuous compounding,

$$i' = R/f' = 12\%/12 = 0.12/12 = 0.01$$

$$i^* = e^{ki'} - 1 = e^{(365/360)(0.01)} - 1 = 0.0102$$

$$R_e = e^{kR} - 1 = e^{(365/360)(0.12)} - 1 = 0.1294$$

From Eq. (6.2-41)

$$V_t = \frac{12000}{12} \left[\frac{0.1294}{0.0102} \right] \left\{ \frac{1 - \left[\dfrac{1.06}{1.1294}\right]^{15}}{0.1294 - 0.06} \right\}$$

$$= \$112,192.65$$

Amortization—Level Payments and Interest Rates

Given that an account is to be amortized as a complex annuity with payments occurring at the ends of payment intervals, the level periodic payment can be determined by

$$p = V_{nc} \left[\frac{(1 + i^*)^c - 1}{1 - (1 + i^*)^{-nc}} \right] \qquad (6.2\text{-}43)$$

where:

I. *Discrete Compounding of Interest*

$$c = f/f'$$

$$n = f't$$

$$i^* = i = R/f$$

II. *Continuous Compounding of Interest*

$$c = 1$$

$$[(1 + i^*)^c - 1] = i^*$$

$$i' = R/f'$$

$$n = f't$$

$$i^* = e^{ki'} - 1$$

For the use of Tables A-2 and A-3,

$$p = V_{nc} \left[\frac{(S/p,i,c)}{(V/p,i,nc)} \right] \qquad (6.2\text{-}44)$$

Example 25.   A \$1,000,000 loan is to be amortized by quarterly payments over a period of 20 years. If the interest rate is 15% compounded annually, the level of payments can be determined as follows. For annual compounding, f = 1 and

$$i^* = i = R/f = 15\%/1 = 15\% = 0.15$$

For quarterly payments, f' = 4 and

$$c = f/f' = 1/4$$

For t = 20 years,

$$n = f't = (4)(20) = 80$$

and

$$nc = (80)(1/4) = 20$$

a)   Using Eq. (6.2-43)

$$p = (1000000) \left[\frac{(1 + 15\%)^{1/4} - 1}{1 - (1 + 15\%)^{-20}} \right]$$

From Tables A-2 and A-4 or the y^x function on the calculator

$$p = (1000000) \left[\frac{1.0355581 - 1}{1 - 0.0611003} \right]$$

$$= \$37,872.10 \text{ every three months}$$

b)   Using Eq. (6.2-44). From Tables A-2 and A-3

$$p = (1000000) \left[\frac{0.23705384}{6.25933147} \right] = \$37,872.06$$

Example 26.   One month before you retire, your IRA contains \$150,000 and earns interest at 12% compounded continuously. Monthly withdrawals for 15 years can be determined as follows. For continuous compounding $c = 1$, and for monthly withdrawals $f' = 12$. Then

$$i' = R/f' = 12\%/12 = 0.12/12 = 0.01$$

and

$$i* = e^{ki'} - 1 = e^{(365/360)(0.01)} - 1 = 0.0102$$

For $t = 15$ years

$$n = f't = (12)(15) = 180$$

and

$$nc = (180)(1) = 180$$

From Eq. (6.2-43)

$$p = (150000) \left[\frac{0.0102}{1 - (1.0102)^{-180}} \right]$$

$$= \$1,823.48 \text{ each month}$$

Amortization—Total Interest over Term

See Eq. (3.2-18).

Amortization—Initial Annual Amount
Annual Amount Changing at a Constant Rate

Given that an account is to be amortized as a complex annuity where the annual amount, payable by f' equal payments equally spaced during the year, is increased at a constant rate of G%, the initial annual amount can be determined as follows.

I.   *Discrete Compounding of Interest*

$$p_o = V_{nc} f' \left[\frac{(1 + i*)^c - 1}{(1 + i*)^f - 1} \right] \left\{ \frac{R - G}{1 - \left[\frac{1 + G}{1 + R} \right]^t} \right\} \tag{6.2-45}$$

where $c = f/f'$ and $i* = i = R/f$. The values of $(1 + i*)^c$ and $(1 + i*)^f$ can be determined from Table A-2 or A-4, but since the ratio $(1 + G)/(1 + R)$ would not normally be an element of either of those tables, Eq. (6.2-45) would be a calculator-oriented formula. If $G = R$, Eq. (6.2-45) reduces to

$$p_o = \frac{V_{nc} f'(1 + R)}{t} \left[\frac{(1 + i*)^c - 1}{(1 + i*)^f - 1} \right] = \frac{V_{nc} f'(1 + R)}{t} \left[\frac{(S/p,i,c)}{(S/p,i,f)} \right] \tag{6.2-46}$$

II. *Continuous Compounding of Interest*

$$p_o = V_t f' \left[\frac{i^*}{R_e} \right] \left\{ \frac{R_e - G}{1 - \left[\dfrac{1 + G}{1 + R_e} \right]^t} \right\} \qquad (6.2\text{-}47)$$

where,

$$i' = R/f'$$
$$i^* = e^{ki'} - 1$$
$$R_e = e^{kR} - 1$$

For $G = R_e$

$$p_o = \frac{V_t f'(1 + R_e)}{t} \left[\frac{i^*}{R_e} \right] \qquad (6.2\text{-}48)$$

Example 27. You own an IRA of $150,000, and plan to make monthly withdrawals beginning in one month. In order to compensate, to some extent, the effects of inflation, you plan to increase the annual amount that is withdrawn by 5% each year. Assuming that the account will not earn less than 12% interest, the initial annual and monthly amounts can be determined as follows for a 15 year term.

Discrete Compounding. Assuming annual compounding, f = 1 and

$$i^* = i = R/f = 12\%/1 = 12\% = 0.12$$

For monthly withdrawals, $f' = 12$ and

$$c = f/f' = 1/12$$

For t = 15 years, and G = 5% = 0.05, Eq. (6.2-45) gives

$$p_o = (150000)\,(12) \left[\frac{(1 + 12\%)^{1/12} - 1}{(1 + 12\%)^1 - 1} \right] \left\{ \frac{0.12 - 0.05}{1 - \left[\dfrac{1.05}{1.12} \right]^{15}} \right\}$$

$$= (150000)\,(12) \left[\frac{(1.12)^{1/12} - 1}{0.12} \right] \left[\frac{0.07}{1 - (0.9375)^{15}} \right]$$

$$= \$16,064.87 \text{ the first year}$$

This initial annual amount will give 16064.87/12 = $1,338.74 per month during the first year. In subsequent years each value could be increased 5% per year for the next 14 years.

Continuous Compounding.

$$i' = R/f' = 12\%/12 = 0.12/12 = 0.01$$
$$i^* = e^{ki'} - 1 = e^{(365/360)\,(0.01)} - 0.0102$$
$$R_e = e^{kR} - 1 = e^{(365/360)\,(0.12)} - 1 = 0.1294$$

From Eq. (6.2-47)

$$p_o = (150000)(12)\left[\frac{0.0102}{0.1294}\right]\left\{\frac{0.1294 - 0.05}{1 - \left[\dfrac{1.05}{1.1294}\right]^{15}}\right\}$$

= \$16,942.46 the first year

and \$1,411.87 per month during the first year.

6.3   COMPLEX ANNUITIES DUE

An annuity was defined in Chapter 4 as "due" when payments are made at the *beginnings of periods*. The same definition applies for complex annuities due except that payments are made at the *beginnings of payment intervals*. The basic computational difference between an ordinary annuity and an annuity due is that the future amount of an annuity due is equal to the future amount of an ordinary annuity multiplied by $(1 + i^*)^c$, or $S_d = (1 + i^*)^c S_{nc}$. This implies that the formulas of Section 6.2 may be appropriately modified by $(1 + i^*)^c$ in order to achieve results for annuities due. Simply replace p by $p(1 + i^*)^c$. When p is to be determined, divide the result by $(1 + i^*)^c$.

Computer Programs—Combination of Increasing and Level Payments to a Sinking Fund

Because of the possibility of a large number of iterations in order to converge to a starting annual amount, computer programs are supplied for the combination of increasing and level payments for annuities due. The necessary data are:

1.   The desired future amount—S.
2.   The desired level payment—p.
3.   The nominal annual interest rate—R.
4.   The nominal annual growth rate—G.
5.   The term of the annuity (sinking fund)—t.
6.   The compounding frequency—f.
7.   The payment frequency—f'.

These values are "read" in statement 0030, and the corresponding values are listed in statement 0040 in the sequence:

$$S, p, R, G, t, f, f'$$

when interest is compounded discretely and in the sequence:

$$S, p, R, G, t, f'$$

when interest is compounded continuously.

The statement PRINT CHR\$(12) appears twice in each of the following programs—statements 0090 and 0510 and statements 0090 and 0530 respectively. This statement is used to advance the paper to the top of the next page. It has no other use in the program.

The symbol, $\wedge$, in statement 0230 and elsewhere is analogous to the upward directed arrow in BASIC.

These programs can be used for the combination of increasing and level payment annuities due which are discussed in Chapter 4. In order to be used for that simple annuity due, the value of f' is made equal to 1. (For an annuity due, the results of Example 18 of Section 6.2 are as follows:)

Discrete Compounding. Program 6-3

```
THE MAXIMUM PAYMENT FOR THE LAST N YEARS IS        7500
THE GROWTH RATE FOR THE FIRST M YEARS IS           8  %
THE NOMINAL ANNUAL INTEREST RATE IS                12  %
THE COMPOUNDING FREQUENCY IS                       1
THE NUMBER OF PAYMENTS PER YEAR IS                 2
THE NUMBER OF YEARS TO ACHIEVE S IS                25
THE DESIRED FUTURE AMOUNT (S) IS                   1000000

FOR DISCRETE COMPOUNDING OF INTEREST

THE NUMBER OF ITERATIONS IS                        5
THE INITIAL ANNUAL AMOUNT IS $                     5336
THE GROWTH OF PO AT   8  % PER YEAR CEASES AT       5
THE VALUE IN THE ACCOUNT THEN IS $                 42575
THE NUMBER OF YEARS AT $  7500  PER YEAR IS         20
THE FUTURE AMOUNT AT THE END OF  25  YEARS IS $     999256
```

```
0010 REM PROGRAM 6-3
0020 REM DISCRETE COMPOUNDING OF INTEREST
0030 READ S, P, R, G, T, F, F1
0040 DATA 1000000, 7500, 12, 8, 25, 1, 2
0050 LET R=R/100
0060 LET I=R/F
0070 LET G=G/100
0080 LET C=F/F1
0090 PRINT CHR$(12)
0100 PRINT
0110 PRINT "THE MAXIMUM PAYMENT FOR THE LAST N YEARS IS ", P
0120 PRINT "THE GROWTH RATE FOR THE FIRST M YEARS IS     ", (100*G);
0130 PRINT " %"
0140 PRINT "THE NOMINAL ANNUAL INTEREST RATE IS          ", (100*R);
0150 PRINT " %"
0160 PRINT "THE COMPOUNDING FREQUENCY IS                 ", F
0170 PRINT "THE NUMBER OF PAYMENTS PER YEAR IS           ", F1
0180 PRINT "THE NUMBER OF YEARS TO ACHIEVE S IS          ", T
0190 PRINT "THE DESIRED FUTURE AMOUNT (S) IS             ", S
0200 PRINT
0210 PRINT "FOR DISCRETE COMPOUNDING OF INTEREST"
0220 LET J=1
0230 LET PO=(F1/(1+I)^C)*S*(((1+I)^C-1)/((1+I)^F-1))*(R-G)/((1+R)^T-(1+G)^T)
0240 LET M=1+LOG(P/PO)/LOG(1+G)
0250 LET T1=T-M
0260 LET N=F1*T1
0270 LET E=N*C
0280 LET SO=S/(1+I)^E-(P/F1)*(1+I)^C/(1+I)^E*((1+I)^E-1)/((1+I)^C-1)
0290 LET QO=F1/(1+I)^C*SO*(((1+I)^C-1)/((1+I)^F-1))*((R-G)/((1+R)^M-(1+G)^M))
0300 LET Q1=PO-QO
0310 IF J=1000 THEN GOTO 0360
0320 IF ABS(Q1)<=1 THEN GOTO 0360
0330 LET PO=QO
```

Program 6-3 (Continued)

```
0340 LET J=J+1
0350 GOTO 0240
0360 PRINT
0370 LET L=INT(T1+.5)
0380 LET K=INT(M+.5)
0390 LET E=INT(E+.5)
0400 LET S0=(P0/F1)*(1+I)^C*((1+I)^F-1)/((1+I)^C-1)*((1+R)^K-(1+G)^K)/(R-G)
0410 LET S1=S0*(1+I)^L+(P/F1)*(1+I)^C*((1+I)^E-1)/((1+I)^C-1)
0420 PRINT "THE NUMBER OF ITERATIONS IS ",,J
0430 PRINT "THE INITIAL ANNUAL AMOUNT IS $ ",,INT(P0+.5)
0440 PRINT "THE GROWTH OF P0 AT ";(100*G);
0450 PRINT " % PER YEAR CEASES AT ",INT(M+.5)
0460 PRINT "THE VALUE IN THE ACCOUNT THEN IS $ ",,INT(S0+.5)
0470 PRINT "THE NUMBER OF YEARS AT $ ";P;
0480 PRINT " PER YEAR IS ",INT(T1+.5)
0490 PRINT "THE FUTURE AMOUNT AT THE END OF ";T;
0500 PRINT " YEARS IS $",INT(S1+.5)
0510 PRINT CHR$(12)
0520 STOP
0530 END
```

Continuous Compounding. Program 6-4

```
THE MAXIMUM PAYMENT FOR THE LAST N YEARS IS          7500
THE GROWTH RATE FOR THE FIRST M YEARS IS             8  %
THE NOMINAL ANNUAL INTEREST RATE IS                  12  %
THE NUMBER OF PAYMENTS PER YEAR IS                   2
THE NUMBER OF YEARS TO ACHIEVE S IS                  25
THE DESIRED FUTURE AMOUNT (S) IS                     1000000

FOR CONTINUOUS COMPOUNDING OF INTEREST

THE NUMBER OF ITERATIONS IS                          4
THE INITIAL ANNUAL AMOUNT IS $                       4015
THE GROWTH OF P0 AT   8   % PER YEAR CEASES AT        9
THE VALUE IN THE ACCOUNT THEN IS $                   88243
THE NUMBER OF YEARS AT $   7500   PER YEAR IS         16
THE FUTURE AMOUNT AT THE END OF   25   YEARS IS $     999732
```

```
0010 REM PROGRAM 6-4
0020 REM CONTINUOUS COMPOUNDING OF INTEREST
0030 READ S,P,R,G,T,F1
0040 DATA 1000000,7500,12,8,25,2
0050 LET R=R/100
0060 LET I=R/F1
0070 LET G=G/100
0080 LET C=1
0090 PRINT CHR$(12)
0100 PRINT
0110 PRINT "THE MAXIMUM PAYMENT FOR THE LAST N YEARS IS ",P
0120 PRINT "THE GROWTH RATE FOR THE FIRST M YEARS IS    ",(100*G);
0130 PRINT " %"
0140 PRINT "THE NOMINAL ANNUAL INTEREST RATE IS         ",(100*R);
0150 PRINT " %"
0160 PRINT "THE NUMBER OF PAYMENTS PER YEAR IS          ",F1
```

Program 6-4 (Continued)

```
0170 PRINT "THE NUMBER OF YEARS TO ACHIEVE S IS          ", T
0180 PRINT "THE DESIRED FUTURE AMOUNT (S) IS             ", S
0190 LET K=365/360
0200 LET R=EXP(K*R)-1
0210 LET I=EXP(K*I)-1
0220 PRINT
0230 PRINT "FOR CONTINUOUS COMPOUNDING OF INTEREST"
0240 LET J=1
0250 LET PO=F1/(1+I)*S*(I/R)*(R-G)/((1+R)^T-(1+G)^T)
0260 LET M=1+LOG(P/PO)/LOG(1+G)
0270 LET T1=T-M
0280 LET N=F1*T1
0290 LET E=N*C
0300 LET SO=S/(1+I)^E-(P/F1)*(1+I)/(1+I)^E*((1+I)^E-1)/I
0310 LET QO=F1/(1+I)*SO*(I/R)*(R-G)/((1+R)^M-(1+G)^M)
0320 LET Q1=PO-QO
0330 IF J=1000 THEN GOTO 0380
0340 IF ABS(Q1)<=1 THEN GOTO 0380
0350 LET PO=QO
0360 LET J=J+1
0370 GOTO 0260
0380 PRINT
0390 LET L=INT(T1+.5)
0400 LET T2=INT(M+.5)
0410 LET E=INT(E+.5)
0420 LET SO=(PO/F1)*(1+I)*(R/I)*((1+R)^T2-(1+G)^T2)/(R-G)
0430 LET S1=SO*(1+R)^L+(P/F1)*(1+I)*(R/I)*((1+R)^L-1)/R
0440 PRINT "THE NUMBER OF ITERATIONS IS ",, J
0450 PRINT "THE INITIAL ANNUAL AMOUNT IS $ ",, INT(PO+.5)
0460 PRINT "THE GROWTH OF PO AT ";(100*G);
0470 PRINT " % PER YEAR CEASES AT ", INT(M+.5)
0480 PRINT "THE VALUE IN THE ACCOUNT THEN IS $ ",, INT(SO+.5)
0490 PRINT "THE NUMBER OF YEARS AT $ ";P;
0500 PRINT " PER YEAR IS ", INT(T1+.5)
0510 PRINT "THE FUTURE AMOUNT AT THE END OF ";T;
0520 PRINT " YEARS IS $", INT(S1+.5)
0530 PRINT CHR$(12)
0540 STOP
0550 END
```

6.4 COMPLEX DEFERRED ANNUITIES

Deferred annuities are defined in Chapter 5 as equally spaced payments which occur at the end of interest conversion periods with the initial payment deferred by a number of interest conversion periods. The same definition applies for complex deferred annuities except that the period of deferment is a number of payment intervals.

Future Amount and Sinking Fund Payments

For a period of deferment, d, Eqs. (6.2-1) through (6.2-32) apply for deferred annuities with the definition

$$d = f't_d \tag{6.4-1}$$

where t_d represents the number of years from the *beginning of the period of deferment* to the beginning of the annuity. Thus, when n is determined by $n = f't$, the resulting values will be the number of payments from the *beginning of the annuity* to its end. These values of n will be the same as those of n in Eqs. (6.2-1) through (6.2-32).

Examples 1–18. For any period of deferment, the results of Section 6.2 will be the same.

In general, the formulas which address the present value and periodic payments of complex deferred annuities are the same as the formulas for present value and periodic payment of complex ordinary annuities appropriately modified by $(1 + i^*)^{-cd}$ for discrete compounding and $(1 + i^*)^{-d}$ for continuous compounding. Thus, the formulas of Section 6.2, beginning with Eq. (6.2-33), apply for this section. Simply replace p by $p(1 + i^*)^{-cd}$. When p is to be determined, multiply the result by $(1 + i^*)^{cd}$.

Period of Deferment—Given Level Payment Amortization

For a given amount of money available "today" and a specified level payment and term of a deferred annuity, the required period of deferment can be determined by

$$d = \frac{1}{c} \left\{ \frac{\log\left\{ \frac{p}{V_{d+n}} \left[\frac{1 - (1 + i^*)^{-nc}}{(1 + i^*)^c - 1} \right] \right\}}{\log(1 + i^*)} \right\} \qquad (6.4\text{-}2)$$

where

I. *Discrete Compounding of Interest*

$$c = f/f'$$

$$n = f't$$

$$i^* = i = R/f$$

II. *Continuous Compounding of Interest*

$$c = 1$$

$$[(1 + i^*)^c - 1] = i^*$$

$$i' = R/f'$$

$$n = f't$$

$$i^* = e^{ki'} - 1$$

Example 19. Suppose you have $20,000 "today" which you would like to use to purchase $10,000 semiannually for 8 years at some future date. If the interest rate does not fall below 12%, the required period of deferment can be determined as follows.

Discrete Compounding. Assuming annual compounding, f = 1 and for semiannual payments, f' = 2. Then

$$i^* = i = R/f = 12\%/1 = 12\% = 0.12$$

$$c = f/f' = 1/2$$

$$n = f't = (2)(8) = 16$$

$$nc = (16)(1/2) = 8$$

From Eq. (6.4-2)

$$d = \frac{1}{1/2} \left\{ \frac{\log\left\{ \left[\frac{10000}{20000}\right] \left[\frac{1 - (1.12)^{-8}}{(1.12)^{1/2} - 1}\right] \right\}}{\log 1.12} \right\}$$

The value of $(1.12)^{-8}$ can be determined by Table A-2, the value of $(1.12)^{1/2}$ can be determined by Table A-4, or both values can be determined by the calculator.

$$d = 2\left\{ \frac{\log\left\{ \left[\frac{10000}{20000}\right] \left[\frac{1 - 0.4038832}{1.0583005 - 1}\right] \right\}}{\log 1.12} \right\}$$

= 28.8 semiannual payment intervals (14.4 years)

Continuous Compounding. For continuous compounding, $c = 1$ and for semiannual payments, $f' = 2$. Then

$$i' = R/f' = 12\%/2 = 0.12/2 = 0.06$$

$$i^* = e^{ki'} - 1 = e^{(365/360)(0.06)} - 1 = 0.0627$$

$$nc = n = f't = (2)(8) = 16$$

From Eq. (6.4-2)

$$d = \frac{\log\left\{ \left[\frac{10000}{20000}\right] \left[\frac{1 - (1.0627)^{-16}}{0.0627}\right] \right\}}{\log 1.0627}$$

$$= \frac{\log\left\{ \left[\frac{10000}{20000}\right] \left[\frac{1 - 0.3779454}{0.0627}\right] \right\}}{\log 1.0627}$$

= 26.34 semiannual payment intervals (13.17 years)

Period of Deferment—Given Initial Annual Amount
Annual Amount Changing at a Constant Rate

For a given amount of money "today," a specified initial annual amount, a specified annual growth rate of payments, and a specified term, the required period of deferment can be determined by

I. Discrete Compounding of Interest

$$d = \frac{1}{c}\left\{\frac{\log\left\{\frac{p_o}{f'V_{d+n}}\left[\frac{(1+i^*)^f-1}{(1+i^*)^c-1}\right]\left\{\frac{1-\left[\frac{1+G}{1+R}\right]^t}{R-G}\right\}\right\}}{\log(1+i^*)}\right\} \qquad (6.4\text{-}3)$$

where $c = f/f'$ and $i^* = i = R/f$. For $G = R$, Eq. (6.4-3) reduces to

$$d = \frac{1}{c}\left\{\frac{\log\left\{\frac{tp_o}{f'(1+G)V_{d+n}}\left[\frac{(1+i^*)^f-1}{(1+i^*)^c-1}\right]\right\}}{\log(1+i^*)}\right\} \qquad (6.4\text{-}4)$$

or for the use of Tables A-2 and A-3

$$d = \frac{1}{c}\left\{\frac{\log\left\{\frac{tp_o}{f'(1+G)V_{d+n}}\left[\frac{(S/p,i,f)}{(S/p,i,c)}\right]\right\}}{\log(1+i^*)}\right\} \qquad (6.4\text{-}5)$$

II. Continuous Compounding of Interest

$$d = \frac{\log\left\{\frac{p_o}{f'V_{d+n}}\left[\frac{R_e}{i^*}\right]\left\{\frac{1-\left[\frac{1+G}{1+R_e}\right]^t}{R_e-G}\right\}\right\}}{\log(1+i^*)} \qquad (6.4\text{-}6)$$

where

$$i' = R/f'$$

$$i^* = e^{ki'} - 1$$

$$R_e = e^{kR} - 1$$

For $G = R_e$, Eq. (6.4-6) reduces to

$$d = \frac{\log\left\{\frac{tp_o}{f'(1+G)V_{d+n}}\left[\frac{R_e}{i^*}\right]\right\}}{\log(1+i^*)} \qquad (6.4\text{-}7)$$

Example 20. Suppose that in Example 19 of this section, you specify that the initial annual amount is to be $15,000, and that the annual amount is to increase by 8% per year. If the interest rate does not fall below 12%, and you specify equal semiannual payments for 8 years, the required period of deferment can be determined as follows.

Discrete Compounding. Assuming annual compounding, f = 1 and for semiannual payments, f' = 2. Then

$$i^* = i = R/f = 12\%/1 = 12\% = 0.12$$

$$c = f/f' = 1/2$$

$$n = f't = (2)(8) = 16$$

$$nc = (16)(1/2) = 8$$

From Eq. (6.4-3)

$$d = \frac{1}{1/2} \left\{ \frac{\log\left\{ \frac{15000}{(2)(20000)} \left[\frac{(1.12)^1 - 1}{(1.12)^{1/2} - 1} \right] \left\{ \frac{1 - \left[\frac{1.08}{1.12} \right]^8}{0.12 - 0.08} \right\} \right\}}{\log 1.12} \right\}$$

$$= 2 \left\{ \frac{\log\left\{ \frac{15000}{(2)(20000)} \left[\frac{0.12}{1.0583005 - 1} \right] \left[\frac{1 - 0.7475597}{0.04} \right] \right\}}{\log 1.12} \right\}$$

$$= 27.94 \text{ semiannual payment intervals (14 years)}$$

Continuous Compounding.

$$i' = R/f' = 12\%/2 = 0.12/2 = 0.06$$

$$i^* = e^{ki'} - 1 = e^{(365/360)(0.06)} - 1 = 0.0627$$

$$R_e = e^{kR} - 1 = e^{(365/360)(0.12)} - 1 = 0.1294$$

From Eq. (6.4-6)

$$d = \frac{\log\left\{ \frac{15000}{(2)(20000)} \left[\frac{0.1294}{0.0627} \right] \left\{ \frac{1 - \left[\frac{1.08}{1.1294} \right]^8}{0.1294 - 0.08} \right\} \right\}}{\log 1.0627}$$

$$= \frac{\log\left\{ \frac{15000}{(2)(20000)} \left[\frac{0.1294}{0.0627} \right] \left[\frac{1 - 0.6992102}{0.0494} \right] \right\}}{\log 1.0627}$$

$$= 25.5 \text{ semiannual payment intervals (12.25 years).}$$

CHAPTER **7**

Formulas for Evaluating
Investment Alternatives

This chapter provides formulas for the evaluation of investment alternatives for assets which can appreciate, depreciate, or remain constant in value. The evaluations are based on present value, rate of return, future value, and perpetual replacement (capitalization) of alternative investments. Within the text are one or more examples which indicate the use of each formulas. The examples include:

1. Determining the present value on a total investment when the cash flow estimate is not a level periodic amount. Page 156
2. Determining the present value on a total investment when the cash flow estimate is a level periodic amount and the cash flow can be considered to be a simple ordinary annuity or it can be considered to be a complex ordinary annuity. Page 156
3. Determining the best alternative based on the present value on a total investment for level periodic cash flow estimates. Page 156
4. Determining the present value on a total investment and the best alternative when the annual cash flow increases at a constant rate for both annual cash flow estimates and periodic cash flow estimates which are not annual. Page 159
5. Determining the periodic equivalent cash flow for the examples cited in 1 through 3 above and the initial periodic equivalent cash flow for the examples in 4 above. Pages 160, 162, 163, 164
6. Determining the rate of return on a total investment for significant and negligible residual values—including a computer program. Pages 165, 169
7. Determining the best alternative based on the rate of returns on an incremental investment. That is, is the additional cost of an alternative advantageous relative to a lower cost alternative? Page 170
8. Determining the necessary appreciation of an asset for the rate of return on the total investment to reach a specified level. These future values are determined for both level periodic and annually increasing cash flows. Page 171
9. Determining the present value (capitalized cost) for an infinite number of replacements of an asset at the end of its useful life for both level replacement costs and replacement costs increasing at a constant rate. Pages 174, 175

155

If you perform the calculations in the examples, your results may differ from the indicated results, depending upon the number of decimal places you carry at each step of the solutions.

The nomenclature for the formulas is as follows:

c—Interest conversions per payment interval (c = f/f′).

C—Capitalized cost.

f—Frequency of compounding (Interest conversions per year).

f′—Frequency of payments (Payment intervals per year).

G—Annual rate of change of cash flow.

i—Periodic interest rate (i = R/f).

i*—Rate of return on total investment (V = 0).

MARR—*Minimum Attractive Rate of Return.* That rate which must be and can be achieved by an investment. It is assumed to be compounded annually.

n—Number of interest conversion periods (n = ft) for cash flows that are simple annuities and the number of payments for cash flows that are complex annuities.

n′—Number of interest conversions for non-uniform cash flow.

p—Periodic cash flow (p = Receipts minus Disbursements).

p′—Non-uniform cash flow.

p_o—Initial periodic cash flow for annually increasing cash flows.

p_e—Periodic equivalent cash flow.

P—First cost of an asset (investment).

R—Annual interest rate.

S—Residual value (future amount) of an asset (investment).

t—Number of years (replacement number of years for capitalized cost).

V—Present value on total investment.

7.1   PRESENT VALUE EVALUATIONS

Present Value on Total Investment—Level Cash Flow

If the cash flow for an investment can be estimated without the effects of inflation over the life of the investment, the present value on the total investment can be determined as follows.

1. If the periodic cash flow is estimated on a non-uniform basis, the present value can be determined by

$$V = -P + \sum p'_j(1 + i)^{-n'_j} + S(1 + i)^{-n} \qquad (7.1\text{-}1)$$

2. If the periodic cash flow is estimated to be a simple ordinary annuity (end-of-period cash flow) with level payments, the present value can be determined by

$$V = -P + p\left[\frac{1 - (1 + i)^{-n}}{i}\right] + S(1 + i)^{-n} \qquad (7.1\text{-}2)$$

If tables are to be used,

$$V = -P + p(V/p,i,n) + S(1 + i)^{-n} \qquad (7.1\text{-}3)$$

3. If the periodic cash flow is estimated to be a complex ordinary annuity (end-of-period cash flow) with level payments, the present value can be determined by,

$$V = -P + p\left[\frac{1 - (1 + i)^{-nc}}{(1 + i)^c - 1}\right] + S(1 + i)^{-nc} \qquad (7.1\text{-}4)$$

If tables are to be used,

$$V = -P + p\left[\frac{(V/p,i,nc)}{(S/p,i,c)}\right] + S(1 + i)^{-nc} \qquad (7.1\text{-}5)$$

Example 1. A revenue generating asset requires an expenditure of $10,000. Its useful life is estimated to be 3 years at the end of which it is expected to have a residual value of $4,000. The MARR is 20%, and the net cash flow is estimated as follows.

End of Year	Net Annual Cash Flow	Residual Value
0	-$10,000	
1	4,000	
2	5,000	
3	3,000	$4,000

The present value on the total investment can be determined as follows. Since the cash flow estimates are different for each year Eq. (7.1-1) is used.

$$V = -10000 + (4000)(1 + 20\%)^{-1} + (5000)(1 + 20\%)^{-2} + (3000)(1 + 20\%)^{-3}$$
$$+ (4000)(1 + 20\%)^{-3}$$

From Table A-2 or the y^x function on the calculator,

$$V = -10000 + (4000)(0.8333333) + (5000)(0.6944444) + (3000)(0.5787037)$$
$$+ (4000)(0.5787037) = -10000 + 10856 = \$856$$

Example 2. Suppose that cash flow of Example 1 is estimated as follows.

End of Year	Net Annual Cash Flow	Residual Value
0	-$10,000	
1	4,000	
2	4,000	
3	4,000	$4,000

Since the cash flow estimates form a simple ordinary annuity with level payments, Eq. (7.1-2) or (7.1-3) is used.

From Eq. (7.1-3)

$$V = -10000 + (4000)\left[\frac{1 - (1.20)^{-3}}{0.20}\right] + (4000)(1.20)^{-3}$$

$$= -10000 + (4000)\left[\frac{1 - 0.5787037}{0.20}\right] + (4000)(0.5787037)$$

$$= -10000 + 8426 + 2315 = \$741$$

From Eq. (7.1-4) and Table A-2

$$V = -10000 + (4000)(V/p,i,3) + (4000)(1 + 20\%)^{-3}$$

$$= -10000 + (4000)(2.10648148) + (4000)(0.5787037)$$

$$= -10000 + 8426 + 2315 = \$741$$

Example 3. Suppose the net cash flow of Example 1 is estimated to be $1,000 per quarter with a $4,000 residual value at the end of 3 years. Since the cash flow estimates form a complex ordinary annuity (the MARR is 20% compounded annually and does not coincide with the frequency of the estimates), Eq. (7.1-5) or (7.1-6) is used. For Eqs. (7.1-4) and (7.1-5)

$$f = 1, \quad f' = 4, \quad \text{and} \quad c = f/f' = 1/4$$

$$n = f't = (4)(3) = 12$$

$$nc = (12)(1/4) = 3$$

$$i = R/f = 20\%/1 = 0.20$$

From Eq. (7.1-5),

$$V = -10000 + (1000)\left[\frac{1 - (1.20)^{-3}}{(1.20)^{1/4} - 1}\right] + (4000)(1.2)^{-3}$$

$$= -10000 + (1000)\left[\frac{1 - 0.5787037}{1.0466351 - 1}\right] + (4000)(0.5787037)$$

$$= -10000 + 9034 + 2315 = \$1,349$$

From Eq. (7.1-6) and tables,

$$V = -10000 + (1000)\left[\frac{(V/p,i,3)}{(S/p,i,1/4)}\right] + (4000)(1 + 20\%)^{-3}$$

$(V/p,i,3)$ can be determined from Table A-2, and $(S/p,i,1/4)$ can be determined from Table A-3.

$$= -10000 + (1000)\left[\frac{2.10648148}{0.2331757}\right] + (4000)(0.5787037)$$

$$= -10000 + 9034 + 2315 = \$1,349$$

Example 4. Three alternatives are presented as viable solutions for a production situation. Each alternative has a useful life of 10 years, and the estimated cash flows are shown below. With a MARR of 20% you must make the decision.

End of Year	A	B	C
0	-$20,000	-$25,000	-$30,000
1-10	5,000	6,000	7,000
Residual Value	2,000	2,500	3,000

Since each of the cash flows forms a simple ordinary annuity, Eq. (7.1-2) or (7.1-3) can be used. Using Eq. (7.1-3) and Table A-2,

$$V = -P + p(V/p,i,10) + S(1 + 20\%)^{-10}$$

$$V_A = -20000 + (5000)(4.1924721) + (2000)(0.1615056) = \$1,285$$

$$V_B = -25000 + (6000)(4.1924721) + (2500)(0.1615056) = \$559$$

$$V_C = -30000 + (7000)(4.1924721) + (3000)(0.1615056) = -\$168$$

Since the present value of alternative A is the largest, A would be the most profitable of the three alternatives if the estimated cash flows prove to be accurate.

Present Value on Total Investment
Annual Cash Flow Changing at a Constant Rate

If the estimated cash flow of an investment includes the effects of inflation over the life of the investment, the present value on the total investment can be determined as follows.

1. If the periodic cash flow is estimated on a non-uniform basis, Eq. (7.1-1) applies.
2. If the annual cash flow is estimated to change at an estimated constant rate over the life of the investment, the cash flow would be a simple ordinary annuity with a changing level of payment. The present value can be determined by

$$V = -P + p_0 \left[\frac{(1 + R)^t - (1 + G)^t}{(R - G)(1 + R)^t} \right] + S(1 + R)^{-t} \qquad (7.1\text{-}6)$$

3. If the annual cash flow, with equal fractions occurring over equal intervals during the year, is estimated to change at an estimated constant rate over the life of the investment, the cash flow would be a complex ordinary annuity with a changing level of the annual amount. The present value can be determined by

$$V = -P + \frac{p_0}{f'} \left[\frac{R}{(1 + R)^c - 1} \right] \left[\frac{(1 + R)^t - (1 + G)^t}{(R - G)(1 + R)^t} \right] + S(1 + R)^{-t} \qquad (7.1\text{-}7)$$

If Table A-3 is to be used

$$V = -P + \frac{p_0}{f'(S/p,i,c)} \left[\frac{(1 + R)^t - (1 + G)^t}{(R - G)(1 + R)^t} \right] + S(1 + R)^{-t} \qquad (7.1\text{-}8)$$

Example 5. Suppose that the estimated cash flows for the alternatives of Example 4 are as shown below.

End of Year	A	B	C
0	-$20,000	-$25,000	-$30,000
1	5,000	6,000	7,000
Residual Value	2,000	2,500	3,000

Each alternative has a useful life of 10 years, and the annual cash flow is estimated to increase 7% per year. The MARR is 20%. Since the cash flow represents a simple ordinary annuity with annual amounts increasing at a constant rate, Eq. (7.1-6) is used. For each alternative

$$\frac{(1 + R)^t - (1 + G)^t}{(R - G)(1 + R)^t} = \frac{(1.20)^{10} - (1.07)^{10}}{(0.20 - 0.07)(1.20)^{10}} = 5.2484159$$

and

$$(1 + R)^{-t} = (1 + 20\%)^{-10} = (1.20)^{-10} = 0.1615056$$

Then,

$$V_A = -20000 + (5000)(5.2484159) + (2000)(0.1615056) = \$6,565$$

$$V_B = -25000 + (6000)(5.2484159) + (2500)(0.1615056) = \$6,894$$

$$V_C = -30000 + (7000)(5.2484159) + (3000)(0.1615056) = \$7,223$$

Since the present value of alternative C is the greatest, C would be the most profitable alternative if the estimates would prove to be accurate.

It should be noted that the effect of estimating a constant growth in cash flows is to change the most profitable alternative as determined in Example 4.

Example 6. Suppose the cash flows of Example 5 are annual representations of estimated quarterly cash flows. As such, these cash flows would represent a complex ordinary annuity with annual amounts changing at a constant rate. Then, Eq. (7.1-7) or (7.1-8) would be used. For an MARR of 20%, f = 1. For quarterly estimates, $f' = 4$. Then $c = f/f' = 1/4$. In order to use Table A-3, Eq. (7.1-8) is used. As in Example 5

$$\frac{(1 + R)^t - (1 + G)^t}{(R - G)(1 + R)^t} = \frac{(1.20)^{10} - (1.07)^{10}}{(0.20 - 0.07)(1.20)^{10}} = 5.2484159$$

$$(1 + R)^{-t} = (1 + 20\%)^{-10} = (1.20)^{-10} = 0.1615056$$

$$(S/p, i, 1/4) = 0.2331757$$

Then

$$V_A = -20000 + \frac{(5000)(5.2484159)}{(4)(0.2331757)} + (2000)(0.1615056) = \$8,459$$

$$V_B = -25000 + \frac{(6000)(5.2484159)}{(4)(0.2331757)} + (2500)(0.1615056) = \$9,166$$

$$V_C = -30000 + \frac{(7000)(5.2484159)}{(4)(0.2331757)} + (3000)(0.1615056) = \$9,874$$

As in Example 5, C would be the most profitable alternative if the estimated cash flow growth rate would prove to be accurate.

Periodic Equivalent Level Cash Flow

If a periodic equivalent level cash flow of an investment is desired, the present value on the total investment can be represented as an ordinary annuity where the periodic equivalent would be the level periodic payment which reduces the present value to zero over the life of the investment. Then:

1. For a simple ordinary annuity periodic equivalent level cash flow,

$$p_e = V\left[\frac{i}{1 - (1 + i)^{-n}}\right] \tag{7.1-9}$$

If tables are to be used,

$$p_e = V(p/V,i,n) \tag{7.1-10}$$

2. For a complex ordinary annuity periodic equivalent level cash flow

$$p_e = V\left[\frac{(1 + i)^c - 1}{1 - (1 + i)^{-nc}}\right] \tag{7.1-11}$$

If tables are to be used,

$$p_e = V\left[\frac{(S/p,i,c)}{(V/p,i,nc)}\right] \tag{7.1-12}$$

Example 7. For a MARR of 20%, the periodic equivalent level cash flows of a) Example 1, b) Example 2, and c) Example 3 are desired.

a) From Example 1, $V = 856$. Since the cash flow is annual, the periodic equivalent cash flow is an annual equivalent amount with $n = 3$. Using Eq. (7.1-10) and Table A-2,

$$p_e = (856) (p/V,i,3)$$

$$= (856) (0.4747253)$$

$$= \$406 \text{ per year}$$

b) From Example 2, $V = 741$. Since the cash flow is annual, the periodic equivalent cash flow is an annual equivalent amount with $n = 3$. Using Eq. (7.1-10) and Table A-2,

$$p_e = (741) (p/V,i,3)$$

$$= (741) (0.4747253)$$

$$= \$352 \text{ per year}$$

c) From Example 3, $V = 1349$. Since the cash flow is quarterly, the periodic equivalent cash flow is the quarterly equivalent amount with $nc = 3$. Using Eq. (7.1-12) and Tables A-2 and A-3 (for $c = 1/4$)

$$p_e = (1349)\left[\frac{(S/p,i,1/4)}{(V/p,i,3)}\right]$$

$$= (1349)\left[\frac{0.2331757}{0.4747253}\right]$$

$$= \$663 \text{ per quarter}$$

Example 8. The annual equivalent cash flows of the alternatives of Example 4 are desired. The MARR = 20% and $n = 10$. From Example 4, $V_A = 1285$, $V_B = 559$, and $V_C = -168$. Using Eq. (7.1-10) and Table A-2

$$p_e = V(p/V,i,10)$$

$$p_{eA} = (1285) (0.2385228) = \$307 \text{ per year}$$

$$p_{eB} = (559) (0.2385228) = \$133 \text{ per year}$$

$$p_{eC} = (-168) (0.2385228) = -\$40 \text{ per year}$$

Initial Periodic Cash Flow
Annual Equivalent Cash Flow Changing at a Constant Rate

If the equivalent annual cash flow, which includes the effects of inflation, is desired, the initial annual amount can be determined as follows:

1. For a simple ordinary annuity annual equivalent cash flow, the initial annual amount can be determined by,

$$p_o = V \left[\frac{(R - G)(1 + R)^t}{(1 + R)^t - (1 + G)^t} \right] \tag{7.1-13}$$

2. For a complex ordinary annuity periodic equivalent cash flow, the initial annual amount can be determined by,

$$p_o = f'V \left[\frac{(1 + R)^c - 1}{R} \right] \left[\frac{(R - G)(1 + R)^t}{(1 + R)^t - (1 + G)^t} \right] \tag{7.1-14}$$

$$p_o = f'V(S/p,i,c) \left[\frac{(R - G)(1 + R)^t}{(1 + R)^t - (1 + G)^t} \right] \tag{7.1-15}$$

Example 9. The annual equivalent cash flows of the alternatives of Example 5 are desired. The MARR is 20% and $t = 10$. From Example 5, $V_A = 6565$, $V_B = 6894$, $V_C = 7223$. Since the estimated cash flow of Example 5 represents a simple ordinary annuity, Eq. (7.1-13) is used to determine the initial annual amount. For each alternative,

$$\frac{(R - G)(1 + R)^t}{(1 + R)^t - (1 + G)^t} = \frac{(0.20 - 0.07)(1.20)^{10}}{(1.20)^{10} - (1.07)^{10}} = 0.1905337$$

Then,

$$p_{oA} = (6565)(0.1905337) = \$1251 \text{ the first year and increasing 7\% per year}$$

$$p_{oB} = (6894)(0.1905337) = \$1314 \text{ the first year and increasing 7\% per year}$$

$$p_{oC} = (7223)(0.1905337) = \$1376 \text{ the first year and increasing 7\% per year}$$

Example 10. The quarterly equivalent cash flows of the alternatives of Example 6 are desired. The MARR is 20% and $t = 10$. From Example 6, $V_A = 8459$, $V_B = 9166$, and $V_C = 9872$. Also, $c = 1/4$. Since the estimated cash flow of Example 6 represents a complex ordinary annuity (annual conversion with quarterly payments), the initial annual amouts can be determined by Eq. (7.1-14) or (7.1-15). For each alternative,

$$\frac{(R - G)(1 + R)^t}{(1 + R)^t - (1 + G)^t} = \frac{(0.20 - 0.07)(1.20)^{10}}{(1.20)^{10} - (1.07)^{10}} = 0.1905337$$

$$(S/p,i,1/4) = 0.2331757$$

Then,

$$p_{oA} = (8459)(0.2331757)(0.1905337) = \$376 \text{ the first year}$$

$$p_{oB} = (9166)(0.2331757)(0.1905337) = \$407 \text{ the first year}$$

$$p_{oC} = (9872)(0.2331757)(0.1905337) = \$439 \text{ the first year}$$

The quarterly equivalent amounts are simply the annual amount divided by $f' = 4$. Then

$$p_{eA}/f' = 376/4 = \$94 \text{ per quarter the first year}$$
$$\text{and increasing 7\% each year.}$$

$$p_{eB}/f' = 407/4 = \$102 \text{ per quarter the first year}$$
$$\text{and increasing 7\% each year.}$$

$$p_{eC}/f' = 439/4 = \$110 \text{ per quarter the first year}$$
$$\text{and increasing 7\% each year.}$$

Capital Recovery With Return—Zero Present Value
Level Cash Flow

Given an estimated residual value of a revenue generating investment, the minimum periodic cash flow that is necessary in order to recover the principal investment and yield a specified rate of return over the useful life of the investment can be determined as follows.

1. If the periodic cash flow is to be a simple ordinary annuity with level payments, the required minimum periodic cash flow can be determined by

$$p = (P - S)\left[\frac{i}{1 - (1 + i)^{-n}}\right] + Si \tag{7.1-16}$$

If tables are to be used,

$$p = (P - S)(p/V,i,n) + Si \tag{7.1-17}$$

2. If the periodic cash flow is to be a complex ordinary annuity with level payments, the required minimum periodic cash flow can be determined by

$$p = \left\{(P - S)\left[\frac{i}{1 - (1 + i)^{-nc}}\right] + Si\right\}\left[\frac{(1 + i)^c - 1}{i}\right] \tag{7.1-18}$$

If tables are to be used

$$p = [(P - S)(p/V,i,nc) + Si](S/p,i,c) \tag{7.1-19}$$

Example 11. For a first cost of $20,000 and an estimated residual value of $2,000 at the end of 10 years, the minimum level, annual cash flow for capital recovery is desired for an MARR of 20%. Since a level, annual cash flow forms a simple ordinary annuity, Eq. (7.1-16) or (7.1-17) can be used. Since R = 20% compounded annually, i = 0.20. Using Eq. (7.1-17) and Table A-2,

$$p = (20000 - 2000)(p/V,i,10) + (2000)(0.20)$$

$$= (18000)(0.2385228) + (2000)(0.20)$$

$$= \$4,693 \text{ per year}$$

Therefore, with a cash flow of $4,693 per year, the present value of alternative A in Example 4 will be, essentially, zero.

Example 12. The minimum quarterly level cash flow is desired for the investment of Example 11.

$$i = R/f = 20\%/1 = 0.20$$

$$f' = 4$$

$$c = f/f' = 1/4$$

$$n = f't = (4)(10) = 40$$

$$nc = (40)(1/4) = 10$$

Using Eq. (7.1-19) and Tables A-2 and A-3

$$p = [(20000 - 2000)(p/V,i,10) + (2000)(0.20)](S/p,i,1/4)$$

$$= [(18000)(0.2385228) + (2000)(0.20)](0.2331757)$$

$$= (4693)(0.2331757)$$

$$= \$1,094 \text{ per quarter}$$

Capital Recovery With Return—Zero Present Value
Initial Annual Cash Flow Amount—Cash Flow Changing at a Constant Rate

Given an estimated residual value of a revenue generating investment, where the annual cash flow is expected to include the effects of inflation, the initial annual cash flow amount that is required in order to recover the principal and yield a specified rate of return over the life of the investment can be determined as follows.

1.   If the annual cash flow is estimated to change at an estimated constant rate over the life of the investment the cash flow would be a simple ordinary annuity with the level of payment changing at a constant rate. The initial annual amount can be determined by

$$p_o = [P(1 + R)^t - S]\left[\frac{R - G}{(1 + R)^t - (1 + G)^t}\right] \qquad (7.1\text{-}20)$$

2.   If the annual cash flow, with equal fractions occurring over equal intervals during the year, is estimated to change at an estimated constant rate over the life of the investment, the cash flow would be a complex ordinary annuity and can be determined by

$$p_o = f'[P(1 + R)^t - S]\left[\frac{(1 + R)^c - 1}{R}\right]\left[\frac{R - G}{(1 + R)^t - (1 + G)^t}\right] \qquad (7.1\text{-}21)$$

$$p_o = f'[P(1 + R)^t - S](S/p,i,c)\left[\frac{R - G}{(1 + R)^t - (1 + G)^t}\right] \qquad (7.1\text{-}22)$$

Example 13.   For a first cost of $30,000 and an estimated residual value of $3,000 at the end of 10 years, if the inflation rate is estimated to be 7% per year and the annual cash flow is expected to increase at the same rate, the initial annual cash flow that is required can be determined by Eq. (7.1-20). If the MARR is 20%

$$p_o = [(30000)(1.20)^{10} - 3000]\left[\frac{0.20 - 0.07}{(1.20)^{10} - (1.07)^{10}}\right]$$

$$= (185752 - 3000)(0.0307723)$$

$$= \$5,624 \text{ the first year and increasing 7\% per year}$$

Therefore, with a cash flow of \$5,624 the first year and a 7% increase each year thereafter, the present value of alternative C of Example 5 will be, essentially, zero.

Example 14. The quarterly cash flow, during the first year, of Example 13 can be determined by Eq. (7.1-21) or (7.1-22).

$$f = 1$$

$$f' = 4$$

$$c = f/f' = 1/4$$

From Eq. (7.1-21)

$$p_o = (4) \, [(30000) \, (1.20)^{10} - 3000] \left[\frac{(1.20)^{1/4} - 1}{0.20} \right] \left[\frac{0.20 - 0.07}{(1.20)^{10} - (1.07)^{10}} \right]$$

$$= (4) \, (185752 - 3000) \, (0.2331757) \, (0.0307723)$$

$$= \$5,245 \text{ the first year.}$$

Then, the required quarterly cash flow would be $5245/4 = \$1,311$ during the first year and must increase 7% per year.

7.2   RATE OF RETURN EVALUATIONS

The rate of return of an investment is defined as that interest rate which reduces the present value of an investment to zero relative to the useful life of the investment. In the general situation, rate of return calculations are trial and error and require computer solutions. However, rate of return can be determined by interpolation of tables.

Rate of Return on Total Investment

The relationship between the present value on the total investment and the interest rate is that as the interest rate increases, the present value decreases. The rate of return is the value of i (i*) that makes V = 0 at n.

Equations (7.1-2) through (7.1-5) reduce as follows:

$$i = 0 \qquad V = -P + np + S \tag{7.2-1}$$

$$i = i^* \qquad V = 0$$

$$i = \infty \qquad V = -P$$

Equations (7.1-6) through (7.1-8) reduce as follows:

$$i = 0 \qquad V = -P + \frac{p_o(1 + G)^t}{cf'G} + S \tag{7.2-2}$$

$$i = i^* \qquad V = 0$$

$$i = \infty \qquad V = -P$$

Given a first cost, estimated cash flow, and estimated residual value, the rate of return on a total investment will be the interest rate that reduces the present value on the total investment to zero. The solution to Eqs. (7.1-1) through (7.1-8) for the value of i that reduces V to zero is a trial-and-error solution. One relatively formalized procedure could be as follows.

1. Solve Eq. (7.2-1) or (7.2-2), as appropriate, for $i = 0$. The value of V for either solution should be positive.
2. As a first trial, determine the general area of i by letting $i = p/P$ or $i = p_o/P$ and solving the appropriate equation of Eqs. (7.1-2) through (7.1-8).
3. If the value of V does not change sign from Step 1, increase i and solve the appropriate equation for V on a continuous basis until the value of V changes signs. Then, interpolate between the last two values of i.

If the value of V does change sign from Step 1, decrease i and solve the appropriate equation for V on a continuous basis until the value of V changes in sign again. Then, interpolate between the last two values of i.

In Step 3, above, the magnitude of the increase or decrease in the value of i depends upon the nearness to zero of the solution in Step 2 and is an arbitrary matter.

Example 1.   The estimated cash flow for an investment is as follows.

End of Year	Cash Flow	Residual Value
0	-$20,000	
1-9	5,000	
10	5,000	$2,000

The rate of return, should the cash flow estimates prove accurate, is determined as follows.

1. $i = 0$. From (7.2-1)

    $$V = -20000 + (10)(5000) + 2000 = \$32,000$$

2. $i = 5000/20000 = 0.25 = 25\%$. From Eq. (7.1-2) or (7.1-3) with $n = 10$

    $$V = -20000 + (5000)(3.57050327) + (2000)(0.10737418)$$

    $$= -\$1,933$$

3. Since V changed signs from Step 1, decrease i by 2% until V approaches zero. For $i = 23\%$

    $$V = -20000 + (5000)(3.79926999) + (2000)(0.1261679)$$

    $$= -\$751$$

    For $i = 21\%$

    $$V = -20000 + (5000)(4.05407796) + (2000)(0.14864363)$$

    $$= \$568$$

Since the sign of V changes for $i = 23\%$ and $i = 21\%$, interpolate between these two values

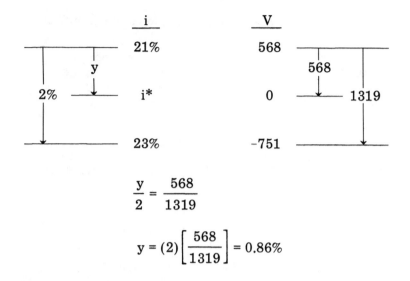

$$\frac{y}{2} = \frac{568}{1319}$$

$$y = (2)\left[\frac{568}{1319}\right] = 0.86\%$$

Then

$$i^* = 21 + y = 21 + 0.86 = 21.86\%$$

As a check for the nearness to zero, using the value of 21.86% in Eq. (7.1-2) gives a V of -18.

Computer Program. Should the need to determine the rate of return on a total investment occur frequently or if a rate which is more accurate than that which is obtained by interpolation, as in Example 1, is desired, a computer is almost mandatory. The following program is a "no frills" BASIC language program which starts with i = 0% per period and increments by 1% to a maximum of 1,000% per period. When there is a change in the sign of the present value and the present value is within $1.00 of V = 0, the program prints the rate of return. Prior to data input, Eq. (7.2-1) should be solved. For i = 0, Eq. (7.2-1) gives

$$V = -P + np + S$$

and if V is negative for the estimated values of p and S, the present value can not reach zero in n periods. The estimated cash flow parameters should be checked. If this calculation is omitted, as it might be by a busy individual, the program will indicate that a problem exists. The solution to Example 1 follows the program.

The statement PRINT CHR$(12) appears twice in the program—statements 0020 and 0590. This statement is used to advance the paper to the top of the next page. It has no other use in the program.

The appropriate data are "read" in statement 0100 in the sequence:

1. First cost—P
2. Annual cash flow—p
3. Residual value—S
4. Compounding frequency—f
5. Payment frequency—f'
6. Useful life—t

These data are supplied in statement 0110. The symbol, ^, in statement 0210 and elsewhere is analogous to the upward directed arrow in BASIC.

Computer Solution to Example 1. Program 7-1.

```
THE INITIAL COST IS                    $    20,000.00
THE RESIDUAL VALUE IS                  $     2,000.00
THE PERIODIC CASH FLOW IS              $     5,000.00
AND IT OCCURS  1  TIMES PER YEAR

FOR AN ASSET LIFE OF  10  YEARS
THE PRESENT VALUE OF THE CASH FLOW IS  $          0.96
THE NOMINAL ANNUAL RATE OF RETURN IS             21.83 %
THE EFFECTIVE ANNUAL RATE OF RETURN  IS          21.83 %
```

```
0010 REM PROGRAM 7-1
0020 PRINT CHR$(12)
0030 REM RATE OF RETURN FOR ZERO PRESENT VALUE
0040 REM P IS THE FIRST COST, P1 IS THE PERIODIC CASH FLOW
0050 REM S IS THE RESIDUAL VALUE, F IS THE COMPOUNDING FREQUENCY
0060 REM F1 IS THE CASH FLOW FREQUENCY, AND T IS THE ASSET LIFE
0070 REM IN NUMBER OF YEARS.
0080 DIM V(1000),V$(20)
0090 LET V$="-###,###.##"
0100 READ P,P1,S,F,F1,T
0110 DATA 20000,5000,2000,1,1,10
0120 LET C=F/F1
0130 LET N=F*T
0140 LET E1=-N*C
0150 LET V(1)=-P+N*P1+S
0160 IF V(1)<=0 THEN GOTO 0550
0170 LET M=100
0180 LET IO=0
0190 FOR K=1 TO 1000
0200    LET I=IO+K/M
0210    LET N1=1-(1+I)^E1
0220    LET D=(1+I)^C-1
0230    LET V1=N1/D
0240    LET S1=(1+I)^E1
0250    LET V(K)=-P+P1*V1+S*S1
0260    IF V(K)<0 THEN GOTO 0300
0270    IF K=1000 THEN GOTO 0550
0280    IF ABS(V(K))<=1 THEN GOTO 0330
0290 NEXT K
0300 LET IO=IO+(K-1)/M
0310 LET M=10*M
0320 GOTO 0190
0330 LET R=F*I
0340 LET R1=(1+I)^F-1
0350 PRINT "THE INITIAL COST IS                    $ ";
0360 PRINT USING V$,P
0370 PRINT "THE RESIDUAL VALUE IS                  $ ";
0380 PRINT USING V$,S
0390 PRINT "THE PERIODIC CASH FLOW IS              $ ";
0400 PRINT USING V$,P1
```

Program 7-1 (Continued)

```
0410 PRINT "AND IT OCCURS ";F1;" TIMES PER YEAR"
0420 PRINT
0430 PRINT "FOR AN ASSET LIFE OF ";
0440 PRINT T;
0450 PRINT " YEARS"
0460 PRINT "THE PRESENT VALUE OF THE CASH FLOW IS $ ";
0470 PRINT USING V$,V(K)
0480 PRINT "THE NOMINAL ANNUAL RATE OF RETURN IS    ";
0490 PRINT USING V$, 100*R;
0500 PRINT " %"
0510 PRINT "THE EFFECTIVE ANNUAL RATE OF RETURN   IS";
0520 PRINT USING V$, 100*R1;
0530 PRINT " %"
0540 GOTO 0590
0550 PRINT "THE PRESENT VALUE HAS NOT CHANGED SIGNS FOR RATES OF RETURN"
0560 PRINT "BETWEEN 0% AND 1000%.   THE CASH FLOW PARAMETERS SHOULD BE"
0570 PRINT "CHECKED AGAINST A POSSIBILTY OF A NEGATIVE PRESENT VALUE"
0580 PRINT "AT 0% OR A RATE OF RETURN IN EXCESS OF 1000% PER PERIOD. "
0590 PRINT CHR$(12)
0600 STOP
0610 END
```

Rate of Return on Total Investment—Negligible Residual Value

If the residual value of a revenue-generating asset can be considered to be negligible, and if the cash flow can be considered to be a simple ordinary annuity a present value equal to zero will occur when

$$(V/p,i,n) = P/p \qquad (7.2\text{-}3)$$

A search of Table A-2 for the value of $(V/p,i,n)$ given by Eq. (7.2-3) will yield the approximate rate of return.

Example 2. The estimated cash flow for an investment is as follows.

End of Year	Cash Flow	Residual Value
0	-$30,000	
1-9	7,000	
10	7,000	$3,000

The approximate rate of return if the residual value is ignored can be determined by Eq. (7.2-3).

$$(V/p,i,n) = 30000/7000 = 4.2857143$$

A search of Table A-2, opposite n = 10, shows that the value 4.2857143 occurs between 19% and 19 1/2% and is closer to 19 1/2%. Then, the approximate rate of return is 19 1/2%. For a more accurate result interpolation is necessary.

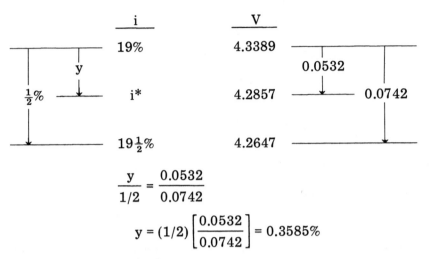

$$\frac{y}{1/2} = \frac{0.0532}{0.0742}$$

$$y = (1/2)\left[\frac{0.0532}{0.0742}\right] = 0.3585\%$$

Then, for a negligible residual value

$$i^* = 19\% + y = 19 + 0.3585 = 19.3585\%$$

Rate of Return on Incremental Investment

If alternative investments are being considered where first costs and estimated cash flows are different, the selection can be made based on the rate of return of the increment of the first cost difference being greater than the minimum attractive rate of return. The procedure would be as follows:

1. List the alternatives in ascending order of first costs.
2. Determine the rate of return on the differences in first cost, cash flow, and residual value.
3. If the rate of return is greater than the MARR, select the alternative with the higher first cost. If the rate of return is less than the MARR, select the alternative with the lower first cost.
4. Repeat Steps 2 and 3 with the increment based on the alternative selected in Step 3 and the alternative with the next higher first cost.

Example 3. For the estimated cash flows shown below and an MARR of 20%, one of the alternatives is to be selected.

End of Year	Do Nothing	A	B	C
0	0	−$20,000	−$25,000	−$30,000
1–10	0	5,000	6,000	7,000
Residual Value	0	2,000	2,500	3,000

For the analysis, Eqs. (7.1-2) and (7.1-3) should be used. However, for simplicity, it is assumed that the residual values are negligible to the analysis. Then, Eq. (7.2-3) may be used with n = 10. Then,

$$(V/p,i,n) = P/p$$

For the alternatives "Do Nothing" and A

End of Year	A - Do Nothing
0	-20,000
1-10	5,000

$$(V/p,i,n) = 20000/5000 = 4$$

From Table A-2, this value occurs between 21% and 21 1/2% and the rate of return of the $20,000 increment over "Do Nothing" is greater than the MARR of 20%. Select A over Do Nothing.

For the alternatives A and B:

End of Year	B - A
0	-5,000
1-10	1,000

Then

$$(V/p,i,n) = 5000/1000 = 5$$

From Table A-2, this value occurs between 15% and 15 1/2% and the rate of return of the $5,000 increment of B over A is less than the MARR of 20%. Select A over B.

For the alternatives A and C:

End of Year	C - A
0	-10,000
1-10	2,000

Then,

$$(V/p,i,n) = 10000/2000 = 5$$

This value occurs between 15% and 15 1/2% and the rate of return of the $10,000 increment of C over A is less than the MARR of 20%. Select A over C.

Then, based on an analysis of rate of return on incremental investment, alternative A should be selected. This conclusion is in agreement with the result of Example 4 in Section 7.1 where the analysis is based on the present value of the total investment.

7.3   FUTURE VALUE EVALUATIONS

Whether assets appreciate or depreciate in value, if the future value is known or can be estimated, the equations of Section 7.1 may be used to determine the present value on the total investment, and the procedures of Section 7.2 may be used to determine the rates of return. This section addresses the situation where it is desired to know the following: If the cash flow of an investment generates a "current" rate of return, what level must the residual value reach in order for the total investment to yield a specified rate of return?

1. If the periodic cash flow is estimated to be a simple ordinary annuity, the present value can be determined as follows:

I. *Level Periodic Cash Flow*

$$S = P(1 + i)^n - p\left[\frac{(1 + i)^n - 1}{i}\right] \qquad (7.3\text{-}1)$$

If tables are to be used,

$$S = P(1 + i)^n - p(S/p,i,n) \qquad (7.3\text{-}2)$$

II. *Annual Cash Flow Changing at a Constant Rate*

$$S = P(1 + R)^t - p_o\left[\frac{(1 + R)^t - (1 + G)^t}{R - G}\right] \qquad (7.3\text{-}3)$$

2. If the periodic cash flow is estimated to be a complex ordinary annuity, the present value can be determined as follows:

I. *Level Periodic Cash Flow*

$$S = P(1 + i)^{nc} - p\left[\frac{(1 + i)^{nc} - 1}{(1 + i)^c - 1}\right] \qquad (7.3\text{-}4)$$

If tables are to be used,

$$S = P(1 + i)^{nc} - p\left[\frac{(S/p,i,nc)}{(S/p,i,c)}\right] \qquad (7.3\text{-}5)$$

II. *Annual Cash Flow Changing at a Constant Rate*

$$S = P(1 + R)^t - \frac{p_o}{f'}\left[\frac{R}{(1 + R)^c - 1}\right]\left[\frac{(1 + R)^t - (1 + G)^t}{R - G}\right] \qquad (7.3\text{-}6)$$

If Table A-3 is to be used

$$S = P(1 + R)^t - \frac{p_o}{f'(S/p,i,c)}\left[\frac{(1 + R)^t - (1 + G)^t}{R - G}\right] \qquad (7.3\text{-}7)$$

Example 1. Twenty years ago $120,000 was invested in the purchase of real estate. The annual cash flow from that investment has been $12,000. It is desired to establish a selling price so that an interest rate of 20% compounded annually will have been realized over the 20-year term. Since this cash flow is a simple ordinary annuity, Eq. (7.3-1) or (7.3-2) can be used.

$$i = R/f = 20\%/1 = 20\% = 0.20$$

$$n = ft = (20)(1) = 20$$

From Eq. (7.3-2) and Table A-2

$$S = (120000)(38.33759992) - (12000)(186.68799962)$$

$$= 4600512 - 2240256$$

$$= \$2,360,256$$

Example 2. Suppose the cash flow of Example 1 was $1,000 per month. Since this cash flow represents a complex ordinary annuity for an interest rate of 20% compounded annually, Eq. (7.3-4) or (7.3-5) can be used.

$$i = R/f = 20\%/1 = 20\% = 0.20$$

$$f' = 12$$

$$c = f/f' = 1/12$$

$$n = f't = (12)(20) = 240$$

$$nc = (240)(1/12) = 20$$

From Eq. (7.3-5) and Tables A-2 and A-3

$$S = (120000)(38.33759992) - (1000)\left[\frac{186.68799962}{0.07654735}\right]$$

$$= 4600512 - 2438858$$

$$= \$2,161,654$$

Example 3. Suppose the annual cash flow of Example 1 started at $12,000 per year and increased 5% per year over the 20-year period. Since this cash flow represents a simple ordinary annuity with uniformly increasing payments, Eq. (7.3-3) can be used with G = 5%. For R = 20% compounded annually

$$S = (120000)(1 + 20\%)^{20} - (12000)\left[\frac{(1 + 20\%)^{20} - (1 + 5\%)^{20}}{20\% - 5\%}\right]$$

From Table A-2 or the y^x function on the calculator

$$S = (120000)(38.33759992) - (12000)\left[\frac{38.33759992 - 2.65329771}{0.15}\right]$$

$$= 4600512 - 2854744$$

$$= \$1,745,768$$

Example 4. Suppose the cash flow of Example 1 started at $1,000 per month with the annual amount increasing 5% per year over the 20-year period. For an interest rate of 20% compounded annually, this cash flow represents a complex ordinary annuity with uniformly increasing annual amounts. Then, Eq. (7.3-6) or (7.3-7) can be used with f = 1 and f' = 12.

$$i = R/f = 20\%/1 = 20\% = 0.20$$

$$c = f/f' = 1/12$$

$$nc = f'tc = (12)(20)(1/12) = 20$$

$$p_0 = (1000)(f') = (1000)(12) = 12000$$

From Eq. (7.3-7) and Tables A-2 and A-3

$$S = (120000)(38.33759992) - \frac{12000}{(12)(0.07654735)} \left[\frac{38.33759992 - 2.65329771}{0.15} \right]$$

$$= 4600512 - 3107822$$

$$= \$1,492,690$$

The long-term capital gain on the real estate of Example 1 would be the difference between the value of S from the appropriate cash flow example above and the original purchase price.

7.4   CAPITALIZATION

Capitalized cost, C, of an asset is defined as the sum of the first cost, P, and the future renewal cost, p, in perpetuity.

Level Future Renewal Costs

1.   If the interest conversion period coincides with the renewal interval,

$$C = P + \frac{p}{i} \qquad (7.4\text{-}1)$$

If the future renewal or replacement cost is the same as the first cost

$$C = \frac{P(1 + i)}{i} \qquad (7.4\text{-}2)$$

2.   If the interest conversion period does not coincide with the renewal interval,

$$C = P + \frac{p}{(1 + i)^c - 1} \qquad (7.4\text{-}3)$$

where $(1 + i)^c$ can be determined from Table A-4. For the use of Table A-2 or A-3,

$$C = P + \frac{p}{i(S/p,i,c)} \qquad (7.4\text{-}4)$$

If the future renewal or replacement cost is the same as the first cost.

$$C = \frac{P}{1 - (1 + i)^{-c}} \qquad (7.4\text{-}5)$$

where $(1 + i)^{-c}$ can be determined from Table A-4. For the use of Table A-2 or A-3 when p = P,

$$C = \frac{P}{i(V/p,i,c)} \qquad (7.4\text{-}6)$$

Example 1.   The cost of machine A is $20,000 and must be renewed every 10 years at the same cost. The cost of machine B is $17,500 and must be renewed every 7 years at the same cost. Which is the better buy based on a MARR of 20%? Since the interest conversion period and the replacement do not coincide, Eqs. (7.4-3) through (7.4-6) apply, and since the replacement costs are the same as the first costs, Eq. (7.4-5) or (7.4-6) apply. For a MARR of 20%,

$$i = R/f = 20\%/1 = 0.20$$

The capitalized cost for machine A: Since machine A requires 1 replacement every 10 years, $f' = 1/10$ and

$$c = \frac{f}{f'} = \frac{1}{1/10} = 10$$

Since c is greater than 1, $(V/p,i,c)$ can be determined by Table A-2 opposite $n = 10$, and from Eq. (7.4-6)

$$C = \frac{20000}{0.20}\left[\frac{1}{4.19247209}\right] = \$23,852$$

The capitalized cost for machine B: Since machine B requires 1 replacement every 7 years, $f' = 1/7$ and

$$c = \frac{f}{f'} = \frac{1}{1/7} = 7$$

Since c is greater than 1, $(V/p,i,c)$ can be determined by Table A-2 opposite $n = 7$, and from Eq. (7.4-6)

$$C = \frac{17500}{0.20}\left[\frac{1}{3.60459176}\right] = \$24,275$$

Since the capitalized cost of machine A is less than that of machine B, A is the better buy. Therefore, committing $23,852, "now" for machine A leaves $3,852 after the purchase. For the replacement in 10 years, the $3,852 will have grown to a future amount given by

$$S = (3852)(1.20)^{10} = 23852$$

from which $20,000 may be used to replace the machine. This leaves $3,852 to grow for the next replacement.

Future Renewal Costs Changing at a Constant Rate

If it can be estimated that the future renewal (replacement) cost of an asset will change (normally increase) at a rate of G% per year, if the minimum attractive rate of return is R%, and if t represents the number of years between renewals, the capitalized cost can be determined by

$$C = \frac{P(1+R)^t}{(1+R)^t - (1+G)^t} \tag{7.4-7}$$

Example 2. The cost of machine A is $20,000, and the machine must be replaced every 10 years. The cost of machine B is $17,500, and the machine must be replaced every 7 years. If it is estimated that the cost of both machines will increase 8% per year, and if the MARR is 20%, Eq. (7.4-7) can be used to determine which machine is the better buy. The capitalized cost of A:

$$C = \frac{(20000)\,(1 + 20\%)^{10}}{(1 + 20\%)^{10} - (1 + 8\%)^{10}}$$

From Table A-2

$$C = \frac{(20000)\,(6.19173642)}{6.19173642 - 2.158925} = \$30,707$$

The capitalized cost of B:

$$C = \frac{(17500)\,(1 + 20\%)^{7}}{(1 + 20\%)^{7} - (1 + 8\%)^{7}}$$

$$C = \frac{(17500)\,(3.5831808)}{3.5831808 - 1.71382427} = \$33,544$$

Since the capitalized cost of machine A is less than that of machine B, A is the better buy. A tabulation for 3 replacements (30 years) of machine A is shown below.

Replacement of Machine A

End of Year	Cost Of Machine A	Committed For Replacement	Balance After Replacement
0	$ 20,000	$ 30,707	$ 10,707
10	43,179	66,295	23,116
20	93,219	143,128	49,909
30	201,253	309,024	107,770

In order to sustain a perpetual growth in the cost, the Balance After Replacement increases by a factor of $(1.08)^{10}$ every 10 years. For the columns above,

Cost of . . . = $(1.08)^{10}$ times previous Cost Of . . .

Committed For . . . = $(1.20)^{10}$ times previous Balance After . . .

Balance After . . . = Committed For . . . - Cost of . . .

CHAPTER 8

How to Use Bond Formulas

This chapter provides formulas for elementary determinations of the various parameters of bonds. Within the text are one or more examples which indicate the use of each formula. The examples include:

1. Determining the cost and quoted price of a bond on an interest payment date. Page 178
2. Determining the amount of a bond issue in order to raise a specified amount of money. Page 179
3. Determining the approximate cost, quote, and face value of long-term bonds. Page 179
4. Determining the cost of a bond between interest payment dates. Page 181
5. Determining the quoted price of a bond between interest payment dates. Page 182
6. Determining the exact yield of a bond. Page 182
7. Determining the approximate yield of a bond by interpolation. Page 183
8. Determining the approximate yield of a bond by the average investment. Page 184
9. Determining the amortization of a bond premium. Page 187
10. Determining the accumulation of a bond discount. Page 188
11. Determining a bond coupon rate. Page 189

If you perform the calculations in the examples, your results may differ from the indicated results, depending upon the number of decimal places you carry at each step of the solutions.

The nomenclature for the formulas is as follows:

B—Annual bond coupon rate.
b—Periodic bond coupon rate.
P—Cost (Price) of a bond on an interest payment date.
P_F—Cost (Flat price) of a bond between interest payment dates.
f—Compounding frequency and bond interest payment frequency per year.
S—Face value of a bond (Future Amount).
i—Periodic bond yield = R/f (see R below).
p—Periodic bond interest.
I_a—Accrued bond interest.

n—Number of interest payment periods until bond maturity date.

V—Present value of S.

Q—Quote price of a bond—usually expressed as percent of face value.

R—Annual yield of a bond.

T—Number of years until bond maturity date.

t—Fraction of a year for accrued interest.

V_i—Present value of periodic bond interest.

$\approx$—Approximately equal to

8.1   THE COST (PRICE) OF BONDS

The cost, or purchase price, of a bond is the sum of the present value of an ordinary annuity formed by the periodic interest, the present value of the face value of the bond, and the accrued interest from the last interest payment date. Then

$$P = V + V_i + I_a \tag{8.1-1}$$

Cost on an Interest Payment Date

If a bond is purchased on an interest payment date, the seller will receive the interest, and there is no accrued interest. Then $I_a = 0$.

$$P = S \left[\frac{B}{R} + \left[1 - \frac{B}{R} \right] (1 + i)^{-n} \right] \tag{8.1-2}$$

and the quote would be determined from

$$Q = \frac{P}{S} \times 100\% \text{ or } P = QS \tag{8.1-3}$$

Then,

$$Q = \left[\frac{B}{R} + \left[1 - \frac{B}{R} \right] (1 + i)^{-n} \right] (\times 100 \text{ for } \%) \tag{8.1-4}$$

Equations (8.1-2) and (8.1-4) assume that the interest conversion period for the yield rate (investor's yield) and the interest payment period coincide. Thus, semiannual interest payments imply semiannual compounding; etc.

Example 1.   A \$10,000 bond with an 8% coupon rate payable semiannually on June 30 and December 31 matures in 10 years. What should be the quoted price on December 31 to yield a nominal 15%? For a nominal 15% and semiannual compounding

$$i = R/f = 15\%/2 = 7.5\% = 0.075$$

$$B = 8\%$$

The number of interest conversion periods in 10 years is

$$n = fT = (2)(10) = 20$$

Then, from Eq. (8.1-4)

$$Q = \left[\frac{8}{15} + \left[1 - \frac{8}{15} \right] (1 + 7.5\%)^{-20} \right] \times 100$$

The value $(1 + 7.5\%)^{-20}$ can be determined by the calculator or Table A-2. Also note that the ratio (B/R) can be expressed with B and R in percent values rather than the corresponding decimals. Then,

$$Q = [0.53333 + (1 - 0.53333)(0.2354132)] \times 100$$

$$= 64.3192\%$$

Then, the cost is (from Eq. (8.1-3))

$$P = QS = (0.643192)(10000) = \$6,431.92$$

The true cost would add any charges or commissions to the quoted price.

Amount of a Bond Issue

If it is desired to issue bonds which yield a rate different from the coupon rate, the cost of the bonds would be the amount of money that is to be generated from the issue. The "face value" would be the amount to be redeemed upon maturity. Then

$$S = \frac{P}{\dfrac{B}{R} + \left[1 - \dfrac{B}{R}\right](1 + i)^{-n}} \qquad (8.1-5)$$

Example 2.   Ten million dollars is to be raised by the issue of a 6% coupon rate bond with the interest to be paid semiannually. The bonds are to mature in 20 years and are to sell at a nominal yield of 12%. The face value of the issue can be determined by Eq. (8.1-5) where:

$$P = 10000000$$

$$i = R/f = 12\%/2 = 6\% = 0.06$$

$$n = ft = (2)(20) = 40$$

Then, with B and R in percent values,

$$S = \frac{10000000}{\dfrac{6}{12} + \left[1 - \dfrac{6}{12}\right](1 + 6\%)^{-40}}$$

$$S = \frac{10000000}{0.5 + (0.5)(0.09722219)}$$

$$= \$18,227,848$$

Therefore, in order to realize $10 million from the sale of the bonds, over $18 million of bonds must be sold to yield 12% with a 6% coupon rate.

Approximate Values for Long-Term Bonds

For extremely long-term bonds, the number of interest conversions would be large and $(1 + i)^{-n}$ could approach a negligibly small value. Thus, the limiting cost, quote, and face value become, respectively,

$$P \approx \frac{SB}{R} \qquad\qquad (8.1\text{-}6)$$

$$Q \approx \frac{B}{R} \times 100\% \qquad\qquad (8.1\text{-}7)$$

$$S \approx \frac{PR}{B} \qquad\qquad (8.1\text{-}8)$$

where the symbol $\approx$ means "approximately."

Example 3.   Compare the actual quote against the approximate quote for 20-year and 30-year bonds for a 3% coupon rate and a 24% nominal yield. Assuming semiannual payments and compounding

$$i = R/f = 24\%/2 = 12\% = 0.12$$

For 20-year bonds:

$$n = ft = (2)(20) = 40$$

From Eq. (8.1-4), the actual quote is

$$Q = \left[\frac{3}{24} + \left[1 - \frac{3}{24}\right](1 + 12\%)^{-40}\right] \times 100 = 13.44\%$$

From Eq. (8.1-7), the approximate quote would be

$$Q = \frac{3}{24} \times 100 = 12.5\%$$

The difference between the actual and approximate is 0.94% and the error of approximation is 6.99%.

For 30-year bonds:

$$n = ft = (2)(30) = 60$$

From Eq. (8.1-4), the actual quote would be

$$Q = \left[\frac{3}{24} + \left[1 - \frac{3}{24}\right](1 + 12\%)^{-60}\right] \times 100 = 12.597\%$$

The approximate quote remains at 12.5% and the difference between the two is 0.0979%. The error of approximation is 0.77%.

For higher coupon rates and lower nominal yields, the approximations of Eqs. (8.1-6), (8.1-7), and (8.1-8) generate smaller errors of approximation (Error = Difference/Exact).

Example 4.   Compare the actual quote against the approximate quote for 20-year and 30-year bonds for a 10% coupon rate and a 16% nominal yield. Assuming semiannual payments and compounding

$$i = R/f = 16\%/2 = 8\%$$

For 20-year bonds:

$$n = ft = (2)(20) = 40$$

From Eq. (8.1-4), the actual quote is

$$Q = \left[\frac{10}{16} + \left[1 - \frac{10}{16}\right](1 + 8\%)^{-40}\right] \times 100 = 64.226\%$$

From Eq. (8.1-7), the approximate quote is

$$Q = \frac{10}{16} \times 100 = 62.5\%$$

The difference between the exact and approximate quotes is 1.726%, and the error of the approximation is 2.69%. For the 20-year bond of Example 3 with a 3% coupon and a 24% nominal yield, the error of the approximation is 6.99%.

For 30-year bonds:

$$n = ft = (2)(30) = 60$$

From Eq. (8.1-4), the actual quote is

$$Q = \left[\frac{10}{16} + \left[1 - \frac{10}{16}\right](1 + 8\%)^{-60}\right] \times 100 = 62.87\%$$

The approximate quote remains at 62.5%. The difference between the two is 0.37%, and the error of the approximation is 0.59%. For the 30-year bonds of Example 3, the error of the approximation is 0.77%.

In both cases of this example the error of the approximation (Error = Difference/ Exact Quote) decreased as the coupon rate increased and the nominal yield decreased from Example 3.

Cost Between Interest Payment Dates

If a bond is purchased between interest payment dates, the cost (purchase price) of the bond is the cost on the immediately previous interest payment date plus accrued interest to the purchase date.

The accrued interest is based on compound interest for a fractional interest conversion period, and the *flat price* (purchase price) would be

$$P_F = P(1 + i)^{ft} \tag{8.1-9}$$

where the values of $(1 + i)^{ft}$ can be determined from Table A-4 or the y^x function on the calculator. t is the fraction of the year of accrued interest. The value of P can be determined by Eq. (8.1-2).

As a reasonably close approximation which is easier to use, the *flat price* (purchase price) would be

$$P_F = P(1 + Rt) \tag{8.1-10}$$

Example 5. A \$10,000, 6% bond is redeemable in 5 years and 2 months. It is purchased at a yield of 15% compounded semiannually. The flat price is determined as follows:

The cost of the bond is determined to the immediately previous interest payment date or 5 years and 6 months prior to maturity. Then,

$$i = R/f = 15\%/2 = 7.5\% = 0.075$$

$$n = ft = (2)(5.5) = 11$$

From Eq. (8.1-2)

$$P = (10000)\left[\frac{6}{15} + \left[1 - \frac{6}{15}\right](1 + 7.5\%)^{-11}\right] = \$6{,}708$$

Using Eq. (8.1-9): Since maturity occurs in 5 years and 2 months and since P was determined for maturity in 5 years and 6 months, accrued interest at the yield rate is needed for 4 months. Then

$$ft = (2)(4/12) = 2/3$$

and

$$P_F = (6708)(1 + 7.5\%)^{2/3}$$

Since Table A-4 does not include 2/3, but does include 1/3

$$P_F = (6708)(1 + 7.5\%)^{1/3}(1 + 7.5\%)^{1/3}$$
$$= (6708)(1.02439981)(1.02439981)$$
$$= \$7{,}039$$

Using Eq. (8.1-10)

$$P_F = (6708)[1 + (0.15)(4/12)]$$
$$= \$7{,}043$$

The error between the two results is \$4.

Quoted Price Between Interest Payment Dates

The quoted price of a bond between interest payment dates is the flat price less the accrued bond interest.

$$Q = \left[\frac{P_F}{S} - Bt\right](\times 100 \text{ for } \%) \qquad (8.1\text{-}11)$$

Example 6. The quotes for the bond of Example 5 would be as follows. The time for the accrued bond interest would be 4/12 years. Then, depending upon the method for determining C_F (Eq. (8.1-9) or Eq. (8.1-10)),

$$Q = \left[\frac{7039}{10000} - (0.06)(4/12)\right] \times 100 = 68.39\%$$

or

$$Q = \left[\frac{7043}{10000} - (0.06)(4/12)\right] \times 100 = 68.43\%.$$

8.2   BOND YIELD

Exact Yield

The "exact" yield of a bond can be determined by Eq. (8.1-2), (8.1-9), or (8.1-10), but the procedure is trial and error. Thus, in general

$$P_F = S\left[\frac{B}{R} + \left[1 - \frac{B}{R}\right](1+i)^{-n}\right](1+i)^{ft} \qquad (8.2\text{-}1)$$

if accrued interest is determined by compounding interest at the yield rate, and

$$P_F = S\left[\frac{B}{R} + \left[1 - \frac{B}{R}\right](1+i)^{-n}\right](1+Rt) \qquad (8.2\text{-}2)$$

if accrued interest is determined by simple interest at the yield rate. Eqs. (8.2-1) and (8.2-2) are general in that the cost, P_F, can include accrued interest and any charges or commissions. If a bond is purchased on an interest payment date, both $(1+i)^{ft}$ and $(1+Rt)$ equal 1. For an "exact" yield, a large number of trials may be necessary, therefore, a computer is almost mandatory (see page 186). Rearranging Eq. (8.1-6) gives a yield that can be used as a starting value of R as

$$R = \frac{SB}{P_F} \qquad (8.2\text{-}3)$$

where P_F is the known cost of the bond. Then, the value of R can be substituted into Eq. (8.2-1) or (8.2-2) which solve for P_F. Now,

1. If the bond was purchased at a discount, repeatedly increase R by some small amount and solve Eq. (8.2-1) or (8.2-2) repeatedly until the actual P_F is bracketed. Then decrease R repeatedly by a smaller amount and solve Eq. (8.2-1) or (8.2-2) repeatedly until the actual P_F is bracketed again. Continue alternating the increase and decrease of R until the calculated P_F and the actual P_F agree to within some specified level (perhaps within $1 or perhaps within 1 cent). See Program 8-1 (page 186).

2. If the bond was purchased at a premium, initially decrease R and then alternate as in Step 1 above.

Approximate Yield by Interpolation

If the yield of a bond is to be determined manually, a reasonable approximation may be determined using the procedure in Steps 1 or 2 above but by increasing or decreasing the initial estimate of R (Eq. (8.2-3)) by a relatively large amount.

Example 1. A $10,000 bond with an 8% coupon rate, payable semiannually on June 30 and December 31, matures in 10 years. The bond is purchased on December 31 for $6,431.92. The yield, neglecting charges and commissions, is desired. Since the bond is purchased on December 31 which is an interest payment date, t = 0 and

$$(1+i)^{ft} = (1+Rt) = 1; \quad i = R/f = R/2; \quad \text{and} \quad n = fT = (2)(10) = 20$$

From Eq. (8.2-3), the initial value of R is

$$R = \frac{(10000)(8)}{6431.92} = 12.44\%$$

Since this value of R is a crude estimate, it may be rounded to 12.5% (for use of tables if desired). Then i = R/2 = 6.25% from Eq. (8.2-1) or (8.2-2)

$$P_F = (10000)\left[\frac{8}{12.5} + \left[1 - \frac{8}{12.5}\right](1+6.25\%)^{-20}\right] = 7470.84$$

Since this bond was purchased for \$6,431.92, which is at a discount, the estimate of R may be increased. Assume an increase of 50% in order to be reasonably sure of bracketing the actual cost. Then

$$R = 12.5\% + (0.50) (12.5\%) = 18.75\%$$

Then $i = R/2 = 9.375\%$ and

$$P_F = (10000) \left[\frac{8}{18.75} + \left[1 - \frac{8}{18.75} \right] (1 + 9.375\%)^{-20} \right]$$

$$= 5221.76$$

Since the values of R (12.5% and 18.75%) cause a bracketing of the actual cost, interpolation may be used for the approximation.

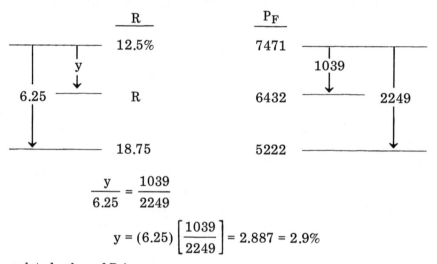

$$\frac{y}{6.25} = \frac{1039}{2249}$$

$$y = (6.25) \left[\frac{1039}{2249} \right] = 2.887 = 2.9\%$$

The interpolated value of R is

$$R = 12.5\% + y = 12.5\% + 2.9\% = 15.4\%$$

Example 1 of Section 8.1 is the same as this example and the cost of \$6,431.92 is obtained with an exact yield of 15%. Then, the error of the approximation is 2.7% (difference is 0.4% with a 15% base).

Approximate Yield by Average Investment

The approximation based on average investment is defined by

$$R = \frac{\text{Annual Income}}{\text{Average Annual Investment}} \qquad (8.2\text{-}4)$$

Two forms of the equation are available.

$$R = \frac{2}{S + P_F} \left[BS + \frac{S - P_F}{T} \right] (\times 100 \text{ for } \%) \qquad (8.2\text{-}5)$$

which utilizes actual dollars, and

$$R = \frac{2}{1 + Q} \left[B + \frac{1 - Q}{T} \right] (\times 100 \text{ for } \%) \qquad (8.2\text{-}6)$$

where $Q = P_F/S$.

Example 2.   Determine the approximate yield by the average investment for Example 1 of this section.   From Example 1, B = 8% = 0.08, S = 10,000, P_F = 6431.92, and T = 10.   Then from Eq. (8.2-5)

$$R = \frac{2}{10000 + 6432} \left[(0.08)(10000) + \frac{(10000 - 6432)}{10} \right] \times 100$$

$$= \frac{2}{16432} \left[800 + \frac{3568}{10} \right] \times 100$$

$$= 14.08\%$$

In order to use Eq. (8.2-6),

$$Q = \frac{P_F}{S} = \frac{6432}{10000} = 0.6432$$

$$= \frac{2}{1.6432} \left[0.08 + \frac{1 - 0.6432}{10} \right] \times 100$$

$$= \frac{2}{1.6432} \left[0.08 + \frac{0.3568}{10} \right] \times 100$$

$$= 14.08\%$$

The exact yield for Example 1 is 15%.

Computer Program.   In order to determine the exact yield to maturity for a bond, a large number of iterations may be necessary.   Therefore, a computer is almost mandatory. Program 8-1 is a "no frills" BASIC language program which starts with i = 0% and increments by 1%, to a maximum of 1,000% per period, in Eq. (8.2-1) modified as:

$$V = -P + \text{Right side of Eq. (8.2-1)}.$$

When the value of V becomes negative and is within $1.00 of V = 0, the bond yield is printed.

The statement PRINT CHR$(12) appears twice in the program—statements 0020 and 0630.   This statement is used to advance the paper to the top of the next page.   It has no other purpose in the program.

The bond purchase data are "read" in statement 0120 and are supplied in statement 0130 in the sequence:

1.   Flat price—P.
2.   Coupon interest—p.
3.   Face value of bond—S.
4.   Compounding frequency—f.
5.   Payment frequency—f'.
6.   Bond life from the immediately preceding coupon payment date—T.
7.   Number of days from the immediately preceding coupon payment date to the actual purchase date of the bond—D.

The symbol, ^, in statement 0250 and elsewhere is analogous to the upward directed arrow in BASIC.

The computer solution for Example 1 of Section 8.1 is shown below from the perspective that the purchase price is known and, it is desired to determine the yield.

Computer Solution to Example 1
Program 8-1

```
THE INITIAL COST IS                          $     6,431.92
THE RESIDUAL VALUE IS                        $    10,000.00
THE PERIODIC CASH FLOW IS                    $       400.00
AND IT OCCURS  2  TIMES PER YEAR

FOR A BOND LIFE OF            10.00 YEARS
THE PRESENT VALUE OF THE CASH FLOW IS $           0.01
THE NOMINAL ANNUAL YIELD TO MATURITY IS         15.00 %
THE EFFECTIVE ANNUAL YIELD TO MATURITY IS       15.56 %
```

```
0010 REM PROGRAM 8-1
0020 PRINT CHR$(12)
0030 REM BOND YIELD
0040 REM P IS THE FIRST COST, P1 IS THE PERIODIC CASH FLOW
0050 REM S IS THE BOND FACE VALUE, F IS THE COMPOUNDING FREQUENCY
0060 REM F1 IS THE CASH FLOW FREQUENCY, AND T IS THE ASSET LIFE,
0070 REM IN NUMBER OF YEARS, FROM PRECEEDING COUPON PAYMENT DATE.
0080 REM D IS THE NUMBER OF DAYS FROM THE PRECEDING COUPON
0090 REM PAYMENT DATE TO THE PURCHASE DATE.
0100 DIM V(1000),V$(20)
0110 LET V$="-###,###.##"
0120 READ P,P1,S,F,F1,T,D
0130 DATA 6431.92,400,10000,2,2,10,0
0140 LET C=F/F1
0150 LET N=F*T
0160 LET T2=D/365
0170 LET N2=F*T2
0180 LET E1=-N*C
0190 LET V(1)=-P+N*P1+S
0200 IF V(1)<=0 THEN GOTO 0590
0210 LET M=100
0220 LET I0=0
0230 FOR K=1 TO 1000
0240    LET I=I0+K/M
0250    LET N1=1-(1+I)^E1
0260    LET N3=(1+I)^C-1
0270    LET V1=N1/N3
0280    LET S1=(1+I)^E1
0290    LET V(K)=-P+(P1*V1+S*S1)*(1+I)^N2
0300    IF V(K)<0 THEN GOTO 0340
0310    IF K=1000 THEN GOTO 0590
0320    IF ABS(V(K))<=1 THEN GOTO 0370
0330 NEXT K
0340 LET I0=I0+(K-1)/M
0350 LET M=10*M
0360 GOTO 0230
0370 LET R=F*I
0380 LET R1=(1+I)^F-1
0390 PRINT "THE INITIAL COST IS                       $ ";
0400 PRINT USING V$,P
0410 PRINT "THE RESIDUAL VALUE IS                     $ ";
0420 PRINT USING V$,S
0430 PRINT "THE PERIODIC CASH FLOW IS                 $ ";
```

Program 8-1 (Continued)

```
0440 PRINT USING V$, P1
0450 PRINT "AND IT OCCURS ";F1;" TIMES PER YEAR"
0460 PRINT
0470 PRINT "FOR A BOND LIFE OF ";
0480 PRINT USING V$, (T-T2);
0490 PRINT " YEARS"
0500 PRINT "THE PRESENT VALUE OF THE CASH FLOW IS $   ";
0510 PRINT USING V$, V(K)
0520 PRINT "THE NOMINAL ANNUAL YIELD TO MATURITY IS   ";
0530 PRINT USING, V$, 100*R;
0540 PRINT " %"
0550 PRINT "THE EFFECTIVE ANNUAL YIELD TO MATURITY IS";
0560 PRINT USING V$, 100*R1;
0570 PRINT " %"
0580 GOTO 0630
0590 PRINT "THE PRESENT VALUE HAS NOT CHANGED SIGNS FOR RATES OF RETURN"
0600 PRINT "BETWEEN 0% AND 1000%.   THE CASH FLOW PARAMETERS SHOULD BE"
0610 PRINT "CHECKED AGAINST A POSSIBILTY OF A NEGATIVE PRESENT VALUE"
0620 PRINT "AT 0% OR A RATE OF RETURN IN EXCESS OF 1000% PER PERIOD. "
0630 PRINT CHR$(12)
0640 STOP
0650 END
```

8.3   BOOK VALUE OF BONDS

The book value of a bond can be kept current by periodically amortizing any premium or accumulating any discount until the face value of the bond is achieved at maturity (if kept until then).

Amortization of a Premium

Example 1.   A $10,000 bond with 12% interest payable semiannually on June 30 and December 31 is purchased on March 31 to yield 10%. The bond matures in 3 years and 9 months. The cost of the bond would be the cost for a 4-year maturity plus accrued interest.

$$i = R/f = 10\%/2 = 5\% = 0.05: \quad B = 12\%/2 = 6\%$$

$$n = fT = 2(4) = 8$$

$$t = 3 \text{ months} \quad \text{and} \quad ft = (2) (3/12) = 1/2$$

From Eq. (8.1-9)

$$P_F = (10000) \left[\frac{12}{10} + \left[1 - \frac{12}{10} \right] (1 + 5\%)^{-8} \right] (1 + 5\%)^{1/2}$$

$$= \$10,909.23$$

Thus, there is a premium of $909.23 which must be amortized over 8 interest payment periods (3 Years, 9 months = 8 interest periods).

For a premium amortization schedule:

Bond Interest = bS.
Investor Yield = iV, where V is the immediately previous book value.

Premium Amortization = bS – iV.
Book Value = V = Previous Book Value minus Premium Amortization.

Amortization Schedule for Bond Premium

S = $10,000:   b = 6%:   i = 5%

(1) End of Interest Period	(2) Bond Interest bS 0.06S	(3) Investor Yield iV 0.05V	(4) Premium Amortization bS – iV (2) – (3)	(5) Book Value of Bond V (5) – (4)
				$10,909.23
1	$600	$269.40	$330.60	10,578.63
2	600	528.93	71.07	10,507.56
3	600	525.38	74.62	10,432.94
4	600	521.65	78.35	10,354.59
5	600	517.73	82.27	10,272.32
6	600	513.62	86.38	10,185.94
7	600	509.30	90.70	10,095.24
8	600	504.76	95.24	10,000.00

Note: Because this bond is purchased between interest payment dates, the "Investor Yield" at the end of the first interest period is determined by compound interest from the purchase date to the bond interest payment date. For this bond, that time is 3 months (0.25 years). Then

$$\text{"}iV_1\text{"} = [(1 + 5\%)^{f(0.5-t)} - 1]\,(10909.23)$$

$$= [(1 + 5\%)^{2(0.5-0.25)} - 1]\,(10909.23)$$

$$= [(1 + 5\%)^{0.5} - 1]\,(10909.23)$$

$$= (0.0246951)\,(10909.23) = \$269.40$$

Accumulation of a Discount

Example 2.   Suppose the bond of Example 1 had been purchased to yield 15%. Then

$$i = R/f = 15\%/2 = 7.5\% = 0.075$$

and

$$P_F = (10000)\left[\frac{12}{15} + \left[1 - \frac{12}{15}\right](1 + 7.5\%)^{-8}\right](1 + 7.5\%)^{1/2}$$

$$= \$9,457.27$$

and the discount of $542.73 is to be accumulated over 8 interest periods.

For a discount accumulation schedule:

Bond Interest = bS.
Investor Yield = iV, where V is the immediately previous book value.
Discount Accumulation = iV – bS
Book Value = V = Previous Book Value plus Discount Accumulation.

Accumulation Schedule for Bond Discount

$$S = \$10,000: \quad b = 6\%: \quad i = 7\,1/2\%$$

(1) End of Interest Period	(2) Bond Interest bS $0.06S$	(3) Investor Yield iV $0.075V$	(4) Discount Accumulation $iV - bS$ (3) – (2)	(5) Book Value V (5) + (4)
				$ 9,457.27
1	$600	$348.24	-$251.76	9,205.51
2	600	690.41	90.41	9,295.92
3	600	697.19	97.19	9,393.11
4	600	704.48	104.48	9,497.59
5	600	712.32	112.32	9,609.91
6	600	720.74	120.74	9,730.65
7	600	729.80	129.80	9,860.45
8	600	739.55*	139.55	10,000.00

*Corrected for 2 cent discrepancy due to rounding.

Note: Because this bond is purchased between interest payment dates, the "Investor Yield" at the end of the first interest period is determined by compound interest from the purchase date to the bond interest payment date. For this bond, that time is 3 months (0.25 years). Then

$$\text{``}iV_1\text{''} = [(1 + 7.5\%)^{f(0.5-t)} - 1]\,(9457.27)$$

$$= [(1 + 7.5\%)^{2(0.5-0.25)} - 1]\,(9457.27)$$

$$= (0.0368221)\,(9457.27) = \$348.24$$

8.4   BOND COUPON RATE

When a specified amount of money, C, is to be raised by a bond issue and the face value, S, of the bond issue is to be limited to a specified amount, a coupon rate which reflects the market rate on the day of the issue can be determined by

$$B = \frac{R[(P/S) - (1 + i)^{-n}]}{1 - (1 + i)^{-n}} \tag{8.4-1}$$

where B will be an annual percent if R is used as an annual percent.

Example 1. Nine million dollars is to be raised by a bond issue which is to be limited to $10 million of bonds. If the term of the bonds is 20 years and interest is to be paid semiannually, the necessary coupon rate for a 12% annual yield can be determined by Eq. (8.4-1). For semiannual interest payments,

$$i = R/f = 12\%/2 = 6\% = 0.06$$

$$n = fT = (2)\,(20) = 40$$

Then

$$B = \frac{(12)\,[(9000000/10000000) - (1 + 6\%)^{-40}]}{1 - (1 + 6\%)^{-40}}$$

$$= \frac{(12)\,(0.9 - 0.0972222)}{1 - 0.0972222} = 10.67\%$$

Thus, investors would quote 90% on the day of issue. Substitution of B, R, and i into Eq. (8.1-4) gives

$$Q = \left[\frac{10.67}{12} + \left[1 - \frac{10.67}{12}\right]\,(1 + 6\%)^{-40}\right] \times 100 = 89.994\%$$

The discrepancy of 0.006% is due to rounding.

CHAPTER 9

Formulas and Tables for Calculating Partial Payments on Short-Term Loans

This chapter provides formulas and tables for determining loan repayments using the United States Rule, the Merchants' Rule, Add-on Interest, and consolidation of debts. Within the text are one or more examples for the use of each formula. The examples include:

1. Determining the final payment, in a series of unequal payments with unequal payment intervals, using the Merchants' Rule. Page 192
2. Determining the equal payment level at equal payment intervals using the Merchants' Rule. Page 193
3. Determining the final payment, in a series of unequal payments with unequal payment intervals, using the United States Rule. Page 199
4. Determining the equal payment level at equal payment intervals using the United States Rule. Page 200
5. Determining the periodic payment for add-on interest. Page 201
6. Determining the true annual interest rate for add-on interest. Page 202
7. Determining an approximate true annual interest rate for add-on interest Page 203
8. Determining the Rule of 78 Interest Rebate Factor. Page 203
9. Determining the periodic payment for consolidating debts at both simple and compound interest. Pages 204 and 206.

If you perform the calculations in the examples, your results may differ from the indicated results, depending upon the number of decimal places you carry at each step of the solutions.

The nomenclature for the formulas is as follows:

Π—Product of
Σ—Summation of
B—The balance due on a loan.
B_0—The initial loan amount.
f—Frequency of compounding interest.
F—Frequency of payments per year.
F_R—Rebate factor—Rule of 78.

F_P—Payment factor—Rule of 78.

i—Periodic interest rate.

I—Interest.

j—Subscript for counting.

L—Number of payments remaining with add-on interest.

n—Number of interest conversion periods.

N—The number of payments.

P—The payment amount.

R—Nominal annual interest rate.

R_t—True annual interest rate.

R_e—True effective annual interest rate.

S—The future amount or maturity value of a loan.

t—Time between payments in U.S. Rule and time from payment to maturity date in Merchants' Rule.

T—Term of a loan in Merchants' Rule and Add-on Interest, and time from maturity and payment dates to the comparison date in consolidation of debts.

v—The present value of $1.

V—The present value of the maturity value of a loan.

9.1   MERCHANTS' RULE

The principal of the Merchants' Rule is that all values are projected forward to the maturity date of a loan. Then, the final payment is the difference between the future amount of the loan on the maturity date and the sum of the future amounts of all partial payments on the maturity date.

Unequal Payments and/or Payment Intervals

If the magnitude of the partial payments is not equal and/or the payment intervals are not equal, the amount of the final payment in a series of payments can be determined by

$$P_N = S - \sum_{j=1}^{N-1} S_j \tag{9.1-1}$$

or

$$P_N = B_0(1 + RT) - \sum_{j=1}^{N-1} P_j(1 + Rt_j) \tag{9.1-2}$$

Example 1.   A $10,000 debt is to be repaid in 6 months. If it is planned that a payment of $4,000 will be made at the end of 3 months, and a payment of $3,000 will be made at the end of 5 months, the amount of the final payment is desired. The interest rate is 18%. The given information is shown in Figure 9-1.

For the calculations:

$$B_0 = 10000, \quad R = 18\% = 0.18, \quad \text{and} \quad T = 6 \text{ months} = 1/2 \text{ year}$$

$$P_1 = 4000 \quad \text{and} \quad t_1 = (T - 3) \text{ months} = (6 - 3)/12 = 3/12 = 1/4 \text{ year}$$

$$P_2 = 3000 \quad \text{and} \quad t_2 = (T - 5) \text{ months} = (6 - 5)/12 = 1/12 \text{ year}$$

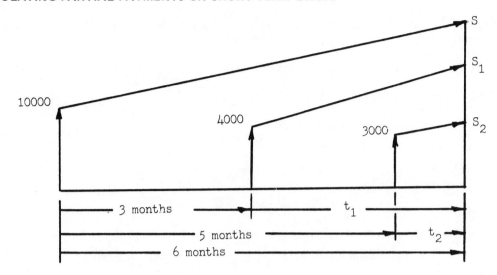

Figure 9-1. Time Chart for 3-Payment Merchants' Rule Calculations.

Then

$$S = B_0(1 + RT) = (10000)[1 + (0.18)(1/2)] = 10900$$

Since $N = 3$

$$S_1 = P_1(1 + Rt_1) = (4000)[1 + (0.18)(1/4)] = 4180$$

$$S_2 = P_2(1 + Rt_2) = (3000)[1 + (0.18)(1/12)] = 3045$$

$$\sum_{j=1}^{2} S_j = 4180 + 3045 = 7225$$

The amount of the final payment will be, from Eq. (9.1-1)

$$P_N = S - \sum_{j=1}^{2} S_j = 10900 - 7225 = 3675$$

Therefore, the amount of the final payment will be \$3,675. The total interest will be the sum of the payments less the original balance, Eq. (9.2-3), or

$$I = 4000 + 3000 + 3675 - 10000 = \$675.00$$

Equal Payments with Equal Payment Intervals

If a debt is to be repaid over a relatively short term with equal payment amounts at equal payment intervals, the equal payment amount can be determined by

$$P = B_0 \left[\frac{1 + (R/F)N}{N + (R/F)(N/2)(N-1)} \right] \tag{9.1-3}$$

Example 2. If it is desired to repay the \$10,000 load of Example 1 with 3 bimonthly equal payments, the amount of each payment can be determined by Eq. (9.1-3). For bimonthly payments, the frequency will be 6 payments per year. Then, $F = 6$. For an interest rate of 18%

$$R/F = (0.18)/6 = 0.03$$

and $N = 3$. From Eq. (9.1-3)

$$P = (10000)\left[\frac{1 + (0.03)(3)}{3 + (0.03)(3/2)(3 - 1)}\right]$$

$$= (10000)\left[\frac{1.09}{3 + (0.03)(3/2)(2)}\right]$$

$$= (10000)[1.09/3.09] = \$3,527.51$$

As a check, the following calculations utilize Eqs. (9.1-1) and (9.1-2)

$$T = 6 \text{ months} = 6/12 = 1/2 \text{ year and } P_1 = P_2 = 3527.51$$

$$t_1 = (T - 2)/12 = (6 - 2)/12 = 4/12 = 1/3 \text{ year}$$

$$t_2 = (T - 4)/12 = (6 - 4)/12 = 2/12 = 1/6 \text{ year}$$

$$S = B_0(1 + RT) = (10000)[1 + (0.18)(1/2)] = 10900$$

$$S_1 = P_1(1 + Rt_1) = (3527.51)[1 + (0.18)(1/3)] = 3739.16$$

$$S_2 = P_2(1 + Rt_2) = (3527.51)[1 + (0.18)(1/6)] = 3633.34$$

Then

$$P_3 = S - \sum_{j=1}^{2} S_j = S - (S_1 + S_2) = 10900 - (3739.16 + 3633.34)$$

$$= 10900 - 7372.50 = \$3,527.50$$

Note: The 1-cent discrepancy is due to rounding

The expression within the brackets is equivalent to the amortization factor, $(p/V, i, n)$ and as such,

$$P = B_0(p/V, i, n)_M \tag{9.1-4}$$

where

$$(p/V, i, n)_M = \frac{1 + (R/F)N}{N + (R/F)(N/2)(N - 1)} \tag{9.1-5}$$

and is provided as Table 9-1.

Example 3.   Use Table 9-1. to determine the equal payment amount for the following.

a)   A \$10,000 loan to be repaid in 3 bimonthly equal payments (Example 2 above). $R = 18\%$

b)   A \$25,000 loan to be repaid in 12 quarterly equal payments. $R = 24\%$

a)   Bimonthly payments indicate 6 payments per year. $F = 6$. Then, opposite 18%, opposite $F = 6$, and under "Number of Equal Payments" = 3, read 0.35275081. Then, from Eq. (9.1-4)

$$P = (10000)(0.35275081) = 3527.5081$$

$$= \$3,527.51$$

b)   Quarterly payments indicate 4 payments per year. $F = 4$. Then, opposite 24%, opposite $F = 4$, and under "Number of Equal Payments" = 12, read 0.10776942. Then, from Eq. (9.1-4)

$$P = (25000)(0.10776942) = 2694.235$$

$$= \$2,694.24$$

Note: The actual final payment will be different by a few cents due to rounding of decimals.

TABLE 9-1

MERCHANTS RULE

NUMBER OF EQUAL PAYMENTS

R	F	1	2	3	4	6	12
6.00	1	1.06000000	.54368932	.37106918	.28440367	.19710145	.10776942
	2	1.03000000	.52216749	.35275081	.26794258	.18294574	.09728183
	3	1.02000000	.51485149	.34640523	.26213592	.17777778	.09309309
	4	1.01500000	.51116625	.34318555	.25916870	.17510040	.09083911
	6	1.01000000	.50746269	.33993399	.25615764	.17235772	.08846761
	12	1.00500000	.50374065	.33665008	.25310174	.16954733	.08596918
7.00	1	1.07000000	.55072464	.37694704	.28959276	.20141844	.11070999
	2	1.03500000	.52579853	.35587762	.27078385	.18544061	.09923131
	3	1.02333333	.51729819	.34853420	.26409018	.17952756	.09453471
	4	1.01750000	.51301115	.34479934	.26065773	.17644711	.09198024
	6	1.01166667	.50869925	.34102142	.25716626	.17327935	.08927173
	12	1.00583333	.50436228	.33719967	.25361421	.17002053	.08639483
8.00	1	1.08000000	.55769231	.38271605	.29464286	.20555556	.11342593
	2	1.04000000	.52941176	.35897436	.27358491	.18787879	.10109290
	3	1.02666667	.51973684	.35064935	.26602564	.18125000	.09593023
	4	1.02000000	.51485149	.34640523	.26213592	.17777778	.09309309
	6	1.01333333	.50993377	.34210526	.25816993	.17419355	.09006211
	12	1.00666667	.50498339	.33774834	.25412541	.17049180	.08681672
9.00	1	1.09000000	.56459330	.38837920	.29955947	.20952381	.11594203
	2	1.04500000	.53300733	.36204147	.27634660	.19026217	.10287241
	3	1.03000000	.52216749	.35275081	.26794258	.18294574	.09728183
	4	1.02250000	.51668727	.34800326	.26360339	.17909270	.09417872
	6	1.01500000	.51116625	.34318555	.25916870	.17510040	.09083911
	12	1.00750000	.50560399	.33829611	.25463535	.17096115	.08723489
10.00	1	1.10000000	.57142857	.39393939	.30434783	.21333333	.11827957
	2	1.05000000	.53658537	.36507937	.27906977	.19259259	.10457516
	3	1.03333333	.52459016	.35483871	.26984127	.18461538	.09859155
	4	1.02500000	.51851852	.34959350	.26506024	.18039216	.09523810
	6	1.01666667	.51239669	.34426230	.26016260	.17600000	.09160305
	12	1.00833333	.50622407	.33884278	.25514403	.17142857	.08764940

CALCULATING PARTIAL PAYMENTS ON SHORT-TERM LOANS

TABLE 9-1

MERCHANTS RULE

NUMBER OF EQUAL PAYMENTS

R	F	1	2	3	4	6	12
11.00	1	1.11000000	.57819905	.39939940	.30901288	.21699346	.12045691
	2	1.05500000	.54014599	.36808847	.28175520	.19487179	.10620601
	3	1.03666667	.52700491	.35691318	.27172196	.18625954	.09986130
	4	1.02750000	.52034525	.35117599	.26650660	.18167641	.09627217
	6	1.01833333	.51362510	.34533552	.26115166	.17689243	.09235428
	12	1.00916667	.50684363	.33938893	.25565146	.17189409	.08806029
12.00	1	1.12000000	.58490566	.40476190	.31355932	.22051282	.12248996
	2	1.06000000	.54368932	.37106918	.28440367	.19710145	.10776942
	3	1.04000000	.52941176	.35897436	.27358491	.18787879	.10109290
	4	1.03000000	.52216749	.35275081	.26794258	.18294574	.09728183
	6	1.02000000	.51485149	.34640523	.26213592	.17777778	.09309309
	12	1.01000000	.50746269	.33993399	.25615764	.17235772	.08846761
13.00	1	1.13000000	.59154930	.41002950	.31799163	.22389937	.12439261
	2	1.06500000	.54721550	.37402191	.28701595	.19928315	.10926949
	3	1.04333333	.53181077	.36102236	.27543036	.18947368	.10228802
	4	1.03250000	.52398524	.35431800	.26936830	.18420039	.09826794
	6	1.02166667	.51607585	.34747145	.26311542	.17865613	.09381981
	12	1.01083333	.50808123	.34047815	.25666257	.17281947	.08887141
14.00	1	1.14000000	.59813084	.41520468	.32231405	.22716049	.12617702
	2	1.07000000	.55072464	.37694704	.28959276	.20141844	.11070999
	3	1.04666667	.53420195	.36305732	.27725857	.19104478	.10344828
	4	1.03500000	.52579853	.35587762	.27078385	.18544061	.09923131
	6	1.02333333	.51729819	.34853420	.26409018	.17952756	.09453471
	12	1.01166667	.50869925	.34102142	.25716626	.17327935	.08927173
15.00	1	1.15000000	.60465116	.42028986	.32653061	.23030303	.12785388
	2	1.07500000	.55421687	.37984496	.29213483	.20350877	.11209440
	3	1.05000000	.53658537	.36507937	.27906977	.19259259	.10457516
	4	1.03750000	.52760736	.35742972	.27218935	.18666667	.10017271
	6	1.02500000	.51851852	.34959350	.26506024	.18039216	.09523810
	12	1.01250000	.50931677	.34156379	.25766871	.17373737	.08966862
16.00	1	1.16000000	.61111111	.42528736	.33064516	.23333333	.12943262
	2	1.08000000	.55769231	.38271605	.29464286	.20555556	.11342593
	3	1.05333333	.53896104	.36708861	.28086420	.19411765	.10567010
	4	1.04000000	.52941176	.35897436	.27358491	.18787879	.10109290
	6	1.02666667	.51973684	.35064935	.26602564	.18125000	.09593023
	12	1.01333333	.50993377	.34210526	.25816993	.17419355	.09006211
17.00	1	1.17000000	.61751152	.43019943	.33466135	.23625731	.13092162
	2	1.08500000	.56115108	.38556068	.29711752	.20756014	.11470755
	3	1.05666667	.54132061	.36908517	.28264209	.19562044	.10673443
	4	1.04250000	.53121175	.36051159	.27497062	.18907721	.10199257
	6	1.02833333	.52095316	.35170178	.26698641	.18210117	.09661139
	12	1.01416667	.51055027	.34264585	.25866993	.17464789	.09045226
18.00	1	1.18000000	.62385321	.43502825	.33858268	.23908046	.13232831
	2	1.09000000	.56459330	.38837920	.29955947	.20952381	.11594203
	3	1.06000000	.54368932	.37106918	.28440367	.19710145	.10776942
	4	1.04500000	.53300733	.36204147	.27634660	.19026217	.10287241
	6	1.03000000	.52216749	.35275081	.26794258	.18294574	.09728183
	12	1.01500000	.51116625	.34318555	.25916870	.17510040	.09083911

TABLE 9-1

MERCHANTS RULE

NUMBER OF EQUAL PAYMENTS

R	F	1	2	3	4	6	12
19.00	1	1.19000000	.63013699	.43977591	.34241245	.24180791	.13365933
	2	1.09500000	.56801909	.39117199	.30196937	.21144781	.11713191
	3	1.06333333	.54604200	.37304075	.28614916	.19856115	.10877627
	4	1.04750000	.53479853	.36356404	.27771295	.19143389	.10373307
	6	1.03166667	.52337982	.35379645	.26889419	.18378378	.09794180
	12	1.01583333	.51178173	.34372436	.25966626	.17555110	.09122269
20.00	1	1.20000000	.63636364	.44444444	.34615385	.24444444	.13492063
	2	1.10000000	.57142857	.39393939	.30434783	.21333333	.11827957
	3	1.06666667	.54838710	.37500000	.28787879	.20000000	.10975610
	4	1.05000000	.53658537	.36507937	.27906977	.19259259	.10457516
	6	1.03333333	.52459016	.35483871	.26984127	.18461538	.09859155
	12	1.01666667	.51239669	.34426230	.26016260	.17600000	.09160305
21.00	1	1.21000000	.64253394	.44903581	.34980989	.24699454	.13611756
	2	1.10500000	.57482185	.39668175	.30669546	.21518152	.11938722
	3	1.07000000	.55072464	.37694704	.28959276	.20141844	.11070999
	4	1.05250000	.53836784	.36658749	.28041715	.19373849	.10539929
	6	1.03500000	.52579853	.35587762	.27078385	.18544061	.09923131
	12	1.01750000	.51301115	.34479934	.26065773	.17644711	.09198024
22.00	1	1.22000000	.64864865	.45355191	.35338346	.24946237	.13725490
	2	1.11000000	.57819905	.39939940	.30901288	.21699346	.12045691
	3	1.07333333	.55305466	.37888199	.29129129	.20281690	.11163895
	4	1.05500000	.54014599	.36808847	.28175520	.19487179	.10620601
	6	1.03666667	.52700491	.35691318	.27172196	.18625954	.09986130
	12	1.01833333	.51362510	.34533552	.26115166	.17689243	.09235428
23.00	1	1.23000000	.65470852	.45799458	.35687732	.25185185	.13833701
	2	1.11500000	.58156028	.40209268	.31130064	.21877023	.12149056
	3	1.07666667	.55537721	.38080495	.29297459	.20419580	.11254396
	4	1.05750000	.54191981	.36958235	.28308400	.19599271	.10699588
	6	1.03833333	.52820932	.35794543	.27265563	.18707224	.10048176
	12	1.01916667	.51423855	.34587081	.26164439	.17733598	.09272522
24.00	1	1.24000000	.66071429	.46236559	.36029412	.25416667	.13936782
	2	1.12000000	.58490566	.40476190	.31355932	.22051282	.12248996
	3	1.08000000	.55769231	.38271605	.29464286	.20555556	.11342593
	4	1.06000000	.54368932	.37106918	.28440367	.19710145	.10776942
	6	1.04000000	.52941176	.35897436	.27358491	.18787879	.10109290
	12	1.02000000	.51485149	.34640523	.26213592	.17777778	.09309309
25.00	1	1.25000000	.66666667	.46666667	.36363636	.25641026	.14035088
	2	1.12500000	.58823529	.40740741	.31578947	.22222222	.12345679
	3	1.08333333	.56000000	.38461538	.29629630	.20689655	.11428571
	4	1.06250000	.54545455	.37254902	.28571429	.19819820	.10852713
	6	1.04166667	.53061224	.36000000	.27450980	.18867925	.10169492
	12	1.02083333	.51546392	.34693878	.26262626	.17821782	.09345794
26.00	1	1.26000000	.67256637	.47089947	.36690647	.25858586	.14128944
	2	1.13000000	.59154930	.41002950	.31799163	.22389937	.12439261
	3	1.08666667	.56230032	.38650307	.29793510	.20821918	.11512415
	4	1.06500000	.54721550	.37402191	.28701595	.19928315	.10926949
	6	1.04333333	.53181077	.36102236	.27543036	.18947368	.10228802
	12	1.02166667	.51607585	.34747145	.26311542	.17865613	.09381981

TABLE 9-1

MERCHANTS RULE

NUMBER OF EQUAL PAYMENTS

R	F	1	2	3	4	6	12
27.00	1	1.27000000	.67841410	.47506562	.37010676	.26069652	.14218645
	2	1.13500000	.59484778	.41262849	.32016632	.22554517	.12529890
	3	1.09000000	.56459330	.38837920	.29955947	.20952381	.11594203
	4	1.06750000	.54897219	.37548790	.28830874	.20035651	.10999696
	6	1.04500000	.53300733	.36204147	.27634660	.19026217	.10287241
	12	1.02250000	.51668727	.34800326	.26360339	.17909270	.09417872
28.00	1	1.28000000	.68421053	.47916667	.37323944	.26274510	.14304462
	2	1.14000000	.59813084	.41520468	.32231405	.22716049	.12617702
	3	1.09333333	.56687898	.39024390	.30116959	.21081081	.11674009
	4	1.07000000	.55072464	.37694704	.28959276	.20141844	.11070999
	6	1.04666667	.53420195	.36305732	.27725857	.19104478	.10344828
	12	1.02333333	.51729819	.34853420	.26409018	.17952756	.09453471
29.00	1	1.29000000	.68995633	.48320413	.37630662	.26473430	.14386641
	2	1.14500000	.60139860	.41775837	.32443532	.22874618	.12702828
	3	1.09666667	.56915739	.39209726	.30276565	.21208054	.11751904
	4	1.07250000	.55247286	.37839938	.29086809	.20246914	.11140900
	6	1.04833333	.53539463	.36406995	.27816628	.19182156	.10401580
	12	1.02416667	.51790860	.34906428	.26457579	.17996071	.09488783
30.00	1	1.30000000	.69565217	.48717949	.37931034	.26666667	.14465409
	2	1.15000000	.60465116	.42028986	.32653061	.23030303	.12785388
	3	1.10000000	.57142857	.39393939	.30434783	.21333333	.11827957
	4	1.07500000	.55421687	.37984496	.29213483	.20350877	.11209440
	6	1.05000000	.53658537	.36507937	.27906977	.19259259	.10457516
	12	1.02500000	.51851852	.34959350	.26506024	.18039216	.09523810
31.00	1	1.31000000	.70129870	.49109415	.38225256	.26854460	.14540974
	2	1.15500000	.60788863	.42279942	.32860041	.23183183	.12865497
	3	1.10333333	.57369255	.39577039	.30591631	.21456954	.11902232
	4	1.07750000	.55595668	.38128384	.29339306	.20453752	.11276658
	6	1.05166667	.53777417	.36608558	.27996906	.19335793	.10512654
	12	1.02583333	.51912793	.35012185	.26554352	.18082192	.09558555
32.00	1	1.32000000	.70689655	.49494949	.38513514	.27037037	.14613527
	2	1.16000000	.61111111	.42528736	.33064516	.23333333	.12943262
	3	1.10666667	.57594937	.39759036	.30747126	.21578947	.11974790
	4	1.08000000	.55769231	.38271605	.29464286	.20555556	.11342593
	6	1.05333333	.53896104	.36708861	.28086420	.19411765	.10567010
	12	1.02666667	.51973684	.35064935	.26602564	.18125000	.09593023
33.00	1	1.33000000	.71244635	.49874687	.38795987	.27214612	.14683245
	2	1.16500000	.61431871	.42775393	.33266533	.23480826	.13018785
	3	1.11000000	.57819905	.39939940	.30901288	.21699346	.12045691
	4	1.08250000	.55942377	.38414165	.29588432	.20656304	.11407280
	6	1.05500000	.54014599	.36808847	.28175520	.19487179	.10620601
	12	1.02750000	.52034525	.35117599	.26650660	.18167641	.09627217

9.2   UNITED STATES RULE

The principle of the United States Rule is that interest is charged on an unpaid balance at a simple interest rate during a payment interval. The mechanics for calculations, using the United States Rule, can be formalized into a "formula" by determining the future amount, of an unpaid balance, on the date a partial payment is made and subtracting the partial payment from that future amount.

Unequal Payments and/or Payment Intervals

If the magnitude of the partial payments is not equal and/or the payment intervals are not equal, the amount of the final payment in a series of payments can be determined by a successive series of

$$B_j = B_{j-1}(1 + Rt_j) - P_j \qquad j = 1, 2, \ldots N \tag{9.2-1}$$

The final payment due will be

$$P_N = B_{N-1}(1 + Rt_N) \tag{9.2-2}$$

Example 1.   A \$10,000 debt is to be repaid in 6 months. If it is planned that a payment of \$4,000 will be made at the end of 3 months, and a payment of \$3,000 will be made at the end of 5 months, the amount of the final payment is desired. The interest rate is 18%. For the calculations,

$$B_0 = 10000 \quad \text{and} \quad R = 18\% = 0.18$$

$$P_1 = 4000 \quad \text{and} \quad t_1 = 3/12 = 1/4 \text{ year}$$

$$P_2 = 3000 \quad \text{and} \quad t_2 = (5 - 3)/12 = 2/12 = 1/6 \text{ year}$$

$$P_3 = ? \quad \text{and} \quad t_3 = (6 - 5)/12 = 1/12 \text{ year}$$

Then, for N = 3

$$B_1 = B_0(1 + Rt_1) - P_1$$
$$= (10000)[1 + (0.18)(1/4)] - 4000$$
$$= 6450$$
$$B_2 = B_1(1 + Rt_2) - P_2$$
$$= (6450)[1 + (0.18)(1/6)] - 3000$$
$$= 3643.50$$
$$P_3 = (3643.50)[1 + (0.18)(1/12)]$$
$$= 3698.15$$

Therefore, the final payment will be \$3,698.15. The total interest will be the sum of the payments less the original balance or

$$I = \sum P_j - B_0 \tag{9.2-3}$$

and equals 4000 + 3000 + 3698.15 - 10000 = \$698.15

For the same conditions, the United States Rule results in a total interest which is slightly greater than the total interest using the Merchants' Rule. Comparing the interests of Example 1 of Section 9.1 and this example shows that $23.15 more interest is required if repayment is by the United States Rule.

If it is not important to know what the interim balances will be, the final payment due can be determined directly from

$$P_N = B_0 \prod_{j=1}^{N} (1 + Rt_j) - P_1 \prod_{j=2}^{N} (1 + Rt_j) - P_2 \prod_{j=3}^{N} (1 + Rt_j) - \cdots - P_{N-1}(1 + Rt_N) \quad (9.2\text{-}4)$$

Example 2. Use Eq. (9.2-4) to solve for the final payment amount in Example 1. For 3 payments, N = 3 and Eq. (9.2-4) becomes

$$P_3 = B_0(1 + Rt_1)(1 + Rt_2)(1 + Rt_3) - P_1(1 + Rt_2)(1 + Rt_3) - P_2(1 + Rt_3)$$

From Example 1:

$$(1 + Rt_3) = [1 + (0.18)(1/12)] = 1.015$$

$$(1 + Rt_2)(1 + Rt_3) = [1 + (0.18)(1/6)](1.015) = (1.03)(1.015) = 1.04545$$

$$(1 + Rt_1)(1 + Rt_2)(1 + Rt_3) = [1 + (0.18)(1/4)](1.04545) = (1.045)(1.04545)$$

$$= 1.0924953$$

Then

$$P_3 = (10000)(1.0924953) - (4000)(1.04545) - 3000(1.015)$$

$$= 10924.95 - 4181.80 - 3045$$

$$= 3698.15$$

Equal Payments with Equal Payment Intervals

If a debt is to be repaid over a relatively short term with equal payment amounts at equal payment intervals, the equal payment amount can be determined by

$$P = B_0 \left[\frac{R/F}{1 - (1 + R/F)^{-N}} \right] \quad (9.2\text{-}5)$$

where F is the frequency of equal payment intervals per year.

Example 3. If it is planned to repay the $10,000 loan of Example 1 with 3 bimonthly equal payments, the amount of each payment can be determined by Eq. (9.2-5). For bimonthly payments, the frequency will be 6 payments per year. Then, F = 6. For an interest rate of 18%,

$$R/F = (0.18)/6 = 0.03$$

and N = 3. From Eq. (9.2-5),

$$P = (10000) \left[\frac{0.03}{1 - (1 + 0.03)^{-3}} \right]$$

$$= (10000)(0.3535304) = \$3,535.30$$

As a check, the following calculations utilize Eqs. (9.2-1) and (9.2-2)

$$B_0 = 10000 \quad \text{and} \quad R = 18\% = 0.18$$

$$P_1 = P_2 = 3535.30 \quad \text{and} \quad t_1 = t_2 = t_3 = 2/12 = 1/6.$$

Then

$$(1 + Rt_1) = (1 + Rt_2) = (1 + Rt_3) = [1 + (0.18)(1/6)] = 1.03$$

$$B_1 = B_0(1 + Rt_1) - P_1 = (10000)(1.03) - 3535.30 = 6764.70$$

$$B_2 = B_1(1 + Rt_2) - P_2 = (6764.70)(1.03) - 3535.30 = 3432.34$$

$$P_3 = B_2(1 + Rt_3) = (3432.34)(1.03) = 3535.31$$

Note: The 1-cent discrepancy in P_3 is due to rounding of decimals.

Equation (9.2-5) is simply the level payment for a simple ordinary annuity where $i = R/F$ and the expression within the bracket is $(p/V, i, n)$ in Table A-2.

9.3   ADD-ON INTEREST

Add-on interest is simple interest for the term of a loan and is added to the principal. Then

$$I = B_0 RT \tag{9.3-1}$$

The amount to be repaid is the future amount of B_0 at simple interest or

$$S = B_0 + I \tag{9.3-2}$$

Then, if the frequency of payments per year is F, the number of payments can be determined by

$$N = FT \tag{9.3-3}$$

Periodic Payment

The periodic payment for add-on interest can be determined by

$$P = \frac{S}{N} \tag{9.3-4}$$

Example 1.   A loan of $7,000, including add-on interest at 10%, is to be repaid in 4 years by monthly payments. From Eq. (9.3-1), the interest is

$$I = (7000)(0.10)(4) = \$2,800$$

The total amount of the loan is, from Eq. (9.3-2)

$$S = 7000 + 2800 = \$9,800$$

The number of monthly payments is, from Eq. (9.3-3)

$$N = (12)(4) = 48$$

Then, from Eq. (9.3-4), the amount of the monthly payment is

$$P = \frac{9800}{48} = 204.17 = \$204.17 \ .$$

True Annual Interest Rate

Since add-on interest is a calculation which assumes that the full amount of the loan is outstanding for the full term of the loan, the interest rate which is used in the calculations is not a true rate. When the first payment is made, the amortization of that payment is partially principal and partially interest, therefore, after the first payment, the amount that is unpaid is less than before the first payment. The true interest rate may be determined by using Table A-2 and the "Present Value of an Annuity Factor," $(V/p, i, n)$.

$$(V/p,i,n) = \frac{B_0}{P} \qquad (9.3\text{-}5)$$

where P will have been determined by Eq. (9.3-4).

Example 2. Determine the true interest rate for the loan of Example 1. From Example 1, $B_0 = 7000$ and $P = 204.17$. From Eq. (9.3-5)

$$(V/p,i,n) = \frac{7000}{204.17} = 34.285155$$

Search Table A-2 opposite $N = 48$ until $(V/p,i,n)$ is found. In the 1-5/12% table, $(V/p,i,n) = 34.65598800$ and in the 1-1/2% table, $(V/p,i,n) = 34.04255365$. The true interest rate is between 1-5/12% and 1-1/2% per month (for Example 1). Then, the nominal annual interest rate is between 17% and 18% respectively ($12 \times 1\text{-}5/12\%$ and $12 \times 1\text{-}1/2\%$).

	R	$(V/p, i, n)$	
	17%	34.655988	
			0.370833
1%	R_t	34.285155	
			0.613434
	18%	34.042554	

$$\frac{y}{1\%} = \frac{0.370833}{0.613434}$$

$$y = \left[\frac{0.370833}{0.613434}\right](1\%) = 0.6045198\%$$

Then, the nominal true annual interest rate is

$$R_t = 17\% + y = 17.605\%$$

Thus, the true annual interest rate (APR) is 17.605% within the accuracy of interpolation. Of course, since

$$(V/p,i,n) = \frac{1 - (1 + i)^{-n}}{i},$$

the exact value of i can be determined by substituting values of i until the expression results in the value of B_0/P.

The effective annual interest rate for $R_t\%$ compounded f times a year is

$$R_e = [(1 + i)^f - 1](\times 100 \text{ for } \%)$$

where

$$i = R_t/f$$

Then

$$i = 0.17605/12 = 0.0146708$$

and

$$R_e = [(1.0146708)^{12} - 1] \times 100 = 19.097\%$$

Approximate True Annual Interest Rate

With add-on interest, a "rule-of-thumb" approximation of the true annual interest rate can be determined by

$$R_t = \frac{2NR}{N + 1} \tag{9.3-6}$$

Example 3. The approximate true annual interest rate for a 48-payment loan with 10% add-on interest is

$$R_t = \frac{2(48)(10)}{48 + 1} = 19.592\%$$

which is reasonably close to the true effective annual interest rate of Example 2.

The factor, $2N/(N + 1)$, exceeds 1.9 for values of N greater than 19. Then, as a crude guess, whenever the repayment period exceeds 19 periods,

$$R_t \approx 2R \tag{9.3-7}$$

Rule of 78 Interest Rebate Factor

Whenever Rule of 78 rebate is used for the early retirement of a debt, the fraction of the original loan that is to be rebated can be determined by

$$F_R = \frac{L(L + 1)}{N(N + 1)} \tag{9.3-8}$$

where L is the number of payments remaining and F_R is the rebate factor.

Example 4. Suppose it is desired to liquidate the 48-payment loan of Example 1 on the date of the 37th payment. The amount of the liquidating payment is needed. From Example 1, the total interest was $2,800, the total to be repaid was $9,800, and the monthly payment was $204.17. After the 36th payment, the remaining balance is

$$9800 - (36)(204.17) = 2449.88$$

The amount of the interest to be rebated can be determined by Eq. (9.3-8). When the 37th payment is due, there are 12 payments remaining (48 - 37 + 1). Then,

$$F_R = \frac{(12)(13)}{(48)(49)} = 0.0663265$$

and the amount of interest to be rebated is

$$(0.0663265)(2800) = \$185.71$$

Then, the liquidating amount is $2449.88 - 185.71 = \$2,264.17$

Rule of 78 Interest Payment Factor

The interest payment factor for Rule of 78 interest rebate is

$$F_P = 1 - F_R \qquad (9.3\text{-}9)$$

9.4   CONSOLIDATION OF DEBTS

When several debts are to be consolidated into a single debt, the present value of all the debts on the consolidation date (comparison or focal date) may be determined and a periodic payment to liquidate the consolidation can be determined. Then,

$$P = \frac{\sum V_j}{\sum v_j} \qquad (9.4\text{-}1)$$

where, on the comparison date,

V_j—is the present value of the maturity value of a debt.
v_j—is the present value of a \$1 per period payment.

Consolidation at Simple Interest

When loans are to be consolidated at simple interest

$$V_j = \frac{S_j}{1 + RT_j} \qquad (9.4\text{-}2)$$

and

$$v_j = \frac{1}{1 + Rt_j} \qquad (9.4\text{-}3)$$

Example 1.   A loan with a maturity of \$1,000 is due in two months and a loan with a maturity of \$4,000 is due in eight months. An agreement to consolidate the two loans into two equal payments at 5-month intervals is entered at an 18% simple interest rate. The level of the payments is desired. A time diagram of the transactions is shown in Figure 9.2.

For the present values of the maturity values of the debts,

$$T_1 = 2 \text{ months} = 2/12 = 1/6 \text{ year}$$
$$T_2 = 8 \text{ months} = 8/12 = 2/3 \text{ year}$$

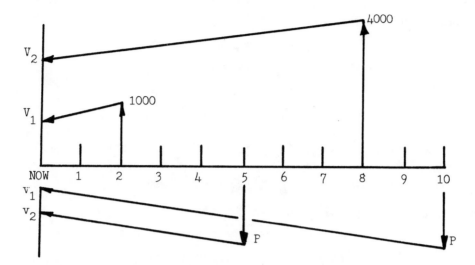

Figure 9-2. A Consolidation of Debts.

For the present values of the payments,

$$T_1 = 5 \text{ months} = 5/12 \text{ year}$$

$$T_2 = 10 \text{ months} = 10/12 = 5/6 \text{ year}$$

Then, for the maturity values of the loans, the present values are:

$$V_1 = \frac{1000}{1 + RT_1} = \frac{1000}{1 + (0.18)(1/6)} = \frac{1000}{1.03} = 970.87$$

$$V_2 = \frac{4000}{1 + RT_2} = \frac{4000}{1 + (0.18)(2/3)} = \frac{4000}{1.12} = 3571.43$$

$$\sum V_j = V_1 + V_2 = 970.87 + 3571.43 = 4542.30$$

For the present values of $1

$$v_1 = \frac{1}{1 + Rt_1} = \frac{1}{1 + (0.18)(5/12)} = \frac{1}{1.075} = 0.9302326$$

$$v_2 = \frac{1}{1 + Rt_2} = \frac{1}{1 + (0.18)(5/6)} = \frac{1}{1.15} = 0.8695652$$

$$\sum v_j = v_1 + v_2 = 0.9302326 + 0.8695652 = 1.7997978$$

and from Eq. (9.4-1)

$$P = \frac{4542.30}{1.7997978} = 2523.78$$

Then, two payments of $2,523.78 at 5-month intervals would replace $1,000 due in 2 months and $4,000 due in 8 months.

Consolidation at Compound Interest

When loans are to be consolidated at compound interest

$$V_j = S_j(1 + i)^{-n_j}$$ (9.4-4)

and

$$v_j = (1 + i)^{-n_j}$$ (9.4-5)

Example 2.   Solve Example 1 if money is worth 18% compounded monthly. For the calculations,

$$i = R/f = 18\%/12 = 1\text{-}1/2\%$$

Since n is in months, $n_1 = 2$ and $n_2 = 8$. Then,

$$V_1 = (1000)(1 + 1\text{-}1/2\%)^{-2} = (1000)(0.97066175) = 970.66$$

$$V_2 = (4000)(1 + 1\text{-}1/2\%)^{-8} = (4000)(0.88771112) = 3550.84$$

$$\sum V_j = V_1 + V_2 = 4521.50$$

For the present value of $1, $n_1 = 5$ and $n_2 = 10$

$$v_1 = (1 + 1\text{-}1/2\%)^{-5} = 0.9282603$$

$$v_2 = (1 + 1\text{-}1/2\%)^{-10} = 0.8616672$$

$$\sum v_j = v_1 + v_2 = 1.7899275$$

From Eq. (9.4-1)

$$P = \frac{4521.50}{1.7899275} = \$2,526.08$$

Example 3.   You wish to consolidate the following debts:

1) $1,000 due 2 months from today.
2) $4,000 due 8 months from today.
3) $564.88 per month for 2 years on an amortization that was at 12% compounded monthly (the present value of this is $12,000).

If money is worth 18% compounded monthly, what monthly payment for 3 years will liquidate all the loans? For the calculation

$$i = R/f = 18\%/12 = 1\text{-}1/2\%$$

For the present loans, $n_1 = 2$, $n_2 = 8$, and $n_3 = 0$. Then, from Eq. (9.4-4) and Table A-2.

$$V_1 = (1000)(1 + 1\text{-}1/2\%)^{-2} = (1000)(0.97066175) = 970.66$$

$$V_2 = (4000)(1 + 1\text{-}1/2\%)^{-8} = (4000)(0.88771112) = 3550.84$$

$$V_3 = 12000$$

$$\sum V_j = V_1 + V_2 + V_3 = 970.66 + 3550.84 + 12000 = 16521.50$$

For level periodic payments equally spaced,

$$\sum v_j = (V/p, i, n)$$ (9.4-6)

Then, for a 3-year liquidation, $n = ft = (12)(3) = 36$ and from Table A-2

$$\sum v_j = 27.66068431$$

From Eq. (9.4-1)

$$P = \frac{16521.50}{27.66068431} = 597.29$$

Then, \$597.29 per month for 3 years will liquidate \$1,000 due in 2 months, \$4,000 due in 8 months, and \$564.88 per month for 2 years.

CHAPTER 10

Formulas for Linear
Break-Even Analysis

This chapter provides formulas for determining when break-even will occur when income and cost are linear (straight line) functions of a number of units. Within the text are one or more examples for the use of each formula. These examples include:

1. Determining the number of units to break-even in a production process when the time value of money is not considered. Page 209
2. Determining a linear profit based on the break-even point. Page 209
3. Determining the time to break-even when the time value of money is not considered. Page 210
4. The manufacture or purchase decision. Page 210
5. Determining the number of units to break-even when the time value of money is considered. Page 210
6. Determining the time to break-even when the time value of money is considered. Page 211
7. The lease or purchase decision. Page 212

The nomenclature for the formulas is as follows:

c—Variable cost per unit.
c_b—Variable purchase cost per unit.
c_l—Variable lease cost per unit.
c_m—Variable manufacturing cost per unit.
C—Fixed Cost.
C_b—Total cost to purchase.
C_m—Total cost to manufacture.
C_M—Periodic maintenance cost.
C_T—General total cost.
I_T—General total income.
i—Periodic interest rate.
n—Number of interest conversion periods.
N—Number of units.
N_0—Break-even number of units.
p—Periodic profit (savings, cash flow, etc.)
p_0—Sustainable production level.

P—Profit.

T_0—Time to break-even.

r—Income (revenue) per unit.

S—Residual value of an asset.

10.1 BREAK-EVEN WITHOUT TIME VALUE OF MONEY

Number of Units to Break-Even

If the total cost of using an income-generating asset is a linear function of a number of units and is in the form

$$C_T = C + cN \qquad (10.1\text{-}1)$$

and the income from that asset is a linear function of a number of units and is in the form

$$I_T = rN \qquad (10.1\text{-}2)$$

the number of units that is necessary in order to recover the fixed and variable costs can be determined by

$$N_0 = \frac{C}{r - c} \qquad (10.1\text{-}3)$$

Example 1. A new product is in the planning stages. In full production, the fixed cost associated with the production is estimated to be $60,000 annually. The variable cost is estimated to be $6 per unit, and the sales department estimates that the product can be sold for $16 per unit. The break-even production level is desired. From Eq. (10.1-3), the annual production must be

$$N_0 = \frac{60000}{16 - 6} = 6{,}000 \text{ units per year}$$

Note: If production at 6,000 units per year cannot be sustained, an annual loss will be realized. If production is at 6,000 units per year, profit will be 0 (by definition of break-even). Profit will be realized only on production levels in excess of 6,000 units per year.

Linear Profit Function

Given linear cost and income functions, a linear profit function would be

$$P = (r - c)N - C \qquad (10.1\text{-}4)$$

Example 2. The profit, in Example 1, is desired if production is at 5000, 6000, 8000 units annually. For N = 5000

$$P = (16 - 6)(5000) - 60000 = -\$10{,}000 \text{ (a \$10,000 loss) per year}$$

For N = 6000

$$P = (16 - 6)(6000) - 60000 = 0 \text{ (definition of break-even)}$$

For N = 8000

$$P = (16 - 6)(8000) - 60000 = \$20{,}000 \text{ per year}$$

Time to Break-Even

Given a number of units capability for a given time period, the time to break-even can be determined by

$$T_0 = \frac{N_0}{p_0} \tag{10.1-5}$$

Example 3. Given the conditions in Example 1, if a production level of 9000 units per year is available, the time to break-even can be determined by Eq. (10.1-5) as

$$T_0 = \frac{6000}{9000} = \frac{2}{3} \text{ year} = 8 \text{ months.}$$

Manufacture or Purchase Decision

If an asset (or component) can be manufactured or purchased and if costs are linear functions of the number of units, such that

$$C_m = C + c_m N \tag{10.1-6}$$

and

$$C_b = c_b N \tag{10.1-7}$$

the number of units for equivalence (break-even) between manufacturing or purchasing is

$$N_0 = \frac{C}{c_b - c_m} \tag{10.1-8}$$

The product should be manufactured if N is greater than N_0.

Example 4. For a fixed cost of $60,000 annually and a variable cost of $6 per unit, if the product can be purchased for $12 per unit, a manufacture or purchase decision is to be made. From Eq. (10.1-8), the number of units for equivalence (break-even) is

$$N_0 = \frac{60000}{12 - 6} = 10,000 \text{ units per year.}$$

Then, if sales are estimated to be greater than 10,000 units per year, the product should be manufactured provided that production at and beyond 10,000 units annually can be sustained.

10.2   BREAK-EVEN WITH TIME VALUE OF MONEY

Number of Units to Break-Even

If the fixed cost of an income-generating asset is incurred at one point in time and is considered to have a time value; if the total cost is a linear function of the number of units in the form

$$C_T = C(1 + i)^n + cN \tag{10.2-1}$$

and if the income is a linear function of the number of units, the number of units that is necessary to recover the fixed and variable costs is

$$N_0 = \frac{C(1 + i)^n}{r - c} \tag{10.2-2}$$

Example 1. A new product is in the planning stages. In full production, the present value at the beginning of each year of the fixed cost associated with the production is estimated to be $60,000. The variable cost per unit is estimated to be $6 per unit, and it is estimated that the product can be sold for $16 per unit. It is argued that the $60,000 that is to be expended annually could be better invested at money-market rates. You must justify the expenditure for the new product. It is assumed that the money-market rate will be in the 15% range for the year. Then $i = 15\%$ and $n = 1$. From Eq. (10.2-2),

$$N_0 = \frac{(60000)(1.15)}{16 - 6} = 6,900 \text{ units per year}$$

Thus, if production and sales exceed 6,900 units annually (rather than 6,000 units annually (as in Example 1 of Section 10.1) the $60,000 annually is better invested in the product than in the money-market.

Time to Break-Even

If a "one-time" expenditure can effect a periodic savings, the number of units to break-even (the recovery of the expenditure) can be determined by

$$T_0 = -\frac{\log\left[1 - \dfrac{Ci}{p}\right]}{\log(1 + i)} \tag{10.2-3}$$

Example 2. A new computer system is proposed. It is estimated that it will save $20,000 per year from current operations. The total cost of the system at the start-up date is estimated to be $25,000. The break-even point is desired for an interest rate of 20% annually.

$$T_0 = -\frac{\log\left[1 - \dfrac{(25000)(0.20)}{20000}\right]}{\log 1.20}$$

$$= -\frac{-0.1249387}{0.0791812} = 1.58$$

Since the $20,000 per year is simply the capital recovery of $25,000 at 20% on the unrecovered balance, the units of T_0 are units which are compatible with i (number of interest periods—years in this example). Then,

$$T_0 = 1.58 \text{ years} \approx 19 \text{ months}$$

Alternatively, the break-even time may be approximated by using Table A-2 with

$$(V/p,i,n) = \frac{C}{p} \tag{10.2-4}$$

Example 3. Use Table A-2 to approximate N_0 of Example 2. From Eq. (10.2-4)

$$(V/p,i,n) = \frac{25000}{20000} = 1.25$$

In the 20% table of Table A-2, in the $(V/p,i,n)$ column, the value 1.25 occurs between $n = 1$ and 2 and the table must be interpolated.

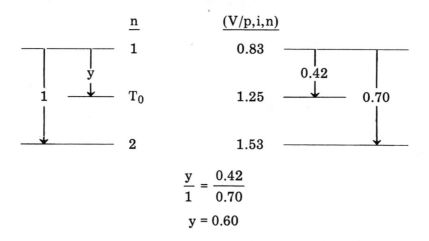

$$\frac{y}{1} = \frac{0.42}{0.70}$$

$$y = 0.60$$

Then $T_0 \approx 1 + y$

≈ 1.60 years ≈ 19.2 months

Lease or Purchase Decision

Given a periodic leasing cost

$$C_l = c_l N \qquad\qquad (10.2\text{-}5)$$

and a periodic cost for purchase

$$C_b = (C - S)(p/V,i,n) + Si + C_M + c_b N \qquad\qquad (10.2\text{-}6)$$

which is simply capital recovery of the fixed cost (see Chapter 7) where S is the residual value and C_M is the periodic maintenance cost (compatible with i) of the asset, the lease or purchase equivalence (break-even) will occur when

$$N_0 = \frac{(C - S)(p/V,i,n) + Si + C_M}{c_l - c_b} \qquad\qquad (10.2\text{-}7)$$

Example 3. A computer system can be leased for $100 per day. Alternatively, the system can be purchased for $20,000. It has a useful life of 5 years with an expected residual value of $4,000. Annual maintenance costs are expected to be $1,500. Whether the system is leased or purchased, operating costs are expected to be $50 per day. The number of operating days to break-even is needed in order to make a lease-purchase decision. The interest rate is 20%. For Eq. (10.2-7)

$$c_l = \$100 + \$50 = \$150 \text{ per day}$$

For Eq. (10.2-7)

$$c_b = \$50 \text{ per day}$$

also, at 20% for 5 years, $(p/V,i,n) = 0.3343797$. Then from Eq. (10.2-7)

$$N_0 = \frac{(20000 - 4000)(0.3343797) + (4000)(0.2) + 1500}{150 - 50}$$

$$= \frac{(16000)(0.3343797) + 800 + 1500}{100}$$

$$= 76.5 = 77 \text{ days per year}$$

If the system will be used more than 77 days (616 hours based on an 8-hour day), the purchase of the system is warranted.

CHAPTER 11

Formulas for Calculating Inventory Models and Minimum Total Cost

This chapter provides formulas for some elementary inventory models for economic purchasing and manufacturing and the associated minimum total cost equations. Within the text are one or more examples for the use of each formula. These examples include:

1. Determining the economic purchase quantity. Page 214 (below)
2. Determining the minimum total purchase cost. Page 215
3. Determining the economic production quantity. Page 216
4. Determining the minimum total production cost. Page 216
5. Determining the equivalence (break-even point) between purchasing and manufacturing. Page 217

The nomenclature for the formulas is as follows:

c_h—Holding cost for 1 unit for 1 year.
c_i—Item cost for purchase or manufacture of 1 unit.
c_{ib}—Item cost for purchase of 1 unit.
c_{im}—Item cost for manufacture of 1 unit.
c_p—Purchase-order cost for each purchase.
c_s—Setup cost per production run.
C_b—Minimum total purchase cost.
C_m—Minimum total manufacturing cost.
D—Annual demand
Q_b—Economic order quantity.
Q_m—Economic production quantity.
R_m—Annual production rate.
t—Time between purchase orders and between production runs.

11.1 ECONOMIC PURCHASE QUANTITY AND MINIMUM PURCHASE COST

Economic Purchase Quantity

Given that an inventory replacement process can be graphed reasonably close to that depicted in Figure 11-1.

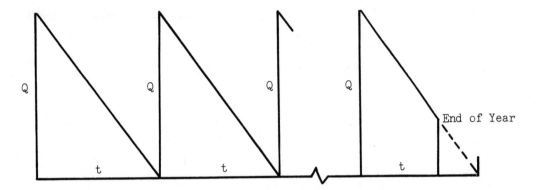

Figure 11-1.   Linear Depletion of Inventory

The economic purchase quantity, based on an assumption that the average inventory level during a year is $Q/2$, can be determined by

$$Q_b = \sqrt{\frac{2c_p D}{c_h}} \qquad (11.1\text{-}1)$$

Example 1.   The annual demand for an item is estimated to be 5,000 units. The cost for issuing a purchase order is estimated to be $10, and the cost for holding 1 unit in inventory for 1 year is estimated to be $1.50. If it is reasonable to expect that each purchased quantity will be depleted over equal periods of time during the year, the economic purchase quantity can be determined by Eq. (11.1-1) as

$$Q_b = \sqrt{\frac{2(10)(5000)}{1.5}} = 258 \text{ units per purchase order}$$

Minimum Total Purchase Cost

Total annual purchase cost is defined as the sum of item cost, purchase cost, and holding cost. Then, the minimum total annual purchase cost, based on the economic order quantity which is modeled by Eq. (11.1-1), would be

$$C_b = c_i D + \frac{c_p D}{Q_b} + \frac{c_h Q_b}{2} \qquad (11.1\text{-}2)$$

Example 2.   If the unit cost for the item of Example 1 is $8, the minimum total purchase cost, annually, for that item would be

$$C_b = (8)(5000) + \frac{(10)(5000)}{258} + \frac{(1.50)(258)}{2}$$

$$= 40000 + 193.80 + 193.50$$

$$= \$40,387 \text{ annually}$$

11.2   ECONOMIC PRODUCTION QUANTITY AND MINIMUM PRODUCTION COST

Economic Production Quantity

Given that an inventory replacement process can be graphed reasonably close to that depicted in Figure 11.2,

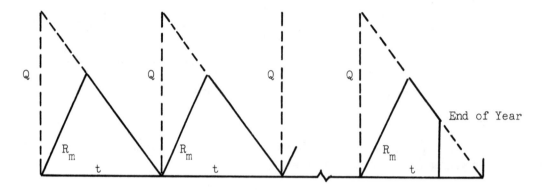

Figure 11.2.   Linear Replacement and Depletion of Inventory

the economic production quantity, based on an assumption that the average inventory level during a year is $Q/2$, can be determined by

$$Q_m = \sqrt{\frac{2c_s R_m D}{c_h (R_m - D)}} \quad (R_m > D) \tag{11.2-1}$$

Example 1.   The annual demand for an item is 5,000 units. The setup cost per production run is estimated at \$75 and the unit holding cost is \$1.50 per year. If the available production rate is 8,000 units per year, the economic production quantity can be determined by Eq. (11.2-1).

$$Q_m = \sqrt{\frac{2(75)(8000)(5000)}{(1.50)(8000 - 5000)}} = 1155 \text{ units per production run}$$

Minimum Total Production Cost

Total annual production cost is defined as the sum of item cost, setup cost, and holding cost. Then, the minimum total annual production cost, based on the economic production quantity which is modeled by Eq. (11.2-1), would be

$$C_m = c_i D + \frac{c_s D}{Q_m} + \frac{c_h (R_m - D) Q_m}{2R_m} \tag{11.2-2}$$

Example 2.   Including variable cost per unit and fixed cost per unit, the unit cost to manufacture the item in Example 1 of this section is \$7.60. Using the economic production quantity of Example 1, the minimum total annual production cost for the item would be

$$C_m = (7.60)(5000) + \frac{(75)(5000)}{1155} + \frac{(1.50)(8000 - 5000)(1155)}{(2)(8000)}$$

$$= 38000 + 324.67 + 324.84$$

$$= \$38,650 \text{ annually}$$

It should be noted that if the annual production capability is less than or equal to the annual demand, the model for the economic production quantity, Eq. (11.2-1) fails in that $R_m - D \leqslant 0$ and Q becomes infinite or imaginary. In this case, the maximum Q would be R_m and Eq. (11.2.2) would reduce to

$$C_m = c_i R_m + c_s \tag{11.2-3}$$

which is not necessarily a minimum.

11.3 MANUFACTURE OR PURCHASE DECISION

Unless other factors will influence the decision, the manufacture or purchase decision depends upon the relative total costs. With economic quantities (purchase and production), that minimum total annual cost which is the least (C_m or C_b) will determine the most economic course of action.

Example 1. Considering Examples 1 and 2 of Section 11.1 and Examples 1 and 2 of Section 11.2,

$$C_b = \$40,387 \text{ annually with quantities purchased in lots of 258 units}$$

$$C_m = \$38,650 \text{ annually with quantities manufactured in production runs of 1,155 units}$$

Then, since the minimum total annual cost to manufacture is less than that to purchase, the product should be manufactured.

Break-even Between Manufacture and Purchase

For an equivalence (break-even) between manufacture and purchase, $C_m = C_b$. Then

$$c_{im} = c_{ib} + \left[\frac{c_p}{Q_b} - \frac{c_s}{Q_m}\right] + \frac{c_h}{2D}\left[Q_b - \frac{(R_m - D)Q_m}{R_m}\right] \tag{11.3-1}$$

Example 2. The following tabulates Examples 1 and 2 each of Sections 11.1 and 11.2.

	Purchase	Manufacture
Item cost	$ 8.00	$ 7.60
Purchase order cost	10.00	—
Setup cost	—	75.00
Holding cost	1.50	1.50
Annual Demand	5,000	5,000
Annual Production Capacity	—	8,000
Economic quantities	258	1,155

It is desired to know the unit cost for manufacturing which is equivalent to purchasing. From Eq. (11.3-1),

$$c_{im} = 8.00 + \left[\frac{10}{258} - \frac{75}{1155}\right] + \frac{1.50}{(2)(5000)}\left[258 - \frac{(8000 - 5000)(1155)}{8000}\right]$$

$$= 8.00 + (0.03876 - 0.06494) + (0.00015)(258 - 433.13)$$

$$= 8.00 + (-0.02618) + (-0.02627)$$

$$= 8.00 - 0.02618 - 0.02627 = 7.94755$$

Thus, manufacturing costs can rise from $7.60 per unit to $7.94755 per unit before purchasing will become economically better than manufacturing.

For an equivalence between purchase and manufacture, $C_b = C_m$. Then

$$c_{ib} = c_{im} - \left[\frac{c_p}{Q_b} - \frac{c_s}{Q_m}\right] - \frac{c_h}{2D}\left[Q_b - \frac{(R_m - D)Q_m}{R_m}\right] \qquad (11.3-2)$$

Example 3. Using the tabulation in Example 2, the unit purchase cost that will give an equivalence (break-even) with manufacturing can be determined by Eq. (11.3-2).

$$c_{ib} = 7.60 - \left[\frac{10}{258} - \frac{75}{1155}\right] - \frac{1.50}{(2)(5000)}\left[258 - \frac{(8000 - 5000)(1155)}{8000}\right]$$

Using the results shown in Example 2, above,

$$c_{ib} = 7.60 - (-0.02618) - (-0.02627)$$

$$= 7.60 + 0.02618 + 0.02627$$

$$= 7.65245$$

Thus, the unit purchase cost must fall from $8.00 per unit to $7.65245 per unit before purchasing will become economically better than manufacturing.

CHAPTER **12**

How to Derive and Use Formulas for Fast Calculations of Corporation Federal Income Taxes

Whenever a decision which affects the taxable income of a corporation must be made, the effect of that decision on the federal income tax can be determined quickly if formulas are available that require only the insertion of the estimated taxable income in order to determine the tax. Given brackets of taxable incomes and tax rates for the respective brackets, a simple formula can be derived for the federal income tax on a specified taxable income. Then, with these simple formulas, the effective tax rate of an increment of additional taxable income, which spans one or more brackets, can be determined quickly. This chapter is a tutorial on the derivation of such formulas and provides some uses of those formulas.

Within the text are examples which include:

1. Determining the tax at the lower limit of each tax bracket. Page 220
2. Deriving the equations in order to determine the tax for taxable income within each bracket. Page 220
3. Determining the tax for taxable income within each bracket. Page 220
4. Deriving the equations in order to determine the effective tax rate for taxable income within a bracket. Page 222
5. Determining the effective tax rate for taxable income within each bracket. Page 222
6. Determining the effective tax rates for incremental taxable incomes across tax brackets. Page 223

If you perform the calculations in the examples, your results may differ from the indicated results, depending upon the number of decimal places you carry at each step of the solutions.

12.1 DERIVATION OF TAX FORMULAS

The nomenclature that is used for the derivation of tax formulas is as follows:

I—Taxable income.
j—Subscript which identifies a tax bracket.
b_j—A constant for the formula in the j-th tax bracket.
L_j—The lower limit of the j-th tax bracket.

R_j—Tax rate within the j-th tax bracket.
T_j'—Tax at the lower limit of j-th bracket.
T_j—Tax for income within the j-th bracket.

Tax at Lower Limit of Tax Bracket

With the tax rates for a given year, the tax at the *lower limits* of each bracket must be calculated. In general,

$$T_1' = R_1 L_1 = 0$$

$$T_j' = T_{j-1}' + R_{j-1}(L_j - L_{j-1}) \qquad j = 2, 3, \ldots, n \tag{12.1-1}$$

Example 1. The corporation income tax rate schedule for tax years beginning in 1983 is as follows.

Bracket	Over	Not Over	Rate
1	0	$ 25,000	15%
2	$ 25,000	50,000	18
3	50,000	75,000	30
4	75,000	100,000	40
5	100,000	—	46

The tax at the *lower limit* of each bracket can be determined as follows: $T_1' = 0$. From Eq. (12.1-1)

$$T_2' = T_1' + R_1(L_2 - L_1) = 0 + (0.15)(25000) = 3750$$

$$T_3' = T_2' + R_2(L_3 - L_2) = 3750 + (0.18)(50000 - 25000) = 8250$$

$$T_4' = T_3' + R_3(L_4 - L_3) = 8250 + (0.30)(75000 - 50000) = 15750$$

$$T_5' = T_4' + R_4(L_5 - L_4) = 15750 + (0.40)(100000 - 75000) = 25750$$

The Tax Equations

For taxable income within each tax bracket, the formula for calculating the tax is the equation of a straight line such as

$$T_j = R_j I_j + b_j \qquad j = 1, 2, \ldots, n \tag{12.1-2}$$

where R_j is the tax rate for the bracket. In order to determine b_j,

$$b_j = T_j' - R_j L_j \qquad j = 1, 2, \ldots, n \tag{12.1-3}$$

and these values are substituted into Eq. (12.1-2).

Example 2. Develop the tax equations for the tax rate schedule in Example 1. From Example 1,

$$T_1' = 0 \qquad R_1 = 0.15 \qquad L_1 = 0$$

$$T_2' = 3750 \qquad R_2 = 0.18 \qquad L_2 = 25000$$

$$T_3' = 8250 \qquad R_3 = 0.30 \qquad L_3 = 50000$$

$$T_4' = 15750 \qquad R_4 = 0.40 \qquad L_4 = 75000$$
$$T_5' = 25750 \qquad R_5 = 0.46 \qquad L_5 = 100000$$

From Eq. (12.1-3)

$$b_1 = T_1' - R_1 L_1 = 0 - (0.15)(0) = 0$$
$$b_2 = T_2' - R_2 L_2 = 3750 - (0.18)(25000) = -750$$
$$b_3 = T_3' - R_3 L_3 = 8250 - (0.30)(50000) = -6750$$
$$b_4 = T_4' - R_4 L_4' = 15750 - (0.40)(75000) = -14250$$
$$b_5 = T_5' - R_5 L_5 = 25750 - (0.46)(100000) = -20250$$

Then, from Eq. (12.1-2)

$$T_1 = 0.15 I_1 \qquad\qquad I \leq 25000$$
$$T_2 = 0.18 I_2 - 750 \qquad 25000 < I \leq 50000$$
$$T_3 = 0.30 I_3 - 6750 \qquad 50000 < I \leq 75000$$
$$T_4 = 0.40 I_4 - 14250 \qquad 75000 < I \leq 100000$$
$$T_5 = 0.46 I_5 - 20250 \qquad I > 100000$$

Example 3. For the tax rate schedule of Example 1, determine the corporation federal income tax for the following taxable incomes: a) \$18,000, b) \$36,000, c) \$68,000, d) \$90,000, and e) \$130,000. The tax equations are developed in Example 2

a)   For I = \$18,000 which is less than \$25,000,

$$T_1 = (0.15)I_1 = (0.15)(18000) = \$2,700.$$

b)   For I = \$36,000 which is between \$25,000 and \$50,000,

$$T_2 = (0.18)I_2 - 750 = (0.18)(36000) - 750 = \$5,730.$$

c)   For I = \$68,000 which is between \$50,000 and \$75,000,

$$T_3 = (0.30)I_3 - 6750 = (0.30)(68000) - 6750 = \$13,650.$$

d)   For I = \$90,000 which is between \$75,000 and \$100,000,

$$T_4 = (0.40)I_4 - 14250 = (0.40)(90000) - 14250 = \$21,750.$$

e)   For I = \$130,000 which is over \$100,000,

$$T_5 = (0.46)I_5 - 20250 = (0.46)(130000) - 20250 = \$39,550.$$

12.2   EFFECTIVE TAX RATES

The nomenclature, in addition to that of Section 12.1, is as follows:

R_{ej}—Effective tax rate for the j-th tax bracket.
R_{ei}—Effective tax rate for an increment of taxable income.

Effective Tax Rate in a Bracket

The effective tax rate, as defined here, is the ratio of a tax to the taxable income which generated the tax ($R_e = T/I$). From Eq. (12.1-2)

$$R_{ej} = R_j + \frac{b_j}{I_j} \quad (\times 100 \text{ for } \%) \tag{12.2-1}$$

Normally, the sign of b_j is negative, therefore, b_j/I_j will subtract from R_j.

Example 1.   For tax years beginning in 1983, the tax rate schedule is as follows.

Bracket	Over	Not Over	Rate
1	0	$ 25,000	15%
2	$ 25,000	50,000	18%
3	50,000	75,000	30%
4	75,000	100,000	40%
5	100,000	—	46%

The tax formulas for this schedule are derived in Example 2 of Section 12.1. From the results of that example, the effective tax rate formulas are as follows:

$$R_{e1} = R_1 + \frac{b_1}{I_1} = 0.15 = 15\% \qquad I \leqslant 25000$$

$$R_{e2} = R_2 + \frac{b_2}{I_2} = 0.18 - \frac{750}{I_2} \qquad 25000 < I \leqslant 50000$$

$$R_{e3} = R_3 + \frac{b_3}{I_3} = 0.30 - \frac{6750}{I_3} \qquad 50000 < I \leqslant 75000$$

$$R_{e4} = R_4 + \frac{b_4}{I_4} = 0.40 - \frac{14250}{I_4} \qquad 75000 < I \leqslant 100000$$

$$R_{e5} = R_5 + \frac{b_5}{I_5} = 0.46 - \frac{20250}{I_5} \qquad I > 100000$$

Example 2.   The tax rate formulas of Example 1 give the following effective tax rates for taxable income of a) \$18,000, b) \$36,000, c) \$68,000, d) \$90,000, and e) \$130,000.

a)   For $I = \$18,000$ which is less than \$25,000,

$$R_{e1} = 0.15 = 15\%$$

b)   For $I = \$36,000$ which is between \$25,000 and \$50,000,

$$R_{e2} = 0.18 - \frac{750}{36000} = 0.15917 \times 100 = 15.917\%$$

Thus, an increase of \$18,000 in taxable income (a 100% increase) increases the effective rate less than 1%.

c)   For $I = \$68,000$ which is between \$50,000 and \$75,000,

$$R_{e3} = 0.30 - \frac{6750}{68000} = 0.20074 \times 100 = 20.074\%$$

Thus, an increase from $36,000 to $68,000 ($32,000 or 89%) of taxable income increases the effective tax rate by 4.157%.

d)   For I = $90,000 which is between $75,000 and $100,000,

$$R_{e4} = 0.40 - \frac{14250}{90000} = 0.24167 \times 100 = 24.167\%$$

Thus, an increase from $68,000 to $90,000 ($22,000 or 32%) of taxable income increases the effective tax rate by 4.093%.

e)   For I = $130,000 which is over $100,000,

$$R_{e5} = 0.46 - \frac{20250}{130000} = 0.30423 \times 100 = 30.423\%$$

Thus, an increase from $90,000 to $130,000 ($40,000 or 44%) of taxable income increases the effective tax rate by 6.256%.

For an increase in taxable income from $18,000 (effective rate = 15%) to $130,000 (effective rate = 30.423%) the taxable income increased $112,000 or 622% while the effective tax rate increased 100% from 15% to 30%.

Effective Tax Rate Across Brackets

The effective tax rate across brackets, as defined here, is the rate at which an additional increment of taxable income will be taxed. It is defined as the change in tax divided by the change in taxable income, or

$$R_{ei} = \frac{T_h - T_l}{I_h - I_l} \qquad (\times \text{ 100 for \%}) \qquad (12.2\text{-}2)$$

where the subscripts h and l are for high and low, respectively, and the values of T_h and T_l can be determined by Eq. (12.1-2). Alternatively,

$$R_{ei} = \frac{R_{eh} I_h - R_{el} I_l}{I_h - I_l} \qquad (\times \text{ 100 for \%}) \qquad (12.2\text{-}3)$$

where R_{eh} and R_{el} can be determined by Eq. (12.2-1).

Example 3.   Determine the effective tax rates for the following increments of taxable income.   a) $18,000 to $36,000, b) $36,000 to $68,000, c) $68,000 to $90,000, d) $90,000 to $130,000 and e) $68,000 to $130,000 using the tax rate schedule of Example 1.   From Example 2 of Section 12.1 and Example 2 of this section:

$$I = \$\ 18,000 \qquad T = \$\ 2,700 \qquad R_e = 15\%$$

$$I = \ \ \ 36,000 \qquad T = \ \ \ 5,730 \qquad R_e = 15.917\%$$

$$I = \ \ \ 68,000 \qquad T = \ \ 13,650 \qquad R_e = 20.074\%$$

$$I = \ \ \ 90,000 \qquad T = \ \ 21,750 \qquad R_e = 24.167\%$$

$$I = \ \ 130,000 \qquad T = \ \ 39,550 \qquad R_e = 30.423\%$$

a)   For an increase from $18,000 to $36,000: Using Eq. (12.2-2),

$$R_{ei} = \frac{5730 - 2700}{36000 - 18000} \times 100 = 16.83\%$$

Using Eq. (12.2-3),

$$R_{ei} = \frac{(0.15917)(36000) - (0.15)(18000)}{36000 - 18000} \times 100 = 16.83\%$$

Thus, the first $18,000 of taxable income is taxed at 15%, and the increment of $18,000 is taxed at 16.83%.

b)   For an increase from $36,000 to $68,000: Using Eq. (12.2-2),

$$R_{ei} = \frac{13650 - 5730}{68000 - 36000} \times 100 = 24.75\%$$

Thus, the first $36,000 of taxable income is taxed at 15.917%, and the increment of $32,000 is taxed at 24.75%.

c)   For an increase from $68,000 to $90,000: Using Eq. (12.2-2),

$$R_{ei} = \frac{21750 - 13650}{90000 - 68000} \times 100 = 36.82\%$$

Thus, the first $68,000 of taxable income is taxed at 20.074%, and the increment of $22,000 is taxed at 36.82%.

d)   For an increase from $90,000 to $130,000: Using Eq. (12.2-2),

$$R_{ei} = \frac{39550 - 21750}{130000 - 90000} \times 100 = 44.5\%$$

Thus, the first $90,000 of taxable income is taxed at 24.167%, and the increment of $40,000 is taxed at 44.5%.

e)   For an increase from $68,000 to $130,000: Using Eq. (12.2-2),

$$R_{ei} = \frac{39550 - 13650}{130000 - 68000} \times 100 = 41.77\%$$

Thus, the first $68,000 of taxable income is taxed at 20.074%, and the increment of $62,000 is taxed at 41.774%.

Note: This example shows that when incremental taxable income places the total taxable income in a higher bracket, the effective tax rate on the increment can be significantly greater than the base tax rate prior to the increment. Such investment opportunities might be deferred to the next tax year.

CHAPTER **13**

Formulas and Tables for
Fast Answers to Depreciation of
"Old" and "New" Assets

The Economic Recovery Tax Act of 1981 included the Accelerated Cost Recovery System for the depreciation of assets which were placed in service after 1980. However, since many assets were placed in service prior to 1981, the "old" methods of depreciation apply to them. Then, in order to take full advantage of Accelerated Cost Recovery System, answers to questions involving an annual depreciation, accumulated depreciation, and book value may be needed, and in order to determine those answers without the need of a depreciation schedule, formulas are necessary. This chapter provides those formulas and rate tables (as appropriate). Within the chapter are one or more examples which indicate the use of each formula. The examples include:

10. Determining the year when the accumulated depreciation is a specified fraction of the original cost with the Accelerated Cost Recovery System of depreciation. Page 244

If you perform the calculations in the examples, your results may differ from the indicated results, depending upon the number of decimal places you carry at each step of the solutions.

The nomenclature for the formulas is as follows:

A—Acceleration factor for accelerated declining balance depreciation.
B_0—Original cost of an asset.
B_n—Book value at the end of year n.
C—Depreciable cost of an asset.
d_1—Depreciation for year 1.
d_n—Depreciation for year n.
D_n—Accumulated depreciation at the end of year n.
F—Fraction of original cost.
M—Maximum allowable additional first-year depreciation.
N—Useful life of an asset.
n—The n-th year of an asset life.
n'—Conversion year—accelerated declining balance to straight-line.
K, L—Simplification factors in sum of the years-digits depreciation.
R_1—Additional first-year depreciation rate.
R—Accelerated declining balance depreciation rate.
V—Residual (salvage) value of an asset.

13.1   STRAIGHT-LINE DEPRECIATION

Basic Formulas

Depreciable cost is defined as the original cost reduced by additional first-year depreciation (if allowed) and estimated residual (salvage) value.

$$C = \begin{cases} B_0 - R_1 B_0 - V & R_1 B_0 < M \\ B_0 - M - V & R_1 B_0 \geqslant M \end{cases} \qquad (13.1\text{-}1)$$

The annual depreciation can be determined by

$$d_n = \frac{C}{N} \qquad (13.1\text{-}2)$$

and the first year depreciation can be determined by

$$d_1 = \begin{cases} R_1 B_0 + d_n & R_1 B_0 < M \\ M + d_n & R_1 B_0 \geqslant M \end{cases} \qquad (13.1\text{-}3)$$

The accumulated depreciation for the n-th year can be determined by

$$D_n = d_1 + \frac{(n-1)\,C}{N} \qquad (13.1\text{-}4)$$

The book value at the end of the n-th year can be determined by

$$B_n = B_0 - D_n \qquad (13.1\text{-}5)$$

Example 1. The estimated useful life of an asset which cost \$15,000 is 10 years at which time a salvage value of \$1,000 is expected. The depreciation, accumulated depreciation, and book value are desired for year 6 of the asset's life using the straight-line method and a 20% additional first-year depreciation. For use in the equations: $B_0 = 15000$, $R_1 = 0.20$, $V = 1000$, $N = 10$, and $n = 6$. The additional first-year depreciation is determined as $R_1 B_0 = (0.20)(15000) = 3000$ and is less then M (10,000).

Then, the depreciable cost can be determined by using Eq. (13.1-1).

$$C = 15000 - 3000 - 1000 = \$11,000$$

The annual depreciation can be determined by using Eq. (13.1-2).

$$d_n = \frac{11000}{10} = \$1,100 \text{ per year}$$

The accumulated depreciation through year 6 can be determined by using Eq. (13.1-4).

$$D_6 = d_1 + \frac{(6-1)(11000)}{10} = d_1 + 5500$$

The first-year depreciation is determined by using Eq. (13.1-3).

$$d_1 = 3000 + 1100 = \$4,100$$

Then,

$$D_6 = 4100 + 5500 = \$9,600$$

The book value at the end of year 6 is determined by using Eq. (13.1-5).

$$B_6 = 15000 - 9600 = \$5,400$$

Year When Accumulated Depreciation Is a Specified Fraction of the Original Cost

If an occasion occurs using straight-line depreciation, where it is desirable to be able to predetermine when the accumulated depreciation will be a specified fraction of the original cost,

$$n = \frac{FB_0 - d_1}{d_n} + 1 \tag{13.1-6}$$

Example 2. The owner of the asset in Example 1 plans to replace it when 80% of the original cost has been depreciated. He would like to know when that will occur in order to establish a sinking fund. Equation (13.1-6) can be used to determine the answer. From Example 1, $d_1 = 4100$, $d = 1100$, $B_0 = 15000$. Then, for $F = 80\% = 0.8$

$$n = \frac{(0.80)(15000) - 4100}{1100} + 1$$

$$= 8.2$$

Then, the accumulated depreciation at the end of the 8th year will be approximately 80% (\$11,800) of the original cost (\$15,000).

Note: In the event of no additional first-year depreciation and/or if the residual (salvage) value is 0 or negligible, R_1 and V would be set to 0 in Eqs. (13.1-1) and (13.1-3).

13.2   SUM OF THE YEARS-DIGITS DEPRECIATION

Basic Formulas

Depreciable cost is defined as the original cost reduced by additional first-year depreciation (if allowed) and estimated residual (salvage) value. As defined by Eq. (13.1-1)

$$C = \begin{cases} B_0 - R_1 B_0 - V & R_1 B_0 < M \\ B_0 - M - V & R_1 B_0 \geqslant M \end{cases} \qquad (13.2\text{-}1)$$

The sum of the years-digits can be determined by

$$S = \frac{N(N + 1)}{2} \qquad (13.2\text{-}2)$$

and the depreciation for the n-th year can be determined by

$$d_n = \frac{(N - n + 1)\,C}{S} \qquad n \geqslant 2 \qquad (13.2\text{-}3)$$

The first-year depreciation can be determined by

$$d_1 = \begin{cases} R_1 B_0 + \dfrac{NC}{S} & R_1 B_0 < M \\[3mm] M + \dfrac{NC}{S} & R_1 B_0 \geqslant M \end{cases} \qquad (13.2\text{-}4)$$

The accumulated depreciation and book value for the n-th year can be determined, respectively, by

$$D_n = d_1 + \frac{(n - 1)(2N - n)\,C}{2S} \qquad (13.2\text{-}5)$$

$$B_n = B_0 - D_n \qquad (13.2\text{-}6)$$

Example 1.   The estimated useful life of an asset which cost \$15,000 is 10 years at which time a salvage of \$1,000 is expected. The depreciation, accumulated depreciation, and book value are desired for year 6 of the asset's life using the sum of the years-digits method and a 20% additional first-year depreciation. For use in the equations: $B_0 = 15000$; $R_1 = 0.20$; $V = 1000$; $N = 10$; and $n = 6$. The additional first-year depreciation is determined as $R_1 B_0 = (0.20)(15000) = 3000$ and is less than M (10,000). Then, the depreciable cost can be determined by using Eq. (13.2-1)

$$C = 15000 - 3000 - 1000 = \$11,000$$

The sum of the years-digits can be determined by using Eq. (13.2-2) with $N = 10$,

$$S = \frac{(10)(10 + 1)}{2} = 55$$

The first-year depreciation can be determined by using Eq. (13.2-4).

$$d_1 = 3000 + \frac{(10)(11000)}{55} = \$5,000$$

The depreciation for the 6-th year can be determined by using Eq. (13.2-3).

$$d_6 = \frac{(10 - 6 + 1)(11000)}{55} = \$1,000$$

The accumulated depreciation through year 6 can be determined by using Eq. (13.2-5).

$$D_6 = 5000 + \frac{(6 - 1)(20 - 6)(11000)}{(2)(55)} = \$12,000$$

The book value at the end of year 6 can be determined by using Eq. (13.2-6).

$$B_6 = 15000 - 12000 = \$3,000$$

Year When Accumulated Depreciation is a Specified Fraction of the Original Cost

If an occasion occurs, using sum of the years-digits depreciation, where it is desirable to be able to predetermine when the accumulated depreciation will be a specified fraction of the original cost, the following equation must be solved.

$$n^2 - (2N + 1)n + \left[2N + \frac{2S(FB_0 - d_1)}{C}\right] = 0 \qquad (13.2\text{-}7)$$

Although Eq. (13.2-7) appears to be formidable, the following substitutions will simplify the solution. Let

$$K = 2N + 1$$

and

$$L = 2N + \frac{2S(FB_0 - d_1)}{C} \left.\vphantom{\frac{2S(FB_0 - d_1)}{C}}\right\} \qquad (13.2\text{-}8)$$

Then, Eq. (13.2-7) reduces to

$$n^2 - Kn + L = 0 \qquad (13.2\text{-}9)$$

which can be solved by the quadratic formula (modified for $-K$) to give

$$n = \frac{K - \sqrt{K^2 - 4L}}{2} \qquad (13.2\text{-}10)$$

Example 2. The owner of the asset in Example 1 plans to replace it when the accumulated depreciation reaches $12,000. He would like to know when that will occur in order to establish a sinking fund. From Example 1, the parameters of the problem are: $B_0 = 15000$; $d_1 = 5000$; $S = 55$. For the accumulated depreciation to reach 12000,

$$F = 12000/15000 = 0.80$$

From Eqs. (13.2-8),

$$K = (2)(10) + 1 = 21$$

$$L = (2)(10) + \frac{(2)(55)[(0.80)(15000) - 5000]}{11000} = 90$$

From Eq. (13.2-10)

$$n = \frac{21 - \sqrt{(21)^2 - (4)(90)}}{2}$$

$$= \frac{21 - \sqrt{441 - 360}}{2}$$

$$= \frac{21 - \sqrt{81}}{2} = \frac{21 - 9}{2}$$

$$= 6$$

which is confirmed by the results of Example 1.

Note: In the event of no additional first-year depreciation, and/or if the residual (salvage) value is 0 or negligible, R_1 and V would be set equal to 0 in Eqs. (13.2-1) and (13.2-4).

13.3   ACCELERATED DECLINING BALANCE

Basic Formulas

Depreciable cost, when accelerated declining balance depreciation is in effect, is the original cost of the asset reduced by additional first-year depreciation (if allowed).

$$C = \begin{cases} B_0(1 - R_1) & R_1 B_0 < M \\ B_0 - M & R_1 B_0 \geqslant M \end{cases} \tag{13.3-1}$$

With A = 1.5 for 150% declining balance (used assets) and A = 2 for 200% (double) declining balance (new assets), the depreciation rate is given by

$$R = \frac{A}{N} \tag{13.3-2}$$

The first-year depreciation can be determined by

$$d_1 = \begin{cases} R_1 B_0 + RC & R_1 B_0 < M \\ M + RC & R_1 B_0 \geqslant M \end{cases} \tag{13.3-3}$$

Then, the depreciation for the n-th year can be determined by

$$d_n = RC(1 - R)^{n-1} \qquad n \geqslant 2 \tag{13.3-4}$$

The accumulated depreciation after the n-th year can be determined by

$$D_n = B_0 - C(1 - R)^n \tag{13.3-5}$$

and the book value at the end of the n-th year can be determined by

$$B_n = C(1 - R)^n \tag{13.3-6}$$

Example 1.   The estimated useful life of an asset which cost $15,000, when new, is 10 years at which time a salvage value of $1,000 is expected. The depreciation, accumulated depreciation, and book value are desired for year 6 of the asset's life. For use in the equations: $B_0 = 15000$; V = 2000; $R_1 = 0.20$; N = 10. Since the asset is new, A = 2.

The additional first-year depreciation is determined as $R_1 B_0 = (0.20)(15000) = 3000$ and is less than $M(10,000)$.

Then, the depreciable cost can be determined by using Eq. (13.3-1).

$$C = (15000)(1 - 0.20) = \$12,000$$

The depreciation for the 6-th year can be determined by using Eq. (13.3-4).

$$d_6 = (0.20)(12000)(1 - 0.20)^5$$
$$= (0.20)(12000)(0.80)^5$$

Using the y^x function on the hand-held calculator

$$d_6 = (0.20)(12000)(0.32768)$$
$$= \$786.43$$

The accumulated depreciation through the 6-th year can be determined by using Eq. (13.3-5)

$$D_6 = 15000 - (12000)(1 - 0.20)^6$$
$$= 15000 - (12000)(0.80)^6$$

Using the y^x function on the hand-held calculator

$$D_6 = 15000 - (12000)(0.262144)$$
$$= \$11,854.27$$

The book value at the end of the 6-th year can be determined by using Eq. (13.3-6).

$$B_6 = (12000)(1 - 0.20)^6$$
$$= (12000)(0.262144)$$
$$= \$3,145.73$$

A depreciation schedule for this example is as follows:

Year	Depreciation	Accumulated Depreciation	Book Value
1	$5,400.00	$ 5,400.00	$9,600.00
2	1,920.00	7,320.00	7,680.00
3	1,536.00	8,856.00	6,144.00
4	1,228.80	10,084.80	4,915.20
5	983.04	11,067.84	3,932.16
6	786.43	11,854.27	3,145.73
7	629.15	12,483.42	2,516.58
8	503.32	12,986.74	2,013.27
9	402.65	13,389.39	1,610.61
10	322.12	13,711.51	1,288.49

Since the salvage value in this example is $2,000, depreciation in year 8 should be $13.27 because depreciation below a reasonable salvage value is not allowed.

Note: In the event of no additional first-year depreciation, R_1 is set equal to 0 in Eqs. (13.3-1), (13.3-4), and (13.3-5).

Conversion to Straight-Line Depreciation

When an asset is depreciated with accelerated declining balance depreciation, conversion to straight-line depreciation is advantageous when that subsequent straight-line depreciation is greater than the declining balance depreciation.

Year of Conversion

Zero or Negligible Salvage Value

When using accelerated declining balance depreciation with a zero or negligible salvage value, the conversion year occurs as follows:

    I.   *150% Declining Balance*

$$n = \frac{N}{3} + 1 \qquad\qquad (13.3\text{-}7)$$

    II.   *200% Declining Balance*

$$n = \frac{N}{2} + 1 \qquad\qquad (13.3\text{-}8)$$

Example 2. A new asset with a useful life of 10 years costing $15,000 has a negligible salvage value. It is to be depreciated using 200% declining balance with a 20% additional first-year depreciation. Develop a depreciation schedule. This is the schedule of Example 1, however, it can be predetermined that conversion to straight-line depreciation will occur for the year determined by using Eq. (13.3-8).

$$n = \frac{10}{2} + 1 = 6$$

In order to confirm the calculations, Eqs. (13.3-4), (13.3-5), and (13.3-6) give, respectively,

$$d_6 = (0.20)(12000)(1 - 0.20)^5 = 786.43$$
$$D_6 = 15000 - (12000)(1 - 0.20)^6 = 11854.27$$
$$B_6 = (12000)(1 - 0.20)^6 = 3145.73$$

The depreciation schedule is shown below.

Year	Depreciation	Accumulated Depreciation	Book Value
1	$5,400.00	$ 5,400.00	$9,600.00
2	1,920.00	7,320.00	7,680.00
3	1,536.00	8,856.00	6,144.00
4	1,228.80	10,084.80	4,915.20
5	983.04	11,067.84	3,932.16
6	786.43	11,854.27	3,145.73
7	786.43	12,640.70	2,359.30
8	786.43	13,427.13	1,572.87
9	786.43	14,213.56	786.44
10	786.43	14,999.99	0.01

Year of Conversion

Significant Salvage Value

When using accelerated declining balance depreciation with a significant salvage value, the following equation must be solved for n.

$$RC(1 - R)^{n-1} = \frac{C(1 - R)^n - V}{N - n + 1} \tag{13.3-9}$$

Because n is both "free" in the denominator of the right side and is "tied up" as an exponent on $(1 - R)$, there is no explicit solution for n. However, Table 13-1 was produced by an implicit solution and provides values of n for given asset lives, N, and given percents of the ratio of the salvage value to the depreciable cost. That is, at the intersection of V/C (expressed as %) and N, read the value of n to the left or right.

Example 3.   Determine the conversion year in Example 4 if the salvage value is expected to be $1,000. For Example 4, C = 12000. Then V/C = 1000/12000 = 8.3%. In the 200% Declining Balance table of Table 13-1, find 8.4 under 10, and read across. The table shows n = 8. Eqs. (13.3-4), (13.3-5) and (13.3-6) give, respectively,

$$d_8 = (0.20)(12000)(1 - 0.20)^7 = 503.32$$

$$D_8 = 15000 - (12000)(1 - 0.20)^8 = 12986.73$$

$$B_8 = (12000)(1 - 0.20)^8 = 2013.27$$

The depreciation schedule is shown below.

Year	Depreciation	Accumulated Depreciation	Book Value
1	$5,400.00	$ 5,400.00	$9,600.00
2	1,920.00	7,320.00	7,680.00
3	1,536.00	8,856.00	6,144.00
4	1,228.80	10,084.80	4,915.20
5	983.04	11,067.84	3,932.16
6	786.43	11,854.27	3,145.73
7	629.15	12,483.42	2,516.58
8	503.31	12,986.74	2,013.27
9	503.31	13,490.05	1,509.96
10	503.31	13,993.36	1,006.65

The discrepancy of $6.65 as the final book value and the discrepancy of $6.64 in the final accumulated depreciation is due to the fact that the value of n that was used for V/C = 8.4% whereas 1000/12000 is not quite 8.4%. This type of error will occur when using the table.

Table 13-1 follows on pages 234 through 240.

TABLE 13-1

CONVERSION YEAR

150 PERCENT DECLINING BALANCE

THE EXTREME LEFT AND RIGHT COLUMNS
GIVE THE YEAR OF THE ASSET LIFE.
THE VALUES IN THE TABLE ARE THE
ESTIMATED RESIDUAL VALUES AS A
PERCENT OF THE ORIGINAL COST.

TABLE 13-1

150 PERCENT DECLINING BALANCE

ASSET LIFE – YEARS

CONVERSION YEAR	5	6	7	8	9	10	11	12	13	14	15	16	17	18
3	5.0	.0												
4	13.8	10.6	7.0	3.4	.0									
5	16.9	15.9	13.7	10.9	8.1	5.3	2.6	.0						
6		17.8	17.2	15.5	13.4	11.1	8.8	6.5	4.2	2.1	.0			
7			18.5	18.0	16.8	15.1	13.3	11.3	9.3	7.3	5.4	3.5	1.7	.0
8				19.0	18.7	17.7	16.3	14.8	13.1	11.4	9.6	7.9	6.2	4.6
9					19.4	19.1	18.3	17.2	15.9	14.5	13.0	11.4	9.9	8.4
10						19.7	19.5	18.8	17.9	16.8	15.5	14.2	12.9	11.5
11							20.0	19.8	19.2	18.4	17.5	16.4	15.2	14.0
12								20.2	20.0	19.6	18.9	18.0	17.1	16.0
13									20.4	20.2	19.8	19.2	18.5	17.6
14										20.5	20.4	20.0	19.5	18.9
15											20.6	20.5	20.2	19.8
16												20.7	20.7	20.4
17													20.8	20.8
18														20.9

234

TABLE 13-1

150 PERCENT DECLINING BALANCE

ASSET LIFE – YEARS

CONVERSION YEAR	19	20	21	22	23	24	25	26	27	28	29	30	31	32
8	.0	1.5	.0	2.6	1.3	.0	2.3	1.2	.0	2.1	1.1	.0	.9	.0
9	3.0	5.4	4.0	6.1	4.8	3.5	5.4	4.3	3.2	4.9	3.9	.9	1.9	1.0
10	6.9	8.7	7.4	9.0	7.8	6.6	8.2	7.1	6.0	7.4	6.4	2.9	4.5	3.6
11	10.1	11.5	10.3	11.5	10.4	9.3	10.5	9.5	8.4	9.7	8.7	5.5	6.8	5.9
12	12.8	13.8	12.7	13.7	12.6	11.6	12.6	11.6	10.6	11.6	10.7	7.8	8.9	8.0
13	15.0	15.7	14.7	15.5	14.5	13.6	14.3	13.4	12.5	13.3	12.5	9.6	10.8	9.9
14	16.7	17.3	16.4	17.0	16.1	15.2	15.9	15.0	14.2	14.8	14.1	11.6	12.5	11.6
15	18.1	18.5	17.8	18.2	17.4	16.7	17.1	16.4	15.6	16.2	15.4	13.3	13.9	13.2
16	19.2	19.5	18.9	19.1	18.5	17.9	18.2	17.6	16.9	17.3	16.6	14.7	15.2	14.5
17	20.0	20.2	19.7	19.9	19.4	18.8	19.1	18.5	17.9	18.2	17.6	15.9	16.4	15.7
18	20.5	20.6	20.3	20.5	20.1	19.6	19.8	19.3	18.8	19.0	18.5	17.0	17.4	16.8
19	20.9	20.9	20.7	20.8	20.6	20.2	20.4	20.0	19.5	19.7	19.3	18.0	18.3	17.7
20	21.0	21.1	21.0	21.1	20.9	20.7	20.8	20.5	20.1	20.3	19.9	18.8	19.0	18.5
21			21.1	21.2	21.1	21.0	21.1	20.9	20.6	20.7	20.4	19.5	19.6	19.2
22				21.2	21.3	21.2	21.3	21.1	20.9	21.0	20.8	20.0	20.2	19.8
23						21.3	21.3	21.3	21.2	21.2	21.1	20.5	20.6	20.3
24								21.4	21.3	21.4	21.3	20.9	20.9	20.7
25									21.4	21.5	21.4	21.1	21.2	21.0
26											21.5	21.3	21.4	21.2
27												21.5	21.5	21.4
28												21.5		21.5
29														21.6
30														
31														
32														

CONVERSION YEAR

235

TABLE 13-1

150 PERCENT DECLINING BALANCE

ASSET LIFE – YEARS

Conversion Year	33	34	35	36	37	38	39	40	41	42	43	44	45	46
12	.0	.8												
13	2.7	1.8	.9	.0										
14	5.0	4.1	3.3	2.4	1.6	.8	.0							
15	7.2	6.3	5.5	4.7	3.8	3.0	2.3	1.5	.8	.0				
16	9.1	8.3	7.5	6.7	5.9	5.1	4.3	3.6	2.8	2.1	1.4	.7	.0	
17	10.8	10.1	9.3	8.5	7.7	7.0	6.2	5.5	4.8	4.0	3.3	2.7	2.0	1.3
18	12.4	11.7	10.9	10.2	9.4	8.7	7.9	7.2	6.5	5.8	5.1	4.5	3.8	3.1
19	13.8	13.1	12.4	11.7	11.0	10.2	9.5	8.8	8.2	7.5	6.8	6.1	5.5	4.8
20	15.1	14.4	13.7	13.0	12.4	11.7	11.0	10.3	9.7	9.0	8.3	7.7	7.1	6.4
21	16.2	15.6	14.9	14.3	13.6	13.0	12.3	11.7	11.0	10.4	9.8	9.1	8.5	7.9
22	17.2	16.6	16.0	15.4	14.8	14.2	13.6	12.9	12.3	11.7	11.1	10.5	9.9	9.3
23	18.0	17.5	16.9	16.4	15.8	15.2	14.7	14.1	13.5	12.9	12.3	11.7	11.1	10.5
24	18.8	18.3	17.8	17.3	16.7	16.2	15.7	15.1	14.5	14.0	13.4	12.8	12.3	11.7
25	19.4	19.0	18.5	18.1	17.6	17.1	16.6	16.0	15.5	15.0	14.4	13.9	13.3	12.8
26	19.9	19.6	19.2	18.7	18.3	17.8	17.4	16.9	16.4	15.9	15.4	14.9	14.3	13.8
27	20.4	20.1	19.7	19.3	18.9	18.5	18.1	17.6	17.2	16.7	16.2	15.7	15.2	14.7
28	20.8	20.5	20.2	19.9	19.5	19.1	18.7	18.3	17.9	17.4	17.0	16.5	16.1	15.6
29	21.0	20.8	20.6	20.3	20.0	19.6	19.3	18.9	18.5	18.1	17.7	17.3	16.8	16.4
30	21.3	21.1	20.9	20.7	20.4	20.1	19.8	19.4	19.1	18.7	18.3	17.9	17.5	17.1
31	21.4	21.3	21.2	21.0	20.7	20.5	20.2	19.9	19.6	19.2	18.9	18.5	18.1	17.7
32	21.5	21.5	21.4	21.2	21.0	20.8	20.6	20.3	20.0	19.7	19.4	19.0	18.7	18.3
33	21.6	21.6	21.5	21.4	21.3	21.1	20.9	20.7	20.4	20.1	19.8	19.5	19.2	18.9
34		21.6	21.6	21.5	21.4	21.3	21.1	20.9	20.7	20.5	20.2	19.9	19.7	19.3
35			21.6	21.6	21.6	21.5	21.3	21.2	21.0	20.8	20.6	20.3	20.1	19.8
36				21.7	21.6	21.6	21.5	21.4	21.2	21.1	20.9	20.6	20.4	20.1
37					21.7	21.7	21.6	21.5	21.4	21.3	21.1	20.9	20.7	20.5
38						21.7	21.7	21.6	21.5	21.4	21.3	21.1	21.0	20.8
39							21.7	21.7	21.6	21.6	21.5	21.3	21.2	21.0
40								21.7	21.7	21.7	21.6	21.5	21.4	21.2
41									21.7	21.7	21.7	21.6	21.5	21.4
42										21.8	21.7	21.7	21.6	21.5
43											21.8	21.8	21.7	21.7
44												21.8	21.8	21.7
45													21.8	21.8
46														21.8

CONVERSION YEAR

TABLE 13-1
150 PERCENT DECLINING BALANCE
ASSET LIFE – YEARS

Conversion Year	47	48	49	50	51	52	53	54	55	56	57	58	59	60
17	.7	.0		.6	.0		.6	.0		.6	.0		.6	.0
18	2.5	1.9	1.3	2.4	1.8	1.2	2.2	1.7	1.1	2.1	1.6	1.1	2.0	1.5
19	4.2	3.6	3.0	4.0	3.4	2.8	3.8	3.2	2.7	3.6	3.1	2.5	3.4	2.9
20	5.8	5.2	4.6	5.5	4.9	4.3	5.2	4.7	4.1	5.0	4.4	3.9	4.7	4.2
21	7.3	6.7	6.1	6.9	6.3	5.8	6.6	6.0	5.5	6.3	5.8	5.2	6.0	5.5
22	8.7	8.1	7.5	8.2	7.7	7.1	7.8	7.3	6.8	7.5	7.0	6.5	7.2	6.7
23	10.0	9.4	8.8	9.5	8.9	8.4	9.0	8.5	8.0	8.7	8.2	7.7	8.3	7.8
24	11.1	10.6	10.0	10.6	10.1	9.6	10.2	9.7	9.2	9.7	9.3	8.8	9.4	8.9
25	12.3	11.7	11.2	11.7	11.2	10.7	11.2	10.7	10.2	10.8	10.3	9.8	10.4	9.9
26	13.3	12.8	12.2	12.7	12.2	11.7	12.2	11.7	11.3	11.7	11.3	10.8	11.3	10.8
27	14.2	13.7	13.2	13.7	13.2	12.7	13.1	12.7	12.2	12.6	12.1	11.7	12.2	11.7
28	15.1	14.6	14.2	14.5	14.1	13.6	14.0	13.6	13.1	13.5	13.1	12.6	13.0	12.6
29	15.9	15.5	15.0	15.3	14.9	14.5	14.8	14.4	13.9	14.3	13.9	13.4	13.8	13.4
30	16.7	16.2	15.8	16.1	15.7	15.2	15.5	15.1	14.7	15.0	14.6	14.2	14.5	14.1
31	17.3	16.9	16.5	16.8	16.4	16.0	16.2	15.8	15.4	15.7	15.3	14.9	15.2	14.8
32	18.0	17.6	17.2	17.4	17.0	16.6	16.9	16.5	16.1	16.4	16.0	15.6	15.9	15.5
33	18.5	18.2	17.8	18.0	17.6	17.3	17.5	17.1	16.7	17.0	16.6	16.2	16.5	16.1
34	19.0	18.7	18.3	18.5	18.2	17.8	18.0	17.7	17.3	17.5	17.2	16.8	17.0	16.7
35	19.5	19.2	18.8	19.0	18.7	18.3	18.5	18.2	17.9	18.0	17.7	17.4	17.6	17.2
36	19.9	19.6	19.3	19.4	19.1	18.8	19.0	18.7	18.4	18.5	18.2	17.9	18.1	17.7
37	20.2	20.0	19.7	19.8	19.5	19.3	19.4	19.1	18.8	18.9	18.7	18.4	18.5	18.2
38	20.6	20.3	20.1	20.2	19.9	19.7	19.8	19.5	19.2	19.3	19.1	18.8	18.9	18.6
39	20.8	20.6	20.4	20.5	20.2	20.0	20.1	19.9	19.6	19.7	19.4	19.2	19.3	19.0
40	21.1	20.9	20.7	20.7	20.5	20.3	20.4	20.2	19.9	20.0	19.8	19.6	19.7	19.4
41	21.3	21.1	20.9	21.0	20.8	20.6	20.7	20.5	20.3	20.3	20.1	19.9	20.0	19.7
42	21.4	21.3	21.1	21.2	21.0	20.9	20.9	20.7	20.5	20.6	20.4	20.2	20.3	20.1
43	21.6	21.5	21.3	21.4	21.2	21.1	21.1	21.0	20.8	20.8	20.7	20.5	20.5	20.3
44	21.7	21.6	21.5	21.5	21.4	21.3	21.3	21.3	21.0	21.0	20.8	20.7	20.8	20.6
45	21.8	21.7	21.6	21.6	21.5	21.4	21.5	21.5	21.2	21.2	21.0	20.9	21.0	20.8
46	21.8	21.8	21.7	21.8	21.7	21.6	21.6	21.6	21.4	21.4	21.3	21.1	21.2	21.0
47	21.8	21.8	21.8	21.8	21.8	21.7	21.7	21.7	21.5	21.5	21.4	21.3	21.5	21.2
48		21.8	21.8	21.8	21.8	21.8	21.8	21.8	21.6	21.6	21.6	21.4	21.6	21.4
49			21.8	21.9	21.9	21.8	21.8	21.8	21.7	21.7	21.7	21.6	21.7	21.5
50				21.9	21.9	21.9	21.9	21.9	21.8	21.8	21.8	21.7	21.8	21.6
51					21.9	21.9	21.9	21.9	21.9	21.9	21.9	21.8	21.8	21.8
52						21.9	21.9	21.9	21.9	21.9	21.9	21.9	21.9	21.9
53							21.9	21.9	21.9	21.9	21.9	21.9	21.9	21.9
54								21.9	21.9	21.9	21.9	21.9	21.9	21.9
55									21.9	21.9	21.9	21.9	21.9	21.9
56										21.9	21.9	21.9	21.9	21.9
57											21.9	21.9	21.9	21.9
58												21.9	21.9	21.9
59													21.9	21.9
60														21.9

TABLE 13-1

CONVERSION YEAR

200 PERCENT DECLINING BALANCE

THE EXTREME LEFT AND RIGHT COLUMNS GIVE THE YEAR OF THE ASSET LIFE. THE VALUES IN THE TABLE ARE THE ESTIMATED RESIDUAL VALUES AS A PERCENT OF THE ORIGINAL COST.

TABLE 13-1

200 PERCENT DECLINING BALANCE

ASSET LIFE – YEARS

CONVERSION YEAR	5	6	7	8	9	10	11	12	13	14	15	16	17	18	CONVERSION YEAR
4	4.4	.0													4
5	7.8	6.6	3.8	.0											5
6		8.8	8.0	6.0	3.2	.0									6
7			9.5	8.9	7.4	5.3	2.8	.0							7
8				10.1	9.6	8.4	6.7	4.7	2.4	.0					8
9					10.5	10.1	9.2	7.8	6.1	4.2	2.2	.0			9
10						10.8	10.5	9.7	8.6	7.2	5.6	3.8	2.0	.0	10
11							11.0	10.8	10.2	9.2	8.0	6.6	5.1	3.5	11
12								11.3	11.1	10.5	9.7	8.7	7.5	6.1	12
13									11.4	11.3	10.8	10.1	9.2	8.2	13
14										11.6	11.5	11.1	10.5	9.7	14
15											11.7	11.6	11.3	10.7	15
16												11.9	11.7	11.4	16
17													12.0	11.9	17
18														12.1	18

238

TABLE 13-1

200 PERCENT DECLINING BALANCE

ASSET LIFE – YEARS

CONVERSION YEAR	19	20	21	22	23	24	25	26	27	28	29	30	31	32
11	1.8	.0												
12	4.7	3.2	1.6	.0										
13	7.0	5.7	4.3	2.9	1.5	.0								
14	8.7	7.7	6.5	5.3	4.0	2.7	1.4	.0						
15	10.0	9.2	8.3	7.2	6.1	5.0	3.8	2.6	1.3	.0				
16	11.0	10.3	9.6	8.8	7.8	6.8	5.8	4.7	3.6	2.4	1.2	.0		
17	11.6	11.2	10.6	9.9	9.2	8.3	7.4	6.5	5.5	4.4	3.3	2.3	1.2	.0
18	12.0	11.7	11.3	10.8	10.2	9.5	8.9	7.9	7.1	6.1	5.2	4.2	3.2	2.1
19	12.1	12.1	11.8	11.5	11.0	10.5	9.9	9.2	8.4	7.6	6.7	5.8	4.9	4.0
20		12.2	12.1	11.9	11.6	11.2	10.7	10.1	9.5	8.8	8.0	7.2	6.4	5.6
21			12.3	12.2	12.0	11.7	11.4	10.9	10.4	9.8	9.1	8.4	7.7	6.9
22				12.3	12.3	12.1	11.9	11.5	11.1	10.6	10.0	9.4	8.8	8.1
23					12.4	12.3	12.2	11.9	11.6	11.2	10.8	10.3	9.7	9.1
24						12.4	12.4	12.3	12.0	11.7	11.4	11.0	10.5	10.0
25							12.5	12.4	12.3	12.1	11.8	11.5	11.1	10.7
26								12.5	12.5	12.4	12.2	11.9	11.6	11.3
27									12.6	12.5	12.4	12.2	12.0	11.7
28										12.6	12.6	12.5	12.3	12.1
29											12.6	12.6	12.5	12.4
30												12.7	12.6	12.6
31													12.7	12.7
32														12.7

CONVERSION YEAR

239

TABLE 13-1

200 PERCENT DECLINING BALANCE

ASSET LIFE – YEARS

Conversion Year	33	34	35	36	37	38	39	40	41	42	43	44	45	46
18	1.1	.0	1.0	.0	1.0									
19	3.0	2.0	.9	.9	.0	.0	.9							
20	4.7	3.8	2.9	1.9	1.0	1.8	2.6	.0	.9					
21	6.1	5.3	4.5	3.6	2.7	3.4	4.1	1.8	2.5	.0	.9			
22	7.4	6.6	5.9	5.1	4.3	4.9	5.4	3.3	3.9	1.7	2.4	.0	.8	
23	8.5	7.8	7.1	6.4	5.6	6.1	6.6	4.7	5.2	3.2	3.8	1.6	2.3	.0
24	9.4	8.8	8.2	7.5	6.8	7.2	7.6	5.9	6.3	4.5	5.1	3.0	3.6	1.5
25	10.2	9.7	9.1	8.5	7.9	8.2	8.5	7.0	7.4	5.7	6.1	4.3	4.8	2.9
26	10.8	10.4	9.6	9.4	8.8	9.1	9.3	8.0	8.3	6.7	7.1	5.5	5.9	4.2
27	11.4	11.0	10.6	10.1	9.6	9.8	10.0	8.8	9.1	7.6	8.0	6.5	6.9	5.3
28	11.8	11.5	11.1	10.7	10.3	10.5	10.6	9.6	9.8	8.6	8.8	7.5	7.8	6.3
29	12.2	11.9	11.6	11.3	10.9	11.0	11.1	10.2	10.4	9.3	9.5	8.3	8.6	7.2
30	12.4	12.2	12.0	11.7	11.4	11.5	11.6	10.8	10.9	10.0	10.1	9.1	9.3	8.1
31	12.6	12.5	12.3	12.1	11.8	11.9	11.9	11.3	11.4	10.5	10.7	9.7	9.9	8.8
32	12.7	12.6	12.5	12.3	12.1	12.2	12.2	11.7	11.8	11.0	11.2	10.3	10.5	9.5
33	12.8	12.7	12.7	12.5	12.4	12.4	12.5	12.0	12.1	11.5	11.6	10.8	10.9	10.1
34	12.	12.8	12.7	12.7	12.6	12.6	12.6	12.3	12.3	11.8	11.9	11.3	11.4	10.6
35			12.8	12.7	12.7	12.7	12.6	12.5	12.5	12.1	12.2	11.6	11.7	11.1
36				12.8	12.8	12.8	12.8	12.7	12.7	12.4	12.4	12.0	12.0	11.5
37					12.	12.9	12.8	12.8	12.8	12.6	12.6	12.2	12.3	11.8
38						12.	12.9	12.9	12.9	12.7	12.8	12.5	12.5	12.1
39							12.	12.9	12.9	12.8	12.9	12.6	12.7	12.3
40								12.	12.9	12.9	12.9	12.8	12.8	12.5
41									12.	12.9	12.9	12.9	12.9	12.7
42										12.	12.9	12.9	12.9	12.8
43											12.	13.0	13.0	12.9
44												12.	12.9	12.9
45													12.	13.0
46														13.0

Example 4. Determine the year of conversion to straight line for the following using Table 13-1.

$$
\begin{array}{llll}
\text{a)} & A = 150\% & N = 20 & V/C = 20 \\
\text{b)} & A = 150\% & N = 20 & V/C = 20.2\% \\
\text{c)} & A = 200\% & N = 20 & V/C = 0 \\
\text{d)} & A = 200\% & N = 20 & V/C = 10.3\%
\end{array}
$$

a) From the 150% table of Table 13-1, at $V/C = 0$ and $N = 20$, $n = 8$ (the smallest value of V/C is 1.5%). Eq. (13.3-9) gives

$$ n = \frac{N}{3} + 1 = \frac{20}{3} + 1 = 7.67 \approx 8 $$

b) From the 150% table of Table 13-1, at $V/C = 20.2\%$ and $N = 20$, $n = 17$.

c) From the 200% table of Table 13-1, at $V/C = 0$ and $N = 20$, $n = 11$. Eq. (13.3-10) gives

$$ n = \frac{N}{2} + 1 = \frac{20}{2} + 1 = 11 $$

d) From the 200% table of Table 13-1, at $V/C = 10.3\%$ and $N = 20$, $n = 16$.

For a given value, N, of an asset life, if the estimated value of V/C is greater than the largest value given under N, then, conversion from accelerated declining balance to straight-line will not be advantageous during the depreciation life of the asset.

Accumulated Depreciation and Book Value

The accumulated depreciation and book value for the n-th year, when straight-line conversion is to occur can be determined by, respectively,

$$ D_n = D_{n'} + (n - n')d_{n'} \qquad n > n' \tag{13.3-10} $$

and

$$ B_n = B_{n'} - (n - n')d_{n'} \qquad n > n' \tag{13.3-11} $$

where n' can be determined by Eq. (13.3-7) or (13.3-8), and $d_{n'}$, $D_{n'}$, and $B_{n'}$ can be determined by Eqs. (13.3-4), (13.3-5), and (13.3-6), respectively. For $n \leq n'$, the basic formulas apply.

Example 5. Confirm the accumulated depreciation and book value for year 8 of the depreciation schedule of Example 2. From Example 2; $B = 15000$; $C = 12000$; $N = 10$; $R = 0.20$; $R_1 = 0.20$. From Eq. (13.3-8)

$$ n' = \frac{10}{2} + 1 = 6 $$

From Eq. (13.3-4)

$$ d_6 = (0.20)(12000)(1 - 0.20)^5 = 786.43 $$

From Eq. (13.3-5)

$$ D_6 = 15000 - (12000)(1 - 0.20)^6 = 11854.27 $$

From Eq. (13.3-6)

$$B_6 = (12000)(1 - 0.20)^6 = 3145.73$$

The accumulated depreciation through year 8 can be determined by Eq. (13.3-10).

$$D_8 = 11854.27 + (8 - 6)(786.43) = \$13,427.13$$

which agrees with the depreciation schedule of Example 2. The book value at the end of year 8 can be determined by Eq. (13.3-11).

$$B_n = 3145.73 - (8 - 6)(786.43) = \$1,572.87$$

which agrees with the depreciation schedule of Example 2

Year When Accumulated Depreciation Is a Specified Fraction of the Original Cost and the Corresponding Book Value

The pre-determination of when the accumulated depreciation will reach a specified fraction of the original cost after conversion to straight-line depreciation can be determined by

$$n = n' + \frac{FB_0 - D_{n'}}{d_{n'}} \qquad FB_0 > D_{n'} \tag{13.3-12}$$

where n' can be determined by Eq. (13.3-7) or (13.3-8), and $d_{n'}$, $D_{n'}$, and $B_{n'}$ can be determined by Eqs. (13.3-4), (13.3-5), and (13.3-6). The corresponding book value will be

$$B_n = B_0 - D_n \qquad FB_0 > D_{n'} \tag{13.3-13}$$

where D_n can be determined by Eq. (13.3-10).

> **Example 6.** An asset with a useful life of 20 years cost \$100,000 when new. Including a 20% additional first-year depreciation, the owner wishes to predetermine the year when the accumulated depreciation reaches 80% of the original cost. For the additional first-year depreciation $R_1 B_0 = (0.20)(100000) = \$20,000$ which is greater than M. Then, from Eq. (13.3-1)
>
> $$C = 100000 - 10000 = 90000$$
>
> Because the asset is new, A = 200% = 2 and
>
> $$R = \frac{2}{20} = 0.10$$
>
> The conversion can be determined by Eq. (13.3-8) as
>
> $$n' = \frac{20}{2} + 1 = 11$$
>
> For use in Eq. (13.3-12), Eqs. (13.3-4) and (13.3-5) give, respectively
>
> $$d_{11} = (0.10)(90000)(0.90)^{10} = 3138.11$$
> $$D_{11} = 100000 - (90000)(0.90)^{11} = 71757.05$$
>
> Because $FB_0 = (0.80)(100000) = 80000$ and is greater than D_{11}, Eq. (13.3-12) can be used.

$$n = 11 + \frac{(0.80)(100000) - 71757.05}{3138.11} = 13.63$$

Thus, at the end of the 14th year, the accumulated depreciation will exceed 80% of the original cost. The corresponding book value (at year 14) is determined by Eqs. (13.3-10) and (13.3-13.) From Eq. (13.3-10)

$$D_{14} = 71757.05 + (14 - 11)(3138.11) = \$81,171.38$$

From Eq. (13.3-13)

$$B_{14} = 100000 - 81171.38 = \$18,828.62$$

For the case where FB_0 is less than or equal to $D_{n'}$ the basic formulas can be rearranged to

$$n = \frac{\log\left[\dfrac{(1 - F)B_0}{C}\right]}{\log (1 - R)} \qquad FB_0 < D_{n'} \qquad (13.3\text{-}14)$$

Example 7. Suppose that the year when 50% of the original cost is desired in accumulated depreciation. From Example 6, $C = 90000$; $R = 0.10$; $n' = 11$; and $D_{n'} = D_{11} = 71757.05$. Because $FB_0 = (0.50)(100000) = 50000$ and is less than D_{11}, Eq. (13.3-14) must be used.

$$n = \frac{\log\left[\dfrac{(1 - 0.50)(100000)}{90000}\right]}{\log (1 - 0.10)}$$

$$= \frac{\log 0.555556}{\log 0.90} = 5.58$$

Thus, at the end of year 6, the accumulated depreciation will be greater than 50% of the original cost. Eq. (13.3-6) gives the corresponding book value (at the end of year 6) as

$$B_6 = (90000)(0.90)^6 = \$47,829.69$$

13.4   THE ACCELERATED COST RECOVERY SYSTEM (ACRS)

Most tangible depreciable assets which are placed in service after 1980 must be depreciated using the ACRS. The rates of depreciation reflect 150% declining balance with conversion to straight-line for 1981 through 1984; 175% declining balance with conversion to straight-line for 1985; and 200% declining balance with conversion to straight-line for 1986 and thereafter. The rates in each first year of the published schedule are 50% of the corresponding full-year depreciation. Thus, the rate each year thereafter is the sum of one-half the preceding year and one-half the current year. The depreciable cost for all categories is the unadjusted basis (original cost) of the property. Then, in general

$$d_1 = RB_0 \qquad\qquad (13.4\text{-}1)$$

and

$$d_n = (0.5)(d_n + d_{n-1}) \qquad\qquad (13.4\text{-}2)$$

where the d's can be determined by Eq. (13.3-4) and:

For 150% declining balance $n' = \dfrac{N}{3} + 1$

For 175% declining balance $n' = \dfrac{3N}{7} + 1$

For 200% declining balance $n' = \dfrac{N}{2} + 1$

Tables 13-2, 13-3, and 13-4 provide the annual and accumulated rates for each of the four ACRS categories.

Example 1. An asset which costs $15,000 and which is in the 5-year category is placed in service in 1983. The depreciation, accumulated depreciation, and book value for year 3 are desired. From Table 13-2, $R_3 = 21\%$ and the cumulative rate is 58%. Then

$$d_3 = (0.21)(15000) = \$3,150$$
$$D_3 = (0.58)(15000) = \$8,700$$
$$B_3 = B_0 - D_3 = 15000 - 8700 = \$6,300$$

Example 2. The year when the accumulated depreciation will reach 80% of the original cost and the corresponding book value are desired for a $100,000 asset which may be classified as 10-year property. The asset is placed in service in 1983. From Table 13-2, under 10-Year Property, a cumulative rate of 80% occurs between years 7 and 8. To find the "exact" point, the table must be interpolated.

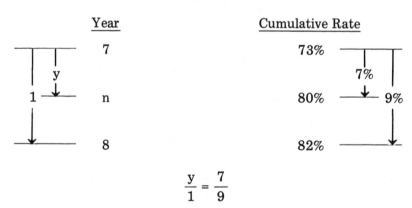

$$\frac{y}{1} = \frac{7}{9}$$

and $y = (7/9)(1) = 7/9$. Then

$$n = 7 + y = 7 + 7/9 = 7.77$$
$$D_n = (0.80)(100000) = \$80,000$$
$$B_n = (0.20)(100000) = \$20,000$$

If the cumulative rate of 80% is a lower limit, then,

$$D_8 = (0.82)(100000) = \$82,000$$
$$B_8 = (0.18)(100000) = \$18,000$$

TABLE 13-2
ACRS STANDARD RECOVERY RATES
1981–1984

3-Year Property

Year	Rate	Cumulative Rate	Book Value Rate
1	25%		75%
2	38	63%	37
3	37	100	0
4	....		
5	....		

5-Year Property

Rate	Cumulative Rate	Book Value Rate
15%		85%
22	37%	63
21	58	42
21	79	21
21	100	0

10-Year Property

Year	Rate	Cumulative Rate	Book Value Rate
1	8%		92%
2	14	22%	78
3	12	34	66
4	10	44	56
5	10	54	46
6	10	64	36
7	9	73	27
8	9	82	18
9	9	91	9
10	9	100	0
11	....		
12	....		
13	....		
14	....		
15	....		

15-Year Property

Rate	Cumulative Rate	Book Value Rate
5%		95%
10	15%	85
9	24	76
8	32	68
7	39	61
7	46	54
6	52	48
6	58	42
6	64	36
6	70	30
6	76	24
6	82	18
6	88	12
6	94	6
6	100	0

TABLE 13-3
ACRS STANDARD RECOVERY RATES
1985

3-Year Property

Year	Rate	Cumulative Rate	Book Value Rate
1	29%		71%
2	47	76%	24
3	24	100	0
4			
5			

5-Year Property

Rate	Cumulative Rate	Book Value Rate
18%		82%
33	51%	49
25	76	24
16	92	8
8	100	0

10-Year Property

Year	Rate	Cumulative Rate	Book Value Rate
1	9%		91%
2	19	28	72
3	16	44	56
4	14	58	42
5	12	70	30
6	10	80	20
7	8	88	12
8	6	94	6
9	4	98	2
10	2	100	0
11			
12			
13			
14			
15			

15-Year Property

Rate	Cumulative Rate	Book Value Rate
6%		94%
12	18%	82
12	30	70
11	41	59
10	51	49
9	60	40
8	68	32
7	75	25
6	81	19
5	86	14
4	90	10
4	94	6
3	97	3
2	99	1
1	100	0

TABLE 13-4
ACRS STANDARD RECOVERY RATES
POST-1985

		3-Year Property			5-Year Property	
Year	Rate	Cumulative Rate	Book Value Rate	Rate	Cumulative Rate	Book Value Rate
1	33%		67%	20%		80%
2	45	78%	22	32	52%	48
3	22	100	0	24	76	24
4	....			16	92	8
5	....			8	100	0

		10-Year Property			15-Year Property	
Year	Rate	Cumulative Rate	Book Value Rate	Rate	Cumulative Rate	Book Value Rate
1	10%		90%	7%		93%
2	18	28%	72	12	19%	81
3	16	44	56	12	31	69
4	14	58	42	11	42	58
5	12	70	30	10	52	48
6	10	80	20	9	61	39
7	8	88	12	8	69	31
8	6	94	6	7	76	24
9	4	98	2	6	82	18
10	2	100	0	5	87	13
11	....			4	91	9
12	....			3	94	6
13	....			3	97	3
14	....			2	99	1
15	....			1	100	0

CHAPTER 14

Accounting Ratios in the Analysis of Financial Statements

This chapter provides some key accounting ratios which can help in the determination of the financial stability of a business. The ratios that are provided are as follows.

DEFINITIONS

Current Assets:	The sum of cash, notes receivable, accounts receivable (reduced by reserves for bad debts), advances on merchandise, inventories, and securities (not in excess of market value).
Current Liabilities:	The total of all liabilities due within one year from the date of a financial statement.
Net Profits:	Net earnings after taxes.
Net Sales:	Total sales dollars reduced by returns, allowances, and cash discounts.
Tangible Net Worth:	The stockholders' equity which is obtained by subtracting total liabilities from total assets and then reducing the difference by intangible assets, such as goodwill.

Net Working Capital:	The difference between Current Assets and Current Liabilities.
Collection Period:	The number of days when notes and accounts receivable are "turned over."
Fixed Assets:	Depreciated book values of building, leasehold improvements, machinery, furniture, fixtures, tools, other physical equipment, and land which is valued at cost or appraised market value.
Total Liabilities:	The sum of total current and long-term liabilities.
Funded Liabilities:	All long-term obligations which can be represented as mortgages, bonds, debentures (unsecured loans), and other liabilities due beyond one year.
Average Inventory:	Beginning plus Ending Inventories divided by 2.

14.1   THE ANALYSIS

All financial statements will include the parameters with which the "key" ratios can be determined. The degree of detail can differ, depending upon the nature and size of the business. Therefore, rather than provide a "typical" financial statement, the key ratio parameters are presented below:

1.	Current Assets:	$22,101,736
2.	Current Liabilities:	$13,474,436
3.	Net Profits:	$ 2,992,321
4.	Net Sales:	$62,019,321
5.	Tangible Net Worth:	$15,332,428
6.	Net Working Capital: (22101736 – 13474436)	$ 8,627,300
7.	Notes and Accounts Receivable	$10,517,436
8.	Fixed Assets:	$30,188,360
9.	Funded Liabilities:	$21,332,555
10.	Total Liabilities:	$36,957,668
11.	Inventory:	$ 1,977,086
12.	Average Inventory:	$ 1,624,126
13.	Cost of Goods Sold:	$52,961,844

Current Ratio

The current ratio is defined as $\dfrac{\text{Current Assets}}{\text{Current Liabilities}}$. As one test for solvency, it should exceed the value 1.

The Current Ratio is:

$$\frac{22101736}{13474436} = 1.64$$

Since this ratio is significantly greater than 1, the current assets appear to be sufficient to cover the current liabilities.

Net Profits on Net Sales

This ratio is obtained by dividing the net profits by the net sales. This ratio, in conjunction with the Net Profits on Tangible Net Worth ratio, is important in viewing the profitability of a business.

The Net Profits on Net Sales ratio is:

$$\frac{2992321}{62019321} = 0.048$$

In effect, this ratio indicates a 4.8%, after taxes, rate of return on sales.

Net Profits on Tangible Net Worth

This ratio is obtained by dividing the after-taxes profits (net profits) by the tangible net worth. A magnitude of at least 10% for this ratio is considered as desirable in order to provide dividends and funds for future growth.

The Net Profits on Tangible Net Worth ratio is:

$$\frac{2992321}{15332428} = 0.195$$

Since this ratio exceeds the desirable 10% level, the relationship between net profits and ownership is satisfactory. In conjunction with the previous ratio, the business appears to be profitable.

Net Profits on Net Working Capital

This ratio is obtained by dividing the net profits by the net working capital. It is a measure of the availability of the funds which are necessary for carrying inventories and receivables and for the financing of daily operations.

The Net Profits on Net Working Capital ratio is:

$$\frac{2992321}{8627300} = 0.347$$

In effect, this ratio indicates that net profits of 34.7% of net working capital is an additional availability for operations.

Net Sales to Tangible Net Worth

This ratio is obtained by dividing net sales by the tangible net worth and is a measure of the number of times per year invested capital is returned and "turned over."

The Net Sales to Tangible Net Worth ratio is:

$$\frac{62019321}{15332428} = 4.05$$

This ratio indicates that the investment of the owners was turned over approximately 4 times during the year.

Net Sales to Net Working Capital

This ratio is obtained by dividing the net sales by the net working capital and is a measure of the number of times per year that the excess of Current Assets over Current Liabilities is "turned over."

The Net Sales to Net Working Capital ratio is:

$$\frac{62019321}{8627300} = 7.20$$

This ratio indicates that the excess of current assets over current liabilities was turned over approximately 7 times during the year.

Collection Period

The value is a "number of days" that the receivables are outstanding. It is obtained by:

$$\text{Period} = \frac{(365)\,(\text{Notes} + \text{Accounts Receivable})}{\text{Net Sales}}\ \text{days}$$

From the Balance Sheet and Income statement, the Collection Period is:

$$\frac{(365)\,(10517436)}{62019321} = 62\ \text{days}$$

The acceptability of this value depends on the nature of a business.

Inventory Turnover

This ratio is obtained by dividing the Cost of Goods Sold by the Average Inventory for the year. It indicates the number of times the inventory was "turned over" during the year. The average inventory can be one-half the sum of beginning and ending inventories for the year.

The Inventory Turnover is:

$$\frac{52961844}{1624126} = 32.6$$

Dividing this number into 365 gives the average duration of each inventory during the year. From above the:

$$\text{Days to Inventory Turnover} = \frac{365}{32.6} = 11.2$$

This value indicates that inventory was "depleted" approximately once each $1\frac{1}{2}$ weeks.

Fixed Assets to Tangible Net Worth

This ratio is obtained by dividing the fixed assets by the tangible net worth. The normal values for this ratio are 1 (100%) for manufacturers and 0.75 (75%) for wholesalers and retailers.

The Fixed Assets to Tangible Net Worth ratio is:

$$\frac{30188360}{15332428} = 1.97$$

Unless a business is normally a debt-leveraged business, such as utilities, this magnitude is a little high.

Current Liabilities to Tangible Net Worth

This ratio is obtained by dividing the current liabilities by the tangible net worth. Normally, if this ratio exceeds and is sustained at a value of 0.80 (80%), financial difficulties are indicated.

The Current Liabilities to Tangible Net Worth ratio is:

$$\frac{13474436}{15332428} = 0.88$$

The magnitude of this ratio indicates a marginal position relative to financial peace.

Total Liabilities to Tangible Net Worth

This ratio is obtained by dividing the total liabilities by the tangible net worth. When this ratio exceeds 1 (100%), the equity of the creditors in the assets exceeds that of the owners.

The Total Liabilities to Tangible Net Worth ratio is:

$$\frac{36957668}{15332428} = 2.41$$

This value appears to be high unless the business is a debt-leveraged business such as utilities.

Inventory to Net Working Capital

This ratio is obtained by dividing the inventory by the net working capital. Normally, this ratio should not exceed 0.80 (80%) in order for an acceptable inventory to be indicated.

The Inventory to Net Working Capital ratio is:

$$\frac{1977086}{8627300} = 0.23$$

Because this value is much smaller than the desirable 0.80, the inventory levels are appropriate.

Current Liabilities to Inventory

This ratio is obtained by dividing the current liabilities by the inventory. It is a measure of the reliance on funds from the disposal of inventory to meet current liabilities.

The Current Liabilities to Inventory ratio is:

$$\frac{13474436}{1977086} = 6.82$$

Since the value of this ratio is approximately 7, the use of inventory to meet current liabilities cannot be relied upon to a great extent.

Funded Liabilities to Net Working Capital

This ratio is obtained by dividing the funded liabilities by the net working capital. It indicates whether long-term obligations are in proper proportion to the net working capital, and normally, it should not exceed 1 (100%).

The Funded Liabilities to Net Working Capital ratio is:

$$\frac{21332555}{8627300} = 2.47$$

Because the value of this ratio exceeds 100%, either current assets are insufficient relative to current liabilities or current liabilities are too high relative to the current assets.

CHAPTER **15**

Formulas for Fast Answers to Trade and Cash Discounts

This chapter provides formulas that enable the determination of those elements which are important to purchasers of goods and the payment for those purchases. Within the text are one or more examples of the use of each formula. The examples include:

1. Determining a cost factor from a chain of discount rates. Page 255
2. Determining the actual cost from a list price where a chain discount series is in effect. Page 255
3. Determining the single equivalent discount rate for a chain discount series. Page 255
4. Determining the effect on cost when one or more rates are removed from a chain discount series. Page 255
5. Determining the net cost after a cash discount. Page 256
6. Determining the balance due after a partial payment when the cash discount applies to partial payments. Page 257
7. Determining the amount of a short-term loan in order to realize a cash discount. Page 257

If you perform the calculations in the examples, your results may differ from the indicated results, depending upon the number of decimal places you carry at each step of the solutions.

15.1   TRADE DISCOUNTS

Because trade discounts are not "real" discounts, a formula which gives *cost* directly from a *list price* is more appropriate than determining the discount and subtracting from the list price to obtain the cost. The nomenclature for trade discounts is as follows.

C—The cost to the purchaser.
d—A discount rate.
d_e—A single equivalent discount rate.
F—The cost factor.
r—The actual increase in cost when one or more discounts are removed from the "chain."
Π—The product of . . .

Chain Discounts, Cost Factor, and Cost

When an item is listed with a series of discounts, the discounts are referred to as chain discounts. Thus, a catalog may indicate the cost of an item as L, less d_1 %, d_2 %, d_3 %, ..., d_N %. In order to determine the actual cost directly, a cost factor F is defined by

$$F = \prod (1 - d_j) \qquad j = 1, 2, 3, \ldots, N \qquad (15.1\text{-}1)$$

Example 1. The cost factor is desired for an item which is listed as $600 less 25%, 20%, 15%, 10%, 10%, 5%, 5%. From Eq. (15.1-1),

$$F = (1 - 0.25)(1 - 0.20)(1 - 0.15)(1 - 0.10)(1 - 0.10)(1 - 0.05)(1 - 0.05)$$

$$= (0.75)(0.80)(0.85)(0.90)(0.90)(0.95)(0.95)$$

$$= 0.3728$$

Note: The *complement* of a number is the difference between the number and 1. Thus, the *cost factor* in a chain discount series is simply the *product of the discount rate complements*.

Cost

The cost of an item, subsequent to a chain discount series, is determined by

$$C = FL \qquad (15.1\text{-}2)$$

Example 2. The cost of the item in Example 1 is

$$C = (0.3728)(600) = \$223.68$$

Single Equivalent Discount Rate

The single equivalent discount rate is a rate that when it is applied to the list, gives the same trade discount as with the chain. It is determined by

$$d_e = 1 - F \quad (\times 100 \text{ for } \%) \qquad (15.1\text{-}3)$$

Example 3. The single equivalent discount rate of the chain in Example 1 is determined by Eq. (15.1-3) as

$$d_e = (1 - 0.3728) \times 100 = 62.72\%$$

As a check, a discount of 62.72% applied to a list of $600 is $376.32. Then, 600 − 376.32 = $223.68 as indicated in Example 2.

Rate of Cost Increase by Removal of Discount Rates from a Series

In order to increase the cost of an item relative to the same list price, when a chain discount series is in effect, one or more of the discount rates may be removed from the chain. The rate of increase in the cost can be determined by

$$r = \frac{1}{\prod (1 - d_k)} - 1 \quad (\times 100 \text{ for } \%) \qquad (15.1\text{-}4)$$

where the d_k are the rates which are *removed* from the chain.

Example 4. For the chain discount series in Example 1, 25%, 20%, 15%, 10%, 10%, 5%, 5%, it is desired to increase the cost of the item by approximately 20% by removing appropriate discounts from the chain. The actual increase in the cost can be determined by Eq. (15.1-4). Removing one 10% and two 5% rates gives a rate of cost increase as

$$r = \frac{1}{(1 - 0.10)(1 - 0.05)(1 - 0.05)} - 1$$

$$= \frac{1}{(0.90)(0.95)(0.95)} - 1$$

$$= 0.231148 = 23.1148\%$$

Removing the 15% rate and one 5% rate gives a rate of cost increase as

$$r = \frac{1}{(0.85)(0.95)} - 1 = 23.8390\%$$

Removing the two 10% rates gives a rate of cost increase as

$$r = \frac{1}{(0.90)(0.90)} - 1 = 23.4568\%$$

Removing the 20% rate gives a rate of cost increase as

$$r = \frac{1}{1 - 0.20} - 1 = 25\%$$

Thus, depending upon which combination of the discount rates is removed from the chain, the actual increase in the cost can range from 23.1148% to 25% for a nominal 20% increase.

15.2   CASH DISCOUNTS

When an invoice for purchased goods indicates a cash discount, and if the cash flow of the business is such that all or part of the cash discount can be lost, a partial payment can be made in order to realize part of the discount (if the terms of the invoice apply to partial payments) or a short-term loan for the net amount due can be secured in order to realize most of the discount. The nomenclature, in addition to that in Section 15.1, is as follows.

B—Balance due after a partial payment.
C_n—Net cost after a cash discount.
n—Number of days of a short-term loan.
P—Partial payment.
R—Interest (discount) rate for loans.
S—Amount of a short-term loan.

Net Cost

The net cost, after a cash discount, can be determined by

$$C_n = (1 - d) C \tag{15.2-1}$$

Example 1. An invoice for $30,000 with a cash discount of 2%, if paid within 10 days with the net due in 30 days, is to be paid on the 10th day. Then, net cost can be determined by Eq. (15.2-1) as

$$C_n = (1 - 0.02)(30000) = \$29,400$$

Thus, a cash discount of $600 is to be realized.

Balance Due After a Partial Payment

If a partial payment on an invoice, with cash discount terms, is credited with the cash discount, the balance due after a partial payment can be determined by

$$B = C - \frac{P}{1 - d} \qquad (15.2\text{-}2)$$

Example 2. The cash flow of the company in Example 1 is such that only $20,000 can be remitted by the 10th day. If the 2% cash discount applies to the partial payment, the balance due can be determined by Eq. (15.2-2) as

$$B = 30000 - \frac{20000}{1 - 0.02} = \$9,591.84$$

A Short-Term Loan in Order to Realize a Cash Discount

If a short-term loan is secured on the last day to which a cash discount applies, some of the cash discount will be realized—even with relatively high interest rates. The proceeds of such a loan must be the net cost. Then, the amount of the loan can be determined by

$$S = \frac{C_n}{1 - Rn/360} \qquad (15.2\text{-}3)$$

where R is a bank discount rate.

Example 3. The $29,400, needed on day 10 in Example 1, will not be available until the end of the month. In order to realize the $600 cash discount, a loan is negotiated on day 10 which is to be repaid on day 30 (a 20-day loan). The bank discount rate is 21%. The amount of the loan can be determined by Eq. (15.2-3) as

$$S = \frac{29400}{1 - (0.21)(20)/360} = \$29,747.05$$

The interest on the loan is $347.05 (29747.05 - 29400). The amount of realized cash discount is $252.95 (600 - 347.05).

CHAPTER 16

Formulas for Fast Answers to Markup on Cost and Selling Price

This chapter provides formulas that enable the determination of selling price when the markup is based on cost or selling price. Additionally, it provides formulas for the equivalence between markup rates based on cost and selling price and it provides a formula to determine a selling price per unit that will cover losses. Within the text are one or more examples of the use of each formula. The examples include:

If you perform the calculations in the examples, your results may differ from the indicated results, depending upon the number of decimal places you carry at each step of the solution.

16.1 MARKUP

The nomenclature for the formulas is as follows.

C—Net cost of an item.
d—Discount rate.
L—List price.
R_c—Markup rate based on cost.
R_s—Markup rate based on selling price.
R_e—Expense Rate.
R_p—Profit rate (before taxes).
S—Selling price of an item.
T—As a subscript, "Total."

Markup Based on Cost

When the expense rate and profit rate are both based on cost of goods, the markup rate is defined by

$$R_c = R_{ec} + R_{pc} \qquad\qquad (16.1\text{-}1)$$

and the selling price of an item can be determined by

$$S = (1 + R_c)\, C \qquad\qquad (16.1\text{-}2)$$

Example 1.   The direct cost of an item is \$200. The operating expenses of your company are 80% of the cost of goods sold. Your company has a policy that profit must be 15% of the cost of goods sold. The selling price of that item can be determined by Eqs. (16.1-1) and (16.1-2). $R_{ec} = 80\% = 0.80$, and $R_{pc} = 15\% = 0.15$. From Eq. (16.1-1)

$$R_c = 0.80 + 0.15 = 0.95$$

and from Eq. (16.1-2)

$$S = (1 + 0.95)(200) = \$390.00$$

Markup Based on Selling Price

When the expense rate and profit rate are both based on selling price, a direct determination of those elements can be made by knowing the total sales. The markup rate is defined by

$$R_s = R_{es} + R_{ps} \qquad\qquad (16.1\text{-}3)$$

and the selling price of an item can be determined by

$$S = \frac{C}{1 - R_s} \qquad R_s \neq 1 \qquad\qquad (16.1\text{-}4)$$

Example 2.   The direct cost of an item is \$200. The operating expenses of your company are 32% of sales and your pre-tax profits are to be 18% of sales. The selling price of that item can be determined by Eqs. (16.1-3) and (16.1-4). $R_{es} = 32\% = 0.32$, and $R_{ps} = 18\% = 0.18$. From Eq. (16.1-3)

$$R_s = 0.32 + 0.18 = 0.50$$

and from Eq. (16.1-4)

$$S = \frac{200}{1 - 0.50} = \$400.00$$

Establishing a List Price

If a trade discount (or an apparent discount) from a list price is to be offered, the list price of an item can be determined by the following.

I. *Markup is Based on Cost*

$$L = \frac{(1 + R_c)\,C}{1 - d} \qquad (16.1\text{-}5)$$

II. *Markup is Based on Selling Price*

$$L = \frac{C}{(1 - R_s)(1 - d)} \qquad (16.1\text{-}6)$$

Example 3. A 50% discount from a list price is to be offered on the item in Example 1. A list price is needed. From Example 1, $R_c = 95\%$ and $C = 200$. From Eq. (16.1-5)

$$L = \frac{(1.95)(200)}{1 - 0.50} = \$780.$$

Example 4. A 50% discount from a list price is to be offered on the item in Example 2. A list price is needed. From Example 2, $R_s = 50\%$ and $C = 200$. From Eq. (16.1-6)

$$L = \frac{200}{(0.50)\,(1 - 0.50)} = \$800$$

Equivalent Selling Price and Cost Markup Rates

The equivalence between markup rates which are based on cost and selling price can be determined by

$$R_s = \frac{R_c}{1 + R_c} \qquad (\times\ 100\ \text{for}\ \%) \qquad (16.1\text{-}7)$$

and

$$R_c = \frac{R_s}{1 - R_s} \qquad (\times\ 100\ \text{for}\ \%) \qquad (16.1\text{-}8)$$

Example 5. The markup rate, based on cost, in Example 1 is 95%. The markup rate, based on selling price, that is equivalent to this can be determined by Eq. (16.1-7).

$$R_s = \frac{0.95}{1.95} \times 100 = 48.72\%$$

Using this rate in Eq. (16.1-4) for Example 1 gives

$$S = \frac{200}{1 - 0.4872} = \$390.00^*$$

*Adjusted by 0.02 due to rounding of R_s.

Example 6. The markup rate, based on selling price, in Example 2 is 50%. The markup rate, based on cost, that is equivalent to this can be determined by Eq. (16.1-8).

$$R_c = \frac{0.50}{1 - 0.50} \times 100 = 100\%$$

Using this rate in Eq. (16.1-2) for Example 2 gives

$$S = (1 + 1)(200) = \$400.00$$

Selling Price to Cover Losses

In situations where the total quantity of an item cannot be sold at a price which is established by the markup policy of a company, a selling price which will return a desired markup rate can be established as follows. The necessary total sales revenue is:

I. *Markup Based on Cost*

$$S_T = (1 + R_c) C_T \qquad (16.1\text{-}9)$$

II. *Markup Based on Selling Price*

$$S_T = \frac{C_T}{1 - R_s} \qquad (16.1\text{-}10)$$

In general, the total sales revenue would be comprised of the sales revenue from the number of items which are sold at a "regular" price and the sales revenue from the number of items which are sold at reduced prices. The regular selling price that is required in order to cover expected losses, is:

$$S = \frac{S_T}{n + \sum n_j (1 - d_j)} \qquad (16.1\text{-}11)$$

where n is the number of items that will be sold at the regular selling price, and the subscript j represents the j-th reduced price.

Example 7. Your company is a retail business. It has just purchased 500 suits for a total cost of \$50,000. Experience has shown that 50% of the suits will be sold at the "regular" price, 30% of them will be sold at "1/3 OFF," 15% of them will be sold at "1/2 PRICE," and 5% of the suits will be unaccounted for. A "regular" price must be determined in order to return a 40% markup on cost. The numbers of suits that are expected to be sold at each price level are as follows:

At regular selling price:	$n = (0.50)(500) = 250$	
At 1/3 OFF:	$n_1 = (0.30)(500) = 150;$	$d_1 = 1/3$
At 1/2 PRICE:	$n_2 = (0.15)(500) = 75;$	$d_2 = 1/2$
Unaccounted for:	$n_3 = (0.05)(500) = 25;$	$d_3 = 1$

The actual total sales revenue that is necessary can be determined by Eq. (16.1-9) with $R_c = 40\% = 0.40$.

$$S_T = (1.40)(50000) = \$70,000$$

Then:

$$n_1 (1 - d_1) = (150)(1 - 1/3) = 100$$

$$n_2 (1 - d_2) = (75)(1 - 1/2) = 38$$

$$n_3 (1 - d_3) = (25)(1 - 1) = 0$$

Summation of $n_j (1 - d_j) = 138$.

The regular selling price per suit can be determined by Eq. (16.1-11) as

$$S = \frac{70000}{250 + 138} = \$180.41$$

Note: The indicated selling price per suit is $140, obtained by dividing $70,000 by 500 suits. In order to cover the losses, the selling prices as indicated in this example return $70,000, as policy required. The arithmetic is as follows:

$$
\begin{aligned}
(250)(180.41) &= \$45,102.50 \\
(150)(2/3)(180.41) &= 18,041.00 \\
(75)(1/2)(180.41) &= \underline{6,765.38} \\
& \$69,908.88
\end{aligned}
$$

The $91.12 discrepancy is due to rounding (75)(0.5) to 38.

Had the 40% markup been based on selling price, S_T would be determined by Eq. (16.1-10) as $83,333.33. From Eq. (16.1-11), the selling price per suit would be

$$S = \frac{83333.33}{388} = \$214.78$$

CHAPTER 17

How to Use Formulas to Determine
an Average and Its
Representation of the Data

The subject of statistics, especially inferential statistics, is too extensive for a handbook of this nature. Therefore, this chapter provides formulas to determine four basic measures of central tendency—the average (mean), the standard deviation, the median, and the mode. These measures are determined for raw data and grouped data. Within the text are one or more examples of the use of each formula. The examples include:

1. Determining the average and standard deviation of raw data. Page 263 (below)
2. Determining the average and standard deviation of grouped data. Page 265
3. Determining the median of grouped data. Page 266
4. Determining the modal group of grouped data. Page 266.

If you perform the calculations in the examples, your results may differ from the indicated results, depending upon the number of decimal places you carry at each step of the solutions.

17.1   THE CENTRAL TENDENCY OF RAW DATA

The nomenclature for the measures of central tendency is:

N—Number of values in a sample.
s—Standard Deviation.
x—Raw statistic.
$\bar{x}$—Average (mean)

The Average and Standard Deviation

With a set of raw data, the average can be determined by

$$\bar{x} = \frac{\sum x_i}{N}$$

(17.1-1)

and the standard deviation can be determined by

$$s = \sqrt{\frac{\sum x_i - N\bar{x}^2}{N - 1}} \qquad (17.1\text{-}2)$$

A small standard deviation signifies that the data is grouped closely around the average and gives strong credibility to the average. As a "rule of thumb," if approximately:

1. 68% of the data is within $\bar{x} - s$ and $\bar{x} + s$,
2. 95% of the data is within $\bar{x} - 2s$ and $\bar{x} + 2s$,
3. 100% of the data is within $\bar{x} - 3s$ and $\bar{x} + 3s$,

or if s is approximately 0, the average can be considered to be representative of the data.

Example 1.   The average and standard deviation of the following set of raw data is desired. The 30 individual values and their respective squares are tabulated.

x	x^2	x	x^2	x	x^2
13.0	169.00	11.3	127.69	14.3	204.49
12.3	151.29	13.2	174.24	11.2	125.44
10.5	110.25	13.1	171.61	13.5	182.25
12.9	166.41	13.0	169.00	13.7	187.69
14.4	207.36	12.0	144.00	11.7	136.89
10.2	104.04	9.4	88.36	10.1	102.01
13.6	184.96	11.7	136.89	14.9	222.01
15.5	240.25	11.9	141.61	13.2	174.24
11.6	134.56	12.6	158.76	10.0	100.00
14.7	216.09	13.5	182.25	10.8	116.64

$$\sum x_i = 373.8$$

$$\sum x_i^2 = 4730.28$$

From Eq. (17.1-1),

$$\bar{x} = \frac{373.8}{30} = 12.46$$

From Eq. (17.1-2),

$$s = \sqrt{\frac{4730.28 - (30)(12.46)^2}{29}} = 1.58$$

From the test for representation:

1. Between 10.88 (12.46 − 1.58) and 14.04 (12.46 + 1.58) are 21 values or 70%.
2. Between 9.3 and 15.62 are 30 values or 100% ($\bar{x} \pm 2s$).

Therefore, this average may be considered as representative of the data.

The Median and Mode

In the order to determine the median, the data must be arranged in ascending or descending order. The value which is exactly in the middle is the median. The mode is that value which occurs most frequently.

For raw data, the time and effort necessary to sort the data may not be worth the results. If a computer is available, a sort routine can be programmed to accomplish the arrangement. For manual efforts, a grouping of the data simplifies the determination of the median and mode.

17.2   THE CENTRAL TENDENCY OF GROUPED DATA

The nomenclature, in addition to that in Section 17.1, for grouped data is as follows.

f—Number of values in each group (frequency of occurrence).
L—Lower boundary of median group.
n—Number of values from median group that is necessary to reach the median.
m—Median value.
M—Mid-point of each group.
f_m—Number of values in the median group.
W—Width of each group.

In order to determine the measures of central tendency, the raw data would be grouped in a convenient number of groups.

The Average and Standard Deviation

For grouped data, the average can be determined by

$$\bar{x} = \frac{\sum f_i M_i}{N} \tag{17.2-1}$$

and the standard deviation can be determined by

$$s = \sqrt{\frac{\sum f_i M_i^2 - N\bar{x}^2}{N - 1}} \tag{17.2-2}$$

Example 1.   With groups from 9–10, 10–11, 11–12, 12–13, 13–14, 14–15, and 15–16, the average and standard deviation are desired. It is stipulated that the upper boundary of each group belongs to the group to the right. A "tally" of the raw data in Example 1 of Section 17.1 shows the following.

Group	Frequency	Mid-point	fM	fM^2
9–10	1	9.5	9.5	90.25
10–11	5	10.5	52.5	551.25
11–12	6	11.5	69.0	793.50
12–13	4	12.5	50.0	625.00
13–14	9	13.5	121.5	1640.25
14–15	4	14.5	58.0	841.00
15–16	1	15.5	15.5	240.25
			376.0	4781.5

$$\sum f_i M_i = 376$$

$$\sum f_i M_i^2 = 4781.50$$

From Eq. (17.2-1)

$$\bar{x} = \frac{376}{30} = 12.53$$

From Eq. (17.2-2)

$$s = \sqrt{\frac{4781.50 - (30)(12.53)^2}{29}} = 1.57$$

The errors caused by grouping the data, relative to the average and standard deviation in Example 1, are approximately 0.6%. The average plus and minus one standard deviation is a spread between 10.96 and 14.1. Considering all group values to be at the mid-point of each group, the range to be used is between 11 and 14.5 in which there are 23 (77%) values. This indicates that the average is representative of the data.

The Median

The median score is the (N/2)th value. Then, the median can be determined by determining the median group and,

$$m = L + \frac{n}{f_m} W \qquad (17.2\text{-}3)$$

Example 2. The median value of Example 1 can be determined as follows. There are 30 values, therefore, the median value is the 15th (30/2) value. Counting from the lowest group, the 15th value occurs in the group 12–13. The number of values to the lower boundary of the median group is 12 (1 + 5 + 6). Then, the number of values of the median group that are needed to reach 15 is 3. From the given information,

$$W = 1$$
$$L = 12$$
$$n = 3$$
$$f_m = 4$$

and from Eq. (17.2-3)

$$m = 12 + \frac{3}{4}(1) = 12.75$$

Thus, half the values are above and half are below 12.75. A check of the raw data of Example 1 in Section 17.1 shows that this value is "exact" (that is 15 values are above 12.75). This degree of exactness cannot always be expected.

The Mode

The mode is the most frequently occurring value. In grouped data the modal group is the group with the most values. In Example, 1, the modal group is 13–14.

APPENDIX

TABLE A-1

JULIAN DATES

DAY OF MONTH	JAN	FEB	MAR	APR	MAY	JUNE	JULY	AUG	SEPT	OCT	NOV	DEC	DAY OF MONTH
1	1	32	60	91	121	152	182	213	244	274	305	335	1
2	2	33	61	92	122	153	183	214	245	275	306	336	2
3	3	34	62	93	123	154	184	215	246	276	307	337	3
4	4	35	63	94	124	155	185	216	247	277	308	338	4
5	5	36	64	95	125	156	186	217	248	278	309	339	5
6	6	37	65	96	126	157	187	218	249	279	310	340	6
7	7	38	66	97	127	158	188	219	250	280	311	341	7
8	8	39	67	98	128	159	189	220	251	281	312	342	8
9	9	40	68	99	129	160	190	221	252	282	313	343	9
10	10	41	69	100	130	161	191	222	253	283	314	344	10
11	11	42	70	101	131	162	192	223	254	284	315	345	11
12	12	43	71	102	132	163	193	224	255	285	316	346	12
13	13	44	72	103	133	164	194	225	256	286	317	347	13
14	14	45	73	104	134	165	195	226	257	287	318	348	14
15	15	46	74	105	135	166	196	227	258	288	319	349	15
16	16	47	75	106	136	167	197	228	259	289	320	350	16
17	17	48	76	107	137	168	198	229	260	290	321	351	17
18	18	49	77	108	138	169	199	230	261	291	322	352	18
19	19	50	78	109	139	170	200	231	262	292	323	353	19
20	20	51	79	110	140	171	201	232	263	293	324	354	20
21	21	52	80	111	141	172	202	233	264	294	325	355	21
22	22	53	81	112	142	173	203	234	265	295	326	356	22
23	23	54	82	113	143	174	204	235	266	296	327	357	23
24	24	55	83	114	144	175	205	236	267	297	328	358	24
25	25	56	84	115	145	176	206	237	268	298	329	359	25
26	26	57	85	116	146	177	207	238	269	299	330	360	26
27	27	58	86	117	147	178	208	239	270	300	331	361	27
28	28	59	87	118	148	179	209	240	271	301	332	362	28
29	29		88	119	149	180	210	241	272	302	333	363	29
30	30		89	120	150	181	211	242	273	303	334	364	30
31	31		90		151		212	243		304		365	31

NOTE: ADD 1 TO EACH DATE AFTER FEB 28 IN LEAP YEARS.

TABLE A-2

COMPOUND INTEREST FOR $1

$\frac{5}{12}$ %

PERIODS n	FUTURE AMOUNT $(1+i)^n$	PRESENT VALUE $(1+i)^{-n}$	AMOUNT OF ANNUITY (S/p,i,n) $\frac{(1+i)^n - 1}{i}$	SINKING FUND (p/S,i,n) $\frac{i}{(1+i)^n - 1}$	PRESENT VALUE OF ANNUITY (V/p,i,n) $\frac{1-(1+i)^{-n}}{i}$	AMORTIZATION (p/V,i,n) $\frac{i}{1-(1+i)^{-n}}$	PERIODS n
1	1.00416667	0.99585062	1.00000000	1.00000000	0.99585062	1.00416667	1
2	1.00835069	0.99171846	2.00416667	0.49896050	1.98756908	0.50312717	2
3	1.01255216	0.98760345	3.01251736	0.33194829	2.97517253	0.33611496	3
4	1.01677112	0.98350551	4.02506952	0.24844291	3.95867804	0.25260958	4
5	1.02100767	0.97942457	5.04184064	0.19834026	4.93810261	0.20250693	5
6	1.02526187	0.97536057	6.06284831	0.16493898	5.91346318	0.16910564	6
7	1.02953379	0.97131343	7.08811018	0.14108133	6.88477661	0.14524800	7
8	1.03382352	0.96728308	8.11764397	0.12318845	7.85205970	0.12735512	8
9	1.03813111	0.96326946	9.15146749	0.10927209	8.81532916	0.11343876	9
10	1.04245666	0.95927249	10.18959860	0.09813929	9.77460165	0.10230596	10
11	1.04680023	0.95529211	11.23205526	0.08903090	10.72989376	0.09319757	11
12	1.05116190	0.95132824	12.27885549	0.08144082	11.68122200	0.08560748	12
13	1.05554174	0.94738082	13.33001739	0.07501866	12.62860283	0.07918532	13
14	1.05993983	0.94344978	14.38555913	0.06951416	13.57205261	0.07368082	14
15	1.06435625	0.93953505	15.44549896	0.06474378	14.51158766	0.06891045	15
16	1.06879106	0.93563657	16.50985520	0.06056988	15.44722422	0.06473655	16
17	1.07324436	0.93175426	17.57864627	0.05688720	16.37897848	0.06105387	17
18	1.07771621	0.92788806	18.65189063	0.05361387	17.30686654	0.05778053	18
19	1.08220670	0.92403790	19.72960684	0.05068525	18.23090443	0.05485191	19
20	1.08671589	0.92020372	20.81181353	0.04804963	19.15110815	0.05221630	20
21	1.09124387	0.91638544	21.89852942	0.04566517	20.06749359	0.04983183	21
22	1.09579072	0.91258301	22.98977330	0.04349760	20.98007661	0.04766427	22
23	1.10035652	0.90879636	24.08556402	0.04151865	21.88887297	0.04568531	23
24	1.10494134	0.90502542	25.18592053	0.03970472	22.79389839	0.04387139	24
25	1.10954526	0.90127013	26.29086187	0.03803603	23.69516853	0.04220270	25
26	1.11416836	0.89753042	27.40040713	0.03649581	24.59269895	0.04066247	26
27	1.11881073	0.89380623	28.51457549	0.03506978	25.48650517	0.03923645	27
28	1.12347244	0.89009749	29.63338622	0.03374572	26.37660266	0.03791239	28
29	1.12815358	0.88640414	30.75685866	0.03251307	27.26300680	0.03667974	29
30	1.13285422	0.88272611	31.88501224	0.03136270	28.14573291	0.03552936	30
31	1.13757444	0.87906335	33.01786646	0.03028663	29.02479626	0.03445330	31
32	1.14231434	0.87541578	34.15544090	0.02927791	29.90021205	0.03344458	32
33	1.14707398	0.87178335	35.29775524	0.02833041	30.77199540	0.03249708	33
34	1.15185346	0.86816599	36.44482922	0.02743873	31.64016139	0.03160540	34
35	1.15665284	0.86456365	37.59668268	0.02659809	32.50472504	0.03076476	35
36	1.16147223	0.86097624	38.75333552	0.02580423	33.36570128	0.02997090	36
37	1.16631170	0.85740373	39.91480775	0.02505336	34.22310501	0.02922003	37
38	1.17117133	0.85384604	41.08111945	0.02434208	35.07695105	0.02850875	38
39	1.17605121	0.85030311	42.25229078	0.02366736	35.92725416	0.02783402	39
40	1.18095142	0.84677488	43.42834199	0.02302644	36.77402904	0.02719310	40

TABLE A-2

COMPOUND INTEREST FOR $1

$\frac{5}{12}$ %

PERIODS n	FUTURE AMOUNT $(1+i)^n$	PRESENT VALUE $(1+i)^{-n}$	AMOUNT OF ANNUITY $(S/p,i,n)$ $\dfrac{(1+i)^n - 1}{i}$	SINKING FUND $(p/S,i,n)$ $\dfrac{i}{(1+i)^n - 1}$	PRESENT VALUE OF ANNUITY $(V/p,i,n)$ $\dfrac{1-(1+i)^{-n}}{i}$	AMORTIZATION $(p/V,i,n)$ $\dfrac{i}{1-(1+i)^{-n}}$	PERIODS n
41	1.18587206	0.84326129	44.60929342	0.02241685	37.61729033	0.02658352	41
42	1.19081319	0.83976228	45.79516547	0.02183637	38.45705261	0.02600303	42
43	1.19577491	0.83627779	46.98597866	0.02128295	39.29333040	0.02544961	43
44	1.20075731	0.83280776	48.18175357	0.02075474	40.12613816	0.02492141	44
45	1.20576046	0.82935212	49.38251088	0.02025008	40.95549028	0.02441675	45
46	1.21078446	0.82591083	50.58827134	0.01976743	41.78140111	0.02393409	46
47	1.21582940	0.82248381	51.79905581	0.01930537	42.60388492	0.02347204	47
48	1.22089536	0.81907102	53.01488521	0.01886263	43.42295594	0.02302929	48
49	1.22598242	0.81567238	54.23578056	0.01843801	44.23862832	0.02260468	49
50	1.23109068	0.81228785	55.46176298	0.01803044	45.05091617	0.02219711	50
51	1.23622022	0.80891736	56.69285366	0.01763891	45.85983353	0.02180557	51
52	1.24137114	0.80556086	57.92907388	0.01726249	46.66539439	0.02142916	52
53	1.24654352	0.80221828	59.17044502	0.01690033	47.46761267	0.02106700	53
54	1.25173745	0.79888957	60.41698854	0.01655164	48.26650224	0.02071830	54
55	1.25695302	0.79557468	61.66872600	0.01621567	49.06207692	0.02038234	55
56	1.26219033	0.79227354	62.92567902	0.01589176	49.85435046	0.02005843	56
57	1.26744946	0.78898610	64.18786935	0.01557927	50.64333656	0.01974593	57
58	1.27273050	0.78571230	65.45531881	0.01527760	51.42904885	0.01944426	58
59	1.27803354	0.78245208	66.72804930	0.01498620	52.21150093	0.01915287	59
60	1.28335868	0.77920539	68.00608284	0.01470457	52.99070632	0.01887123	60
61	1.28870601	0.77597217	69.28944152	0.01443221	53.76667850	0.01859888	61
62	1.29407561	0.77275237	70.57814753	0.01416869	54.53943087	0.01833536	62
63	1.29946760	0.76954593	71.87222314	0.01391358	55.30897680	0.01808025	63
64	1.30488204	0.76635279	73.17169074	0.01366649	56.07532959	0.01783315	64
65	1.31031905	0.76317291	74.47657278	0.01342704	56.83850250	0.01759371	65
66	1.31577872	0.76000621	75.78689183	0.01319489	57.59850871	0.01736156	66
67	1.32126113	0.75685266	77.10267055	0.01296972	58.35536137	0.01713639	67
68	1.32676638	0.75371219	78.42393168	0.01275121	59.10907357	0.01691788	68
69	1.33229458	0.75058476	79.75069806	0.01253908	59.85965832	0.01670574	69
70	1.33784580	0.74747030	81.08299264	0.01233304	60.60712862	0.01649971	70
71	1.34342016	0.74436876	82.42083844	0.01213285	61.35149738	0.01629952	71
72	1.34901774	0.74128009	83.76425860	0.01193827	62.09277748	0.01610493	72
73	1.35463865	0.73820424	85.11327634	0.01174905	62.83098172	0.01591572	73
74	1.36028298	0.73514115	86.46791499	0.01156498	63.56612287	0.01573165	74
75	1.36595082	0.73209078	87.82819797	0.01138586	64.29821365	0.01555253	75
76	1.37164229	0.72905306	89.19414880	0.01121150	65.02726670	0.01537816	76
77	1.37735746	0.72602794	90.56579108	0.01104170	65.75329464	0.01520836	77
78	1.38309645	0.72301537	91.94314855	0.01087629	66.47631002	0.01504295	78
79	1.38885935	0.72001531	93.32624500	0.01071510	67.19632533	0.01488177	79
80	1.39464627	0.71702770	94.71510435	0.01055798	67.91335303	0.01472464	80

PERIODS n	FUTURE AMOUNT $(1+i)^n$	PRESENT VALUE $(1+i)^{-n}$	AMOUNT OF ANNUITY (S/p,i,n) $\frac{(1+i)^n-1}{i}$	SINKING FUND (p/S,i,n) $\frac{i}{(1+i)^n-1}$	PRESENT VALUE OF ANNUITY (V/p,i,n) $\frac{1-(1+i)^{-n}}{i}$	AMORTIZATION (p/V,i,n) $\frac{i}{1-(1+i)^{-n}}$	PERIODS n
81	1.40045729	0.71405248	96.10975062	0.01040477	68.62740550	0.01457144	81
82	1.40629253	0.71108960	97.51020792	0.01025534	69.33849511	0.01442200	82
83	1.41215209	0.70813902	98.91650045	0.01010954	70.04663413	0.01427620	83
84	1.41803605	0.70520069	100.32865253	0.00996724	70.75183482	0.01413391	84
85	1.42394454	0.70227454	101.74668859	0.00982833	71.45410936	0.01399500	85
86	1.42987764	0.69936054	103.17063312	0.00969268	72.15346991	0.01385935	86
87	1.43583546	0.69645863	104.60051076	0.00956018	72.84992854	0.01372685	87
88	1.44181811	0.69356876	106.03634622	0.00943073	73.54349730	0.01359740	88
89	1.44782568	0.69069088	107.47816433	0.00930422	74.23418818	0.01347088	89
90	1.45385829	0.68782495	108.92599002	0.00918055	74.92201313	0.01334721	90
91	1.45991603	0.68497090	110.37984831	0.00905962	75.60698403	0.01322629	91
92	1.46599902	0.68212870	111.83976434	0.00894136	76.28911272	0.01310803	92
93	1.47210735	0.67929829	113.30576336	0.00882568	76.96841101	0.01299234	93
94	1.47824113	0.67647962	114.77787071	0.00871248	77.64489063	0.01287915	94
95	1.48440047	0.67367265	116.25611184	0.00860170	78.31856329	0.01276836	95
96	1.49058547	0.67087733	117.74051230	0.00849325	78.98944062	0.01265992	96
97	1.49679624	0.66809361	119.23109777	0.00838707	79.65753422	0.01255374	97
98	1.50303289	0.66532143	120.72789401	0.00828309	80.32285566	0.01244976	98
99	1.50929553	0.66256076	122.23092690	0.00818124	80.98541642	0.01234790	99
100	1.51558426	0.65981155	123.74022243	0.00808145	81.64522797	0.01224811	100
101	1.52189919	0.65707374	125.25580669	0.00798366	82.30230172	0.01215033	101
102	1.52824044	0.65434730	126.77770589	0.00788782	82.95664901	0.01205449	102
103	1.53460811	0.65163216	128.30594633	0.00779387	83.60828117	0.01196054	103
104	1.54100231	0.64892829	129.84055444	0.00770175	84.25720947	0.01186842	104
105	1.54742315	0.64623565	131.38155675	0.00761142	84.90344511	0.01177809	105
106	1.55387075	0.64355417	132.92897990	0.00752281	85.54699928	0.01168948	106
107	1.56034521	0.64088382	134.48285065	0.00743589	86.18788310	0.01160256	107
108	1.56684665	0.63822455	136.04319586	0.00735061	86.82610765	0.01151727	108
109	1.57337518	0.63557632	137.61004251	0.00726691	87.46168397	0.01143358	109
110	1.57993091	0.63293907	139.18341769	0.00718476	88.09462304	0.01135143	110
111	1.58651395	0.63031277	140.76334859	0.00710412	88.72493581	0.01127079	111
112	1.59312443	0.62769736	142.34986255	0.00702495	89.35263317	0.01119161	112
113	1.59976245	0.62509281	143.94298697	0.00694720	89.97772598	0.01111386	113
114	1.60642812	0.62249906	145.54274942	0.00687083	90.60022504	0.01103750	114
115	1.61312157	0.61991608	147.14917754	0.00679582	91.22014112	0.01096249	115
116	1.61984291	0.61734381	148.76229911	0.00672213	91.83748493	0.01088880	116
117	1.62659226	0.61478222	150.38214203	0.00664973	92.45226715	0.01081639	117
118	1.63336973	0.61223126	152.00873429	0.00657857	93.06449841	0.01074524	118
119	1.64017543	0.60969088	153.64210401	0.00650863	93.67418929	0.01067530	119
120	1.64700950	0.60716104	155.28227945	0.00643988	94.28135033	0.01060655	120

TABLE A-2

COMPOUND INTEREST FOR $1

$\frac{5}{12}\%$

PERIODS n	FUTURE AMOUNT $(1+i)^n$	PRESENT VALUE $(1+i)^{-n}$	AMOUNT OF ANNUITY $(S/p,i,n)$ $\dfrac{(1+i)^n-1}{i}$	SINKING FUND $(p/S,i,n)$ $\dfrac{i}{(1+i)^n-1}$	PRESENT VALUE OF ANNUITY $(V/p,i,n)$ $\dfrac{1-(1+i)^{-n}}{i}$	AMORTIZATION $(p/V,i,n)$ $\dfrac{i}{1-(1+i)^{-n}}$	PERIODS n
121	1.65387204	0.60464170	156.92928894	0.00637230	94.88599203	0.01053896	121
122	1.66076317	0.60213281	158.58316098	0.00630584	95.48812484	0.01047251	122
123	1.66768302	0.59963434	160.24392415	0.00624049	96.08775918	0.01040715	123
124	1.67463170	0.59714623	161.91160717	0.00617621	96.68490541	0.01034288	124
125	1.68160933	0.59466844	163.58623887	0.00611298	97.27957385	0.01027965	125
126	1.68861603	0.59220094	165.26784819	0.00605078	97.87177479	0.01021745	126
127	1.69565193	0.58974367	166.95646423	0.00598959	98.46151846	0.01015625	127
128	1.70271715	0.58729660	168.65211616	0.00592937	99.04881506	0.01009603	128
129	1.70981181	0.58485969	170.35483331	0.00587010	99.63367475	0.01003677	129
130	1.71693602	0.58243288	172.06464512	0.00581177	100.21610764	0.00997844	130
131	1.72408992	0.58001615	173.78158114	0.00575435	100.79612379	0.00992102	131
132	1.73127363	0.57760944	175.50567106	0.00569782	101.37373323	0.00986449	132
133	1.73848727	0.57521273	177.23694469	0.00564216	101.94894596	0.00980883	133
134	1.74573097	0.57282595	178.97543196	0.00558736	102.52177191	0.00975403	134
135	1.75300485	0.57044908	180.72116293	0.00553339	103.09222099	0.00970005	135
136	1.76030903	0.56808207	182.47416772	0.00548023	103.66030306	0.00964689	136
137	1.76764365	0.56572488	184.23447680	0.00542787	104.22602794	0.00959453	137
138	1.77500884	0.56337748	186.00212046	0.00537628	104.78940542	0.00954295	138
139	1.78240471	0.56103981	187.77712929	0.00532546	105.35044523	0.00949213	139
140	1.78983139	0.55871185	189.55953400	0.00527539	105.90915708	0.00944205	140
141	1.79728902	0.55639354	191.34936539	0.00522604	106.46555061	0.00939271	141
142	1.80477773	0.55408485	193.14665441	0.00517741	107.01963547	0.00934408	142
143	1.81229763	0.55178574	194.95143214	0.00512948	107.57142121	0.00929615	143
144	1.81984887	0.54949618	196.76372977	0.00508224	108.12091739	0.00924890	144
145	1.82743158	0.54721611	198.58357865	0.00503566	108.66813350	0.00920233	145
146	1.83504588	0.54494550	200.41101022	0.00498975	109.21307900	0.00915641	146
147	1.84269190	0.54268432	202.24605610	0.00494447	109.75576332	0.00911114	147
148	1.85036978	0.54043252	204.08874800	0.00489983	110.29619584	0.00906650	148
149	1.85807966	0.53819006	205.93911778	0.00485580	110.83438590	0.00902247	149
150	1.86582166	0.53595690	207.79719744	0.00481238	111.37034280	0.00897905	150
151	1.87359591	0.53373302	209.66301910	0.00476956	111.90407582	0.00893623	151
152	1.88140256	0.53151836	211.53661501	0.00472731	112.43559418	0.00889398	152
153	1.88924174	0.52931289	213.41801757	0.00468564	112.96490707	0.00885231	153
154	1.89711358	0.52711657	215.30725931	0.00464453	113.49202364	0.00881119	154
155	1.90501822	0.52492936	217.20437289	0.00460396	114.01695300	0.00877063	155
156	1.91295580	0.52275123	219.10939111	0.00456393	114.53970423	0.00873060	156
157	1.92092645	0.52058214	221.02234691	0.00452443	115.06028637	0.00869110	157
158	1.92893031	0.51842205	222.94327336	0.00448545	115.57870842	0.00865211	158
159	1.93696752	0.51627092	224.87220366	0.00444697	116.09497934	0.00861364	159
160	1.94503821	0.51412872	226.80917118	0.00440899	116.60910805	0.00857566	160

TABLE A-2

COMPOUND INTEREST FOR $1

$\frac{5}{12}$ %

PERIODS n	FUTURE AMOUNT $(1+i)^n$	PRESENT VALUE $(1+i)^{-n}$	AMOUNT OF ANNUITY $(S/p,i,n)$ $\dfrac{(1+i)^n - 1}{i}$	SINKING FUND $(p/S,i,n)$ $\dfrac{i}{(1+i)^n - 1}$	PRESENT VALUE OF ANNUITY $(V/p,i,n)$ $\dfrac{1-(1+i)^{-n}}{i}$	AMORTIZATION $(p/V,i,n)$ $\dfrac{i}{1-(1+i)^{-n}}$	PERIODS n
161	1.95314254	0.511199540	228.75420939	0.00437150	117.12110346	0.00853817	161
162	1.96128063	0.50987094	230.70735193	0.00433450	117.63097440	0.00850116	162
163	1.96945264	0.50775529	232.66863256	0.00429796	118.13872969	0.00846462	163
164	1.97765869	0.50564842	234.63808520	0.00426188	118.64437811	0.00842855	164
165	1.98589893	0.50355030	236.61574389	0.00422626	119.14792841	0.00839293	165
166	1.99417351	0.50146088	238.60164282	0.00419109	119.64938929	0.00835775	166
167	2.00248257	0.49938013	240.59581633	0.00415635	120.14876942	0.00832301	167
168	2.01082625	0.49730801	242.59829890	0.00412204	120.64607743	0.00828871	168
169	2.01920469	0.49524449	244.60912514	0.00408815	121.14132192	0.00825482	169
170	2.02761804	0.49318954	246.62832983	0.00405468	121.63451146	0.00822135	170
171	2.03606645	0.49114311	248.65594787	0.00402162	122.12565456	0.00818829	171
172	2.04455006	0.48910517	250.69201432	0.00398896	122.61475973	0.00815563	172
173	2.05306902	0.48707569	252.73656438	0.00395669	123.10183542	0.00812336	173
174	2.06162347	0.48505462	254.78963340	0.00392481	123.58689004	0.00809147	174
175	2.07021357	0.48304195	256.85125687	0.00389330	124.06993199	0.00805997	175
176	2.07883946	0.48103763	258.92147044	0.00386217	124.55096962	0.00802884	176
177	2.08750129	0.47904162	261.00030990	0.00383141	125.03001124	0.00799808	177
178	2.09619921	0.47705390	263.08781120	0.00380101	125.50706513	0.00796768	178
179	2.10493338	0.47507442	265.18401041	0.00377097	125.98213955	0.00793763	179
180	2.11370393	0.47310316	267.28894379	0.00374127	126.45524271	0.00790794	180
181	2.12251103	0.47114007	269.40264772	0.00371192	126.92638278	0.00787858	181
182	2.13135483	0.46918513	271.52515875	0.00368290	127.39556791	0.00784957	182
183	2.14023547	0.46723831	273.65651358	0.00365422	127.86280622	0.00782088	183
184	2.14915312	0.46529956	275.79674905	0.00362586	128.32810578	0.00779253	184
185	2.15810793	0.46336886	277.94590217	0.00359782	128.79147463	0.00776449	185
186	2.16710004	0.46144616	280.10401010	0.00357010	129.25292080	0.00773677	186
187	2.17612963	0.45953145	282.27111014	0.00354269	129.71245225	0.00770936	187
188	2.18519683	0.45762468	284.44723977	0.00351559	130.17007693	0.00768226	188
189	2.19430182	0.45572582	286.63243660	0.00348879	130.62580275	0.00765546	189
190	2.20344474	0.45383484	288.82673842	0.00346228	131.07963759	0.00762895	190
191	2.21262576	0.45195171	291.03018316	0.00343607	131.53158930	0.00760274	191
192	2.22184504	0.45007639	293.24280892	0.00341014	131.98166570	0.00757681	192
193	2.23110272	0.44820886	295.46465396	0.00338450	132.42987455	0.00755117	193
194	2.24039899	0.44634907	297.69575669	0.00335913	132.87622362	0.00752580	194
195	2.24973398	0.44449700	299.93615567	0.00333404	133.32072062	0.00750071	195
196	2.25910787	0.44265261	302.18588965	0.00330922	133.76337323	0.00747589	196
197	2.26852082	0.44081588	304.44499753	0.00328467	134.20418911	0.00745133	197
198	2.27797299	0.43898677	306.71351835	0.00326037	134.64317587	0.00742704	198
199	2.28746455	0.43716525	308.99149134	0.00323634	135.08034112	0.00740300	199
200	2.29699565	0.43535128	311.27895589	0.00321255	135.51569240	0.00737922	200

273

TABLE A-2

COMPOUND INTEREST FOR $1

$\frac{5}{12}$ %

PERIODS n	FUTURE AMOUNT $(1+i)^n$	PRESENT VALUE $(1+i)^{-n}$	AMOUNT OF ANNUITY $(S/p,i,n)$ $\dfrac{(1+i)^n-1}{i}$	SINKING FUND $(p/S,i,n)$ $\dfrac{i}{(1+i)^n-1}$	PRESENT VALUE OF ANNUITY $(V/p,i,n)$ $\dfrac{1-(1+i)^{-n}}{i}$	AMORTIZATION $(p/V,i,n)$ $\dfrac{i}{1-(1+i)^{-n}}$	PERIODS n
201	2.30656646	0.43354484	313.57595154	0.00318902	135.94923725	0.00735569	201
202	2.31617716	0.43174590	315.88251801	0.00316573	136.38098315	0.00733240	202
203	2.32582790	0.42995443	318.19869516	0.00314269	136.81093758	0.00730936	203
204	2.33551885	0.42817038	320.52452306	0.00311989	137.23910796	0.00728655	204
205	2.34525017	0.42639374	322.86004191	0.00309732	137.66550170	0.00726398	205
206	2.35502205	0.42462447	325.20529208	0.00307498	138.09012618	0.00724165	206
207	2.36483464	0.42286255	327.56031413	0.00305287	138.51298872	0.00721954	207
208	2.37468812	0.42110793	329.92514877	0.00303099	138.93409665	0.00719766	208
209	2.38458265	0.41936059	332.29983689	0.00300933	139.35345725	0.00717600	209
210	2.39451841	0.41762051	334.68441955	0.00298789	139.77107776	0.00715456	210
211	2.40449557	0.41588764	337.07893796	0.00296666	140.18696540	0.00713333	211
212	2.41451431	0.41416197	339.48343354	0.00294565	140.60112737	0.00711232	212
213	2.42457478	0.41244345	341.89794784	0.00292485	141.01357083	0.00709152	213
214	2.43467718	0.41073207	344.32252263	0.00290425	141.42430290	0.00707092	214
215	2.44482167	0.40902779	346.75719980	0.00288386	141.83333069	0.00705053	215
216	2.45500842	0.40733058	349.20202147	0.00286367	142.24066127	0.00703034	216
217	2.46523762	0.40564041	351.65702989	0.00284368	142.64630167	0.00701035	217
218	2.47550945	0.40395725	354.12226752	0.00282388	143.05025893	0.00699055	218
219	2.48582407	0.40228108	356.59777696	0.00280428	143.45254001	0.00697095	219
220	2.49618167	0.40061187	359.08360104	0.00278487	143.85315188	0.00695153	220
221	2.50658243	0.39894958	361.57978271	0.00276564	144.25210146	0.00693231	221
222	2.51702652	0.39729418	364.08636513	0.00274660	144.64939564	0.00691327	222
223	2.52751413	0.39564566	366.60339166	0.00272774	145.04504130	0.00689441	223
224	2.53804544	0.39400398	369.13090579	0.00270907	145.43904528	0.00687573	224
225	2.54862063	0.39236911	371.66895123	0.00269057	145.83141439	0.00685723	225
226	2.55923988	0.39074102	374.21757186	0.00267224	146.22215541	0.00683891	226
227	2.56990338	0.38911969	376.77681174	0.00265409	146.61127509	0.00682076	227
228	2.58061131	0.38750508	379.34671512	0.00263611	146.99878018	0.00680278	228
229	2.59136386	0.38589718	381.92732644	0.00261830	147.38467735	0.00678497	229
230	2.60216121	0.38429594	384.51869030	0.00260065	147.76897330	0.00676732	230
231	2.61300355	0.38270136	387.12085151	0.00258317	148.15167465	0.00674984	231
232	2.62389106	0.38111338	389.73385505	0.00256585	148.53278804	0.00673252	232
233	2.63482394	0.37953200	392.35774612	0.00254869	148.91232004	0.00671536	233
234	2.64580238	0.37795718	394.99257006	0.00253169	149.29027722	0.00669836	234
235	2.65682655	0.37638889	397.63837243	0.00251485	149.66666611	0.00668151	235
236	2.66789666	0.37482711	400.29519899	0.00249816	150.04149322	0.00666482	236
237	2.67901290	0.37327181	402.96309565	0.00248162	150.41476503	0.00664828	237
238	2.69017545	0.37172297	405.64210855	0.00246523	150.78648800	0.00663189	238
239	2.70138452	0.37018055	408.33228400	0.00244899	151.15666855	0.00661565	239
240	2.71264029	0.36864453	411.03366852	0.00243289	151.52531307	0.00659956	240

TABLE A-2

COMPOUND INTEREST FOR $1

$\frac{1}{2}\%$

PERIODS n	FUTURE AMOUNT $(1+i)^n$	PRESENT VALUE $(1+i)^{-n}$	AMOUNT OF ANNUITY $(S/p,i,n)$ $\dfrac{(1+i)^n-1}{i}$	SINKING FUND $(p/S,i,n)$ $\dfrac{i}{(1+i)^n-1}$	PRESENT VALUE OF ANNUITY $(V/p,i,n)$ $\dfrac{1-(1+i)^{-n}}{i}$	AMORTIZATION $(p/V,i,n)$ $\dfrac{i}{1-(1+i)^{-n}}$	PERIODS n
1	1.00500000	0.99502488	1.00000000	1.00000000	0.99502488	1.00500000	1
2	1.01002500	0.99007450	2.00500000	0.49875312	1.98509938	0.50375312	2
3	1.01507512	0.98514876	3.01502500	0.33167221	2.97024814	0.33667221	3
4	1.02015050	0.98024752	4.03010012	0.24813279	3.95049566	0.25313279	4
5	1.02525125	0.97537067	5.05025063	0.19800997	4.92586633	0.20300997	5
6	1.03037751	0.97051808	6.07550188	0.16459546	5.89638441	0.16959546	6
7	1.03552940	0.96568963	7.10587939	0.14072854	6.86207404	0.14572854	7
8	1.04070704	0.96088520	8.14140879	0.12282886	7.82295924	0.12782886	8
9	1.04591058	0.95610468	9.18211583	0.10890736	8.77906392	0.11390736	9
10	1.05114013	0.95134794	10.22802641	0.09777057	9.73041186	0.10277057	10
11	1.05639583	0.94661487	11.27916654	0.08865903	10.67702673	0.09365903	11
12	1.06167781	0.94190534	12.33556237	0.08106643	11.61893207	0.08606643	12
13	1.06698620	0.93721924	13.39724018	0.07464224	12.55615131	0.07964224	13
14	1.07232113	0.93255646	14.46422639	0.06913609	13.48870777	0.07413609	14
15	1.07768274	0.92791688	15.53654752	0.06436436	14.41662465	0.06936436	15
16	1.08307115	0.92330037	16.61423026	0.06018937	15.33992502	0.06518937	16
17	1.08848651	0.91870684	17.69730141	0.05650579	16.25863186	0.06150579	17
18	1.09392894	0.91413616	18.78578791	0.05323173	17.17276802	0.05823173	18
19	1.09939858	0.90958822	19.87971685	0.05030253	18.08235624	0.05530253	19
20	1.10489558	0.90506290	20.97911544	0.04766645	18.98741915	0.05266645	20
21	1.11042006	0.90056010	22.08401101	0.04528163	19.88797925	0.05028163	21
22	1.11597216	0.89607971	23.19443107	0.04311380	20.78405896	0.04811380	22
23	1.12155202	0.89162160	24.31040322	0.04113465	21.67568055	0.04613465	23
24	1.12715978	0.88718567	25.43195524	0.03932061	22.56286622	0.04432061	24
25	1.13279558	0.88277181	26.55911502	0.03765186	23.44563803	0.04265186	25
26	1.13845955	0.87837991	27.69191059	0.03611163	24.32401794	0.04111163	26
27	1.14415185	0.87400986	28.83037015	0.03468565	25.19802780	0.03968565	27
28	1.14987261	0.86966155	29.97452200	0.03336167	26.06768936	0.03836167	28
29	1.15562197	0.86533488	31.12439461	0.03212914	26.93302423	0.03712914	29
30	1.16140008	0.86102973	32.28001658	0.03097892	27.79405397	0.03597892	30
31	1.16720708	0.85674600	33.44141666	0.02990304	28.65079997	0.03490304	31
32	1.17304312	0.85248358	34.60862375	0.02889453	29.50328355	0.03389453	32
33	1.17890833	0.84824237	35.78166686	0.02794727	30.35152592	0.03294727	33
34	1.18480288	0.84402226	36.96057520	0.02705586	31.19554818	0.03205586	34
35	1.19072689	0.83982314	38.14537807	0.02621550	32.03537132	0.03121550	35
36	1.19668052	0.83564492	39.33610496	0.02542194	32.87101624	0.03042194	36
37	1.20266393	0.83148748	40.53278549	0.02467139	33.70250372	0.02967139	37
38	1.20867725	0.82735073	41.73544942	0.02396045	34.52985445	0.02896045	38
39	1.21472063	0.82323455	42.94412666	0.02328607	35.35308900	0.02828607	39
40	1.22079424	0.81913886	44.15884730	0.02264552	36.17222786	0.02764552	40

TABLE A-2

COMPOUND INTEREST FOR $1

$\frac{1}{2}\%$

PERIODS n	FUTURE AMOUNT $(1+i)^n$	PRESENT VALUE $(1+i)^{-n}$	AMOUNT OF ANNUITY (S/p,i,n) $\dfrac{(1+i)^n - 1}{i}$	SINKING FUND (p/S,i,n) $\dfrac{i}{(1+i)^n - 1}$	PRESENT VALUE OF ANNUITY (V/p,i,n) $\dfrac{1-(1+i)^{-n}}{i}$	AMORTIZATION (p/V,i,n) $\dfrac{i}{1-(1+i)^{-n}}$	PERIODS n
41	1.22689821	0.81506354	45.37964153	0.02203631	36.98729141	0.02703631	41
42	1.23303270	0.81100850	46.60653974	0.02145622	37.79829991	0.02645622	42
43	1.23919786	0.80697363	47.83957244	0.02090320	38.60527354	0.02590320	43
44	1.24539385	0.80295884	49.07877030	0.02037541	39.40823238	0.02537541	44
45	1.25162082	0.79896402	50.32416415	0.01987117	40.20719640	0.02487117	45
46	1.25787892	0.79498907	51.57578497	0.01938894	41.00218547	0.02438894	46
47	1.26416832	0.79103390	52.83366390	0.01892733	41.79321937	0.02392733	47
48	1.27049916	0.78709841	54.09783222	0.01848503	42.58031778	0.02348503	48
49	1.27684161	0.78318250	55.36832138	0.01806087	43.36350028	0.02306087	49
50	1.28322581	0.77928607	56.64516299	0.01765376	44.14278635	0.02265376	50
51	1.28964194	0.77540902	57.92838880	0.01726269	44.91819537	0.02226269	51
52	1.29609015	0.77155127	59.21803075	0.01688675	45.68974664	0.02188675	52
53	1.30257060	0.76771270	60.51412090	0.01652507	46.45745934	0.02152507	53
54	1.30908346	0.76389324	61.81669150	0.01617686	47.22135258	0.02117686	54
55	1.31562887	0.76009277	63.12577496	0.01584139	47.98144535	0.02084139	55
56	1.32220702	0.75631122	64.44140384	0.01551797	48.73775657	0.02051797	56
57	1.32881805	0.75254847	65.76361086	0.01520598	49.49030505	0.02020598	57
58	1.33546214	0.74880445	67.09242891	0.01490481	50.23910950	0.01990481	58
59	1.34213946	0.74507906	68.42789105	0.01461392	50.98418855	0.01961392	59
60	1.34885015	0.74137220	69.77003051	0.01433280	51.72556075	0.01933280	60
61	1.35559440	0.73768378	71.11888066	0.01406096	52.46324453	0.01906096	61
62	1.36237238	0.73401371	72.47447507	0.01379796	53.19725824	0.01879796	62
63	1.36918424	0.73036190	73.83684744	0.01354337	53.92762014	0.01854337	63
64	1.37603016	0.72672826	75.20603168	0.01329681	54.65434839	0.01829681	64
65	1.38291031	0.72311269	76.58206184	0.01305789	55.37746109	0.01805789	65
66	1.38982486	0.71951512	77.96497215	0.01282627	56.09697621	0.01782627	66
67	1.39677399	0.71593544	79.35479701	0.01260163	56.81291165	0.01760163	67
68	1.40375785	0.71237357	80.75157099	0.01238366	57.52528522	0.01738366	68
69	1.41077664	0.70882943	82.15532885	0.01217206	58.23411465	0.01717206	69
70	1.41783053	0.70530291	83.56610549	0.01196657	58.93941756	0.01696657	70
71	1.42491968	0.70179394	84.98393602	0.01176693	59.64121151	0.01676693	71
72	1.43204428	0.69830243	86.40885570	0.01157289	60.33951394	0.01657289	72
73	1.43920450	0.69482829	87.84089998	0.01138422	61.03434222	0.01638422	73
74	1.44640052	0.69137143	89.28010448	0.01120070	61.72571366	0.01620070	74
75	1.45363252	0.68793177	90.72650500	0.01102214	62.41364543	0.01602214	75
76	1.46090069	0.68450923	92.18013752	0.01084832	63.09815466	0.01584832	76
77	1.46820519	0.68110371	93.64103821	0.01067908	63.77925836	0.01567908	77
78	1.47554622	0.67771513	95.10924340	0.01051423	64.45697350	0.01551423	78
79	1.48292395	0.67434342	96.58478962	0.01035360	65.13131691	0.01535360	79
80	1.49033857	0.67098847	98.06771357	0.01019704	65.80230538	0.01519704	80

TABLE A-2

COMPOUND INTEREST FOR $1

$\frac{1}{2}\%$

PERIODS n	FUTURE AMOUNT $(1+i)^n$	PRESENT VALUE $(1+i)^{-n}$	AMOUNT OF ANNUITY $(S/p,i,n)$ $\dfrac{(1+i)^n-1}{i}$	SINKING FUND $(p/S,i,n)$ $\dfrac{i}{(1+i)^n-1}$	PRESENT VALUE OF ANNUITY $(V/p,i,n)$ $\dfrac{1-(1+i)^{-n}}{i}$	AMORTIZATION $(p/V,i,n)$ $\dfrac{i}{1-(1+i)^{-n}}$	PERIODS n
81	1.49779026	0.66765022	99.55805214	0.01004439	66.46995561	0.01504439	81
82	1.50527921	0.66432858	101.05584240	0.00989552	67.13428419	0.01489552	82
83	1.51280561	0.66102346	102.56112161	0.00975028	67.79530765	0.01475028	83
84	1.52036964	0.65773479	104.07392722	0.00960855	68.45304244	0.01460855	84
85	1.52797148	0.65446248	105.59429685	0.00947021	69.10750491	0.01447021	85
86	1.53561134	0.65120644	107.12226834	0.00933513	69.75871135	0.01433513	86
87	1.54328940	0.64796661	108.65787968	0.00920320	70.40667796	0.01420320	87
88	1.55100585	0.64474290	110.20116908	0.00907431	71.05142086	0.01407431	88
89	1.55876087	0.64153522	111.75217492	0.00894837	71.69295608	0.01394837	89
90	1.56655468	0.63834350	113.31093580	0.00882527	72.33129958	0.01382527	90
91	1.57438745	0.63516766	114.87749048	0.00870493	72.96646725	0.01370493	91
92	1.58225939	0.63200763	116.45187793	0.00858724	73.59847487	0.01358724	92
93	1.59017069	0.62886331	118.03413732	0.00847213	74.22733818	0.01347213	93
94	1.59812154	0.62573464	119.62430800	0.00835950	74.85307282	0.01335950	94
95	1.60611215	0.62262153	121.22242954	0.00824930	75.47569434	0.01324930	95
96	1.61414271	0.61952391	122.82854169	0.00814143	76.09521825	0.01314143	96
97	1.62221342	0.61644170	124.44268440	0.00803583	76.71165995	0.01303583	97
98	1.63032449	0.61337483	126.06489782	0.00793242	77.32503478	0.01293242	98
99	1.63847611	0.61032321	127.69522231	0.00783115	77.93535799	0.01283115	99
100	1.64666849	0.60728678	129.33369842	0.00773194	78.54264477	0.01273194	100
101	1.65490183	0.60426545	130.98036692	0.00763473	79.14691021	0.01263473	101
102	1.66317634	0.60125915	132.63526875	0.00753947	79.74816937	0.01253947	102
103	1.67149223	0.59826781	134.29844509	0.00744610	80.34643718	0.01244610	103
104	1.67984969	0.59529136	135.96993732	0.00735457	80.94172854	0.01235457	104
105	1.68824894	0.59232971	137.64978701	0.00726481	81.53405825	0.01226481	105
106	1.69669018	0.58938279	139.33803594	0.00717679	82.12344104	0.01217679	106
107	1.70517363	0.58645054	141.03472612	0.00709045	82.70989158	0.01209045	107
108	1.71369950	0.58353288	142.73989975	0.00700575	83.29342446	0.01200575	108
109	1.72226800	0.58062973	144.45359925	0.00692264	83.87405419	0.01192264	109
110	1.73087934	0.57774102	146.17586725	0.00684107	84.45179522	0.01184107	110
111	1.73953373	0.57486669	147.90674658	0.00676102	85.02666191	0.01176102	111
112	1.74823140	0.57200666	149.64628032	0.00668242	85.59866856	0.01168242	112
113	1.75697256	0.56916085	151.39451172	0.00660526	86.16782942	0.01160526	113
114	1.76575742	0.56632921	153.15148428	0.00652948	86.73415862	0.01152948	114
115	1.77458621	0.56351165	154.91724170	0.00645506	87.29767027	0.01145506	115
116	1.78345914	0.56070811	156.69182791	0.00638195	87.85837838	0.01138195	116
117	1.79237644	0.55791852	158.47528704	0.00631013	88.41629690	0.01131013	117
118	1.80133832	0.55514280	160.26766348	0.00623956	88.97143970	0.01123956	118
119	1.81034501	0.55238090	162.06900180	0.00617021	89.52382059	0.01117021	119
120	1.81939673	0.54963273	163.87934681	0.00610205	90.07345333	0.01110205	120

TABLE A-2

COMPOUND INTEREST FOR $1

$\frac{1}{2}$ %

PERIODS n	FUTURE AMOUNT $(1+i)^n$	PRESENT VALUE $(1+i)^{-n}$	AMOUNT OF ANNUITY (S/p,i,n) $\dfrac{(1+i)^n - 1}{i}$	SINKING FUND (p/S,i,n) $\dfrac{i}{(1+i)^n - 1}$	PRESENT VALUE OF ANNUITY (V/p,i,n) $\dfrac{1-(1+i)^{-n}}{i}$	AMORTIZATION (p/V,i,n) $\dfrac{i}{1-(1+i)^{-n}}$	PERIODS n
121	1.82849372	0.54689824	165.69874354	0.00603505	90.62035157	0.01103505	121
122	1.83763619	0.54417736	167.52723726	0.00596918	91.16452892	0.01096918	122
123	1.84682437	0.54147001	169.36487344	0.00590441	91.70599893	0.01090441	123
124	1.85605849	0.53877612	171.21169781	0.00584072	92.24477505	0.01084072	124
125	1.86533878	0.53609565	173.06775630	0.00577808	92.78087070	0.01077808	125
126	1.87466548	0.53342850	174.93309508	0.00571647	93.31429921	0.01071647	126
127	1.88403880	0.53077463	176.80776056	0.00565586	93.84507384	0.01065586	127
128	1.89345900	0.52813396	178.69179936	0.00559623	94.37320780	0.01059623	128
129	1.90292629	0.52550643	180.58525836	0.00553755	94.89871423	0.01053755	129
130	1.91244092	0.52289197	182.48818465	0.00547981	95.42160619	0.01047981	130
131	1.92200313	0.52029052	184.40062557	0.00542298	95.94189671	0.01042298	131
132	1.93161314	0.51770201	186.32262870	0.00536703	96.45959872	0.01036703	132
133	1.94127121	0.51512637	188.25424184	0.00531197	96.97472509	0.01031197	133
134	1.95097757	0.51256356	190.19551305	0.00525775	97.48728865	0.01025775	134
135	1.96073245	0.51001349	192.14649062	0.00520436	97.99730214	0.01020436	135
136	1.97053611	0.50747611	194.10722307	0.00515179	98.50477825	0.01015179	136
137	1.98038880	0.50495135	196.07775919	0.00510002	99.00972960	0.01010002	137
138	1.99029074	0.50243916	198.05814798	0.00504902	99.51216876	0.01004902	138
139	2.00024219	0.49993946	200.04843872	0.00499879	100.01210821	0.00999879	139
140	2.01024340	0.49745220	202.04868092	0.00494930	100.50956041	0.00994930	140
141	2.02029462	0.49497731	204.05892432	0.00490055	101.00453772	0.00990055	141
142	2.03039609	0.49251474	206.07921894	0.00485250	101.49705246	0.00985250	142
143	2.04054808	0.49006442	208.10961504	0.00480516	101.98711688	0.00980516	143
144	2.05075082	0.48762628	210.15016311	0.00475850	102.47474316	0.00975850	144
145	2.06100457	0.48520028	212.20091393	0.00471252	102.95994344	0.00971252	145
146	2.07130959	0.48278635	214.26191850	0.00466718	103.44272979	0.00966718	146
147	2.08166614	0.48038443	216.33322809	0.00462250	103.92311422	0.00962250	147
148	2.09207447	0.47799447	218.41489423	0.00457844	104.40110868	0.00957844	148
149	2.10253484	0.47561637	220.50696870	0.00453500	104.87672506	0.00953500	149
150	2.11304752	0.47325012	222.60950354	0.00449217	105.34997518	0.00949217	150
151	2.12361276	0.47089565	224.72255106	0.00444993	105.82087083	0.00944993	151
152	2.13423082	0.46855288	226.84616382	0.00440827	106.28942371	0.00940827	152
153	2.14490197	0.46622177	228.98039464	0.00436719	106.75564548	0.00936719	153
154	2.15562648	0.46390226	231.12529661	0.00432666	107.21954774	0.00932666	154
155	2.16640462	0.46159429	233.28092309	0.00428668	107.68114203	0.00928668	155
156	2.17723664	0.45929780	235.44732771	0.00424723	108.14043983	0.00924723	156
157	2.18812282	0.45701274	237.62456435	0.00420832	108.59745257	0.00920832	157
158	2.19906344	0.45473904	239.81268717	0.00416992	109.05219161	0.00916992	158
159	2.21005875	0.45247666	242.01175060	0.00413203	109.50466827	0.00913203	159
160	2.22110905	0.45022553	244.22180936	0.00409464	109.95489380	0.00909464	160

COMPOUND INTEREST FOR $1

$\frac{1}{2}\%$

PERIODS n	FUTURE AMOUNT $(1+i)^n$	PRESENT VALUE $(1+i)^{-n}$	AMOUNT OF ANNUITY $(S/p,i,n)$ $\dfrac{(1+i)^n-1}{i}$	SINKING FUND $(p/S,i,n)$ $\dfrac{i}{(1+i)^n-1}$	PRESENT VALUE OF ANNUITY $(V/p,i,n)$ $\dfrac{1-(1+i)^{-n}}{i}$	AMORTIZATION $(p/V,i,n)$ $\dfrac{i}{1-(1+i)^{-n}}$	PERIODS n
161	2.23221459	0.44798560	246.44291840	0.00405773	110.40287940	0.00905773	161
162	2.24337566	0.44575682	248.67513300	0.00402131	110.84863622	0.00902131	162
163	2.25459254	0.44353912	250.91850866	0.00398536	111.29217535	0.00898536	163
164	2.26586551	0.44133246	253.17310121	0.00394987	111.73350781	0.00894987	164
165	2.27719483	0.43913678	255.43896671	0.00391483	112.17264458	0.00891483	165
166	2.28858081	0.43695202	257.71616154	0.00388024	112.60959660	0.00888024	166
167	2.30002371	0.43477813	260.00474235	0.00384608	113.04437473	0.00884608	167
168	2.31152383	0.43261505	262.30476606	0.00381236	113.47698978	0.00881236	168
169	2.32308145	0.43046274	264.61628989	0.00377906	113.90745252	0.00877906	169
170	2.33469686	0.42832113	266.93937134	0.00374617	114.33577365	0.00874617	170
171	2.34637034	0.42619018	269.27406820	0.00371369	114.76196383	0.00871369	171
172	2.35810219	0.42406983	271.62043854	0.00368161	115.18603366	0.00868161	172
173	2.36989270	0.42196003	273.97854073	0.00364992	115.60799369	0.00864992	173
174	2.38174217	0.41986073	276.34843344	0.00361862	116.02785442	0.00861862	174
175	2.39365088	0.41777187	278.73017561	0.00358770	116.44562629	0.00858770	175
176	2.40561913	0.41569340	281.12382648	0.00355715	116.86131969	0.00855715	176
177	2.41764723	0.41362528	283.52944562	0.00352697	117.27494496	0.00852697	177
178	2.42973546	0.41156744	285.94709284	0.00349715	117.68651240	0.00849715	178
179	2.44188414	0.40951984	288.37682831	0.00346768	118.09603224	0.00846768	179
180	2.45409356	0.40748243	290.81871245	0.00343857	118.50351467	0.00843857	180
181	2.46636403	0.40545515	293.27280601	0.00340979	118.90896982	0.00840979	181
182	2.47869585	0.40343796	295.73917004	0.00338136	119.31240778	0.00838136	182
183	2.49108933	0.40143081	298.21786589	0.00335325	119.71383859	0.00835325	183
184	2.50354478	0.39943364	300.70895522	0.00332547	120.11327223	0.00832547	184
185	2.51606250	0.39744641	303.21250000	0.00329802	120.51071863	0.00829802	185
186	2.52864281	0.39546906	305.72856250	0.00327088	120.90618769	0.00827088	186
187	2.54128603	0.39350155	308.25720531	0.00324404	121.29968925	0.00824404	187
188	2.55399246	0.39154383	310.79849134	0.00321752	121.69123308	0.00821752	188
189	2.56676242	0.38959586	313.35248379	0.00319129	122.08082894	0.00819129	189
190	2.57959623	0.38765757	315.91924621	0.00316537	122.46848651	0.00816537	190
191	2.59249421	0.38572892	318.49884244	0.00313973	122.85421543	0.00813973	191
192	2.60545668	0.38380987	321.09133666	0.00311438	123.23802530	0.00811438	192
193	2.61848397	0.38190037	323.69679334	0.00308931	123.61992567	0.00808931	193
194	2.63157639	0.38000037	326.31527731	0.00306452	123.99992604	0.00806452	194
195	2.64473427	0.37810982	328.94685369	0.00304000	124.37803586	0.00804000	195
196	2.65795794	0.37622868	331.59158796	0.00301576	124.75426454	0.00801576	196
197	2.67124773	0.37435689	334.24954590	0.00299178	125.12862143	0.00799178	197
198	2.68460397	0.37249442	336.92079363	0.00296806	125.50111585	0.00796806	198
199	2.69802699	0.37064121	339.60539760	0.00294459	125.87175707	0.00794459	199
200	2.71151712	0.36879723	342.30342459	0.00292138	126.24055430	0.00792138	200

COMPOUND INTEREST FOR $1

$\frac{1}{2}$%

PERIODS n	FUTURE AMOUNT $(1+i)^n$	PRESENT VALUE $(1+i)^{-n}$	AMOUNT OF ANNUITY $(S/p,i,n)$ $\dfrac{(1+i)^n - 1}{i}$	SINKING FUND $(p/S,i,n)$ $\dfrac{i}{(1+i)^n - 1}$	PRESENT VALUE OF ANNUITY $(V/p,i,n)$ $\dfrac{1-(1+i)^{-n}}{i}$	AMORTIZATION $(p/V,i,n)$ $\dfrac{i}{1-(1+i)^{-n}}$	PERIODS n
201	2.72507471	0.36696242	345.01494171	0.00289843	126.60751671	0.00789843	201
202	2.73870008	0.36513673	347.74001642	0.00287571	126.97265345	0.00787571	202
203	2.75239358	0.36332013	350.47871650	0.00285324	127.33597358	0.00785324	203
204	2.76615555	0.36151257	353.23111008	0.00283101	127.69748615	0.00783101	204
205	2.77998633	0.35971400	355.99726563	0.00280901	128.05720015	0.00780901	205
206	2.79388626	0.35792438	358.77725196	0.00278724	128.41512452	0.00778724	206
207	2.80785569	0.35614366	361.57113822	0.00276571	128.77126818	0.00776571	207
208	2.82189497	0.35437180	364.37899391	0.00274440	129.12563998	0.00774440	208
209	2.83600444	0.35260876	367.20088888	0.00272330	129.47824874	0.00772330	209
210	2.85018447	0.35085448	370.03689333	0.00270243	129.82910322	0.00770243	210
211	2.86443539	0.34910894	372.88707779	0.00268178	130.17821216	0.00768178	211
212	2.87875757	0.34737208	375.75151318	0.00266133	130.52558424	0.00766133	212
213	2.89315135	0.34564386	378.63027075	0.00264110	130.87122810	0.00764110	213
214	2.90761711	0.34392424	381.52342210	0.00262107	131.21515234	0.00762107	214
215	2.92215520	0.34221317	384.43103921	0.00260125	131.55736551	0.00760125	215
216	2.93676597	0.34051062	387.35319441	0.00258162	131.89787613	0.00758162	216
217	2.95144980	0.33881654	390.28996038	0.00256220	132.23669267	0.00756220	217
218	2.96620705	0.33713088	393.24141018	0.00254297	132.57382355	0.00754297	218
219	2.98103809	0.33545361	396.20761723	0.00252393	132.90927716	0.00752393	219
220	2.99594328	0.33378469	399.18865532	0.00250508	133.24306186	0.00750508	220
221	3.01092299	0.33212407	402.18459859	0.00248642	133.57518593	0.00748642	221
222	3.02597761	0.33047171	405.19552159	0.00246794	133.90565764	0.00746794	222
223	3.04110750	0.32882757	408.22149920	0.00244965	134.23448521	0.00744965	223
224	3.05631303	0.32719162	411.26260669	0.00243154	134.56167683	0.00743154	224
225	3.07159460	0.32556380	414.31891973	0.00241360	134.88724062	0.00741360	225
226	3.08695257	0.32394408	417.39051432	0.00239584	135.21118470	0.00739584	226
227	3.10238733	0.32233241	420.47746690	0.00237825	135.53351712	0.00737825	227
228	3.11789927	0.32072877	423.57985423	0.00236083	135.85424589	0.00736083	228
229	3.13348877	0.31913311	426.69775350	0.00234358	136.17337899	0.00734358	229
230	3.14915621	0.31754538	429.83124227	0.00232649	136.49092437	0.00732649	230
231	3.16490199	0.31596555	432.98039848	0.00230957	136.80688992	0.00730957	231
232	3.18072650	0.31439358	436.14530047	0.00229281	137.12128350	0.00729281	232
233	3.19663013	0.31282944	439.32602697	0.00227621	137.43411294	0.00727621	233
234	3.21261329	0.31127307	442.52265711	0.00225977	137.74538601	0.00725977	234
235	3.22867635	0.30972445	445.73527039	0.00224348	138.05511045	0.00724348	235
236	3.24481973	0.30818353	448.96394675	0.00222735	138.36329398	0.00722735	236
237	3.26104383	0.30665028	452.20876648	0.00221137	138.66994426	0.00721137	237
238	3.27734905	0.30512466	455.46981031	0.00219554	138.97506892	0.00719554	238
239	3.29373580	0.30360662	458.74715936	0.00217985	139.27867554	0.00717985	239
240	3.31020448	0.30209614	462.04089516	0.00216431	139.58077168	0.00716431	240

TABLE A-2

COMPOUND INTEREST FOR $1

$\frac{7}{12}\%$

PERIODS n	FUTURE AMOUNT $(1+i)^n$	PRESENT VALUE $(1+i)^{-n}$	AMOUNT OF ANNUITY (S/p,i,n) $\dfrac{(1+i)^n-1}{i}$	SINKING FUND (p/S,i,n) $\dfrac{i}{(1+i)^n-1}$	PRESENT VALUE OF ANNUITY (V/p,i,n) $\dfrac{1-(1+i)^{-n}}{i}$	AMORTIZATION (p/V,i,n) $\dfrac{i}{1-(1+i)^{-n}}$	PERIODS n
1	1.00583333	0.99420050	1.00000000	1.00000000	0.99420050	1.00583333	1
2	1.01170069	0.98843463	2.00583333	0.49854591	1.98263513	0.50437924	2
3	1.01760228	0.98270220	3.01753403	0.33139643	2.96533732	0.33722976	3
4	1.02353830	0.97700301	4.03513631	0.24782310	3.94234034	0.25365644	4
5	1.02950894	0.97133688	5.05867460	0.19768024	4.91367722	0.20351357	5
6	1.03551440	0.96570361	6.08818354	0.16425260	5.87938083	0.17008594	6
7	1.04155490	0.96010301	7.12369794	0.14037653	6.83948384	0.14620986	7
8	1.04763064	0.95453489	8.16525285	0.12247018	7.79401874	0.12830352	8
9	1.05374182	0.94899906	9.21288349	0.10854365	8.74301780	0.11437698	9
10	1.05988865	0.94349534	10.26662531	0.09740299	9.68651314	0.10323632	10
11	1.06607133	0.93802354	11.32651396	0.08828842	10.62453667	0.09412175	11
12	1.07229008	0.93258347	12.39258529	0.08069341	11.55712014	0.08652675	12
13	1.07854511	0.92717495	13.46487537	0.07426730	12.48429509	0.08010064	13
14	1.08483662	0.92179779	14.54342048	0.06875962	13.40609288	0.07459295	14
15	1.09116483	0.91645182	15.62825710	0.06398666	14.32254470	0.06982000	15
16	1.09752996	0.91113686	16.71942193	0.05981068	15.23368156	0.06564401	16
17	1.10393222	0.90585272	17.81695189	0.05612632	16.13953427	0.06195966	17
18	1.11037182	0.90059922	18.92088411	0.05285165	17.04013350	0.05868499	18
19	1.11684899	0.89537619	20.03125593	0.04992198	17.93550969	0.05575532	19
20	1.12336395	0.89018346	21.14810493	0.04728556	18.82569315	0.05311889	20
21	1.12991690	0.88502084	22.27146887	0.04490050	19.71071398	0.05073383	21
22	1.13650808	0.87988815	23.40138577	0.04273251	20.59060213	0.04856585	22
23	1.14313771	0.87478524	24.53789386	0.04075329	21.46538738	0.04658663	23
24	1.14980602	0.86971192	25.68103157	0.03893925	22.33509930	0.04477258	24
25	1.15651322	0.86466802	26.83083759	0.03727055	23.19976732	0.04310388	25
26	1.16325955	0.85965338	27.98735081	0.03573043	24.05942070	0.04156376	26
27	1.17004523	0.85466782	29.15061036	0.03430460	24.91408852	0.04013793	27
28	1.17687049	0.84971117	30.32065558	0.03298082	25.76379968	0.03881415	28
29	1.18373557	0.84478327	31.49752607	0.03174853	26.60858295	0.03758186	29
30	1.19064069	0.83988394	32.68126164	0.03059857	27.44846689	0.03643191	30
31	1.19758610	0.83501303	33.87190233	0.02952299	28.28347993	0.03535633	31
32	1.20457202	0.83017037	35.06948843	0.02851482	29.11365030	0.03434815	32
33	1.21159869	0.82535580	36.27406045	0.02756791	29.93900610	0.03340124	33
34	1.21866634	0.82056914	37.48565913	0.02667687	30.75957524	0.03251020	34
35	1.22577523	0.81581025	38.70432548	0.02583691	31.57538549	0.03167024	35
36	1.23292559	0.81107896	39.93010071	0.02504376	32.38646445	0.03087710	36
37	1.24011765	0.80637510	41.16302630	0.02429365	33.19283955	0.03012698	37
38	1.24735167	0.80169853	42.40314395	0.02358316	33.99453808	0.02941649	38
39	1.25462789	0.79704907	43.65049562	0.02290925	34.79158716	0.02874258	39
40	1.26194655	0.79242659	44.90512352	0.02226917	35.58401374	0.02810251	40

COMPOUND INTEREST FOR $1

$\frac{7}{12}\%$

PERIODS n	FUTURE AMOUNT $(1+i)^n$	PRESENT VALUE $(1+i)^{-n}$	AMOUNT OF ANNUITY $(S/p,i,n)$ $\dfrac{(1+i)^n-1}{i}$	SINKING FUND $(p/S,i,n)$ $\dfrac{i}{(1+i)^n-1}$	PRESENT VALUE OF ANNUITY $(V/p,i,n)$ $\dfrac{1-(1+i)^{-n}}{i}$	AMORTIZATION $(p/V,i,n)$ $\dfrac{i}{1-(1+i)^{-n}}$	PERIODS n
41	1.26930791	0.78783091	46.16707007	0.02166046	36.37184465	0.02749379	41
42	1.27671220	0.78326188	47.43637798	0.02108087	37.15510653	0.02691420	42
43	1.28415969	0.77871935	48.71309018	0.02052836	37.93382588	0.02636170	43
44	1.29165062	0.77420316	49.99724988	0.02000110	38.70802904	0.02583443	44
45	1.29918525	0.76971317	51.28890050	0.01949740	39.47774221	0.02533073	45
46	1.30676383	0.76524922	52.58808575	0.01901571	40.24299143	0.02484905	46
47	1.31438662	0.76081115	53.89484959	0.01855465	41.00380258	0.02438798	47
48	1.32205388	0.75639883	55.20923621	0.01811291	41.76020141	0.02394624	48
49	1.32976586	0.75201209	56.53129009	0.01768932	42.51221349	0.02352265	49
50	1.33752283	0.74765079	57.86105595	0.01728278	43.25986428	0.02311612	50
51	1.34532504	0.74331479	59.19857877	0.01689230	44.00317907	0.02272563	51
52	1.35317277	0.73900393	60.54390381	0.01651694	44.74218301	0.02235027	52
53	1.36106628	0.73471808	61.89707659	0.01615585	45.47690108	0.02198919	53
54	1.36900583	0.73045708	63.25814287	0.01580824	46.20735816	0.02164157	54
55	1.37699170	0.72622079	64.62714870	0.01547337	46.93357895	0.02130671	55
56	1.38502415	0.72200907	66.00414040	0.01515056	47.65558802	0.02098390	56
57	1.39310346	0.71782178	67.38916455	0.01483918	48.37340980	0.02067251	57
58	1.40122990	0.71365877	68.78226801	0.01453863	49.08706856	0.02037196	58
59	1.40940374	0.70951990	70.18349791	0.01424836	49.79658846	0.02008170	59
60	1.41762526	0.70540504	71.59290165	0.01396787	50.50199350	0.01980120	60
61	1.42589474	0.70131404	73.01052691	0.01369666	51.20330754	0.01952999	61
62	1.43421246	0.69724677	74.43642165	0.01343428	51.90055431	0.01926762	62
63	1.44257870	0.69320308	75.87063411	0.01318033	52.59375739	0.01901366	63
64	1.45099374	0.68918285	77.31321281	0.01293440	53.28294024	0.01876773	64
65	1.45945787	0.68518593	78.76420655	0.01269612	53.96812617	0.01852946	65
66	1.46797138	0.68121219	80.22366442	0.01246515	54.64933836	0.01829848	66
67	1.47653454	0.67726150	81.69163580	0.01224116	55.32659986	0.01807449	67
68	1.48514766	0.67333372	83.16817034	0.01202383	55.99993358	0.01785716	68
69	1.49381102	0.66942872	84.65331800	0.01181289	56.66936230	0.01764622	69
70	1.50252492	0.66554637	86.14712902	0.01160805	57.33490867	0.01744138	70
71	1.51128965	0.66168653	87.64965394	0.01140906	57.99659520	0.01724239	71
72	1.52010550	0.65784908	89.16094359	0.01121567	58.65444427	0.01704901	72
73	1.52897279	0.65403388	90.68104909	0.01102766	59.30847815	0.01686100	73
74	1.53789179	0.65024081	92.21002188	0.01084481	59.95871896	0.01667814	74
75	1.54686283	0.64646973	93.74791367	0.01066690	60.60518869	0.01650024	75
76	1.55588620	0.64272053	95.29477650	0.01049375	61.24790922	0.01632709	76
77	1.56496220	0.63899307	96.85066270	0.01032517	61.88690229	0.01615851	77
78	1.57409115	0.63528723	98.41562490	0.01016099	62.52218952	0.01599432	78
79	1.58327334	0.63160288	99.98971604	0.01000103	63.15379239	0.01583436	79
80	1.59250910	0.62793989	101.57298939	0.00984514	63.78173229	0.01567847	80

COMPOUND INTEREST FOR $1

$\frac{7}{12}$ %

PERIODS n	FUTURE AMOUNT $(1+i)^n$	PRESENT VALUE $(1+i)^{-n}$	AMOUNT OF ANNUITY (S/p,i,n) $\frac{(1+i)^n - 1}{i}$	SINKING FUND (p/S,i,n) $\frac{i}{(1+i)^n - 1}$	PRESENT VALUE OF ANNUITY (V/p,i,n) $\frac{1-(1+i)^{-n}}{i}$	AMORTIZATION (p/V,i,n) $\frac{i}{1-(1+i)^{-n}}$	PERIODS n
81	1.60179874	0.62429816	103.16549849	0.00969316	64.40603044	0.01552650	81
82	1.61114257	0.62067754	104.76729723	0.00954496	65.02670798	0.01537830	82
83	1.62054090	0.61707792	106.37843980	0.00940040	65.64378590	0.01523373	83
84	1.62999405	0.61349917	107.99898070	0.00925935	66.25728507	0.01509268	84
85	1.63950235	0.60994118	109.62897475	0.00912168	66.86722625	0.01495501	85
86	1.64906612	0.60640382	111.26847710	0.00898727	67.47363007	0.01482060	86
87	1.65868567	0.60288698	112.91754322	0.00885602	68.07651706	0.01468935	87
88	1.66836134	0.59939054	114.57622889	0.00872781	68.67590759	0.01456115	88
89	1.67809344	0.59591437	116.24459022	0.00860255	69.27182197	0.01443588	89
90	1.68788232	0.59245836	117.92268367	0.00848013	69.86428033	0.01431347	90
91	1.69772830	0.58902240	119.61056599	0.00836047	70.45330273	0.01419380	91
92	1.70763172	0.58560636	121.30829429	0.00824346	71.03890910	0.01407679	92
93	1.71759290	0.58221014	123.01592601	0.00812903	71.62111923	0.01396236	93
94	1.72761219	0.57883361	124.73351891	0.00801709	72.19995284	0.01385042	94
95	1.73768993	0.57547666	126.46113110	0.00790757	72.77542950	0.01374090	95
96	1.74782646	0.57213918	128.19882103	0.00780038	73.34756869	0.01363372	96
97	1.75802211	0.56882106	129.94664749	0.00769547	73.91638975	0.01352880	97
98	1.76827724	0.56552218	131.70466960	0.00759275	74.48191193	0.01342608	98
99	1.77859219	0.56224243	133.47294684	0.00749215	75.04415436	0.01332549	99
100	1.78896731	0.55898171	135.25153903	0.00739363	75.60313606	0.01322696	100
101	1.79940295	0.55573989	137.04050634	0.00729711	76.15887596	0.01313045	101
102	1.80989947	0.55251688	138.83990929	0.00720254	76.71139283	0.01303587	102
103	1.82045722	0.54931255	140.64980877	0.00710986	77.26070538	0.01294319	103
104	1.83107655	0.54612681	142.47026598	0.00701901	77.80683219	0.01285234	104
105	1.84175783	0.54295955	144.30134253	0.00692994	78.34979174	0.01276328	105
106	1.85250142	0.53981065	146.14310037	0.00684261	78.88960240	0.01267594	106
107	1.86330768	0.53668002	147.99560178	0.00675696	79.42628241	0.01259029	107
108	1.87417697	0.53356754	149.85890946	0.00667294	79.95984996	0.01250628	108
109	1.88510967	0.53047312	151.73308643	0.00659052	80.49032307	0.01242385	109
110	1.89610614	0.52739664	153.61819610	0.00650965	81.01771971	0.01234298	110
111	1.90716676	0.52433800	155.51430225	0.00643028	81.54205770	0.01226361	111
112	1.91829190	0.52129710	157.42146901	0.00635237	82.06335480	0.01218571	112
113	1.92948194	0.51827383	159.33976091	0.00627590	82.58162863	0.01210923	113
114	1.94073725	0.51526810	161.26924285	0.00620081	83.09689674	0.01203414	114
115	1.95205822	0.51227980	163.20998010	0.00612708	83.60917654	0.01196041	115
116	1.96344522	0.50930884	165.16203832	0.00605466	84.11848537	0.01188799	116
117	1.97489865	0.50635510	167.12548354	0.00598353	84.62484047	0.01181686	117
118	1.98641890	0.50341849	169.10038220	0.00591365	85.12825896	0.01174698	118
119	1.99800634	0.50049891	171.08680109	0.00584499	85.62875787	0.01167832	119
120	2.00966138	0.49759627	173.08480743	0.00577751	86.12635414	0.01161085	120

COMPOUND INTEREST FOR $1

$\frac{7}{12}$%

PERIODS n	FUTURE AMOUNT $(1+i)^n$	PRESENT VALUE $(1+i)^{-n}$	AMOUNT OF ANNUITY (S/p,i,n) $\frac{(1+i)^n - 1}{i}$	SINKING FUND (p/S,i,n) $\frac{i}{(1+i)^n - 1}$	PRESENT VALUE OF ANNUITY (V/p,i,n) $\frac{1-(1+i)^{-n}}{i}$	AMORTIZATION (p/V,i,n) $\frac{i}{1-(1+i)^{-n}}$	PERIODS n
121	2.02138440	0.49471046	175.09446881	0.00571120	86.62106460	0.01154454	121
122	2.03317581	0.49184138	177.11585321	0.00564602	87.11290598	0.01147936	122
123	2.04503600	0.48898895	179.14902902	0.00558194	87.60189493	0.01141528	123
124	2.05696538	0.48615305	181.19406502	0.00551894	88.08804798	0.01135228	124
125	2.06896434	0.48333361	183.25103040	0.00545700	88.57138159	0.01129033	125
126	2.08103330	0.48053051	185.31999475	0.00539607	89.05191210	0.01122941	126
127	2.09317266	0.47774367	187.40102805	0.00533615	89.52965577	0.01116948	127
128	2.10538284	0.47497300	189.49420071	0.00527721	90.00462877	0.01111054	128
129	2.11766424	0.47221839	191.59958355	0.00521922	90.47684716	0.01105255	129
130	2.13001728	0.46947976	193.71724779	0.00516216	90.94632692	0.01099550	130
131	2.14244238	0.46675701	195.84726507	0.00510602	91.41308393	0.01093935	131
132	2.15493996	0.46405005	197.98970745	0.00505077	91.87713399	0.01088410	132
133	2.16751044	0.46135879	200.14464741	0.00499639	92.33849278	0.01082972	133
134	2.18015425	0.45868314	202.31215785	0.00494286	92.79717592	0.01077619	134
135	2.19287182	0.45602301	204.49231210	0.00489016	93.25319893	0.01072349	135
136	2.20566357	0.45337830	206.68518393	0.00483828	93.70657722	0.01067161	136
137	2.21852994	0.45074893	208.89084750	0.00478719	94.15732616	0.01062052	137
138	2.23147137	0.44813481	211.10937744	0.00473688	94.60546097	0.01057021	138
139	2.24448828	0.44553585	213.34084881	0.00468733	95.05099682	0.01052067	139
140	2.25758113	0.44295197	215.58533710	0.00463853	95.49394878	0.01047187	140
141	2.27075036	0.44038306	217.84291823	0.00459046	95.93433185	0.01042380	141
142	2.28399640	0.43782906	220.11366858	0.00454311	96.37216091	0.01037644	142
143	2.29731971	0.43528987	222.39766498	0.00449645	96.80745078	0.01032978	143
144	2.31072074	0.43276541	224.69498470	0.00445048	97.24021619	0.01028381	144
145	2.32419995	0.43025558	227.00570544	0.00440518	97.67047177	0.01023851	145
146	2.33775778	0.42776031	229.32990539	0.00436053	98.09823208	0.01019386	146
147	2.35139470	0.42527952	231.66766317	0.00431653	98.52351160	0.01014986	147
148	2.36511117	0.42281311	234.01905787	0.00427316	98.94632470	0.01010649	148
149	2.37890765	0.42036100	236.38416904	0.00423040	99.36668570	0.01006374	149
150	2.39278461	0.41792312	238.76307670	0.00418825	99.78460882	0.01002159	150
151	2.40674252	0.41549937	241.15586131	0.00414670	100.20010819	0.00998003	151
152	2.42078186	0.41308968	243.56260384	0.00410572	100.61319786	0.00993905	152
153	2.43490308	0.41069396	245.98338569	0.00406532	101.02389183	0.00989865	153
154	2.44910668	0.40831214	248.41828877	0.00402547	101.43220397	0.00985880	154
155	2.46339314	0.40594414	250.86739546	0.00398617	101.83814811	0.00981950	155
156	2.47776293	0.40358986	253.33078860	0.00394741	102.24173797	0.00978074	156
157	2.49221655	0.40124924	255.80855153	0.00390917	102.64298721	0.00974251	157
158	2.50675448	0.39892220	258.30076808	0.00387146	103.04190941	0.00970479	158
159	2.52137721	0.39660864	260.80752256	0.00383425	103.43851805	0.00966758	159
160	2.53608525	0.39430851	263.32889978	0.00379753	103.83282656	0.00963087	160

TABLE A-2

COMPOUND INTEREST FOR $1

$\frac{7}{12}\%$

PERIODS n	FUTURE AMOUNT $(1+i)^n$	PRESENT VALUE $(1+i)^{-n}$	AMOUNT OF ANNUITY $(S/p,i,n)$ $\dfrac{(1+i)^n-1}{i}$	SINKING FUND $(p/S,i,n)$ $\dfrac{i}{(1+i)^n-1}$	PRESENT VALUE OF ANNUITY $(V/p,i,n)$ $\dfrac{1-(1+i)^{-n}}{i}$	AMORTIZATION $(p/V,i,n)$ $\dfrac{i}{1-(1+i)^{-n}}$	PERIODS n
161	2.55087908	0.39202172	265.86498503	0.00376131	104.22484828	0.00959464	161
162	2.56575921	0.38974819	268.41586411	0.00372556	104.61459647	0.00955890	162
163	2.58072614	0.38748784	270.98162331	0.00369029	105.00208431	0.00952362	163
164	2.59578037	0.38524060	273.56234945	0.00365547	105.38732491	0.00948881	164
165	2.61092242	0.38300640	276.15812982	0.00362111	105.77033132	0.00945445	165
166	2.62615280	0.38078515	278.76905225	0.00358720	106.15111647	0.00942053	166
167	2.64147203	0.37857679	281.39520505	0.00355372	106.52969326	0.00938705	167
168	2.65688062	0.37638123	284.03667708	0.00352067	106.90607449	0.00935401	168
169	2.67237909	0.37419841	286.69355770	0.00348804	107.28027290	0.00932138	169
170	2.68796796	0.37202824	289.36593678	0.00345583	107.65230114	0.00928917	170
171	2.70364778	0.36987066	292.05390475	0.00342403	108.02217181	0.00925736	171
172	2.71941906	0.36772560	294.75755252	0.00339262	108.38989741	0.00922595	172
173	2.73528233	0.36559297	297.47697158	0.00336160	108.75549038	0.00919494	173
174	2.75123815	0.36347272	300.21225392	0.00333098	109.11896309	0.00916431	174
175	2.76728704	0.36136475	302.96349206	0.00330073	109.48032785	0.00913406	175
176	2.78342954	0.35926902	305.73077910	0.00327085	109.83959687	0.00910418	176
177	2.79966622	0.35718544	308.51420864	0.00324134	110.19678230	0.00907468	177
178	2.81599760	0.35511394	311.31387486	0.00321219	110.55189624	0.00904553	178
179	2.83242426	0.35305445	314.12987247	0.00318340	110.90495070	0.00901673	179
180	2.84894673	0.35100691	316.96229672	0.00315495	111.25595761	0.00898828	180
181	2.86556559	0.34897125	319.81124345	0.00312684	111.60492886	0.00896018	181
182	2.88228139	0.34694739	322.67680904	0.00309908	111.95187625	0.00893241	182
183	2.89909469	0.34493527	325.55909043	0.00307164	112.29681151	0.00890497	183
184	2.91600608	0.34293481	328.45818512	0.00304453	112.63974633	0.00887786	184
185	2.93301612	0.34094596	331.37419120	0.00301774	112.98069229	0.00885107	185
186	2.95012538	0.33896864	334.30720731	0.00299126	113.31966093	0.00882459	186
187	2.96733444	0.33700279	337.25733269	0.00296509	113.65666373	0.00879843	187
188	2.98464389	0.33504835	340.22466713	0.00293923	113.99171207	0.00877257	188
189	3.00205431	0.33310523	343.20931102	0.00291367	114.32481731	0.00874701	189
190	3.01956630	0.33117339	346.21136534	0.00288841	114.65599069	0.00872174	190
191	3.03718043	0.32925275	349.23093163	0.00286343	114.98524344	0.00869677	191
192	3.05489732	0.32734324	352.26811207	0.00283875	115.31258668	0.00867208	192
193	3.07271755	0.32544482	355.32300939	0.00281434	115.63803150	0.00864767	193
194	3.09064174	0.32355740	358.39572694	0.00279021	115.96158890	0.00862355	194
195	3.10867048	0.32168093	361.48636868	0.00276636	116.28326982	0.00859969	195
196	3.12680440	0.31981534	364.59503917	0.00274277	116.60308516	0.00857610	196
197	3.14504409	0.31796057	367.72184356	0.00271945	116.92104573	0.00855278	197
198	3.16339018	0.31611655	370.86688765	0.00269639	117.23716228	0.00852972	198
199	3.18184329	0.31428323	374.03027783	0.00267358	117.55144552	0.00850691	199
200	3.20040404	0.31246055	377.21212112	0.00265103	117.86390606	0.00848436	200

TABLE A-2

COMPOUND INTEREST FOR $1

$\frac{7}{12}$ %

PERIODS n	FUTURE AMOUNT $(1+i)^n$	PRESENT VALUE $(1+i)^{-n}$	AMOUNT OF ANNUITY $(S/p,i,n)$ $\frac{(1+i)^n - 1}{i}$	SINKING FUND $(p/S,i,n)$ $\frac{i}{(1+i)^n - 1}$	PRESENT VALUE OF ANNUITY $(V/p,i,n)$ $\frac{1-(1+i)^{-n}}{i}$	AMORTIZATION $(p/V,i,n)$ $\frac{i}{1-(1+i)^{-n}}$	PERIODS n
201	3.21907306	0.31064843	380.41252516	0.00262873	118.17455450	0.00846206	201
202	3.23785099	0.30884683	383.63159822	0.00260667	118.48340132	0.00844000	202
203	3.25673845	0.30705567	386.86944921	0.00258485	118.79045699	0.00841818	203
204	3.27573609	0.30527490	390.12618766	0.00256327	119.09573189	0.00839661	204
205	3.29484456	0.30350445	393.40192376	0.00254193	119.39923634	0.00837526	205
206	3.31406448	0.30174428	396.69676831	0.00252082	119.70098062	0.00835415	206
207	3.33339652	0.29999431	400.01083280	0.00249993	120.00097493	0.00833327	207
208	3.35284134	0.29825450	403.34422932	0.00247927	120.29922943	0.00831261	208
209	3.37239958	0.29652477	406.69707066	0.00245883	120.59575420	0.00829217	209
210	3.39207191	0.29480507	410.06947024	0.00243861	120.89055927	0.00827194	210
211	3.41185900	0.29309535	413.46154215	0.00241860	121.18365461	0.00825194	211
212	3.43176151	0.29139554	416.87340114	0.00239881	121.47505016	0.00823214	212
213	3.45178012	0.28970559	420.30516265	0.00237922	121.76475575	0.00821256	213
214	3.47191550	0.28802544	423.75694276	0.00235984	122.05278119	0.00819318	214
215	3.49216834	0.28635504	427.22885826	0.00234067	122.33913623	0.00817400	215
216	3.51253932	0.28469432	430.72102660	0.00232169	122.62383055	0.00815502	216
217	3.53302913	0.28304324	434.23356593	0.00230291	122.90687379	0.00813624	217
218	3.55363847	0.28140173	437.76659506	0.00228432	123.18827551	0.00811766	218
219	3.57436803	0.27976974	441.32023353	0.00226593	123.46804525	0.00809926	219
220	3.59521851	0.27814721	444.89460156	0.00224772	123.74619246	0.00808106	220
221	3.61619062	0.27653410	448.48982007	0.00222971	124.02272655	0.00806304	221
222	3.63728506	0.27493033	452.10601069	0.00221187	124.29765689	0.00804520	222
223	3.65850256	0.27333588	455.74329575	0.00219422	124.57099276	0.00802755	223
224	3.67984382	0.27175066	459.40179831	0.00217674	124.84274343	0.00801008	224
225	3.70130958	0.27017464	463.08164213	0.00215945	125.11291807	0.00799278	225
226	3.72290055	0.26860777	466.78295171	0.00214232	125.38152584	0.00797566	226
227	3.74461747	0.26704997	470.50585226	0.00212537	125.64857581	0.00795871	227
228	3.76646107	0.26550122	474.25046973	0.00210859	125.91407703	0.00794192	228
229	3.78843210	0.26396144	478.01693081	0.00209198	126.17803847	0.00792531	229
230	3.81053128	0.26243060	481.80536290	0.00207553	126.44046907	0.00790886	230
231	3.83275938	0.26090863	485.61589419	0.00205924	126.70137770	0.00789257	231
232	3.85511715	0.25939549	489.44865357	0.00204312	126.96077319	0.00787645	232
233	3.87760533	0.25789112	493.30377071	0.00202715	127.21866431	0.00786048	233
234	3.90022469	0.25639548	497.18137604	0.00201134	127.47505980	0.00784467	234
235	3.92297600	0.25490852	501.08160074	0.00199568	127.72996832	0.00782902	235
236	3.94586003	0.25343018	505.00457674	0.00198018	127.98339849	0.00781351	236
237	3.96887755	0.25196041	508.95043677	0.00196483	128.23535890	0.00779816	237
238	3.99202933	0.25049916	512.91931432	0.00194962	128.48585806	0.00778296	238
239	4.01531617	0.24904639	516.91134365	0.00193457	128.73490445	0.00776790	239
240	4.03873885	0.24760205	520.92665983	0.00191966	128.98250650	0.00775299	240

TABLE A-2

COMPOUND INTEREST FOR $1

$\frac{2}{3}\%$

PERIODS n	FUTURE AMOUNT $(1+i)^n$	PRESENT VALUE $(1+i)^{-n}$	AMOUNT OF ANNUITY $(S/p,i,n)$ $\dfrac{(1+i)^n-1}{i}$	SINKING FUND $(p/S,i,n)$ $\dfrac{i}{(1+i)^n-1}$	PRESENT VALUE OF ANNUITY $(V/p,i,n)$ $\dfrac{1-(1+i)^{-n}}{i}$	AMORTIZATION $(p/V,i,n)$ $\dfrac{i}{1-(1+i)^{-n}}$	PERIODS n
1	1.00666667	0.99337748	1.00000000	1.00000000	0.99337748	1.00666667	1
2	1.01337778	0.98679882	2.00666667	0.49833887	1.98017631	0.50500554	2
3	1.02013363	0.98026373	3.02004444	0.33112095	2.96044004	0.33778762	3
4	1.02693452	0.97377192	4.04017807	0.24751384	3.93421196	0.25418051	4
5	1.03378075	0.96732310	5.06711259	0.19735105	4.90153506	0.20401772	5
6	1.04067262	0.96091699	6.10089335	0.16391042	5.86245205	0.17057709	6
7	1.04761044	0.95455330	7.14156597	0.14002531	6.81700535	0.14669198	7
8	1.05459451	0.94823175	8.18917641	0.12211240	7.76523710	0.12877907	8
9	1.06162514	0.94195207	9.24377092	0.10818096	8.70718917	0.11484763	9
10	1.06870264	0.93571398	10.30539606	0.09703654	9.64290315	0.10370321	10
11	1.07582732	0.92951720	11.37409870	0.08791905	10.57242035	0.09458572	11
12	1.08299951	0.92336145	12.44992602	0.08032176	11.49578180	0.08698843	12
13	1.09021950	0.91724648	13.53292553	0.07389385	12.41302828	0.08056052	13
14	1.09748763	0.91117200	14.62314503	0.06838474	13.32420028	0.07505141	14
15	1.10480422	0.90513775	15.72063266	0.06361067	14.22933802	0.07027734	15
16	1.11216958	0.89914346	16.82543688	0.05943382	15.12848148	0.06610049	16
17	1.11958404	0.89318886	17.93760646	0.05574880	16.02167035	0.06241546	17
18	1.12704794	0.88727371	19.05719051	0.05247363	16.90894405	0.05914030	18
19	1.13456159	0.88139772	20.18423844	0.04954361	17.79034177	0.05621027	19
20	1.14212533	0.87556065	21.31880003	0.04690696	18.66590242	0.05357362	20
21	1.14973950	0.86976224	22.46092536	0.04452176	19.53566466	0.05118843	21
22	1.15740443	0.86400222	23.61066487	0.04235374	20.39966688	0.04902041	22
23	1.16512046	0.85828035	24.76806930	0.04037456	21.25794723	0.04704123	23
24	1.17288793	0.85259638	25.93318976	0.03856062	22.11054361	0.04522729	24
25	1.18070718	0.84695004	27.10607769	0.03689210	22.95749365	0.04355876	25
26	1.18857857	0.84134110	28.28678488	0.03535220	23.79883475	0.04201886	26
27	1.19650242	0.83576931	29.47536344	0.03392664	24.63460406	0.04059331	27
28	1.20447911	0.83023441	30.67186587	0.03260317	25.46483847	0.03926983	28
29	1.21250897	0.82473617	31.87634497	0.03137123	26.28957464	0.03803789	29
30	1.22059236	0.81927434	33.08885394	0.03022166	27.10884898	0.03688832	30
31	1.22872964	0.81384868	34.30944630	0.02914649	27.92269766	0.03581316	31
32	1.23692117	0.80845896	35.53817594	0.02813875	28.73115662	0.03480542	32
33	1.24516731	0.80310492	36.77509711	0.02719231	29.53426154	0.03385898	33
34	1.25346843	0.79778635	38.02026443	0.02630176	30.33204789	0.03296843	34
35	1.26182489	0.79250299	39.27373286	0.02546231	31.12455088	0.03212898	35
36	1.27023705	0.78725463	40.53555774	0.02466970	31.91180551	0.03133637	36
37	1.27870530	0.78204102	41.80579479	0.02392013	32.69384653	0.03058680	37
38	1.28723000	0.77686194	43.08450009	0.02321020	33.47070848	0.02987687	38
39	1.29581153	0.77171716	44.37173009	0.02253687	34.24242564	0.02920354	39
40	1.30445028	0.76660645	45.66754163	0.02189739	35.00903209	0.02856406	40

TABLE A-2

COMPOUND INTEREST FOR $1

$\frac{2}{3}\%$

PERIODS n	FUTURE AMOUNT $(1+i)^n$	PRESENT VALUE $(1+i)^{-n}$	AMOUNT OF ANNUITY (S/p,i,n) $\dfrac{(1+i)^n - 1}{i}$	SINKING FUND (p/S,i,n) $\dfrac{i}{(1+i)^n - 1}$	PRESENT VALUE OF ANNUITY (V/p,i,n) $\dfrac{1-(1+i)^{-n}}{i}$	AMORTIZATION (p/V,i,n) $\dfrac{i}{1-(1+i)^{-n}}$	PERIODS n
41	1.31314661	0.76152959	46.97199191	0.02128928	35.77056168	0.02795595	41
42	1.32190092	0.75648635	48.28513852	0.02071031	36.52704803	0.02737697	42
43	1.33071360	0.75147650	49.60703944	0.02015843	37.27852453	0.02682510	43
44	1.33958502	0.74649984	50.93775304	0.01963180	38.02502437	0.02629847	44
45	1.34851559	0.74155613	52.27733806	0.01912875	38.76658050	0.02579541	45
46	1.35750569	0.73664516	53.62585365	0.01864772	39.50322566	0.02531439	46
47	1.36655573	0.73176672	54.98335934	0.01818732	40.23499238	0.02485399	47
48	1.37566610	0.72692058	56.34991507	0.01774626	40.96191296	0.02441292	48
49	1.38483721	0.72210654	57.72558117	0.01732334	41.68401949	0.02399001	49
50	1.39406946	0.71732437	59.11041837	0.01691749	42.40134387	0.02358416	50
51	1.40336325	0.71257388	60.50448783	0.01652770	43.11391775	0.02319437	51
52	1.41271901	0.70785485	61.90785108	0.01615304	43.82177260	0.02281971	52
53	1.42213713	0.70316707	63.32057009	0.01579266	44.52493967	0.02245932	53
54	1.43161805	0.69851033	64.74270722	0.01544576	45.22345000	0.02211242	54
55	1.44116217	0.69388444	66.17432527	0.01511160	45.91733444	0.02177827	55
56	1.45076992	0.68928918	67.61548744	0.01478951	46.60662361	0.02145618	56
57	1.46044172	0.68472435	69.06625736	0.01447885	47.29134796	0.02114552	57
58	1.47017799	0.68018975	70.52669907	0.01417903	47.97153771	0.02084569	58
59	1.47997918	0.67568518	71.99687706	0.01388949	48.64722289	0.02055616	59
60	1.48984571	0.67121044	73.47685625	0.01360973	49.31843334	0.02027639	60
61	1.49977801	0.66676534	74.96670195	0.01333926	49.98519868	0.02000592	61
62	1.50977653	0.66234968	76.46647997	0.01307763	50.64754836	0.01974429	62
63	1.51984171	0.65796326	77.97625650	0.01282442	51.30551161	0.01949108	63
64	1.52997399	0.65360588	79.49609821	0.01257923	51.95911749	0.01924590	64
65	1.54017381	0.64927737	81.02607220	0.01234171	52.60839486	0.01900837	65
66	1.55044164	0.64497752	82.56624601	0.01211149	53.25337238	0.01877815	66
67	1.56077792	0.64070614	84.11668765	0.01188825	53.89407852	0.01855491	67
68	1.57118310	0.63646306	85.67746557	0.01167168	54.53054158	0.01833835	68
69	1.58165766	0.63224807	87.24864867	0.01146150	55.16278965	0.01812816	69
70	1.59220204	0.62806100	88.83030633	0.01125742	55.79085064	0.01792409	70
71	1.60281672	0.62390165	90.42250837	0.01105919	56.41475230	0.01772586	71
72	1.61350217	0.61976985	92.02532510	0.01086657	57.03452215	0.01753324	72
73	1.62425885	0.61566542	93.63882726	0.01067933	57.65018756	0.01734600	73
74	1.63508724	0.61158816	95.26308611	0.01049725	58.26177573	0.01716391	74
75	1.64598782	0.60753791	96.89817335	0.01032011	58.86931363	0.01698678	75
76	1.65696107	0.60351448	98.54416118	0.01014773	59.47282811	0.01681440	76
77	1.66800748	0.59951769	100.20112225	0.00997993	60.07234581	0.01664659	77
78	1.67912753	0.59554738	101.86912973	0.00981652	60.66789319	0.01648318	78
79	1.69032172	0.59160336	103.54825726	0.00965733	61.25949654	0.01632400	79
80	1.70159053	0.58768545	105.23857898	0.00950222	61.84718200	0.01616889	80

TABLE A-2

COMPOUND INTEREST FOR $1

$\frac{2}{3}\%$

PERIODS n	FUTURE AMOUNT $(1+i)^n$	PRESENT VALUE $(1+i)^{-n}$	AMOUNT OF ANNUITY $(S/p,i,n)$ $\dfrac{(1+i)^n - 1}{i}$	SINKING FUND $(p/S,i,n)$ $\dfrac{i}{(1+i)^n - 1}$	PRESENT VALUE OF ANNUITY $(V/p,i,n)$ $\dfrac{1-(1+i)^{-n}}{i}$	AMORTIZATION $(p/V,i,n)$ $\dfrac{i}{1-(1+i)^{-n}}$	PERIODS n
81	1.71293446	0.58379350	106.94016950	0.00935102	62.43097549	0.01601769	81
82	1.72435403	0.57992731	108.65310397	0.00920360	63.01090281	0.01587027	82
83	1.73584972	0.57608674	110.37745799	0.00905982	63.58698954	0.01572649	83
84	1.74742205	0.57227159	112.11330771	0.00891955	64.15926114	0.01558621	84
85	1.75907153	0.56848171	113.86072966	0.00878266	64.72774285	0.01544933	85
86	1.77079868	0.56471693	115.61980130	0.00864904	65.29245979	0.01531570	86
87	1.78260400	0.56097709	117.39059997	0.00851857	65.85343687	0.01518524	87
88	1.79448803	0.55726201	119.17320397	0.00839115	66.41069888	0.01505781	88
89	1.80645128	0.55357153	120.96769200	0.00826667	66.96427041	0.01493334	89
90	1.81849429	0.54990549	122.77414328	0.00814504	67.51417591	0.01481170	90
91	1.83061758	0.54626374	124.59263757	0.00802616	68.06043964	0.01469282	91
92	1.84282170	0.54264610	126.42325515	0.00790994	68.60308574	0.01457660	92
93	1.85510718	0.53905241	128.26607685	0.00779629	69.14213815	0.01446296	93
94	1.86747456	0.53548253	130.12118403	0.00768514	69.67762068	0.01435181	94
95	1.87992439	0.53193629	131.98865859	0.00757641	70.20955696	0.01424308	95
96	1.89245722	0.52841353	133.86858298	0.00747001	70.73797049	0.01413668	96
97	1.90507360	0.52491410	135.76104020	0.00736588	71.26288460	0.01403255	97
98	1.91777409	0.52143785	137.66611380	0.00726395	71.78432245	0.01393062	98
99	1.93055925	0.51798462	139.58388790	0.00716415	72.30230707	0.01383082	99
100	1.94342965	0.51455426	141.51444715	0.00706642	72.81686133	0.01373308	100
101	1.95638585	0.51114661	143.45787680	0.00697069	73.32800794	0.01363735	101
102	1.96942842	0.50776154	145.41426264	0.00687690	73.83576948	0.01354357	102
103	1.98255794	0.50439888	147.38369106	0.00678501	74.34016835	0.01345168	103
104	1.99577499	0.50105849	149.36624900	0.00669495	74.84122684	0.01336162	104
105	2.00908016	0.49774022	151.36202399	0.00660668	75.33896706	0.01327334	105
106	2.02247403	0.49444393	153.37110415	0.00652013	75.83341099	0.01318680	106
107	2.03595719	0.49116946	155.39357818	0.00643527	76.32458045	0.01310194	107
108	2.04953024	0.48791669	157.42953537	0.00635205	76.81249714	0.01301871	108
109	2.06319377	0.48468545	159.47906560	0.00627042	77.29718259	0.01293708	109
110	2.07694840	0.48147561	161.54225937	0.00619033	77.77865820	0.01285700	110
111	2.09079472	0.47828703	163.61920777	0.00611175	78.25694523	0.01277842	111
112	2.10473335	0.47511957	165.71000249	0.00603464	78.73206480	0.01270131	112
113	2.11876491	0.47197308	167.81473584	0.00595895	79.20403788	0.01262562	113
114	2.13289000	0.46884743	169.93350074	0.00588465	79.67288531	0.01255132	114
115	2.14710927	0.46574248	172.06639075	0.00581171	80.13862779	0.01247838	115
116	2.16142333	0.46265809	174.21350002	0.00574008	80.60128589	0.01240675	116
117	2.17583282	0.45959413	176.37492335	0.00566974	81.06088002	0.01233641	117
118	2.19033837	0.45655046	178.55075618	0.00560065	81.51743048	0.01226732	118
119	2.20494063	0.45352695	180.74109455	0.00553278	81.97095743	0.01219944	119
120	2.21964023	0.45052346	182.94603518	0.00546609	82.42148089	0.01213276	120

TABLE A-2

COMPOUND INTEREST FOR $1

$\frac{2}{3}\%$

PERIODS n	FUTURE AMOUNT $(1+i)^n$	PRESENT VALUE $(1+i)^{-n}$	AMOUNT OF ANNUITY $(S/p,i,n)$ $\dfrac{(1+i)^n - 1}{i}$	SINKING FUND $(p/S,i,n)$ $\dfrac{i}{(1+i)^n - 1}$	PRESENT VALUE OF ANNUITY $(V/p,i,n)$ $\dfrac{1-(1+i)^{-n}}{i}$	AMORTIZATION $(p/V,i,n)$ $\dfrac{i}{1-(1+i)^{-n}}$	PERIODS n
121	2.23443784	0.44753986	185.16567542	0.00540057	82.86902076	0.01206724	121
122	2.24933409	0.44457602	187.40011325	0.00533618	83.31359678	0.01200284	122
123	2.26432965	0.44163181	189.64944734	0.00527289	83.75522859	0.01193955	123
124	2.27942518	0.43870710	191.91377699	0.00521067	84.19393568	0.01187734	124
125	2.29462135	0.43580175	194.19320217	0.00514951	84.62973743	0.01181618	125
126	2.30991882	0.43291565	196.48782352	0.00508937	85.06265308	0.01175604	126
127	2.32531828	0.43004866	198.79774234	0.00503024	85.49270173	0.01169690	127
128	2.34082040	0.42720065	201.12306062	0.00497208	85.91990238	0.01163875	128
129	2.35642587	0.42437151	203.46388103	0.00491488	86.34427389	0.01158154	129
130	2.37213538	0.42156110	205.82030690	0.00485861	86.76583499	0.01152527	130
131	2.38794962	0.41876930	208.19244228	0.00480325	87.18460430	0.01146991	131
132	2.40386928	0.41599600	210.58039190	0.00474878	87.60060029	0.01141545	132
133	2.41989507	0.41324106	212.98426117	0.00469518	88.01384135	0.01136185	133
134	2.43602771	0.41050436	215.40415625	0.00464244	88.42434571	0.01130910	134
135	2.45226789	0.40778579	217.84018396	0.00459052	88.83213150	0.01125719	135
136	2.46861635	0.40508522	220.29245185	0.00453942	89.23721673	0.01120609	136
137	2.48507379	0.40240254	222.76106820	0.00448911	89.63961926	0.01115578	137
138	2.50164095	0.39973762	225.24614198	0.00443959	90.03935688	0.01110625	138
139	2.51831855	0.39709035	227.74778293	0.00439082	90.43644724	0.01105749	139
140	2.53510734	0.39446061	230.26610148	0.00434280	90.83090785	0.01100947	140
141	2.55200806	0.39184829	232.80120883	0.00429551	91.22275614	0.01096218	141
142	2.56902145	0.38925327	235.35321689	0.00424893	91.61200941	0.01091560	142
143	2.58614826	0.38667543	237.92223833	0.00420305	91.99868485	0.01086972	143
144	2.60338924	0.38411467	240.50838659	0.00415786	92.38279952	0.01082453	144
145	2.62074517	0.38157086	243.11177583	0.00411333	92.76437038	0.01078000	145
146	2.63821681	0.37904390	245.73252100	0.00406947	93.14341429	0.01073613	146
147	2.65580492	0.37653368	248.37073781	0.00402624	93.51994797	0.01069291	147
148	2.67351028	0.37404008	251.02654273	0.00398364	93.89398805	0.01065031	148
149	2.69133369	0.37156299	253.70005301	0.00394166	94.26555104	0.01060833	149
150	2.70927591	0.36910231	256.39138670	0.00390029	94.63465335	0.01056695	150
151	2.72733775	0.36665792	259.10066261	0.00385950	95.00131128	0.01052617	151
152	2.74552000	0.36422973	261.82800036	0.00381930	95.36554100	0.01048597	152
153	2.76382347	0.36181761	264.57352036	0.00377967	95.72735861	0.01044633	153
154	2.78224896	0.35942147	267.33734383	0.00374059	96.08678008	0.01040726	154
155	2.80079729	0.35704119	270.11959279	0.00370206	96.44382127	0.01036873	155
156	2.81946927	0.35467668	272.92039008	0.00366407	96.79849795	0.01033074	156
157	2.83826573	0.35232783	275.73985935	0.00362661	97.15082578	0.01029327	157
158	2.85718750	0.34999453	278.57812507	0.00358966	97.50082031	0.01025632	158
159	2.87623542	0.34767669	281.43531257	0.00355321	97.84849700	0.01021988	159
160	2.89541032	0.34537419	284.31154799	0.00351727	98.19387119	0.01018393	160

TABLE A-2

COMPOUND INTEREST FOR $1

$\frac{2}{3}\%$

PERIODS	FUTURE AMOUNT	PRESENT VALUE	AMOUNT OF ANNUITY	SINKING FUND	PRESENT VALUE OF ANNUITY	AMORTIZATION	PERIODS
n	$(1+i)^n$	$(1+i)^{-n}$	$(S/p,i,n)$ $\dfrac{(1+i)^n - 1}{i}$	$(p/S,i,n)$ $\dfrac{i}{(1+i)^n - 1}$	$(V/p,i,n)$ $\dfrac{1-(1+i)^{-n}}{i}$	$(p/V,i,n)$ $\dfrac{i}{1-(1+i)^{-n}}$	n
161	2.91471306	0.34308695	287.20695831	0.00348181	98.53695813	0.01014848	161
162	2.93414448	0.34081485	290.12167137	0.00344683	98.87777298	0.01011350	162
163	2.95370544	0.33855779	293.05581584	0.00341232	99.21633077	0.01007899	163
164	2.97339681	0.33631569	296.00952128	0.00337827	99.55264647	0.01004494	164
165	2.99321945	0.33408843	298.98291809	0.00334467	99.88673490	0.01001134	165
166	3.01317425	0.33187593	301.97613754	0.00331152	100.21861083	0.00997819	166
167	3.03326208	0.32967807	304.98931179	0.00327880	100.54828890	0.00994547	167
168	3.05348383	0.32749478	308.02257387	0.00324652	100.87578368	0.00991318	168
169	3.07384038	0.32532594	311.07605770	0.00321465	101.20110961	0.00988131	169
170	3.09433265	0.32317146	314.14989808	0.00318319	101.52428107	0.00984986	170
171	3.11496154	0.32103125	317.24423074	0.00315215	101.84531232	0.00981881	171
172	3.13572795	0.31890522	320.35919228	0.00312150	102.16421754	0.00978816	172
173	3.15663280	0.31679326	323.49492022	0.00309124	102.48101080	0.00975791	173
174	3.17767702	0.31469529	326.65155303	0.00306137	102.79570609	0.00972803	174
175	3.19886153	0.31261122	329.82923005	0.00303187	103.10831731	0.00969854	175
176	3.22018728	0.31054094	333.02809158	0.00300275	103.41885826	0.00966942	176
177	3.24165519	0.30848438	336.24827886	0.00297399	103.72734264	0.00964066	177
178	3.26326623	0.30644144	339.48993405	0.00294560	104.03378408	0.00961226	178
179	3.28502134	0.30441203	342.75320028	0.00291755	104.33819610	0.00958422	179
180	3.30692148	0.30239605	346.03822161	0.00288985	104.64059216	0.00955652	180
181	3.32896762	0.30039343	349.34514309	0.00286250	104.94098559	0.00952917	181
182	3.35116074	0.29840407	352.67411071	0.00283548	105.23938965	0.00950215	182
183	3.37350181	0.29642788	356.02527145	0.00280879	105.53581754	0.00947546	183
184	3.39599182	0.29446478	359.39877326	0.00278242	105.83028232	0.00944909	184
185	3.41863177	0.29251469	362.79476508	0.00275638	106.12279701	0.00942305	185
186	3.44142265	0.29057750	366.21339685	0.00273065	106.41337451	0.00939731	186
187	3.46436546	0.28865315	369.65481949	0.00270523	106.70202766	0.00937189	187
188	3.48746123	0.28674154	373.11918496	0.00268011	106.98876920	0.00934678	188
189	3.51071097	0.28484259	376.60664619	0.00265529	107.27361179	0.00932196	189
190	3.53411571	0.28295621	380.11735716	0.00263077	107.55656800	0.00929743	190
191	3.55767649	0.28108233	383.65147288	0.00260653	107.83765033	0.00927320	191
192	3.58139433	0.27922086	387.20914936	0.00258258	108.11687119	0.00924925	192
193	3.60527029	0.27737171	390.79054369	0.00255892	108.39424291	0.00922558	193
194	3.62930543	0.27553482	394.39581398	0.00253552	108.66977772	0.00920219	194
195	3.65350080	0.27371008	398.02511941	0.00251240	108.94348780	0.00917907	195
196	3.67785747	0.27189743	401.67862021	0.00248955	109.21538523	0.00915622	196
197	3.70237652	0.27009679	405.35647767	0.00246696	109.48548202	0.00913363	197
198	3.72705903	0.26830807	409.05885419	0.00244464	109.75379009	0.00911130	198
199	3.75190609	0.26653119	412.78591322	0.00242256	110.02032128	0.00908923	199
200	3.77691880	0.26476608	416.53781931	0.00240074	110.28508736	0.00906741	200

TABLE A-2

COMPOUND INTEREST FOR $1

$\frac{2}{3}$ %

PERIODS n	FUTURE AMOUNT $(1+i)^n$	PRESENT VALUE $(1+i)^{-n}$	AMOUNT OF ANNUITY (S/p,i,n) $\frac{(1+i)^n-1}{i}$	SINKING FUND (p/S,i,n) $\frac{i}{(1+i)^n-1}$	PRESENT VALUE OF ANNUITY (V/p,i,n) $\frac{1-(1+i)^{-n}}{i}$	AMORTIZATION (p/V,i,n) $\frac{i}{1-(1+i)^{-n}}$	PERIODS n
201	3.80209825	0.26301267	420.31473810	0.00237917	110.54810003	0.00904584	201
202	3.82744558	0.26127086	424.11683636	0.00235784	110.80937089	0.00902451	202
203	3.85296188	0.25954059	427.94428193	0.00233675	111.06891148	0.00900342	203
204	3.87864829	0.25782178	431.79724381	0.00231590	111.32673326	0.00898257	204
205	3.90450595	0.25611435	435.67589210	0.00229528	111.58284761	0.00896195	205
206	3.93053599	0.25441823	439.58039805	0.00227490	111.83726583	0.00894156	206
207	3.95673956	0.25273334	443.51093404	0.00225474	112.08999917	0.00892140	207
208	3.98311782	0.25105961	447.46767360	0.00223480	112.34105878	0.00890146	208
209	4.00967194	0.24939696	451.45079142	0.00221508	112.59045574	0.00888175	209
210	4.03640309	0.24774533	455.46046337	0.00219558	112.83820107	0.00886225	210
211	4.06331244	0.24610463	459.49686646	0.00217629	113.08430570	0.00884296	211
212	4.09040119	0.24447480	463.56017890	0.00215722	113.32878049	0.00882388	212
213	4.11767053	0.24285576	467.65058009	0.00213835	113.57163625	0.00880502	213
214	4.14512167	0.24124744	471.76825062	0.00211968	113.81288370	0.00878635	214
215	4.17275582	0.23964978	475.91337230	0.00210122	114.05253347	0.00876789	215
216	4.20057419	0.23806269	480.08612811	0.00208296	114.29059616	0.00874963	216
217	4.22857802	0.23648612	484.28670230	0.00206489	114.52708228	0.00873156	217
218	4.25676854	0.23491998	488.51528031	0.00204702	114.76200227	0.00871369	218
219	4.28514699	0.23336422	492.77204885	0.00202934	114.99536649	0.00869600	219
220	4.31371464	0.23181876	497.05719584	0.00201184	115.22718526	0.00867851	220
221	4.34247274	0.23028354	501.37091048	0.00199453	115.45746880	0.00866120	221
222	4.37142255	0.22875848	505.71338322	0.00197740	115.68622728	0.00864407	222
223	4.40056537	0.22724353	510.08480577	0.00196046	115.91347081	0.00862712	223
224	4.42990247	0.22573860	514.48537114	0.00194369	116.13920941	0.00861036	224
225	4.45943516	0.22424365	518.91527362	0.00192710	116.36345306	0.00859376	225
226	4.48916473	0.22275859	523.37470878	0.00191068	116.58621165	0.00857734	226
227	4.51909249	0.22128337	527.86387350	0.00189443	116.80749502	0.00856109	227
228	4.54921977	0.21981791	532.38296599	0.00187835	117.02731293	0.00854501	228
229	4.57954791	0.21836217	536.93218576	0.00186243	117.24567510	0.00852910	229
230	4.61007822	0.21691606	541.51173367	0.00184668	117.46259115	0.00851335	230
231	4.64081208	0.21547973	546.12181189	0.00183109	117.67807068	0.00849776	231
232	4.67175083	0.21405251	550.76262397	0.00181566	117.89212320	0.00848233	232
233	4.70289583	0.21263495	555.43437480	0.00180039	118.10475814	0.00846706	233
234	4.73424847	0.21122677	560.13727063	0.00178528	118.31598491	0.00845194	234
235	4.76581013	0.20982791	564.87151910	0.00177031	118.52581282	0.00843698	235
236	4.79758219	0.20843833	569.63732923	0.00175550	118.73425115	0.00842217	236
237	4.82956608	0.20705794	574.43491142	0.00174084	118.94130909	0.00840751	237
238	4.86176318	0.20568669	579.26447750	0.00172633	119.14699578	0.00839299	238
239	4.89417494	0.20432453	584.12624068	0.00171196	119.35132031	0.00837863	239
240	4.92680277	0.20297139	589.02041562	0.00169773	119.55429170	0.00836440	240

TABLE A-2

COMPOUND INTEREST FOR $1

$\frac{3}{4}$ %

PERIODS n	FUTURE AMOUNT $(1+i)^n$	PRESENT VALUE $(1+i)^{-n}$	AMOUNT OF ANNUITY (S/p,i,n) $\dfrac{(1+i)^n-1}{i}$	SINKING FUND (p/S,i,n) $\dfrac{i}{(1+i)^n-1}$	PRESENT VALUE OF ANNUITY (V/p,i,n) $\dfrac{1-(1+i)^{-n}}{i}$	AMORTIZATION (p/V,i,n) $\dfrac{i}{1-(1+i)^{-n}}$	PERIODS n
1	1.00750000	0.99255583	1.00000000	1.00000000	0.99255583	1.00750000	1
2	1.01505625	0.98516708	2.00750000	0.49813200	1.97772291	0.50563200	2
3	1.02266917	0.97783333	3.02255625	0.33084579	2.95555624	0.33834579	3
4	1.03033919	0.97055417	4.04522542	0.24720501	3.92611041	0.25470501	4
5	1.03806673	0.96332920	5.07556461	0.19702242	4.88943961	0.20452242	5
6	1.04585224	0.95615802	6.11363135	0.16356891	5.84559763	0.17106891	6
7	1.05369613	0.94904022	7.15948358	0.13967488	6.79463785	0.14717488	7
8	1.06159885	0.94197540	8.21317971	0.12175552	7.73661325	0.12925552	8
9	1.06956084	0.93496318	9.27477856	0.10781929	8.67157642	0.11531929	9
10	1.07758255	0.92800315	10.34433940	0.09667123	9.59957958	0.10417123	10
11	1.08566441	0.92109494	11.42192194	0.08755094	10.52067452	0.09505094	11
12	1.09380690	0.91423815	12.50758636	0.07995148	11.43491267	0.08745148	12
13	1.10201045	0.90743241	13.60139325	0.07352188	12.34234508	0.08102188	13
14	1.11027553	0.90067733	14.70340370	0.06801146	13.24302242	0.07551146	14
15	1.11860259	0.89397254	15.81367923	0.06323639	14.13699495	0.07073639	15
16	1.12699211	0.88731766	16.93228183	0.05905879	15.02431261	0.06655879	16
17	1.13544455	0.88071231	18.05927394	0.05537321	15.90502492	0.06287321	17
18	1.14396039	0.87415614	19.19471849	0.05209766	16.77918107	0.05959766	18
19	1.15254009	0.86764878	20.33867888	0.04916740	17.64682984	0.05666740	19
20	1.16118414	0.86118985	21.49121897	0.04653063	18.50801969	0.05403063	20
21	1.16989302	0.85477901	22.65240312	0.04414543	19.36279870	0.05164543	21
22	1.17866722	0.84841589	23.82229614	0.04197748	20.21121459	0.04947748	22
23	1.18750723	0.84210014	25.00096336	0.03999846	21.05331473	0.04749846	23
24	1.19641353	0.83583140	26.18847059	0.03818474	21.88914614	0.04568474	24
25	1.20538663	0.82960933	27.38488412	0.03651650	22.71875547	0.04401650	25
26	1.21442703	0.82343358	28.59027075	0.03497693	23.54218905	0.04247693	26
27	1.22353523	0.81730380	29.80469778	0.03355176	24.35949286	0.04105176	27
28	1.23271175	0.81121966	31.02823301	0.03222871	25.17071251	0.03972871	28
29	1.24195709	0.80518080	32.26094476	0.03099723	25.97589331	0.03849723	29
30	1.25127176	0.79918690	33.50290184	0.02984816	26.77508021	0.03734816	30
31	1.26065630	0.79323762	34.75417361	0.02877352	27.56831783	0.03627352	31
32	1.27011122	0.78733262	36.01482991	0.02776634	28.35565045	0.03526634	32
33	1.27963706	0.78147158	37.28494113	0.02682048	29.13712203	0.03432048	33
34	1.28923434	0.77565418	38.56457819	0.02593053	29.91277621	0.03343053	34
35	1.29890359	0.76988008	39.85381253	0.02509170	30.68265629	0.03259170	35
36	1.30864537	0.76414896	41.15271612	0.02429973	31.44680525	0.03179973	36
37	1.31846021	0.75846051	42.46136149	0.02355082	32.20526576	0.03105082	37
38	1.32834866	0.75281440	43.77982170	0.02284157	32.95808016	0.03034157	38
39	1.33831128	0.74721032	45.10817037	0.02216893	33.70529048	0.02966893	39
40	1.34834861	0.74164796	46.44648164	0.02153016	34.44693844	0.02903016	40

TABLE A-2

COMPOUND INTEREST FOR $1

$\frac{3}{4}$ %

PERIODS n	FUTURE AMOUNT $(1+i)^n$	PRESENT VALUE $(1+i)^{-n}$	AMOUNT OF ANNUITY (S/p,i,n) $\dfrac{(1+i)^n - 1}{i}$	SINKING FUND (p/S,i,n) $\dfrac{i}{(1+i)^n - 1}$	PRESENT VALUE OF ANNUITY (V/p,i,n) $\dfrac{1-(1+i)^{-n}}{i}$	AMORTIZATION (p/V,i,n) $\dfrac{i}{1-(1+i)^{-n}}$	PERIODS n
41	1.35846123	0.73612701	47.79483026	0.02092276	35.18306545	0.02842276	41
42	1.36864969	0.73064716	49.15329148	0.02034452	35.91371260	0.02784452	42
43	1.37891456	0.72520809	50.52194117	0.01979338	36.63892070	0.02729338	43
44	1.38925642	0.71980952	51.90085573	0.01926751	37.35873022	0.02676751	44
45	1.39967584	0.71445114	53.29011215	0.01876521	38.07318136	0.02626521	45
46	1.41017341	0.70913264	54.68978799	0.01828495	38.78231401	0.02578495	46
47	1.42074971	0.70385374	56.09996140	0.01782532	39.48616775	0.02532532	47
48	1.43140533	0.69861414	57.52071111	0.01738504	40.18478189	0.02488504	48
49	1.44214087	0.69341353	58.95211644	0.01696292	40.87819542	0.02446292	49
50	1.45295693	0.68825165	60.39425732	0.01655787	41.56644707	0.02405787	50
51	1.46385411	0.68312819	61.84721424	0.01616888	42.24957525	0.02366888	51
52	1.47483301	0.67804286	63.31106835	0.01579503	42.92761812	0.02329503	52
53	1.48589426	0.67299540	64.78590136	0.01543546	43.60061351	0.02293546	53
54	1.49703847	0.66798551	66.27179562	0.01508938	44.26859902	0.02258938	54
55	1.50826626	0.66301291	67.76883409	0.01475605	44.93161193	0.02225605	55
56	1.51957825	0.65807733	69.27710035	0.01443478	45.58968926	0.02193478	56
57	1.53097509	0.65317849	70.79667860	0.01412496	46.24286776	0.02162496	57
58	1.54245740	0.64831612	72.32765369	0.01382597	46.89118388	0.02132597	58
59	1.55402583	0.64348995	73.87011109	0.01353727	47.53467382	0.02103727	59
60	1.56568103	0.63869970	75.42413693	0.01325836	48.17337352	0.02075836	60
61	1.57742363	0.63394511	76.98981795	0.01298873	48.80731863	0.02048873	61
62	1.58925431	0.62922592	78.56724159	0.01272795	49.43654455	0.02022795	62
63	1.60117372	0.62454185	80.15649590	0.01247560	50.06108640	0.01997560	63
64	1.61318252	0.61989266	81.75766962	0.01223127	50.68097906	0.01973127	64
65	1.62528139	0.61527807	83.37085214	0.01199460	51.29625713	0.01949460	65
66	1.63747100	0.61069784	84.99613353	0.01176524	51.90695497	0.01926524	66
67	1.64975203	0.60615170	86.63360453	0.01154286	52.51310667	0.01904286	67
68	1.66212517	0.60163940	88.28335657	0.01132716	53.11474607	0.01882716	68
69	1.67459111	0.59716070	89.94548174	0.01111785	53.71190677	0.01861785	69
70	1.68715055	0.59271533	91.62007285	0.01091464	54.30462210	0.01841464	70
71	1.69980418	0.58830306	93.30722340	0.01071728	54.89292516	0.01821728	71
72	1.71255271	0.58392363	95.00702758	0.01052554	55.47684880	0.01802554	72
73	1.72539685	0.57957681	96.71958028	0.01033917	56.05642561	0.01783917	73
74	1.73833733	0.57526234	98.44497714	0.01015796	56.63168795	0.01765796	74
75	1.75137486	0.57097999	100.18331446	0.00998170	57.20266794	0.01748170	75
76	1.76451017	0.56672952	101.93468932	0.00981020	57.76939746	0.01731020	76
77	1.77774400	0.56251069	103.69919949	0.00964328	58.33190815	0.01714328	77
78	1.79107708	0.55832326	105.47694349	0.00948074	58.89023141	0.01698074	78
79	1.80451015	0.55416701	107.26802056	0.00932244	59.44439842	0.01682244	79
80	1.81804398	0.55004170	109.07253072	0.00916821	59.99444012	0.01666821	80

TABLE A-2

COMPOUND INTEREST FOR $1

$\frac{3}{4}\%$

PERIODS n	FUTURE AMOUNT $(1+i)^n$	PRESENT VALUE $(1+i)^{-n}$	AMOUNT OF ANNUITY $(S/p,i,n)$ $\frac{(1+i)^n-1}{i}$	SINKING FUND $(p/S,i,n)$ $\frac{i}{(1+i)^n-1}$	PRESENT VALUE OF ANNUITY $(V/p,i,n)$ $\frac{1-(1+i)^{-n}}{i}$	AMORTIZATION $(p/V,i,n)$ $\frac{i}{1-(1+i)^{-n}}$	PERIODS n
81	1.83167931	0.54594710	110.89057470	0.00901790	60.54038722	0.01651790	81
82	1.84541691	0.54188297	112.72225401	0.00887136	61.08227019	0.01637136	82
83	1.85925753	0.53784911	114.56767091	0.00872847	61.62011930	0.01622847	83
84	1.87320196	0.53384527	116.42692845	0.00858908	62.15396456	0.01608908	84
85	1.88725098	0.52987123	118.30013041	0.00845308	62.68383579	0.01595308	85
86	1.90140536	0.52592678	120.18738139	0.00832034	63.20976257	0.01582034	86
87	1.91566590	0.52201169	122.08878675	0.00819076	63.73177427	0.01569076	87
88	1.93003339	0.51812575	124.00445265	0.00806423	64.24990002	0.01556423	88
89	1.94450865	0.51426873	125.93448604	0.00794064	64.76416875	0.01544064	89
90	1.95909246	0.51044043	127.87899469	0.00781989	65.27460918	0.01531989	90
91	1.97378565	0.50664063	129.83808715	0.00770190	65.78124981	0.01520190	91
92	1.98858905	0.50286911	131.81187280	0.00758657	66.28411892	0.01508657	92
93	2.00350346	0.49912567	133.80046185	0.00747382	66.78324458	0.01497382	93
94	2.01852974	0.49541009	135.80396531	0.00736356	67.27865467	0.01486356	94
95	2.03366871	0.49172217	137.82249505	0.00725571	67.77037685	0.01475571	95
96	2.04892123	0.48806171	139.85616377	0.00715020	68.25843856	0.01465020	96
97	2.06428814	0.48442850	141.90508499	0.00704696	68.74286705	0.01454696	97
98	2.07977030	0.48082233	143.96937313	0.00694592	69.22368938	0.01444592	98
99	2.09536858	0.47724301	146.04914343	0.00684701	69.70093239	0.01434701	99
100	2.11108384	0.47369033	148.14451201	0.00675017	70.17462272	0.01425017	100
101	2.12691697	0.47016410	150.25559585	0.00665533	70.64478682	0.01415533	101
102	2.14286885	0.46666412	152.38251281	0.00656243	71.11145094	0.01406243	102
103	2.15894036	0.46319019	154.52538166	0.00647143	71.57464113	0.01397143	103
104	2.17513242	0.45974213	156.68432202	0.00638226	72.03438325	0.01388226	104
105	2.19144591	0.45631973	158.85945444	0.00629487	72.49070298	0.01379487	105
106	2.20788175	0.45292281	161.05090035	0.00620922	72.94362579	0.01370922	106
107	2.22444087	0.44955117	163.25878210	0.00612524	73.39317696	0.01362524	107
108	2.24112417	0.44620464	165.48322296	0.00604291	73.83938160	0.01354291	108
109	2.25793260	0.44288302	167.72434714	0.00596216	74.28226461	0.01346216	109
110	2.27486710	0.43958612	169.98227974	0.00588297	74.72185073	0.01338297	110
111	2.29192860	0.43631377	172.25714684	0.00580527	75.15816450	0.01330527	111
112	2.30911807	0.43306577	174.54907544	0.00572905	75.59123027	0.01322905	112
113	2.32643645	0.42984196	176.85819351	0.00565425	76.02107223	0.01315425	113
114	2.34388472	0.42664214	179.18462996	0.00558084	76.44771437	0.01308084	114
115	2.36146386	0.42346615	181.52851468	0.00550878	76.87118052	0.01300878	115
116	2.37917484	0.42031379	183.88997854	0.00543803	77.29149431	0.01293803	116
117	2.39701865	0.41718491	186.26915338	0.00536858	77.70867922	0.01286858	117
118	2.41499629	0.41407931	188.66617203	0.00530037	78.12275853	0.01280037	118
119	2.43310876	0.41099683	191.08116832	0.00523338	78.53375536	0.01273338	119
120	2.45135708	0.40793730	193.51427708	0.00516758	78.94169267	0.01266758	120

COMPOUND INTEREST FOR $1

$\frac{3}{4}$%

PERIODS n	FUTURE AMOUNT $(1+i)^n$	PRESENT VALUE $(1+i)^{-n}$	AMOUNT OF ANNUITY (S/p,i,n) $\dfrac{(1+i)^n-1}{i}$	SINKING FUND (p/S,i,n) $\dfrac{i}{(1+i)^n-1}$	PRESENT VALUE OF ANNUITY (V/p,i,n) $\dfrac{1-(1+i)^{-n}}{i}$	AMORTIZATION (p/V,i,n) $\dfrac{i}{1-(1+i)^{-n}}$	PERIODS n
121	2.46974226	0.40490055	195.96563416	0.00510294	79.34659322	0.01260294	121
122	2.48826532	0.40188640	198.43537642	0.00503942	79.74847962	0.01253942	122
123	2.50692731	0.39889469	200.92364174	0.00497702	80.14737432	0.01247702	123
124	2.52572927	0.39592525	203.43056905	0.00491568	80.54329957	0.01241568	124
125	2.54467224	0.39297792	205.95629832	0.00485540	80.93627749	0.01235540	125
126	2.56375728	0.39005252	208.50097056	0.00479614	81.32633001	0.01229614	126
127	2.58298546	0.38714891	211.06472784	0.00473788	81.71347892	0.01223788	127
128	2.60235785	0.38426691	213.64771330	0.00468060	82.09774583	0.01218060	128
129	2.62187553	0.38140636	216.25007115	0.00462428	82.47915219	0.01212428	129
130	2.64153960	0.37856711	218.87194668	0.00456888	82.85771929	0.01206888	130
131	2.66135115	0.37574899	221.51348628	0.00451440	83.23346828	0.01201440	131
132	2.68131128	0.37295185	224.17483743	0.00446080	83.60642013	0.01196080	132
133	2.70142112	0.37017553	226.85614871	0.00440808	83.97659566	0.01190808	133
134	2.72168177	0.36741988	229.55756982	0.00435621	84.34401554	0.01185621	134
135	2.74209439	0.36468475	232.27925160	0.00430516	84.70870029	0.01180516	135
136	2.76266009	0.36196997	235.02134598	0.00425493	85.07067026	0.01175493	136
137	2.78338005	0.35927541	237.78400608	0.00420550	85.42994567	0.01170550	137
138	2.80425540	0.35660090	240.56738612	0.00415684	85.78654657	0.01165684	138
139	2.82528731	0.35394630	243.37164152	0.00410894	86.14049288	0.01160894	139
140	2.84647697	0.35131147	246.19692883	0.00406179	86.49180434	0.01156179	140
141	2.86782554	0.34869625	249.04340580	0.00401536	86.84050059	0.01151536	141
142	2.88933424	0.34610049	251.91123134	0.00396965	87.18660108	0.01146965	142
143	2.91100424	0.34352406	254.80056558	0.00392464	87.53012514	0.01142464	143
144	2.93283677	0.34096681	257.71156982	0.00388031	87.87109195	0.01138031	144
145	2.95483305	0.33842860	260.64440659	0.00383664	88.20952055	0.01133664	145
146	2.97699430	0.33590928	263.59923964	0.00379364	88.54542982	0.01129364	146
147	2.99932175	0.33340871	266.57623394	0.00375127	88.87883854	0.01125127	147
148	3.02181667	0.33092676	269.57555569	0.00370954	89.20976530	0.01120954	148
149	3.04448029	0.32846329	272.59737236	0.00366841	89.53822858	0.01116841	149
150	3.06731389	0.32601815	275.64185265	0.00362790	89.86424673	0.01112790	150
151	3.09031875	0.32359122	278.70916655	0.00358797	90.18783795	0.01108797	151
152	3.11349614	0.32118235	281.79948530	0.00354862	90.50902029	0.01104862	152
153	3.13684736	0.31879141	284.91298144	0.00350984	90.82781171	0.01100984	153
154	3.16037372	0.31641828	288.04982880	0.00347162	91.14422998	0.01097162	154
155	3.18407652	0.31406280	291.21020251	0.00343395	91.45829279	0.01093395	155
156	3.20795709	0.31172487	294.39427903	0.00339681	91.77001765	0.01089681	156
157	3.23201677	0.30940434	297.60223613	0.00336019	92.07942199	0.01086019	157
158	3.25625690	0.30710108	300.83425290	0.00332409	92.38652307	0.01082409	158
159	3.28067882	0.30481496	304.09050979	0.00328849	92.69133803	0.01078849	159
160	3.30528391	0.30254587	307.37118862	0.00325340	92.99388390	0.01075340	160

TABLE A-2

COMPOUND INTEREST FOR $1

$\frac{3}{4}$%

PERIODS	FUTURE AMOUNT	PRESENT VALUE	AMOUNT OF ANNUITY	SINKING FUND	PRESENT VALUE OF ANNUITY	AMORTIZATION	PERIODS
n	$(1+i)^n$	$(1+i)^{-n}$	$(S/p,i,n)$ $\dfrac{(1+i)^n-1}{i}$	$(p/S,i,n)$ $\dfrac{i}{(1+i)^n-1}$	$(V/p,i,n)$ $\dfrac{1-(1+i)^{-n}}{i}$	$(p/V,i,n)$ $\dfrac{i}{1-(1+i)^{-n}}$	n
161	3.33007354	0.30029367	310.67647253	0.00321878	93.29417757	0.01071878	161
162	3.35504910	0.29805823	314.00654608	0.00318465	93.59223580	0.01068465	162
163	3.38021196	0.29583944	317.36159517	0.00315098	93.88807524	0.01065098	163
164	3.40556355	0.29363716	320.74180714	0.00311777	94.18171239	0.01061777	164
165	3.43110528	0.29145127	324.14737069	0.00308502	94.47316367	0.01058502	165
166	3.45683857	0.28928166	327.57847597	0.00305270	94.76244533	0.01055270	166
167	3.48276486	0.28712820	331.03531454	0.00302083	95.04957352	0.01052083	167
168	3.50888560	0.28499077	334.51807940	0.00298938	95.33456429	0.01048938	168
169	3.53520224	0.28286925	338.02696499	0.00295834	95.61743354	0.01045834	169
170	3.56171625	0.28076352	341.56216723	0.00292772	95.89819706	0.01042772	170
171	3.58842913	0.27867347	345.12388349	0.00289751	96.17687053	0.01039751	171
172	3.61534235	0.27659898	348.71231261	0.00286769	96.45346951	0.01036769	172
173	3.64245741	0.27453993	352.32765496	0.00283827	96.72800944	0.01033827	173
174	3.66977584	0.27249621	355.97011237	0.00280922	97.00050565	0.01030922	174
175	3.69729916	0.27046770	359.63988821	0.00278056	97.27097335	0.01028056	175
176	3.72502891	0.26845429	363.33718737	0.00275226	97.53942764	0.01025226	176
177	3.75296662	0.26645587	367.06221628	0.00272433	97.80588352	0.01022433	177
178	3.78111387	0.26447233	370.81518290	0.00269676	98.07035585	0.01019676	178
179	3.80947223	0.26250355	374.59629677	0.00266954	98.33285940	0.01016954	179
180	3.83804327	0.26054943	378.40576900	0.00264267	98.59340884	0.01014267	180
181	3.86682859	0.25860986	382.24381226	0.00261613	98.85201869	0.01011613	181
182	3.89582981	0.25668472	386.11064086	0.00258993	99.10870342	0.01008993	182
183	3.92504853	0.25477392	390.00647066	0.00256406	99.36347734	0.01006406	183
184	3.95448639	0.25287734	393.93151919	0.00253851	99.61635468	0.01003851	184
185	3.98414504	0.25099488	397.88600559	0.00251328	99.86734956	0.01001328	185
186	4.01402613	0.24912643	401.87015063	0.00248837	100.11647599	0.00998837	186
187	4.04413133	0.24727189	405.88417676	0.00246376	100.36374788	0.00996376	187
188	4.07446231	0.24543116	409.92830808	0.00243945	100.60917904	0.00993945	188
189	4.10502078	0.24360413	414.00277039	0.00241544	100.85278316	0.00991544	189
190	4.13580843	0.24179070	418.10779117	0.00239173	101.09457386	0.00989173	190
191	4.16682700	0.23999077	422.24359961	0.00236830	101.33456462	0.00986830	191
192	4.19807820	0.23820423	426.41042660	0.00234516	101.57276886	0.00984516	192
193	4.22956379	0.23643100	430.60850480	0.00232230	101.80919986	0.00982230	193
194	4.26128551	0.23467097	434.83806859	0.00229971	102.04387083	0.00979971	194
195	4.29324516	0.23292404	439.09935410	0.00227739	102.27679487	0.00977739	195
196	4.32544449	0.23119011	443.39259926	0.00225534	102.50798498	0.00975534	196
197	4.35788533	0.22946909	447.71804375	0.00223355	102.73745407	0.00973355	197
198	4.39056947	0.22776089	452.07592908	0.00221202	102.96521496	0.00971202	198
199	4.42349874	0.22606540	456.46649855	0.00219074	103.19128036	0.00969074	199
200	4.45667498	0.22438253	460.88999729	0.00216972	103.41566289	0.00966972	200

TABLE A-2

COMPOUND INTEREST FOR $1

$\frac{3}{4}$ %

PERIODS n	FUTURE AMOUNT $(1+i)^n$	PRESENT VALUE $(1+i)^{-n}$	AMOUNT OF ANNUITY $(S/p,i,n)$ $\frac{(1+i)^n - 1}{i}$	SINKING FUND $(p/S,i,n)$ $\frac{i}{(1+i)^n - 1}$	PRESENT VALUE OF ANNUITY $(V/p,i,n)$ $\frac{1-(1+i)^{-n}}{i}$	AMORTIZATION $(p/V,i,n)$ $\frac{i}{1-(1+i)^{-n}}$	PERIODS n
201	4.49010004	0.22271219	465.34667227	0.00214894	103.63837507	0.00964894	201
202	4.52377579	0.22105428	469.83677231	0.00212840	103.85942935	0.00962840	202
203	4.55770411	0.21940871	474.36054810	0.00210810	104.07883807	0.00960810	203
204	4.59188689	0.21777540	478.91825221	0.00208804	104.29661347	0.00958804	204
205	4.62632604	0.21615424	483.51013911	0.00206821	104.51276771	0.00956821	205
206	4.66102349	0.21454515	488.13646515	0.00204861	104.72731286	0.00954861	206
207	4.69598116	0.21294804	492.79748864	0.00202923	104.94026091	0.00952923	207
208	4.73120282	0.21136282	497.49346980	0.00201008	105.15162373	0.00951008	208
209	4.76668503	0.20978940	502.22467083	0.00199114	105.36141313	0.00949114	209
210	4.80243517	0.20822769	506.99135586	0.00197242	105.56964082	0.00947242	210
211	4.83845343	0.20667761	511.79379103	0.00195391	105.77631843	0.00945391	211
212	4.87474183	0.20513907	516.63224446	0.00193561	105.98145750	0.00943561	212
213	4.91130240	0.20361198	521.50698629	0.00191752	106.18506948	0.00941752	213
214	4.94813717	0.20209626	526.41828869	0.00189963	106.38716574	0.00939963	214
215	4.98524818	0.20059182	531.36642585	0.00188194	106.58775756	0.00938194	215
216	5.02263756	0.19909858	536.35167405	0.00186445	106.78685614	0.00936445	216
217	5.06030734	0.19761646	541.37431160	0.00184715	106.98447259	0.00934715	217
218	5.09825964	0.19614537	546.43461894	0.00183005	107.18061796	0.00933005	218
219	5.13649659	0.19468523	551.53287858	0.00181313	107.37530318	0.00931313	219
220	5.17502031	0.19323596	556.66937517	0.00179640	107.56853914	0.00929640	220
221	5.21383297	0.19179748	561.84439549	0.00177985	107.76033661	0.00927985	221
222	5.25293671	0.19036970	567.05822845	0.00176349	107.95070632	0.00926349	222
223	5.29233374	0.18895256	572.31116517	0.00174730	108.13965888	0.00924730	223
224	5.33202624	0.18754596	577.60349890	0.00173129	108.32720484	0.00923129	224
225	5.37201644	0.18614984	582.93552515	0.00171546	108.51335468	0.00921546	225
226	5.41230656	0.18476411	588.30754158	0.00169979	108.69811879	0.00919979	226
227	5.45289886	0.18338869	593.71984815	0.00168430	108.88150748	0.00918430	227
228	5.49379560	0.18202352	599.17274701	0.00166897	109.06353100	0.00916897	228
229	5.53499907	0.18066850	604.66654261	0.00165380	109.24419950	0.00915380	229
230	5.57651156	0.17932358	610.20154168	0.00163880	109.42352308	0.00913880	230
231	5.61833540	0.17798866	615.77805324	0.00162396	109.60151174	0.00912396	231
232	5.66047291	0.17666368	621.39638864	0.00160928	109.77817543	0.00910928	232
233	5.70292646	0.17534857	627.05686156	0.00159475	109.95352400	0.00909475	233
234	5.74569841	0.17404325	632.75978802	0.00158038	110.12756724	0.00908038	234
235	5.78879115	0.17274764	638.50548643	0.00156616	110.30031488	0.00906616	235
236	5.83220708	0.17146168	644.29427758	0.00155209	110.47177656	0.00905209	236
237	5.87594863	0.17018529	650.12648466	0.00153816	110.64196184	0.00903816	237
238	5.92001825	0.16891840	656.00243329	0.00152438	110.81088024	0.00902438	238
239	5.96441839	0.16766094	661.92245154	0.00151075	110.97854118	0.00901075	239
240	6.00915152	0.16641284	667.88686993	0.00149726	111.14495403	0.00899726	240

TABLE A-2

COMPOUND INTEREST FOR $1

$\frac{5}{6}$ %

PERIODS n	FUTURE AMOUNT $(1+i)^n$	PRESENT VALUE $(1+i)^{-n}$	AMOUNT OF ANNUITY $(S/p,i,n)$ $\dfrac{(1+i)^n - 1}{i}$	SINKING FUND $(p/S,i,n)$ $\dfrac{i}{(1+i)^n - 1}$	PRESENT VALUE OF ANNUITY $(V/p,i,n)$ $\dfrac{1-(1+i)^{-n}}{i}$	AMORTIZATION $(p/V,i,n)$ $\dfrac{i}{1-(1+i)^{-n}}$	PERIODS n
1	1.00833333	0.99173554	1.00000000	1.00000000	0.99173554	1.00833333	1
2	1.01673611	0.98353938	2.00833333	0.49792531	1.97527491	0.50625864	2
3	1.02520891	0.97541095	3.02506944	0.33057092	2.95068586	0.33890426	3
4	1.03375232	0.96734970	4.05027836	0.24689661	3.91803557	0.25522994	4
5	1.04236692	0.95935508	5.08403068	0.19669433	4.87739065	0.20502766	5
6	1.05105331	0.95142652	6.12639760	0.16322806	5.82881717	0.17156139	6
7	1.05981209	0.94356349	7.17745091	0.13932523	6.77238066	0.14765856	7
8	1.06864386	0.93576545	8.23726300	0.12139955	7.70814611	0.12973288	8
9	1.07754922	0.92803185	9.30590686	0.10745863	8.63617796	0.11579196	9
10	1.08652880	0.92036217	10.38345608	0.09630705	9.55654013	0.10464038	10
11	1.09558321	0.91275587	11.46998489	0.08718407	10.46929600	0.09551741	11
12	1.10471307	0.90521243	12.56556809	0.07958255	11.37450843	0.08791589	12
13	1.11391901	0.89773134	13.67028116	0.07315138	12.27223976	0.08148472	13
14	1.12320167	0.89031207	14.78420017	0.06763978	13.16255183	0.07597311	14
15	1.13256168	0.88295412	15.90740184	0.06286382	14.04550595	0.07119715	15
16	1.14199970	0.87565698	17.03996352	0.05868557	14.92116292	0.06701890	16
17	1.15151636	0.86842014	18.18196322	0.05499956	15.78958306	0.06333289	17
18	1.16111233	0.86124312	19.33347958	0.05172375	16.65082618	0.06005708	18
19	1.17078827	0.85412540	20.49459191	0.04879336	17.50495158	0.05712669	19
20	1.18054483	0.84706652	21.66538017	0.04615659	18.35201810	0.05448992	20
21	1.19038271	0.84006597	22.84592501	0.04377148	19.19208406	0.05210482	21
22	1.20030256	0.83312327	24.03630772	0.04160373	20.02520734	0.04993706	22
23	1.21030509	0.82623796	25.23661028	0.03962497	20.85144529	0.04795831	23
24	1.22039096	0.81940954	26.44691537	0.03781159	21.67085483	0.04614493	24
25	1.23056089	0.81263756	27.66730633	0.03614374	22.48349240	0.04447708	25
26	1.24081556	0.80592155	28.89786721	0.03460463	23.28941395	0.04293796	26
27	1.25115569	0.79926104	30.13868277	0.03317995	24.08867499	0.04151328	27
28	1.26158199	0.79265558	31.38983846	0.03185744	24.88133057	0.04019078	28
29	1.27209517	0.78610471	32.65142045	0.03062654	25.66743527	0.03895987	29
30	1.28269596	0.77960797	33.92351562	0.02947808	26.44704325	0.03781141	30
31	1.29338510	0.77316493	35.20621158	0.02840408	27.22020818	0.03673741	31
32	1.30416331	0.76677514	36.49959668	0.02739756	27.98698332	0.03573090	32
33	1.31503133	0.76043815	37.80375999	0.02645240	28.74742147	0.03478573	33
34	1.32598993	0.75415354	39.11879132	0.02556316	29.50157501	0.03389650	34
35	1.33703984	0.74792087	40.44478125	0.02472507	30.24949588	0.03305840	35
36	1.34818184	0.74173970	41.78182109	0.02393385	30.99123559	0.03226719	36
37	1.35941669	0.73560962	43.13000293	0.02318572	31.72684521	0.03151905	37
38	1.37074516	0.72953020	44.48941962	0.02247725	32.45637541	0.03081059	38
39	1.38216804	0.72350103	45.86016479	0.02180542	33.17987644	0.03013875	39
40	1.39368611	0.71752168	47.24233283	0.02116746	33.89739813	0.02950079	40

TABLE A-2

COMPOUND INTEREST FOR $1

$\frac{5}{6}$%

PERIODS n	FUTURE AMOUNT $(1+i)^n$	PRESENT VALUE $(1+i)^{-n}$	AMOUNT OF ANNUITY $(S/p,i,n)$ $\dfrac{(1+i)^n-1}{i}$	SINKING FUND $(p/S,i,n)$ $\dfrac{i}{(1+i)^n-1}$	PRESENT VALUE OF ANNUITY $(V/p,i,n)$ $\dfrac{1-(1+i)^{-n}}{i}$	AMORTIZATION $(p/V,i,n)$ $\dfrac{i}{1-(1+i)^{-n}}$	PERIODS n
41	1.40530016	0.71159175	48.63601893	0.02056089	34.60898988	0.02889423	41
42	1.41701099	0.70571083	50.04131909	0.01998349	35.31470070	0.02831682	42
43	1.42881942	0.69987851	51.45833008	0.01943320	36.01457921	0.02776653	43
44	1.44072625	0.69409439	52.88714950	0.01890818	36.70867360	0.02724152	44
45	1.45273230	0.68835807	54.32787575	0.01840676	37.39703167	0.02674009	45
46	1.46483840	0.68266916	55.78060805	0.01792738	38.07970083	0.02626071	46
47	1.47704539	0.67702727	57.24544645	0.01746864	38.75672809	0.02580197	47
48	1.48935410	0.67143200	58.72249183	0.01702925	39.42816009	0.02536258	48
49	1.50176538	0.66588297	60.21184593	0.01660803	40.09404307	0.02494136	49
50	1.51428009	0.66037981	61.71361131	0.01620388	40.75442288	0.02453721	50
51	1.52689910	0.65492212	63.22789141	0.01581580	41.40934500	0.02414914	51
52	1.53962325	0.64950955	64.75479050	0.01544287	42.05885455	0.02377621	52
53	1.55245345	0.64414170	66.29441376	0.01508423	42.70299624	0.02341756	53
54	1.56539056	0.63881821	67.84686721	0.01473907	43.34181446	0.02307241	54
55	1.57843548	0.63353872	69.41225777	0.01440668	43.97535318	0.02274001	55
56	1.59158911	0.62830287	70.99069325	0.01408635	44.60365605	0.02241969	56
57	1.60485235	0.62311028	72.58228236	0.01377747	45.22676633	0.02211080	57
58	1.61822612	0.61796061	74.18713471	0.01347943	45.84472694	0.02181276	58
59	1.63171134	0.61285350	75.80536083	0.01319168	46.45758043	0.02152501	59
60	1.64530893	0.60778859	77.43707217	0.01291371	47.06536902	0.02124704	60
61	1.65901984	0.60276555	79.08238111	0.01264504	47.66813457	0.02097837	61
62	1.67284501	0.59778401	80.74140095	0.01238522	48.26591858	0.02071855	62
63	1.68678538	0.59284365	82.41424596	0.01213382	48.85876223	0.02046716	63
64	1.70084193	0.58794411	84.10103134	0.01189046	49.44670634	0.02022379	64
65	1.71501561	0.58308507	85.80187327	0.01165476	50.02979141	0.01998809	65
66	1.72930741	0.57826619	87.51688888	0.01142637	50.60805760	0.01975970	66
67	1.74371830	0.57348713	89.24619629	0.01120496	51.18154473	0.01953829	67
68	1.75824929	0.56874756	90.98991459	0.01099023	51.75029229	0.01932356	68
69	1.77290137	0.56404717	92.74816388	0.01078188	52.31433946	0.01911522	69
70	1.78767554	0.55938562	94.52106524	0.01057965	52.87372509	0.01891299	70
71	1.80257284	0.55476260	96.30874079	0.01038327	53.42848769	0.01871661	71
72	1.81759428	0.55017779	98.11131363	0.01019250	53.97866548	0.01852584	72
73	1.83274090	0.54563086	99.92890791	0.01000711	54.52429634	0.01834045	73
74	1.84801374	0.54112152	101.76164881	0.00982688	55.06541786	0.01816022	74
75	1.86341385	0.53664944	103.60966255	0.00965161	55.60206730	0.01798494	75
76	1.87894230	0.53221432	105.47307640	0.00948109	56.13428162	0.01781443	76
77	1.89460016	0.52781585	107.35201870	0.00931515	56.66209747	0.01764848	77
78	1.91038849	0.52345374	109.24661886	0.00915360	57.18555121	0.01748693	78
79	1.92630839	0.51912768	111.15700735	0.00899628	57.70467889	0.01732962	79
80	1.94236096	0.51483736	113.08331575	0.00884304	58.21951625	0.01717637	80

COMPOUND INTEREST FOR $1

$\frac{5}{6}$ %

PERIODS n	FUTURE AMOUNT $(1+i)^n$	PRESENT VALUE $(1+i)^{-n}$	AMOUNT OF ANNUITY (S/p,i,n) $\frac{(1+i)^n - 1}{i}$	SINKING FUND (p/S,i,n) $\frac{i}{(1+i)^n - 1}$	PRESENT VALUE OF ANNUITY (V/p,i,n) $\frac{1-(1+i)^{-n}}{i}$	AMORTIZATION (p/V,i,n) $\frac{i}{1-(1+i)^{-n}}$	PERIODS n
81	1.95854731	0.51058251	115.02567671	0.00869371	58.73009876	0.01702704	81
82	1.97486853	0.50636282	116.98422402	0.00854816	59.23646158	0.01688149	82
83	1.99132577	0.50217800	118.95909255	0.00840625	59.73863959	0.01673958	83
84	2.00792015	0.49802777	120.95041832	0.00826785	60.23666736	0.01660118	84
85	2.02465282	0.49391184	122.95833847	0.00813284	60.73057920	0.01646617	85
86	2.04152493	0.48982992	124.98299109	0.00800109	61.22040912	0.01633442	86
87	2.05853764	0.48578174	127.02451622	0.00787250	61.70619087	0.01620583	87
88	2.07569212	0.48176702	129.08305386	0.00774695	62.18795788	0.01608028	88
89	2.09298955	0.47778547	131.15874597	0.00762435	62.66574336	0.01595768	89
90	2.11043113	0.47383683	133.25173552	0.00750459	63.13958019	0.01583793	90
91	2.12801806	0.46992082	135.36216665	0.00738759	63.60950101	0.01572092	91
92	2.14575154	0.46603718	137.49018471	0.00727325	64.07553819	0.01560658	92
93	2.16363280	0.46218563	139.63593625	0.00716148	64.53772383	0.01549481	93
94	2.18166308	0.45836592	141.79956905	0.00705221	64.99608975	0.01538554	94
95	2.19984360	0.45457777	143.98123212	0.00694535	65.45066752	0.01527868	95
96	2.21817563	0.45082093	146.18107572	0.00684083	65.90148845	0.01517416	96
97	2.23666043	0.44709514	148.39925136	0.00673858	66.34858358	0.01507191	97
98	2.25529926	0.44340014	150.63591178	0.00663852	66.79198372	0.01497186	98
99	2.27409343	0.43973567	152.89121105	0.00654060	67.23171939	0.01487393	99
100	2.29304420	0.43610149	155.16530447	0.00644474	67.66782088	0.01477807	100
101	2.31215291	0.43249735	157.45834868	0.00635089	68.10031823	0.01468422	101
102	2.33142085	0.42892299	159.77050158	0.00625898	68.52924122	0.01459231	102
103	2.35084935	0.42537817	162.10192243	0.00616896	68.95461939	0.01450229	103
104	2.37043976	0.42186265	164.45277178	0.00608077	69.37648204	0.01441411	104
105	2.39019343	0.41837618	166.82321155	0.00599437	69.79485823	0.01432770	105
106	2.41011171	0.41491853	169.21340498	0.00590970	70.20977675	0.01424303	106
107	2.43019597	0.41148945	171.62351669	0.00582671	70.62126620	0.01416004	107
108	2.45044761	0.40808871	174.05371266	0.00574535	71.02935491	0.01407869	108
109	2.47086800	0.40471608	176.50416026	0.00566559	71.43407099	0.01399892	109
110	2.49145857	0.40137131	178.97502827	0.00558737	71.83544230	0.01392070	110
111	2.51222072	0.39805420	181.46648684	0.00551066	72.23349650	0.01384399	111
112	2.53315590	0.39476449	183.97870756	0.00543541	72.62826099	0.01376874	112
113	2.55426553	0.39150198	186.51186346	0.00536159	73.01976296	0.01369492	113
114	2.57555107	0.38826642	189.06612898	0.00528915	73.40802938	0.01362249	114
115	2.59701400	0.38505107	191.64168006	0.00521807	73.79308699	0.01355140	115
116	2.61865578	0.38187531	194.23869406	0.00514830	74.17496231	0.01348164	116
117	2.64047792	0.37871932	196.85734984	0.00507982	74.55368163	0.01341315	117
118	2.66248190	0.37558941	199.49782776	0.00501259	74.92927103	0.01334592	118
119	2.68466925	0.37248536	202.16030966	0.00494657	75.30175640	0.01327990	119
120	2.70704149	0.36940697	204.84497890	0.00488174	75.67116337	0.01321507	120

COMPOUND INTEREST FOR $1

$\frac{5}{6}$%

PERIODS n	FUTURE AMOUNT $(1+i)^n$	PRESENT VALUE $(1+i)^{-n}$	AMOUNT OF ANNUITY (S/p,i,n) $\dfrac{(1+i)^n - 1}{i}$	SINKING FUND (p/S,i,n) $\dfrac{i}{(1+i)^n - 1}$	PRESENT VALUE OF ANNUITY (V/p,i,n) $\dfrac{1-(1+i)^{-n}}{i}$	AMORTIZATION (p/V,i,n) $\dfrac{i}{1-(1+i)^{-n}}$	PERIODS n
121	2.72960017	0.36635402	207.55202039	0.00481807	76.037751739	0.01315140	121
122	2.75234684	0.36332630	210.28162056	0.00475553	76.40084369	0.01308886	122
123	2.77528306	0.36032361	213.03396740	0.00469409	76.76116730	0.01302742	123
124	2.79841042	0.35734572	215.80925046	0.00463372	77.11851302	0.01296706	124
125	2.82173051	0.35439245	218.60766088	0.00457441	77.47290548	0.01290774	125
126	2.84524493	0.35146359	221.42939139	0.00451611	77.82436907	0.01284945	126
127	2.86895530	0.34855893	224.27463632	0.00445882	78.17292800	0.01279215	127
128	2.89286326	0.34567828	227.14359162	0.00440250	78.51860628	0.01273583	128
129	2.91697046	0.34282144	230.03645489	0.00434714	78.86142772	0.01268047	129
130	2.94127854	0.33998820	232.95342534	0.00429270	79.20141592	0.01262604	130
131	2.96578920	0.33717838	235.89470389	0.00423918	79.53859430	0.01257251	131
132	2.99050411	0.33439178	238.86049309	0.00418654	79.87298608	0.01251988	132
133	3.01542498	0.33162821	241.85099720	0.00413478	80.20461430	0.01246811	133
134	3.04055352	0.32888749	244.86642217	0.00408386	80.53350178	0.01241719	134
135	3.06589146	0.32616941	247.90697569	0.00403377	80.85967119	0.01236710	135
136	3.09144056	0.32347379	250.97286716	0.00398449	81.18314498	0.01231783	136
137	3.11720256	0.32080045	254.06430771	0.00393601	81.50394544	0.01226934	137
138	3.14317925	0.31814921	257.18151028	0.00388830	81.82209465	0.01222164	138
139	3.16937241	0.31551988	260.32468953	0.00384136	82.13761453	0.01217469	139
140	3.19578385	0.31291228	263.49406194	0.00379515	82.45052680	0.01212849	140
141	3.22241538	0.31032622	266.68984579	0.00374967	82.76085303	0.01208301	141
142	3.24926884	0.30776155	269.91226118	0.00370491	83.06861457	0.01203824	142
143	3.27634608	0.30521806	273.16153002	0.00366084	83.37383263	0.01199417	143
144	3.30364897	0.30269560	276.43787610	0.00361745	83.67652823	0.01195078	144
145	3.33117938	0.30019398	279.74152507	0.00357473	83.97672221	0.01190806	145
146	3.35893920	0.29771304	283.07270445	0.00353266	84.27443525	0.01186599	146
147	3.38693036	0.29525260	286.43164365	0.00349123	84.56968786	0.01182457	147
148	3.41515478	0.29281250	289.81857401	0.00345043	84.86250035	0.01178377	148
149	3.44361441	0.29039256	293.23372880	0.00341025	85.15289291	0.01174358	149
150	3.47231119	0.28799262	296.67734320	0.00337067	85.44088553	0.01170400	150
151	3.50124712	0.28561252	300.14965440	0.00333167	85.72649805	0.01166500	151
152	3.53042418	0.28325208	303.65090152	0.00329326	86.00975013	0.01162659	152
153	3.55984438	0.28091116	307.18132570	0.00325541	86.29066129	0.01158874	153
154	3.58950975	0.27858958	310.74117008	0.00321811	86.56925086	0.01155145	154
155	3.61942233	0.27628718	314.33067983	0.00318136	86.84553805	0.01151470	155
156	3.64958418	0.27400382	317.95010216	0.00314515	87.11954186	0.01147848	156
157	3.67999739	0.27173932	321.59968634	0.00310946	87.39128119	0.01144279	157
158	3.71066403	0.26949354	325.27968373	0.00307428	87.66077473	0.01140761	158
159	3.74158623	0.26726632	328.99034776	0.00303960	87.92804106	0.01137294	159
160	3.77276612	0.26505751	332.73193399	0.00300542	88.19309857	0.01133876	160

TABLE A-2

COMPOUND INTEREST FOR $1

$\frac{5}{6}$ %

PERIODS n	FUTURE AMOUNT $(1+i)^n$	PRESENT VALUE $(1+i)^{-n}$	AMOUNT OF ANNUITY $(S/p,i,n)$ $\dfrac{(1+i)^n - 1}{i}$	SINKING FUND $(p/S,i,n)$ $\dfrac{i}{(1+i)^n - 1}$	PRESENT VALUE OF ANNUITY $(V/p,i,n)$ $\dfrac{1-(1+i)^{-n}}{i}$	AMORTIZATION $(p/V,i,n)$ $\dfrac{i}{1-(1+i)^{-n}}$	PERIODS n
161	3.80420583	0.26286695	336.50470011	0.00297173	88.45596552	0.01130506	161
162	3.83590755	0.26069450	340.30890594	0.00293851	88.71666002	0.01127184	162
163	3.86787345	0.25854000	344.14481349	0.00290575	88.97520002	0.01123909	163
164	3.90010572	0.25640331	348.01268694	0.00287346	89.23160333	0.01120679	164
165	3.93260661	0.25428427	351.91279266	0.00284161	89.48588760	0.01117495	165
166	3.96537833	0.25218275	355.84539927	0.00281021	89.73807034	0.01114354	166
167	3.99842315	0.25009859	359.81077760	0.00277924	89.98816894	0.01111257	167
168	4.03174334	0.24803166	363.80920074	0.00274869	90.23620060	0.01108203	168
169	4.06534120	0.24598181	367.84094408	0.00271857	90.48218241	0.01105190	169
170	4.09921904	0.24394891	371.90628528	0.00268885	90.72613132	0.01102218	170
171	4.13337920	0.24193280	376.00550433	0.00265954	90.96806412	0.01099287	171
172	4.16782403	0.23993335	380.13888353	0.00263062	91.20799747	0.01096395	172
173	4.20255590	0.23795043	384.30670756	0.00260209	91.44594790	0.01093542	173
174	4.23757720	0.23598390	388.50926345	0.00257394	91.68193181	0.01090727	174
175	4.27289034	0.23403362	392.74684065	0.00254617	91.91596543	0.01087950	175
176	4.30849776	0.23209946	397.01973099	0.00251877	92.14806489	0.01085210	176
177	4.34440191	0.23018128	401.32822875	0.00249173	92.37824617	0.01082506	177
178	4.38060526	0.22827896	405.67263065	0.00246504	92.60652513	0.01079838	178
179	4.41711030	0.22639235	410.05323591	0.00243871	92.83291748	0.01077204	179
180	4.45391955	0.22452134	414.47034621	0.00241272	93.05743882	0.01074605	180
181	4.49103555	0.22266579	418.92426576	0.00238707	93.28010462	0.01072040	181
182	4.52846084	0.22082558	423.41530131	0.00236175	93.50093020	0.01069508	182
183	4.56619802	0.21900058	427.94376215	0.00233676	93.71993078	0.01067009	183
184	4.60424967	0.21719065	432.50996017	0.00231209	93.93712143	0.01064542	184
185	4.64261842	0.21539569	437.11420984	0.00228773	94.15251712	0.01062106	185
186	4.68130690	0.21361556	441.75682825	0.00226369	94.36613268	0.01059702	186
187	4.72031779	0.21185014	446.43813516	0.00223995	94.57798283	0.01057329	187
188	4.75965377	0.21009932	451.15845295	0.00221652	94.78808214	0.01054985	188
189	4.79931756	0.20836296	455.91810672	0.00219338	94.99644510	0.01052671	189
190	4.83931187	0.20664095	460.71742428	0.00217053	95.20308605	0.01050386	190
191	4.87963947	0.20493317	465.55673615	0.00214797	95.40801922	0.01048130	191
192	4.92030313	0.20323951	470.43637562	0.00212569	95.61125873	0.01045902	192
193	4.96130566	0.20155985	475.35667875	0.00210368	95.81281858	0.01043702	193
194	5.00264987	0.19989406	480.31798440	0.00208195	96.01271264	0.01041529	194
195	5.04433862	0.19824204	485.32063427	0.00206049	96.21095468	0.01039383	195
196	5.08637477	0.19660368	490.36497289	0.00203930	96.40755836	0.01037263	196
197	5.12876123	0.19497886	495.45134767	0.00201836	96.60253722	0.01035169	197
198	5.17150091	0.19336746	500.58010890	0.00199768	96.79590468	0.01033102	198
199	5.21459675	0.19176938	505.75160980	0.00197726	96.98767406	0.01031059	199
200	5.25805172	0.19018451	510.96620655	0.00195708	97.17785858	0.01029041	200

TABLE A-2

COMPOUND INTEREST FOR $1

$\frac{5}{6}$%

PERIODS n	FUTURE AMOUNT $(1+i)^n$	PRESENT VALUE $(1+i)^{-n}$	AMOUNT OF ANNUITY $(S/p,i,n)$ $\dfrac{(1+i)^n-1}{i}$	SINKING FUND $(p/S,i,n)$ $\dfrac{i}{(1+i)^n-1}$	PRESENT VALUE OF ANNUITY $(V/p,i,n)$ $\dfrac{1-(1+i)^{-n}}{i}$	AMORTIZATION $(p/V,i,n)$ $\dfrac{i}{1-(1+i)^{-n}}$	PERIODS n
201	5.30186882	0.18861274	516.22425827	0.00193714	97.36647131	0.01027048	201
202	5.34605106	0.18705396	521.52612709	0.00191745	97.55352527	0.01025078	202
203	5.39060148	0.18550806	526.87217815	0.00189799	97.73903333	0.01023133	203
204	5.43552316	0.18397493	532.26277964	0.00187877	97.92300826	0.01021210	204
205	5.48081919	0.18245448	537.69830280	0.00185978	98.10546273	0.01019311	205
206	5.52649268	0.18094659	543.17912199	0.00184101	98.28640932	0.01017435	206
207	5.57254679	0.17945116	548.70561467	0.00182247	98.46586049	0.01015580	207
208	5.61898468	0.17796810	554.27816146	0.00180415	98.64382858	0.01013748	208
209	5.66580955	0.17649728	559.89714614	0.00178604	98.82032587	0.01011938	209
210	5.71302463	0.17503863	565.56295569	0.00176815	98.99536450	0.01010148	210
211	5.76063317	0.17359203	571.27598032	0.00175047	99.16895652	0.01008380	211
212	5.80863845	0.17215738	577.03661349	0.00173299	99.34111391	0.01006633	212
213	5.85704377	0.17073460	582.84525194	0.00171572	99.51184850	0.01004905	213
214	5.90585246	0.16932357	588.70229570	0.00169865	99.68117207	0.01003198	214
215	5.95506790	0.16792420	594.60814817	0.00168178	99.84909627	0.01001511	215
216	6.00469347	0.16653639	600.56321607	0.00166510	100.01563266	0.00999844	216
217	6.05473258	0.16516006	606.56790954	0.00164862	100.18079272	0.00998195	217
218	6.10518868	0.16379510	612.62264212	0.00163233	100.34458782	0.00996566	218
219	6.15606526	0.16244142	618.72783080	0.00161622	100.50702925	0.00994955	219
220	6.20736580	0.16109893	624.88389606	0.00160030	100.66812818	0.00993363	220
221	6.25909385	0.15976754	631.09126186	0.00158456	100.82789571	0.00991789	221
222	6.31125296	0.15844714	637.35035571	0.00156900	100.98634286	0.00990233	222
223	6.36384674	0.15713766	643.66160867	0.00155361	101.14348052	0.00988694	223
224	6.41687880	0.15583900	650.02545541	0.00153840	101.29931952	0.00987173	224
225	6.47035279	0.15455108	656.44233420	0.00152336	101.45387060	0.00985670	225
226	6.52427239	0.15327380	662.91268699	0.00150849	101.60714440	0.00984183	226
227	6.57864133	0.15200707	669.43695938	0.00149379	101.75915147	0.00982713	227
228	6.63346334	0.15075081	676.01560071	0.00147926	101.90990228	0.00981259	228
229	6.68874220	0.14950494	682.64906405	0.00146488	102.05940722	0.00979821	229
230	6.74448172	0.14826936	689.33780625	0.00145067	102.20767659	0.00978400	230
231	6.80068573	0.14704400	696.08228797	0.00143661	102.35472058	0.00976995	231
232	6.85735811	0.14582876	702.88297370	0.00142271	102.50054934	0.00975605	232
233	6.91450277	0.14462356	709.74033181	0.00140897	102.64517290	0.00974230	233
234	6.97212362	0.14342832	716.65483458	0.00139537	102.78860122	0.00972871	234
235	7.03022465	0.14224297	723.62695820	0.00138193	102.93084418	0.00971526	235
236	7.08880986	0.14106740	730.65718285	0.00136863	103.07191159	0.00970196	236
237	7.14788327	0.13990156	737.74599271	0.00135548	103.21181314	0.00968881	237
238	7.20744897	0.13874535	744.89387598	0.00134247	103.35055849	0.00967581	238
239	7.26751104	0.13759869	752.10132495	0.00132961	103.48815718	0.00966294	239
240	7.32807363	0.13646151	759.36883599	0.00131688	103.62461869	0.00965022	240

TABLE A-2

COMPOUND INTEREST FOR $1

$\frac{11}{12}\%$

PERIODS n	FUTURE AMOUNT $(1+i)^n$	PRESENT VALUE $(1+i)^{-n}$	AMOUNT OF ANNUITY $(S/p,i,n)$ $\dfrac{(1+i)^n-1}{i}$	SINKING FUND $(p/S,i,n)$ $\dfrac{i}{(1+i)^n-1}$	PRESENT VALUE OF ANNUITY $(V/p,i,n)$ $\dfrac{1-(1+i)^{-n}}{i}$	AMORTIZATION $(p/V,i,n)$ $\dfrac{i}{1-(1+i)^{-n}}$	PERIODS n
1	1.00916667	0.99091660	1.00000000	1.00000000	0.99091660	1.00916667	1
2	1.01841736	0.98191570	2.00916667	0.49771879	1.97283230	0.50688546	2
3	1.02775285	0.97299657	3.02758403	0.33029637	2.94582887	0.33946303	3
4	1.03717392	0.96415845	4.05533688	0.24658864	3.90998732	0.25575531	4
5	1.04668135	0.95540061	5.09251080	0.19636679	4.86538793	0.20553346	5
6	1.05627593	0.94672232	6.13919215	0.16288788	5.81211025	0.17205455	6
7	1.06595846	0.93812286	7.19546808	0.13897637	6.75023312	0.14814303	7
8	1.07572974	0.92960152	8.26142654	0.12104447	7.67983463	0.13021114	8
9	1.08559060	0.92115757	9.33715628	0.10709899	8.60099220	0.11626566	9
10	1.09554185	0.91279033	10.42274688	0.09594400	9.51378253	0.10511066	10
11	1.10558431	0.90449909	11.51828873	0.08681845	10.41828162	0.09598512	11
12	1.11571884	0.89628316	12.62387304	0.07921499	11.31456477	0.08838166	12
13	1.12594626	0.88814186	13.73959188	0.07278237	12.20270663	0.08194903	13
14	1.13626743	0.88007451	14.86553813	0.06726968	13.08278113	0.07643635	14
15	1.14668322	0.87208044	16.00180557	0.06249295	13.95486157	0.07165961	15
16	1.15719448	0.86415898	17.14848879	0.05831418	14.81902055	0.06748084	16
17	1.16780210	0.85630947	18.30568327	0.05462784	15.67533002	0.06379451	17
18	1.17850695	0.84853127	19.47348536	0.05135188	16.52386129	0.06051854	18
19	1.18930993	0.84082372	20.65199231	0.04842148	17.36468502	0.05758815	19
20	1.20021194	0.83318618	21.84130224	0.04578482	18.19787120	0.05495148	20
21	1.21121388	0.82561802	23.04151418	0.04339993	19.02348921	0.05256659	21
22	1.22231667	0.81811860	24.25272806	0.04123247	19.84160781	0.05039914	22
23	1.23352124	0.81068729	25.47504473	0.03925410	20.65229510	0.04842077	23
24	1.24482852	0.80332350	26.70856598	0.03744117	21.45561860	0.04660784	24
25	1.25623945	0.79602659	27.95339450	0.03577383	22.25164518	0.04494050	25
26	1.26775498	0.78879596	29.20963395	0.03423528	23.04044114	0.04340195	26
27	1.27937607	0.78163101	30.47738892	0.03281121	23.82207214	0.04197788	27
28	1.29110368	0.77453114	31.75676499	0.03148935	24.59660328	0.04065602	28
29	1.30293880	0.76749576	33.04786867	0.03025914	25.36409904	0.03942580	29
30	1.31488240	0.76052429	34.35080746	0.02911140	26.12462333	0.03827806	30
31	1.32693549	0.75361614	35.66568987	0.02803815	26.87823946	0.03720482	31
32	1.33909907	0.74677074	36.99262536	0.02703241	27.62501020	0.03619908	32
33	1.35137414	0.73998752	38.33172442	0.02608805	28.36499773	0.03525472	33
34	1.36376174	0.73326592	39.68309856	0.02519965	29.09826364	0.03436631	34
35	1.37626289	0.72660537	41.04686030	0.02436240	29.82486901	0.03352907	35
36	1.38887863	0.72000532	42.42312319	0.02357205	30.54487433	0.03273872	36
37	1.40161002	0.71346522	43.81200182	0.02282480	31.25833955	0.03199146	37
38	1.41445811	0.70698453	45.21361183	0.02211723	31.96532408	0.03128390	38
39	1.42742397	0.70056270	46.62806994	0.02144631	32.66588678	0.03061298	39
40	1.44050869	0.69419921	48.05549391	0.02080928	33.36008599	0.02997594	40

TABLE A-2

COMPOUND INTEREST FOR $1

$\frac{11}{12}\%$

PERIODS n	FUTURE AMOUNT $(1+i)^n$	PRESENT VALUE $(1+i)^{-n}$	AMOUNT OF ANNUITY $(S/p,i,n)$ $\frac{(1+i)^n - 1}{i}$	SINKING FUND $(p/S,i,n)$ $\frac{i}{(1+i)^n - 1}$	PRESENT VALUE OF ANNUITY $(V/p,i,n)$ $\frac{1 - (1+i)^{-n}}{i}$	AMORTIZATION $(p/V,i,n)$ $\frac{i}{1 - (1+i)^{-n}}$	PERIODS n
41	1.45371336	0.68789352	49.49600261	0.02020365	34.04797952	0.02937032	41
42	1.46703906	0.68164511	50.94971597	0.01962719	34.72962462	0.02879386	42
43	1.48048692	0.67545345	52.41675503	0.01907787	35.40507807	0.02824454	43
44	1.49405805	0.66931804	53.89724195	0.01855383	36.07439611	0.02772049	44
45	1.50775358	0.66323835	55.39130000	0.01805338	36.73763446	0.02722004	45
46	1.52157466	0.65721389	56.89905358	0.01757498	37.39484835	0.02674165	46
47	1.53552243	0.65124415	58.42062824	0.01711724	38.04609250	0.02628391	47
48	1.54959805	0.64532864	59.95615067	0.01667886	38.69142114	0.02584552	48
49	1.56380270	0.63946686	61.50574872	0.01625864	39.33088800	0.02542531	49
50	1.57813755	0.63365833	63.06955141	0.01585551	39.96454633	0.02502218	50
51	1.59260382	0.62790255	64.64768897	0.01546846	40.59244888	0.02463512	51
52	1.60720268	0.62219906	66.24029278	0.01509655	41.21464794	0.02426322	52
53	1.62193538	0.61654738	67.84749547	0.01473894	41.83119532	0.02390560	53
54	1.63680312	0.61094703	69.46943084	0.01439482	42.44214234	0.02356149	54
55	1.65180714	0.60539755	71.10623396	0.01406346	43.04753990	0.02323013	55
56	1.66694871	0.59989848	72.75804110	0.01374419	43.64743838	0.02291085	56
57	1.68222907	0.59444936	74.42498981	0.01343635	44.24188774	0.02260301	57
58	1.69764951	0.58904974	76.10721889	0.01313936	44.83093748	0.02230602	58
59	1.71321270	0.58369916	77.80486839	0.01285267	45.41463664	0.02201933	59
60	1.72891573	0.57839719	79.51807969	0.01257576	45.99303383	0.02174242	60
61	1.74476412	0.57314338	81.24699542	0.01230815	46.56617721	0.02147481	61
62	1.76075780	0.56793728	82.99175954	0.01204939	47.13411449	0.02121606	62
63	1.77689808	0.56277848	84.75251734	0.01179906	47.69689297	0.02096573	63
64	1.79318631	0.55766654	86.52941541	0.01155676	48.25455951	0.02072343	64
65	1.80962385	0.55260103	88.32260172	0.01132213	48.80716054	0.02048880	65
66	1.82621207	0.54758153	90.13222557	0.01109481	49.35474207	0.02026148	66
67	1.84295235	0.54260763	91.95843764	0.01087448	49.89734970	0.02004114	67
68	1.85984607	0.53767890	93.80138998	0.01066082	50.43502860	0.01982749	68
69	1.87689466	0.53279495	95.66123606	0.01045356	50.96782355	0.01962022	69
70	1.89409953	0.52795536	97.53813072	0.01025240	51.49577891	0.01941907	70
71	1.91146211	0.52315973	99.43223025	0.01005710	52.01893864	0.01922377	71
72	1.92898385	0.51840766	101.34369236	0.00986741	52.53734630	0.01903408	72
73	1.94666620	0.51369875	103.27267621	0.00968310	53.05104506	0.01884977	73
74	1.96451064	0.50903262	105.21934241	0.00950396	53.56007768	0.01867062	74
75	1.98251865	0.50440887	107.18385305	0.00932976	54.06448655	0.01849643	75
76	2.00069174	0.49982712	109.16637170	0.00916033	54.56431367	0.01832700	76
77	2.01903141	0.49528699	111.16706344	0.00899547	55.05960067	0.01816214	77
78	2.03753920	0.49078810	113.18609486	0.00883501	55.55038877	0.01800167	78
79	2.05621665	0.48633008	115.22363406	0.00867878	56.03671885	0.01784544	79
80	2.07506530	0.48191255	117.27985070	0.00852661	56.51863139	0.01769328	80

COMPOUND INTEREST FOR $1

$\frac{11}{12}\%$

PERIODS n	FUTURE AMOUNT $(1+i)^n$	PRESENT VALUE $(1+i)^{-n}$	AMOUNT OF ANNUITY (S/p,i,n) $\dfrac{(1+i)^n-1}{i}$	SINKING FUND (p/S,i,n) $\dfrac{i}{(1+i)^n-1}$	PRESENT VALUE OF ANNUITY (V/p,i,n) $\dfrac{1-(1+i)^{-n}}{i}$	AMORTIZATION (p/V,i,n) $\dfrac{i}{1-(1+i)^{-n}}$	PERIODS n
81	2.09408673	0.47753514	119.35491600	0.00837837	56.99616653	0.01754504	81
82	2.11328253	0.47319750	121.44900273	0.00823391	57.46936403	0.01740058	82
83	2.13265428	0.46889925	123.56228526	0.00809308	57.93826328	0.01725975	83
84	2.15220361	0.46464005	125.69493954	0.00795577	58.40290334	0.01712244	84
85	2.17193215	0.46041954	127.84714315	0.00782184	58.86332288	0.01698851	85
86	2.19184152	0.45623736	130.01907530	0.00769118	59.31956024	0.01685785	86
87	2.21193340	0.45209318	132.21091682	0.00756367	59.77165342	0.01673034	87
88	2.23220946	0.44798663	134.42285022	0.00743921	60.21964005	0.01660588	88
89	2.25267138	0.44391739	136.65505968	0.00731769	60.66355744	0.01648436	89
90	2.27332087	0.43988511	138.90773107	0.00719902	61.10344255	0.01636569	90
91	2.29415964	0.43588946	141.18105193	0.00708310	61.53933201	0.01624977	91
92	2.31518944	0.43193010	143.47521158	0.00696985	61.97126211	0.01613651	92
93	2.33641201	0.42800670	145.79040102	0.00685916	62.39926881	0.01602583	93
94	2.35782912	0.42411895	148.12681302	0.00675097	62.82338775	0.01591764	94
95	2.37944255	0.42026650	150.48464214	0.00664520	63.24365426	0.01581186	95
96	2.40125411	0.41644905	152.86408470	0.00654176	63.66010331	0.01570843	96
97	2.42326561	0.41266628	155.26533881	0.00644059	64.07276959	0.01560725	97
98	2.44547887	0.40891787	157.68860441	0.00634161	64.48168745	0.01550828	98
99	2.46789576	0.40520350	160.13408329	0.00624477	64.88689095	0.01541143	99
100	2.49051814	0.40152287	162.60197905	0.00614999	65.28841383	0.01531665	100
101	2.51334789	0.39787568	165.09249719	0.00605721	65.68628951	0.01522388	101
102	2.53638691	0.39426161	167.60584508	0.00596638	66.08055112	0.01513305	102
103	2.55963713	0.39068038	170.14223200	0.00587744	66.47123150	0.01504410	103
104	2.58310047	0.38713167	172.70186912	0.00579033	66.85836317	0.01495699	104
105	2.60677889	0.38361520	175.28496959	0.00570500	67.24197837	0.01487166	105
106	2.63067436	0.38013067	177.89174848	0.00562140	67.62210903	0.01478806	106
107	2.65478888	0.37667779	180.52442284	0.00553948	67.99878682	0.01470614	107
108	2.67912444	0.37325627	183.17721171	0.00545919	68.37204309	0.01462586	108
109	2.70368308	0.36986583	185.85633615	0.00538050	68.74190893	0.01454717	109
110	2.72846684	0.36650619	188.56001924	0.00530335	69.10841512	0.01447002	110
111	2.75347779	0.36317707	191.28848608	0.00522771	69.47159219	0.01439437	111
112	2.77871800	0.35987819	194.04196387	0.00515352	69.83147038	0.01432019	112
113	2.80418958	0.35660927	196.82068187	0.00508077	70.18807965	0.01424743	113
114	2.82989465	0.35337004	199.62487145	0.00500940	70.54144970	0.01417606	114
115	2.85583536	0.35016024	202.45476611	0.00493937	70.89160994	0.01410604	115
116	2.88201385	0.34697960	205.31060146	0.00487067	71.23858954	0.01403734	116
117	2.90843231	0.34382784	208.19261531	0.00480324	71.58241738	0.01396991	117
118	2.93509294	0.34070471	211.10104762	0.00473707	71.92312209	0.01390373	118
119	2.96199796	0.33760996	214.03614056	0.00467211	72.26073205	0.01383877	119
120	2.98914960	0.33454331	216.99813851	0.00460833	72.59527536	0.01377500	120

TABLE A-2

COMPOUND INTEREST FOR $1

$\frac{11}{12}\%$

PERIODS n	FUTURE AMOUNT $(1+i)^n$	PRESENT VALUE $(1+i)^{-n}$	AMOUNT OF ANNUITY $(S/p,i,n)$ $\dfrac{(1+i)^n-1}{i}$	SINKING FUND $(p/S,i,n)$ $\dfrac{i}{(1+i)^n-1}$	PRESENT VALUE OF ANNUITY $(V/p,i,n)$ $\dfrac{1-(1+i)^{-n}}{i}$	AMORTIZATION $(p/V,i,n)$ $\dfrac{i}{1-(1+i)^{-n}}$	PERIODS n
121	3.01655014	0.33150452	219.98728811	0.00454572	72.92677987	0.01371238	121
122	3.04420185	0.32849333	223.00383825	0.00448423	73.25527320	0.01365089	122
123	3.07210703	0.32550949	226.04804010	0.00442384	73.58078269	0.01359051	123
124	3.10026802	0.32255276	229.12014714	0.00436452	73.90333545	0.01353119	124
125	3.12868714	0.31962288	232.22041515	0.00430625	74.22295833	0.01347292	125
126	3.15736677	0.31671962	235.34910229	0.00424901	74.53967795	0.01341567	126
127	3.18630930	0.31384273	238.50646906	0.00419276	74.85352068	0.01335943	127
128	3.21551714	0.31099197	241.69277836	0.00413748	75.16451265	0.01330415	128
129	3.24499271	0.30816710	244.90829550	0.00408316	75.47267975	0.01324983	129
130	3.27473848	0.30536790	248.15328821	0.00402977	75.77804765	0.01319643	130
131	3.30475691	0.30259412	251.42802668	0.00397728	76.08064176	0.01314395	131
132	3.33505052	0.29984553	254.73278359	0.00392568	76.38048730	0.01309235	132
133	3.36562181	0.29712192	258.06783411	0.00387495	76.67760921	0.01304162	133
134	3.39647335	0.29442304	261.43345592	0.00382507	76.97203225	0.01299173	134
135	3.42760768	0.29174867	264.82992927	0.00377601	77.26378093	0.01294267	135
136	3.45902742	0.28909860	268.25753695	0.00372776	77.55287953	0.01289443	136
137	3.49073517	0.28647261	271.71656438	0.00368031	77.83935214	0.01284697	137
138	3.52273358	0.28387046	275.20729955	0.00363362	78.12322259	0.01280029	138
139	3.55502530	0.28129195	278.73003313	0.00358770	78.40451454	0.01275437	139
140	3.58761304	0.27873686	282.28505843	0.00354252	78.68325141	0.01270919	140
141	3.62049949	0.27620498	285.87267147	0.00349806	78.95945639	0.01266473	141
142	3.65368740	0.27369610	289.49317096	0.00345431	79.23315249	0.01262098	142
143	3.68717953	0.27121001	293.14685836	0.00341126	79.50436250	0.01257793	143
144	3.72097868	0.26874650	296.83403789	0.00336889	79.77310900	0.01253555	144
145	3.75508765	0.26630537	300.55501657	0.00332718	80.03941437	0.01249384	145
146	3.78950929	0.26388641	304.31010422	0.00328612	80.30330078	0.01245279	146
147	3.82424646	0.26148942	308.09961351	0.00324570	80.56479020	0.01241237	147
148	3.85930205	0.25911421	311.92385997	0.00320591	80.82390441	0.01237258	148
149	3.89467899	0.25676057	315.78316202	0.00316673	81.08066498	0.01233340	149
150	3.93038021	0.25442831	319.67784101	0.00312815	81.33509330	0.01229482	150
151	3.96640869	0.25211724	323.60822121	0.00309016	81.58721053	0.01225682	151
152	4.00276744	0.24982715	327.57462991	0.00305274	81.83703769	0.01221941	152
153	4.03945948	0.24755787	331.57739735	0.00301589	82.08459556	0.01218255	153
154	4.07648785	0.24530921	335.61685683	0.00297959	82.32990477	0.01214625	154
155	4.11385566	0.24308096	339.69334468	0.00294383	82.57298573	0.01211050	155
156	4.15156600	0.24087296	343.80720034	0.00290861	82.81385869	0.01207527	156
157	4.18962202	0.23868502	347.95876634	0.00287390	83.05254371	0.01204057	157
158	4.22802689	0.23651694	352.14838837	0.00283971	83.28906065	0.01200638	158
159	4.26678381	0.23436857	356.37641526	0.00280602	83.52342922	0.01197269	159
160	4.30589599	0.23223970	360.64319907	0.00277282	83.75566892	0.01193949	160

TABLE A-2

COMPOUND INTEREST FOR $1

$\frac{11}{12}$ %

PERIODS n	FUTURE AMOUNT $(1+i)^n$	PRESENT VALUE $(1+i)^{-n}$	AMOUNT OF ANNUITY (S/p,i,n) $\frac{(1+i)^n-1}{i}$	SINKING FUND (p/S,i,n) $\frac{i}{(1+i)^n-1}$	PRESENT VALUE OF ANNUITY (V/p,i,n) $\frac{1-(1+i)^{-n}}{i}$	AMORTIZATION (p/V,i,n) $\frac{i}{1-(1+i)^{-n}}$	PERIODS n
161	4.34536670	0.23013017	364.94909506	0.00274011	83.98579910	0.01190677	161
162	4.38519923	0.22803981	369.29446176	0.00270787	84.21383891	0.01187453	162
163	4.42539689	0.22596843	373.67966100	0.00267609	84.43980734	0.01184276	163
164	4.46596303	0.22391587	378.10505789	0.00264477	84.66372321	0.01181143	164
165	4.50690103	0.22188195	382.57102092	0.00261389	84.88560516	0.01178056	165
166	4.54821428	0.21986651	387.07792194	0.00258346	85.10547167	0.01175013	166
167	4.58990625	0.21786937	391.62613623	0.00255346	85.32334105	0.01172012	167
168	4.63198039	0.21589038	396.21604248	0.00252388	85.53923142	0.01169054	168
169	4.67444021	0.21392936	400.84802287	0.00249471	85.75316078	0.01166138	169
170	4.71728924	0.21198615	405.52246308	0.00246595	85.96514694	0.01163262	170
171	4.76053106	0.21006060	410.23975232	0.00243760	86.17520753	0.01160427	171
172	4.80416926	0.20815253	415.00028338	0.00240964	86.38336007	0.01157630	172
173	4.84820748	0.20626180	419.80445265	0.00238206	86.58962187	0.01154873	173
174	4.89264938	0.20438824	424.65266013	0.00235487	86.79401011	0.01152153	174
175	4.93749867	0.20253170	429.54530952	0.00232804	86.99654181	0.01149471	175
176	4.98275908	0.20069202	434.48280819	0.00230159	87.19723383	0.01146825	176
177	5.02843437	0.19886906	439.46556726	0.00227549	87.39610289	0.01144216	177
178	5.07452835	0.19706265	444.49400163	0.00224975	87.59316554	0.01141642	178
179	5.12104486	0.19527265	449.56852998	0.00222435	87.78843819	0.01139102	179
180	5.16798777	0.19349891	454.68975484	0.00219930	87.98193710	0.01136597	180
181	5.21536099	0.19174128	459.85756260	0.00217459	88.17367838	0.01134125	181
182	5.26316847	0.18999962	465.07292359	0.00215020	88.36367800	0.01131687	182
183	5.31141418	0.18827378	470.33609206	0.00212614	88.55195177	0.01129281	183
184	5.36010214	0.18656361	475.64750624	0.00210240	88.73851538	0.01126906	184
185	5.40923641	0.18486898	481.00760838	0.00207897	88.92338436	0.01124564	185
186	5.45882108	0.18318974	486.41684479	0.00205585	89.10657409	0.01122252	186
187	5.50886027	0.18152575	491.87566587	0.00203303	89.28809985	0.01119970	187
188	5.55935816	0.17987688	497.38452614	0.00201052	89.46797673	0.01117718	188
189	5.61031894	0.17824299	502.94388429	0.00198829	89.64621971	0.01115496	189
190	5.66174686	0.17662393	508.55420323	0.00196636	89.82284365	0.01113303	190
191	5.71364621	0.17501959	514.21595010	0.00194471	89.99786323	0.01111137	191
192	5.76602130	0.17342981	519.92959630	0.00192334	90.17129305	0.01109000	192
193	5.81887649	0.17185448	525.69561760	0.00190224	90.34314753	0.01106891	193
194	5.87221620	0.17029346	531.51449410	0.00188142	90.51344098	0.01104808	194
195	5.92604484	0.16874661	537.38671029	0.00186086	90.68218760	0.01102752	195
196	5.98036692	0.16721382	543.31275514	0.00184056	90.84940142	0.01100723	196
197	6.03518695	0.16569495	549.29312206	0.00182052	91.01509637	0.01098719	197
198	6.09050950	0.16418988	555.32830901	0.00180074	91.17928624	0.01096740	198
199	6.14633917	0.16269847	561.41881851	0.00178120	91.34198472	0.01094787	199
200	6.20268061	0.16122062	567.56515768	0.00176191	91.50320534	0.01092858	200

TABLE A-2

COMPOUND INTEREST FOR $1

$\frac{11}{12}$ %

PERIODS n	FUTURE AMOUNT $(1+i)^n$	PRESENT VALUE $(1+i)^{-n}$	AMOUNT OF ANNUITY (S/p,i,n) $\frac{(1+i)^n - 1}{i}$	SINKING FUND (p/S,i,n) $\frac{i}{(1+i)^n - 1}$	PRESENT VALUE OF ANNUITY (V/p,i,n) $\frac{1-(1+i)^{-n}}{i}$	AMORTIZATION (p/V,i,n) $\frac{i}{1-(1+i)^{-n}}$	PERIODS n
201	6.25953852	0.15975619	573.76783829	0.00174287	91.66296152	0.01090953	201
202	6.31691762	0.15830506	580.02737681	0.00172406	91.82126658	0.01089072	202
203	6.37482270	0.15686711	586.34429443	0.00170548	91.97813369	0.01087215	203
204	6.43325857	0.15544222	592.71911713	0.00168714	92.13357591	0.01085381	204
205	6.49223011	0.15403028	599.15237571	0.00166902	92.28760618	0.01083569	205
206	6.55174222	0.15263116	605.64460582	0.00165113	92.44023734	0.01081780	206
207	6.61179986	0.15124475	612.19634804	0.00163346	92.59148209	0.01080013	207
208	6.67240802	0.14987093	618.80814789	0.00161601	92.74135302	0.01078268	208
209	6.73357176	0.14850959	625.48055592	0.00159877	92.88986261	0.01076544	209
210	6.79529617	0.14716062	632.21412768	0.00158174	93.03702323	0.01074841	210
211	6.85758639	0.14582390	639.00942385	0.00156492	93.18284713	0.01073159	211
212	6.92044759	0.14449932	645.86701023	0.00154831	93.32734646	0.01071497	212
213	6.98388503	0.14318678	652.78745783	0.00153189	93.47053324	0.01069856	213
214	7.04790398	0.14188616	659.77134286	0.00151568	93.61241939	0.01068234	214
215	7.11250976	0.14059735	666.81924683	0.00149966	93.75301674	0.01066632	215
216	7.17770777	0.13932024	673.93175660	0.00148383	93.89233698	0.01065050	216
217	7.24350342	0.13805474	681.10946437	0.00146819	94.03039173	0.01063486	217
218	7.30990220	0.13680074	688.35296779	0.00145274	94.16719246	0.01061941	218
219	7.37690964	0.13555812	695.66286999	0.00143748	94.30275058	0.01060414	219
220	7.44453131	0.13432679	703.03977963	0.00142239	94.43707737	0.01058906	220
221	7.51277285	0.13310665	710.48431095	0.00140749	94.57018402	0.01057416	221
222	7.58163993	0.13189759	717.99708380	0.00139276	94.70208160	0.01055943	222
223	7.65113830	0.13069951	725.57872373	0.00137821	94.83278111	0.01054488	223
224	7.72127374	0.12951231	733.22986203	0.00136383	94.96229342	0.01053050	224
225	7.79205208	0.12833590	740.95113577	0.00134962	95.09062932	0.01051628	225
226	7.86347922	0.12717017	748.74318785	0.00133557	95.21779949	0.01050224	226
227	7.93556111	0.12601503	756.60666707	0.00132169	95.34381452	0.01048836	227
228	8.00830376	0.12487039	764.54222818	0.00130797	95.46868491	0.01047464	228
229	8.08171321	0.12373614	772.55053194	0.00129441	95.59242105	0.01046108	229
230	8.15579558	0.12261220	780.63224515	0.00128101	95.71503325	0.01044768	230
231	8.23055704	0.12149846	788.78804073	0.00126777	95.83653171	0.01043443	231
232	8.30600381	0.12039484	797.01859777	0.00125468	95.95692655	0.01042134	232
233	8.38214218	0.11930125	805.32460159	0.00124174	96.07622779	0.01040840	233
234	8.45897848	0.11821758	813.70674377	0.00122894	96.19444538	0.01039561	234
235	8.53651942	0.11714377	822.16572225	0.00121630	96.31158914	0.01038297	235
236	8.61477055	0.11607970	830.70224137	0.00120380	96.42766884	0.01037047	236
237	8.69373928	0.11502530	839.31701192	0.00119144	96.54269415	0.01035811	237
238	8.77343189	0.11398048	848.01075119	0.00117923	96.65667463	0.01034590	238
239	8.85385501	0.11294515	856.78418308	0.00116716	96.76961978	0.01033382	239
240	8.93501535	0.11191923	865.63803809	0.00115522	96.88153901	0.01032188	240

TABLE A-2

COMPOUND INTEREST FOR $1

1%

PERIODS n	FUTURE AMOUNT $(1+i)^n$	PRESENT VALUE $(1+i)^{-n}$	AMOUNT OF ANNUITY $(S/p,i,n)$ $\dfrac{(1+i)^n - 1}{i}$	SINKING FUND $(p/S,i,n)$ $\dfrac{i}{(1+i)^n - 1}$	PRESENT VALUE OF ANNUITY $(V/p,i,n)$ $\dfrac{1-(1+i)^{-n}}{i}$	AMORTIZATION $(p/V,i,n)$ $\dfrac{i}{1-(1+i)^{-n}}$	PERIODS n
1	1.01000000	0.99009901	1.00000000	1.00000000	0.99009901	1.01000000	1
2	1.02010000	0.98029605	2.01000000	0.49751244	1.97039506	0.50751244	2
3	1.03030100	0.97059015	3.03010000	0.33002211	2.94098521	0.34002211	3
4	1.04060401	0.96098034	4.06040100	0.24628109	3.90196555	0.25628109	4
5	1.05101005	0.95146569	5.10100501	0.19603980	4.85343124	0.20603980	5
6	1.06152015	0.94204524	6.15201506	0.16254837	5.79547647	0.17254837	6
7	1.07213535	0.93271805	7.21353521	0.13862828	6.72819453	0.14862828	7
8	1.08285671	0.92348322	8.28567056	0.12069029	7.65167775	0.13069029	8
9	1.09368527	0.91433982	9.36852727	0.10674036	8.56601758	0.11674036	9
10	1.10462213	0.90528695	10.46221254	0.09558208	9.47130453	0.10558208	10
11	1.11566835	0.89632372	11.56683467	0.08645408	10.36762825	0.09645408	11
12	1.12682503	0.88744923	12.68250301	0.07884879	11.25507747	0.08884879	12
13	1.13809328	0.87866260	13.80932804	0.07241482	12.13374007	0.08241482	13
14	1.14947421	0.86996297	14.94742132	0.06690117	13.00370304	0.07690117	14
15	1.16096896	0.86134947	16.09689554	0.06212378	13.86505252	0.07212378	15
16	1.17257864	0.85282126	17.25786449	0.05794460	14.71787378	0.06794460	16
17	1.18430443	0.84437749	18.43044314	0.05425806	15.56225127	0.06425806	17
18	1.19614748	0.83601731	19.61474757	0.05098205	16.39826858	0.06098205	18
19	1.20810895	0.82773992	20.81089504	0.04805175	17.22600850	0.05805175	19
20	1.22019004	0.81954447	22.01900399	0.04541531	18.04555297	0.05541531	20
21	1.23239194	0.81143017	23.23919403	0.04303075	18.85698313	0.05303075	21
22	1.24471586	0.80339621	24.47158598	0.04086372	19.66037934	0.05086372	22
23	1.25716302	0.79544179	25.71630183	0.03888584	20.45582113	0.04888584	23
24	1.26973465	0.78756613	26.97346485	0.03707347	21.24338726	0.04707347	24
25	1.28243200	0.77976844	28.24319950	0.03540675	22.02315570	0.04540675	25
26	1.29525631	0.77204796	29.52563150	0.03386888	22.79520366	0.04386888	26
27	1.30820888	0.76440392	30.82088781	0.03244553	23.55960759	0.04244553	27
28	1.32129097	0.75683557	32.12909669	0.03112444	24.31644316	0.04112444	28
29	1.33450388	0.74934215	33.45038766	0.02989502	25.06578530	0.03989502	29
30	1.34784892	0.74192292	34.78489153	0.02874811	25.80770822	0.03874811	30
31	1.36132740	0.73457715	36.13274045	0.02767573	26.54228537	0.03767573	31
32	1.37494068	0.72730411	37.49406785	0.02667089	27.26958947	0.03667089	32
33	1.38869009	0.72010307	38.86900853	0.02572744	27.98969255	0.03572744	33
34	1.40257699	0.71297334	40.25769862	0.02483997	28.70266589	0.03483997	34
35	1.41660276	0.70591420	41.66027560	0.02400368	29.40858009	0.03400368	35
36	1.43076878	0.69892495	43.07687836	0.02321431	30.10750504	0.03321431	36
37	1.44507647	0.69200490	44.50764714	0.02246805	30.79950994	0.03246805	37
38	1.45952724	0.68515337	45.95272361	0.02176150	31.48466330	0.03176150	38
39	1.47412251	0.67836967	47.41225085	0.02109160	32.16303298	0.03109160	39
40	1.48886373	0.67165314	48.88637336	0.02045560	32.83468611	0.03045560	40

311

TABLE A-2

COMPOUND INTEREST FOR $1

1%

PERIODS n	FUTURE AMOUNT $(1+i)^n$	PRESENT VALUE $(1+i)^{-n}$	AMOUNT OF ANNUITY $(S/p,i,n)$ $\dfrac{(1+i)^n - 1}{i}$	SINKING FUND $(p/S,i,n)$ $\dfrac{i}{(1+i)^n - 1}$	PRESENT VALUE OF ANNUITY $(V/p,i,n)$ $\dfrac{1-(1+i)^{-n}}{i}$	AMORTIZATION $(p/V,i,n)$ $\dfrac{i}{1-(1+i)^{-n}}$	PERIODS n
41	1.50375237	0.66500311	50.37523709	0.01985102	33.49968922	0.02985102	41
42	1.51878989	0.65841892	51.87898946	0.01927563	34.15810814	0.02927563	42
43	1.53397779	0.65189992	53.39777936	0.01872737	34.81000806	0.02872737	43
44	1.54931757	0.64544546	54.93175715	0.01820441	35.45545352	0.02820441	44
45	1.56481075	0.63905492	56.48107472	0.01770505	36.09450844	0.02770505	45
46	1.58045885	0.63272764	58.04588547	0.01722775	36.72723608	0.02722775	46
47	1.59626344	0.62646301	59.62634432	0.01677111	37.35369909	0.02677111	47
48	1.61222608	0.62026041	61.22260777	0.01633384	37.97395949	0.02633384	48
49	1.62834834	0.61411921	62.83483385	0.01591474	38.58807871	0.02591474	49
50	1.64463182	0.60803882	64.46318218	0.01551273	39.19611753	0.02551273	50
51	1.66107814	0.60201864	66.10781401	0.01512680	39.79813617	0.02512680	51
52	1.67768892	0.59605806	67.76889215	0.01475603	40.39419423	0.02475603	52
53	1.69446581	0.59015649	69.44658107	0.01439956	40.98435072	0.02439956	53
54	1.71141047	0.58431336	71.14104688	0.01405658	41.56866408	0.02405658	54
55	1.72852457	0.57852808	72.85245735	0.01372637	42.14719216	0.02372637	55
56	1.74580982	0.57280008	74.58098192	0.01340824	42.71999224	0.02340824	56
57	1.76326792	0.56712879	76.32679174	0.01310156	43.28712102	0.02310156	57
58	1.78090060	0.56151365	78.09005966	0.01280573	43.84863468	0.02280573	58
59	1.79870960	0.55595411	79.87096025	0.01252020	44.40458879	0.02252020	59
60	1.81669670	0.55044962	81.66966986	0.01224445	44.95503841	0.02224445	60
61	1.83486367	0.54499962	83.48636655	0.01197800	45.50003803	0.02197800	61
62	1.85321230	0.53960358	85.32123022	0.01172041	46.03964161	0.02172041	62
63	1.87174443	0.53426097	87.17444252	0.01147125	46.57390258	0.02147125	63
64	1.89046187	0.52897126	89.04618695	0.01123013	47.10287385	0.02123013	64
65	1.90936649	0.52373392	90.93664882	0.01099667	47.62660777	0.02099667	65
66	1.92846015	0.51854844	92.84601531	0.01077052	48.14515621	0.02077052	66
67	1.94774475	0.51341429	94.77447546	0.01055136	48.65857050	0.02055136	67
68	1.96722220	0.50833099	96.72222021	0.01033889	49.16690149	0.02033889	68
69	1.98689442	0.50329801	98.68944242	0.01013280	49.67019949	0.02013280	69
70	2.00676337	0.49831486	100.67633684	0.00993282	50.16851435	0.01993282	70
71	2.02683100	0.49338105	102.68310021	0.00973870	50.66189539	0.01973870	71
72	2.04709931	0.48849609	104.70993121	0.00955019	51.15039148	0.01955019	72
73	2.06757031	0.48365949	106.75703052	0.00936706	51.63405097	0.01936706	73
74	2.08824601	0.47887078	108.82460083	0.00918910	52.11292175	0.01918910	74
75	2.10912847	0.47412949	110.91284684	0.00901609	52.58705124	0.01901609	75
76	2.13021975	0.46943514	113.02197530	0.00884784	53.05648638	0.01884784	76
77	2.15152195	0.46478726	115.15219506	0.00868416	53.52127364	0.01868416	77
78	2.17303717	0.46018541	117.30371701	0.00852488	53.98145905	0.01852488	78
79	2.19476754	0.45562912	119.47675418	0.00836983	54.43708817	0.01836983	79
80	2.21671522	0.45111794	121.67152172	0.00821885	54.88820611	0.01821885	80

TABLE A-2

COMPOUND INTEREST FOR $1

1%

PERIODS n	FUTURE AMOUNT $(1+i)^n$	PRESENT VALUE $(1+i)^{-n}$	AMOUNT OF ANNUITY $(S/p,i,n)$ $\dfrac{(1+i)^n - 1}{i}$	SINKING FUND $(p/S,i,n)$ $\dfrac{i}{(1+i)^n - 1}$	PRESENT VALUE OF ANNUITY $(V/p,i,n)$ $\dfrac{1-(1+i)^{-n}}{i}$	AMORTIZATION $(p/V,i,n)$ $\dfrac{i}{1-(1+i)^{-n}}$	PERIODS n
81	2.23888237	0.44665142	123.88823694	0.00807179	55.33485753	0.01807179	81
82	2.26127119	0.44222913	126.12711931	0.00792851	55.77708666	0.01792851	82
83	2.28388390	0.43785063	128.38839050	0.00778887	56.21493729	0.01778887	83
84	2.30672274	0.43351547	130.67227440	0.00765273	56.64845276	0.01765273	84
85	2.32978997	0.42922324	132.97899715	0.00751998	57.07767600	0.01751998	85
86	2.35308787	0.42497350	135.30878712	0.00739050	57.50264951	0.01739050	86
87	2.37661875	0.42076585	137.66187499	0.00726418	57.92341535	0.01726418	87
88	2.40038494	0.41659985	140.03849374	0.00714089	58.34001520	0.01714089	88
89	2.42438879	0.41247510	142.43887868	0.00702056	58.75249030	0.01702056	89
90	2.44863267	0.40839119	144.86326746	0.00690306	59.16088148	0.01690306	90
91	2.47311900	0.40434771	147.31190014	0.00678832	59.56522919	0.01678832	91
92	2.49785019	0.40034427	149.78501914	0.00667624	59.96557346	0.01667624	92
93	2.52282869	0.39638046	152.28286933	0.00656673	60.36195392	0.01656673	93
94	2.54805698	0.39245590	154.80569803	0.00645971	60.75440982	0.01645971	94
95	2.57353755	0.38857020	157.35375501	0.00635511	61.14298002	0.01635511	95
96	2.59927293	0.38472297	159.92729256	0.00625284	61.52770299	0.01625284	96
97	2.62526565	0.38091383	162.52656548	0.00615284	61.90861682	0.01615284	97
98	2.65151831	0.37714241	165.15183114	0.00605503	62.28575923	0.01605503	98
99	2.67803349	0.37340832	167.80334945	0.00595936	62.65916755	0.01595936	99
100	2.70481383	0.36971121	170.48138294	0.00586574	63.02887877	0.01586574	100
101	2.73186197	0.36605071	173.18619677	0.00577413	63.39492947	0.01577413	101
102	2.75918059	0.36242644	175.91805874	0.00568446	63.75735591	0.01568446	102
103	2.78677239	0.35883806	178.67723933	0.00559668	64.11619397	0.01559668	103
104	2.81464012	0.35528521	181.46401172	0.00551073	64.47147918	0.01551073	104
105	2.84278652	0.35176753	184.27865184	0.00542656	64.82324671	0.01542656	105
106	2.87121438	0.34828469	187.12143836	0.00534412	65.17153140	0.01534412	106
107	2.89992653	0.34483632	189.99265274	0.00526336	65.51636772	0.01526336	107
108	2.92892579	0.34142210	192.89257927	0.00518423	65.85778983	0.01518423	108
109	2.95821505	0.33804168	195.82150506	0.00510669	66.19583151	0.01510669	109
110	2.98779720	0.33469474	198.77972011	0.00503069	66.53052625	0.01503069	110
111	3.01767517	0.33138093	201.76751731	0.00495620	66.86190718	0.01495620	111
112	3.04785192	0.32809993	204.78519248	0.00488317	67.19000710	0.01488317	112
113	3.07833044	0.32485141	207.83304441	0.00481155	67.51485852	0.01481155	113
114	3.10911375	0.32163506	210.91137485	0.00474133	67.83649358	0.01474133	114
115	3.14020489	0.31845056	214.02048860	0.00467245	68.15494414	0.01467245	115
116	3.17160693	0.31529758	217.16069349	0.00460488	68.47024172	0.01460488	116
117	3.20332300	0.31217582	220.33230042	0.00453860	68.78241755	0.01453860	117
118	3.23535623	0.30908497	223.53562343	0.00447356	69.09150252	0.01447356	118
119	3.26770980	0.30602473	226.77097966	0.00440974	69.39752725	0.01440974	119
120	3.30038689	0.30299478	230.03868946	0.00434709	69.70052203	0.01434709	120

TABLE A-2

COMPOUND INTEREST FOR $1

1%

PERIODS	FUTURE AMOUNT	PRESENT VALUE	AMOUNT OF ANNUITY	SINKING FUND	PRESENT VALUE OF ANNUITY	AMORTIZATION	PERIODS
n	$(1+i)^n$	$(1+i)^{-n}$	$\dfrac{(S/p,i,n)}{(1+i)^n - 1}{i}$	$\dfrac{(p/S,i,n)}{i}{(1+i)^n - 1}$	$\dfrac{(V/p,i,n)}{1-(1+i)^{-n}}{i}$	$\dfrac{(p/V,i,n)}{i}{1-(1+i)^{-n}}$	n
121	3.33339076	0.29999483	233.33907635	0.00428561	70.00051686	0.01428561	121
122	3.36672467	0.29702459	236.67246712	0.00422525	70.29754145	0.01422525	122
123	3.40039192	0.29408375	240.03919179	0.00416599	70.59162520	0.01416599	123
124	3.43439584	0.29117203	243.43958370	0.00410780	70.88279722	0.01410780	124
125	3.46873980	0.28828914	246.87397954	0.00405065	71.17108636	0.01405065	125
126	3.50342719	0.28543479	250.34271934	0.00399452	71.45652115	0.01399452	126
127	3.53846147	0.28260870	253.84614653	0.00393939	71.73912985	0.01393939	127
128	3.57384608	0.27981060	257.38460800	0.00388524	72.01894045	0.01388524	128
129	3.60958454	0.27704019	260.95845408	0.00383203	72.29598064	0.01383203	129
130	3.64568039	0.27429722	264.56803862	0.00377975	72.57027786	0.01377975	130
131	3.68213719	0.27158141	268.21371900	0.00372837	72.84185927	0.01372837	131
132	3.71895856	0.26889248	271.89585619	0.00367788	73.11075175	0.01367788	132
133	3.75614815	0.26623018	275.61481475	0.00362825	73.37698193	0.01362825	133
134	3.79370963	0.26359424	279.37096290	0.00357947	73.64057617	0.01357947	134
135	3.83164673	0.26098439	283.16467253	0.00353151	73.90156056	0.01353151	135
136	3.86996319	0.25840039	286.99631926	0.00348437	74.15996095	0.01348437	136
137	3.90866282	0.25584197	290.86628245	0.00343801	74.41580293	0.01343801	137
138	3.94774945	0.25330888	294.77494527	0.00339242	74.66911181	0.01339242	138
139	3.98722695	0.25080087	298.72269473	0.00334759	74.91991268	0.01334759	139
140	4.02709922	0.24831770	302.70992167	0.00330349	75.16823038	0.01330349	140
141	4.06737021	0.24585911	306.73702089	0.00326012	75.41408948	0.01326012	141
142	4.10804391	0.24342486	310.80439110	0.00321746	75.65751434	0.01321746	142
143	4.14912435	0.24101471	314.91243501	0.00317549	75.89852905	0.01317549	143
144	4.19061559	0.23862843	319.06155936	0.00313419	76.13715747	0.01313419	144
145	4.23252175	0.23626577	323.25217495	0.00309356	76.37342324	0.01309356	145
146	4.27484697	0.23392650	327.48469670	0.00305358	76.60734974	0.01305358	146
147	4.31759544	0.23161040	331.75954367	0.00301423	76.83896014	0.01301423	147
148	4.36077139	0.22931723	336.07713911	0.00297551	77.06827737	0.01297551	148
149	4.40437910	0.22704676	340.43791050	0.00293739	77.29532413	0.01293739	149
150	4.44842290	0.22479877	344.84228960	0.00289988	77.52012290	0.01289988	150
151	4.49290712	0.22257304	349.29071250	0.00286294	77.74269594	0.01286294	151
152	4.53783620	0.22036935	353.78361962	0.00282659	77.96306529	0.01282659	152
153	4.58321456	0.21818747	358.32145582	0.00279079	78.18125276	0.01279079	153
154	4.62904670	0.21602720	362.90467038	0.00275554	78.39727996	0.01275554	154
155	4.67533717	0.21388832	367.53371708	0.00272084	78.61116828	0.01272084	155
156	4.72209054	0.21177061	372.20905425	0.00268666	78.82293889	0.01268666	156
157	4.76931145	0.20967387	376.93114480	0.00265300	79.03261276	0.01265300	157
158	4.81700456	0.20759789	381.70045624	0.00261986	79.24021065	0.01261986	158
159	4.86517461	0.20554247	386.51746081	0.00258721	79.44575312	0.01258721	159
160	4.91382635	0.20350739	391.38263541	0.00255504	79.64926052	0.01255504	160

TABLE A-2

COMPOUND INTEREST FOR $1

1%

PERIODS n	FUTURE AMOUNT $(1+i)^n$	PRESENT VALUE $(1+i)^{-n}$	AMOUNT OF ANNUITY (S/p,i,n) $\dfrac{(1+i)^n - 1}{i}$	SINKING FUND (p/S,i,n) $\dfrac{i}{(1+i)^n - 1}$	PRESENT VALUE OF ANNUITY (V/p,i,n) $\dfrac{1-(1+i)^{-n}}{i}$	AMORTIZATION (p/V,i,n) $\dfrac{i}{1-(1+i)^{-n}}$	PERIODS n
161	4.96296462	0.20149247	396.29646177	0.00252336	79.85075299	0.01252336	161
162	5.01259426	0.19949750	401.25942639	0.00249215	80.05025048	0.01249215	162
163	5.06272021	0.19752227	406.27202065	0.00246141	80.24777275	0.01246141	163
164	5.11334741	0.19556661	411.33474086	0.00243111	80.44333936	0.01243111	164
165	5.16448088	0.19363030	416.44808826	0.00240126	80.63696966	0.01240126	165
166	5.21612569	0.19171317	421.61256915	0.00237185	80.82868284	0.01237185	166
167	5.26828695	0.18981502	426.82869484	0.00234286	81.01849786	0.01234286	167
168	5.32096982	0.18793566	432.09698179	0.00231430	81.20643352	0.01231430	168
169	5.37417952	0.18607492	437.41795161	0.00228614	81.39250844	0.01228614	169
170	5.42792131	0.18423259	442.79213112	0.00225840	81.57674103	0.01225840	170
171	5.48220052	0.18240850	448.22005243	0.00223105	81.75914953	0.01223105	171
172	5.53702253	0.18060248	453.70225296	0.00220409	81.93975201	0.01220409	172
173	5.59239275	0.17881434	459.23927549	0.00217751	82.11856635	0.01217751	173
174	5.64831668	0.17704390	464.83166824	0.00215132	82.29561025	0.01215132	174
175	5.70479985	0.17529099	470.47998492	0.00212549	82.47090123	0.01212549	175
176	5.76184785	0.17355543	476.18478477	0.00210003	82.64445667	0.01210003	176
177	5.81946633	0.17183706	481.94663262	0.00207492	82.81629373	0.01207492	177
178	5.87766099	0.17013571	487.76609895	0.00205016	82.98642944	0.01205016	178
179	5.93643760	0.16845119	493.64375994	0.00202575	83.15488063	0.01202575	179
180	5.99580198	0.16678336	499.58019754	0.00200168	83.32166399	0.01200168	180
181	6.05576000	0.16513204	505.57599951	0.00197794	83.48679603	0.01197794	181
182	6.11631760	0.16349707	511.63175951	0.00195453	83.65029310	0.01195453	182
183	6.17748077	0.16187829	517.74807710	0.00193144	83.81217138	0.01193144	183
184	6.23925558	0.16027553	523.92555787	0.00190867	83.97244691	0.01190867	184
185	6.30164813	0.15868864	530.16481345	0.00188621	84.13113556	0.01188621	185
186	6.36466462	0.15711747	536.46646159	0.00186405	84.28825303	0.01186405	186
187	6.42831126	0.15556185	542.83112620	0.00184219	84.44381488	0.01184219	187
188	6.49259437	0.15402163	549.25943746	0.00182063	84.59783651	0.01182063	188
189	6.55752032	0.15249667	555.75203184	0.00179936	84.75033318	0.01179936	189
190	6.62309552	0.15098680	562.30955216	0.00177838	84.90131998	0.01177838	190
191	6.68932648	0.14949188	568.93264768	0.00175768	85.05081186	0.01175768	191
192	6.75621974	0.14801176	575.62197415	0.00173725	85.19882363	0.01173725	192
193	6.82378194	0.14654630	582.37819390	0.00171710	85.34536993	0.01171710	193
194	6.89201976	0.14509535	589.20197584	0.00169721	85.49046528	0.01169721	194
195	6.96093996	0.14365876	596.09399559	0.00167759	85.63412404	0.01167759	195
196	7.03054936	0.14223640	603.05493555	0.00165822	85.77636043	0.01165822	196
197	7.10085485	0.14082811	610.08548490	0.00163911	85.91718855	0.01163911	197
198	7.17186340	0.13943378	617.18633975	0.00162026	86.05662232	0.01162026	198
199	7.24358203	0.13805324	624.35820315	0.00160164	86.19467557	0.01160164	199
200	7.31601785	0.13668638	631.60178518	0.00158328	86.33136195	0.01158328	200

TABLE A-2

COMPOUND INTEREST FOR $1

1%

PERIODS n	FUTURE AMOUNT $(1+i)^n$	PRESENT VALUE $(1+i)^{-n}$	AMOUNT OF ANNUITY $(S/p,i,n)$ $\dfrac{(1+i)^n - 1}{i}$	SINKING FUND $(p/S,i,n)$ $\dfrac{i}{(1+i)^n - 1}$	PRESENT VALUE OF ANNUITY $(V/p,i,n)$ $\dfrac{1-(1+i)^{-n}}{i}$	AMORTIZATION $(p/V,i,n)$ $\dfrac{i}{1-(1+i)^{-n}}$	PERIODS n
201	7.38917803	0.13533305	638.91780303	0.00156515	86.46669500	0.01156515	201
202	7.46306981	0.13399312	646.30698107	0.00154725	86.60068812	0.01154725	202
203	7.53770051	0.13266645	653.77005088	0.00152959	86.73335457	0.01152959	203
204	7.61307751	0.13135293	661.30775138	0.00151216	86.86470750	0.01151216	204
205	7.68920829	0.13005240	668.92082890	0.00149495	86.99475990	0.01149495	205
206	7.76610037	0.12876475	676.61003719	0.00147796	87.12352465	0.01147796	206
207	7.84376138	0.12748985	684.37613756	0.00146118	87.25101451	0.01146118	207
208	7.92219899	0.12622758	692.21989893	0.00144463	87.37724208	0.01144463	208
209	8.00142098	0.12497780	700.14209792	0.00142828	87.50221989	0.01142828	209
210	8.08143519	0.12374040	708.14351890	0.00141214	87.62596028	0.01141214	210
211	8.16224954	0.12251524	716.22495409	0.00139621	87.74847553	0.01139621	211
212	8.24387204	0.12130222	724.38720363	0.00138048	87.86977775	0.01138048	212
213	8.32631076	0.12010121	732.63107567	0.00136494	87.98987896	0.01136494	213
214	8.40957386	0.11891209	740.95738643	0.00134961	88.10879105	0.01134961	214
215	8.49366960	0.11773474	749.36696029	0.00133446	88.22652579	0.01133446	215
216	8.57860630	0.11656905	757.86062989	0.00131950	88.34309484	0.01131950	216
217	8.66439236	0.11541490	766.43923619	0.00130473	88.45850975	0.01130473	217
218	8.75103629	0.11427218	775.10362855	0.00129015	88.57278193	0.01129015	218
219	8.83854665	0.11314077	783.85466484	0.00127575	88.68592270	0.01127575	219
220	8.92693211	0.11202057	792.69321149	0.00126152	88.79794327	0.01126152	220
221	9.01620144	0.11091145	801.62014360	0.00124747	88.90885472	0.01124747	221
222	9.10636345	0.10981332	810.63634504	0.00123360	89.01866804	0.01123360	222
223	9.19742708	0.10872606	819.74270849	0.00121989	89.12739410	0.01121989	223
224	9.28940136	0.10764956	828.94013557	0.00120636	89.23504366	0.01120636	224
225	9.38229537	0.10658373	838.22953693	0.00119299	89.34162739	0.01119299	225
226	9.47611832	0.10552844	847.61183230	0.00117979	89.44715583	0.01117979	226
227	9.57087951	0.10448361	857.08795062	0.00116674	89.55163944	0.01116674	227
228	9.66658830	0.10344911	866.65883013	0.00115386	89.65508855	0.01115386	228
229	9.76325418	0.10242487	876.32541843	0.00114113	89.75751342	0.01114113	229
230	9.86088673	0.10141076	886.08867261	0.00112856	89.85892417	0.01112856	230
231	9.95949559	0.10040669	895.94955934	0.00111613	89.95933087	0.01111613	231
232	10.05909055	0.09941257	905.90905493	0.00110386	90.05874343	0.01110386	232
233	10.15968145	0.09842828	915.96814548	0.00109174	90.15717171	0.01109174	233
234	10.26127827	0.09745375	926.12782694	0.00107976	90.25462546	0.01107976	234
235	10.36389105	0.09648886	936.38910521	0.00106793	90.35111432	0.01106793	235
236	10.46752996	0.09553352	946.75299626	0.00105624	90.44664784	0.01105624	236
237	10.57220526	0.09458765	957.22052622	0.00104469	90.54123548	0.01104469	237
238	10.67792731	0.09365113	967.79273148	0.00103328	90.63488662	0.01103328	238
239	10.78470659	0.09272389	978.47065880	0.00102200	90.72761051	0.01102200	239
240	10.89255365	0.09180584	989.25536539	0.00101086	90.81941635	0.01101086	240

TABLE A-2

COMPOUND INTEREST FOR $1

$1\frac{1}{12}\%$

PERIODS n	FUTURE AMOUNT $(1+i)^n$	PRESENT VALUE $(1+i)^{-n}$	AMOUNT OF ANNUITY $(S/p,i,n)$ $\frac{(1+i)^n-1}{i}$	SINKING FUND $(p/S,i,n)$ $\frac{i}{(1+i)^n-1}$	PRESENT VALUE OF ANNUITY $(V/p,i,n)$ $\frac{1-(1+i)^{-n}}{i}$	AMORTIZATION $(p/V,i,n)$ $\frac{i}{1-(1+i)^{-n}}$	PERIODS n
1	1.01083333	0.98928277	1.00000000	1.00000000	0.98928277	1.01083333	1
2	1.02178403	0.97868040	2.01083333	0.49730626	1.96796317	0.50813959	2
3	1.03285335	0.96819166	3.03261736	0.32974816	2.93615483	0.34058150	3
4	1.04404260	0.95781532	4.06547072	0.24597398	3.89397015	0.25680731	4
5	1.05535306	0.94755020	5.10951332	0.19571336	4.84152034	0.20654669	5
6	1.06678605	0.93739508	6.16486638	0.16220952	5.77891543	0.17304285	6
7	1.07834290	0.92734880	7.23165243	0.13828098	6.70626423	0.14911432	7
8	1.09002495	0.91741019	8.30999533	0.12033701	7.62367443	0.13117034	8
9	1.10183355	0.90757810	9.40002028	0.10638275	8.53125252	0.11721608	9
10	1.11377008	0.89785137	10.50185383	0.09522128	9.42910390	0.10605462	10
11	1.12583593	0.88822889	11.61562392	0.08609094	10.31733279	0.09692427	11
12	1.13803248	0.87870954	12.74145984	0.07848394	11.19604233	0.08931728	12
13	1.15036117	0.86929221	13.87949232	0.07204874	12.06533454	0.08288208	13
14	1.16282341	0.85997580	15.02985349	0.06653425	12.92531035	0.07736758	14
15	1.17542067	0.85075925	16.19267690	0.06175631	13.77606959	0.07258964	15
16	1.18815439	0.84164146	17.36809757	0.05757683	14.61771106	0.06841016	16
17	1.20102606	0.83262140	18.56625196	0.05389019	15.45033246	0.06472353	17
18	1.21403718	0.82369800	19.75727802	0.05061426	16.27403046	0.06144759	18
19	1.22718925	0.81487024	20.97131520	0.04768418	17.08890070	0.05851751	19
20	1.24048380	0.80613709	22.19850445	0.04504808	17.89503779	0.05588141	20
21	1.25392237	0.79749753	23.43898825	0.04266396	18.69253533	0.05349729	21
22	1.26750653	0.78895057	24.69291062	0.04049745	19.48148590	0.05133079	22
23	1.28123785	0.78049520	25.96041715	0.03852018	20.26198110	0.04935352	23
24	1.29511793	0.77213046	27.24165500	0.03670849	21.03411156	0.04754182	24
25	1.30914837	0.76385536	28.53677293	0.03504250	21.79796692	0.04587584	25
26	1.32333081	0.75566894	29.84592131	0.03350542	22.55363586	0.04433875	26
27	1.33766690	0.74757027	31.16925212	0.03208290	23.30120613	0.04291623	27
28	1.35215829	0.73955838	32.50691902	0.03076268	24.04076451	0.04159601	28
29	1.36680667	0.73163237	33.85907731	0.02953418	24.77239688	0.04036751	29
30	1.38161374	0.72379129	35.22588398	0.02838822	25.49618817	0.03922155	30
31	1.39658123	0.71603426	36.60749772	0.02731681	26.21222243	0.03815014	31
32	1.41171086	0.70836035	38.00407895	0.02631297	26.92058278	0.03714630	32
33	1.42700439	0.70076869	39.41578980	0.02537054	27.62135148	0.03620388	33
34	1.44246360	0.69325839	40.84279419	0.02448412	28.31460987	0.03531746	34
35	1.45809029	0.68582858	42.28525780	0.02364890	29.00043845	0.03448224	35
36	1.47388627	0.67847840	43.74334809	0.02286062	29.67891685	0.03369395	36
37	1.48985337	0.67120699	45.21723436	0.02211546	30.35012385	0.03294879	37
38	1.50599345	0.66401351	46.70708773	0.02141003	31.01413736	0.03224336	38
39	1.52230838	0.65689713	48.21308118	0.02074126	31.67103448	0.03157459	39
40	1.53880005	0.64985701	49.73538956	0.02010641	32.32089149	0.03093974	40

TABLE A-2

COMPOUND INTEREST FOR $1

$1\frac{1}{12}\%$

PERIODS n	FUTURE AMOUNT $(1+i)^n$	PRESENT VALUE $(1+i)^{-n}$	AMOUNT OF ANNUITY $(S/p,i,n)$ $\dfrac{(1+i)^n-1}{i}$	SINKING FUND $(p/S,i,n)$ $\dfrac{i}{(1+i)^n-1}$	PRESENT VALUE OF ANNUITY $(V/p,i,n)$ $\dfrac{1-(1+i)^{-n}}{i}$	AMORTIZATION $(p/V,i,n)$ $\dfrac{i}{1-(1+i)^{-n}}$	PERIODS n
41	1.55547039	0.64289234	51.27418962	0.01950299	32.96378383	0.03033632	41
42	1.57232132	0.63600232	52.82966000	0.01892876	33.59978615	0.02976209	42
43	1.58935480	0.62918613	54.40198132	0.01838168	34.22897229	0.02921502	43
44	1.60657281	0.62244300	55.99133612	0.01785991	34.85141529	0.02869324	44
45	1.62397735	0.61577214	57.59790892	0.01736165	35.46718742	0.02819507	45
46	1.64157043	0.60917276	59.22188627	0.01688565	36.07636019	0.02771898	46
47	1.65935411	0.60264412	60.86345671	0.01643022	36.67900431	0.02726355	47
48	1.67733045	0.59618544	62.52281082	0.01599416	37.27518975	0.02682750	48
49	1.69550153	0.58979599	64.20014127	0.01557629	37.86498574	0.02640962	49
50	1.71386946	0.58347501	65.89564280	0.01517551	38.44846075	0.02600884	50
51	1.73243638	0.57722177	67.60951227	0.01479082	39.02568252	0.02562415	51
52	1.75120444	0.57103555	69.34194865	0.01442128	39.59671807	0.02525462	52
53	1.77017583	0.56491563	71.09315309	0.01406605	40.16163371	0.02489939	53
54	1.78935273	0.55886130	72.86332892	0.01372432	40.72049501	0.02455766	54
55	1.80873738	0.55287186	74.65268165	0.01339537	41.27336687	0.02422870	55
56	1.82833204	0.54694660	76.46141903	0.01307849	41.82031348	0.02391182	56
57	1.84813897	0.54108485	78.28975107	0.01277306	42.36139833	0.02360640	57
58	1.86816048	0.53528592	80.13789004	0.01247849	42.89668425	0.02331183	58
59	1.88839888	0.52954914	82.00605052	0.01219422	43.42623339	0.02302756	59
60	1.90885654	0.52387384	83.89444940	0.01191974	43.95010723	0.02275307	60
61	1.92953581	0.51825936	85.80330593	0.01165456	44.46836659	0.02248790	61
62	1.95043912	0.51270506	87.73284175	0.01139824	44.98107164	0.02223157	62
63	1.97156888	0.50721028	89.68328087	0.01115035	45.48828192	0.02198368	63
64	1.99292754	0.50177439	91.65484974	0.01091050	45.99005631	0.02174383	64
65	2.01451759	0.49639676	93.64777728	0.01067831	46.48645307	0.02151164	65
66	2.03634153	0.49107676	95.66229487	0.01045344	46.97752983	0.02128677	66
67	2.05840189	0.48581378	97.69863640	0.01023556	47.46334361	0.02106889	67
68	2.08070125	0.48060720	99.75703829	0.01002436	47.94395081	0.02085769	68
69	2.10324218	0.47545642	101.83773954	0.00981954	48.41940723	0.02065288	69
70	2.12602730	0.47036085	103.94098172	0.00962084	48.88976808	0.02045418	70
71	2.14905926	0.46531988	106.06700902	0.00942800	49.35508796	0.02026134	71
72	2.17234074	0.46033294	108.21606828	0.00924077	49.81542090	0.02007411	72
73	2.19587443	0.45539945	110.38840902	0.00905892	50.27082034	0.01989226	73
74	2.21966307	0.45051883	112.58428345	0.00888223	50.72133917	0.01971557	74
75	2.24370942	0.44569051	114.80394652	0.00871050	51.16702968	0.01954384	75
76	2.26801627	0.44091394	117.04765594	0.00854353	51.60794363	0.01937686	76
77	2.29258645	0.43618857	119.31567222	0.00838113	52.04413219	0.01921446	77
78	2.31742280	0.43151383	121.60825867	0.00822313	52.47564603	0.01905646	78
79	2.34252822	0.42688920	123.92568147	0.00806935	52.90253523	0.01890269	79
80	2.36790560	0.42231413	126.26820968	0.00791965	53.32484936	0.01875298	80

318

TABLE A-2

COMPOUND INTEREST FOR $1

$1\frac{1}{12}\%$

PERIODS n	FUTURE AMOUNT $(1+i)^n$	PRESENT VALUE $(1+i)^{-n}$	AMOUNT OF ANNUITY $(S/p,i,n)$ $\dfrac{(1+i)^n-1}{i}$	SINKING FUND $(p/S,i,n)$ $\dfrac{i}{(1+i)^n-1}$	PRESENT VALUE OF ANNUITY $(V/p,i,n)$ $\dfrac{1-(1+i)^{-n}}{i}$	AMORTIZATION $(p/V,i,n)$ $\dfrac{i}{1-(1+i)^{-n}}$	PERIODS n
81	2.39355792	0.41778809	128.63611529	0.00777387	53.74263746	0.01860720	81
82	2.41948813	0.41331056	131.02967320	0.00763186	54.15594802	0.01846519	82
83	2.44569925	0.40888102	133.44916133	0.00749349	54.56482904	0.01832682	83
84	2.47219432	0.40449895	135.89486058	0.00735863	54.96932798	0.01819196	84
85	2.49897643	0.40016384	138.36705490	0.00722715	55.36949182	0.01806049	85
86	2.52604867	0.39587519	140.86603133	0.00709894	55.76536701	0.01793228	86
87	2.55341420	0.39163251	143.39208000	0.00697389	56.15699952	0.01780722	87
88	2.58107619	0.38743529	145.94549420	0.00685187	56.54443481	0.01768521	88
89	2.60903785	0.38328306	148.52657039	0.00673280	56.92771786	0.01756614	89
90	2.63730242	0.37917532	151.13560824	0.00661657	57.30689319	0.01744991	90
91	2.66587320	0.37511161	153.77291066	0.00650310	57.68200480	0.01733643	91
92	2.69475349	0.37109146	156.43878386	0.00639228	58.05309626	0.01722561	92
93	2.72394665	0.36711438	159.13353735	0.00628403	58.42021065	0.01711736	93
94	2.75345608	0.36317994	161.85794008	0.00617827	58.78339058	0.01701161	94
95	2.78328518	0.35928765	164.61094008	0.00607493	59.14267823	0.01690826	95
96	2.81343744	0.35543708	167.39422526	0.00597392	59.49811532	0.01680726	96
97	2.84391635	0.35162778	170.20766270	0.00587518	59.84974310	0.01670851	97
98	2.87472544	0.34785931	173.05157905	0.00577862	60.19760241	0.01661196	98
99	2.90586830	0.34413122	175.92630449	0.00568420	60.54173363	0.01651753	99
100	2.93734854	0.34044309	178.83217279	0.00559183	60.88217671	0.01642517	100
101	2.96916981	0.33679448	181.76952133	0.00550147	61.21897119	0.01633481	101
102	3.00133582	0.33318497	184.73869114	0.00541305	61.55215617	0.01624638	102
103	3.03385029	0.32961415	187.74002696	0.00532651	61.88177032	0.01615985	103
104	3.06671700	0.32608160	190.77387725	0.00524181	62.20785192	0.01607514	104
105	3.09993977	0.32258691	193.84059426	0.00515888	62.53043884	0.01599221	105
106	3.13352245	0.31912967	196.94053403	0.00507767	62.84956851	0.01591101	106
107	3.16746895	0.31570949	200.07405648	0.00499815	63.16527800	0.01583148	107
108	3.20178319	0.31232596	203.24152543	0.00492025	63.47760396	0.01575359	108
109	3.23646918	0.30897869	206.44330862	0.00484394	63.78658265	0.01567728	109
110	3.27153093	0.30566729	209.67977780	0.00476918	64.09224994	0.01560251	110
111	3.30697251	0.30239139	212.95130872	0.00469591	64.39464132	0.01552924	111
112	3.34279805	0.29915059	216.25828123	0.00462411	64.69379191	0.01545743	112
113	3.37901169	0.29594452	219.60107928	0.00455371	64.98973643	0.01538705	113
114	3.41561765	0.29277282	222.98009097	0.00448471	65.28250925	0.01531804	114
115	3.45262018	0.28963510	226.39570862	0.00441704	65.57214435	0.01525038	115
116	3.49002356	0.28653102	229.84832880	0.00435070	65.85867537	0.01518403	116
117	3.52783215	0.28346020	233.33835236	0.00428562	66.14213557	0.01511896	117
118	3.56605033	0.28042229	236.86618451	0.00422179	66.42255786	0.01505513	118
119	3.60468254	0.27741694	240.43223485	0.00415918	66.69997480	0.01499251	119
120	3.64373327	0.27444380	244.03691739	0.00409774	66.97441860	0.01493107	120

COMPOUND INTEREST FOR $1

$1\frac{1}{12}\%$

PERIODS n	FUTURE AMOUNT $(1+i)^n$	PRESENT VALUE $(1+i)^{-n}$	AMOUNT OF ANNUITY $(S/p,i,n)$ $\dfrac{(1+i)^n-1}{i}$	SINKING FUND $(p/S,i,n)$ $\dfrac{i}{(1+i)^n-1}$	PRESENT VALUE OF ANNUITY $(V/p,i,n)$ $\dfrac{1-(1+i)^{-n}}{i}$	AMORTIZATION $(p/V,i,n)$ $\dfrac{i}{1-(1+i)^{-n}}$	PERIODS n
121	3.68320705	0.27150252	247.68065066	0.00403746	67.24592112	0.01487079	121
122	3.72310846	0.26859277	251.36385771	0.00397830	67.51451388	0.01481163	122
123	3.76344213	0.26571420	255.08696617	0.00392023	67.78022808	0.01475356	123
124	3.80421276	0.26286648	258.85040830	0.00386324	68.04309455	0.01469657	124
125	3.84542506	0.26004928	262.65462106	0.00380728	68.30314383	0.01464061	125
126	3.88708383	0.25726227	266.50004612	0.00375234	68.56040610	0.01458568	126
127	3.92919391	0.25450513	270.38712995	0.00369840	68.81491123	0.01453173	127
128	3.97176018	0.25177754	274.31632386	0.00364543	69.06668876	0.01447876	128
129	4.01478758	0.24907918	278.28808404	0.00359340	69.31576794	0.01442673	129
130	4.05828111	0.24640974	282.30287161	0.00354229	69.56217769	0.01437563	130
131	4.10224582	0.24376891	286.36115272	0.00349209	69.80594660	0.01432543	131
132	4.14668682	0.24115638	290.46339854	0.00344277	70.04710298	0.01427611	132
133	4.19160926	0.23857186	294.61008536	0.00339432	70.28567484	0.01422765	133
134	4.23701836	0.23601503	298.80169462	0.00334670	70.52168986	0.01418003	134
135	4.28291939	0.23348560	303.03871298	0.00329991	70.75517546	0.01413324	135
136	4.32931768	0.23098328	307.32163237	0.00325392	70.98615874	0.01408725	136
137	4.37621863	0.22850778	311.65095005	0.00320872	71.21466652	0.01404205	137
138	4.42362766	0.22605881	316.02716868	0.00316428	71.44072533	0.01399762	138
139	4.47155029	0.22363608	320.45079634	0.00312060	71.66436142	0.01395394	139
140	4.51999209	0.22123933	324.92234663	0.00307766	71.88560074	0.01391099	140
141	4.56895867	0.21886825	329.44233872	0.00303543	72.10446899	0.01386877	141
142	4.61845572	0.21652259	334.01129739	0.00299391	72.32099159	0.01382724	142
143	4.66848899	0.21420207	338.62975311	0.00295308	72.53519365	0.01378641	143
144	4.71906429	0.21190642	343.29824210	0.00291292	72.74710007	0.01374625	144
145	4.77018749	0.20963537	348.01730639	0.00287342	72.95673544	0.01370675	145
146	4.82186452	0.20738866	352.78749388	0.00283457	73.16412409	0.01366790	146
147	4.87410138	0.20516602	357.60935840	0.00279635	73.36929012	0.01362968	147
148	4.92690415	0.20296721	362.48345978	0.00275875	73.57225733	0.01359208	148
149	4.98027894	0.20079197	367.41036393	0.00272175	73.77304929	0.01355509	149
150	5.03423196	0.19864003	372.39064287	0.00268535	73.97168933	0.01351869	150
151	5.08876948	0.19651116	377.42487483	0.00264953	74.16820049	0.01348287	151
152	5.14389781	0.19440511	382.51364431	0.00261429	74.36260559	0.01344762	152
153	5.19962337	0.19232162	387.65754212	0.00257960	74.55492722	0.01341293	153
154	5.25595263	0.19026047	392.85716550	0.00254545	74.74518768	0.01337879	154
155	5.31289211	0.18822140	398.11311812	0.00251185	74.93340908	0.01334518	155
156	5.37044844	0.18620419	403.42601024	0.00247877	75.11961327	0.01331210	156
157	5.42862830	0.18420860	408.79645868	0.00244621	75.30382187	0.01327954	157
158	5.48743844	0.18223439	414.22508698	0.00241415	75.48605626	0.01324748	158
159	5.54688569	0.18028134	419.71252543	0.00238258	75.66633760	0.01321592	159
160	5.60697695	0.17834923	425.25941112	0.00235151	75.84468683	0.01318484	160

COMPOUND INTEREST FOR $1

$1\frac{1}{12}\%$

PERIODS n	FUTURE AMOUNT $(1+i)^n$	PRESENT VALUE $(1+i)^{-n}$	AMOUNT OF ANNUITY (S/p,i,n) $\frac{(1+i)^n-1}{i}$	SINKING FUND (p/S,i,n) $\frac{i}{(1+i)^n-1}$	PRESENT VALUE OF ANNUITY (V/p,i,n) $\frac{1-(1+i)^{-n}}{i}$	AMORTIZATION (p/V,i,n) $\frac{i}{1-(1+i)^{-n}}$	PERIODS n
161	5.66771920	0.17643782	430.86638807	0.00232091	76.02112465	0.01315424	161
162	5.72911950	0.17454689	436.53410728	0.00229077	76.19567154	0.01312411	162
163	5.79118496	0.17267623	442.26322677	0.00226110	76.36834777	0.01309443	163
164	5.85392279	0.17082562	448.05441173	0.00223187	76.53917339	0.01306521	164
165	5.91734029	0.16899484	453.90833452	0.00220309	76.70816824	0.01303642	165
166	5.98144481	0.16718369	459.82567481	0.00217474	76.87535192	0.01300807	166
167	6.04624380	0.16539194	465.80711962	0.00214681	77.04074386	0.01298014	167
168	6.11174477	0.16361940	471.85336342	0.00211930	77.20436326	0.01295264	168
169	6.17795534	0.16186585	477.96510819	0.00209220	77.36622911	0.01292554	169
170	6.24488319	0.16013110	484.14306353	0.00206551	77.52636021	0.01289884	170
171	6.31253609	0.15841494	490.38794672	0.00203920	77.68477515	0.01287254	171
172	6.38092190	0.15671717	496.70048281	0.00201329	77.84149231	0.01284662	172
173	6.45004855	0.15503759	503.08140470	0.00198775	77.99652991	0.01282108	173
174	6.51992408	0.15337602	509.53145325	0.00196259	78.14990593	0.01279592	174
175	6.59055659	0.15173225	516.05137733	0.00193779	78.30163818	0.01277112	175
176	6.66195428	0.15010610	522.64193392	0.00191336	78.45174428	0.01274669	176
177	6.73412546	0.14849738	529.30388820	0.00188927	78.60024166	0.01272261	177
178	6.80707848	0.14690590	536.03801366	0.00186554	78.74714757	0.01269887	178
179	6.88082183	0.14533148	542.84509214	0.00184215	78.89247904	0.01267548	179
180	6.95536407	0.14377393	549.72591397	0.00181909	79.03625297	0.01265242	180
181	7.03071385	0.14223307	556.68127804	0.00179636	79.17848604	0.01262969	181
182	7.10687991	0.14070872	563.71199188	0.00177396	79.31919476	0.01260729	182
183	7.18387111	0.13920072	570.81887180	0.00175187	79.45839548	0.01258520	183
184	7.26169638	0.13770887	578.00274291	0.00173010	79.59610435	0.01256343	184
185	7.34036476	0.13623301	585.26443929	0.00170863	79.73233736	0.01254196	185
186	7.41988538	0.13477297	592.60480405	0.00168747	79.86711033	0.01252080	186
187	7.50026747	0.13332858	600.02468942	0.00166660	80.00043891	0.01249993	187
188	7.58152037	0.13189967	607.52495689	0.00164602	80.13233857	0.01247936	188
189	7.66365350	0.13048607	615.10647726	0.00162573	80.26282464	0.01245907	189
190	7.74667642	0.12908762	622.77013076	0.00160573	80.39191226	0.01243906	190
191	7.83059874	0.12770416	630.51680718	0.00158600	80.51961641	0.01241933	191
192	7.91543023	0.12633552	638.34740592	0.00156655	80.64595193	0.01239988	192
193	8.00118073	0.12498155	646.26283615	0.00154736	80.77093349	0.01238069	193
194	8.08786018	0.12364210	654.26401688	0.00152843	80.89457558	0.01236177	194
195	8.17547867	0.12231700	662.35187706	0.00150977	81.01689258	0.01234310	195
196	8.26404635	0.12100610	670.52735573	0.00149136	81.13789868	0.01232470	196
197	8.35357352	0.11970925	678.79140208	0.00147321	81.25760793	0.01230654	197
198	8.44407057	0.11842630	687.14497561	0.00145530	81.37603422	0.01228863	198
199	8.53554800	0.11715709	695.58904618	0.00143763	81.49319132	0.01227096	199
200	8.62801644	0.11590149	704.12459418	0.00142020	81.60909281	0.01225354	200

TABLE A-2

COMPOUND INTEREST FOR $1

$1\frac{1}{12}\%$

PERIODS n	FUTURE AMOUNT $(1+i)^n$	PRESENT VALUE $(1+i)^{-n}$	AMOUNT OF ANNUITY (S/p,i,n) $\dfrac{(1+i)^n - 1}{i}$	SINKING FUND (p/S,i,n) $\dfrac{i}{(1+i)^n - 1}$	PRESENT VALUE OF ANNUITY (V/p,i,n) $\dfrac{1-(1+i)^{-n}}{i}$	AMORTIZATION (p/V,i,n) $\dfrac{i}{1-(1+i)^{-n}}$	PERIODS n
201	8.72148661	0.11465935	712.75261061	0.00140301	81.72375216	0.01223634	201
202	8.81596939	0.11343052	721.47409723	0.00138605	81.83718268	0.01221938	202
203	8.91147572	0.11221486	730.29006662	0.00136932	81.94939754	0.01220265	203
204	9.00801671	0.11101223	739.20154234	0.00135281	82.06040977	0.01218614	204
205	9.10560356	0.10982248	748.20955905	0.00133652	82.17023226	0.01216986	205
206	9.20424759	0.10864549	757.31516260	0.00132045	82.27887775	0.01215379	206
207	9.30396028	0.10748111	766.51941020	0.00130460	82.38635886	0.01213793	207
208	9.40475318	0.10632921	775.82337047	0.00128895	82.49268807	0.01212229	208
209	9.50663801	0.10518966	785.22812365	0.00127352	82.59787773	0.01210685	209
210	9.60962658	0.10406232	794.73476166	0.00125828	82.70194005	0.01209161	210
211	9.71373087	0.10294706	804.34438824	0.00124325	82.80488710	0.01207658	211
212	9.81896296	0.10184375	814.05811912	0.00122841	82.90673085	0.01206175	212
213	9.92533506	0.10075227	823.87708207	0.00121377	83.00748312	0.01204711	213
214	10.03285952	0.09967248	833.80241713	0.00119932	83.10715560	0.01203266	214
215	10.14154883	0.09860427	843.83527665	0.00118507	83.20575987	0.01201840	215
216	10.25141561	0.09754750	853.97682548	0.00117099	83.30330737	0.01200433	216
217	10.36247261	0.09650206	864.22824109	0.00115710	83.39980943	0.01199044	217
218	10.47473273	0.09546783	874.59071370	0.00114339	83.49527726	0.01197673	218
219	10.58820900	0.09444468	885.06544643	0.00112986	83.58972194	0.01196319	219
220	10.70291460	0.09343249	895.65365544	0.00111650	83.68315444	0.01194984	220
221	10.81886284	0.09243116	906.35657004	0.00110332	83.77558559	0.01193665	221
222	10.93606719	0.09144055	917.17543288	0.00109030	83.86702614	0.01192364	222
223	11.05454125	0.09046056	928.11150007	0.00107746	83.95748670	0.01191079	223
224	11.17429878	0.08949107	939.16604132	0.00106477	84.04697778	0.01189811	224
225	11.29535368	0.08853198	950.34034010	0.00105225	84.13550975	0.01188559	225
226	11.41772002	0.08758316	961.63569378	0.00103989	84.22309291	0.01187323	226
227	11.54141198	0.08664451	973.05341380	0.00102769	84.30973743	0.01186103	227
228	11.66644395	0.08571592	984.59482578	0.00101565	84.39545335	0.01184898	228
229	11.79283042	0.08479728	996.26126973	0.00100375	84.48025063	0.01183709	229
230	11.92058608	0.08388849	1008.05410015	0.00099201	84.56413913	0.01182534	230
231	12.04972577	0.08298944	1019.97468624	0.00098042	84.64712857	0.01181375	231
232	12.18026446	0.08210002	1032.02441200	0.00096897	84.72922859	0.01180230	232
233	12.31221733	0.08122014	1044.20467647	0.00095767	84.81044873	0.01179100	233
234	12.44559968	0.08034968	1056.51689380	0.00094651	84.89079841	0.01177984	234
235	12.58042701	0.07948856	1068.96249348	0.00093549	84.97028697	0.01176882	235
236	12.71671497	0.07863666	1081.54292049	0.00092461	85.04892363	0.01175794	236
237	12.85447938	0.07779389	1094.25963546	0.00091386	85.12671752	0.01174719	237
238	12.99373624	0.07696016	1107.11411485	0.00090325	85.20367768	0.01173658	238
239	13.13450172	0.07613536	1120.10785109	0.00089277	85.27981304	0.01172610	239
240	13.27679216	0.07531940	1133.24235281	0.00088242	85.35513244	0.01171576	240

TABLE A-2

COMPOUND INTEREST FOR $1

$1\frac{1}{6}\%$

PERIODS n	AMORTIZATION $(p/V,i,n)$ $\dfrac{i}{1-(1+i)^{-n}}$	PRESENT VALUE OF ANNUITY $(V/p,i,n)$ $\dfrac{1-(1+i)^{-n}}{i}$	SINKING FUND $(p/S,i,n)$ $\dfrac{i}{(1+i)^{n}-1}$	AMOUNT OF ANNUITY $(S/p,i,n)$ $\dfrac{(1+i)^{n}-1}{i}$	PRESENT VALUE $(1+i)^{-n}$	FUTURE AMOUNT $(1+i)^{n}$	PERIODS n
1	1.01166667	0.98846787	1.00000000	1.00000000	0.98846787	1.01166667	1
2	0.50876692	1.96553661	0.49710025	2.01166667	0.97706874	1.02346944	2
3	0.34114118	2.93133767	0.32947452	3.03513611	0.96580106	1.03540992	3
4	0.25733395	3.88600100	0.24566729	4.07054603	0.95466332	1.04748970	4
5	0.20705413	4.82965502	0.19538746	5.11803574	0.94365402	1.05971042	5
6	0.17353800	5.76242671	0.16187133	6.17774615	0.93277169	1.07207371	6
7	0.14960113	6.68444156	0.13793446	7.24981986	0.92201485	1.08458123	7
8	0.13165129	7.59582362	0.11998463	8.33440109	0.91138206	1.09723468	8
9	0.11769281	8.49669550	0.10602615	9.43163577	0.90087189	1.11003575	9
10	0.10652828	9.38717842	0.09486162	10.54167152	0.89048292	1.12298617	10
11	0.09739571	10.26739218	0.08572905	11.66465769	0.88021376	1.13608767	11
12	0.08978712	11.13745520	0.07812045	12.80074536	0.87006302	1.14934203	12
13	0.08335081	11.99748455	0.07168414	13.95008739	0.86002935	1.16275102	13
14	0.07783557	12.84759593	0.06616891	15.11283841	0.85011138	1.17631645	14
15	0.07305721	13.68790372	0.06139054	16.28915486	0.84030779	1.19004014	15
16	0.06887754	14.51852097	0.05721087	17.47919500	0.83061726	1.20392394	16
17	0.06519092	15.33955945	0.05352425	18.68311894	0.82103847	1.21796972	17
18	0.06191517	16.15112960	0.05024851	19.90108866	0.81157015	1.23217937	18
19	0.05898542	16.95334063	0.04731876	21.13326803	0.80221103	1.24655479	19
20	0.05634977	17.74630046	0.04468311	22.37982282	0.79295983	1.26109793	20
21	0.05396620	18.53011577	0.04229954	23.64092075	0.78381532	1.27581074	21
22	0.05180034	19.30489203	0.04013367	24.91673150	0.77477626	1.29069520	22
23	0.04982379	20.07073347	0.03815712	26.20742670	0.76584144	1.30575331	23
24	0.04801288	20.82774314	0.03634622	27.51318001	0.75700966	1.32098710	24
25	0.04634774	21.57602287	0.03468108	28.83416711	0.74827973	1.33639862	25
26	0.04481155	22.31567335	0.03314489	30.17056573	0.73965048	1.35198993	26
27	0.04338998	23.04679408	0.03172332	31.52255566	0.73112074	1.36776315	27
28	0.04207075	23.76948344	0.03040408	32.89031881	0.72268936	1.38372039	28
29	0.04084327	24.48383866	0.02917660	34.27403919	0.71435522	1.39986379	29
30	0.03969836	25.18995584	0.02803170	35.67390298	0.70611718	1.41619553	30
31	0.03862804	25.88792999	0.02696137	37.09097852	0.69797415	1.43271782	31
32	0.03762531	26.57785502	0.02595864	38.52281634	0.68992502	1.44943286	32
33	0.03668402	27.25982374	0.02501736	39.97224919	0.68196872	1.46634291	33
34	0.03579876	27.93392791	0.02413209	41.43859210	0.67410417	1.48345024	34
35	0.03496472	28.60025823	0.02329805	42.92204234	0.66633032	1.50075716	35
36	0.03417763	29.25890435	0.02251096	44.42279805	0.65864612	1.51826599	36
37	0.03343368	29.90995488	0.02176702	45.94106550	0.65105053	1.53597910	37
38	0.03272948	30.55349741	0.02106281	47.47704459	0.64354253	1.55389885	38
39	0.03206195	31.18961852	0.02039528	49.03094345	0.63612112	1.57202767	39
40	0.03142835	31.81840381	0.01976169	50.60297112	0.62878529	1.59036800	40

TABLE A-2

COMPOUND INTEREST FOR $1

$1\frac{1}{6}$ %

PERIODS n	FUTURE AMOUNT $(1+i)^n$	PRESENT VALUE $(1+i)^{-n}$	AMOUNT OF ANNUITY $(S/p,i,n)$ $\dfrac{(1+i)^n-1}{i}$	SINKING FUND $(p/S,i,n)$ $\dfrac{i}{(1+i)^n-1}$	PRESENT VALUE OF ANNUITY $(V/p,i,n)$ $\dfrac{1-(1+i)^{-n}}{i}$	AMORTIZATION $(p/V,i,n)$ $\dfrac{i}{1-(1+i)^{-n}}$	PERIODS n
41	1.60892229	0.62153406	52.19333912	0.01915953	32.43993787	0.03082620	41
42	1.62769305	0.61436645	53.80226141	0.01858658	33.05430432	0.03025325	42
43	1.64668280	0.60728150	55.42995446	0.01804079	33.66158582	0.02970745	43
44	1.66589410	0.60027825	57.07663726	0.01752030	34.26186407	0.02918697	44
45	1.68532953	0.59335577	58.74253136	0.01702344	34.85521984	0.02869011	45
46	1.70499171	0.58651312	60.42786089	0.01654866	35.44173296	0.02821532	46
47	1.72488328	0.57974937	62.13285260	0.01609455	36.02148233	0.02776121	47
48	1.74500692	0.57306363	63.85773588	0.01565981	36.59454596	0.02732648	48
49	1.76536533	0.56645499	65.60274280	0.01524327	37.16100095	0.02690993	49
50	1.78596126	0.55992256	67.36810813	0.01484382	37.72092351	0.02651049	50
51	1.80679748	0.55346546	69.15406940	0.01446046	38.27438897	0.02612713	51
52	1.82787678	0.54708283	70.96086687	0.01409227	38.82147180	0.02575894	52
53	1.84920201	0.54077380	72.78874365	0.01373839	39.36224560	0.02540505	53
54	1.87077603	0.53453753	74.63794566	0.01339801	39.89678313	0.02506468	54
55	1.89260175	0.52837318	76.50872169	0.01307041	40.42515631	0.02473707	55
56	1.91468211	0.52227991	78.40132345	0.01275489	40.94743622	0.02442155	56
57	1.93702006	0.51625691	80.31600555	0.01245082	41.46369313	0.02411749	57
58	1.95961863	0.51030337	82.25302562	0.01215761	41.97399650	0.02382427	58
59	1.98248085	0.50441849	84.21264425	0.01187470	42.47841500	0.02354137	59
60	2.00560979	0.49860147	86.19512510	0.01160158	42.97701647	0.02326825	60
61	2.02900857	0.49285154	88.20073489	0.01133777	43.46986801	0.02300444	61
62	2.05268034	0.48716791	90.22974347	0.01108282	43.95703592	0.02274949	62
63	2.07662828	0.48154983	92.28242381	0.01083630	44.43858576	0.02250297	63
64	2.10085561	0.47599654	94.35905209	0.01059782	44.91458230	0.02226448	64
65	2.12536559	0.47050729	96.45990769	0.01036700	45.38508959	0.02203367	65
66	2.15016152	0.46508134	98.58527328	0.01014350	45.85017092	0.02181017	66
67	2.17524674	0.45971796	100.73543480	0.00992699	46.30988889	0.02159366	67
68	2.20062462	0.45441644	102.91068154	0.00971716	46.76430533	0.02138383	68
69	2.22629857	0.44917605	105.11130616	0.00951372	47.21348138	0.02118039	69
70	2.25227206	0.44399610	107.33760473	0.00931640	47.65747747	0.02098307	70
71	2.27854856	0.43887588	109.58987679	0.00912493	48.09635335	0.02079160	71
72	2.30513163	0.43381471	111.86842535	0.00893907	48.53016806	0.02060574	72
73	2.33202483	0.42881190	114.17355698	0.00875860	48.95897996	0.02042526	73
74	2.35923179	0.42386679	116.50558181	0.00858328	49.38284674	0.02024995	74
75	2.38675616	0.41897870	118.86481360	0.00841292	49.80182545	0.02007959	75
76	2.41460165	0.41414699	121.25156976	0.00824732	50.21597244	0.01991398	76
77	2.44277200	0.40937099	123.66617141	0.00808629	50.62534343	0.01975295	77
78	2.47127101	0.40465008	126.10894341	0.00792965	51.02999351	0.01959632	78
79	2.50010250	0.39998360	128.58021441	0.00777725	51.42997711	0.01944391	79
80	2.52927036	0.39537094	131.08031691	0.00762891	51.82534804	0.01929558	80

COMPOUND INTEREST FOR $1

$1\frac{1}{6}\%$

PERIODS n	FUTURE AMOUNT $(1+i)^n$	PRESENT VALUE $(1+i)^{-n}$	AMOUNT OF ANNUITY $(S/p,i,n)$ $\dfrac{(1+i)^n-1}{i}$	SINKING FUND $(p/S,i,n)$ $\dfrac{i}{(1+i)^n-1}$	PRESENT VALUE OF ANNUITY $(V/p,i,n)$ $\dfrac{1-(1+i)^{-n}}{i}$	AMORTIZATION $(p/V,i,n)$ $\dfrac{i}{1-(1+i)^{-n}}$	PERIODS n
81	2.55877852	0.39081147	133.60758728	0.00748449	52.21615952	0.01915116	81
82	2.58863093	0.38630459	136.16836580	0.00734385	52.60246410	0.01901052	82
83	2.61883163	0.38184967	138.75699673	0.00720684	52.98431378	0.01887351	83
84	2.64938466	0.37744613	141.37582836	0.00707334	53.36175991	0.01874001	84
85	2.68029415	0.37309338	144.02521302	0.00694323	53.73485329	0.01860990	85
86	2.71156425	0.36879082	146.70550718	0.00681638	54.10364411	0.01848304	86
87	2.74319917	0.36453788	149.41707143	0.00669268	54.46818198	0.01835934	87
88	2.77520316	0.36033398	152.16027059	0.00657202	54.82851596	0.01823868	88
89	2.80758053	0.35617856	154.93547375	0.00645430	55.18469453	0.01812097	89
90	2.84033563	0.35207107	157.74305428	0.00633942	55.53676560	0.01800609	90
91	2.87347288	0.34801094	160.58338991	0.00622729	55.88477654	0.01789396	91
92	2.90699673	0.34399763	163.45686279	0.00611782	56.22877417	0.01778449	92
93	2.94091169	0.34003061	166.36385952	0.00601092	56.56880478	0.01767759	93
94	2.97522233	0.33610934	169.30477122	0.00590651	56.90491412	0.01757317	94
95	3.00993326	0.33223328	172.27999355	0.00580450	57.23714740	0.01747117	95
96	3.04504915	0.32840192	175.28992681	0.00570483	57.56554932	0.01737150	96
97	3.08057472	0.32461475	178.33497595	0.00560742	57.89016407	0.01727409	97
98	3.11651476	0.32087125	181.41555067	0.00551221	58.21103533	0.01717887	98
99	3.15287410	0.31717093	184.53206543	0.00541911	58.52820626	0.01708578	99
100	3.18965763	0.31351327	187.68493953	0.00532808	58.84171953	0.01699474	100
101	3.22687030	0.30989780	190.87459716	0.00523904	59.15161733	0.01690571	101
102	3.26451712	0.30632402	194.10146746	0.00515194	59.45794134	0.01681861	102
103	3.30260315	0.30279145	197.36598458	0.00506673	59.76073279	0.01673340	103
104	3.34113352	0.29929962	200.66858773	0.00498334	60.06003242	0.01665001	104
105	3.38011341	0.29584806	204.00972125	0.00490173	60.35588048	0.01656839	105
106	3.41954807	0.29243630	207.38983467	0.00482184	60.64831678	0.01648850	106
107	3.45944280	0.28906389	210.80938274	0.00474362	60.93738067	0.01641029	107
108	3.49980296	0.28573037	214.26882554	0.00466703	61.22311104	0.01633370	108
109	3.54063400	0.28243529	217.76862850	0.00459203	61.50554634	0.01625870	109
110	3.58194140	0.27917821	221.30926250	0.00451856	61.78472455	0.01618523	110
111	3.62373071	0.27595870	224.89120390	0.00444659	62.06068325	0.01611326	111
112	3.66600757	0.27277631	228.51493461	0.00437608	62.33345955	0.01604275	112
113	3.70877766	0.26963061	232.18094218	0.00430699	62.60309017	0.01597365	113
114	3.75204673	0.26652120	235.88971984	0.00423927	62.86961137	0.01590594	114
115	3.79582061	0.26344764	239.64176657	0.00417290	63.13305901	0.01583956	115
116	3.84010518	0.26040953	243.43758718	0.00410783	63.39346855	0.01577450	116
117	3.88490641	0.25740646	247.27769236	0.00404404	63.65087500	0.01571070	117
118	3.93023032	0.25443801	251.16259877	0.00398148	63.90531302	0.01564815	118
119	3.97608301	0.25150380	255.09282909	0.00392014	64.15681682	0.01558681	119
120	4.02247064	0.24860343	259.06891210	0.00385998	64.40542025	0.01552664	120

PERIODS n	FUTURE AMOUNT $(1+i)^n$	PRESENT VALUE $(1+i)^{-n}$	AMOUNT OF ANNUITY $(S/p,i,n)$ $\dfrac{(1+i)^n - 1}{i}$	SINKING FUND $(p/S,i,n)$ $\dfrac{i}{(1+i)^n - 1}$	PRESENT VALUE OF ANNUITY $(V/p,i,n)$ $\dfrac{1-(1+i)^{-n}}{i}$	AMORTIZATION $(p/V,i,n)$ $\dfrac{i}{1-(1+i)^{-n}}$	PERIODS n
121	4.06939947	0.24573650	263.09138274	0.00380096	64.65115676	0.01546763	121
122	4.11687579	0.24290264	267.16078221	0.00374306	64.89405940	0.01540973	122
123	4.16490601	0.24010146	271.27765800	0.00368626	65.13416085	0.01535293	123
124	4.21349658	0.23733258	275.44256401	0.00363052	65.37149343	0.01529719	124
125	4.26265404	0.23459563	279.65606059	0.00357582	65.60608906	0.01524249	125
126	4.31238500	0.23189024	283.91871463	0.00352213	65.83797930	0.01518880	126
127	4.36269616	0.22921605	288.23109963	0.00346944	66.06719535	0.01513610	127
128	4.41359428	0.22657271	292.59379579	0.00341771	66.29376806	0.01508437	128
129	4.46508622	0.22395984	297.00739008	0.00336692	66.51772790	0.01503359	129
130	4.51717889	0.22137711	301.47247630	0.00331705	66.73910501	0.01498372	130
131	4.56987931	0.21882416	305.98965519	0.00326808	66.95792917	0.01493475	131
132	4.62319457	0.21630065	310.55953450	0.00321999	67.17422982	0.01488666	132
133	4.67713184	0.21380625	315.18272907	0.00317276	67.38803607	0.01483943	133
134	4.73169838	0.21134061	319.85986091	0.00312637	67.59937667	0.01479304	134
135	4.78690152	0.20890340	324.59155928	0.00308079	67.80828007	0.01474746	135
136	4.84274871	0.20649430	329.37846081	0.00303602	68.01477437	0.01470269	136
137	4.89924744	0.20411298	334.22120952	0.00299203	68.21888735	0.01465870	137
138	4.95640533	0.20175912	339.12045696	0.00294880	68.42064648	0.01461547	138
139	5.01423006	0.19943241	344.07686229	0.00290633	68.62007889	0.01457299	139
140	5.07272941	0.19713253	349.09109235	0.00286458	68.81721142	0.01453125	140
141	5.13191125	0.19485918	354.16382176	0.00282355	69.01207060	0.01449022	141
142	5.19178355	0.19261204	359.29573302	0.00278322	69.20468264	0.01444989	142
143	5.25235436	0.19039081	364.48751657	0.00274358	69.39507344	0.01441024	143
144	5.31363183	0.18819520	369.73987093	0.00270460	69.58326864	0.01437127	144
145	5.37562420	0.18602491	375.05350276	0.00266629	69.76929355	0.01433295	145
146	5.43833981	0.18387965	380.42912696	0.00262861	69.95317320	0.01429528	146
147	5.50178711	0.18175912	385.86746677	0.00259156	70.13493232	0.01425823	147
148	5.56597463	0.17966305	391.36925388	0.00255513	70.31459538	0.01422180	148
149	5.63091100	0.17759116	396.93522851	0.00251930	70.49218653	0.01418597	149
150	5.69660496	0.17554315	402.56613951	0.00248406	70.66772969	0.01415073	150
151	5.76306535	0.17351877	408.26274447	0.00244940	70.84124845	0.01411607	151
152	5.83030111	0.17151773	414.02580982	0.00241531	71.01276618	0.01408198	152
153	5.89832129	0.16953976	419.85611094	0.00238177	71.18230595	0.01404844	153
154	5.96713504	0.16758461	425.75443223	0.00234877	71.34989056	0.01401544	154
155	6.03675162	0.16565200	431.72156728	0.00231631	71.51554256	0.01398297	155
156	6.10718039	0.16374168	437.75831889	0.00228437	71.67928424	0.01395103	156
157	6.17843082	0.16185339	443.86549928	0.00225293	71.84113764	0.01391960	157
158	6.25051252	0.15998688	450.04393011	0.00222201	72.00112452	0.01388867	158
159	6.32343516	0.15814189	456.29444262	0.00219157	72.15926641	0.01385823	159
160	6.39720857	0.15631818	462.61787779	0.00216161	72.31558459	0.01382828	160

TABLE A-2
COMPOUND INTEREST FOR $1
$1\frac{1}{6}\%$

PERIODS n	FUTURE AMOUNT $(1+i)^n$	PRESENT VALUE $(1+i)^{-n}$	AMOUNT OF ANNUITY $(S/p,i,n)$ $\dfrac{(1+i)^n-1}{i}$	SINKING FUND $(p/S,i,n)$ $\dfrac{i}{(1+i)^n-1}$	PRESENT VALUE OF ANNUITY $(V/p,i,n)$ $\dfrac{1-(1+i)^{-n}}{i}$	AMORTIZATION $(p/V,i,n)$ $\dfrac{i}{1-(1+i)^{-n}}$	PERIODS n
161	6.47184267	0.15451550	469.01508636	0.00213213	72.47010009	0.01379879	161
162	6.54734751	0.15273361	475.48692904	0.00210311	72.62283370	0.01376977	162
163	6.62373323	0.15097226	482.03427654	0.00207454	72.77380596	0.01374121	163
164	6.70101011	0.14923123	488.65800977	0.00204642	72.92303719	0.01371309	164
165	6.77918857	0.14751028	495.35901988	0.00201874	73.07054747	0.01368540	165
166	6.85827917	0.14580917	502.13820845	0.00199148	73.21635664	0.01365815	166
167	6.93829235	0.14412768	508.99648755	0.00196465	73.36048433	0.01363132	167
168	7.01923910	0.14246558	515.93477990	0.00193823	73.50294991	0.01360490	168
169	7.10113022	0.14082265	522.95401900	0.00191221	73.64377257	0.01357888	169
170	7.18397674	0.13919867	530.05514922	0.00188660	73.78297123	0.01355326	170
171	7.26778980	0.13759341	537.23912596	0.00186137	73.92056465	0.01352804	171
172	7.35258068	0.13600667	544.50691576	0.00183652	74.05657131	0.01350319	172
173	7.43836079	0.13443822	551.85949645	0.00181206	74.19100954	0.01347872	173
174	7.52514167	0.13288786	559.29785724	0.00178796	74.32389740	0.01345462	174
175	7.61293499	0.13135538	566.82299891	0.00176422	74.45525278	0.01343089	175
176	7.70175256	0.12984058	574.43593389	0.00174084	74.58509336	0.01340750	176
177	7.79160634	0.12834324	582.13768646	0.00171781	74.71343660	0.01338447	177
178	7.88250842	0.12686317	589.92929280	0.00169512	74.84029977	0.01336179	178
179	7.97447101	0.12540017	597.81180121	0.00167277	74.96569994	0.01333943	179
180	8.06750651	0.12395404	605.78627223	0.00165075	75.08965398	0.01331741	180
181	8.16162742	0.12252458	613.85377874	0.00162905	75.21217856	0.01329572	181
182	8.25684641	0.12111161	622.01540616	0.00160768	75.33329017	0.01327434	182
183	8.35317628	0.11971494	630.27225256	0.00158662	75.45300511	0.01325328	183
184	8.45063000	0.11833437	638.62542884	0.00156586	75.57133949	0.01323253	184
185	8.54922069	0.11696973	647.07605885	0.00154541	75.68830921	0.01321208	185
186	8.64896159	0.11562082	655.62527953	0.00152526	75.80393003	0.01319193	186
187	8.74986615	0.11428746	664.27424113	0.00150540	75.91821749	0.01317207	187
188	8.85194792	0.11296949	673.02410727	0.00148583	76.03118698	0.01315250	188
189	8.95522064	0.11166671	681.87605519	0.00146654	76.14285368	0.01313321	189
190	9.05969822	0.11037895	690.83127583	0.00144753	76.25323264	0.01311420	190
191	9.16539470	0.10910605	699.89097405	0.00142879	76.36233868	0.01309546	191
192	9.27232430	0.10784782	709.05636875	0.00141033	76.47018651	0.01307699	192
193	9.38050142	0.10660411	718.32869305	0.00139212	76.57679062	0.01305879	193
194	9.48994060	0.10537474	727.70919447	0.00137418	76.68216536	0.01304084	194
195	9.60065658	0.10415954	737.19913507	0.00135649	76.78632490	0.01302315	195
196	9.71266424	0.10295836	746.79979165	0.00133905	76.88928326	0.01300571	196
197	9.82597865	0.10177103	756.51245589	0.00132186	76.99105429	0.01298852	197
198	9.94061507	0.10059740	766.33843454	0.00130491	77.09165169	0.01297157	198
199	10.05658891	0.09943730	776.27904961	0.00128820	77.19108899	0.01295486	199
200	10.17391578	0.09829057	786.33563852	0.00127172	77.28937956	0.01293839	200

TABLE A-2

COMPOUND INTEREST FOR $1

$1\frac{1}{6}\%$

PERIODS n	FUTURE AMOUNT $(1+i)^n$	PRESENT VALUE $(1+i)^{-n}$	AMOUNT OF ANNUITY $(S/p,i,n)$ $\frac{(1+i)^n-1}{i}$	SINKING FUND $(p/S,i,n)$ $\frac{i}{(1+i)^n-1}$	PRESENT VALUE OF ANNUITY $(V/p,i,n)$ $\frac{1-(1+i)^{-n}}{i}$	AMORTIZATION $(p/V,i,n)$ $\frac{i}{1-(1+i)^{-n}}$	PERIODS n
201	10.29261147	0.09715707	796.50955430	0.00125548	77.38653663	0.01292214	201
202	10.41269193	0.09603665	806.80216577	0.00123946	77.48257328	0.01290613	202
203	10.53417334	0.09492914	817.21485770	0.00122367	77.57750241	0.01289034	203
204	10.65707203	0.09383440	827.74903104	0.00120810	77.67133682	0.01287476	204
205	10.78140454	0.09275229	838.40610307	0.00119274	77.76408911	0.01285941	205
206	10.90718759	0.09168266	849.18750761	0.00117760	77.85577177	0.01284426	206
207	11.03443811	0.09062537	860.09469520	0.00116266	77.94639714	0.01282933	207
208	11.16317322	0.08958026	871.12913331	0.00114794	78.03597740	0.01281460	208
209	11.29341024	0.08854721	882.29230653	0.00113341	78.12452462	0.01280008	209
210	11.42516670	0.08752608	893.58571677	0.00111909	78.21205069	0.01278575	210
211	11.55846031	0.08651671	905.01088347	0.00110496	78.29856741	0.01277163	211
212	11.69330901	0.08551899	916.56934377	0.00109102	78.38408640	0.01275769	212
213	11.82973095	0.08453278	928.26265278	0.00107728	78.46861917	0.01274395	213
214	11.96774448	0.08355793	940.09238373	0.00106373	78.55217711	0.01273039	214
215	12.10736816	0.08259433	952.06012821	0.00105035	78.63477144	0.01271702	215
216	12.24862079	0.08164184	964.16749637	0.00103716	78.71641329	0.01270383	216
217	12.39152137	0.08070034	976.41611716	0.00102415	78.79711363	0.01269082	217
218	12.53608912	0.07976969	988.80763853	0.00101132	78.87688332	0.01267799	218
219	12.68234349	0.07884978	1001.34372765	0.00099866	78.95573310	0.01266532	219
220	12.83030416	0.07794047	1014.02607114	0.00098617	79.03367358	0.01265283	220
221	12.97999105	0.07704166	1026.85637530	0.00097385	79.11071523	0.01264051	221
222	13.13142427	0.07615320	1039.83636634	0.00096169	79.18686843	0.01262836	222
223	13.28462422	0.07527499	1052.96779062	0.00094970	79.26214343	0.01261636	223
224	13.43961151	0.07440691	1066.25241484	0.00093786	79.33655034	0.01260453	224
225	13.59640697	0.07354884	1079.69202635	0.00092619	79.41009918	0.01259286	225
226	13.75503172	0.07270067	1093.28843332	0.00091467	79.48279985	0.01258134	226
227	13.91550709	0.07186228	1107.04346505	0.00090331	79.55466213	0.01256997	227
228	14.07785467	0.07103355	1120.95897214	0.00089209	79.62569568	0.01255876	228
229	14.24209631	0.07021438	1135.03682681	0.00088103	79.69591006	0.01254770	229
230	14.40825410	0.06940466	1149.27892313	0.00087011	79.76531472	0.01253678	230
231	14.57635040	0.06860428	1163.68717723	0.00085934	79.83391900	0.01252600	231
232	14.74640782	0.06781313	1178.26352763	0.00084871	79.90173213	0.01251537	232
233	14.91844925	0.06703110	1193.00993545	0.00083822	79.96876322	0.01250488	233
234	15.09249782	0.06625808	1207.92838470	0.00082786	80.03502131	0.01249453	234
235	15.26857696	0.06549399	1223.02088252	0.00081765	80.10051529	0.01248431	235
236	15.44671036	0.06473870	1238.28945948	0.00080757	80.16525400	0.01247423	236
237	15.62692198	0.06399213	1253.73616984	0.00079762	80.22924613	0.01246428	237
238	15.80923607	0.06325416	1269.36309183	0.00078780	80.29250029	0.01245446	238
239	15.99367716	0.06252471	1285.17232790	0.00077811	80.35502500	0.01244477	239
240	16.18027006	0.06180367	1301.16600506	0.00076854	80.41682866	0.01243521	240

COMPOUND INTEREST FOR $1

$1\frac{1}{4}\%$

PERIODS n	FUTURE AMOUNT $(1+i)^n$	PRESENT VALUE $(1+i)^{-n}$	AMOUNT OF ANNUITY $(S/p,i,n)$ $\dfrac{(1+i)^n-1}{i}$	SINKING FUND $(p/S,i,n)$ $\dfrac{i}{(1+i)^n-1}$	PRESENT VALUE OF ANNUITY $(V/p,i,n)$ $\dfrac{1-(1+i)^{-n}}{i}$	AMORTIZATION $(p/V,i,n)$ $\dfrac{i}{1-(1+i)^{-n}}$	PERIODS n
1	1.01250000	0.98765432	1.00000000	1.00000000	0.98765432	1.01250000	1
2	1.02515625	0.97546106	2.01250000	0.49689441	1.96311538	0.50939441	2
3	1.03797070	0.96341833	3.03765625	0.32920117	2.92653371	0.34170117	3
4	1.05094534	0.95152428	4.07562695	0.24536102	3.87805798	0.25786102	4
5	1.06408215	0.93977706	5.12657229	0.19506211	4.81783504	0.20756211	5
6	1.07738318	0.92817488	6.19065444	0.16153381	5.74600992	0.17403381	6
7	1.09085047	0.91671593	7.26803762	0.13758872	6.66272585	0.15008872	7
8	1.10448610	0.90539845	8.35888809	0.11963314	7.56812429	0.13213314	8
9	1.11829218	0.89422069	9.46337420	0.10567055	8.46234498	0.11817055	9
10	1.13227083	0.88318093	10.58166637	0.09450307	9.34552591	0.10700307	10
11	1.14642422	0.87227746	11.71393720	0.08536839	10.21780337	0.09786839	11
12	1.16075452	0.86150860	12.86036142	0.07775831	11.07931197	0.09025831	12
13	1.17526395	0.85087269	14.02111594	0.07132100	11.93018466	0.08382100	13
14	1.18995475	0.84036809	15.19637988	0.06580515	12.77055275	0.07830515	14
15	1.20482918	0.82999318	16.38633463	0.06102646	13.60054592	0.07352646	15
16	1.21988955	0.81974635	17.59116382	0.05684672	14.42029227	0.06934672	16
17	1.23513817	0.80962602	18.81105336	0.05316023	15.22991829	0.06566023	17
18	1.25057739	0.79963064	20.04619153	0.04988479	16.02954893	0.06238479	18
19	1.26620961	0.78975866	21.29676893	0.04695548	16.81930759	0.05945548	19
20	1.28203723	0.78000855	22.56297854	0.04432039	17.59931613	0.05682039	20
21	1.29806270	0.77037881	23.84501577	0.04193749	18.36969495	0.05443749	21
22	1.31428848	0.76086796	25.14307847	0.03977238	19.13056291	0.05227238	22
23	1.33071709	0.75147453	26.45736695	0.03779666	19.88203744	0.05029666	23
24	1.34735105	0.74219707	27.78808403	0.03598665	20.62423451	0.04848665	24
25	1.36419294	0.73303414	29.13543508	0.03432247	21.35726865	0.04682247	25
26	1.38124535	0.72398434	30.49962802	0.03278729	22.08125299	0.04528729	26
27	1.39851092	0.71504626	31.88087337	0.03136677	22.79629925	0.04386677	27
28	1.41599230	0.70621853	33.27938429	0.03004863	23.50251778	0.04254863	28
29	1.43369221	0.69749978	34.69537659	0.02882228	24.20001756	0.04132228	29
30	1.45161336	0.68888867	36.12906880	0.02767854	24.88890623	0.04017854	30
31	1.46975853	0.68038387	37.58068216	0.02660942	25.56929010	0.03910942	31
32	1.48813051	0.67198407	39.05044069	0.02560791	26.24127418	0.03810791	32
33	1.50673214	0.66368797	40.53857120	0.02466786	26.90496215	0.03716786	33
34	1.52556629	0.65549429	42.04530334	0.02378387	27.56045644	0.03628387	34
35	1.54463587	0.64740177	43.57086963	0.02295111	28.20785822	0.03545111	35
36	1.56394382	0.63940916	45.11550550	0.02216533	28.84726737	0.03466533	36
37	1.58349312	0.63151522	46.67944932	0.02142270	29.47878259	0.03392270	37
38	1.60328678	0.62371873	48.26294243	0.02071983	30.10250133	0.03321983	38
39	1.62332787	0.61601850	49.86622921	0.02005365	30.71851983	0.03255365	39
40	1.64361946	0.60841334	51.48955708	0.01942141	31.32693316	0.03192141	40

TABLE A-2

COMPOUND INTEREST FOR $1

$1\frac{1}{4}$%

PERIODS n	FUTURE AMOUNT $(1+i)^n$	PRESENT VALUE $(1+i)^{-n}$	AMOUNT OF ANNUITY (S/p,i,n) $\dfrac{(1+i)^n-1}{i}$	SINKING FUND (p/S,i,n) $\dfrac{i}{(1+i)^n-1}$	PRESENT VALUE OF ANNUITY (V/p,i,n) $\dfrac{1-(1+i)^{-n}}{i}$	AMORTIZATION (p/V,i,n) $\dfrac{i}{1-(1+i)^{-n}}$	PERIODS n
41	1.66416471	0.60090206	53.13317654	0.01882063	31.92783522	0.03132063	41
42	1.68496677	0.59348352	54.79734125	0.01824906	32.52131874	0.03074906	42
43	1.70602885	0.58615656	56.48230801	0.01770466	33.10747530	0.03020466	43
44	1.72735421	0.57892006	58.18833687	0.01718557	33.68639536	0.02968557	44
45	1.74894614	0.57177290	59.91569108	0.01669012	34.25816825	0.02919012	45
46	1.77080797	0.56471397	61.66463721	0.01621675	34.82288222	0.02871675	46
47	1.79294306	0.55774219	63.43544518	0.01576406	35.38062442	0.02826406	47
48	1.81535485	0.55085649	65.22838824	0.01533075	35.93148091	0.02783075	48
49	1.83804679	0.54405579	67.04374310	0.01491563	36.47553670	0.02741563	49
50	1.86102237	0.53733905	68.88178989	0.01451763	37.01287575	0.02701763	50
51	1.88428515	0.53070524	70.74281226	0.01413571	37.54358099	0.02663571	51
52	1.90783872	0.52415332	72.62709741	0.01376897	38.06773431	0.02626897	52
53	1.93168670	0.51768229	74.53493613	0.01341653	38.58541660	0.02591653	53
54	1.95583279	0.51129115	76.46662283	0.01307760	39.09670776	0.02557760	54
55	1.98028070	0.50497892	78.42245562	0.01275145	39.60168667	0.02525145	55
56	2.00503420	0.49874461	80.40273631	0.01243739	40.10043128	0.02493739	56
57	2.03009713	0.49258727	82.40777052	0.01213478	40.59301855	0.02463478	57
58	2.05547335	0.48650594	84.43786765	0.01184303	41.07952449	0.02434303	58
59	2.08116676	0.48049970	86.49334099	0.01156158	41.56002419	0.02406158	59
60	2.10718135	0.47456760	88.57450776	0.01128993	42.03459179	0.02378993	60
61	2.13352111	0.46870874	90.68168910	0.01102758	42.50330054	0.02352758	61
62	2.16019013	0.46292222	92.81521022	0.01077410	42.96622275	0.02327410	62
63	2.18719250	0.45720713	94.97540034	0.01052904	43.42342988	0.02302904	63
64	2.21453241	0.45156259	97.16259285	0.01029203	43.87499247	0.02279203	64
65	2.24221407	0.44598775	99.37712526	0.01006268	44.32098022	0.02256268	65
66	2.27024174	0.44048173	101.61933933	0.00984065	44.76146195	0.02234065	66
67	2.29861976	0.43504368	103.88958107	0.00962560	45.19650563	0.02212560	67
68	2.32735251	0.42967277	106.18820083	0.00941724	45.62617840	0.02191724	68
69	2.35644442	0.42436817	108.51555334	0.00921527	46.05054656	0.02171527	69
70	2.38589997	0.41912905	110.87199776	0.00901941	46.46967562	0.02151941	70
71	2.41572372	0.41395462	113.25789773	0.00882941	46.88363024	0.02132941	71
72	2.44592027	0.40884407	115.67362145	0.00864501	47.29247431	0.02114501	72
73	2.47649427	0.40379661	118.11954172	0.00846600	47.69627093	0.02096600	73
74	2.50745045	0.39881147	120.59603599	0.00829215	48.09508240	0.02079215	74
75	2.53879358	0.39388787	123.10348644	0.00812325	48.48897027	0.02062325	75
76	2.57052850	0.38902506	125.64228002	0.00795910	48.87799533	0.02045910	76
77	2.60266011	0.38422228	128.21280852	0.00779953	49.26221761	0.02029953	77
78	2.63519336	0.37947879	130.81546863	0.00764436	49.64169640	0.02014436	78
79	2.66813336	0.37479387	133.45066199	0.00749341	50.01649027	0.01999341	79
80	2.70148494	0.37016679	136.11879526	0.00734652	50.38665706	0.01984652	80

TABLE A-2

COMPOUND INTEREST FOR $1

$1\frac{1}{4}$%

PERIODS n	FUTURE AMOUNT $(1+i)^n$	PRESENT VALUE $(1+i)^{-n}$	AMOUNT OF ANNUITY (S/p,i,n) $\frac{(1+i)^n - 1}{i}$	SINKING FUND (p/S,i,n) $\frac{i}{(1+i)^n - 1}$	PRESENT VALUE OF ANNUITY (V/p,i,n) $\frac{1-(1+i)^{-n}}{i}$	AMORTIZATION (p/V,i,n) $\frac{i}{1-(1+i)^{-n}}$	PERIODS n
81	2.73525350	0.36559683	138.82028020	0.00720356	50.75225389	0.01970356	81
82	2.76944417	0.36108329	141.55553370	0.00706437	51.11333717	0.01956437	82
83	2.80406222	0.35662547	144.32497787	0.00692881	51.46996264	0.01942881	83
84	2.83911300	0.35222268	147.12904010	0.00679675	51.82218532	0.01929675	84
85	2.87460191	0.34787426	149.96815310	0.00666808	52.17005958	0.01916808	85
86	2.91053444	0.34357951	152.84275501	0.00654267	52.51363909	0.01904267	86
87	2.94691612	0.33933779	155.75328945	0.00642041	52.85297688	0.01892041	87
88	2.98375257	0.33514843	158.70020557	0.00630119	53.18812531	0.01880119	88
89	3.02104948	0.33101080	161.68395814	0.00618491	53.51913611	0.01868491	89
90	3.05881260	0.32692425	164.70500762	0.00607146	53.84606036	0.01857146	90
91	3.09704775	0.32288814	167.76382021	0.00596076	54.16894850	0.01846076	91
92	3.13576085	0.31890187	170.86086796	0.00585272	54.48785037	0.01835272	92
93	3.17495786	0.31496481	173.99662881	0.00574724	54.80281518	0.01824724	93
94	3.21464483	0.31107636	177.17158667	0.00564425	55.11389154	0.01814425	94
95	3.25482789	0.30723591	180.38623151	0.00554366	55.42112744	0.01804366	95
96	3.29551324	0.30344287	183.64105940	0.00544541	55.72457031	0.01794541	96
97	3.33670716	0.29969666	186.93657264	0.00534941	56.02426698	0.01784941	97
98	3.37841600	0.29599670	190.27327980	0.00525560	56.32026368	0.01775560	98
99	3.42064620	0.29234242	193.65169580	0.00516391	56.61260610	0.01766391	99
100	3.46340427	0.28873326	197.07234200	0.00507428	56.90133936	0.01757428	100
101	3.50669683	0.28516865	200.53574627	0.00498664	57.18650801	0.01748664	101
102	3.55053054	0.28164805	204.04244310	0.00490094	57.46815606	0.01740094	102
103	3.59491217	0.27817091	207.59297364	0.00481712	57.74632697	0.01731712	103
104	3.63984857	0.27473670	211.18788581	0.00473512	58.02106368	0.01723512	104
105	3.68534668	0.27134489	214.82773438	0.00465489	58.29240857	0.01715489	105
106	3.73141351	0.26799496	218.51308106	0.00457639	58.56040353	0.01707639	106
107	3.77805618	0.26468638	222.24449457	0.00449955	58.82508990	0.01699955	107
108	3.82528188	0.26141864	226.02255076	0.00442434	59.08650855	0.01692434	108
109	3.87309791	0.25819125	229.84783264	0.00435070	59.34469980	0.01685070	109
110	3.92151163	0.25500371	233.72093055	0.00427861	59.59970350	0.01677861	110
111	3.97053053	0.25185551	237.64244218	0.00420800	59.85155902	0.01670800	111
112	4.02016216	0.24874618	241.61297271	0.00413885	60.10030520	0.01663885	112
113	4.07041419	0.24567524	245.63313487	0.00407111	60.34598045	0.01657111	113
114	4.12129436	0.24264222	249.70354905	0.00400475	60.58862266	0.01650475	114
115	4.17281054	0.23964663	253.82484342	0.00393972	60.82826930	0.01643972	115
116	4.22497067	0.23668803	257.99765396	0.00387600	61.06495733	0.01637600	116
117	4.27778281	0.23376596	262.22262463	0.00381355	61.29872329	0.01631355	117
118	4.33125509	0.23087996	266.50040744	0.00375234	61.52960325	0.01625234	118
119	4.38539578	0.22802959	270.83166253	0.00369233	61.75763284	0.01619233	119
120	4.44021323	0.22521441	275.21705832	0.00363350	61.98284725	0.01613350	120

TABLE A-2

COMPOUND INTEREST FOR $1

$1\tfrac{1}{4}\%$

PERIODS n	FUTURE AMOUNT $(1+i)^n$	PRESENT VALUE $(1+i)^{-n}$	AMOUNT OF ANNUITY $(S/p,i,n)$ $\dfrac{(1+i)^n-1}{i}$	SINKING FUND $(p/S,i,n)$ $\dfrac{i}{(1+i)^n-1}$	PRESENT VALUE OF ANNUITY $(V/p,i,n)$ $\dfrac{1-(1+i)^{-n}}{i}$	AMORTIZATION $(p/V,i,n)$ $\dfrac{i}{1-(1+i)^{-n}}$	PERIODS n
121	4.49571589	0.22243398	279.65727154	0.00357581	62.20528123	0.01607581	121
122	4.55191234	0.21968789	284.15298744	0.00351923	62.42496912	0.01601923	122
123	4.60881125	0.21697569	288.70489978	0.00346374	62.64194481	0.01596374	123
124	4.66642139	0.21429698	293.31371103	0.00340932	62.85624179	0.01590932	124
125	4.72475166	0.21165134	297.98013242	0.00335593	63.06789312	0.01585593	125
126	4.78381105	0.20903836	302.70488407	0.00330355	63.27693148	0.01580355	126
127	4.84360869	0.20645764	307.48869512	0.00325215	63.48338911	0.01575215	127
128	4.90415380	0.20390878	312.33230381	0.00320172	63.68729789	0.01570172	128
129	4.96545572	0.20139138	317.23645761	0.00315222	63.88868927	0.01565222	129
130	5.02752392	0.19890507	322.20191333	0.00310364	64.08759435	0.01560364	130
131	5.09036797	0.19644945	327.22943725	0.00305596	64.28404380	0.01555596	131
132	5.15399757	0.19402415	332.31980521	0.00300915	64.47806795	0.01550915	132
133	5.21842253	0.19162879	337.47380278	0.00296319	64.66969674	0.01546319	133
134	5.28365282	0.18926300	342.69222531	0.00291807	64.85895974	0.01541807	134
135	5.34969848	0.18692642	347.97587813	0.00287376	65.04588617	0.01537376	135
136	5.41656971	0.18461869	353.32557660	0.00283025	65.23050485	0.01533025	136
137	5.48427683	0.18233945	358.74214631	0.00278752	65.41284430	0.01528752	137
138	5.55283029	0.18008834	364.22642314	0.00274554	65.59293264	0.01524554	138
139	5.62224067	0.17786503	369.77925343	0.00270432	65.77079767	0.01520432	139
140	5.69251868	0.17566916	375.40149410	0.00266381	65.94646684	0.01516381	140
141	5.76367516	0.17350041	381.09401277	0.00262402	66.11996725	0.01512402	141
142	5.83572110	0.17135843	386.85768793	0.00258493	66.29132568	0.01508493	142
143	5.90866761	0.16924289	392.69340903	0.00254652	66.46056857	0.01504652	143
144	5.98252596	0.16715347	398.60207665	0.00250877	66.62772204	0.01500877	144
145	6.05730753	0.16508985	404.58460260	0.00247167	66.79281189	0.01497167	145
146	6.13302388	0.16305171	410.64191014	0.00243521	66.95586360	0.01493521	146
147	6.20968668	0.16103872	416.77493401	0.00239938	67.11690232	0.01489938	147
148	6.28730776	0.15905059	422.98462069	0.00236415	67.27595291	0.01486415	148
149	6.36589911	0.15708700	429.27192845	0.00232953	67.43303991	0.01482953	149
150	6.44547284	0.15514766	435.63782755	0.00229548	67.58818756	0.01479548	150
151	6.52604125	0.15323225	442.08330040	0.00226202	67.74141982	0.01476202	151
152	6.60761677	0.15134050	448.60934165	0.00222911	67.89276031	0.01472911	152
153	6.69021198	0.14947209	455.21695842	0.00219675	68.04223241	0.01469675	153
154	6.77383963	0.14762676	461.90717040	0.00216494	68.18985917	0.01466494	154
155	6.85851263	0.14580421	468.68101003	0.00213365	68.33566338	0.01463365	155
156	6.94424403	0.14400416	475.53952266	0.00210287	68.47966753	0.01460287	156
157	7.03104708	0.14222633	482.48376669	0.00207261	68.62189386	0.01457261	157
158	7.11893517	0.14047045	489.51481378	0.00204284	68.76236431	0.01454284	158
159	7.20792186	0.13873624	496.63374895	0.00201356	68.90110055	0.01451356	159
160	7.29802089	0.13702345	503.84167081	0.00198475	69.03812400	0.01448475	160

COMPOUND INTEREST FOR $1

$1\frac{1}{4}\%$

PERIODS n	FUTURE AMOUNT $(1+i)^n$	PRESENT VALUE $(1+i)^{-n}$	AMOUNT OF ANNUITY (S/p,i,n) $\dfrac{(1+i)^n-1}{i}$	SINKING FUND (p/S,i,n) $\dfrac{i}{(1+i)^n-1}$	PRESENT VALUE OF ANNUITY (V/p,i,n) $\dfrac{1-(1+i)^{-n}}{i}$	AMORTIZATION (p/V,i,n) $\dfrac{i}{1-(1+i)^{-n}}$	PERIODS n
161	7.38924615	0.13533180	511.13969169	0.00195641	69.17345580	0.01445641	161
162	7.48161172	0.13366104	518.52893784	0.00192853	69.30711684	0.01442853	162
163	7.57513187	0.13201090	526.01054956	0.00190110	69.43912774	0.01440110	163
164	7.66982102	0.13038114	533.58568143	0.00187411	69.56950888	0.01437411	164
165	7.76569378	0.12877150	541.25550245	0.00184756	69.69828038	0.01434756	165
166	7.86276495	0.12718172	549.02119623	0.00182142	69.82546210	0.01432142	166
167	7.96104951	0.12561158	556.88396118	0.00179571	69.95107368	0.01429571	167
168	8.06056263	0.12406082	564.84501070	0.00177040	70.07513450	0.01427040	168
169	8.16131967	0.12252920	572.90557333	0.00174549	70.19766370	0.01424549	169
170	8.26333616	0.12101650	581.06689300	0.00172097	70.31868020	0.01422097	170
171	8.36662786	0.11952247	589.33022916	0.00169684	70.43820267	0.01419684	171
172	8.47121071	0.11804688	597.69685703	0.00167309	70.55624955	0.01417309	172
173	8.57710085	0.11658951	606.16806774	0.00164971	70.67283906	0.01414971	173
174	8.68431461	0.11515014	614.74516859	0.00162669	70.78798919	0.01412669	174
175	8.79286854	0.11372853	623.42948319	0.00160403	70.90171772	0.01410403	175
176	8.90277940	0.11232447	632.22235173	0.00158172	71.01404220	0.01408172	176
177	9.01406414	0.11093775	641.12513113	0.00155976	71.12497995	0.01405976	177
178	9.12673994	0.10956815	650.13919527	0.00153813	71.23454810	0.01403813	178
179	9.24082419	0.10821546	659.26593521	0.00151684	71.34276355	0.01401684	179
180	9.35633449	0.10687946	668.50675940	0.00149587	71.44964301	0.01399587	180
181	9.47328867	0.10555996	677.86309389	0.00147522	71.55520298	0.01397522	181
182	9.59170478	0.10425675	687.33638257	0.00145489	71.65945973	0.01395489	182
183	9.71160109	0.10296963	696.92808735	0.00143487	71.76242936	0.01393487	183
184	9.83299611	0.10169840	706.63968844	0.00141515	71.86412777	0.01391515	184
185	9.95590856	0.10044287	716.47268455	0.00139573	71.96457063	0.01389573	185
186	10.08035741	0.09920283	726.42859310	0.00137660	72.06377346	0.01387660	186
187	10.20636188	0.09797811	736.50895052	0.00135776	72.16175157	0.01385776	187
188	10.33394140	0.09676850	746.71531240	0.00133920	72.25852007	0.01383920	188
189	10.46311567	0.09557383	757.04925380	0.00132092	72.35409389	0.01382092	189
190	10.59390462	0.09439390	767.51236948	0.00130291	72.44848780	0.01380291	190
191	10.72632843	0.09322855	778.10627409	0.00128517	72.54171634	0.01378517	191
192	10.86040753	0.09207758	788.83260252	0.00126770	72.63379392	0.01376770	192
193	10.99616263	0.09094082	799.69301005	0.00125048	72.72473473	0.01375048	193
194	11.13361466	0.08981809	810.68917268	0.00123352	72.81455282	0.01373352	194
195	11.27278484	0.08870922	821.82278734	0.00121681	72.90326205	0.01371681	195
196	11.41369465	0.08761405	833.09557218	0.00120034	72.99087610	0.01370034	196
197	11.55636584	0.08653239	844.50926683	0.00118412	73.07740849	0.01368412	197
198	11.70082041	0.08546409	856.06563267	0.00116813	73.16287258	0.01366813	198
199	11.84708066	0.08440898	867.76645307	0.00115238	73.24728156	0.01365238	199
200	11.99516917	0.08336689	879.61353374	0.00113686	73.33064846	0.01363686	200

TABLE A-2

COMPOUND INTEREST FOR $1

$1\frac{1}{4}$%

PERIODS n	FUTURE AMOUNT $(1+i)^n$	PRESENT VALUE $(1+i)^{-n}$	AMOUNT OF ANNUITY $(S/p,i,n)$ $\dfrac{(1+i)^n - 1}{i}$	SINKING FUND $(p/S,i,n)$ $\dfrac{i}{(1+i)^n - 1}$	PRESENT VALUE OF ANNUITY $(V/p,i,n)$ $\dfrac{1-(1+i)^{-n}}{i}$	AMORTIZATION $(p/V,i,n)$ $\dfrac{i}{1-(1+i)^{-n}}$	PERIODS n
201	12.14510879	0.08233767	891.60870291	0.00112157	73.41298613	0.01362157	201
202	12.29692265	0.08132116	903.75381170	0.00110650	73.49430729	0.01360650	202
203	12.45063418	0.08031719	916.05073434	0.00109164	73.57462449	0.01359164	203
204	12.60626711	0.07932562	928.50136852	0.00107700	73.65395011	0.01357700	204
205	12.76384545	0.07834629	941.10763563	0.00106258	73.73229640	0.01356258	205
206	12.92339351	0.07737906	953.87148107	0.00104836	73.80967546	0.01354836	206
207	13.08493593	0.07642376	966.79487459	0.00103435	73.88609922	0.01353435	207
208	13.24849763	0.07548026	979.87981052	0.00102053	73.96157948	0.01352053	208
209	13.41410385	0.07454840	993.12830815	0.00100692	74.03612788	0.01350692	209
210	13.58178015	0.07362805	1006.54241200	0.00099350	74.10975593	0.01349350	210
211	13.75155240	0.07271906	1020.12419215	0.00098027	74.18247499	0.01348027	211
212	13.92344681	0.07182130	1033.87574455	0.00096723	74.25429629	0.01346723	212
213	14.09748989	0.07093461	1047.79919136	0.00095438	74.32523090	0.01345438	213
214	14.27370852	0.07005888	1061.89668125	0.00094171	74.39528978	0.01344171	214
215	14.45212987	0.06919395	1076.17038977	0.00092922	74.46448373	0.01342922	215
216	14.63278150	0.06833971	1090.62251964	0.00091691	74.53282344	0.01341691	216
217	14.81569126	0.06749601	1105.25530114	0.00090477	74.60031945	0.01340477	217
218	15.00088740	0.06666272	1120.07099240	0.00089280	74.66698217	0.01339280	218
219	15.18839850	0.06583973	1135.07187980	0.00088100	74.73282190	0.01338100	219
220	15.37825348	0.06502689	1150.26027830	0.00086937	74.79784879	0.01336937	220
221	15.57048165	0.06422409	1165.63853178	0.00085790	74.86207288	0.01335790	221
222	15.76511267	0.06343120	1181.20901343	0.00084659	74.92550407	0.01334659	222
223	15.96217658	0.06264810	1196.97412610	0.00083544	74.98815217	0.01333544	223
224	16.16170378	0.06187466	1212.93630267	0.00082445	75.05002684	0.01332445	224
225	16.36372508	0.06111078	1229.09800646	0.00081360	75.11113762	0.01331360	225
226	16.56827164	0.06035633	1245.46173154	0.00080292	75.17149394	0.01330292	226
227	16.77537504	0.05961119	1262.03000318	0.00079237	75.23110513	0.01329237	227
228	16.98506723	0.05887525	1278.80537822	0.00078198	75.28998037	0.01328198	228
229	17.19738057	0.05814839	1295.79044545	0.00077173	75.34812876	0.01327173	229
230	17.41234783	0.05743051	1312.98782602	0.00076162	75.40555927	0.01326162	230
231	17.63000217	0.05672149	1330.40017384	0.00075165	75.46228076	0.01325165	231
232	17.85037720	0.05602123	1348.03017601	0.00074182	75.51830199	0.01324182	232
233	18.07350692	0.05532961	1365.88055321	0.00073213	75.57363159	0.01323213	233
234	18.29942575	0.05464652	1383.95406013	0.00072257	75.62827812	0.01322257	234
235	18.52816857	0.05397188	1402.25348588	0.00071314	75.68224999	0.01321314	235
236	18.75977068	0.05330556	1420.78165446	0.00070384	75.73555555	0.01320384	236
237	18.99426781	0.05264746	1439.54142514	0.00069467	75.78820301	0.01319467	237
238	19.23169616	0.05199749	1458.53569295	0.00068562	75.84020050	0.01318562	238
239	19.47209236	0.05135555	1477.76738911	0.00067670	75.89155605	0.01317670	239
240	19.71549352	0.05072153	1497.23948148	0.00066790	75.94227758	0.01316790	240

COMPOUND INTEREST FOR $1

$1\frac{1}{3}$%

PERIODS n	FUTURE AMOUNT $(1+i)^n$	PRESENT VALUE $(1+i)^{-n}$	AMOUNT OF ANNUITY $(S/p,i,n)$ $\dfrac{(1+i)^n-1}{i}$	SINKING FUND $(p/S,i,n)$ $\dfrac{i}{(1+i)^n-1}$	PRESENT VALUE OF ANNUITY $(V/p,i,n)$ $\dfrac{1-(1+i)^{-n}}{i}$	AMORTIZATION $(p/V,i,n)$ $\dfrac{i}{1-(1+i)^{-n}}$	PERIODS n
1	1.01333333	0.98684211	1.00000000	1.00000000	0.98684211	1.01333333	1
2	1.02684444	0.97385734	2.01333333	0.49668874	1.96069945	0.51002208	2
3	1.04053570	0.96104343	3.04017778	0.32892813	2.92174287	0.34226147	3
4	1.05440951	0.94839812	4.08071348	0.24505519	3.87014099	0.25838852	4
5	1.06846831	0.93591920	5.13512299	0.19473730	4.80606019	0.20807064	5
6	1.08271455	0.92360447	6.20359130	0.16119695	5.72966466	0.17453028	6
7	1.09715074	0.91145178	7.28630585	0.13724376	6.64111644	0.15057709	7
8	1.11177942	0.89945899	8.38345660	0.11928254	7.54057544	0.13261587	8
9	1.12660315	0.88762401	9.49523602	0.10531597	8.42819945	0.11864930	9
10	1.14162452	0.87594474	10.62183916	0.09414565	9.30414419	0.10747899	10
11	1.15684618	0.86441916	11.76346369	0.08500898	10.16856334	0.09834231	11
12	1.17227080	0.85304522	12.92030987	0.07739752	11.02160856	0.09073086	12
13	1.18790108	0.84182094	14.09258067	0.07095932	11.86342950	0.08429266	13
14	1.20373976	0.83074435	15.28048174	0.06544296	12.69417385	0.07877630	14
15	1.21978962	0.81981350	16.48422150	0.06066407	13.51398735	0.07399741	15
16	1.23605348	0.80902648	17.70401112	0.05648437	14.32301384	0.06981771	16
17	1.25253419	0.79838140	18.94046460	0.05279813	15.12139523	0.06613146	17
18	1.26923465	0.78787638	20.19259880	0.04952310	15.90927161	0.06285643	18
19	1.28615778	0.77750958	21.46183345	0.04659434	16.68678120	0.05992767	19
20	1.30330655	0.76727919	22.74799123	0.04395993	17.45406039	0.05729326	20
21	1.32068397	0.75718342	24.05129778	0.04157780	18.21124381	0.05491113	21
22	1.33829309	0.74722048	25.37198175	0.03941356	18.95846428	0.05274689	22
23	1.35613700	0.73738863	26.71027484	0.03743878	19.69585291	0.05077211	23
24	1.37421882	0.72768615	28.06641183	0.03562978	20.42353906	0.04896311	24
25	1.39254174	0.71811133	29.44063066	0.03396666	21.14165039	0.04730000	25
26	1.41110897	0.70866249	30.83317240	0.03243260	21.85031288	0.04576594	26
27	1.42992375	0.69933799	32.24428137	0.03101325	22.54965087	0.04434658	27
28	1.44898940	0.69013617	33.67420512	0.02969632	23.23978704	0.04302965	28
29	1.46830926	0.68105543	35.12319452	0.02847121	23.92084247	0.04180455	29
30	1.48788672	0.67209418	36.59150378	0.02732875	24.59293665	0.04066208	30
31	1.50772521	0.66325083	38.07939050	0.02626092	25.25618749	0.03959426	31
32	1.52782821	0.65452385	39.58711570	0.02526074	25.91071134	0.03859408	32
33	1.54819925	0.64591169	41.11494391	0.02432206	26.55662303	0.03765539	33
34	1.56884191	0.63741285	42.66314316	0.02343944	27.19403588	0.03677277	34
35	1.58975980	0.62902584	44.23198507	0.02260807	27.82306173	0.03594141	35
36	1.61095660	0.62074919	45.82174487	0.02182370	28.44381091	0.03515703	36
37	1.63243602	0.61258144	47.43270147	0.02108250	29.05639235	0.03441583	37
38	1.65420183	0.60452115	49.06513749	0.02038107	29.66091350	0.03371440	38
39	1.67625786	0.59656693	50.71933933	0.01971635	30.25748043	0.03304968	39
40	1.69860796	0.58871736	52.39559718	0.01908557	30.84619779	0.03241891	40

TABLE A-2

COMPOUND INTEREST FOR $1

$1\frac{1}{3}\%$

PERIODS n	FUTURE AMOUNT $(1+i)^n$	PRESENT VALUE $(1+i)^{-n}$	AMOUNT OF ANNUITY $(S/p,i,n)$ $\dfrac{(1+i)^n-1}{i}$	SINKING FUND $(p/S,i,n)$ $\dfrac{i}{(1+i)^n-1}$	PRESENT VALUE OF ANNUITY $(V/p,i,n)$ $\dfrac{1-(1+i)^{-n}}{i}$	AMORTIZATION $(p/V,i,n)$ $\dfrac{i}{1-(1+i)^{-n}}$	PERIODS n
41	1.72125607	0.58097108	54.09420515	0.01848627	31.42716888	0.03181960	41
42	1.74420615	0.57332673	55.81546121	0.01791618	32.00049560	0.03124952	42
43	1.76746223	0.56578295	57.55966736	0.01737328	32.56627855	0.03070661	43
44	1.79102839	0.55833844	59.32712959	0.01685569	33.12461699	0.03018903	44
45	1.81490877	0.55099188	61.11815799	0.01636175	33.67560887	0.02969508	45
46	1.83910756	0.54374199	62.93306676	0.01588990	34.21935086	0.02922323	46
47	1.86362899	0.53658749	64.77217432	0.01543873	34.75593835	0.02877206	47
48	1.88847738	0.52952713	66.63580331	0.01500695	35.28546548	0.02834028	48
49	1.91365708	0.52255966	68.52428069	0.01459337	35.80802514	0.02792670	49
50	1.93917250	0.51568388	70.43793776	0.01419689	36.32370902	0.02753023	50
51	1.96502814	0.50889857	72.37711027	0.01381652	36.83260759	0.02714986	51
52	1.99122851	0.50220253	74.34213840	0.01345132	37.33481012	0.02678465	52
53	2.01777823	0.49559460	76.33336692	0.01310043	37.83040472	0.02643376	53
54	2.04468194	0.48907362	78.35114514	0.01276306	38.31947835	0.02609639	54
55	2.07194436	0.48263844	80.39582708	0.01243846	38.80211679	0.02577179	55
56	2.09957029	0.47628794	82.46777144	0.01212595	39.27840473	0.02545928	56
57	2.12756456	0.47002099	84.56734172	0.01182490	39.74842572	0.02515823	57
58	2.15593208	0.46383650	86.69490628	0.01153470	40.21226222	0.02486804	58
59	2.18467784	0.45773339	88.85083836	0.01125470	40.66999561	0.02458815	59
60	2.21380688	0.45171058	91.03551621	0.01098472	41.12170620	0.02431806	60
61	2.24332431	0.44576702	93.24932309	0.01072394	41.56747322	0.02405727	61
62	2.27323530	0.43990167	95.49264740	0.01047201	42.00737489	0.02380534	62
63	2.30354510	0.43411349	97.76588270	0.01022852	42.44148838	0.02356185	63
64	2.33425904	0.42840147	100.06942780	0.00999306	42.86989985	0.02332640	64
65	2.36538249	0.42276461	102.40368684	0.00976527	43.29265445	0.02309861	65
66	2.39692092	0.41720192	104.76906933	0.00954480	43.70985637	0.02287814	66
67	2.42887987	0.41171242	107.16599025	0.00933132	44.12156878	0.02266465	67
68	2.46126493	0.40629515	109.59487012	0.00912451	44.52786393	0.02245785	68
69	2.49408180	0.40094916	112.05613506	0.00892410	44.92881309	0.02225743	69
70	2.52733622	0.39567351	114.55021686	0.00872980	45.32448660	0.02206313	70
71	2.56103404	0.39046728	117.07755308	0.00854139	45.71495388	0.02187468	71
72	2.59518116	0.38532955	119.63858713	0.00835851	46.10028344	0.02169184	72
73	2.62978358	0.38025943	122.23376829	0.00818105	46.48054287	0.02151438	73
74	2.66484736	0.37525601	124.86355186	0.00800874	46.85579888	0.02134208	74
75	2.70037866	0.37031844	127.52839922	0.00784139	47.22611732	0.02117472	75
76	2.73638371	0.36544582	130.22877788	0.00767879	47.59156314	0.02101213	76
77	2.77286882	0.36063733	132.96516158	0.00752077	47.95220047	0.02085410	77
78	2.80984041	0.35589210	135.73803041	0.00736713	48.30809257	0.02070047	78
79	2.84730494	0.35120931	138.54787081	0.00721772	48.65930188	0.02055106	79
80	2.88526901	0.34658813	141.39517575	0.00707238	49.00589001	0.02040571	80

COMPOUND INTEREST FOR $1

$1\frac{1}{3}\%$

PERIODS n	FUTURE AMOUNT $(1+i)^n$	PRESENT VALUE $(1+i)^{-n}$	AMOUNT OF ANNUITY $(S/p,i,n)$ $\frac{(1+i)^n - 1}{i}$	SINKING FUND $(p/S,i,n)$ $\frac{i}{(1+i)^n - 1}$	PRESENT VALUE OF ANNUITY $(V/p,i,n)$ $\frac{1-(1+i)^{-n}}{i}$	AMORTIZATION $(p/V,i,n)$ $\frac{i}{1-(1+i)^{-n}}$	PERIODS n
81	2.92373926	0.34202776	144.28044476	0.00693095	49.34791777	0.02026428	81
82	2.96272245	0.33752740	147.20418403	0.00679329	49.68544517	0.02012662	82
83	3.00222542	0.33308625	150.16690648	0.00665926	50.01853142	0.01999259	83
84	3.04225509	0.32870353	153.16913190	0.00652873	50.34723495	0.01986206	84
85	3.08281849	0.32437849	156.21138699	0.00640158	50.67161344	0.01973492	85
86	3.12392274	0.32011035	159.29420549	0.00627769	50.99172379	0.01961103	86
87	3.16557504	0.31589837	162.41812823	0.00615695	51.30762216	0.01949028	87
88	3.20778271	0.31174181	165.58370327	0.00603924	51.61936397	0.01937257	88
89	3.25055315	0.30763995	168.79148598	0.00592447	51.92700392	0.01925780	89
90	3.29389386	0.30359205	172.04203913	0.00581253	52.23059598	0.01914587	90
91	3.33781244	0.29959742	175.33593298	0.00570334	52.53019340	0.01903667	91
92	3.38231661	0.29565535	178.67374542	0.00559679	52.82584875	0.01893013	92
93	3.42741416	0.29176515	182.05606203	0.00549281	53.11761389	0.01882615	93
94	3.47311302	0.28792613	185.48347619	0.00539132	53.40554003	0.01872465	94
95	3.51942119	0.28413763	188.95658920	0.00529222	53.68967766	0.01862555	95
96	3.56634681	0.28039898	192.47601039	0.00519545	53.97007664	0.01852879	96
97	3.61389810	0.27670952	196.04235742	0.00510094	54.24678615	0.01843427	97
98	3.66208340	0.27306860	199.65625529	0.00500861	54.51985476	0.01834194	98
99	3.71091118	0.26947560	203.31833870	0.00491840	54.78933035	0.01825173	99
100	3.76039000	0.26592986	207.02924988	0.00483024	55.05526022	0.01816357	100
101	3.81052853	0.26243079	210.78963988	0.00474407	55.31769100	0.01807740	101
102	3.86133558	0.25897775	214.60016841	0.00465983	55.57666875	0.01799316	102
103	3.91282005	0.25557015	218.46150399	0.00457747	55.83223890	0.01791080	103
104	3.96499099	0.25220738	222.37432404	0.00449692	56.08444628	0.01783026	104
105	4.01785753	0.24888886	226.33931503	0.00441815	56.33333515	0.01775148	105
106	4.07142897	0.24561401	230.35717256	0.00434108	56.57894916	0.01767442	106
107	4.12571469	0.24238225	234.42860153	0.00426569	56.82133141	0.01759902	107
108	4.18072422	0.23919301	238.55431622	0.00419192	57.06052442	0.01752525	108
109	4.23646721	0.23604573	242.73504043	0.00411972	57.29657015	0.01745305	109
110	4.29295344	0.23293987	246.97150764	0.00404905	57.52951001	0.01738238	110
111	4.35019281	0.22987487	251.26446107	0.00397987	57.75938488	0.01731320	111
112	4.40819539	0.22685020	255.61465389	0.00391214	57.98623508	0.01724547	112
113	4.46697132	0.22386533	260.02284927	0.00384582	58.21010041	0.01717915	113
114	4.52653094	0.22091973	264.48982060	0.00378086	58.43102014	0.01711420	114
115	4.58688469	0.21801289	269.01635154	0.00371725	58.64903303	0.01705058	115
116	4.64804315	0.21514430	273.60323623	0.00365493	58.86417734	0.01698826	116
117	4.71001706	0.21231346	278.25127938	0.00359387	59.07649079	0.01692721	117
118	4.77281729	0.20951986	282.96129643	0.00353405	59.28601065	0.01686739	118
119	4.83645485	0.20676302	287.73411372	0.00347543	59.49277367	0.01680876	119
120	4.90094091	0.20404245	292.57056857	0.00341798	59.69681612	0.01675131	120

COMPOUND INTEREST FOR $1

$1\frac{1}{3}\%$

PERIODS	FUTURE AMOUNT	PRESENT VALUE	AMOUNT OF ANNUITY	SINKING FUND	PRESENT VALUE OF ANNUITY	AMORTIZATION	PERIODS
n	$(1+i)^n$	$(1+i)^{-n}$	$\dfrac{(S/p,i,n)}{\dfrac{(1+i)^n-1}{i}}$	$\dfrac{(p/S,i,n)}{\dfrac{i}{(1+i)^n-1}}$	$\dfrac{(V/p,i,n)}{\dfrac{1-(1+i)^{-n}}{i}}$	$\dfrac{(p/V,i,n)}{\dfrac{i}{1-(1+i)^{-n}}}$	n
121	4.96628679	0.20135768	297.47150948	0.00336167	59.89817380	0.01669500	121
122	5.03250395	0.19870824	302.43779628	0.00330647	60.09688204	0.01663980	122
123	5.09960400	0.19609366	307.47030023	0.00325235	60.29297570	0.01658568	123
124	5.16759872	0.19351348	312.56990423	0.00319928	60.48648918	0.01653262	124
125	5.23650004	0.19096725	317.73750295	0.00314725	60.67745642	0.01648059	125
126	5.30632004	0.18845452	322.97400299	0.00309622	60.86591094	0.01642956	126
127	5.37707097	0.18597486	328.28032303	0.00304618	61.05188580	0.01637951	127
128	5.44876525	0.18352782	333.65739401	0.00299709	61.23541362	0.01633042	128
129	5.52141546	0.18111298	339.10615926	0.00294893	61.41652660	0.01628226	129
130	5.59503433	0.17872991	344.62757472	0.00290168	61.59525651	0.01623502	130
131	5.66963479	0.17637820	350.22260905	0.00285533	61.77163471	0.01618866	131
132	5.74522992	0.17405744	355.89224383	0.00280984	61.94569215	0.01614317	132
133	5.82183298	0.17176721	361.63747375	0.00276520	62.11745936	0.01609853	133
134	5.89945742	0.16950711	367.45930674	0.00272139	62.28696647	0.01605472	134
135	5.97811686	0.16727676	373.35876416	0.00267839	62.45424323	0.01601172	135
136	6.05782508	0.16507575	379.33688101	0.00263618	62.61931898	0.01596951	136
137	6.13859608	0.16290370	385.39470609	0.00259474	62.78222268	0.01592808	137
138	6.22044403	0.16076023	391.53330218	0.00255406	62.94298290	0.01588739	138
139	6.30338328	0.15864496	397.75374620	0.00251412	63.10162787	0.01584745	139
140	6.38742839	0.15655753	404.05712949	0.00247490	63.25818539	0.01580823	140
141	6.47259411	0.15449756	410.44455788	0.00243638	63.41268295	0.01576972	141
142	6.55889536	0.15246470	416.91715199	0.00239856	63.56514765	0.01573189	142
143	6.64634730	0.15045858	423.47604735	0.00236141	63.71560624	0.01569474	143
144	6.73496526	0.14847887	430.12239464	0.00232492	63.86408510	0.01565825	144
145	6.82476480	0.14652520	436.85735990	0.00228908	64.01061030	0.01562241	145
146	6.91576166	0.14459723	443.68212470	0.00225387	64.15520753	0.01558720	146
147	7.00797182	0.14269464	450.59788637	0.00221927	64.29790217	0.01555261	147
148	7.10141144	0.14081708	457.60585818	0.00218529	64.43871925	0.01551862	148
149	7.19609693	0.13896422	464.70726963	0.00215189	64.57768347	0.01548523	149
150	7.29204489	0.13713574	471.90336656	0.00211908	64.71481921	0.01545241	150
151	7.38927215	0.13533133	479.19541144	0.00208683	64.85015054	0.01542016	151
152	7.48779578	0.13355065	486.58468360	0.00205514	64.98370119	0.01538847	152
153	7.58763306	0.13179341	494.07247938	0.00202399	65.11549459	0.01535733	153
154	7.68880150	0.13005928	501.66011243	0.00199338	65.24555387	0.01532671	154
155	7.79131885	0.12834798	509.34891393	0.00196329	65.37390185	0.01529662	155
156	7.89520310	0.12665919	517.14023279	0.00193371	65.50056104	0.01526704	156
157	8.00047248	0.12499262	525.03543589	0.00190463	65.62555365	0.01523797	157
158	8.10714544	0.12334798	533.03590837	0.00187605	65.74890163	0.01520938	158
159	8.21524072	0.12172498	541.14305381	0.00184794	65.87062661	0.01518127	159
160	8.32477726	0.12012333	549.35829453	0.00182031	65.99074994	0.01515364	160

TABLE A-2

COMPOUND INTEREST FOR $1

$1\frac{1}{3}\%$

PERIODS n	FUTURE AMOUNT $(1+i)^n$	PRESENT VALUE $(1+i)^{-n}$	AMOUNT OF ANNUITY $(S/p,i,n)$ $\frac{(1+i)^n-1}{i}$	SINKING FUND $(p/S,i,n)$ $\frac{i}{(1+i)^n-1}$	PRESENT VALUE OF ANNUITY $(V/p,i,n)$ $\frac{1-(1+i)^{-n}}{i}$	AMORTIZATION $(p/V,i,n)$ $\frac{i}{1-(1+i)^{-n}}$	PERIODS n
161	8.43577429	0.11854276	557.68307179	0.00179313	66.10929271	0.01512647	161
162	8.54825128	0.11698299	566.11884608	0.00176641	66.22627570	0.01509975	162
163	8.66222796	0.11544374	574.66709736	0.00174014	66.34171944	0.01507347	163
164	8.77772434	0.11392474	583.32932533	0.00171430	66.45564418	0.01504763	164
165	8.89476066	0.11242573	592.10704967	0.00168888	66.56806992	0.01502222	165
166	9.01335747	0.11094645	601.00181033	0.00166389	66.67901637	0.01499722	166
167	9.13353557	0.10948663	610.01516780	0.00163930	66.78850299	0.01497264	167
168	9.25531604	0.10804601	619.14870337	0.00161512	66.89654901	0.01494845	168
169	9.37872026	0.10662436	628.40401941	0.00159133	67.00317336	0.01492467	169
170	9.50376986	0.10522140	637.78273967	0.00156793	67.10839476	0.01490127	170
171	9.63048679	0.10383691	647.28650954	0.00154491	67.21223168	0.01487824	171
172	9.75889328	0.10247064	656.91696633	0.00152226	67.31470231	0.01485560	172
173	9.88901186	0.10112234	666.67588961	0.00149998	67.41582465	0.01483331	173
174	10.02086535	0.09979178	676.56490148	0.00147805	67.51561643	0.01481139	174
175	10.15447689	0.09847873	686.58576683	0.00145648	67.61409516	0.01478982	175
176	10.28986992	0.09718296	696.74024372	0.00143526	67.71127812	0.01476859	176
177	10.42706818	0.09590424	707.03011364	0.00141437	67.80718236	0.01474770	177
178	10.56609576	0.09464234	717.45718182	0.00139381	67.90182469	0.01472714	178
179	10.70697703	0.09339704	728.02327758	0.00137358	67.99522174	0.01470692	179
180	10.84973673	0.09216814	738.73025461	0.00135367	68.08738987	0.01468701	180
181	10.99439988	0.09095540	749.57999134	0.00133408	68.17834527	0.01466741	181
182	11.14099188	0.08975861	760.57439122	0.00131480	68.26810388	0.01464813	182
183	11.28953844	0.08857758	771.71538311	0.00129581	68.35668146	0.01462915	183
184	11.44006562	0.08741209	783.00492155	0.00127713	68.44409355	0.01461046	184
185	11.59259983	0.08626193	794.44498717	0.00125874	68.53035548	0.01459207	185
186	11.74716783	0.08512690	806.03758700	0.00124064	68.61548238	0.01457397	186
187	11.90379673	0.08400681	817.78475482	0.00122282	68.69948919	0.01455615	187
188	12.06251402	0.08290146	829.68855155	0.00120527	68.78239065	0.01453860	188
189	12.22334754	0.08181065	841.75106557	0.00118800	68.86420130	0.01452133	189
190	12.38632551	0.08073419	853.97441312	0.00117100	68.94493549	0.01450433	190
191	12.55147651	0.07967190	866.36073862	0.00115425	69.02460739	0.01448759	191
192	12.71882954	0.07862359	878.91221514	0.00113777	69.10323098	0.01447110	192
193	12.88841393	0.07758907	891.63104467	0.00112154	69.18082004	0.01445487	193
194	13.06025945	0.07656816	904.51945860	0.00110556	69.25738820	0.01443889	194
195	13.23439624	0.07556068	917.57971805	0.00108982	69.33294888	0.01442316	195
196	13.41085486	0.07456646	930.81411429	0.00107433	69.40751534	0.01440766	196
197	13.58966626	0.07358532	944.22496915	0.00105907	69.48110067	0.01439240	197
198	13.77086181	0.07261710	957.81463540	0.00104404	69.55371777	0.01437738	198
199	13.95447330	0.07166161	971.58549721	0.00102925	69.62537937	0.01436258	199
200	14.14053294	0.07071869	985.53997051	0.00101467	69.69609807	0.01434801	200

COMPOUND INTEREST FOR $1

$1\frac{1}{3}\%$

PERIODS n	FUTURE AMOUNT $(1+i)^n$	PRESENT VALUE $(1+i)^{-n}$	AMOUNT OF ANNUITY $(S/p,i,n)$ $\dfrac{(1+i)^n-1}{i}$	SINKING FUND $(p/S,i,n)$ $\dfrac{i}{(1+i)^n-1}$	PRESENT VALUE OF ANNUITY $(V/p,i,n)$ $\dfrac{1-(1+i)^{-n}}{i}$	AMORTIZATION $(p/V,i,n)$ $\dfrac{i}{1-(1+i)^{-n}}$	PERIODS n
201	14.32907338	0.06978818	999.68050345	0.00100032	69.76588625	0.01433365	201
202	14.52012769	0.06886992	1014.00957683	0.00098618	69.83475617	0.01431952	202
203	14.71372939	0.06796373	1028.52970452	0.00097226	69.90271990	0.01430559	203
204	14.90991245	0.06706947	1043.24343391	0.00095855	69.96978938	0.01429188	204
205	15.10871128	0.06618698	1058.15334636	0.00094504	70.03597636	0.01427838	205
206	15.31016077	0.06531610	1073.26205765	0.00093174	70.10129246	0.01426507	206
207	15.51429625	0.06445668	1088.57221842	0.00091863	70.16574914	0.01425197	207
208	15.72115353	0.06360856	1104.08651466	0.00090573	70.22935770	0.01423906	208
209	15.93076891	0.06277161	1119.80766819	0.00089301	70.29212931	0.01422634	209
210	16.14317916	0.06194567	1135.73843710	0.00088048	70.35407498	0.01421382	210
211	16.35842155	0.06113059	1151.88161626	0.00086814	70.41520557	0.01420148	211
212	16.57653384	0.06032624	1168.24003781	0.00085599	70.47553181	0.01418932	212
213	16.79755429	0.05953248	1184.81657165	0.00084401	70.53506429	0.01417735	213
214	17.02152168	0.05874915	1201.61412594	0.00083221	70.59381344	0.01416555	214
215	17.24847530	0.05797614	1218.63564762	0.00082059	70.65178958	0.01415392	215
216	17.47845497	0.05721329	1235.88412292	0.00080914	70.70900288	0.01414247	216
217	17.71150104	0.05646049	1253.36257789	0.00079785	70.76546337	0.01413119	217
218	17.94765439	0.05571759	1271.07407893	0.00078674	70.82118095	0.01412007	218
219	18.18695644	0.05498446	1289.02173331	0.00077578	70.87616541	0.01410912	219
220	18.42944920	0.05426098	1307.20868976	0.00076499	70.93042640	0.01409832	220
221	18.67517519	0.05354702	1325.63813895	0.00075435	70.98397342	0.01408769	221
222	18.92417752	0.05284246	1344.31331414	0.00074387	71.03681587	0.01407721	222
223	19.17649989	0.05214716	1363.23749166	0.00073355	71.08896303	0.01406688	223
224	19.43218655	0.05146101	1382.41399155	0.00072337	71.14042404	0.01405671	224
225	19.69128237	0.05078389	1401.84617811	0.00071335	71.19120794	0.01404668	225
226	19.95383281	0.05011569	1421.53746048	0.00070346	71.24132362	0.01403680	226
227	20.21988391	0.04945627	1441.49129329	0.00069373	71.29077989	0.01402706	227
228	20.48948236	0.04880553	1461.71117720	0.00068413	71.33958542	0.01401746	228
229	20.76267546	0.04816335	1482.20065956	0.00067467	71.38774877	0.01400801	229
230	21.03951113	0.04752962	1502.96333502	0.00066535	71.43527839	0.01399869	230
231	21.32003795	0.04690423	1524.00284615	0.00065616	71.48218262	0.01398950	231
232	21.60430512	0.04628707	1545.32288410	0.00064711	71.52846969	0.01398045	232
233	21.89236252	0.04567803	1566.92718922	0.00063819	71.57414772	0.01397153	233
234	22.18426069	0.04507700	1588.81955175	0.00062940	71.61922473	0.01396273	234
235	22.48005083	0.04448389	1611.00381244	0.00062073	71.66370861	0.01395406	235
236	22.77978484	0.04389857	1633.48386327	0.00061219	71.70760718	0.01394552	236
237	23.08351531	0.04332096	1656.26364811	0.00060377	71.75092814	0.01393710	237
238	23.39129551	0.04275095	1679.34716342	0.00059547	71.79367909	0.01392880	238
239	23.70317945	0.04218843	1702.73845893	0.00058729	71.83586752	0.01392062	239
240	24.01922185	0.04163332	1726.44163839	0.00057923	71.87750084	0.01391256	240

TABLE A-2

COMPOUND INTEREST FOR $1

$1\frac{5}{12}\%$

PERIODS n	FUTURE AMOUNT $(1+i)^n$	PRESENT VALUE $(1+i)^{-n}$	AMOUNT OF ANNUITY $(S/p,i,n)$ $\frac{(1+i)^n-1}{i}$	SINKING FUND $(p/S,i,n)$ $\frac{i}{(1+i)^n-1}$	PRESENT VALUE OF ANNUITY $(V/p,i,n)$ $\frac{1-(1+i)^{-n}}{i}$	AMORTIZATION $(p/V,i,n)$ $\frac{i}{1-(1+i)^{-n}}$	PERIODS n
1	1.01416667	0.98603122	1.00000000	1.00000000	0.98603122	1.01416667	1
2	1.02853403	0.97225758	2.01416667	0.49648324	1.95828880	0.51064991	2
3	1.04310493	0.95867633	3.04270069	0.32865540	2.91696513	0.34282206	3
4	1.05788225	0.94528479	4.08580562	0.24474977	3.86224992	0.25891644	4
5	1.07286891	0.93208032	5.14368787	0.19441304	4.79433024	0.20857971	5
6	1.08806789	0.91906030	6.21655678	0.16086075	5.71339054	0.17502742	6
7	1.10348218	0.90622215	7.30462467	0.13689957	6.61961270	0.15106624	7
8	1.11911485	0.89356334	8.40810685	0.11893284	7.51317604	0.13309950	8
9	1.13496897	0.88108135	9.52722170	0.10496239	8.39425739	0.11912906	9
10	1.15104770	0.86877373	10.66219067	0.09378936	9.26303111	0.10795602	10
11	1.16735421	0.85663802	11.81323837	0.08465079	10.11966914	0.09881746	11
12	1.18389173	0.84467184	12.98059258	0.07703809	10.96434097	0.09120475	12
13	1.20066353	0.83287280	14.16448431	0.07059911	11.79721378	0.08476578	13
14	1.21767293	0.82123859	15.36514784	0.06508235	12.61845237	0.07924902	14
15	1.23492329	0.80976689	16.58282077	0.06030337	13.42821926	0.07447004	15
16	1.25241804	0.79845544	17.81774406	0.05612383	14.22667470	0.07029049	16
17	1.27016063	0.78730200	19.07016210	0.05243794	15.01397670	0.06660461	17
18	1.28815457	0.77630435	20.34032273	0.04916343	15.79028105	0.06333010	18
19	1.30640343	0.76546033	21.62847730	0.04623534	16.55574138	0.06040201	19
20	1.32491081	0.75476779	22.93488073	0.04360171	17.31050917	0.05776838	20
21	1.34368038	0.74422460	24.25979154	0.04122047	18.05473377	0.05538714	21
22	1.36271585	0.73382870	25.60347192	0.03905720	18.78856247	0.05322387	22
23	1.38202099	0.72357801	26.96618777	0.03708348	19.51214048	0.05125014	23
24	1.40159962	0.71347051	28.34820877	0.03527560	20.22561099	0.04944226	24
25	1.42145562	0.70350420	29.74980839	0.03361366	20.92911519	0.04778033	25
26	1.44159291	0.69367711	31.17126401	0.03208083	21.62279230	0.04624750	26
27	1.46201547	0.68398729	32.61285692	0.03066275	22.30677959	0.04482942	27
28	1.48272736	0.67443282	34.07487239	0.02934714	22.98121242	0.04351381	28
29	1.50373266	0.66501182	35.55759975	0.02812338	23.64622424	0.04229005	29
30	1.52503554	0.65572242	37.06133241	0.02698230	24.30194666	0.04114897	30
31	1.54664021	0.64656278	38.58636795	0.02591589	24.94850944	0.04008255	31
32	1.56855095	0.63753109	40.13300817	0.02491715	25.58604054	0.03908381	32
33	1.59077209	0.62862556	41.70155912	0.02397992	26.21466610	0.03814659	33
34	1.61330803	0.61984443	43.29233120	0.02309878	26.83451053	0.03726545	34
35	1.63616322	0.61118597	44.90563923	0.02226892	27.44569650	0.03643558	35
36	1.65934220	0.60264845	46.54180245	0.02148606	28.04834495	0.03565273	36
37	1.68284955	0.59423019	48.20114465	0.02074640	28.64257513	0.03491306	37
38	1.70668992	0.58592952	49.88399420	0.02004651	29.22850465	0.03421318	38
39	1.73086803	0.57774480	51.59068412	0.01938334	29.80624945	0.03355001	39
40	1.75538866	0.56967441	53.32155214	0.01875414	30.37592386	0.03292081	40

TABLE A-2

COMPOUND INTEREST FOR $1

$1\frac{5}{12}\%$

PERIODS n	FUTURE AMOUNT $(1+i)^n$	PRESENT VALUE $(1+i)^{-n}$	AMOUNT OF ANNUITY $(S/p,i,n)$ $\dfrac{(1+i)^n-1}{i}$	SINKING FUND $(p/S,i,n)$ $\dfrac{i}{(1+i)^n-1}$	PRESENT VALUE OF ANNUITY $(V/p,i,n)$ $\dfrac{1-(1+i)^{-n}}{i}$	AMORTIZATION $(p/V,i,n)$ $\dfrac{i}{1-(1+i)^{-n}}$	PERIODS n
41	1.78025666	0.56171676	55.07694080	0.01815642	30.93764062	0.03232309	41
42	1.80547696	0.55387026	56.85719746	0.01758792	31.49151088	0.03175459	42
43	1.83105455	0.54613337	58.66267443	0.01704661	32.03764426	0.03121328	43
44	1.85699449	0.53850456	60.49372898	0.01653064	32.57614881	0.03069731	44
45	1.88330192	0.53098231	62.35072347	0.01603831	33.10713112	0.03020497	45
46	1.90998203	0.52356514	64.23402539	0.01556807	33.63069626	0.02973474	46
47	1.93704011	0.51625157	66.14400742	0.01511853	34.14694783	0.02928519	47
48	1.96448151	0.50904017	68.08104752	0.01468838	34.65598800	0.02885504	48
49	1.99231166	0.50192950	70.04552903	0.01427643	35.15791750	0.02844310	49
50	2.02053608	0.49491816	72.03784069	0.01388159	35.65283567	0.02804826	50
51	2.04916034	0.48800476	74.05837676	0.01350286	36.14084043	0.02766953	51
52	2.07819011	0.48118793	76.10753710	0.01313930	36.62202836	0.02730597	52
53	2.10763114	0.47446633	78.18572721	0.01279006	37.09649468	0.02695672	53
54	2.13748924	0.46783861	80.29335835	0.01245433	37.56433329	0.02662100	54
55	2.16777034	0.46130348	82.43084759	0.01213138	38.02563677	0.02629805	55
56	2.19848042	0.45485963	84.59861793	0.01182052	38.48049641	0.02598719	56
57	2.22962556	0.44850580	86.79709835	0.01152112	38.92900221	0.02568779	57
58	2.26121192	0.44224073	89.02672391	0.01123258	39.37124293	0.02539925	58
59	2.29324576	0.43606316	91.28793583	0.01095435	39.80730610	0.02512102	59
60	2.32573341	0.42997190	93.58118159	0.01068591	40.23727799	0.02485258	60
61	2.35868130	0.42396571	95.90691500	0.01042678	40.66124371	0.02459344	61
62	2.39209595	0.41804343	98.26596629	0.01017650	41.07928714	0.02434317	62
63	2.42598397	0.41220388	100.65769224	0.00993466	41.49149102	0.02410133	63
64	2.46035208	0.40644589	103.08367621	0.00970086	41.89793691	0.02386752	64
65	2.49520707	0.40076834	105.54402829	0.00947472	42.29870525	0.02364139	65
66	2.53055583	0.39517010	108.03923536	0.00925590	42.69387535	0.02342256	66
67	2.56640538	0.38965006	110.56979120	0.00904406	43.08352541	0.02321073	67
68	2.60276278	0.38420712	113.13619657	0.00883890	43.46773253	0.02300557	68
69	2.63963526	0.37884022	115.73895936	0.00864013	43.84657275	0.02280680	69
70	2.67703009	0.37354929	118.37859461	0.00844747	44.22012104	0.02261414	70
71	2.71495468	0.36833027	121.05562470	0.00826067	44.58845131	0.02242733	71
72	2.75341654	0.36318515	123.77057939	0.00807946	44.95163646	0.02224613	72
73	2.79242328	0.35811190	126.52399593	0.00790364	45.30974836	0.02207031	73
74	2.83198261	0.35310951	129.31641920	0.00773297	45.66285787	0.02189964	74
75	2.87210236	0.34817701	132.14840181	0.00756725	46.01103488	0.02173392	75
76	2.91279048	0.34331340	135.02050417	0.00740628	46.35434828	0.02157295	76
77	2.95405501	0.33851773	137.93329464	0.00724988	46.69286601	0.02141655	77
78	2.99590412	0.33378905	140.88734965	0.00709787	47.02665506	0.02126454	78
79	3.03834610	0.32912643	143.88325377	0.00695008	47.35578149	0.02111675	79
80	3.08138933	0.32452894	146.92159987	0.00680635	47.68031043	0.02097302	80

COMPOUND INTEREST FOR $1

$1\frac{5}{12}\%$

PERIODS n	FUTURE AMOUNT $(1+i)^n$	PRESENT VALUE $(1+i)^{-n}$	AMOUNT OF ANNUITY (S/p,i,n) $\dfrac{(1+i)^n-1}{i}$	SINKING FUND (p/S,i,n) $\dfrac{i}{(1+i)^n-1}$	PRESENT VALUE OF ANNUITY (V/p,i,n) $\dfrac{1-(1+i)^{-n}}{i}$	AMORTIZATION (p/V,i,n) $\dfrac{i}{1-(1+i)^{-n}}$	PERIODS n
81	3.12504235	0.31999566	150.00298920	0.00666653	48.00030609	0.02083320	81
82	3.16931378	0.31552572	153.12803154	0.00653048	48.31583181	0.02069715	82
83	3.21421239	0.31111821	156.29734532	0.00639806	48.62695001	0.02056473	83
84	3.25974707	0.30677227	159.51155772	0.00626914	48.93372228	0.02043580	84
85	3.30592682	0.30248703	162.77130478	0.00614359	49.23620932	0.02031026	85
86	3.35276078	0.29826166	166.07723160	0.00602129	49.53447098	0.02018796	86
87	3.40025823	0.29409531	169.42999238	0.00590214	49.82856629	0.02006881	87
88	3.44842855	0.28998716	172.83025061	0.00578602	50.11855345	0.01995269	88
89	3.49728129	0.28593639	176.27867916	0.00567284	50.40448984	0.01983950	89
90	3.54682611	0.28194221	179.77596045	0.00556248	50.68643205	0.01972915	90
91	3.59707281	0.27800383	183.32278655	0.00545486	50.96443588	0.01962153	91
92	3.64803134	0.27412045	186.91985936	0.00534989	51.23855633	0.01951655	92
93	3.69971178	0.27029132	190.56789070	0.00524747	51.50884766	0.01941414	93
94	3.75212437	0.26651569	194.26760249	0.00514754	51.77536334	0.01931421	94
95	3.80527946	0.26279279	198.01972686	0.00505000	52.03815613	0.01921667	95
96	3.85918759	0.25912189	201.82506632	0.00495479	52.29727802	0.01912145	96
97	3.91385941	0.25550228	205.68419391	0.00486182	52.55278030	0.01902849	97
98	3.96930576	0.25193323	209.59805332	0.00477104	52.80471353	0.01893770	98
99	4.02553759	0.24841403	213.56735908	0.00468236	53.05312756	0.01884903	99
100	4.08256604	0.24494399	217.59289667	0.00459574	53.29807154	0.01876240	100
101	4.14040239	0.24152242	221.67546270	0.00451110	53.53959396	0.01867777	101
102	4.19905809	0.23814865	225.81586509	0.00442839	53.77774261	0.01859505	102
103	4.25854475	0.23482200	230.01492318	0.00434754	54.01256461	0.01851421	103
104	4.31887413	0.23154183	234.27346793	0.00426852	54.24410643	0.01843518	104
105	4.38005818	0.22830747	238.59234205	0.00419125	54.47241390	0.01835792	105
106	4.44210900	0.22511829	242.97240023	0.00411569	54.69753220	0.01828236	106
107	4.50503888	0.22197367	247.41450924	0.00404180	54.91950586	0.01820847	107
108	4.56886027	0.21887297	251.91954812	0.00396952	55.13837883	0.01813619	108
109	4.63358579	0.21581558	256.48840838	0.00389881	55.35419441	0.01806548	109
110	4.69922825	0.21280090	261.12199417	0.00382963	55.56699531	0.01799629	110
111	4.76580065	0.20982833	265.82122242	0.00376193	55.77682364	0.01792859	111
112	4.83331616	0.20689729	270.58702307	0.00369567	55.98372093	0.01786234	112
113	4.90178814	0.20400719	275.42033923	0.00363081	56.18772811	0.01779748	113
114	4.97123014	0.20115745	280.32212737	0.00356732	56.38888557	0.01773399	114
115	5.04165590	0.19834753	285.29335751	0.00350516	56.58723310	0.01767183	115
116	5.11307936	0.19557686	290.33501340	0.00344430	56.78280996	0.01761096	116
117	5.18551465	0.19284489	295.44809276	0.00338469	56.97565485	0.01755136	117
118	5.25897610	0.19015108	300.63360741	0.00332631	57.16580593	0.01749297	118
119	5.33347827	0.18749490	305.89258351	0.00326912	57.35330084	0.01743579	119
120	5.40903588	0.18487583	311.22606178	0.00321310	57.53817667	0.01737977	120

TABLE A-2

COMPOUND INTEREST FOR $1

$1\tfrac{5}{12}\%$

PERIODS n	FUTURE AMOUNT $(1+i)^n$	PRESENT VALUE $(1+i)^{-n}$	AMOUNT OF ANNUITY $(S/p,i,n)$ $\dfrac{(1+i)^n-1}{i}$	SINKING FUND $(p/S,i,n)$ $\dfrac{i}{(1+i)^n-1}$	PRESENT VALUE OF ANNUITY $(V/p,i,n)$ $\dfrac{1-(1+i)^{-n}}{i}$	AMORTIZATION $(p/V,i,n)$ $\dfrac{i}{1-(1+i)^{-n}}$	PERIODS n
121	5.48566388	0.18229334	316.63509766	0.00315821	57.72047001	0.01732488	121
122	5.56337746	0.17974693	322.12076154	0.00310443	57.90021693	0.01727109	122
123	5.64219197	0.17723608	327.68413899	0.00305172	58.07745302	0.01721839	123
124	5.72212302	0.17476031	333.32633096	0.00300006	58.25221333	0.01716673	124
125	5.80318643	0.17231912	339.04845399	0.00294943	58.42453245	0.01711610	125
126	5.88539824	0.16991204	344.85164042	0.00289980	58.59444449	0.01706646	126
127	5.96877471	0.16753857	350.73703866	0.00285114	58.76198306	0.01701781	127
128	6.05333236	0.16519826	356.70581337	0.00280343	58.92718133	0.01697010	128
129	6.13908790	0.16289065	362.75914573	0.00275665	59.09007197	0.01692332	129
130	6.22605831	0.16061526	368.89823362	0.00271077	59.25068724	0.01687744	130
131	6.31426080	0.15837167	375.12429193	0.00266578	59.40905890	0.01683245	131
132	6.40371283	0.15615941	381.43855274	0.00262165	59.56521831	0.01678832	132
133	6.49443210	0.15397805	387.84226557	0.00257837	59.71919636	0.01674503	133
134	6.58643655	0.15182717	394.33669766	0.00253590	59.87102353	0.01670257	134
135	6.67974440	0.14970633	400.92313421	0.00249424	60.02072985	0.01666091	135
136	6.77437411	0.14761511	407.60287861	0.00245337	60.16834497	0.01662004	136
137	6.87034441	0.14555311	414.37725273	0.00241326	60.31389808	0.01657993	137
138	6.96767429	0.14351991	421.24759714	0.00237390	60.45741799	0.01654057	138
139	7.06638301	0.14151511	428.21527143	0.00233527	60.59893310	0.01650194	139
140	7.16649010	0.13953832	435.28165445	0.00229736	60.73847143	0.01646403	140
141	7.26801538	0.13758914	442.44814455	0.00226015	60.87606057	0.01642682	141
142	7.37097893	0.13566719	449.71615993	0.00222362	61.01172776	0.01639029	142
143	7.47540113	0.13377209	457.08713886	0.00218777	61.14549984	0.01635443	143
144	7.58130265	0.13190345	464.56254000	0.00215256	61.27740330	0.01631923	144
145	7.68870444	0.13006092	472.14384265	0.00211800	61.40746422	0.01628467	145
146	7.79762775	0.12824413	479.83254709	0.00208406	61.53570835	0.01625073	146
147	7.90809414	0.12645272	487.63017484	0.00205073	61.66216107	0.01621740	147
148	8.02012548	0.12468633	495.53826898	0.00201801	61.78684740	0.01618467	148
149	8.13374392	0.12294461	503.55839446	0.00198587	61.90979201	0.01615253	149
150	8.24897196	0.12122723	511.69213838	0.00195430	62.03101924	0.01612097	150
151	8.36583240	0.11953383	519.94111034	0.00192329	62.15055307	0.01608996	151
152	8.48434836	0.11786409	528.30694273	0.00189284	62.26841716	0.01605951	152
153	8.60454329	0.11621767	536.79129109	0.00186292	62.38463483	0.01602959	153
154	8.72644099	0.11459425	545.39583438	0.00183353	62.49922909	0.01600020	154
155	8.85006557	0.11299351	554.12227537	0.00180466	62.61222260	0.01597132	155
156	8.97544150	0.11141513	562.97234094	0.00177629	62.72363773	0.01594295	156
157	9.10259358	0.10985880	571.94778243	0.00174841	62.83349653	0.01591508	157
158	9.23154699	0.10832421	581.05037602	0.00172102	62.94182074	0.01588769	158
159	9.36232724	0.10681105	590.28192301	0.00169411	63.04863179	0.01586077	159
160	9.49496021	0.10531903	599.64425025	0.00166766	63.15395082	0.01583432	160

TABLE A-2

COMPOUND INTEREST FOR $1

$1\frac{5}{12}\%$

PERIODS n	FUTURE AMOUNT $(1+i)^n$	PRESENT VALUE $(1+i)^{-n}$	AMOUNT OF ANNUITY (S/p,i,n) $\frac{(1+i)^n-1}{i}$	SINKING FUND (p/S,i,n) $\frac{i}{(1+i)^n-1}$	PRESENT VALUE OF ANNUITY (V/p,i,n) $\frac{1-(1+i)^{-n}}{i}$	AMORTIZATION (p/V,i,n) $\frac{i}{1-(1+i)^{-n}}$	PERIODS n
161	9.62947215	0.10384785	609.13921046	0.00164166	63.25779867	0.01580833	161
162	9.76588967	0.10239722	618.76868261	0.00161611	63.36019590	0.01578278	162
163	9.90423977	0.10096686	628.53457228	0.00159100	63.46116276	0.01575767	163
164	10.04454984	0.09955648	638.43881206	0.00156632	63.56071923	0.01573299	164
165	10.18684763	0.09816580	648.48336189	0.00154206	63.65888503	0.01570873	165
166	10.33116130	0.09679454	658.67020952	0.00151821	63.75567957	0.01568488	166
167	10.47751942	0.09544244	669.00137082	0.00149477	63.85112201	0.01566143	167
168	10.62595095	0.09410922	679.47889024	0.00147172	63.94523123	0.01563838	168
169	10.77648525	0.09279463	690.10484119	0.00144906	64.03802587	0.01561572	169
170	10.92915212	0.09149841	700.88132644	0.00142678	64.12952427	0.01559344	170
171	11.08398178	0.09022029	711.81047856	0.00140487	64.21974456	0.01557153	171
172	11.24100485	0.08896002	722.89446034	0.00138333	64.30870458	0.01554999	172
173	11.40025242	0.08771736	734.13546520	0.00136215	64.39642193	0.01552881	173
174	11.56175600	0.08649205	745.53571762	0.00134132	64.48291398	0.01550798	174
175	11.72554754	0.08528386	757.09747362	0.00132083	64.56819785	0.01548750	175
176	11.89165947	0.08409255	768.82302116	0.00130069	64.65229040	0.01546736	176
177	12.06012464	0.08291788	780.71468063	0.00128088	64.73520828	0.01544754	177
178	12.23097641	0.08175962	792.77480527	0.00126139	64.81696790	0.01542806	178
179	12.40424857	0.08061754	805.00578168	0.00124223	64.89758544	0.01540889	179
180	12.57997543	0.07949141	817.41003025	0.00122338	64.97707685	0.01539004	180
181	12.75819175	0.07838101	829.99000568	0.00120483	65.05545787	0.01537150	181
182	12.93893280	0.07728613	842.74819743	0.00118659	65.13274399	0.01535326	182
183	13.12223434	0.07620653	855.68713023	0.00116865	65.20895053	0.01533532	183
184	13.30813266	0.07514202	868.80936457	0.00115100	65.28409255	0.01531767	184
185	13.49666454	0.07409238	882.11749724	0.00113364	65.35818493	0.01530030	185
186	13.68786729	0.07305740	895.61416178	0.00111655	65.43124233	0.01528322	186
187	13.88177875	0.07203688	909.30202907	0.00109974	65.50327921	0.01526641	187
188	14.07843728	0.07103061	923.18380782	0.00108321	65.57430982	0.01524987	188
189	14.27788181	0.07003840	937.26224509	0.00106694	65.64434822	0.01523360	189
190	14.48015180	0.06906005	951.54012690	0.00105093	65.71340827	0.01521759	190
191	14.68528728	0.06809537	966.02027870	0.00103517	65.78150364	0.01520184	191
192	14.89332885	0.06714416	980.70556598	0.00101967	65.84864779	0.01518634	192
193	15.10431768	0.06620623	995.59889483	0.00100442	65.91485403	0.01517109	193
194	15.31829551	0.06528141	1010.70321251	0.00098941	65.98013544	0.01515608	194
195	15.53530470	0.06436951	1026.02150802	0.00097464	66.04450495	0.01514131	195
196	15.75538818	0.06347035	1041.55681271	0.00096010	66.10797530	0.01512677	196
197	15.97858951	0.06258375	1057.31220090	0.00094579	66.17055905	0.01511246	197
198	16.20495286	0.06170953	1073.29079041	0.00093171	66.23226858	0.01509838	198
199	16.43452303	0.06084752	1089.49574327	0.00091786	66.29311610	0.01508452	199
200	16.66734544	0.05999756	1105.93026630	0.00090422	66.35311366	0.01507088	200

COMPOUND INTEREST FOR $1

$1\frac{5}{12}\%$

PERIODS n	FUTURE AMOUNT $(1+i)^n$	PRESENT VALUE $(1+i)^{-n}$	AMOUNT OF ANNUITY $(S/p,i,n)$ $\dfrac{(1+i)^n - 1}{i}$	SINKING FUND $(p/S,i,n)$ $\dfrac{i}{(1+i)^n - 1}$	PRESENT VALUE OF ANNUITY $(V/p,i,n)$ $\dfrac{1-(1+i)^{-n}}{i}$	AMORTIZATION $(p/V,i,n)$ $\dfrac{i}{1-(1+i)^{-n}}$	PERIODS n
201	16.90346617	0.05915946	1122.59761174	0.00089079	66.41227312	0.01505746	201
202	17.14293194	0.05833308	1139.50107791	0.00087758	66.47060620	0.01504424	202
203	17.38579014	0.05751824	1156.64400984	0.00086457	66.52812444	0.01503124	203
204	17.63208883	0.05671478	1174.02979998	0.00085177	66.58483922	0.01501843	204
205	17.88187676	0.05592254	1191.66188882	0.00083916	66.64076176	0.01500583	205
206	18.13520335	0.05514137	1209.54376558	0.00082676	66.69590313	0.01499342	206
207	18.39211873	0.05437111	1227.67896892	0.00081455	66.75027424	0.01498121	207
208	18.65267374	0.05361162	1246.07108765	0.00080252	66.80388586	0.01496919	208
209	18.91691995	0.05286273	1264.72376139	0.00079069	66.85674859	0.01495735	209
210	19.18490965	0.05212430	1283.64068134	0.00077903	66.90887289	0.01494570	210
211	19.45669587	0.05139619	1302.82559099	0.00076756	66.96026908	0.01493423	211
212	19.73233240	0.05067825	1322.28228687	0.00075627	67.01094732	0.01492293	212
213	20.01187377	0.04997033	1342.01461926	0.00074515	67.06091766	0.01491182	213
214	20.29537532	0.04927231	1362.02649304	0.00073420	67.11018997	0.01490087	214
215	20.58289314	0.04858403	1382.32186835	0.00072342	67.15877400	0.01489009	215
216	20.87448412	0.04790538	1402.90476149	0.00071281	67.20667938	0.01487947	216
217	21.17020598	0.04723620	1423.77924561	0.00070236	67.25391557	0.01486902	217
218	21.47011723	0.04657636	1444.94945159	0.00069207	67.30049194	0.01485873	218
219	21.77427722	0.04592575	1466.41956882	0.00068193	67.34641769	0.01484860	219
220	22.08274615	0.04528422	1488.19384605	0.00067196	67.39170191	0.01483862	220
221	22.39558506	0.04465166	1510.27659220	0.00066213	67.43635357	0.01482880	221
222	22.71285584	0.04402793	1532.67217725	0.00065246	67.48038150	0.01481912	222
223	23.03462130	0.04341291	1555.38503310	0.00064293	67.52379441	0.01480959	223
224	23.36094510	0.04280649	1578.41965440	0.00063355	67.56660090	0.01480021	224
225	23.69189183	0.04220853	1601.78059951	0.00062431	67.60880943	0.01479097	225
226	24.02752696	0.04161893	1625.47249133	0.00061521	67.65042836	0.01478187	226
227	24.36791693	0.04103757	1649.50001829	0.00060624	67.69146593	0.01477291	227
228	24.71312908	0.04046432	1673.86793522	0.00059742	67.73193025	0.01476409	228
229	25.06323174	0.03989908	1698.58106430	0.00058873	67.77182933	0.01475539	229
230	25.41829419	0.03934174	1723.64429604	0.00058017	67.81117108	0.01474683	230
231	25.77838670	0.03879219	1749.06259024	0.00057173	67.84996326	0.01473840	231
232	26.14358051	0.03825031	1774.84097693	0.00056343	67.88821357	0.01473010	232
233	26.51394790	0.03771600	1800.98455744	0.00055525	67.92592957	0.01472192	233
234	26.88956216	0.03718915	1827.49850534	0.00054720	67.96311872	0.01471386	234
235	27.27049762	0.03666966	1854.38806750	0.00053926	67.99978838	0.01470593	235
236	27.65682967	0.03615743	1881.65856512	0.00053145	68.03594582	0.01469811	236
237	28.04863476	0.03565236	1909.31539479	0.00052375	68.07159818	0.01469041	237
238	28.44599042	0.03515434	1937.36402955	0.00051617	68.10675252	0.01468283	238
239	28.84897528	0.03466328	1965.81001997	0.00050870	68.14141579	0.01467536	239
240	29.25766910	0.03417907	1994.65899525	0.00050134	68.17559487	0.01466801	240

TABLE A-2

COMPOUND INTEREST FOR $1

$1\frac{1}{2}\%$

PERIODS n	FUTURE AMOUNT $(1+i)^n$	PRESENT VALUE $(1+i)^{-n}$	AMOUNT OF ANNUITY $(S/p,i,n)$ $\dfrac{(1+i)^n-1}{i}$	SINKING FUND $(p/S,i,n)$ $\dfrac{i}{(1+i)^n-1}$	PRESENT VALUE OF ANNUITY $(V/p,i,n)$ $\dfrac{1-(1+i)^{-n}}{i}$	AMORTIZATION $(p/V,i,n)$ $\dfrac{i}{1-(1+i)^{-n}}$	PERIODS n
1	1.01500000	0.98522167	1.00000000	1.00000000	0.98522167	1.01500000	1
2	1.03022500	0.97066175	2.01500000	0.49627792	1.95588342	0.51127792	2
3	1.04567837	0.95631699	3.04522500	0.32838296	2.91220042	0.34338296	3
4	1.06136355	0.94218423	4.09090337	0.24444479	3.85438465	0.25944479	4
5	1.07728400	0.92826033	5.15226693	0.19408932	4.78264497	0.20908932	5
6	1.09344326	0.91454219	6.22955093	0.16052521	5.69718717	0.17552521	6
7	1.10984491	0.90102679	7.32299419	0.13655616	6.59821396	0.15155616	7
8	1.12649259	0.88771112	8.43283911	0.11858402	7.48592508	0.13358402	8
9	1.14338998	0.87459224	9.55933169	0.10460982	8.36051732	0.11960982	9
10	1.16054083	0.86166723	10.70272167	0.09343418	9.22218455	0.10843418	10
11	1.17794894	0.84893323	11.86326249	0.08429384	10.07111779	0.09929384	11
12	1.19561817	0.83638742	13.04121143	0.07667999	10.90750521	0.09167999	12
13	1.21355244	0.82402702	14.23682960	0.07024036	11.73153222	0.08524036	13
14	1.23175573	0.81184928	15.45038205	0.06472332	12.54338150	0.07972332	14
15	1.25023207	0.79985150	16.68213778	0.05994436	13.34323301	0.07494436	15
16	1.26898555	0.78803104	17.93236984	0.05576508	14.13126405	0.07076508	16
17	1.28802033	0.77638526	19.20135539	0.05207966	14.90764931	0.06707966	17
18	1.30734064	0.76491159	20.48937572	0.04880578	15.67256089	0.06380578	18
19	1.32695075	0.75360747	21.79671636	0.04587847	16.42616837	0.06087847	19
20	1.34685501	0.74247042	23.12366710	0.04324574	17.16863879	0.05824574	20
21	1.36705783	0.73149795	24.47052211	0.04086550	17.90013673	0.05586550	21
22	1.38756370	0.72068763	25.83757994	0.03870332	18.62082437	0.05370332	22
23	1.40837715	0.71003708	27.22514364	0.03673075	19.33086145	0.05173075	23
24	1.42950281	0.69954392	28.63352080	0.03492410	20.03040537	0.04992410	24
25	1.45094535	0.68920583	30.06302361	0.03326345	20.71961120	0.04826345	25
26	1.47270953	0.67902052	31.51396896	0.03173196	21.39863172	0.04673196	26
27	1.49480018	0.66898574	32.98667850	0.03031527	22.06761746	0.04531527	27
28	1.51722218	0.65909925	34.48147867	0.02900108	22.72671671	0.04400108	28
29	1.53998051	0.64935887	35.99870085	0.02777878	23.37607558	0.04277878	29
30	1.56308022	0.63976243	37.53868137	0.02663919	24.01583801	0.04163919	30
31	1.58652642	0.63030781	39.10176159	0.02557430	24.64614582	0.04057430	31
32	1.61032432	0.62099292	40.68828801	0.02457710	25.26713874	0.03957710	32
33	1.63447918	0.61181568	42.29861233	0.02364144	25.87895442	0.03864144	33
34	1.65899637	0.60277407	43.93309152	0.02276189	26.48172849	0.03776189	34
35	1.68388132	0.59386608	45.59208789	0.02193363	27.07559458	0.03693363	35
36	1.70913954	0.58508974	47.25596921	0.02115240	27.66068431	0.03615240	36
37	1.73477663	0.57644309	48.98510874	0.02041437	28.23712740	0.03541437	37
38	1.76079828	0.56792423	50.71988538	0.01971613	28.80505163	0.03471613	38
39	1.78721025	0.55953126	52.48068366	0.01905463	29.36458288	0.03405463	39
40	1.81401841	0.55126232	54.26789391	0.01842710	29.91584520	0.03342710	40

TABLE A-2

COMPOUND INTEREST FOR $1

$1\frac{1}{2}\%$

PERIODS n	FUTURE AMOUNT $(1+i)^n$	PRESENT VALUE $(1+i)^{-n}$	AMOUNT OF ANNUITY $(S/p,i,n)$ $\dfrac{(1+i)^n-1}{i}$	SINKING FUND $(p/S,i,n)$ $\dfrac{i}{(1+i)^n-1}$	PRESENT VALUE OF ANNUITY $(V/p,i,n)$ $\dfrac{1-(1+i)^{-n}}{i}$	AMORTIZATION $(p/V,i,n)$ $\dfrac{i}{1-(1+i)^{-n}}$	PERIODS n
41	1.84122868	0.54311559	56.08191232	0.01783106	30.45896079	0.03283106	41
42	1.86884712	0.53508925	57.92314100	0.01726426	30.99405004	0.03226426	42
43	1.89687982	0.52718153	59.79198812	0.01672465	31.52123157	0.03172465	43
44	1.92533302	0.51939067	61.68886794	0.01621038	32.04062223	0.03121038	44
45	1.95421301	0.51171494	63.61420096	0.01571976	32.55233718	0.03071976	45
46	1.98352621	0.50415265	65.56841398	0.01525125	33.05648983	0.03025125	46
47	2.01327910	0.49670212	67.55194018	0.01480342	33.55319195	0.02980342	47
48	2.04347829	0.48936170	69.56521929	0.01437500	34.04255365	0.02937500	48
49	2.07413046	0.48212975	71.60869758	0.01396478	34.52468339	0.02896478	49
50	2.10524242	0.47500468	73.68282804	0.01357168	34.99968807	0.02857168	50
51	2.13682106	0.46798491	75.78807046	0.01319469	35.46767298	0.02819469	51
52	2.16887337	0.46106887	77.92489152	0.01283287	35.92874185	0.02783287	52
53	2.20140647	0.45425505	80.09376489	0.01248537	36.38299690	0.02748537	53
54	2.23442757	0.44754192	82.29517136	0.01215138	36.83053882	0.02715138	54
55	2.26794398	0.44092800	84.52959893	0.01183018	37.27146681	0.02683018	55
56	2.30196314	0.43441182	86.79754292	0.01152106	37.70587863	0.02652106	56
57	2.33649259	0.42799194	89.09950606	0.01122341	38.13387058	0.02622341	57
58	2.37153998	0.42166694	91.43599865	0.01093661	38.55553751	0.02593661	58
59	2.40711308	0.41543541	93.80753863	0.01066012	38.97097292	0.02566012	59
60	2.44321978	0.40929597	96.21465171	0.01039343	39.38026889	0.02539343	60
61	2.47986807	0.40324726	98.65787149	0.01013604	39.78351614	0.02513604	61
62	2.51706609	0.39728794	101.13773956	0.00988751	40.18080408	0.02488751	62
63	2.55482208	0.39141669	103.65480565	0.00964741	40.57222077	0.02464741	63
64	2.59314442	0.38563221	106.20962774	0.00941534	40.95785298	0.02441534	64
65	2.63204158	0.37993321	108.80277215	0.00919094	41.33778618	0.02419094	65
66	2.67152221	0.37431843	111.43481374	0.00897386	41.71210461	0.02397386	66
67	2.71159504	0.36878663	114.10633594	0.00876376	42.08089125	0.02376376	67
68	2.75226896	0.36333658	116.81793098	0.00856033	42.44422783	0.02356033	68
69	2.79355300	0.35796708	119.57019995	0.00836329	42.80219490	0.02336329	69
70	2.83545629	0.35267692	122.36375295	0.00817235	43.15487183	0.02317235	70
71	2.87798814	0.34746495	125.19920924	0.00798727	43.50233678	0.02298727	71
72	2.92115796	0.34233000	128.07719738	0.00780779	43.84466677	0.02280779	72
73	2.96497533	0.33727093	130.99835534	0.00763368	44.18193771	0.02263368	73
74	3.00944996	0.33228663	133.96333067	0.00746473	44.51422434	0.02246473	74
75	3.05459171	0.32737599	136.97278063	0.00730072	44.84160034	0.02230072	75
76	3.10041059	0.32253793	140.02737234	0.00714146	45.16413826	0.02214146	76
77	3.14691674	0.31777136	143.12778292	0.00698676	45.48190962	0.02198676	77
78	3.19412050	0.31307523	146.27469967	0.00683645	45.79498485	0.02183645	78
79	3.24203230	0.30844850	149.46882016	0.00669036	46.10343335	0.02169036	79
80	3.29066279	0.30389015	152.71085247	0.00654832	46.40732349	0.02154832	80

COMPOUND INTEREST FOR $1

$1\frac{1}{2}\%$

PERIODS n	FUTURE AMOUNT $(1+i)^n$	PRESENT VALUE $(1+i)^{-n}$	AMOUNT OF ANNUITY $(S/p,i,n)$ $\frac{(1+i)^n-1}{i}$	SINKING FUND $(p/S,i,n)$ $\frac{i}{(1+i)^n-1}$	PRESENT VALUE OF ANNUITY $(V/p,i,n)$ $\frac{1-(1+i)^{-n}}{i}$	AMORTIZATION $(p/V,i,n)$ $\frac{i}{1-(1+i)^{-n}}$	PERIODS n
81	3.34002273	0.29939916	156.00151525	0.00641019	46.70672265	0.02141019	81
82	3.39012307	0.29497454	159.34153798	0.00627583	47.00169720	0.02127583	82
83	3.44097492	0.29061531	162.73166105	0.00614509	47.29231251	0.02114509	83
84	3.49258954	0.28632050	166.17263597	0.00601784	47.57863301	0.02101784	84
85	3.54497838	0.28208917	169.66522551	0.00589396	47.86072218	0.02089396	85
86	3.59815306	0.27792036	173.21020389	0.00577333	48.13864254	0.02077333	86
87	3.65212535	0.27381316	176.80835695	0.00565584	48.41245571	0.02065584	87
88	3.70690723	0.26976666	180.46048230	0.00554138	48.68222237	0.02054138	88
89	3.76250084	0.26577996	184.16738954	0.00542984	48.94800234	0.02042984	89
90	3.81894851	0.26185218	187.92990038	0.00532113	49.20985452	0.02032113	90
91	3.87623273	0.25798245	191.74884889	0.00521516	49.46783696	0.02021516	91
92	3.93437622	0.25416990	195.62508162	0.00511182	49.72200686	0.02011182	92
93	3.99339187	0.25041369	199.55945784	0.00501104	49.97242055	0.02001104	93
94	4.05329275	0.24671300	203.55284971	0.00491273	50.21913355	0.01991273	94
95	4.11409214	0.24306699	207.60614246	0.00481681	50.46220054	0.01981681	95
96	4.17580352	0.23947487	211.72023459	0.00472321	50.70167541	0.01972321	96
97	4.23844057	0.23593583	215.89603811	0.00463186	50.93761124	0.01963186	97
98	4.30201718	0.23244909	220.13447868	0.00454268	51.17006034	0.01954268	98
99	4.36654744	0.22901389	224.43649586	0.00445560	51.39907422	0.01945560	99
100	4.43204565	0.22562944	228.80304330	0.00437057	51.62470367	0.01937057	100
101	4.49852633	0.22229502	233.23508895	0.00428752	51.84699869	0.01928752	101
102	4.56600423	0.21900987	237.73361529	0.00420639	52.06600856	0.01920639	102
103	4.63449429	0.21577327	242.29961951	0.00412712	52.28178183	0.01912712	103
104	4.70401171	0.21258450	246.93411381	0.00404966	52.49436634	0.01904966	104
105	4.77457188	0.20944286	251.63812551	0.00397396	52.70380920	0.01897396	105
106	4.84619046	0.20634765	256.41269740	0.00389996	52.91015685	0.01889996	106
107	4.91888332	0.20329817	261.25888786	0.00382762	53.11345502	0.01882762	107
108	4.99266657	0.20029377	266.17777118	0.00375689	53.31374879	0.01875689	108
109	5.06755657	0.19733376	271.17043774	0.00368772	53.51108255	0.01868772	109
110	5.14356991	0.19441750	276.23799431	0.00362007	53.70550005	0.01862007	110
111	5.22072346	0.19154433	281.38156422	0.00355389	53.89704438	0.01855389	111
112	5.29903432	0.18871363	286.60228769	0.00348916	54.08575801	0.01848916	112
113	5.37851983	0.18592476	291.90132200	0.00342582	54.27168277	0.01842582	113
114	5.45919763	0.18317710	297.27984183	0.00336383	54.45485987	0.01836383	114
115	5.54108559	0.18047005	302.73903946	0.00330317	54.63532993	0.01830317	115
116	5.62420188	0.17780301	308.28012505	0.00324380	54.81313293	0.01824380	116
117	5.70856490	0.17517538	313.90432693	0.00318568	54.98830831	0.01818568	117
118	5.79419338	0.17258658	319.61289183	0.00312878	55.16089488	0.01812878	118
119	5.88110628	0.17003604	325.40708521	0.00307307	55.33093092	0.01807307	119
120	5.96932287	0.16752319	331.28819149	0.00301852	55.49845411	0.01801852	120

TABLE A-2

COMPOUND INTEREST FOR $1

$1\frac{1}{2}\%$

PERIODS n	FUTURE AMOUNT $(1+i)^n$	PRESENT VALUE $(1+i)^{-n}$	AMOUNT OF ANNUITY $(S/p,i,n)$ $\dfrac{(1+i)^n-1}{i}$	SINKING FUND $(p/S,i,n)$ $\dfrac{i}{(1+i)^n-1}$	PRESENT VALUE OF ANNUITY $(V/p,i,n)$ $\dfrac{1-(1+i)^{-n}}{i}$	AMORTIZATION $(p/V,i,n)$ $\dfrac{i}{1-(1+i)^{-n}}$	PERIODS n
121	6.05886272	0.16504748	337.25751436	0.00296509	55.66350158	0.01796509	121
122	6.14974566	0.16260835	343.31637708	0.00291277	55.82610994	0.01791277	122
123	6.24199184	0.16020527	349.46612273	0.00286151	55.98631521	0.01786151	123
124	6.33562172	0.15783771	355.70811457	0.00281129	56.14415291	0.01781129	124
125	6.43065604	0.15550513	362.04373629	0.00276210	56.29965804	0.01776210	125
126	6.52711589	0.15320702	368.47439234	0.00271389	56.45286507	0.01771389	126
127	6.62502262	0.15094288	375.00150822	0.00266666	56.60380795	0.01766666	127
128	6.72439796	0.14871220	381.62653084	0.00262036	56.75252015	0.01762036	128
129	6.82526393	0.14651448	388.35092881	0.00257499	56.89903463	0.01757499	129
130	6.92764289	0.14434924	395.17619274	0.00253052	57.04338387	0.01753052	130
131	7.03155753	0.14221600	402.10383563	0.00248692	57.18559987	0.01748692	131
132	7.13703090	0.14011429	409.13539316	0.00244418	57.32571416	0.01744418	132
133	7.24408636	0.13804363	416.27242406	0.00240227	57.46375779	0.01740227	133
134	7.35274766	0.13600358	423.51651042	0.00236118	57.59976137	0.01736118	134
135	7.46303887	0.13399367	430.86925808	0.00232089	57.73375504	0.01732089	135
136	7.57498445	0.13201347	438.33229695	0.00228137	57.86576852	0.01728137	136
137	7.68860922	0.13006253	445.90728140	0.00224262	57.99583105	0.01724262	137
138	7.80393836	0.12814043	453.59589063	0.00220461	58.12397148	0.01720461	138
139	7.92099743	0.12624673	461.39982899	0.00216732	58.25021821	0.01716732	139
140	8.03981240	0.12438101	469.32082642	0.00213074	58.37459922	0.01713074	140
141	8.16040958	0.12254287	477.36063882	0.00209485	58.49714209	0.01709485	141
142	8.28281573	0.12073189	485.52104840	0.00205964	58.61787398	0.01705964	142
143	8.40705796	0.11894768	493.80386412	0.00202510	58.73682165	0.01702510	143
144	8.53316383	0.11718983	502.21092209	0.00199120	58.85401148	0.01699120	144
145	8.66116129	0.11545796	510.74408592	0.00195793	58.96946944	0.01695793	145
146	8.79107871	0.11375168	519.40524721	0.00192528	59.08322112	0.01692528	146
147	8.92294489	0.11207062	528.19632591	0.00189324	59.19529175	0.01689324	147
148	9.05678906	0.11041441	537.11927080	0.00186178	59.30570615	0.01686178	148
149	9.19264090	0.10878267	546.17605987	0.00183091	59.41448882	0.01683091	149
150	9.33053051	0.10717504	555.36870076	0.00180061	59.52166386	0.01680061	150
151	9.47048847	0.10559117	564.69923127	0.00177085	59.62725504	0.01677085	151
152	9.61254580	0.10403071	574.16971974	0.00174165	59.73128575	0.01674165	152
153	9.75673398	0.10249331	583.78226554	0.00171297	59.83377906	0.01671297	153
154	9.90308499	0.10097863	593.53899952	0.00168481	59.93475770	0.01668481	154
155	10.05163127	0.09948634	603.44208452	0.00165716	60.03424404	0.01665716	155
156	10.20240574	0.09801610	613.49371578	0.00163001	60.13226014	0.01663001	156
157	10.35544182	0.09656758	623.69612152	0.00160334	60.22882772	0.01660334	157
158	10.51077345	0.09514048	634.05156334	0.00157716	60.32396820	0.01657716	158
159	10.66843505	0.09373446	644.56233679	0.00155144	60.41770266	0.01655144	159
160	10.82846158	0.09234922	655.23077185	0.00152618	60.51005188	0.01652618	160

PERIODS n	FUTURE AMOUNT $(1+i)^n$	PRESENT VALUE $(1+i)^{-n}$	AMOUNT OF ANNUITY $(S/p,i,n)$ $\dfrac{(1+i)^n-1}{i}$	SINKING FUND $(p/S,i,n)$ $\dfrac{i}{(1+i)^n-1}$	PRESENT VALUE OF ANNUITY $(V/p,i,n)$ $\dfrac{1-(1+i)^{-n}}{i}$	AMORTIZATION $(p/V,i,n)$ $\dfrac{i}{1-(1+i)^{-n}}$	PERIODS n
161	10.99088850	0.09098445	666.05923342	0.00150137	60.60103633	0.01650137	161
162	11.15575183	0.08963986	677.05012192	0.00147700	60.69067619	0.01647700	162
163	11.32308811	0.08831513	688.20587375	0.00145305	60.77899132	0.01645305	163
164	11.49293443	0.08700998	699.52896186	0.00142953	60.86600130	0.01642953	164
165	11.66532844	0.08572412	711.02189629	0.00140643	60.95172542	0.01640643	165
166	11.84030837	0.08445726	722.68722473	0.00138372	61.03618268	0.01638372	166
167	12.01791300	0.08320912	734.52753310	0.00136142	61.11939180	0.01636142	167
168	12.19818169	0.08197943	746.54544610	0.00133950	61.20137124	0.01633950	168
169	12.38115442	0.08076791	758.74362779	0.00131797	61.28213915	0.01631797	169
170	12.56687173	0.07957430	771.12478221	0.00129681	61.36171345	0.01629681	170
171	12.75537481	0.07839832	783.69165394	0.00127601	61.44011177	0.01627601	171
172	12.94670543	0.07723973	796.44702875	0.00125558	61.51735150	0.01625558	172
173	13.14090601	0.07609825	809.39373418	0.00123549	61.59344975	0.01623549	173
174	13.33801960	0.07497365	822.53464019	0.00121575	61.66842340	0.01621575	174
175	13.53808990	0.07386566	835.87265980	0.00119635	61.74228906	0.01619635	175
176	13.74116125	0.07277405	849.41074969	0.00117729	61.81506312	0.01617729	176
177	13.94727866	0.07169857	863.15191094	0.00115854	61.88676169	0.01615854	177
178	14.15648784	0.07063899	877.09918960	0.00114012	61.95740068	0.01614012	178
179	14.36883516	0.06959506	891.25567745	0.00112201	62.02699575	0.01612201	179
180	14.58436769	0.06856657	905.62451261	0.00110421	62.09556231	0.01610421	180
181	14.80313320	0.06755327	920.20888030	0.00108671	62.16311558	0.01608671	181
182	15.02518020	0.06655494	935.01201350	0.00106950	62.22967052	0.01606950	182
183	15.25055791	0.06557137	950.03719370	0.00105259	62.29524189	0.01605259	183
184	15.47931627	0.06460234	965.28775161	0.00103596	62.35984423	0.01603596	184
185	15.71150602	0.06364762	980.76706788	0.00101961	62.42349185	0.01601961	185
186	15.94717861	0.06270702	996.47857390	0.00100353	62.48619887	0.01600353	186
187	16.18638629	0.06178031	1012.42575251	0.00098773	62.54797918	0.01598773	187
188	16.42918208	0.06086730	1028.61213880	0.00097218	62.60884648	0.01597218	188
189	16.67561981	0.05996779	1045.04132088	0.00095690	62.66881427	0.01595690	189
190	16.92575411	0.05908156	1061.71694069	0.00094187	62.72789583	0.01594187	190
191	17.17964042	0.05820844	1078.64269480	0.00092709	62.78610427	0.01592709	191
192	17.43733503	0.05734821	1095.82233523	0.00091256	62.84345248	0.01591256	192
193	17.69889505	0.05650070	1113.25967026	0.00089826	62.89995318	0.01589826	193
194	17.96437848	0.05566572	1130.95856531	0.00088421	62.95561890	0.01588421	194
195	18.23384416	0.05484307	1148.92294379	0.00087038	63.01046197	0.01587038	195
196	18.50735182	0.05403258	1167.15678795	0.00085678	63.06449455	0.01585678	196
197	18.78496210	0.05323407	1185.66413976	0.00084341	63.11772862	0.01584341	197
198	19.06673653	0.05244736	1204.44910186	0.00083026	63.17017598	0.01583026	198
199	19.35273758	0.05167228	1223.51583839	0.00081732	63.22184826	0.01581732	199
200	19.64302864	0.05090865	1242.86857596	0.00080459	63.27275690	0.01580459	200

TABLE A-2

COMPOUND INTEREST FOR $1

$1\frac{1}{2}\%$

PERIODS n	FUTURE AMOUNT $(1+i)^n$	PRESENT VALUE $(1+i)^{-n}$	AMOUNT OF ANNUITY $(S/p,i,n)$ $\dfrac{(1+i)^n-1}{i}$	SINKING FUND $(p/S,i,n)$ $\dfrac{i}{(1+i)^n-1}$	PRESENT VALUE OF ANNUITY $(V/p,i,n)$ $\dfrac{1-(1+i)^{-n}}{i}$	AMORTIZATION $(p/V,i,n)$ $\dfrac{i}{1-(1+i)^{-n}}$	PERIODS n
201	19.93767407	0.05015630	1262.51160460	0.00079207	63.32291321	0.01579207	201
202	20.23673918	0.04941508	1282.44927867	0.00077976	63.37232828	0.01577976	202
203	20.54029027	0.04868480	1302.68601785	0.00076764	63.42101309	0.01576764	203
204	20.84839462	0.04796532	1322.22630812	0.00075573	63.46897841	0.01575573	204
205	21.16112054	0.04725648	1344.07470274	0.00074401	63.51623489	0.01574401	205
206	21.47853735	0.04655811	1365.23582328	0.00073247	63.56279299	0.01573247	206
207	21.80071541	0.04587005	1386.71436063	0.00072113	63.60866305	0.01572113	207
208	22.12772614	0.04519217	1408.51507604	0.00070997	63.65385522	0.01570997	208
209	22.45964203	0.04452431	1430.64280218	0.00069899	63.69837952	0.01569899	209
210	22.79653666	0.04386631	1453.10244422	0.00068818	63.74224584	0.01568818	210
211	23.13848471	0.04321804	1475.89898088	0.00067755	63.78546388	0.01567755	211
212	23.48556198	0.04257935	1499.03746559	0.00066709	63.82804323	0.01566709	212
213	23.83784541	0.04195010	1522.52302758	0.00065680	63.86999333	0.01565680	213
214	24.19541309	0.04133015	1546.36087299	0.00064668	63.91132348	0.01564668	214
215	24.55834429	0.04071936	1570.55628609	0.00063672	63.95204284	0.01563672	215
216	24.92671946	0.04011759	1595.11463038	0.00062691	63.99216043	0.01562691	216
217	25.30062025	0.03952472	1620.04134983	0.00061727	64.03168515	0.01561727	217
218	25.68012955	0.03894061	1645.34197008	0.00060778	64.07062577	0.01560778	218
219	26.06533149	0.03836514	1671.02209963	0.00059844	64.10899090	0.01559844	219
220	26.45631147	0.03779816	1697.08743113	0.00058924	64.14678907	0.01558924	220
221	26.85315614	0.03723957	1723.54374259	0.00058020	64.18402864	0.01558020	221
222	27.25595348	0.03668923	1750.39689873	0.00057130	64.22071787	0.01557130	222
223	27.66479278	0.03614703	1777.65285221	0.00056254	64.25686489	0.01556254	223
224	28.07976467	0.03561283	1805.31764500	0.00055392	64.29247773	0.01555392	224
225	28.50096115	0.03508654	1833.39740967	0.00054544	64.32756426	0.01554544	225
226	28.92847556	0.03456802	1861.89837082	0.00053709	64.36213228	0.01553709	226
227	29.36240270	0.03405716	1890.82684638	0.00052887	64.39618944	0.01552887	227
228	29.80283874	0.03355385	1920.18924907	0.00052078	64.42974329	0.01552078	228
229	30.24988132	0.03305798	1949.99208781	0.00051282	64.46280127	0.01551282	229
230	30.70362954	0.03256944	1980.24196913	0.00050499	64.49537071	0.01550499	230
231	31.16418398	0.03208812	2010.94559866	0.00049728	64.52745883	0.01549728	231
232	31.63164674	0.03161391	2042.10978264	0.00048969	64.55907274	0.01548969	232
233	32.10612144	0.03114671	2073.74142938	0.00048222	64.59021944	0.01548222	233
234	32.58771326	0.03068641	2105.84755082	0.00047487	64.62090586	0.01547487	234
235	33.07652896	0.03023292	2138.43526409	0.00046763	64.65113878	0.01546763	235
236	33.57267690	0.02978613	2171.51179305	0.00046051	64.68092490	0.01546051	236
237	34.07626705	0.02934594	2205.08446994	0.00045350	64.71027084	0.01545350	237
238	34.58741105	0.02891225	2239.16073699	0.00044660	64.73918309	0.01544660	238
239	35.10622222	0.02848498	2273.74814805	0.00043980	64.76766807	0.01543980	239
240	35.63281555	0.02806402	2308.85437027	0.00043312	64.79573209	0.01543312	240

TABLE A-2

COMPOUND INTEREST FOR $1

$1\frac{7}{12}\%$

PERIODS n	FUTURE AMOUNT $(1+i)^n$	PRESENT VALUE $(1+i)^{-n}$	AMOUNT OF ANNUITY $(S/p,i,n)$ $\dfrac{(1+i)^n-1}{i}$	SINKING FUND $(p/S,i,n)$ $\dfrac{i}{(1+i)^n-1}$	PRESENT VALUE OF ANNUITY $(V/p,i,n)$ $\dfrac{1-(1+i)^{-n}}{i}$	AMORTIZATION $(p/V,i,n)$ $\dfrac{i}{1-(1+i)^{-n}}$	PERIODS n
1	1.01583333	0.98441345	1.00000000	1.00000000	0.98441345	1.01583333	1
2	1.03191736	0.96906985	2.01583333	0.49607276	1.95348330	0.51190609	2
3	1.04825605	0.95396540	3.04775069	0.32811083	2.90744870	0.34394416	3
4	1.06485344	0.93909637	4.09600675	0.24414022	3.84654507	0.25997356	4
5	1.08171362	0.92445910	5.16086019	0.19376615	4.77100417	0.20959948	5
6	1.09884075	0.91004998	6.24257381	0.16019034	5.68105414	0.17602367	6
7	1.11623906	0.89586544	7.34141456	0.13621353	6.57691958	0.15204686	7
8	1.13391285	0.88190199	8.45765362	0.11823610	7.45882158	0.13406944	8
9	1.15186647	0.86815619	9.59156647	0.10425826	8.32697776	0.12009159	9
10	1.17010435	0.85462463	10.74343294	0.09308012	9.18160239	0.10891345	10
11	1.18863101	0.84130398	11.91353730	0.08393813	10.02290637	0.09977146	11
12	1.20745100	0.82819096	13.10216830	0.07632324	10.85109733	0.09215658	12
13	1.22656897	0.81528232	14.30961930	0.06988306	11.66637965	0.08571619	13
14	1.24598965	0.80257489	15.53618827	0.06436585	12.46895454	0.08019917	14
15	1.26571782	0.79006552	16.78217792	0.05958702	13.25902006	0.07542036	15
16	1.28575835	0.77775112	18.04789574	0.05540812	14.03677118	0.07124145	16
17	1.30611619	0.76562867	19.33365409	0.05172328	14.80239985	0.06755661	17
18	1.32679636	0.75369516	20.63977028	0.04845015	15.55609501	0.06428348	18
19	1.34780397	0.74194766	21.96656664	0.04552373	16.29804267	0.06135706	19
20	1.36914420	0.73038326	23.31437061	0.04289200	17.02842592	0.05872533	20
21	1.39082232	0.71899910	24.68351481	0.04051287	17.74742503	0.05634620	21
22	1.41284367	0.70779239	26.07433713	0.03835189	18.45521742	0.05418522	22
23	1.43521370	0.69676035	27.48718080	0.03638060	19.15197777	0.05221393	23
24	1.45793791	0.68590026	28.92239450	0.03457528	19.83787803	0.05040862	24
25	1.48102193	0.67520945	30.38033241	0.03291603	20.51308748	0.04874937	25
26	1.50447144	0.66468526	31.86135434	0.03138599	21.17777275	0.04721932	26
27	1.52829224	0.65432512	33.36582578	0.02997079	21.83209786	0.04580412	27
28	1.55249020	0.64412645	34.89411803	0.02865813	22.47622431	0.04449146	28
29	1.57707130	0.63408674	36.44660823	0.02743740	23.11031105	0.04327073	29
30	1.60204159	0.62420352	38.02367953	0.02629940	23.73451457	0.04213273	30
31	1.62740725	0.61447434	39.62572112	0.02523613	24.34898892	0.04106947	31
32	1.65317453	0.60489681	41.25312837	0.02424059	24.95388573	0.04007392	32
33	1.67934980	0.59546856	42.90630290	0.02330660	25.54935428	0.03913993	33
34	1.70593950	0.58618726	44.58565270	0.02242874	26.13554154	0.03826207	34
35	1.73295021	0.57705062	46.29159220	0.02160219	26.71259217	0.03743553	35
36	1.76038859	0.56805640	48.02454241	0.02082269	27.28064856	0.03665602	36
37	1.78826141	0.55920236	49.78493100	0.02008640	27.83985092	0.03591973	37
38	1.81657555	0.55048633	51.57319240	0.01938992	28.39033725	0.03522325	38
39	1.84533799	0.54190615	53.38976795	0.01873018	28.93224340	0.03456351	39
40	1.87455584	0.53345970	55.23510594	0.01810443	29.46570310	0.03393776	40

TABLE A-2

COMPOUND INTEREST FOR $1

$1\frac{7}{12}\%$

PERIODS n	FUTURE AMOUNT $(1+i)^n$	PRESENT VALUE $(1+i)^{-n}$	AMOUNT OF ANNUITY $(S/p,i,n)$ $\dfrac{(1+i)^n - 1}{i}$	SINKING FUND $(p/S,i,n)$ $\dfrac{i}{(1+i)^n - 1}$	PRESENT VALUE OF ANNUITY $(V/p,i,n)$ $\dfrac{1-(1+i)^{-n}}{i}$	AMORTIZATION $(p/V,i,n)$ $\dfrac{i}{1-(1+i)^{-n}}$	PERIODS n
41	1.90423631	0.52514491	57.10966179	0.01751017	29.99084800	0.03334351	41
42	1.93438672	0.51695971	59.01389810	0.01694516	30.50780772	0.03277849	42
43	1.96501451	0.50890209	60.94828482	0.01640735	31.01670981	0.03224069	43
44	1.99612724	0.50097007	62.91329933	0.01589489	31.51767988	0.03172822	44
45	2.02773259	0.49316168	64.90942657	0.01540608	32.01084155	0.03123942	45
46	2.05983835	0.48547499	66.93715915	0.01493939	32.49631654	0.03077272	46
47	2.09245246	0.47790811	68.99699751	0.01449338	32.97422465	0.03032672	47
48	2.12558296	0.47045917	71.08944997	0.01406678	33.44468382	0.02990012	48
49	2.15923802	0.46312634	73.21503293	0.01365840	33.90781016	0.02949173	49
50	2.19342596	0.45590780	75.37427095	0.01326713	34.36371796	0.02910046	50
51	2.22815520	0.44880177	77.56769690	0.01289196	34.81251973	0.02872530	51
52	2.26343432	0.44180650	79.79585210	0.01253198	35.25432623	0.02836531	52
53	2.29927204	0.43492026	82.05928643	0.01218631	35.68924650	0.02801964	53
54	2.33567718	0.42814136	84.35855846	0.01185416	36.11738786	0.02768750	54
55	2.37265873	0.42146811	86.69423564	0.01153479	36.53885597	0.02736813	55
56	2.41022583	0.41489888	89.06689437	0.01122752	36.95375485	0.02706085	56
57	2.44838204	0.40843204	91.47712020	0.01093170	37.36218689	0.02676503	57
58	2.48715388	0.40206600	93.92550794	0.01064674	37.76425289	0.02648007	58
59	2.52653381	0.39579918	96.41266181	0.01037208	38.16005207	0.02620541	59
60	2.56653726	0.38963003	98.93919562	0.01010722	38.54968210	0.02594055	60
61	2.60717410	0.38355705	101.50573289	0.00985166	38.93323915	0.02568499	61
62	2.64845436	0.37757872	104.11290699	0.00960496	39.31081786	0.02543829	62
63	2.69038822	0.37169357	106.76136135	0.00936668	39.68251143	0.02520002	63
64	2.73298603	0.36590015	109.45174957	0.00913645	40.04841158	0.02496978	64
65	2.77625831	0.36019703	112.18473561	0.00891387	40.40860861	0.02474720	65
66	2.82021574	0.35458280	114.96099392	0.00869860	40.76319141	0.02453194	66
67	2.86486915	0.34905608	117.78120966	0.00849032	41.11224750	0.02432365	67
68	2.91022958	0.34361550	120.64607881	0.00828871	41.45586300	0.02412204	68
69	2.95630822	0.33825972	123.55630839	0.00809348	41.79412272	0.02392681	69
70	3.00311643	0.33298742	126.51261661	0.00790435	42.12711014	0.02373768	70
71	3.05066577	0.32779730	129.51573304	0.00772107	42.45490744	0.02355440	71
72	3.09896798	0.32268807	132.56639881	0.00754339	42.77759551	0.02337672	72
73	3.14803497	0.31765848	135.66536679	0.00737108	43.09525399	0.02320441	73
74	3.19787886	0.31270728	138.81340177	0.00720392	43.40796127	0.02303725	74
75	3.24851194	0.30783325	142.01128063	0.00704169	43.71579453	0.02287503	75
76	3.29994672	0.30303520	145.25979257	0.00688422	44.01882972	0.02271755	76
77	3.35219587	0.29831192	148.55973929	0.00673130	44.31714165	0.02256463	77
78	3.40527231	0.29366227	151.91193516	0.00658276	44.61080392	0.02241609	78
79	3.45918912	0.28908509	155.31720747	0.00643844	44.89988901	0.02227177	79
80	3.51395961	0.28457925	158.77639659	0.00629817	45.18446826	0.02213150	80

TABLE A-2

COMPOUND INTEREST FOR $1

$1\frac{7}{12}\%$

PERIODS n	FUTURE AMOUNT $(1+i)^n$	PRESENT VALUE $(1+i)^{-n}$	AMOUNT OF ANNUITY (S/p,i,n) $\dfrac{(1+i)^n - 1}{i}$	SINKING FUND (p/S,i,n) $\dfrac{i}{(1+i)^n - 1}$	PRESENT VALUE OF ANNUITY (V/p,i,n) $\dfrac{1-(1+i)^{-n}}{i}$	AMORTIZATION (p/V,i,n) $\dfrac{i}{1-(1+i)^{-n}}$	PERIODS n
81	3.56959731	0.28014364	162.29035620	0.00616180	45.46461191	0.02199513	81
82	3.62611593	0.27577717	165.85995350	0.00602918	45.74038908	0.02186252	82
83	3.68352943	0.27147876	169.48606943	0.00590019	46.01186784	0.02173352	83
84	3.74185198	0.26724734	173.16959887	0.00577469	46.27911518	0.02160802	84
85	3.80109797	0.26308188	176.91145085	0.00565255	46.54219706	0.02148588	85
86	3.86128202	0.25898134	180.71254882	0.00553365	46.80117840	0.02136698	86
87	3.92241899	0.25494472	184.57383084	0.00541789	47.05612312	0.02125122	87
88	3.98452396	0.25097101	188.49624983	0.00530515	47.30709413	0.02113848	88
89	4.04761225	0.24705924	192.48077379	0.00519532	47.55415337	0.02102866	89
90	4.11169945	0.24320844	196.52838604	0.00508832	47.79736181	0.02092166	90
91	4.17680135	0.23941766	200.64008549	0.00498405	48.03677946	0.02081738	91
92	4.24293404	0.23568596	204.81688684	0.00488241	48.27246543	0.02071574	92
93	4.31011383	0.23201243	209.05982088	0.00478332	48.50447786	0.02061665	93
94	4.37835730	0.22839616	213.36993471	0.00468670	48.73287402	0.02052003	94
95	4.44768129	0.22483625	217.74829201	0.00459246	48.95771028	0.02042579	95
96	4.51810291	0.22133183	222.19597330	0.00450053	49.17904211	0.02033386	96
97	4.58963954	0.21788203	226.71407621	0.00441084	49.39692415	0.02024418	97
98	4.66230883	0.21448601	231.30371575	0.00432332	49.61141015	0.02015665	98
99	4.73612872	0.21114291	235.96602458	0.00423790	49.82255306	0.02007123	99
100	4.81111743	0.20785192	240.70215331	0.00415451	50.03040498	0.01998785	100
101	4.88729345	0.20461223	245.51327073	0.00407310	50.23501721	0.01990643	101
102	4.96467560	0.20142303	250.40056419	0.00399360	50.43644024	0.01982693	102
103	5.04328296	0.19828354	255.36523979	0.00391596	50.63472378	0.01974929	103
104	5.12313494	0.19519298	260.40852275	0.00384012	50.82991676	0.01967345	104
105	5.20425125	0.19215060	265.53165769	0.00376603	51.02206736	0.01959936	105
106	5.28665189	0.18915564	270.73590894	0.00369364	51.21122300	0.01952697	106
107	5.37035721	0.18620735	276.02256083	0.00362289	51.39743035	0.01945623	107
108	5.45538787	0.18330502	281.39291805	0.00355375	51.58073538	0.01938708	108
109	5.54176484	0.18044793	286.84830591	0.00348616	51.76118331	0.01931950	109
110	5.62950945	0.17763537	292.39007076	0.00342009	51.93881868	0.01925342	110
111	5.71864335	0.17486665	298.01958021	0.00335548	52.11368533	0.01918882	111
112	5.80918854	0.17214108	303.73822357	0.00329231	52.28582641	0.01912564	112
113	5.90116736	0.16945800	309.54741211	0.00323052	52.45528441	0.01906386	113
114	5.99460251	0.16681673	315.44857946	0.00317009	52.62210114	0.01900342	114
115	6.08951705	0.16421664	321.44318197	0.00311097	52.78631777	0.01894430	115
116	6.18593440	0.16165707	327.53269902	0.00305313	52.94797484	0.01888646	116
117	6.28387836	0.15913739	333.71863342	0.00299654	53.10711223	0.01882987	117
118	6.38337310	0.15665699	340.00251178	0.00294115	53.26376921	0.01877449	118
119	6.48444318	0.15421525	346.38588489	0.00288695	53.41798446	0.01872029	119
120	6.58711353	0.15181156	352.87032806	0.00283390	53.56979602	0.01866724	120

TABLE A-2

COMPOUND INTEREST FOR $1

$1\frac{7}{12}\%$

PERIODS n	FUTURE AMOUNT $(1+i)^n$	PRESENT VALUE $(1+i)^{-n}$	AMOUNT OF ANNUITY (S/p,i,n) $\dfrac{(1+i)^n-1}{i}$	SINKING FUND (p/S,i,n) $\dfrac{i}{(1+i)^n-1}$	PRESENT VALUE OF ANNUITY (V/p,i,n) $\dfrac{1-(1+i)^{-n}}{i}$	AMORTIZATION (p/V,i,n) $\dfrac{i}{1-(1+i)^{-n}}$	PERIODS n
121	6.69140949	0.14944534	359.45744159	0.00278197	53.71924137	0.01861530	121
122	6.79735681	0.14711601	366.14885108	0.00273113	53.86635738	0.01856446	122
123	6.90498162	0.14482298	372.94620789	0.00268135	54.01118035	0.01851469	123
124	7.01431050	0.14256569	379.85118952	0.00263261	54.15374604	0.01846594	124
125	7.12537042	0.14034358	386.86550002	0.00258488	54.29408962	0.01841821	125
126	7.23818878	0.13815611	393.99087043	0.00253813	54.43224573	0.01837146	126
127	7.35279344	0.13600273	401.22905922	0.00249234	54.56824847	0.01832568	127
128	7.46921267	0.13388292	408.58185265	0.00244749	54.70213139	0.01828082	128
129	7.58747520	0.13179615	416.05106532	0.00240355	54.83392753	0.01823688	129
130	7.70761022	0.12974190	423.63854052	0.00236050	54.96366943	0.01819384	130
131	7.82964739	0.12771967	431.34615075	0.00231832	55.09138911	0.01815166	131
132	7.95361680	0.12572896	439.17579813	0.00227699	55.21711807	0.01811033	132
133	8.07954907	0.12376928	447.12941494	0.00223649	55.34088735	0.01806982	133
134	8.20747526	0.12184015	455.20896401	0.00219679	55.46272750	0.01803013	134
135	8.33742696	0.11994108	463.41643927	0.00215789	55.58266858	0.01799122	135
136	8.46943622	0.11807161	471.75386623	0.00211975	55.70074020	0.01795308	136
137	8.60353562	0.11623128	480.22330244	0.00208236	55.81697148	0.01791570	137
138	8.73975827	0.11441964	488.82683806	0.00204571	55.93139112	0.01787905	138
139	8.87813778	0.11263623	497.56659633	0.00200978	56.04402735	0.01784311	139
140	9.01870829	0.11088062	506.44473411	0.00197455	56.15490798	0.01780788	140
141	9.16150450	0.10915238	515.46344240	0.00194000	56.26406036	0.01777334	141
142	9.30656166	0.10745107	524.62494690	0.00190612	56.37151142	0.01773946	142
143	9.45391555	0.10577628	533.93150856	0.00187290	56.47728770	0.01770623	143
144	9.60360255	0.10412759	543.38542411	0.00184031	56.58141529	0.01767365	144
145	9.75565959	0.10250460	552.98902666	0.00180835	56.68391990	0.01764169	145
146	9.91012420	0.10090691	562.74468625	0.00177700	56.78482680	0.01761034	146
147	10.06703450	0.09933412	572.65481045	0.00174625	56.88416092	0.01757959	147
148	10.22642921	0.09778584	582.72184495	0.00171608	56.98194677	0.01754942	148
149	10.38834767	0.09626170	592.94827416	0.00168649	57.07820847	0.01751982	149
150	10.55282985	0.09476131	603.33662184	0.00165745	57.17296978	0.01749078	150
151	10.71991632	0.09328431	613.88945168	0.00162896	57.26625409	0.01746229	151
152	10.88964833	0.09183033	624.60936800	0.00160100	57.35808442	0.01743433	152
153	11.06206776	0.09039901	635.49901633	0.00157357	57.44848343	0.01740690	153
154	11.23721716	0.08898900	646.56108408	0.00154664	57.53747343	0.01737998	154
155	11.41513977	0.08760296	657.79830125	0.00152022	57.62507639	0.01735356	155
156	11.59587948	0.08623753	669.21344102	0.00149429	57.71131392	0.01732762	156
157	11.77948091	0.08489338	680.80932050	0.00146884	57.79620731	0.01730217	157
158	11.96598936	0.08357019	692.58880141	0.00144386	57.87977749	0.01727719	158
159	12.15545085	0.08226762	704.55479077	0.00141934	57.96204511	0.01725267	159
160	12.34791216	0.08098535	716.71024162	0.00139526	58.04303046	0.01722860	160

COMPOUND INTEREST FOR $1

$1\frac{7}{12}\%$

PERIODS n	FUTURE AMOUNT $(1+i)^n$	PRESENT VALUE $(1+i)^{-n}$	AMOUNT OF ANNUITY $(S/p,i,n)$ $\dfrac{(1+i)^n - 1}{i}$	SINKING FUND $(p/S,i,n)$ $\dfrac{i}{(1+i)^n - 1}$	PRESENT VALUE OF ANNUITY $(V/p,i,n)$ $\dfrac{1-(1+i)^{-n}}{i}$	AMORTIZATION $(p/V,i,n)$ $\dfrac{i}{1-(1+i)^{-n}}$	PERIODS n
161	12.54342077	0.07972307	729.05815378	0.00137163	58.12275353	0.01720497	161
162	12.74202493	0.07848046	741.60157455	0.00134843	58.20123400	0.01718177	162
163	12.94377366	0.07725722	754.34359948	0.00132566	58.27849122	0.01715899	163
164	13.14871674	0.07605305	767.28737314	0.00130329	58.35454427	0.01713663	164
165	13.35690476	0.07486764	780.43608988	0.00128133	58.42941191	0.01711467	165
166	13.56838908	0.07370072	793.79299463	0.00125977	58.50311263	0.01709311	166
167	13.78322191	0.07255198	807.36138371	0.00123860	58.57566461	0.01707194	167
168	14.00145626	0.07142114	821.14460562	0.00121781	58.64708575	0.01705115	168
169	14.22314598	0.07030793	835.14606188	0.00119740	58.71739368	0.01703073	169
170	14.44834579	0.06921208	849.36920786	0.00117734	58.78660576	0.01701068	170
171	14.67711127	0.06813330	863.81755365	0.00115765	58.85473906	0.01699099	171
172	14.90949886	0.06707134	878.49466492	0.00113831	58.92181039	0.01697164	172
173	15.14556593	0.06602593	893.40416378	0.00111931	58.98783632	0.01695265	173
174	15.38537072	0.06499681	908.54972970	0.00110066	59.05283312	0.01693399	174
175	15.62897242	0.06398373	923.93510042	0.00108233	59.11681686	0.01691566	175
176	15.87643115	0.06298645	939.56407285	0.00106432	59.17980331	0.01689766	176
177	16.12780798	0.06200471	955.44050400	0.00104664	59.24180801	0.01687997	177
178	16.38316494	0.06103827	971.56831198	0.00102926	59.30284628	0.01686260	178
179	16.64256505	0.06008689	987.95147692	0.00101220	59.36293317	0.01684553	179
180	16.90607233	0.05915034	1004.59404197	0.00099543	59.42208351	0.01682876	180
181	17.17375181	0.05822839	1021.50011430	0.00097895	59.48031191	0.01681229	181
182	17.44566955	0.05732082	1038.67386611	0.00096277	59.53763272	0.01679610	182
183	17.72189265	0.05642738	1056.11953566	0.00094686	59.59406011	0.01678020	183
184	18.00248928	0.05554787	1073.84142831	0.00093124	59.64960798	0.01676457	184
185	18.28752870	0.05468207	1091.84391759	0.00091588	59.70429005	0.01674922	185
186	18.57708123	0.05382977	1110.13144628	0.00090079	59.75811982	0.01673413	186
187	18.87121835	0.05299075	1128.70852752	0.00088597	59.81111057	0.01671930	187
188	19.17001264	0.05216481	1147.57974587	0.00087140	59.86327538	0.01670473	188
189	19.47353784	0.05135174	1166.74975851	0.00085708	59.91462712	0.01669042	189
190	19.78186886	0.05055134	1186.22329636	0.00084301	59.96517846	0.01667634	190
191	20.09508178	0.04976342	1206.00516521	0.00082918	60.01494188	0.01666252	191
192	20.41325391	0.04898778	1226.10024700	0.00081559	60.06392966	0.01664893	192
193	20.73646376	0.04822423	1246.51350091	0.00080224	60.11215389	0.01663557	193
194	21.06479111	0.04747258	1267.24996467	0.00078911	60.15962647	0.01662244	194
195	21.39831697	0.04673265	1288.31475578	0.00077621	60.20635912	0.01660954	195
196	21.73712365	0.04600425	1309.71307275	0.00076353	60.25236336	0.01659686	196
197	22.08129478	0.04528720	1331.45019640	0.00075106	60.29765056	0.01658439	197
198	22.43091528	0.04458133	1353.53149117	0.00073881	60.34223189	0.01657214	198
199	22.78607144	0.04388646	1375.96240645	0.00072676	60.38611835	0.01656010	199
200	23.14685090	0.04320242	1398.74847789	0.00071492	60.42932077	0.01654826	200

COMPOUND INTEREST FOR $1

$1\frac{7}{12}$ %

PERIODS n	FUTURE AMOUNT $(1+i)^n$	PRESENT VALUE $(1+i)^{-n}$	AMOUNT OF ANNUITY $(S/p,i,n)$ $\dfrac{(1+i)^n - 1}{i}$	SINKING FUND $(p/S,i,n)$ $\dfrac{i}{(1+i)^n - 1}$	PRESENT VALUE OF ANNUITY $(V/p,i,n)$ $\dfrac{1-(1+i)^{-n}}{i}$	AMORTIZATION $(p/V,i,n)$ $\dfrac{i}{1-(1+i)^{-n}}$	PERIODS n
201	23.51334271	0.04252904	1421.89532879	0.00070329	60.47184982	0.01653662	201
202	23.88563730	0.04186616	1445.40867149	0.00069185	60.51371598	0.01652518	202
203	24.26382656	0.04121361	1469.29430879	0.00068060	60.55492959	0.01651393	203
204	24.64800381	0.04057124	1493.55813535	0.00066954	60.59550083	0.01650288	204
205	25.03826387	0.03993887	1518.20613916	0.00065867	60.63543970	0.01649201	205
206	25.43470305	0.03931636	1543.24440303	0.00064799	60.67475607	0.01648132	206
207	25.83741918	0.03870356	1568.67910607	0.00063748	60.71345962	0.01647081	207
208	26.24651165	0.03810030	1594.51652525	0.00062715	60.75155992	0.01646048	208
209	26.66208142	0.03750645	1620.76303690	0.00061699	60.78906637	0.01645033	209
210	27.08423104	0.03692185	1647.42511832	0.00060701	60.82598822	0.01644034	210
211	27.51306470	0.03634637	1674.50934936	0.00059719	60.86233459	0.01643052	211
212	27.94868822	0.03577985	1702.02241406	0.00058754	60.89811445	0.01642087	212
213	28.39120912	0.03522217	1729.97110228	0.00057804	60.93333662	0.01641138	213
214	28.84073660	0.03467318	1758.36231140	0.00056871	60.96800980	0.01640204	214
215	29.29738159	0.03413274	1787.20304800	0.00055953	61.00214254	0.01639287	215
216	29.76125680	0.03360073	1816.50042959	0.00055051	61.03574327	0.01638384	216
217	30.23247670	0.03307701	1846.26168639	0.00054164	61.06882028	0.01637497	217
218	30.71115758	0.03256146	1876.49416309	0.00053291	61.10138174	0.01636624	218
219	31.19741758	0.03205394	1907.20532068	0.00052433	61.13343567	0.01635766	219
220	31.69137669	0.03155433	1938.40273825	0.00051589	61.16499000	0.01634922	220
221	32.19315682	0.03106250	1970.09411494	0.00050759	61.19605250	0.01634092	221
222	32.70288180	0.03057834	2002.28727176	0.00049943	61.22663085	0.01633276	222
223	33.22067743	0.03010173	2034.99015357	0.00049140	61.25673258	0.01632474	223
224	33.74667149	0.02963255	2068.21083100	0.00048351	61.28636513	0.01631684	224
225	34.28099379	0.02917068	2101.95750249	0.00047575	61.31553582	0.01630908	225
226	34.82377619	0.02871601	2136.23849628	0.00046811	61.34425183	0.01630145	226
227	35.37515265	0.02826843	2171.06227247	0.00046060	61.37252026	0.01629394	227
228	35.93525923	0.02782782	2206.43742512	0.00045322	61.40034808	0.01628655	228
229	36.50423417	0.02739408	2242.37268435	0.00044596	61.42774216	0.01627929	229
230	37.08221788	0.02696710	2278.87691852	0.00043881	61.45470927	0.01627215	230
231	37.66935299	0.02654678	2315.95913639	0.00043179	61.48125604	0.01626512	231
232	38.26578442	0.02613301	2353.62848939	0.00042488	61.50738905	0.01625821	232
233	38.87165934	0.02572568	2391.89427380	0.00041808	61.53311473	0.01625141	233
234	39.48712727	0.02532471	2430.76593314	0.00041139	61.55843944	0.01624473	234
235	40.11234012	0.02492998	2470.25306041	0.00040482	61.58336943	0.01623815	235
236	40.74745218	0.02454141	2510.36540053	0.00039835	61.60791084	0.01623168	236
237	41.39262017	0.02415890	2551.11285271	0.00039199	61.63206974	0.01622532	237
238	42.04800332	0.02378234	2592.50547288	0.00038573	61.65585208	0.01621906	238
239	42.71376337	0.02341166	2634.55347620	0.00037957	61.67926373	0.01621290	239
240	43.39006463	0.02304675	2677.26723957	0.00037352	61.70231049	0.01620685	240

TABLE A-2

COMPOUND INTEREST FOR $1

$1\frac{2}{3}\%$

PERIODS n	FUTURE AMOUNT $(1+i)^n$	PRESENT VALUE $(1+i)^{-n}$	AMOUNT OF ANNUITY (S/p,i,n) $\dfrac{(1+i)^n-1}{i}$	SINKING FUND (p/S,i,n) $\dfrac{i}{(1+i)^n-1}$	PRESENT VALUE OF ANNUITY (V/p,i,n) $\dfrac{1-(1+i)^{-n}}{i}$	AMORTIZATION (p/V,i,n) $\dfrac{i}{1-(1+i)^{-n}}$	PERIODS n
1	1.01666667	0.98360656	1.00000000	1.00000000	0.98360656	1.01666667	1
2	1.03361111	0.96748186	2.01666667	0.49586777	1.95108842	0.51253444	2
3	1.05083796	0.95162150	3.05027778	0.32783899	2.90270992	0.34450566	3
4	1.06835193	0.93602115	4.10111574	0.24383608	3.83873107	0.26050275	4
5	1.08615779	0.92067654	5.16946767	0.19344352	4.75940761	0.21011018	5
6	1.10426042	0.90558348	6.25562546	0.15985612	5.66499109	0.17652278	6
7	1.12266476	0.89073785	7.35988589	0.13587167	6.55572894	0.15253834	7
8	1.14137584	0.87613559	8.48255065	0.11788907	7.43186453	0.13455574	8
9	1.16039877	0.86177271	9.62392650	0.10390769	8.29363724	0.12057436	9
10	1.17973875	0.84764529	10.78432527	0.09272717	9.14128253	0.10939384	10
11	1.19940107	0.83374947	11.96406403	0.08358364	9.97503200	0.10025030	11
12	1.21939108	0.82008144	13.16346509	0.07596784	10.79511344	0.09263451	12
13	1.23971427	0.80663748	14.38285618	0.06952722	11.60175093	0.08619389	13
14	1.26037617	0.79341392	15.62257045	0.06400995	12.39516485	0.08067662	14
15	1.28138244	0.78040713	16.88294662	0.05923137	13.17557198	0.07589803	15
16	1.30273882	0.76761357	18.16432907	0.05505296	13.94318556	0.07171962	16
17	1.32445113	0.75502974	19.46706788	0.05136880	14.69821530	0.06803547	17
18	1.34652532	0.74265221	20.79151902	0.04809653	15.44086751	0.06476320	18
19	1.36896741	0.73047758	22.13804433	0.04517111	16.17134509	0.06183778	19
20	1.39178353	0.71850254	23.50701174	0.04254050	16.88984763	0.05920717	20
21	1.41497992	0.70672381	24.89799527	0.04016259	17.59657144	0.05682925	21
22	1.43856292	0.69513817	26.31377519	0.03800291	18.29170961	0.05466958	22
23	1.46253897	0.68374247	27.75233811	0.03603300	18.97545208	0.05269967	23
24	1.48691462	0.67253357	29.21487708	0.03422914	19.64798565	0.05089580	24
25	1.51169653	0.66150843	30.70179169	0.03257137	20.30949408	0.04923806	25
26	1.53689147	0.65066403	32.21348822	0.03104290	20.96015811	0.04770956	26
27	1.56250633	0.63999741	33.75037969	0.02962930	21.60015552	0.04629596	27
28	1.58854810	0.62950565	35.31288602	0.02831827	22.22966117	0.04498494	28
29	1.61502390	0.61918588	36.90143412	0.02709922	22.84884705	0.04376588	29
30	1.64194097	0.60903529	38.51645802	0.02596293	23.45788235	0.04262959	30
31	1.66930665	0.59905111	40.15839899	0.02490139	24.05693345	0.04156806	31
32	1.69712843	0.58923060	41.82770564	0.02390760	24.64616405	0.04057427	32
33	1.72541390	0.57957108	43.52483407	0.02297539	25.22573513	0.03964206	33
34	1.75417080	0.57006992	45.25024797	0.02209933	25.79580505	0.03876599	34
35	1.78340698	0.56072451	47.00441877	0.02127460	26.35652956	0.03794126	35
36	1.81313043	0.55153230	48.78782575	0.02049692	26.90806184	0.03716358	36
37	1.84334927	0.54249079	50.60095618	0.01976247	27.45055265	0.03642914	37
38	1.87407176	0.53359750	52.44430545	0.01906785	27.98415015	0.03573451	38
39	1.90530629	0.52485000	54.31837720	0.01840998	28.50900014	0.03507664	39
40	1.93706139	0.51624590	56.22368349	0.01778610	29.02524604	0.03445277	40

TABLE A-2

COMPOUND INTEREST FOR $1

$1\frac{2}{3}\%$

PERIODS n	FUTURE AMOUNT $(1+i)^n$	PRESENT VALUE $(1+i)^{-n}$	AMOUNT OF ANNUITY (S/p,i,n) $\frac{(1+i)^n - 1}{i}$	SINKING FUND (p/S,i,n) $\frac{i}{(1+i)^n - 1}$	PRESENT VALUE OF ANNUITY (V/p,i,n) $\frac{1-(1+i)^{-n}}{i}$	AMORTIZATION (p/V,i,n) $\frac{i}{1-(1+i)^{-n}}$	PERIODS n
41	1.96934575	0.50778285	58.16074488	0.01719373	29.53302890	0.03386039	41
42	2.00216818	0.49945854	60.13009063	0.01663061	30.03248744	0.03329728	42
43	2.03553765	0.49127070	62.13225881	0.01609470	30.52375814	0.03276137	43
44	2.06946327	0.48321708	64.16779645	0.01558414	31.00697522	0.03225081	44
45	2.10395433	0.47529549	66.23725973	0.01509724	31.48227070	0.03176391	45
46	2.13902023	0.46750376	68.34121406	0.01463246	31.94977446	0.03129913	46
47	2.17467057	0.45983976	70.48023429	0.01418838	32.40961423	0.03085504	47
48	2.21091508	0.45230141	72.65490486	0.01376370	32.86191563	0.03043036	48
49	2.24776367	0.44488663	74.86581994	0.01335723	33.30680226	0.03002390	49
50	2.28522639	0.43759341	77.11358361	0.01296788	33.74439567	0.02963455	50
51	2.32331350	0.43041974	79.39881000	0.01259465	34.17481541	0.02926131	51
52	2.36203539	0.42336368	81.72212350	0.01223659	34.59817909	0.02890326	52
53	2.40140265	0.41642329	84.08415890	0.01189285	35.01460239	0.02855951	53
54	2.44142603	0.40959668	86.48556154	0.01156262	35.42419907	0.02822929	54
55	2.48211646	0.40288198	88.92698757	0.01124518	35.82708105	0.02791185	55
56	2.52348507	0.39627736	91.40910403	0.01093983	36.22335841	0.02760650	56
57	2.56554315	0.38978101	93.93258910	0.01064593	36.61313942	0.02731260	57
58	2.60830220	0.38339116	96.49813225	0.01036289	36.99653058	0.02702956	58
59	2.65177391	0.37710606	99.10643445	0.01009016	37.37363663	0.02675683	59
60	2.69597014	0.37092399	101.75820836	0.00982722	37.74456062	0.02649388	60
61	2.74090297	0.36484327	104.45417850	0.00957358	38.10940389	0.02624024	61
62	2.78658469	0.35886223	107.19508147	0.00932879	38.46826612	0.02599545	62
63	2.83302777	0.35297924	109.98166617	0.00909242	38.82124537	0.02575909	63
64	2.88024490	0.34719270	112.81469393	0.00886409	39.16843806	0.02553076	64
65	2.92824898	0.34150102	115.69493883	0.00864342	39.50993908	0.02531009	65
66	2.97705313	0.33590264	118.62318781	0.00843006	39.84584172	0.02509672	66
67	3.02667068	0.33039604	121.60024094	0.00822367	40.17623776	0.02489033	67
68	3.07711519	0.32497971	124.62691163	0.00802395	40.50121746	0.02469062	68
69	3.12840045	0.31965217	127.70402682	0.00783061	40.82086964	0.02449727	69
70	3.18054045	0.31441197	130.83242727	0.00764337	41.13528161	0.02431003	70
71	3.23354946	0.30925768	134.01296772	0.00746196	41.44453929	0.02412863	71
72	3.28744195	0.30418788	137.24651718	0.00728616	41.74872717	0.02395283	72
73	3.34223265	0.29920119	140.53395914	0.00711572	42.04792836	0.02378238	73
74	3.39793653	0.29429626	143.87619179	0.00695042	42.34222462	0.02361709	74
75	3.45456881	0.28947173	147.27412832	0.00679006	42.63169635	0.02345673	75
76	3.51214495	0.28472629	150.72869712	0.00663444	42.91642264	0.02330110	76
77	3.57068070	0.28005865	154.24084208	0.00648337	43.19648128	0.02315003	77
78	3.63019205	0.27546752	157.81152278	0.00633667	43.47194880	0.02300334	78
79	3.69069525	0.27095166	161.44171482	0.00619419	43.74290046	0.02286085	79
80	3.75220683	0.26650983	165.13241007	0.00605575	44.00941029	0.02272241	80

TABLE A-2

COMPOUND INTEREST FOR $1

1⅓%

PERIODS n	FUTURE AMOUNT $(1+i)^n$	PRESENT VALUE $(1+i)^{-n}$	AMOUNT OF ANNUITY $(S/p,i,n)$ $\dfrac{(1+i)^n-1}{i}$	SINKING FUND $(p/S,i,n)$ $\dfrac{i}{(1+i)^n-1}$	PRESENT VALUE OF ANNUITY $(V/p,i,n)$ $\dfrac{1-(1+i)^{-n}}{i}$	AMORTIZATION $(p/V,i,n)$ $\dfrac{i}{1-(1+i)^{-n}}$	PERIODS n
81	3.81474362	0.26214081	168.88461691	0.00592120	44.27155110	0.02258787	81
82	3.87832268	0.25784342	172.69936052	0.00579041	44.52939453	0.02245708	82
83	3.94296139	0.25361648	176.57768320	0.00566323	44.78301101	0.02232990	83
84	4.00867741	0.24945884	180.52064458	0.00553953	45.03246985	0.02220620	84
85	4.07548870	0.24536935	184.52932199	0.00541919	45.27783919	0.02208586	85
86	4.14341351	0.24134690	188.60481069	0.00530209	45.51918609	0.02196876	86
87	4.21247040	0.23739039	192.74822420	0.00518812	45.75657649	0.02185478	87
88	4.28267824	0.23349875	196.96069461	0.00507716	45.99007523	0.02174382	88
89	4.35405621	0.22967090	201.24337285	0.00496911	46.21974613	0.02163577	89
90	4.42662382	0.22590580	205.59742907	0.00486387	46.44565193	0.02153054	90
91	4.50040088	0.22220243	210.02405288	0.00476136	46.66785436	0.02142803	91
92	4.57540756	0.21855976	214.52445376	0.00466147	46.88641412	0.02132814	92
93	4.65166436	0.21497682	219.09986133	0.00456413	47.10139094	0.02123080	93
94	4.72919209	0.21145261	223.75152568	0.00446924	47.31284355	0.02113591	94
95	4.80801196	0.20798617	228.48071778	0.00437674	47.52082972	0.02104340	95
96	4.88814550	0.20457656	233.28872974	0.00428653	47.72540628	0.02095320	96
97	4.96961459	0.20122285	238.17687524	0.00419856	47.92662913	0.02086523	97
98	5.05244150	0.19792411	243.14648982	0.00411275	48.12455324	0.02077941	98
99	5.13664886	0.19467946	248.19893132	0.00402903	48.31923270	0.02069569	99
100	5.22225967	0.19148799	253.33558018	0.00394733	48.51072068	0.02061400	100
101	5.30929733	0.18834884	258.55783985	0.00386761	48.69906953	0.02053427	101
102	5.39778562	0.18526116	263.86713718	0.00378979	48.88433068	0.02045645	102
103	5.48774871	0.18222409	269.26492280	0.00371381	49.06655477	0.02038048	103
104	5.57921119	0.17923681	274.75267151	0.00363964	49.24579158	0.02030630	104
105	5.67219805	0.17629850	280.33188270	0.00356720	49.42209007	0.02023387	105
106	5.76673468	0.17340836	286.00408075	0.00349645	49.59549843	0.02016312	106
107	5.86284692	0.17056560	291.77081542	0.00342735	49.76606403	0.02009401	107
108	5.96056104	0.16776944	297.63366235	0.00335984	49.93383348	0.02002650	108
109	6.05990372	0.16501912	303.59422339	0.00329387	50.09885260	0.01996054	109
110	6.16090212	0.16231389	309.65412711	0.00322941	50.26116649	0.01989608	110
111	6.26358382	0.15965301	315.81502923	0.00316641	50.42081950	0.01983308	111
112	6.36797688	0.15703575	322.07861305	0.00310483	50.57785524	0.01977150	112
113	6.47410983	0.15446139	328.44658993	0.00304464	50.73231663	0.01971130	113
114	6.58201166	0.15192924	334.92069977	0.00298578	50.88424587	0.01965245	114
115	6.69171186	0.14943859	341.50271143	0.00292823	51.03368446	0.01959490	115
116	6.80324039	0.14698878	348.19442329	0.00287196	51.18067324	0.01953863	116
117	6.91662773	0.14457913	354.99766367	0.00281692	51.32525237	0.01948359	117
118	7.03190486	0.14220898	361.91429140	0.00276309	51.46746135	0.01942975	118
119	7.14910327	0.13987768	368.94619626	0.00271042	51.60733903	0.01937709	119
120	7.26825499	0.13758461	376.09529953	0.00265890	51.74492364	0.01932557	120

TABLE A-2

COMPOUND INTEREST FOR $1

$1\frac{2}{3}\%$

PERIODS n	FUTURE AMOUNT $(1+i)^n$	PRESENT VALUE $(1+i)^{-n}$	AMOUNT OF ANNUITY $(S/p,i,n)$ $\dfrac{(1+i)^n-1}{i}$	SINKING FUND $(p/S,i,n)$ $\dfrac{i}{(1+i)^n-1}$	PRESENT VALUE OF ANNUITY $(V/p,i,n)$ $\dfrac{1-(1+i)^{-n}}{i}$	AMORTIZATION $(p/V,i,n)$ $\dfrac{i}{1-(1+i)^{-n}}$	PERIODS n
121	7.38939258	0.13532912	383.36355452	0.00260849	51.88025276	0.01927516	121
122	7.51254912	0.13311061	390.75294710	0.00255916	52.01336337	0.01922583	122
123	7.63775827	0.13092847	398.26549622	0.00251089	52.14429184	0.01917755	123
124	7.76505424	0.12878210	405.90325449	0.00246364	52.27307394	0.01913031	124
125	7.89447181	0.12667092	413.66830873	0.00241740	52.39974486	0.01908406	125
126	8.02604634	0.12459435	421.56278054	0.00237213	52.52433920	0.01903879	126
127	8.15981378	0.12255182	429.58882688	0.00232781	52.64689102	0.01899447	127
128	8.29581068	0.12054277	437.74864066	0.00228442	52.76743379	0.01895108	128
129	8.43407419	0.11856666	446.04445134	0.00224193	52.88600045	0.01890860	129
130	8.57464209	0.11662294	454.47852553	0.00220032	53.00262339	0.01886699	130
131	8.71755279	0.11471109	463.05316762	0.00215958	53.11733448	0.01882625	131
132	8.86284534	0.11283058	471.77072042	0.00211967	53.23016507	0.01878634	132
133	9.01055943	0.11098090	480.63356576	0.00208059	53.34114597	0.01874725	133
134	9.16073542	0.10916154	489.64412519	0.00204230	53.45030751	0.01870897	134
135	9.31341434	0.10737201	498.80486060	0.00200479	53.55767952	0.01867146	135
136	9.46863792	0.10561181	508.11827495	0.00196805	53.66329133	0.01863471	136
137	9.62644855	0.10388047	517.58691286	0.00193204	53.76717180	0.01859871	137
138	9.78688936	0.10217751	527.21336141	0.00189677	53.86934931	0.01856343	138
139	9.95000418	0.10050247	537.00025077	0.00186220	53.96985178	0.01852886	139
140	10.11583758	0.09885489	546.95025495	0.00182832	54.06870667	0.01849499	140
141	10.28443488	0.09723432	557.06609253	0.00179512	54.16594098	0.01846179	141
142	10.45584212	0.09564031	567.35052741	0.00176258	54.26158130	0.01842925	142
143	10.63010616	0.09407244	577.80636953	0.00173068	54.35565373	0.01839735	143
144	10.80727459	0.09253027	588.43647569	0.00169942	54.44818400	0.01836609	144
145	10.98739584	0.09101338	599.24375028	0.00166877	54.53919738	0.01833544	145
146	11.17051910	0.08952135	610.23114612	0.00163872	54.62871873	0.01830539	146
147	11.35669442	0.08805379	621.40166522	0.00160927	54.71677252	0.01827593	147
148	11.54597266	0.08661029	632.75835964	0.00158038	54.80338281	0.01824705	148
149	11.73840554	0.08519045	644.30433230	0.00155206	54.88857326	0.01821873	149
150	11.93404563	0.08379388	656.04273784	0.00152429	54.97236714	0.01819096	150
151	12.13294639	0.08242021	667.97678347	0.00149706	55.05478735	0.01816372	151
152	12.33516216	0.08106906	680.10972986	0.00147035	55.13585641	0.01813702	152
153	12.54074820	0.07974006	692.44489203	0.00144416	55.21559647	0.01811082	153
154	12.74976067	0.07843284	704.98564023	0.00141847	55.29402931	0.01808514	154
155	12.96225668	0.07714706	717.73540090	0.00139327	55.37117637	0.01805994	155
156	13.17829429	0.07588235	730.69765758	0.00136856	55.44705873	0.01803522	156
157	13.39793253	0.07463838	743.87595187	0.00134431	55.52169711	0.01801098	157
158	13.62123141	0.07341480	757.27388441	0.00132053	55.59511191	0.01798719	158
159	13.84825193	0.07221128	770.89511581	0.00129719	55.66732319	0.01796386	159
160	14.07905613	0.07102749	784.74336774	0.00127430	55.73835068	0.01794097	160

TABLE A-2

COMPOUND INTEREST FOR $1

$1\frac{2}{3}\%$

PERIODS n	FUTURE AMOUNT $(1+i)^n$	PRESENT VALUE $(1+i)^{-n}$	AMOUNT OF ANNUITY $(S/p,i,n)$ $\dfrac{(1+i)^n-1}{i}$	SINKING FUND $(p/S,i,n)$ $\dfrac{i}{(1+i)^n-1}$	PRESENT VALUE OF ANNUITY $(V/p,i,n)$ $\dfrac{1-(1+i)^{-n}}{i}$	AMORTIZATION $(p/V,i,n)$ $\dfrac{i}{1-(1+i)^{-n}}$	PERIODS n
161	14.31370706	0.06986310	798.82242387	0.00125184	55.80821378	0.01791851	161
162	14.55226885	0.06871781	813.13613094	0.00122981	55.87693159	0.01789647	162
163	14.79480666	0.06759129	827.68839979	0.00120818	55.94452287	0.01787485	163
164	15.04138677	0.06648323	842.48320645	0.00118697	56.01100611	0.01785363	164
165	15.29207655	0.06539334	857.52459322	0.00116615	56.07639945	0.01783281	165
166	15.54694450	0.06432132	872.81666978	0.00114572	56.14072077	0.01781238	166
167	15.80606024	0.06326687	888.36361427	0.00112567	56.20398764	0.01779233	167
168	16.06949458	0.06222971	904.16967451	0.00110599	56.26621735	0.01777265	168
169	16.33731948	0.06120955	920.23916909	0.00108667	56.32742690	0.01775334	169
170	16.60960814	0.06020612	936.57648857	0.00106772	56.38763302	0.01773439	170
171	16.88643495	0.05921913	953.18609671	0.00104911	56.44685215	0.01771578	171
172	17.16787553	0.05824833	970.07253166	0.00103085	56.50510048	0.01769752	172
173	17.45400679	0.05729343	987.24040719	0.00101292	56.56239391	0.01767959	173
174	17.74490690	0.05635420	1004.69441397	0.00099533	56.61874811	0.01766199	174
175	18.04065535	0.05543036	1022.43932087	0.00097805	56.67417847	0.01764472	175
176	18.34133294	0.05452166	1040.47997622	0.00096109	56.72870013	0.01762776	176
177	18.64702182	0.05362787	1058.82130916	0.00094445	56.78232800	0.01761111	177
178	18.95780552	0.05274872	1077.46833098	0.00092810	56.83507672	0.01759477	178
179	19.27376894	0.05188399	1096.42613649	0.00091205	56.88696071	0.01757872	179
180	19.59499842	0.05103343	1115.69990543	0.00089630	56.93799414	0.01756297	180
181	19.92158173	0.05019682	1135.29490386	0.00088083	56.98819096	0.01754750	181
182	20.25360809	0.04937392	1155.21648559	0.00086564	57.03756488	0.01753231	182
183	20.59116823	0.04856451	1175.47009368	0.00085072	57.08612939	0.01751739	183
184	20.93435437	0.04776837	1196.06126191	0.00083608	57.13389776	0.01750274	184
185	21.28326027	0.04698528	1216.99561628	0.00082170	57.18088304	0.01748836	185
186	21.63798128	0.04621503	1238.27887655	0.00080757	57.22709807	0.01747424	186
187	21.99861430	0.04545741	1259.91685782	0.00079370	57.27255548	0.01746037	187
188	22.36525787	0.04471221	1281.91547212	0.00078008	57.31726769	0.01744675	188
189	22.73801217	0.04397922	1304.28072999	0.00076671	57.36124690	0.01743337	189
190	23.11697904	0.04325825	1327.01874215	0.00075357	57.40450515	0.01742024	190
191	23.50226202	0.04254910	1350.13572119	0.00074067	57.44705425	0.01740733	191
192	23.89396639	0.04185157	1373.63798321	0.00072799	57.48890582	0.01739466	192
193	24.29219916	0.04116548	1397.53194960	0.00071555	57.53007130	0.01738221	193
194	24.69706915	0.04049063	1421.82414876	0.00070332	57.57056193	0.01736999	194
195	25.10868697	0.03982685	1446.52121790	0.00069131	57.61038878	0.01735798	195
196	25.52716508	0.03917395	1471.62990487	0.00067952	57.64956274	0.01734619	196
197	25.95261783	0.03853176	1497.15706995	0.00066793	57.68809450	0.01733460	197
198	26.38516146	0.03790009	1523.10968778	0.00065655	57.72599459	0.01732322	198
199	26.82491415	0.03727878	1549.49484924	0.00064537	57.76327336	0.01731204	199
200	27.27199606	0.03666765	1576.31976340	0.00063439	57.79994101	0.01730106	200

PERIODS n	FUTURE AMOUNT $(1+i)^n$	PRESENT VALUE $(1+i)^{-n}$	AMOUNT OF ANNUITY $(S/p,i,n)$ $\frac{(1+i)^n-1}{i}$	SINKING FUND $(p/S,i,n)$ $\frac{i}{(1+i)^n-1}$	PRESENT VALUE OF ANNUITY $(V/p,i,n)$ $\frac{1-(1+i)^{-n}}{i}$	AMORTIZATION $(p/V,i,n)$ $\frac{i}{1-(1+i)^{-n}}$	PERIODS n
201	27.72652932	0.03606654	1603.59175946	0.00062360	57.83600755	0.01729027	201
202	28.18863815	0.03547529	1631.31828878	0.00061300	57.87148284	0.01727967	202
203	28.65844878	0.03489372	1659.50692693	0.00060259	57.90637656	0.01726926	203
204	29.13608960	0.03432170	1688.16537571	0.00059236	57.94069826	0.01725903	204
205	29.62169109	0.03375904	1717.30146530	0.00058231	57.97445730	0.01724898	205
206	30.11538594	0.03320562	1746.92315639	0.00057244	58.00766292	0.01723910	206
207	30.61730904	0.03266126	1777.03854233	0.00056273	58.04032419	0.01722940	207
208	31.12759752	0.03212583	1807.65585137	0.00055320	58.07245002	0.01721987	208
209	31.64639081	0.03159918	1838.78344889	0.00054384	58.10404920	0.01721050	209
210	32.17383066	0.03108116	1870.42983971	0.00053464	58.13513036	0.01720130	210
211	32.71006117	0.03057163	1902.60367037	0.00052560	58.16570199	0.01719226	211
212	33.25522886	0.03007046	1935.31373154	0.00051671	58.19577245	0.01718338	212
213	33.80948267	0.02957750	1968.56896040	0.00050798	58.22534995	0.01717465	213
214	34.37297405	0.02909262	2002.37844308	0.00049941	58.25444258	0.01716607	214
215	34.94585695	0.02861570	2036.75141713	0.00049098	58.28305827	0.01715764	215
216	35.52828790	0.02814659	2071.69727408	0.00048270	58.31120486	0.01714936	216
217	36.12042603	0.02768517	2107.22556198	0.00047456	58.33889002	0.01714122	217
218	36.72243313	0.02723131	2143.34598801	0.00046656	58.36612134	0.01713323	218
219	37.33447369	0.02678490	2180.06842115	0.00045870	58.39290623	0.01712537	219
220	37.95671491	0.02634580	2217.40289483	0.00045098	58.41925203	0.01711764	220
221	38.58932683	0.02591390	2255.35960975	0.00044339	58.44516593	0.01711005	221
222	39.23248228	0.02548908	2293.94893658	0.00043593	58.47065502	0.01710260	222
223	39.88635698	0.02507123	2333.18141885	0.00042860	58.49572624	0.01709527	223
224	40.55112960	0.02466023	2373.06777583	0.00042140	58.52038647	0.01708806	224
225	41.22698176	0.02425596	2413.61890543	0.00041432	58.54464243	0.01708098	225
226	41.91409812	0.02385832	2454.84588719	0.00040736	58.56850075	0.01707402	226
227	42.61266642	0.02346720	2496.75998531	0.00040052	58.59196795	0.01706719	227
228	43.32287753	0.02308249	2539.37265173	0.00039380	58.61505044	0.01706046	228
229	44.04492549	0.02270409	2582.69552926	0.00038719	58.63775454	0.01705386	229
230	44.77900758	0.02233189	2626.74045474	0.00038070	58.66008643	0.01704737	230
231	45.52532437	0.02196580	2671.51946232	0.00037432	58.68205222	0.01704099	231
232	46.28407978	0.02160570	2717.04478670	0.00036805	58.70365793	0.01703471	232
233	47.05548111	0.02125151	2763.32886647	0.00036188	58.72490943	0.01702855	233
234	47.83973913	0.02090312	2810.38434758	0.00035582	58.74581256	0.01702249	234
235	48.63706811	0.02056045	2858.22408671	0.00034987	58.76637301	0.01701653	235
236	49.44768591	0.02022339	2906.86115482	0.00034401	58.78659640	0.01701068	236
237	50.27181401	0.01989186	2956.30884073	0.00033826	58.80648826	0.01700493	237
238	51.10967758	0.01956577	3006.58065475	0.00033260	58.82605403	0.01699927	238
239	51.96150554	0.01924502	3057.69033232	0.00032704	58.84529905	0.01699371	239
240	52.82753063	0.01892952	3109.65183786	0.00032158	58.86422857	0.01698825	240

TABLE A-2

COMPOUND INTEREST FOR $1

$1\frac{3}{4}\%$

PERIODS n	FUTURE AMOUNT $(1+i)^n$	PRESENT VALUE $(1+i)^{-n}$	AMOUNT OF ANNUITY $(S/p,i,n)$ $\dfrac{(1+i)^n-1}{i}$	SINKING FUND $(p/S,i,n)$ $\dfrac{i}{(1+i)^n-1}$	PRESENT VALUE OF ANNUITY $(V/p,i,n)$ $\dfrac{1-(1+i)^{-n}}{i}$	AMORTIZATION $(p/V,i,n)$ $\dfrac{i}{1-(1+i)^{-n}}$	PERIODS n
1	1.01750000	0.98280098	1.00000000	1.00000000	0.98280098	1.01750000	1
2	1.03530625	0.96589777	2.01750000	0.49566295	1.94869875	0.51316295	2
3	1.05342411	0.94928528	3.05280625	0.32756746	2.89798403	0.34506746	3
4	1.07185903	0.93295851	4.10623036	0.24353237	3.83094254	0.26103237	4
5	1.09061656	0.91691254	5.17808939	0.19312142	4.74785508	0.21062142	5
6	1.10970235	0.90114254	6.26870596	0.15952256	5.64899762	0.17702256	6
7	1.12912215	0.88564378	7.37840831	0.13553059	6.53464139	0.15303059	7
8	1.14888178	0.87041157	8.50753045	0.11754292	7.40505297	0.13504292	8
9	1.16898721	0.85544135	9.65641224	0.10355813	8.26049432	0.12105813	9
10	1.18944449	0.84072860	10.82539945	0.09237534	9.10122291	0.10987534	10
11	1.21025977	0.82626889	12.01484394	0.08323038	9.92749181	0.10073038	11
12	1.23143931	0.81205788	13.22510371	0.07561377	10.73954969	0.09311377	12
13	1.25298950	0.79809128	14.45654303	0.06917283	11.53764097	0.08667283	13
14	1.27491682	0.78436490	15.70953253	0.06365562	12.32200587	0.08115562	14
15	1.29722786	0.77087459	16.98444935	0.05887739	13.09288046	0.07637739	15
16	1.31992935	0.75761631	18.28167721	0.05469958	13.85049677	0.07219958	16
17	1.34302811	0.74458605	19.60160656	0.05101623	14.59508282	0.06851623	17
18	1.36653111	0.73177990	20.94463468	0.04774492	15.32686272	0.06524492	18
19	1.39044540	0.71919401	22.31116578	0.04482061	16.04605673	0.06232061	19
20	1.41477820	0.70682458	23.70161119	0.04219122	16.75288130	0.05969122	20
21	1.43953681	0.69466789	25.11638938	0.03981464	17.44754919	0.05731464	21
22	1.46472028	0.68272028	26.55592620	0.03765638	18.13026948	0.05515638	22
23	1.49036146	0.67097817	28.02065490	0.03568796	18.80124764	0.05318796	23
24	1.51644279	0.65943800	29.51101637	0.03388565	19.46068565	0.05138565	24
25	1.54298054	0.64809632	31.02745915	0.03222952	20.10878196	0.04972952	25
26	1.56998269	0.63694970	32.57043969	0.03070269	20.74573166	0.04820269	26
27	1.59745739	0.62599479	34.14042238	0.02929079	21.37172644	0.04679079	27
28	1.62541290	0.61522829	35.73787977	0.02798151	21.98695474	0.04548151	28
29	1.65385762	0.60464697	37.36329267	0.02676424	22.59160171	0.04426424	29
30	1.68280013	0.59424764	39.01715029	0.02562975	23.18584934	0.04312975	30
31	1.71224913	0.58402716	40.69995042	0.02457005	23.76987650	0.04207005	31
32	1.74221349	0.57398247	42.41219955	0.02357812	24.34385897	0.04107812	32
33	1.77270223	0.56411053	44.15441305	0.02264779	24.90796951	0.04014779	33
34	1.80372452	0.55440839	45.92711527	0.02177363	25.46237789	0.03927363	34
35	1.83528970	0.54487311	47.73083979	0.02095082	26.00725100	0.03845082	35
36	1.86740727	0.53550183	49.56612949	0.02017507	26.54275283	0.03767507	36
37	1.90008689	0.52629172	51.43353675	0.01944257	27.06904455	0.03694257	37
38	1.93333841	0.51724002	53.33362365	0.01874990	27.58628457	0.03624990	38
39	1.96717184	0.50834400	55.26696206	0.01809399	28.09462857	0.03559399	39
40	2.00159734	0.49960098	57.23413390	0.01747209	28.59422955	0.03497209	40

TABLE A-2

COMPOUND INTEREST FOR $1

$1\frac{3}{4}\%$

PERIODS	FUTURE AMOUNT	PRESENT VALUE	AMOUNT OF ANNUITY	SINKING FUND	PRESENT VALUE OF ANNUITY	AMORTIZATION	PERIODS
n	$(1+i)^n$	$(1+i)^{-n}$	$(S/p,i,n)$ $\dfrac{(1+i)^n-1}{i}$	$(p/S,i,n)$ $\dfrac{i}{(1+i)^n-1}$	$(V/p,i,n)$ $\dfrac{1-(1+i)^{-n}}{i}$	$(p/V,i,n)$ $\dfrac{i}{1-(1+i)^{-n}}$	n
41	2.03662530	0.49100834	59.23573124	0.01688170	29.08523789	0.03438170	41
42	2.07226624	0.48256348	61.27235654	0.01632057	29.56780136	0.03382057	42
43	2.10853090	0.47426386	63.34462278	0.01578666	30.04206522	0.03328666	43
44	2.14543019	0.46610699	65.45315367	0.01527810	30.50817221	0.03277810	44
45	2.18297522	0.45809040	67.59858386	0.01479321	30.96626261	0.03229321	45
46	2.22117728	0.45021170	69.78155908	0.01433043	31.41647431	0.03183043	46
47	2.26004789	0.44246850	72.00273637	0.01388836	31.85894281	0.03138836	47
48	2.29959872	0.43485848	74.26278425	0.01346569	32.29380129	0.03096569	48
49	2.33984170	0.42737934	76.56238298	0.01306124	32.72118063	0.03056124	49
50	2.38078893	0.42002883	78.90222468	0.01267391	33.14120946	0.03017391	50
51	2.42245274	0.41280475	81.28301361	0.01230269	33.55401421	0.02980269	51
52	2.46484566	0.40570492	83.70546635	0.01194665	33.95971913	0.02944665	52
53	2.50798046	0.39872719	86.17031201	0.01160492	34.35844632	0.02910492	53
54	2.55187012	0.39186947	88.67829247	0.01127672	34.75031579	0.02877672	54
55	2.59652785	0.38512970	91.23016259	0.01096129	35.13544550	0.02846129	55
56	2.64196708	0.37850585	93.82669043	0.01065795	35.51395135	0.02815795	56
57	2.68820151	0.37199592	96.46865752	0.01036606	35.88594727	0.02786606	57
58	2.73524503	0.36559796	99.15685902	0.01008503	36.25154523	0.02758503	58
59	2.78311182	0.35931003	101.89210405	0.00981430	36.61085526	0.02731430	59
60	2.83181628	0.35313025	104.67521588	0.00955336	36.96398552	0.02705336	60
61	2.88137306	0.34705676	107.50703215	0.00930172	37.31104228	0.02680172	61
62	2.93179709	0.34108772	110.38840522	0.00905892	37.65213000	0.02655892	62
63	2.98310354	0.33522135	113.32020231	0.00882455	37.98735135	0.02632455	63
64	3.03530785	0.32945587	116.30330585	0.00859821	38.31680723	0.02609821	64
65	3.08842574	0.32378956	119.33861370	0.00837952	38.64059678	0.02587952	65
66	3.14247319	0.31822069	122.42703944	0.00816813	38.95881748	0.02566813	66
67	3.19746647	0.31274761	125.56951263	0.00796372	39.27156509	0.02546372	67
68	3.25342213	0.30736866	128.76697910	0.00776597	39.57893375	0.02526597	68
69	3.31035702	0.30208222	132.02040124	0.00757459	39.88101597	0.02507459	69
70	3.36828827	0.29688670	135.33075826	0.00738930	40.17790267	0.02488930	70
71	3.42723331	0.29178054	138.69904653	0.00720985	40.46968321	0.02470985	71
72	3.48720990	0.28676221	142.12627984	0.00703600	40.75644542	0.02453600	72
73	3.54823607	0.28183018	145.61348974	0.00686750	41.03827560	0.02436750	73
74	3.61033020	0.27698298	149.16172581	0.00670413	41.31525857	0.02420413	74
75	3.67351098	0.27221914	152.77205601	0.00654570	41.58747771	0.02404570	75
76	3.73779742	0.26753724	156.44556699	0.00639200	41.85501495	0.02389200	76
77	3.80320888	0.26293586	160.18336441	0.00624285	42.11795081	0.02374285	77
78	3.86976503	0.25841362	163.98657329	0.00609806	42.37636443	0.02359806	78
79	3.93748592	0.25396916	167.85633832	0.00595748	42.63033359	0.02345748	79
80	4.00639192	0.24960114	171.79382424	0.00582093	42.87993474	0.02332093	80

TABLE A-2

COMPOUND INTEREST FOR $1

$1\frac{3}{4}\%$

PERIODS n	FUTURE AMOUNT $(1+i)^n$	PRESENT VALUE $(1+i)^{-n}$	AMOUNT OF ANNUITY $(S/p,i,n)$ $\dfrac{(1+i)^n - 1}{i}$	SINKING FUND $(p/S,i,n)$ $\dfrac{i}{(1+i)^n - 1}$	PRESENT VALUE OF ANNUITY $(V/p,i,n)$ $\dfrac{1-(1+i)^{-n}}{i}$	AMORTIZATION $(p/V,i,n)$ $\dfrac{i}{1-(1+i)^{-n}}$	PERIODS n
81	4.07650378	0.24530825	175.80021617	0.00568828	43.12524298	0.02318828	81
82	4.14784260	0.24108919	179.87671995	0.00555936	43.36633217	0.02305936	82
83	4.22042984	0.23694269	184.02456255	0.00543406	43.60327486	0.02293406	83
84	4.29428737	0.23286751	188.24499239	0.00531223	43.83614237	0.02281223	84
85	4.36943740	0.22886242	192.53927976	0.00519375	44.06500479	0.02269375	85
86	4.44590255	0.22492621	196.90871716	0.00507850	44.28993099	0.02257850	86
87	4.52370584	0.22105770	201.35461971	0.00496636	44.51098869	0.02246636	87
88	4.60287070	0.21725572	205.87832555	0.00485724	44.72824441	0.02235724	88
89	4.68342093	0.21351914	210.48119625	0.00475102	44.94176355	0.02225102	89
90	4.76538080	0.20984682	215.16461718	0.00464760	45.15161037	0.02214760	90
91	4.84877496	0.20623766	219.92999798	0.00454690	45.35784803	0.02204690	91
92	4.93362853	0.20269057	224.77877295	0.00444882	45.56053860	0.02194882	92
93	5.01996703	0.19920450	229.71240148	0.00435327	45.75974310	0.02185327	93
94	5.10781645	0.19577837	234.73236850	0.00426017	45.95552147	0.02176017	94
95	5.19720324	0.19241118	239.84018495	0.00416944	46.14793265	0.02166944	95
96	5.28815429	0.18910190	245.03738819	0.00408101	46.33703455	0.02158101	96
97	5.38069699	0.18584953	250.32554248	0.00399480	46.52288408	0.02149480	97
98	5.47485919	0.18265310	255.70623947	0.00391074	46.70553718	0.02141074	98
99	5.57066923	0.17951165	261.18109866	0.00382876	46.88504882	0.02132876	99
100	5.66815594	0.17642422	266.75176789	0.00374880	47.06147304	0.02124880	100
101	5.76734867	0.17338990	272.41992383	0.00367080	47.23486294	0.02117080	101
102	5.86827727	0.17040776	278.18727250	0.00359470	47.40527071	0.02109470	102
103	5.97097212	0.16747692	284.05554976	0.00352044	47.57274762	0.02102044	103
104	6.07546413	0.16459648	290.02652188	0.00344796	47.73734410	0.02094796	104
105	6.18178476	0.16176558	296.10198602	0.00337721	47.89910968	0.02087721	105
106	6.28996599	0.15898337	302.28377077	0.00330815	48.05809305	0.02080815	106
107	6.40004039	0.15624901	308.57373676	0.00324072	48.21434207	0.02074072	107
108	6.51204110	0.15356168	314.97377716	0.00317487	48.36790375	0.02067487	108
109	6.62600182	0.15092057	321.48581826	0.00311056	48.51882432	0.02061056	109
110	6.74195685	0.14832489	328.11182007	0.00304774	48.66714921	0.02054774	110
111	6.85994110	0.14577385	334.85377693	0.00298638	48.81292306	0.02048638	111
112	6.97999007	0.14326668	341.71371802	0.00292643	48.95618974	0.02042643	112
113	7.10213989	0.14080263	348.69370809	0.00286785	49.09699237	0.02036785	113
114	7.22642734	0.13838097	355.79584798	0.00281060	49.23537334	0.02031060	114
115	7.35288982	0.13600095	363.02227532	0.00275465	49.37137429	0.02025465	115
116	7.48156539	0.13366187	370.37516514	0.00269997	49.50503616	0.02019997	116
117	7.61249278	0.13136301	377.85673053	0.00264651	49.63639917	0.02014651	117
118	7.74571141	0.12910370	385.46922331	0.00259424	49.76550287	0.02009424	118
119	7.88126136	0.12688324	393.21493472	0.00254314	49.89238611	0.02004314	119
120	8.01918343	0.12470098	401.09619608	0.00249317	50.01708709	0.01999317	120

TABLE A-2

COMPOUND INTEREST FOR $1

$1\frac{3}{4}\%$

PERIODS n	FUTURE AMOUNT $(1+i)^n$	PRESENT VALUE $(1+i)^{-n}$	AMOUNT OF ANNUITY $(S/p,i,n)$ $\dfrac{(1+i)^n-1}{i}$	SINKING FUND $(p/S,i,n)$ $\dfrac{i}{(1+i)^n-1}$	PRESENT VALUE OF ANNUITY $(V/p,i,n)$ $\dfrac{1-(1+i)^{-n}}{i}$	AMORTIZATION $(p/V,i,n)$ $\dfrac{i}{1-(1+i)^{-n}}$	PERIODS n
121	8.15951914	0.12255624	409.11537951	0.00244430	50.13964333	0.01994430	121
122	8.30231073	0.12044839	417.27489865	0.00239865	50.26009173	0.01989650	122
123	8.44760116	0.11837680	425.57720938	0.00234975	50.37846853	0.01984975	123
124	8.59543418	0.11634084	434.02481054	0.00230402	50.49480936	0.01980402	124
125	8.74585428	0.11433989	442.62024472	0.00225927	50.60914925	0.01975927	125
126	8.89890673	0.11237335	451.36609901	0.00221550	50.72152261	0.01971550	126
127	9.05463760	0.11044064	460.26500574	0.00217266	50.83196325	0.01967266	127
128	9.21309376	0.10854117	469.31964334	0.00213074	50.94050442	0.01963074	128
129	9.37432290	0.10667437	478.53273710	0.00208972	51.04717879	0.01958972	129
130	9.53837355	0.10483968	487.90706000	0.00204957	51.15201847	0.01954957	130
131	9.70529509	0.10303654	497.44543355	0.00201027	51.25505501	0.01951027	131
132	9.87513775	0.10126441	507.15072863	0.00197180	51.35631942	0.01947180	132
133	10.04795266	0.09952276	517.02586639	0.00193414	51.45584218	0.01943414	133
134	10.22379183	0.09781107	527.07381905	0.00189727	51.55365325	0.01939727	134
135	10.40270819	0.09612881	537.29761088	0.00186117	51.64978206	0.01936117	135
136	10.58475558	0.09447549	547.70031907	0.00182582	51.74425755	0.01932582	136
137	10.76998881	0.09285061	558.28507465	0.00179120	51.83710816	0.01929120	137
138	10.95846361	0.09125367	569.05506346	0.00175730	51.92836183	0.01925730	138
139	11.15023672	0.08968419	580.01352707	0.00172410	52.01804602	0.01922410	139
140	11.34536587	0.08814171	591.16376380	0.00169158	52.10618774	0.01919158	140
141	11.54390977	0.08662576	602.50912966	0.00165973	52.19281350	0.01915973	141
142	11.74592819	0.08513589	614.05303943	0.00162852	52.27794939	0.01912852	142
143	11.95148193	0.08367163	625.79896762	0.00159796	52.36162102	0.01909796	143
144	12.16063287	0.08223256	637.75044955	0.00156801	52.44385358	0.01906801	144
145	12.37344394	0.08081824	649.91108242	0.00153867	52.52467183	0.01903867	145
146	12.58997921	0.07942825	662.28452636	0.00150993	52.60410007	0.01900993	146
147	12.81030385	0.07806216	674.87450558	0.00148176	52.68216223	0.01898176	147
148	13.03448416	0.07671957	687.68480942	0.00145415	52.75888180	0.01895415	148
149	13.26258764	0.07540007	700.71929359	0.00142710	52.83428187	0.01892710	149
150	13.49468292	0.07410326	713.98188123	0.00140060	52.90838513	0.01890060	150
151	13.73083987	0.07282876	727.47656415	0.00137461	52.98121389	0.01887461	151
152	13.97112957	0.07157617	741.20740402	0.00134915	53.05279006	0.01884915	152
153	14.21562434	0.07034513	755.17853359	0.00132419	53.12313520	0.01882419	153
154	14.46439776	0.06913527	769.39415793	0.00129972	53.19227046	0.01879972	154
155	14.71752472	0.06794621	783.85855569	0.00127574	53.26021667	0.01877574	155
156	14.97508141	0.06677760	798.57608042	0.00125223	53.32699427	0.01875223	156
157	15.23714533	0.06562909	813.55116182	0.00122918	53.39262336	0.01872918	157
158	15.50379538	0.06450034	828.78830716	0.00120658	53.45712370	0.01870658	158
159	15.77511179	0.06339099	844.29210253	0.00118442	53.52051469	0.01868442	159
160	16.05117625	0.06230073	860.06721433	0.00116270	53.58281542	0.01866270	160

TABLE A-2

COMPOUND INTEREST FOR $1

$1\frac{3}{4}\%$

PERIODS n	FUTURE AMOUNT $(1+i)^n$	PRESENT VALUE $(1+i)^{-n}$	AMOUNT OF ANNUITY $(S/p,i,n)$ $\dfrac{(1+i)^n - 1}{i}$	SINKING FUND $(p/S,i,n)$ $\dfrac{i}{(1+i)^n - 1}$	PRESENT VALUE OF ANNUITY $(V/p,i,n)$ $\dfrac{1-(1+i)^{-n}}{i}$	AMORTIZATION $(p/V,i,n)$ $\dfrac{i}{1-(1+i)^{-n}}$	PERIODS n
161	16.33207184	0.06122922	876.11839058	0.00114140	53.64404464	0.01864140	161
162	16.61788309	0.06017614	892.45046241	0.00112051	53.70422078	0.01862051	162
163	16.90869605	0.05914117	909.06834550	0.00110003	53.76336194	0.01860003	163
164	17.20459823	0.05812400	925.97704155	0.00107994	53.82148594	0.01857994	164
165	17.50567870	0.05712432	943.18163978	0.00106024	53.87861026	0.01856024	165
166	17.81202807	0.05614184	960.68731847	0.00104092	53.93475210	0.01854092	166
167	18.12373856	0.05517625	978.49934655	0.00102197	53.98992835	0.01852197	167
168	18.44090399	0.05422728	996.62308511	0.00100339	54.04415563	0.01850339	168
169	18.76361981	0.05329462	1015.06398910	0.00098516	54.09745025	0.01848516	169
170	19.09198316	0.05237801	1033.82760891	0.00096728	54.14982825	0.01846728	170
171	19.42609286	0.05147716	1052.91959207	0.00094974	54.20130541	0.01844974	171
172	19.76604949	0.05059180	1072.34568493	0.00093254	54.25189721	0.01843254	172
173	20.11195535	0.04972167	1092.11173441	0.00091566	54.30161888	0.01841566	173
174	20.46391457	0.04886651	1112.22368976	0.00089910	54.35048538	0.01839910	174
175	20.82203308	0.04802605	1132.68760434	0.00088286	54.39851143	0.01838286	175
176	21.18641865	0.04720005	1153.50963741	0.00086692	54.44571148	0.01836692	176
177	21.55718098	0.04638825	1174.69605607	0.00085128	54.49209974	0.01835128	177
178	21.93443165	0.04559042	1196.25323705	0.00083594	54.53769016	0.01833594	178
179	22.31828420	0.04480631	1218.18766870	0.00082089	54.58249647	0.01832089	179
180	22.70885418	0.04403569	1240.50595290	0.00080612	54.62653216	0.01830612	180
181	23.10625912	0.04327832	1263.21480707	0.00079163	54.66981047	0.01829163	181
182	23.51061866	0.04253397	1286.32106620	0.00077741	54.71234445	0.01827741	182
183	23.92205448	0.04180243	1309.83168486	0.00076346	54.75414688	0.01826346	183
184	24.34069044	0.04108347	1333.75373934	0.00074976	54.79523035	0.01824976	184
185	24.76665252	0.04037687	1358.09442978	0.00073633	54.83560722	0.01823633	185
186	25.20006894	0.03968243	1382.86108230	0.00072314	54.87528965	0.01822314	186
187	25.64107015	0.03899993	1408.06115124	0.00071020	54.91428958	0.01821020	187
188	26.08978887	0.03832917	1433.70222139	0.00069749	54.95261875	0.01819749	188
189	26.54636018	0.03766995	1459.79201026	0.00068503	54.99028870	0.01818503	189
190	27.01092148	0.03702206	1486.33837044	0.00067279	55.02731076	0.01817279	190
191	27.48361261	0.03638532	1513.34929192	0.00066079	55.06369608	0.01816079	191
192	27.96457583	0.03575953	1540.83290453	0.00064900	55.09945561	0.01814900	192
193	28.45395591	0.03514450	1568.79748036	0.00063743	55.13460011	0.01813743	193
194	28.95190013	0.03454005	1597.25143627	0.00062608	55.16914015	0.01812608	194
195	29.45855839	0.03394599	1626.20333640	0.00061493	55.20308615	0.01811493	195
196	29.97408316	0.03336215	1655.66189479	0.00060399	55.23644830	0.01810399	196
197	30.49862961	0.03278836	1685.63597795	0.00059325	55.26923666	0.01809325	197
198	31.03235563	0.03222443	1716.13460756	0.00058270	55.30146109	0.01808270	198
199	31.57542186	0.03167020	1747.16696320	0.00057236	55.33313129	0.01807236	199
200	32.12799174	0.03112551	1778.74238505	0.00056219	55.36425680	0.01806219	200

TABLE A-2

COMPOUND INTEREST FOR $1

$1\frac{3}{4}\%$

PERIODS n	FUTURE AMOUNT $(1+i)^n$	PRESENT VALUE $(1+i)^{-n}$	AMOUNT OF ANNUITY (S/p,i,n) $\dfrac{(1+i)^n-1}{i}$	SINKING FUND (p/S,i,n) $\dfrac{i}{(1+i)^n-1}$	PRESENT VALUE OF ANNUITY (V/p,i,n) $\dfrac{1-(1+i)^{-n}}{i}$	AMORTIZATION (p/V,i,n) $\dfrac{i}{1-(1+i)^{-n}}$	PERIODS n
201	32.69023159	0.03059018	1810.87037679	0.00055222	55.39484698	0.01805222	201
202	33.26231065	0.03006406	1843.56060838	0.00054243	55.42491103	0.01804243	202
203	33.84440108	0.02954698	1876.82291903	0.00053282	55.45445802	0.01803282	203
204	34.43667810	0.02903881	1910.66732011	0.00052338	55.48349682	0.01802338	204
205	35.03931997	0.02853937	1945.10399821	0.00051411	55.51203619	0.01801411	205
206	35.65250807	0.02804852	1980.14331818	0.00050501	55.54008471	0.01800501	206
207	36.27642696	0.02756611	2015.79582625	0.00049608	55.56765082	0.01799608	207
208	36.91126443	0.02709200	2052.07225321	0.00048731	55.59474282	0.01798731	208
209	37.55721156	0.02662604	2088.98351764	0.00047870	55.62136886	0.01797870	209
210	38.21446276	0.02616810	2126.54072920	0.00047025	55.64753697	0.01797025	210
211	38.88321586	0.02571804	2164.75519196	0.00046195	55.67325501	0.01796195	211
212	39.56367214	0.02527571	2203.63840782	0.00045379	55.69853072	0.01795379	212
213	40.25603640	0.02484100	2243.20207996	0.00044579	55.72337171	0.01794579	213
214	40.96051704	0.02441375	2283.45811636	0.00043793	55.74778547	0.01793793	214
215	41.67732608	0.02399386	2324.41863339	0.00043022	55.77177933	0.01793022	215
216	42.40667929	0.02358119	2366.09595948	0.00042264	55.79536052	0.01792264	216
217	43.14879618	0.02317562	2408.50263877	0.00041520	55.81853614	0.01791520	217
218	43.90390011	0.02277702	2451.65143495	0.00040789	55.84131316	0.01790789	218
219	44.67221836	0.02238528	2495.55533506	0.00040071	55.86369843	0.01790071	219
220	45.45398218	0.02200027	2540.22755342	0.00039367	55.88569871	0.01789367	220
221	46.24942687	0.02162189	2585.68153561	0.00038675	55.90732060	0.01788675	221
222	47.05879184	0.02125001	2631.93096248	0.00037995	55.92857061	0.01787995	222
223	47.88232070	0.02088453	2678.98975432	0.00037328	55.94945515	0.01787328	223
224	48.72026131	0.02052534	2726.87207502	0.00036672	55.96998049	0.01786672	224
225	49.57286589	0.02017233	2775.59233634	0.00036028	55.99015281	0.01786028	225
226	50.44039104	0.01982538	2825.16520222	0.00035396	56.00997819	0.01785396	226
227	51.32309788	0.01948440	2875.60559326	0.00034775	56.02946260	0.01784775	227
228	52.22125210	0.01914929	2926.92869114	0.00034166	56.04861189	0.01784166	228
229	53.13512401	0.01881994	2979.14994324	0.00033567	56.06743183	0.01783567	229
230	54.06498868	0.01849626	3032.28506725	0.00032978	56.08592809	0.01782978	230
231	55.01112598	0.01817814	3086.35005592	0.00032401	56.10410623	0.01782401	231
232	55.97382068	0.01786549	3141.36118190	0.00031833	56.12197173	0.01781833	232
233	56.95336255	0.01755823	3197.33500259	0.00031276	56.13952995	0.01781276	233
234	57.95004639	0.01725624	3254.28836513	0.00030729	56.15678620	0.01780729	234
235	58.96417220	0.01695945	3312.23841152	0.00030191	56.17374565	0.01780191	235
236	59.99604522	0.01666777	3371.20202587	0.00029663	56.19041341	0.01779663	236
237	61.04597601	0.01638110	3431.19862894	0.00029144	56.20679451	0.01779144	237
238	62.11428059	0.01609936	3492.24460494	0.00028635	56.22289387	0.01778635	238
239	63.20128050	0.01582246	3554.35888553	0.00028134	56.23871633	0.01778134	239
240	64.30730291	0.01555033	3617.56016603	0.00027643	56.25426666	0.01777643	240

TABLE A-2

COMPOUND INTEREST FOR $1

$1\frac{5}{6}\%$

PERIODS n	FUTURE AMOUNT $(1+i)^n$	PRESENT VALUE $(1+i)^{-n}$	AMOUNT OF ANNUITY $(S/p,i,n)$ $\dfrac{(1+i)^n-1}{i}$	SINKING FUND $(p/S,i,n)$ $\dfrac{i}{(1+i)^n-1}$	PRESENT VALUE OF ANNUITY $(V/p,i,n)$ $\dfrac{1-(1+i)^{-n}}{i}$	AMORTIZATION $(p/V,i,n)$ $\dfrac{i}{1-(1+i)^{-n}}$	PERIODS n
1	1.01833333	0.98199673	1.00000000	1.00000000	0.98199673	1.01833333	1
2	1.03700278	0.96431757	2.01833333	0.49545830	1.94631430	0.51379163	2
3	1.05601450	0.94695670	3.05533611	0.32729623	2.89327100	0.34562957	3
4	1.07537476	0.92990838	4.11135061	0.24322907	3.82317937	0.26156241	4
5	1.09508997	0.91316698	5.18672537	0.19279987	4.73634636	0.21113321	5
6	1.11516661	0.89672699	6.28181533	0.15919865	5.63307335	0.17752299	6
7	1.13561134	0.88058297	7.39698195	0.13519027	6.51365631	0.15352361	7
8	1.15643088	0.86472959	8.53259328	0.11719766	7.37838591	0.13553100	8
9	1.17763211	0.84916163	9.68902416	0.10320957	8.22754753	0.12154290	9
10	1.19922203	0.83387394	10.86665627	0.09202463	9.06142147	0.11035796	10
11	1.22120777	0.81886148	12.06587830	0.08287834	9.88028295	0.10121168	11
12	1.24359658	0.80411929	13.28708607	0.07526105	10.68440225	0.09359438	12
13	1.26639585	0.78964251	14.53068265	0.06881989	11.47404476	0.08715322	13
14	1.28961311	0.77542636	15.79707850	0.06330284	12.24947112	0.08163618	14
15	1.31325601	0.76146615	17.08669160	0.05852508	13.01093727	0.07685841	15
16	1.33733237	0.74775727	18.39994761	0.05434798	13.75869454	0.07268131	16
17	1.36185013	0.73429519	19.73727999	0.05066554	14.49298973	0.06899888	17
18	1.38681739	0.72107547	21.09913012	0.04739532	15.21406520	0.06572865	18
19	1.41224237	0.70809375	22.48594751	0.04447222	15.92215895	0.06280555	19
20	1.43813348	0.69534575	23.89818988	0.04184417	16.61750470	0.06017751	20
21	1.46449926	0.68282725	25.33632336	0.03946903	17.30033194	0.05780236	21
22	1.49134841	0.67053412	26.80082262	0.03731229	17.97086607	0.05564562	22
23	1.51868980	0.65846231	28.29217103	0.03534547	18.62932838	0.05367880	23
24	1.54653245	0.64660784	29.81086084	0.03354482	19.27593622	0.05187815	24
25	1.57488554	0.63496678	31.35739329	0.03189041	19.91090299	0.05022374	25
26	1.60375845	0.62353530	32.93227883	0.03036534	20.53443829	0.04869868	26
27	1.63316068	0.61230962	34.53603727	0.02895526	21.14674791	0.04728860	27
28	1.66310196	0.60128604	36.16919796	0.02764783	21.74803396	0.04598117	28
29	1.69359217	0.59046093	37.83229992	0.02643244	22.33849489	0.04476577	29
30	1.72464135	0.57983070	39.52589209	0.02529987	22.91832558	0.04363321	30
31	1.75625978	0.56939185	41.25053344	0.02424211	23.48771743	0.04257544	31
32	1.78845788	0.55914093	43.00679322	0.02325214	24.04685836	0.04158547	32
33	1.82124627	0.54907456	44.79525110	0.02232379	24.59593292	0.04065713	33
34	1.85463579	0.53918942	46.61649737	0.02145163	25.13512235	0.03978497	34
35	1.88863744	0.52948225	48.47113315	0.02063084	25.66460460	0.03896417	35
36	1.92326246	0.51994984	50.35977059	0.01985712	26.18455443	0.03819045	36
37	1.95852227	0.51058904	52.28303305	0.01912666	26.69514347	0.03746000	37
38	1.99442851	0.50139676	54.24155533	0.01843605	27.19654023	0.03676938	38
39	2.03099304	0.49236998	56.23598384	0.01778221	27.68891021	0.03611554	39
40	2.06822791	0.48350571	58.26697688	0.01716238	28.17241592	0.03549571	40

COMPOUND INTEREST FOR $1

$1\frac{5}{16}\%$

PERIODS n	FUTURE AMOUNT $(1+i)^n$	PRESENT VALUE $(1+i)^{-n}$	AMOUNT OF ANNUITY $(S/p,i,n)$ $\dfrac{(1+i)^n - 1}{i}$	SINKING FUND $(p/S,i,n)$ $\dfrac{i}{(1+i)^n - 1}$	PRESENT VALUE OF ANNUITY $(V/p,i,n)$ $\dfrac{1-(1+i)^{-n}}{i}$	AMORTIZATION $(p/V,i,n)$ $\dfrac{i}{1-(1+i)^{-n}}$	PERIODS n
41	2.10614542	0.47480102	60.33520479	0.01657407	28.64721694	0.03490740	41
42	2.14475809	0.46625305	62.44135021	0.01601503	29.11346999	0.03434836	42
43	2.18407865	0.45785897	64.58610829	0.01548321	29.57132896	0.03381654	43
44	2.22412009	0.44961601	66.77018695	0.01497674	30.02094497	0.03331008	44
45	2.26489563	0.44152145	68.99430704	0.01449395	30.46246642	0.03282728	45
46	2.30641872	0.43357262	71.25920267	0.01403328	30.89603904	0.03236661	46
47	2.34870306	0.42576689	73.56562139	0.01359331	31.32180593	0.03192664	47
48	2.39176261	0.41810169	75.91432444	0.01317274	31.73990762	0.03150608	48
49	2.43561160	0.41057449	78.30608706	0.01277040	32.15048211	0.03110373	49
50	2.48026448	0.40318281	80.74169865	0.01238517	32.55366492	0.03071851	50
51	2.52573599	0.39592420	83.22196313	0.01201606	32.94958912	0.03034939	51
52	2.57204115	0.38879627	85.74769912	0.01166212	33.33838539	0.02999545	52
53	2.61919524	0.38179666	88.31974027	0.01132250	33.72018205	0.02965583	53
54	2.66721382	0.37492307	90.93893551	0.01099639	34.09510513	0.02932972	54
55	2.71611274	0.36817323	93.60614933	0.01068306	34.46327836	0.02901639	55
56	2.76590814	0.36154491	96.32226207	0.01038182	34.82482326	0.02871515	56
57	2.81661645	0.35503592	99.08817020	0.01009202	35.17985918	0.02842536	57
58	2.86825442	0.34864411	101.90478666	0.00981308	35.52850329	0.02814642	58
59	2.92083909	0.34236737	104.77304108	0.00954444	35.87087066	0.02787777	59
60	2.97438780	0.33620364	107.69388017	0.00928558	36.20707429	0.02761891	60
61	3.02891825	0.33015087	110.66826797	0.00903601	36.53722517	0.02736935	61
62	3.08444841	0.32420708	113.69718621	0.00879529	36.86143224	0.02712863	62
63	3.14099663	0.31837029	116.78163463	0.00856299	37.17980253	0.02689632	63
64	3.19858157	0.31263858	119.92263126	0.00833871	37.49244111	0.02667204	64
65	3.25722224	0.30701006	123.12121284	0.00812208	37.79945117	0.02645541	65
66	3.31693798	0.30148288	126.37843507	0.00791274	38.10093405	0.02624608	66
67	3.37774851	0.29605520	129.69537305	0.00771038	38.39698924	0.02604371	67
68	3.43967390	0.29072523	133.07312155	0.00751467	38.68771448	0.02584800	68
69	3.50273458	0.28549123	136.51279545	0.00732532	38.97320571	0.02565865	69
70	3.56695138	0.28035145	140.01553003	0.00714206	39.25355716	0.02547540	70
71	3.63234549	0.27530421	143.58248142	0.00696464	39.52886137	0.02529797	71
72	3.69893849	0.27034783	147.21482691	0.00679279	39.79920920	0.02512613	72
73	3.76675237	0.26548069	150.91376540	0.00662630	40.06468988	0.02495963	73
74	3.83580949	0.26070116	154.68051777	0.00646494	40.32539105	0.02479827	74
75	3.90613267	0.25600769	158.51632726	0.00630850	40.58139874	0.02464183	75
76	3.97774510	0.25139871	162.42245993	0.00615678	40.83279745	0.02449012	76
77	4.05067043	0.24687271	166.40020503	0.00600961	41.07967017	0.02434294	77
78	4.12493272	0.24242820	170.45087545	0.00586679	41.32209836	0.02420013	78
79	4.20055648	0.23806370	174.57580817	0.00572817	41.56016206	0.02406150	79
80	4.27756669	0.23377777	178.77636465	0.00559358	41.79393983	0.02392691	80

COMPOUND INTEREST FOR $1

$1\frac{5}{6}$%

PERIODS n	FUTURE AMOUNT $(1+i)^n$	PRESENT VALUE $(1+i)^{-n}$	AMOUNT OF ANNUITY $(S/p,i,n)$ $\dfrac{(1+i)^n-1}{i}$	SINKING FUND $(p/S,i,n)$ $\dfrac{i}{(1+i)^n-1}$	PRESENT VALUE OF ANNUITY $(V/p,i,n)$ $\dfrac{1-(1+i)^{-n}}{i}$	AMORTIZATION $(p/V,i,n)$ $\dfrac{i}{1-(1+i)^{-n}}$	PERIODS n
81	4.35598874	0.22956900	183.05393134	0.00546287	42.02350883	0.02379620	81
82	4.43584853	0.22543601	187.40992008	0.00533590	42.24894484	0.02366923	82
83	4.51717242	0.22137743	191.84576861	0.00521252	42.47032227	0.02354585	83
84	4.59998725	0.21739191	196.36294104	0.00509261	42.68771418	0.02342594	84
85	4.68432035	0.21347814	200.96292829	0.00497604	42.90119232	0.02330938	85
86	4.77019956	0.20963484	205.64724864	0.00486270	43.11082715	0.02319603	86
87	4.85765322	0.20586072	210.41744820	0.00475246	43.31668787	0.02308579	87
88	4.94671019	0.20215456	215.27510142	0.00464522	43.51884243	0.02297855	88
89	5.03739988	0.19851511	220.22181161	0.00454088	43.71735754	0.02287421	89
90	5.12975221	0.19494119	225.25921149	0.00443933	43.91229873	0.02277266	90
91	5.22379767	0.19143161	230.38896370	0.00434049	44.10373034	0.02267382	91
92	5.31956729	0.18798521	235.61276137	0.00424425	44.29171556	0.02257759	92
93	5.41709269	0.18460087	240.92232866	0.00415054	44.47631642	0.02248388	93
94	5.51640606	0.18127745	246.34942135	0.00405927	44.65759387	0.02239261	94
95	5.61754017	0.17801386	251.86582741	0.00397037	44.83560773	0.02230370	95
96	5.72052841	0.17480903	257.48336758	0.00388375	45.01041675	0.02221708	96
97	5.82540476	0.17166189	263.20389598	0.00379934	45.18207864	0.02213267	97
98	5.93220385	0.16857142	269.02930074	0.00371707	45.35065006	0.02205040	98
99	6.04096092	0.16553658	274.96150459	0.00363687	45.51618664	0.02197021	99
100	6.15171187	0.16255638	281.00246551	0.00355869	45.67874302	0.02189202	100
101	6.26449325	0.15962983	287.15417737	0.00348245	45.83837285	0.02181578	101
102	6.37934229	0.15675597	293.41867063	0.00340810	45.99512882	0.02174143	102
103	6.49629690	0.15393385	299.79801292	0.00333558	46.14906267	0.02166891	103
104	6.61539568	0.15116254	306.29430982	0.00326483	46.30022521	0.02159817	104
105	6.73667793	0.14844112	312.90970550	0.00319581	46.44866632	0.02152914	105
106	6.86018370	0.14576869	319.64638344	0.00312846	46.59443502	0.02146179	106
107	6.98595373	0.14314438	326.50656714	0.00306273	46.73757939	0.02139606	107
108	7.11402955	0.14056731	333.49252087	0.00299857	46.87814670	0.02133190	108
109	7.24445342	0.13803664	340.60655042	0.00293594	47.01618334	0.02126927	109
110	7.37726840	0.13555153	347.85100384	0.00287479	47.15173487	0.02120813	110
111	7.51251832	0.13311116	355.22827224	0.00281509	47.28484603	0.02114842	111
112	7.65024783	0.13071472	362.74079057	0.00275679	47.41556075	0.02109012	112
113	7.79050237	0.12836143	370.39103840	0.00269985	47.54392217	0.02103318	113
114	7.93332825	0.12605050	378.18154077	0.00264423	47.66997267	0.02097757	114
115	8.07877260	0.12378118	386.11486901	0.00258990	47.79375385	0.02092324	115
116	8.22688343	0.12155271	394.19364161	0.00253682	47.91530657	0.02087016	116
117	8.37770963	0.11936437	402.42052504	0.00248496	48.03467093	0.02081830	117
118	8.53130097	0.11721542	410.79823467	0.00243429	48.15188635	0.02076762	118
119	8.68770815	0.11510516	419.32953564	0.00238476	48.26699151	0.02071809	119
120	8.84698280	0.11303289	428.01724379	0.00233635	48.38002439	0.02066969	120

TABLE A-2

COMPOUND INTEREST FOR $1

1⅝%

PERIODS n	FUTURE AMOUNT $(1+i)^n$	PRESENT VALUE $(1+i)^{-n}$	AMOUNT OF ANNUITY $(S/p,i,n)$ $\dfrac{(1+i)^n-1}{i}$	SINKING FUND $(p/S,i,n)$ $\dfrac{i}{(1+i)^n-1}$	PRESENT VALUE OF ANNUITY $(V/p,i,n)$ $\dfrac{1-(1+i)^{-n}}{i}$	AMORTIZATION $(p/V,i,n)$ $\dfrac{i}{1-(1+i)^{-n}}$	PERIODS n
121	9.00917749	0.11099792	436.86422659	0.00228904	48.49102232	0.02062237	121
122	9.17434574	0.10899960	445.87340408	0.00224279	48.60002191	0.02057612	122
123	9.34254208	0.10703725	455.04774982	0.00219757	48.70705916	0.02053090	123
124	9.51382202	0.10511023	464.39029190	0.00215336	48.81216939	0.02048669	124
125	9.68824209	0.10321790	473.90411392	0.00211013	48.91538729	0.02044346	125
126	9.86585986	0.10135964	483.59235601	0.00206786	49.01674693	0.02040119	126
127	10.04673396	0.09953483	493.45821587	0.00202651	49.11628176	0.02035985	127
128	10.23092408	0.09774288	503.50494983	0.00198608	49.21402465	0.02031941	128
129	10.41849102	0.09598319	513.73587391	0.00194653	49.31000784	0.02027986	129
130	10.60949669	0.09425518	524.15436493	0.00190783	49.40426301	0.02024117	130
131	10.80400413	0.09255828	534.76386162	0.00186998	49.49682129	0.02020332	131
132	11.00207754	0.09089192	545.56786575	0.00183295	49.58771321	0.02016629	132
133	11.20378229	0.08925557	556.56994329	0.00179672	49.67696879	0.02013005	133
134	11.40918497	0.08764868	567.77372558	0.00176127	49.76461747	0.02009460	134
135	11.61835336	0.08607072	579.18291055	0.00172657	49.85068818	0.02005990	135
136	11.83135650	0.08452116	590.80126391	0.00169262	49.93520934	0.02002595	136
137	12.04826471	0.08299950	602.63262041	0.00165939	50.01820885	0.01999272	137
138	12.26914956	0.08150524	614.68088512	0.00162686	50.09971409	0.01996019	138
139	12.49408397	0.08003788	626.95003468	0.00159502	50.17975197	0.01992836	139
140	12.72314218	0.07859694	639.44411865	0.00156386	50.25834891	0.01989719	140
141	12.95639978	0.07718193	652.16726083	0.00153335	50.33553084	0.01986668	141
142	13.19393378	0.07579241	665.12366061	0.00150348	50.41132325	0.01983681	142
143	13.43582256	0.07442790	678.31759439	0.00147424	50.48575115	0.01980757	143
144	13.68214598	0.07308795	691.75341695	0.00144560	50.55883910	0.01977894	144
145	13.93298532	0.07177213	705.43556293	0.00141756	50.63061122	0.01975090	145
146	14.18842338	0.07047999	719.36854825	0.00139011	50.70109122	0.01972344	146
147	14.44854448	0.06921112	733.55697163	0.00136322	50.77030234	0.01969655	147
148	14.71343446	0.06796510	748.00551611	0.00133689	50.83826744	0.01967022	148
149	14.98318076	0.06674150	762.71895057	0.00131110	50.90500894	0.01964443	149
150	15.25787241	0.06553994	777.70213133	0.00128584	50.97054888	0.01961917	150
151	15.53760007	0.06436000	792.96000374	0.00126110	51.03490888	0.01959443	151
152	15.82245607	0.06320131	808.49760381	0.00123686	51.09811019	0.01957020	152
153	16.11253443	0.06206348	824.32005988	0.00121312	51.16017368	0.01954645	153
154	16.40793090	0.06094614	840.43259431	0.00118986	51.22111981	0.01952320	154
155	16.70874296	0.05984891	856.84052521	0.00116708	51.28096872	0.01950041	155
156	17.01506992	0.05877143	873.54926817	0.00114476	51.33974015	0.01947809	156
157	17.32701286	0.05771335	890.56433809	0.00112288	51.39745350	0.01945622	157
158	17.64467477	0.05667432	907.89135095	0.00110145	51.45412783	0.01943479	158
159	17.96816047	0.05565400	925.53602572	0.00108045	51.50978183	0.01941379	159
160	18.29757675	0.05465205	943.50418619	0.00105988	51.56443387	0.01939321	160

TABLE A-2

COMPOUND INTEREST FOR $1

$1\tfrac{5}{16}\%$

PERIODS n	FUTURE AMOUNT $(1+i)^n$	PRESENT VALUE $(1+i)^{-n}$	AMOUNT OF ANNUITY $(S/p,i,n)$ $\dfrac{(1+i)^n-1}{i}$	SINKING FUND $(p/S,i,n)$ $\dfrac{i}{(1+i)^n-1}$	PRESENT VALUE OF ANNUITY $(V/p,i,n)$ $\dfrac{1-(1+i)^{-n}}{i}$	AMORTIZATION $(p/V,i,n)$ $\dfrac{i}{1-(1+i)^{-n}}$	PERIODS n
161	18.63303232	0.05366813	961.80176294	0.00103972	51.61810200	0.01937305	161
162	18.97463791	0.05270193	980.43479526	0.00101996	51.67080393	0.01935329	162
163	19.32250627	0.05175312	999.40943317	0.00100059	51.72255705	0.01933392	163
164	19.67675222	0.05082140	1018.73193944	0.00098161	51.77337845	0.01931495	164
165	20.03749268	0.04990644	1038.40869167	0.00096301	51.82328489	0.01929635	165
166	20.40484671	0.04900796	1058.44618435	0.00094478	51.87229285	0.01927811	166
167	20.77893555	0.04812566	1078.85103106	0.00092691	51.92041851	0.01926025	167
168	21.15988272	0.04725924	1099.62996663	0.00090940	51.96767776	0.01924273	168
169	21.54781390	0.04640842	1120.78984935	0.00089223	52.01408618	0.01922556	169
170	21.94285716	0.04557292	1142.33766326	0.00087540	52.05965909	0.01920873	170
171	22.34514287	0.04475245	1164.28052042	0.00085890	52.10441155	0.01919223	171
172	22.75480383	0.04394676	1186.62566329	0.00084273	52.14835831	0.01917606	172
173	23.17197523	0.04315558	1209.38046712	0.00082687	52.19151389	0.01916020	173
174	23.59679478	0.04237864	1232.55244235	0.00081132	52.23389253	0.01914466	174
175	24.02940268	0.04161568	1256.14923712	0.00079608	52.27550821	0.01912942	175
176	24.46994173	0.04086646	1280.17863981	0.00078114	52.31637467	0.01911447	176
177	24.91855733	0.04013073	1304.64858154	0.00076649	52.35650541	0.01909982	177
178	25.37539755	0.03940825	1329.56713886	0.00075212	52.39591366	0.01908546	178
179	25.84061317	0.03869877	1354.94253641	0.00073804	52.43461243	0.01907137	179
180	26.31435774	0.03800207	1380.78314958	0.00072423	52.47261450	0.01905756	180
181	26.79678763	0.03731791	1407.09750732	0.00071068	52.50993240	0.01904402	181
182	27.28806207	0.03664606	1433.89429495	0.00069740	52.54657847	0.01903073	182
183	27.78834321	0.03598631	1461.18235703	0.00068438	52.58256478	0.01901771	183
184	28.29779617	0.03533844	1488.97070024	0.00067160	52.61790322	0.01900494	184
185	28.81658910	0.03470223	1517.26849641	0.00065908	52.65260545	0.01899241	185
186	29.34489323	0.03407748	1546.08508551	0.00064679	52.68668293	0.01898013	186
187	29.88288294	0.03346397	1575.42997875	0.00063475	52.72014691	0.01896808	187
188	30.43073580	0.03286151	1605.31286169	0.00062293	52.75300842	0.01895626	188
189	30.98863262	0.03226990	1635.74359749	0.00061134	52.78527832	0.01894468	189
190	31.55675755	0.03168893	1666.73223011	0.00059998	52.81696725	0.01893331	190
191	32.13529811	0.03111843	1698.28898766	0.00058883	52.84808568	0.01892216	191
192	32.72444524	0.03055820	1730.42428577	0.00057789	52.87864387	0.01891123	192
193	33.32439340	0.03000805	1763.14873101	0.00056717	52.90865192	0.01890050	193
194	33.93534061	0.02946781	1796.47312441	0.00055665	52.93811973	0.01888998	194
195	34.55748853	0.02893729	1830.40846502	0.00054633	52.96705702	0.01887966	195
196	35.19104248	0.02841632	1864.96595355	0.00053620	52.99547334	0.01886954	196
197	35.83621159	0.02790474	1900.15699603	0.00052627	53.02337807	0.01885961	197
198	36.49320881	0.02740236	1935.99320762	0.00051653	53.05078043	0.01884986	198
199	37.16225097	0.02690903	1972.48641643	0.00050697	53.07768946	0.01884031	199
200	37.84355890	0.02642458	2009.64866740	0.00049760	53.10411403	0.01883093	200

TABLE A-2

COMPOUND INTEREST FOR $1

$1\frac{5}{6}\%$

PERIODS n	FUTURE AMOUNT $(1+i)^n$	PRESENT VALUE $(1+i)^{-n}$	AMOUNT OF ANNUITY (S/p,i,n) $\frac{(1+i)^n-1}{i}$	SINKING FUND (p/S,i,n) $\frac{i}{(1+i)^n-1}$	PRESENT VALUE OF ANNUITY (V/p,i,n) $\frac{1-(1+i)^{-n}}{i}$	AMORTIZATION (p/V,i,n) $\frac{i}{1-(1+i)^{-n}}$	PERIODS n
201	38.53735748	0.02594885	2047.49222630	0.00048840	53.13006288	0.01882174	201
202	39.24387570	0.02548168	2086.02958378	0.00047938	53.15554456	0.01881271	202
203	39.96334676	0.02502293	2125.27345948	0.00047053	53.18056749	0.01880386	203
204	40.69600811	0.02457243	2165.23680624	0.00046184	53.20513993	0.01879518	204
205	41.44210160	0.02413005	2205.93281436	0.00045332	53.22926998	0.01878666	205
206	42.20187346	0.02369563	2247.37491595	0.00044496	53.25296561	0.01877830	206
207	42.97557447	0.02326903	2289.57678941	0.00043676	53.27623464	0.01877010	207
208	43.76346000	0.02285011	2332.55236388	0.00042871	53.29908475	0.01876205	208
209	44.56579010	0.02243874	2376.31582389	0.00042082	53.32152349	0.01875415	209
210	45.38282959	0.02203477	2420.88161399	0.00041307	53.34355825	0.01874641	210
211	46.21484813	0.02163807	2466.26444358	0.00040547	53.36519632	0.01873880	211
212	47.06212035	0.02124851	2512.47929172	0.00039801	53.38644483	0.01873135	212
213	47.92492589	0.02086597	2559.54141206	0.00039069	53.40731080	0.01872403	213
214	48.80354953	0.02049031	2607.46633795	0.00038351	53.42780112	0.01871685	214
215	49.69828127	0.02012142	2656.26988748	0.00037647	53.44792254	0.01870980	215
216	50.60941643	0.01975917	2705.96816875	0.00036955	53.46768170	0.01870289	216
217	51.53725573	0.01940344	2756.57758518	0.00036277	53.48708514	0.01869610	217
218	52.48210542	0.01905411	2808.11484091	0.00035611	53.50613926	0.01868944	218
219	53.44427735	0.01871108	2860.59694632	0.00034958	53.52485033	0.01868291	219
220	54.42408910	0.01837422	2914.04122367	0.00034317	53.54322455	0.01867650	220
221	55.42186407	0.01804342	2968.46531277	0.00033687	53.56126797	0.01867021	221
222	56.43793158	0.01771858	3023.88717684	0.00033070	53.57898655	0.01866403	222
223	57.47262699	0.01739959	3080.32510842	0.00032464	53.59638614	0.01865797	223
224	58.52629182	0.01708634	3137.79773540	0.00031869	53.61347248	0.01865203	224
225	59.59927383	0.01677873	3196.32402722	0.00031286	53.63025120	0.01864619	225
226	60.69192719	0.01647666	3255.92330105	0.00030713	53.64672786	0.01864047	226
227	61.80461252	0.01618002	3316.61522824	0.00030151	53.66290788	0.01863485	227
228	62.93769708	0.01588873	3378.41984075	0.00029600	53.67879661	0.01862933	228
229	64.09155486	0.01560268	3441.35753784	0.00029058	53.69439929	0.01862392	229
230	65.26656670	0.01532178	3505.44909270	0.00028527	53.70972107	0.01861860	230
231	66.46312042	0.01504594	3570.71565939	0.00028006	53.72476701	0.01861339	231
232	67.68161096	0.01477506	3637.17877982	0.00027494	53.73954207	0.01860827	232
233	68.92244050	0.01450906	3704.86039078	0.00026992	53.75405113	0.01860325	233
234	70.18601857	0.01424785	3773.78283128	0.00026499	53.76829899	0.01859832	234
235	71.47276225	0.01399134	3843.96884985	0.00026015	53.78229033	0.01859348	235
236	72.78309622	0.01373945	3915.44161210	0.00025540	53.79602978	0.01858873	236
237	74.11745299	0.01349210	3988.22470832	0.00025074	53.80952188	0.01858407	237
238	75.47627296	0.01324920	4062.34216131	0.00024616	53.82277108	0.01857950	238
239	76.86000463	0.01301067	4137.81843426	0.00024167	53.83578175	0.01857501	239
240	78.26910471	0.01277643	4214.67843889	0.00023727	53.84855818	0.01857060	240

TABLE A-2

COMPOUND INTEREST FOR $1

$1\frac{11}{12}\%$

PERIODS n	FUTURE AMOUNT $(1+i)^n$	PRESENT VALUE $(1+i)^{-n}$	AMOUNT OF ANNUITY $(S/p,i,n)$ $\dfrac{(1+i)^n - 1}{i}$	SINKING FUND $(p/S,i,n)$ $\dfrac{i}{(1+i)^n - 1}$	PRESENT VALUE OF ANNUITY $(V/p,i,n)$ $\dfrac{1-(1+i)^{-n}}{i}$	AMORTIZATION $(p/V,i,n)$ $\dfrac{i}{1-(1+i)^{-n}}$	PERIODS n
1	1.01916667	0.98119379	1.00000000	1.00000000	0.98119379	1.01916667	1
2	1.03870069	0.96274125	2.01916667	0.49525382	1.94393503	0.51442048	2
3	1.05860912	0.94463573	3.05786736	0.32702530	2.88857076	0.34619197	3
4	1.07889913	0.92687071	4.11647649	0.24292620	3.81544146	0.26209287	4
5	1.09957803	0.90943978	5.19537562	0.19247886	4.72488124	0.21164553	5
6	1.12065328	0.89233666	6.29495365	0.15885740	5.61721790	0.17802407	6
7	1.14213247	0.87555518	7.41560693	0.13485073	6.49277308	0.15401740	7
8	1.16402334	0.85908930	8.55773940	0.11686200	7.35186238	0.13601996	8
9	1.18633309	0.84293309	9.72176273	0.10286200	8.19479547	0.12202867	9
10	1.20907185	0.82708071	10.90809652	0.09167502	9.02187618	0.11084169	10
11	1.23224573	0.81152645	12.11716837	0.08252753	9.83340263	0.10169420	11
12	1.25586377	0.79626471	13.34941410	0.07490965	10.62966734	0.09407632	12
13	1.27993449	0.78128998	14.60527787	0.06846840	11.41095732	0.08763507	13
14	1.30446657	0.76659688	15.88521236	0.06295163	12.17755420	0.08211830	14
15	1.32946885	0.75218009	17.18967893	0.05817444	12.92973429	0.07734111	15
16	1.35495033	0.73803443	18.51914778	0.05399817	13.66776872	0.07316483	16
17	1.38092021	0.72415480	19.87409811	0.05031675	14.39192352	0.06948342	17
18	1.40738785	0.71053619	21.25501832	0.04704771	15.10245971	0.06621438	18
19	1.43436278	0.69717369	22.66240617	0.04414594	15.79963341	0.06329261	19
20	1.46185278	0.68406250	24.09676896	0.04149934	16.48369590	0.06066601	20
21	1.48987362	0.67119787	25.55862370	0.03912574	17.15489377	0.05829240	21
22	1.51842953	0.65857518	27.04849732	0.03697063	17.81346895	0.05613730	22
23	1.54753276	0.64618987	28.56692685	0.03500552	18.45965882	0.05417218	23
24	1.57719381	0.63403749	30.11445961	0.03320664	19.09369631	0.05237331	24
25	1.60742336	0.62211364	31.69165342	0.03155405	19.71580995	0.05072072	25
26	1.63823230	0.61041404	33.29907678	0.03003086	20.32622399	0.04919753	26
27	1.66963176	0.59893446	34.93730908	0.02862270	20.92515845	0.04778936	27
28	1.70163303	0.58767077	36.60694084	0.02731722	21.51282923	0.04648389	28
29	1.73424767	0.57661891	38.30857388	0.02610382	22.08944814	0.04527048	29
30	1.76748741	0.56577489	40.04282154	0.02497327	22.65522303	0.04413993	30
31	1.80136425	0.55513481	41.81030895	0.02391755	23.21035784	0.04308421	31
32	1.83589040	0.54469482	43.61167321	0.02292964	23.75505266	0.04209631	32
33	1.87107830	0.53445118	45.44756361	0.02200338	24.28950384	0.04117005	33
34	1.90694064	0.52440017	47.31864191	0.02113332	24.81390401	0.04029999	34
35	1.94349033	0.51453819	49.22558255	0.02031464	25.32844220	0.03948131	35
36	1.98074056	0.50486168	51.16907288	0.01954305	25.83330388	0.03870972	36
37	2.01870476	0.49536714	53.14981345	0.01881474	26.32867102	0.03798141	37
38	2.05739660	0.48605116	55.16851820	0.01812628	26.81472218	0.03729295	38
39	2.09683003	0.47691038	57.22591480	0.01747460	27.29163255	0.03664127	39
40	2.13701928	0.46794150	59.32274484	0.01685694	27.75957405	0.03602361	40

TABLE A-2

COMPOUND INTEREST FOR $1

$1\frac{11}{12}\%$

PERIODS n	FUTURE AMOUNT $(1+i)^n$	PRESENT VALUE $(1+i)^{-n}$	AMOUNT OF ANNUITY (S/p,i,n) $\dfrac{(1+i)^n - 1}{i}$	SINKING FUND (p/S,i,n) $\dfrac{i}{(1+i)^n - 1}$	PRESENT VALUE OF ANNUITY (V/p,i,n) $\dfrac{1-(1+i)^{-n}}{i}$	AMORTIZATION (p/V,i,n) $\dfrac{i}{1-(1+i)^{-n}}$	PERIODS n
41	2.17797881	0.45914129	61.45976411	0.01627081	28.21871534	0.03543747	41
42	2.21972341	0.45050658	63.63774293	0.01571395	28.66922192	0.03488061	42
43	2.26226810	0.44203426	65.85746633	0.01518431	29.11125617	0.03435097	43
44	2.30562824	0.43372127	68.11973444	0.01468003	29.54497744	0.03384670	44
45	2.34981945	0.42556461	70.42536268	0.01419943	29.97054205	0.03336610	45
46	2.39485766	0.41756135	72.77518213	0.01374095	30.38810340	0.03290761	46
47	2.44075910	0.40970860	75.17003979	0.01330317	30.79781201	0.03246984	47
48	2.48754031	0.40200354	77.61079888	0.01288480	31.19981554	0.03205147	48
49	2.53521817	0.39444337	80.09833920	0.01248465	31.59425891	0.03165132	49
50	2.58380985	0.38702538	82.63355736	0.01210162	31.98128430	0.03126829	50
51	2.63333287	0.37974690	85.21736721	0.01173470	32.36103120	0.03090136	51
52	2.68380508	0.37260530	87.85070009	0.01138295	32.73363650	0.03054962	52
53	2.73524468	0.36559801	90.53450517	0.01104551	33.09923450	0.03021218	53
54	2.78767021	0.35872249	93.26974985	0.01072159	33.45795700	0.02988826	54
55	2.84110055	0.35197628	96.05742006	0.01041044	33.80993327	0.02957711	55
56	2.89555498	0.34535694	98.89852061	0.01011137	34.15529021	0.02927804	56
57	2.95105312	0.33886208	101.79407559	0.00982375	34.49415229	0.02899042	57
58	3.00761497	0.33248937	104.74512870	0.00954698	34.82664166	0.02871365	58
59	3.06526092	0.32623650	107.75274367	0.00928051	35.15287816	0.02844717	59
60	3.12401175	0.32010123	110.81800459	0.00902380	35.47297939	0.02819047	60
61	3.18388865	0.31408134	113.94201635	0.00877639	35.78706073	0.02794306	61
62	3.24491318	0.30817466	117.12590499	0.00853782	36.09523538	0.02770449	62
63	3.30710735	0.30237906	120.37081817	0.00830766	36.39761444	0.02747433	63
64	3.37049357	0.29669245	123.67792552	0.00808552	36.69430689	0.02725218	64
65	3.43509470	0.29111279	127.04841909	0.00787101	36.98541968	0.02703768	65
66	3.50093401	0.28563806	130.48351379	0.00766380	37.27105774	0.02683047	66
67	3.56803525	0.28026629	133.98444781	0.00746355	37.55132403	0.02663022	67
68	3.63642259	0.27499554	137.55248306	0.00726995	37.82631957	0.02643662	68
69	3.70612069	0.26982392	141.18890565	0.00708271	38.09614349	0.02624938	69
70	3.77715467	0.26474955	144.89502634	0.00690155	38.36089304	0.02606821	70
71	3.84955014	0.25977061	148.67218101	0.00672621	38.62066365	0.02589287	71
72	3.92333318	0.25488531	152.52173115	0.00655644	38.87554896	0.02572311	72
73	3.99853040	0.25009188	156.44506433	0.00639202	39.12564085	0.02555869	73
74	4.07516890	0.24538860	160.44359473	0.00623272	39.37102945	0.02539939	74
75	4.15327630	0.24077377	164.51876362	0.00607833	39.61180322	0.02524500	75
76	4.23288077	0.23624573	168.67203993	0.00592866	39.84804895	0.02509533	76
77	4.31401098	0.23180284	172.90492069	0.00578353	40.07985179	0.02495019	77
78	4.39669619	0.22744351	177.21893167	0.00564274	40.30729530	0.02480940	78
79	4.48096620	0.22316616	181.61562786	0.00550613	40.53046145	0.02467280	79
80	4.56685139	0.21896924	186.09659406	0.00537355	40.74943070	0.02454022	80

TABLE A-2

COMPOUND INTEREST FOR $1

$1\frac{11}{12}\%$

PERIODS n	FUTURE AMOUNT $(1+i)^n$	PRESENT VALUE $(1+i)^{-n}$	AMOUNT OF ANNUITY (S/p,i,n) $\dfrac{(1+i)^n-1}{i}$	SINKING FUND (p/S,i,n) $\dfrac{i}{(1+i)^n-1}$	PRESENT VALUE OF ANNUITY (V/p,i,n) $\dfrac{1-(1+i)^{-n}}{i}$	AMORTIZATION (p/V,i,n) $\dfrac{i}{1-(1+i)^{-n}}$	PERIODS n
81	4.65438270	0.21485126	190.66344545	0.00524484	40.96428196	0.02441151	81
82	4.74359171	0.21081072	195.31782815	0.00511986	41.17509268	0.02428653	82
83	4.83451055	0.20684617	200.06141986	0.00499846	41.38193885	0.02416513	83
84	4.92717200	0.20295618	204.89593041	0.00488053	41.58489503	0.02404719	84
85	5.02160946	0.19913934	209.82310241	0.00476592	41.78403437	0.02393259	85
86	5.11785698	0.19539428	214.84471187	0.00465452	41.97942866	0.02382119	86
87	5.21594924	0.19171966	219.96256885	0.00454623	42.17114832	0.02371289	87
88	5.31592160	0.18811414	225.17851808	0.00444092	42.35926245	0.02360759	88
89	5.41781009	0.18457642	230.49443968	0.00433850	42.54383887	0.02350517	89
90	5.52165145	0.18110524	235.91224977	0.00423886	42.72494411	0.02340553	90
91	5.62748311	0.17769933	241.43390123	0.00414192	42.90264345	0.02330859	91
92	5.73534320	0.17435748	247.06138434	0.00404758	43.07700093	0.02321424	92
93	5.84527061	0.17107848	252.79672754	0.00395575	43.24807941	0.02312241	93
94	5.95730496	0.16786114	258.64199815	0.00386635	43.41594055	0.02303301	94
95	6.07148664	0.16470431	264.59930311	0.00377930	43.58064485	0.02294597	95
96	6.18785680	0.16160684	270.67078975	0.00369453	43.74225169	0.02286119	96
97	6.30645739	0.15856763	276.85864656	0.00361195	43.90081932	0.02277862	97
98	6.42733116	0.15558557	283.16510395	0.00353151	44.05640490	0.02269818	98
99	6.55052167	0.15265960	289.59243511	0.00345313	44.20906449	0.02261980	99
100	6.67607334	0.14978865	296.14295678	0.00337675	44.35885314	0.02254341	100
101	6.80403141	0.14697169	302.81903012	0.00330230	44.50582483	0.02246897	101
102	6.93444201	0.14420771	309.62306153	0.00322973	44.65003254	0.02239640	102
103	7.06735215	0.14149571	316.55750354	0.00315898	44.79152825	0.02232565	103
104	7.20280973	0.13883471	323.62485569	0.00309000	44.93036296	0.02225666	104
105	7.34086359	0.13622375	330.82766543	0.00302272	45.06658672	0.02218939	105
106	7.48156347	0.13366190	338.16852902	0.00295711	45.20024862	0.02212377	106
107	7.62496011	0.13114823	345.65009249	0.00289310	45.33139684	0.02205977	107
108	7.77110517	0.12868183	353.27505260	0.00283066	45.46007867	0.02199732	108
109	7.92005136	0.12626181	361.04615777	0.00276973	45.58634048	0.02193640	109
110	8.07185234	0.12388730	368.96620913	0.00271028	45.71022778	0.02187694	110
111	8.22656284	0.12155745	377.03806147	0.00265225	45.83178523	0.02181892	111
112	8.38423863	0.11927141	385.26462431	0.00259562	45.95105664	0.02176229	112
113	8.54493654	0.11702837	393.64886295	0.00254034	46.06808501	0.02170700	113
114	8.70871449	0.11482751	402.19379949	0.00248636	46.18291252	0.02165303	114
115	8.87563152	0.11266804	410.90251398	0.00243367	46.29558056	0.02160033	115
116	9.04574779	0.11054918	419.77814549	0.00238221	46.40612974	0.02154888	116
117	9.21912462	0.10847017	428.82389328	0.00233196	46.51459991	0.02149863	117
118	9.39582451	0.10643026	438.04301790	0.00228288	46.62103017	0.02144955	118
119	9.57591115	0.10442870	447.43884241	0.00223494	46.72545887	0.02140161	119
120	9.75944944	0.10246480	457.01475356	0.00218811	46.82792367	0.02135478	120

TABLE A-2

COMPOUND INTEREST FOR $1

$1\frac{11}{12}\%$

PERIODS n	FUTURE AMOUNT $(1+i)^n$	PRESENT VALUE $(1+i)^{-n}$	AMOUNT OF ANNUITY $(S/p,i,n)$ $\dfrac{(1+i)^n-1}{i}$	SINKING FUND $(p/S,i,n)$ $\dfrac{i}{(1+i)^n-1}$	PRESENT VALUE OF ANNUITY $(V/p,i,n)$ $\dfrac{1-(1+i)^{-n}}{i}$	AMORTIZATION $(p/V,i,n)$ $\dfrac{i}{1-(1+i)^{-n}}$	PERIODS n
121	9. 94650556	0. 10053782	466. 77420300	0. 00214236	46. 92846149	0. 02130903	121
122	10. 13714691	0. 09864709	476. 72070856	0. 00209766	47. 02710857	0. 02126433	122
123	10. 33144223	0. 09679191	486. 75785548	0. 00205399	47. 12390048	0. 02122065	123
124	10. 52946154	0. 09497162	497. 18929771	0. 00201131	47. 21887210	0. 02117797	124
125	10. 73127622	0. 09318556	507. 71875924	0. 00196959	47. 31205766	0. 02113626	125
126	10. 93695901	0. 09143309	518. 45003546	0. 00192883	47. 40349076	0. 02109549	126
127	11. 14658406	0. 08971358	529. 38699448	0. 00188898	47. 49320434	0. 02105564	127
128	11. 36022692	0. 08802641	540. 53357854	0. 00185002	47. 58123075	0. 02101669	128
129	11. 57796460	0. 08637097	551. 89380546	0. 00181194	47. 66760172	0. 02097861	129
130	11. 79987559	0. 08474666	563. 47177006	0. 00177471	47. 75234837	0. 02094138	130
131	12. 02603988	0. 08315289	575. 27164566	0. 00173831	47. 83550126	0. 02090498	131
132	12. 25653897	0. 08158910	587. 29768553	0. 00170271	47. 91709037	0. 02086938	132
133	12. 49145597	0. 08005472	599. 55422450	0. 00166791	47. 99714509	0. 02083457	133
134	12. 73087554	0. 07854919	612. 04568047	0. 00163386	48. 07569428	0. 02080053	134
135	12. 97488399	0. 07707198	624. 77655602	0. 00160057	48. 15276626	0. 02076724	135
136	13. 22356927	0. 07562255	637. 75144001	0. 00156801	48. 22838881	0. 02073468	136
137	13. 47702101	0. 07420037	650. 97500927	0. 00153616	48. 30258918	0. 02070282	137
138	13. 73533058	0. 07280495	664. 45203028	0. 00150500	48. 37539413	0. 02067167	138
139	13. 99859108	0. 07143576	678. 18736087	0. 00147452	48. 44682989	0. 02064119	139
140	14. 266899741	0. 07009232	692. 18595195	0. 00144470	48. 51692221	0. 02061137	140
141	14. 54034628	0. 06877415	706. 45284936	0. 00141552	48. 58569636	0. 02058219	141
142	14. 81903625	0. 06748077	720. 99319564	0. 00138698	48. 65317714	0. 02055364	142
143	15. 10306778	0. 06621171	735. 81223189	0. 00135904	48. 71938885	0. 02052571	143
144	15. 39254324	0. 06496652	750. 91529967	0. 00133171	48. 78435537	0. 02049837	144
145	15. 68756699	0. 06374475	766. 30784291	0. 00130496	48. 84810012	0. 02047163	145
146	15. 98824536	0. 06254595	781. 99540990	0. 00127878	48. 91064607	0. 02044545	146
147	16. 29468673	0. 06136970	797. 98365526	0. 00125316	48. 97201577	0. 02041983	147
148	16. 60700155	0. 06021557	814. 27834198	0. 00122808	49. 032231133	0. 02039475	148
149	16. 92530242	0. 05908314	830. 88534354	0. 00120354	49. 09131447	0. 02037020	149
150	17. 24970405	0. 05797201	847. 81064596	0. 00117951	49. 14928648	0. 02034618	150
151	17. 58032338	0. 05688178	865. 06035000	0. 00115599	49. 20616826	0. 02032266	151
152	17. 91727957	0. 05581204	882. 64067338	0. 00113296	49. 26198030	0. 02029963	152
153	18. 26069410	0. 05476243	900. 55795295	0. 00111042	49. 31674273	0. 02027709	153
154	18. 61069074	0. 05373256	918. 81864705	0. 00108835	49. 37047529	0. 02025502	154
155	18. 96739564	0. 05272205	937. 42933778	0. 00106675	49. 42319734	0. 02023341	155
156	19. 33093739	0. 05173055	956. 39673343	0. 00104559	49. 47492789	0. 02021226	156
157	19. 70144702	0. 05075769	975. 72767082	0. 00102488	49. 52568558	0. 02019154	157
158	20. 07905809	0. 04980313	995. 42911784	0. 00100459	49. 57548871	0. 02017126	158
159	20. 46390671	0. 04886652	1015. 50817593	0. 00098473	49. 62435524	0. 02015140	159
160	20. 85613158	0. 04794753	1035. 97208264	0. 00096528	49. 67230277	0. 02013194	160

TABLE A-2

COMPOUND INTEREST FOR $1

$1\frac{11}{12}\%$

PERIODS n	FUTURE AMOUNT $(1+i)^n$	PRESENT VALUE $(1+i)^{-n}$	AMOUNT OF ANNUITY $(S/p,i,n)$ $\dfrac{(1+i)^n - 1}{i}$	SINKING FUND $(p/S,i,n)$ $\dfrac{i}{(1+i)^n - 1}$	PRESENT VALUE OF ANNUITY $(V/p,i,n)$ $\dfrac{1-(1+i)^{-n}}{i}$	AMORTIZATION $(p/V,i,n)$ $\dfrac{i}{1-(1+i)^{-n}}$	PERIODS n
161	21.25587411	0.04704582	1056.82821422	0.00094623	49.71934859	0.02011289	161
162	21.66327836	0.04616106	1078.08408833	0.00092757	49.76550965	0.02009424	162
163	22.07849119	0.04529295	1099.74736669	0.00090930	49.81080260	0.02007597	163
164	22.50166228	0.04444116	1121.82585788	0.00089140	49.85524376	0.02005807	164
165	22.93294414	0.04360539	1144.32752016	0.00087388	49.89884916	0.02004054	165
166	23.37249223	0.04278534	1167.26046429	0.00085671	49.94163449	0.02002337	166
167	23.82046500	0.04198071	1190.63295653	0.00083989	49.98361520	0.02000656	167
168	24.27702391	0.04119121	1214.45342153	0.00082342	50.02480641	0.01999008	168
169	24.74233354	0.04041656	1238.73044544	0.00080728	50.06522297	0.01997394	169
170	25.21656160	0.03965648	1263.47277898	0.00079147	50.10487945	0.01995814	170
171	25.69987903	0.03891069	1288.68934057	0.00077598	50.14379014	0.01994265	171
172	26.19246004	0.03817893	1314.38921960	0.00076081	50.18196907	0.01992748	172
173	26.69448219	0.03746093	1340.58167964	0.00074594	50.21942999	0.01991261	173
174	27.20612644	0.03675643	1367.27616184	0.00073138	50.25618642	0.01989805	174
175	27.72757719	0.03606518	1394.48228827	0.00071711	50.29225160	0.01988378	175
176	28.25902242	0.03538693	1422.20986546	0.00070313	50.32763852	0.01986980	176
177	28.80065368	0.03472143	1450.46888788	0.00068943	50.36235996	0.01985610	177
178	29.35266621	0.03406846	1479.26954157	0.00067601	50.39642841	0.01984268	178
179	29.91525898	0.03342776	1508.62220778	0.00066286	50.42985617	0.01982952	179
180	30.48863478	0.03279911	1538.53746677	0.00064997	50.46265528	0.01981663	180
181	31.07300028	0.03218228	1569.02610154	0.00063734	50.49483756	0.01980400	181
182	31.66856612	0.03157705	1600.09910182	0.00062496	50.52641461	0.01979163	182
183	32.27554697	0.03098321	1631.76766794	0.00061283	50.55739782	0.01977950	183
184	32.89416162	0.03040053	1664.04321491	0.00060095	50.58779835	0.01976761	184
185	33.52463305	0.02982881	1696.93737653	0.00058930	50.61762716	0.01975596	185
186	34.16718852	0.02926785	1730.46200958	0.00057788	50.64689501	0.01974455	186
187	34.82205963	0.02871743	1764.62919810	0.00056669	50.67561244	0.01973336	187
188	35.48948244	0.02817736	1799.45125773	0.00055572	50.70378980	0.01972239	188
189	36.16969752	0.02764745	1834.94074017	0.00054498	50.73143725	0.01971164	189
190	36.86295006	0.02712751	1871.11043769	0.00053444	50.75856476	0.01970111	190
191	37.56948993	0.02661734	1907.97338774	0.00052412	50.78518210	0.01969078	191
192	38.28957182	0.02611677	1945.54287768	0.00051400	50.81129888	0.01968066	192
193	39.02345528	0.02562561	1983.83244950	0.00050407	50.83692449	0.01967074	193
194	39.77140484	0.02514369	2022.85590478	0.00049435	50.86206818	0.01966102	194
195	40.53369010	0.02467084	2062.62730962	0.00048482	50.88673902	0.01965149	195
196	41.31058583	0.02420687	2103.16099972	0.00047547	50.91094589	0.01964214	196
197	42.10237206	0.02375163	2144.47158555	0.00046632	50.93469752	0.01963298	197
198	42.90933419	0.02330495	2186.57395761	0.00045734	50.95800247	0.01962400	198
199	43.73176309	0.02286667	2229.48329179	0.00044853	50.98086915	0.01961520	199
200	44.56995522	0.02243664	2273.21505489	0.00043991	51.00330579	0.01960657	200

TABLE A-2

COMPOUND INTEREST FOR $1

$1\frac{11}{12}\%$

PERIODS n	FUTURE AMOUNT $(1+i)^n$	PRESENT VALUE $(1+i)^{-n}$	AMOUNT OF ANNUITY $(S/p,i,n)$ $\frac{(1+i)^n - 1}{i}$	SINKING FUND $(p/S,i,n)$ $\frac{i}{(1+i)^n - 1}$	PRESENT VALUE OF ANNUITY $(V/p,i,n)$ $\frac{1-(1+i)^{-n}}{i}$	AMORTIZATION $(p/V,i,n)$ $\frac{i}{1-(1+i)^{-n}}$	PERIODS n
201	45.42421269	0.02201469	2317.78501011	0.00043145	51.02532048	0.01959811	201
202	46.29484344	0.02160068	2363.20922280	0.00042315	51.04692115	0.01958982	202
203	47.18216127	0.02119445	2409.50406624	0.00041502	51.06811561	0.01958169	203
204	48.08648603	0.02079586	2456.68622751	0.00040705	51.08891147	0.01957372	204
205	49.00814368	0.02040477	2504.77271353	0.00039924	51.10931624	0.01956590	205
206	49.94746643	0.02002104	2553.78085721	0.00039158	51.12933728	0.01955824	206
207	50.90479287	0.01964452	2603.72832364	0.00038406	51.14898179	0.01955073	207
208	51.88046807	0.01927508	2654.63311651	0.00037670	51.16825687	0.01954337	208
209	52.87484370	0.01891259	2706.51358457	0.00036948	51.18716945	0.01953615	209
210	53.88827821	0.01855691	2759.38842828	0.00036240	51.20572637	0.01952907	210
211	54.92113687	0.01820793	2813.27670649	0.00035546	51.22393429	0.01952212	211
212	55.97379200	0.01786550	2868.19784336	0.00034865	51.24179980	0.01951532	212
213	57.04662301	0.01752952	2924.17163536	0.00034198	51.25932932	0.01950864	213
214	58.14001662	0.01719986	2981.21825837	0.00033543	51.27652917	0.01950210	214
215	59.25436694	0.01687639	3039.35827499	0.00032902	51.29340557	0.01949568	215
216	60.39007564	0.01655901	3098.61264193	0.00032273	51.30996458	0.01948939	216
217	61.54755209	0.01624760	3159.00271756	0.00031656	51.32621218	0.01948322	217
218	62.72721350	0.01594204	3220.55026965	0.00031051	51.34215422	0.01947717	218
219	63.92948509	0.01564223	3283.27748315	0.00030457	51.35779646	0.01947124	219
220	65.15480022	0.01534806	3347.20696825	0.00029876	51.37314452	0.01946542	220
221	66.40360056	0.01505942	3412.36176847	0.00029305	51.38820395	0.01945972	221
222	67.67633624	0.01477621	3478.76536903	0.00028746	51.40298016	0.01945412	222
223	68.97346602	0.01449833	3546.44170527	0.00028197	51.41747849	0.01944864	223
224	70.29545745	0.01422567	3615.41517129	0.00027659	51.43170416	0.01944326	224
225	71.64278705	0.01395814	3685.71062874	0.00027132	51.44566230	0.01943798	225
226	73.01594047	0.01369564	3757.35341579	0.00026614	51.45935794	0.01943281	226
227	74.41541266	0.01343808	3830.36935626	0.00026107	51.47279601	0.01942774	227
228	75.84170807	0.01318536	3904.78476892	0.00025610	51.48598137	0.01942276	228
229	77.29534081	0.01293739	3980.62647699	0.00025122	51.49891876	0.01941788	229
230	78.77683484	0.01269409	4057.92181780	0.00024643	51.51161285	0.01941310	230
231	80.28672418	0.01245536	4136.69865264	0.00024174	51.52406821	0.01940841	231
232	81.82555306	0.01222112	4216.98537682	0.00023714	51.53628933	0.01940380	232
233	83.39387616	0.01199129	4298.81092987	0.00023262	51.54828062	0.01939929	233
234	84.99225878	0.01176578	4382.20480603	0.00022820	51.56004640	0.01939486	234
235	86.62127708	0.01154451	4467.19706481	0.00022385	51.57159090	0.01939052	235
236	88.28151822	0.01132740	4553.81834189	0.00021960	51.58291830	0.01938626	236
237	89.97358065	0.01111437	4642.09986011	0.00021542	51.59403268	0.01938209	237
238	91.69807428	0.01090535	4732.07344076	0.00021132	51.60493803	0.01937799	238
239	93.45562070	0.01070027	4823.77151504	0.00020731	51.61563830	0.01937397	239
240	95.24685344	0.01049903	4917.22713575	0.00020337	51.62613733	0.01937003	240

TABLE A-2

COMPOUND INTEREST FOR $1

2%

PERIODS n	FUTURE AMOUNT $(1+i)^n$	PRESENT VALUE $(1+i)^{-n}$	AMOUNT OF ANNUITY (S/p,i,n) $\dfrac{(1+i)^n - 1}{i}$	SINKING FUND (p/S,i,n) $\dfrac{i}{(1+i)^n - 1}$	PRESENT VALUE OF ANNUITY (V/p,i,n) $\dfrac{1-(1+i)^{-n}}{i}$	AMORTIZATION (p/V,i,n) $\dfrac{i}{1-(1+i)^{-n}}$	PERIODS n
1	1.02000000	0.98039216	1.00000000	1.00000000	0.98039216	1.02000000	1
2	1.04040000	0.96116878	2.02000000	0.49504950	1.94156094	0.51504950	2
3	1.06120800	0.94232233	3.06040000	0.32675467	2.88388327	0.34675467	3
4	1.08243216	0.92384543	4.12160800	0.24262375	3.80772870	0.26262375	4
5	1.10408080	0.90573081	5.20404016	0.19215839	4.71345951	0.21215839	5
6	1.12616242	0.88797138	6.30812096	0.15852581	5.60143089	0.17852581	6
7	1.14868567	0.87056018	7.43428338	0.13451196	6.47199107	0.15451196	7
8	1.17165938	0.85349037	8.58296905	0.11650980	7.32548144	0.13650980	8
9	1.19509257	0.83675527	9.75462843	0.10251544	8.16223671	0.12251544	9
10	1.21899442	0.82034830	10.94972100	0.09132653	8.98258501	0.11132653	10
11	1.24337431	0.80426304	12.16871542	0.08217794	9.78684805	0.10217794	11
12	1.26824179	0.78849318	13.41208973	0.07455960	10.57534122	0.09455960	12
13	1.29360663	0.77303253	14.68033152	0.06811835	11.34837375	0.08811835	13
14	1.31947876	0.75787502	15.97393815	0.06260197	12.10624877	0.08260197	14
15	1.34586834	0.74301473	17.29341692	0.05782547	12.84926350	0.07782547	15
16	1.37278571	0.72844581	18.63928525	0.05365013	13.57770931	0.07365013	16
17	1.40024142	0.71416256	20.01207096	0.04996984	14.29187188	0.06996984	17
18	1.42824625	0.70015937	21.41231238	0.04670210	14.99203125	0.06670210	18
19	1.45681117	0.68643076	22.84055863	0.04378177	15.67846201	0.06378177	19
20	1.48594740	0.67297133	24.29736980	0.04115672	16.35143334	0.06115672	20
21	1.51566634	0.65977582	25.78331719	0.03878477	17.01120916	0.05878477	21
22	1.54597967	0.64683904	27.29898354	0.03663140	17.65804820	0.05663140	22
23	1.57689926	0.63415592	28.84496321	0.03466810	18.29220412	0.05466810	23
24	1.60843725	0.62172149	30.42186247	0.03287110	18.91392560	0.05287110	24
25	1.64060599	0.60953087	32.03029972	0.03122044	19.52345647	0.05122044	25
26	1.67341811	0.59757928	33.67090572	0.02969923	20.12103576	0.04969923	26
27	1.70688648	0.58586204	35.34432383	0.02829309	20.70689780	0.04829309	27
28	1.74102421	0.57437455	37.05121031	0.02698967	21.28127236	0.04698967	28
29	1.77584469	0.56311231	38.79223451	0.02577836	21.84438466	0.04577836	29
30	1.81136158	0.55207089	40.56807921	0.02464992	22.39645555	0.04464992	30
31	1.84758882	0.54124597	42.37944079	0.02359635	22.93770152	0.04359635	31
32	1.88454059	0.53063330	44.22702961	0.02261061	23.46833482	0.04261061	32
33	1.92223140	0.52022873	46.11157020	0.02168653	23.98856355	0.04168653	33
34	1.96067603	0.51002817	48.03380160	0.02081867	24.49859172	0.04081867	34
35	1.99988955	0.50002761	49.99447763	0.02000221	24.99861933	0.04000221	35
36	2.03988734	0.49022315	51.99436719	0.01923285	25.48884248	0.03923285	36
37	2.08068509	0.48061093	54.03425453	0.01850678	25.96945341	0.03850678	37
38	2.12229879	0.47118719	56.11493962	0.01782057	26.44064060	0.03782057	38
39	2.16474477	0.46194822	58.23723841	0.01717114	26.90258883	0.03717114	39
40	2.20803966	0.45289042	60.40198318	0.01655575	27.35547924	0.03655575	40

TABLE A-2

COMPOUND INTEREST FOR $1

2%

PERIODS n	FUTURE AMOUNT $(1+i)^n$	PRESENT VALUE $(1+i)^{-n}$	AMOUNT OF ANNUITY (S/p,i,n) $\frac{(1+i)^n - 1}{i}$	SINKING FUND (p/S,i,n) $\frac{i}{(1+i)^n - 1}$	PRESENT VALUE OF ANNUITY (V/p,i,n) $\frac{1-(1+i)^{-n}}{i}$	AMORTIZATION (p/V,i,n) $\frac{i}{1-(1+i)^{-n}}$	PERIODS n
41	2.25220046	0.44401021	62.61002284	0.01597188	27.79948945	0.03597188	41
42	2.29724447	0.43530413	64.86222330	0.01541729	28.23479358	0.03541729	42
43	2.34318936	0.42676875	67.15946777	0.01488993	28.66156233	0.03488993	43
44	2.39005314	0.41840074	69.50265712	0.01438794	29.07996307	0.03438794	44
45	2.43785421	0.41019680	71.89271027	0.01390962	29.49015987	0.03390962	45
46	2.48661129	0.40215373	74.33056447	0.01345342	29.89231360	0.03345342	46
47	2.53634352	0.39426836	76.81717576	0.01301792	30.28658196	0.03301792	47
48	2.58707039	0.38653761	79.35351927	0.01260184	30.67311957	0.03260184	48
49	2.63881179	0.37895844	81.94058966	0.01220396	31.05207801	0.03220396	49
50	2.69158803	0.37152788	84.57940145	0.01182321	31.42360589	0.03182321	50
51	2.74541979	0.36424302	87.27098948	0.01145856	31.78784892	0.03145856	51
52	2.80032819	0.35710100	90.01640927	0.01110909	32.14494992	0.03110909	52
53	2.85633475	0.35009902	92.81673746	0.01077392	32.49504894	0.03077392	53
54	2.91346144	0.34323433	95.67307221	0.01045226	32.83828327	0.03045226	54
55	2.97173067	0.33650425	98.58653365	0.01014337	33.17478752	0.03014337	55
56	3.03116529	0.32990613	101.55826432	0.00984656	33.50469365	0.02984656	56
57	3.09178859	0.32343738	104.58942961	0.00956120	33.82813103	0.02956120	57
58	3.15362436	0.31709547	107.68121820	0.00928667	34.14522650	0.02928667	58
59	3.21669685	0.31087791	110.83484257	0.00902243	34.45610441	0.02902243	59
60	3.28103079	0.30478227	114.05153942	0.00876797	34.76088668	0.02876797	60
61	3.34665140	0.29880614	117.33257021	0.00852278	35.05969282	0.02852278	61
62	3.41358443	0.29294720	120.67922161	0.00828643	35.35264002	0.02828643	62
63	3.48185612	0.28720314	124.09280604	0.00805848	35.63984316	0.02805848	63
64	3.55149324	0.28157170	127.57466216	0.00783855	35.92141486	0.02783855	64
65	3.62252311	0.27605069	131.12615541	0.00762624	36.19746555	0.02762624	65
66	3.69497357	0.27063793	134.74867852	0.00742122	36.46810348	0.02742122	66
67	3.76887304	0.26533130	138.44365209	0.00722316	36.73343478	0.02722316	67
68	3.84425050	0.26012873	142.21252513	0.00703173	36.99356351	0.02703173	68
69	3.92113551	0.25502817	146.05677563	0.00684665	37.24859168	0.02684665	69
70	3.99955822	0.25002761	149.97791114	0.00666765	37.49861929	0.02666765	70
71	4.07954939	0.24512511	153.97746937	0.00649446	37.74374441	0.02649446	71
72	4.16114038	0.24031874	158.05701875	0.00632683	37.98406314	0.02632683	72
73	4.24436318	0.23560661	162.21815913	0.00616454	38.21966975	0.02616454	73
74	4.32925045	0.23098687	166.46252231	0.00600736	38.45065662	0.02600736	74
75	4.41583546	0.22645771	170.79177276	0.00585508	38.67711433	0.02585508	75
76	4.50415216	0.22201737	175.20760821	0.00570751	38.89913170	0.02570751	76
77	4.59423521	0.21766408	179.71176038	0.00556447	39.11679578	0.02556447	77
78	4.68611991	0.21339616	184.30599558	0.00542576	39.33019194	0.02542576	78
79	4.77984231	0.20921192	188.99211549	0.00529123	39.53940386	0.02529123	79
80	4.87543916	0.20510973	193.77195780	0.00516071	39.74451359	0.02516071	80

TABLE A-2

COMPOUND INTEREST FOR $1

2%

PERIODS	FUTURE AMOUNT	PRESENT VALUE	AMOUNT OF ANNUITY	SINKING FUND	PRESENT VALUE OF ANNUITY	AMORTIZATION	PERIODS
n	$(1+i)^n$	$(1+i)^{-n}$	$(S/p,i,n)$ $\dfrac{(1+i)^n-1}{i}$	$(p/S,i,n)$ $\dfrac{i}{(1+i)^n-1}$	$(V/p,i,n)$ $\dfrac{1-(1+i)^{-n}}{i}$	$(p/V,i,n)$ $\dfrac{i}{1-(1+i)^{-n}}$	n
81	4.97294794	0.20108797	198.64739696	0.00503405	39.94560156	0.02503405	81
82	5.07240690	0.19714507	203.62034490	0.00491110	40.14274663	0.02491110	82
83	5.17385504	0.19327948	208.69275180	0.00479173	40.33602611	0.02479173	83
84	5.27733214	0.18948968	213.86660683	0.00467581	40.52551579	0.02467581	84
85	5.38287878	0.18577420	219.14393897	0.00456321	40.71128999	0.02456321	85
86	5.49053636	0.18213157	224.52681775	0.00445381	40.89342156	0.02445381	86
87	5.60034708	0.17856036	230.01735411	0.00434708	41.07198192	0.02434708	87
88	5.71235402	0.17505918	235.61770119	0.00424416	41.24704110	0.02424416	88
89	5.82660110	0.17162665	241.33005521	0.00414370	41.41866774	0.02414370	89
90	5.94313313	0.16826142	247.15665632	0.00404602	41.58692916	0.02404602	90
91	6.06199579	0.16496217	253.09978944	0.00395101	41.75189133	0.02395101	91
92	6.18323570	0.16172762	259.16178523	0.00385859	41.91361895	0.02385859	92
93	6.30690042	0.15855649	265.34502094	0.00376868	42.07217545	0.02376868	93
94	6.43303843	0.15544754	271.65192135	0.00368118	42.22762299	0.02368118	94
95	6.56169920	0.15239955	278.08495978	0.00359602	42.38002254	0.02359602	95
96	6.69293318	0.14941132	284.64665898	0.00351313	42.52943386	0.02351313	96
97	6.82679184	0.14648169	291.33959216	0.00343242	42.67591555	0.02343242	97
98	6.96332768	0.14360950	298.16638400	0.00335383	42.81952505	0.02335383	98
99	7.10259423	0.14079363	305.12971168	0.00327729	42.96031867	0.02327729	99
100	7.24464612	0.13803297	312.23230591	0.00320274	43.09835164	0.02320274	100
101	7.38953904	0.13532644	319.47695203	0.00313012	43.23367808	0.02313012	101
102	7.53732982	0.13267298	326.86649107	0.00305935	43.36635106	0.02305935	102
103	7.68807642	0.13007155	334.40382089	0.00299040	43.49642261	0.02299040	103
104	7.84183795	0.12752113	342.09189731	0.00292319	43.62394373	0.02292319	104
105	7.99867471	0.12502071	349.93373526	0.00285768	43.74896444	0.02285768	105
106	8.15864820	0.12256932	357.93240996	0.00279382	43.87153377	0.02279382	106
107	8.32182116	0.12016600	366.09105816	0.00273156	43.99169977	0.02273156	107
108	8.48825759	0.11780981	374.41287932	0.00267085	44.10950958	0.02267085	108
109	8.65802274	0.11549981	382.90113691	0.00261164	44.22500939	0.02261164	109
110	8.83118319	0.11323511	391.55915965	0.00255389	44.33824450	0.02255389	110
111	9.00780686	0.11101481	400.39034284	0.00249756	44.44925932	0.02249756	111
112	9.18796299	0.10883805	409.39814970	0.00244261	44.55809737	0.02244261	112
113	9.37172225	0.10670397	418.58611269	0.00238899	44.66480134	0.02238899	113
114	9.55915670	0.10461174	427.95783495	0.00233668	44.76941308	0.02233668	114
115	9.75028983	0.10256053	437.51699165	0.00228563	44.87197361	0.02228563	115
116	9.94534663	0.10054954	447.26733148	0.00223580	44.97252314	0.02223580	116
117	10.14425356	0.09857798	457.21267811	0.00218717	45.07110112	0.02218717	117
118	10.34713863	0.09664508	467.35693167	0.00213969	45.16774620	0.02213969	118
119	10.55408141	0.09475007	477.70407030	0.00209335	45.26249627	0.02209335	119
120	10.76516303	0.09289223	488.25815171	0.00204810	45.35538850	0.02204810	120

TABLE A-2

COMPOUND INTEREST FOR $1

2%

PERIODS n	FUTURE AMOUNT $(1+i)^n$	PRESENT VALUE $(1+i)^{-n}$	AMOUNT OF ANNUITY $(S/p,i,n)$ $\dfrac{(1+i)^n-1}{i}$	SINKING FUND $(p/S,i,n)$ $\dfrac{i}{(1+i)^n-1}$	PRESENT VALUE OF ANNUITY $(V/p,i,n)$ $\dfrac{1-(1+i)^{-n}}{i}$	AMORTIZATION $(p/V,i,n)$ $\dfrac{i}{1-(1+i)^{-n}}$	PERIODS n
121	10.98046629	0.09107081	499.02331474	0.00200391	45.44645932	0.02200391	121
122	11.20007562	0.08928511	510.00378104	0.00196077	45.53574443	0.02196077	122
123	11.42407713	0.08753442	521.20385666	0.00191864	45.62327885	0.02191864	123
124	11.65255868	0.08581806	532.62793379	0.00187748	45.70909691	0.02187748	124
125	11.88560985	0.08413535	544.28049247	0.00183729	45.79323227	0.02183729	125
126	12.12332205	0.08248564	556.16610232	0.00179802	45.87571791	0.02179802	126
127	12.36578849	0.08086828	568.28942436	0.00175967	45.95658619	0.02175967	127
128	12.61310426	0.07928262	580.65521285	0.00172219	46.03586881	0.02172219	128
129	12.86536634	0.07772806	593.26831711	0.00168558	46.11359687	0.02168558	129
130	13.12267367	0.07620398	606.13368345	0.00164980	46.18980085	0.02164980	130
131	13.38512714	0.07470979	619.25635712	0.00161484	46.26451064	0.02161484	131
132	13.65282969	0.07324489	632.64148426	0.00158067	46.33775553	0.02158067	132
133	13.92588628	0.07180872	646.29431395	0.00154728	46.40956425	0.02154728	133
134	14.20440400	0.07040070	660.22020023	0.00151465	46.47996495	0.02151465	134
135	14.48849208	0.06902030	674.42460423	0.00148275	46.54898524	0.02148275	135
136	14.77826193	0.06766696	688.91309632	0.00145156	46.61665220	0.02145156	136
137	15.07382716	0.06634015	703.69135824	0.00142108	46.68299235	0.02142108	137
138	15.37530371	0.06503937	718.76518541	0.00139127	46.74803172	0.02139127	138
139	15.68280978	0.06376408	734.14048912	0.00136214	46.81179580	0.02136214	139
140	15.99646598	0.06251381	749.82329890	0.00133365	46.87430961	0.02133365	140
141	16.31639530	0.06128805	765.81976488	0.00130579	46.93559766	0.02130579	141
142	16.64272320	0.06008632	782.13616017	0.00127855	46.99568398	0.02127855	142
143	16.97557767	0.05890816	798.77888338	0.00125191	47.05459213	0.02125191	143
144	17.31508922	0.05775310	815.75446104	0.00122586	47.11234523	0.02122586	144
145	17.66139101	0.05662068	833.06955027	0.00120038	47.16896591	0.02120038	145
146	18.01461883	0.05551047	850.73094127	0.00117546	47.22447638	0.02117546	146
147	18.37491120	0.05442203	868.74556010	0.00115109	47.27889841	0.02115109	147
148	18.74240943	0.05335493	887.12047130	0.00112724	47.33225335	0.02112724	148
149	19.11725761	0.05230876	905.86288072	0.00110392	47.38456211	0.02110392	149
150	19.49960277	0.05128310	924.98013834	0.00108110	47.43584520	0.02108110	150
151	19.88959482	0.05027755	944.47974110	0.00105878	47.48612275	0.02105878	151
152	20.28738672	0.04929171	964.36933593	0.00103695	47.53541446	0.02103695	152
153	20.69313445	0.04832521	984.65672265	0.00101558	47.58373966	0.02101558	153
154	21.10699714	0.04737765	1005.34985710	0.00099468	47.63111732	0.02099468	154
155	21.52913708	0.04644868	1026.45685424	0.00097423	47.67756600	0.02097423	155
156	21.95971983	0.04553792	1047.98599133	0.00095421	47.72310392	0.02095421	156
157	22.39891422	0.04464502	1069.94571115	0.00093463	47.76774894	0.02093463	157
158	22.84689251	0.04376963	1092.34462537	0.00091546	47.81151857	0.02091546	158
159	23.30383036	0.04291140	1115.19151788	0.00089671	47.85442997	0.02089671	159
160	23.76990696	0.04207000	1138.49534824	0.00087835	47.89649997	0.02087835	160

TABLE A-2

COMPOUND INTEREST FOR $1

2%

PERIODS n	FUTURE AMOUNT $(1+i)^n$	PRESENT VALUE $(1+i)^{-n}$	AMOUNT OF ANNUITY $(S/p,i,n)$ $\dfrac{(1+i)^n-1}{i}$	SINKING FUND $(p/S,i,n)$ $\dfrac{i}{(1+i)^n-1}$	PRESENT VALUE OF ANNUITY $(V/p,i,n)$ $\dfrac{1-(1+i)^{-n}}{i}$	AMORTIZATION $(p/V,i,n)$ $\dfrac{i}{1-(1+i)^{-n}}$	PERIODS n
161	24.24530510	0.04124510	1162.26525520	0.00086039	47.93774507	0.02086039	161
162	24.73021121	0.04043637	1186.51056031	0.00084281	47.97818144	0.02084281	162
163	25.22481543	0.03964350	1211.24077151	0.00082560	48.01782494	0.02082560	163
164	25.72931174	0.03886618	1236.46558695	0.00080876	48.05669112	0.02080876	164
165	26.24389797	0.03810410	1262.19489868	0.00079227	48.09479521	0.02079227	165
166	26.76877593	0.03735696	1288.43879666	0.00077613	48.13215217	0.02077613	166
167	27.30415145	0.03662447	1315.20757259	0.00076034	48.16877664	0.02076034	167
168	27.85023448	0.03590634	1342.51172404	0.00074487	48.20468298	0.02074487	168
169	28.40723917	0.03520229	1370.36195852	0.00072973	48.23988527	0.02072973	169
170	28.97538395	0.03451205	1398.76919769	0.00071491	48.27439733	0.02071491	170
171	29.55489163	0.03383535	1427.74458165	0.00070041	48.30823267	0.02070041	171
172	30.14598947	0.03317191	1457.29947328	0.00068620	48.34140458	0.02068620	172
173	30.74890925	0.03252148	1487.44546275	0.00067229	48.37392606	0.02067229	173
174	31.36388744	0.03188380	1518.19437200	0.00065868	48.40580986	0.02065868	174
175	31.99116519	0.03125863	1549.55825944	0.00064535	48.43706849	0.02064535	175
176	32.63098849	0.03064572	1581.54942463	0.00063229	48.46771421	0.02063229	176
177	33.28360826	0.03004482	1614.18041312	0.00061951	48.49775903	0.02061951	177
178	33.94928043	0.02945571	1647.46402139	0.00060699	48.52721473	0.02060699	178
179	34.62826604	0.02887814	1681.41330181	0.00059474	48.55609288	0.02059474	179
180	35.32083136	0.02831190	1716.04156785	0.00058274	48.58440478	0.02058274	180
181	36.02724798	0.02775677	1751.36239921	0.00057098	48.61216155	0.02057098	181
182	36.74779294	0.02721252	1787.38964719	0.00055948	48.63937407	0.02055948	182
183	37.48274880	0.02667894	1824.13744013	0.00054820	48.66605301	0.02054820	183
184	38.23240378	0.02615582	1861.62018894	0.00053717	48.69220883	0.02053717	184
185	38.99705185	0.02564296	1899.85259272	0.00052636	48.71785180	0.02052636	185
186	39.77699289	0.02514016	1938.84964457	0.00051577	48.74299196	0.02051577	186
187	40.57253275	0.02464722	1978.62663746	0.00050540	48.76763917	0.02050540	187
188	41.38398340	0.02416394	2019.19917021	0.00049525	48.79180311	0.02049525	188
189	42.21166307	0.02369014	2060.58315361	0.00048530	48.81549325	0.02048530	189
190	43.05589633	0.02322562	2102.79481669	0.00047556	48.83871887	0.02047556	190
191	43.91701426	0.02277022	2145.85071302	0.00046602	48.86148909	0.02046602	191
192	44.79535455	0.02232374	2189.76772728	0.00045667	48.88381283	0.02045667	192
193	45.69126164	0.02188602	2234.56308183	0.00044751	48.90569885	0.02044751	193
194	46.60508687	0.02145689	2280.25434346	0.00043855	48.92715574	0.02043855	194
195	47.53718861	0.02103616	2326.85943033	0.00042976	48.94819190	0.02042976	195
196	48.48793238	0.02062369	2374.39661894	0.00042116	48.96881559	0.02042116	196
197	49.45769103	0.02021930	2422.88455132	0.00041273	48.98903489	0.02041273	197
198	50.44684485	0.01982285	2472.34224234	0.00040447	49.00885774	0.02040447	198
199	51.45578174	0.01943416	2522.78908719	0.00039639	49.02829190	0.02039639	199
200	52.48489738	0.01905310	2574.24486894	0.00038846	49.04734500	0.02038846	200

COMPOUND INTEREST FOR $1

2%

PERIODS	FUTURE AMOUNT	PRESENT VALUE	AMOUNT OF ANNUITY	SINKING FUND	PRESENT VALUE OF ANNUITY	AMORTIZATION	PERIODS
n	$(1+i)^n$	$(1+i)^{-n}$	$(S/p,i,n)$ $\dfrac{(1+i)^n - 1}{i}$	$(p/S,i,n)$ $\dfrac{i}{(1+i)^n - 1}$	$(V/p,i,n)$ $\dfrac{1-(1+i)^{-n}}{i}$	$(p/V,i,n)$ $\dfrac{i}{1-(1+i)^{-n}}$	n
201	53.53459533	0.01867951	2626.72976631	0.00038070	49.06602451	0.02038070	201
202	54.60528723	0.01831324	2680.26436164	0.00037310	49.08433775	0.02037310	202
203	55.69739298	0.01795416	2734.86964887	0.00036565	49.10229191	0.02036565	203
204	56.81134084	0.01760212	2790.56704185	0.00035835	49.11989403	0.02035835	204
205	57.94756765	0.01725698	2847.37838269	0.00035120	49.13715101	0.02035120	205
206	59.10651901	0.01691861	2905.32595034	0.00034420	49.15406962	0.02034420	206
207	60.28864939	0.01658687	2964.43246935	0.00033733	49.17065649	0.02033733	207
208	61.49442237	0.01626164	3024.72111874	0.00033061	49.18691813	0.02033061	208
209	62.72431082	0.01594278	3086.21554111	0.00032402	49.20286091	0.02032402	209
210	63.97879704	0.01563018	3148.93985193	0.00031757	49.21849109	0.02031757	210
211	65.25837298	0.01532370	3212.91864897	0.00031124	49.23381479	0.02031124	211
212	66.56354044	0.01502324	3278.17702195	0.00030505	49.24883803	0.02030505	212
213	67.89481125	0.01472867	3344.74056239	0.00029898	49.26356670	0.02029898	213
214	69.25270747	0.01443987	3412.63537364	0.00029303	49.27800657	0.02029303	214
215	70.63776162	0.01415673	3481.88808111	0.00028720	49.29216330	0.02028720	215
216	72.05051685	0.01387915	3552.52584273	0.00028149	49.30604245	0.02028149	216
217	73.49152719	0.01360701	3624.57635959	0.00027589	49.31964946	0.02027589	217
218	74.96135774	0.01334021	3698.06788678	0.00027041	49.33298967	0.02027041	218
219	76.46058489	0.01307863	3773.02924451	0.00026504	49.34606830	0.02026504	219
220	77.98979659	0.01282219	3849.48982940	0.00025977	49.35889049	0.02025977	220
221	79.54959252	0.01257077	3927.47962599	0.00025462	49.37146127	0.02025462	221
222	81.14058437	0.01232429	4007.02921851	0.00024956	49.38378556	0.02024956	222
223	82.76339606	0.01208264	4088.16980288	0.00024461	49.39586819	0.02024461	223
224	84.41866398	0.01184572	4170.93319894	0.00023975	49.40771391	0.02023975	224
225	86.10703726	0.01161345	4255.35186292	0.00023500	49.41932737	0.02023500	225
226	87.82917800	0.01138574	4341.45890018	0.00023034	49.43071311	0.02023034	226
227	89.58576156	0.01116249	4429.28807818	0.00022577	49.44187559	0.02022577	227
228	91.37747679	0.01094362	4518.87383974	0.00022129	49.45281921	0.02022129	228
229	93.20502633	0.01072904	4610.25131654	0.00021691	49.46354824	0.02021691	229
230	95.06912686	0.01051866	4703.45634287	0.00021261	49.47406691	0.02021261	230
231	96.97050939	0.01031241	4798.52546973	0.00020840	49.48437932	0.02020840	231
232	98.90991958	0.01011021	4895.49597912	0.00020427	49.49448953	0.02020427	232
233	100.88811797	0.00991197	4994.40589870	0.00020022	49.50440150	0.02020022	233
234	102.90588033	0.00971762	5095.29401668	0.00019626	49.51411912	0.02019626	234
235	104.96399794	0.00952708	5198.19989701	0.00019237	49.52364619	0.02019237	235
236	107.06327790	0.00934027	5303.16389495	0.00018857	49.53298646	0.02018857	236
237	109.20454346	0.00915713	5410.22717285	0.00018484	49.54214359	0.02018484	237
238	111.38863433	0.00897758	5519.43171631	0.00018118	49.55112117	0.02018118	238
239	113.61640701	0.00880155	5630.82035063	0.00017759	49.55992271	0.02017759	239
240	115.88873515	0.00862897	5744.43675765	0.00017408	49.56855168	0.02017408	240

TABLE A-2

COMPOUND INTEREST FOR $1

$2\frac{1}{2}\%$

PERIODS n	FUTURE AMOUNT $(1+i)^n$	PRESENT VALUE $(1+i)^{-n}$	AMOUNT OF ANNUITY $(S/p,i,n)$ $\dfrac{(1+i)^n - 1}{i}$	SINKING FUND $(p/S,i,n)$ $\dfrac{i}{(1+i)^n - 1}$	PRESENT VALUE OF ANNUITY $(V/p,i,n)$ $\dfrac{1-(1+i)^{-n}}{i}$	AMORTIZATION $(p/V,i,n)$ $\dfrac{i}{1-(1+i)^{-n}}$	PERIODS n
1	1.02500000	0.97560976	1.00000000	1.00000000	0.97560976	1.02500000	1
2	1.05062500	0.95181440	2.02500000	0.49382716	1.92742415	0.51882716	2
3	1.07689062	0.92859941	3.07562500	0.32513717	2.85602356	0.35013717	3
4	1.10381289	0.90595064	4.15251562	0.24081788	3.76197421	0.26581788	4
5	1.13140821	0.88385429	5.25632852	0.19024686	4.64582850	0.21524686	5
6	1.15969342	0.86229687	6.38773673	0.15654997	5.50812536	0.18154997	6
7	1.18868575	0.84126524	7.54743015	0.13249543	6.34939060	0.15749543	7
8	1.21840290	0.82074657	8.73611590	0.11446735	7.17013717	0.13946735	8
9	1.24886297	0.80072836	9.95451880	0.10045689	7.97086553	0.12545689	9
10	1.28008454	0.78119840	11.20338177	0.08925876	8.75206393	0.11425876	10
11	1.31208666	0.76214478	12.48346631	0.08010596	9.51420871	0.10510596	11
12	1.34488882	0.74355589	13.79555297	0.07248713	10.25776460	0.09748713	12
13	1.37851104	0.72542038	15.14044179	0.06604827	10.98318497	0.09104827	13
14	1.41297382	0.70772720	16.51895284	0.06053652	11.69091217	0.08553652	14
15	1.44829817	0.69046556	17.93192666	0.05576646	12.38137773	0.08076646	15
16	1.48450562	0.67362493	19.38022483	0.05159899	13.05500266	0.07659899	16
17	1.52161826	0.65719506	20.86473045	0.04792777	13.71219772	0.07292777	17
18	1.55965872	0.64116591	22.38634871	0.04467008	14.35336363	0.06967008	18
19	1.59865019	0.62552772	23.94600743	0.04176062	14.97889134	0.06676062	19
20	1.63861644	0.61027094	25.54465761	0.03914713	15.58916229	0.06414713	20
21	1.67958185	0.59538629	27.18327405	0.03678733	16.18454857	0.06178733	21
22	1.72157140	0.58086467	28.86285590	0.03464661	16.76541324	0.05964661	22
23	1.76461068	0.56669724	30.58442730	0.03269638	17.33211048	0.05769638	23
24	1.80872595	0.55287535	32.34903798	0.03091282	17.88498583	0.05591282	24
25	1.85394410	0.53939059	34.15776393	0.02927592	18.42437642	0.05427592	25
26	1.90029270	0.52623472	36.01170803	0.02776875	18.95061114	0.05276875	26
27	1.94780002	0.51339973	37.91200073	0.02637687	19.46401087	0.05137687	27
28	1.99649502	0.50087778	39.85980075	0.02508793	19.96488866	0.05008793	28
29	2.04640739	0.48866125	41.85629577	0.02389127	20.45354991	0.04889127	29
30	2.09756758	0.47674269	43.90270316	0.02277764	20.93029259	0.04777764	30
31	2.15000677	0.46511481	46.00027074	0.02173900	21.39540741	0.04673900	31
32	2.20375694	0.45377055	48.15027751	0.02076831	21.84917796	0.04576831	32
33	2.25885086	0.44270298	50.35403445	0.01985938	22.29188094	0.04485938	33
34	2.31532213	0.43190534	52.61288531	0.01900675	22.72378628	0.04400675	34
35	2.37320519	0.42137107	54.92820744	0.01820558	23.14515734	0.04320558	35
36	2.43253532	0.41109372	57.30141263	0.01745158	23.55625107	0.04245158	36
37	2.49334870	0.40106705	59.73394794	0.01674090	23.95731812	0.04174090	37
38	2.55568242	0.39128492	62.22729664	0.01607012	24.34860304	0.04107012	38
39	2.61957448	0.38174139	64.78297906	0.01543615	24.73034443	0.04043615	39
40	2.68506384	0.37243062	67.40255354	0.01483623	25.10277505	0.03983623	40

TABLE A-2

COMPOUND INTEREST FOR $1

$2\frac{1}{2}\%$

PERIODS n	FUTURE AMOUNT $(1+i)^n$	PRESENT VALUE $(1+i)^{-n}$	AMOUNT OF ANNUITY $(S/p,i,n)$ $\dfrac{(1+i)^n-1}{i}$	SINKING FUND $(p/S,i,n)$ $\dfrac{i}{(1+i)^n-1}$	PRESENT VALUE OF ANNUITY $(V/p,i,n)$ $\dfrac{1-(1+i)^{-n}}{i}$	AMORTIZATION $(p/V,i,n)$ $\dfrac{i}{1-(1+i)^{-n}}$	PERIODS n
41	2.75219043	0.36334695	70.08761737	0.01426786	25.46612200	0.03926786	41
42	2.82099520	0.35448483	72.83980781	0.01372876	25.82060683	0.03872876	42
43	2.89152008	0.34583886	75.66080300	0.01321688	26.16644569	0.03821688	43
44	2.96380808	0.33740376	78.55232308	0.01273037	26.50384945	0.03773037	44
45	3.03790328	0.32917440	81.51613116	0.01226751	26.83302386	0.03726751	45
46	3.11385086	0.32114576	84.55403443	0.01182676	27.15416962	0.03682676	46
47	3.19169713	0.31331294	87.66788530	0.01140669	27.46748255	0.03640669	47
48	3.27148956	0.30567116	90.85958243	0.01100599	27.77315371	0.03600599	48
49	3.35327680	0.29821576	94.13107199	0.01062348	28.07136947	0.03562348	49
50	3.43710872	0.29094221	97.48434879	0.01025806	28.36231168	0.03525806	50
51	3.52303644	0.28384606	100.92145751	0.00990870	28.64615774	0.03490870	51
52	3.61111235	0.27692298	104.44449395	0.00957446	28.92308072	0.03457446	52
53	3.70139016	0.27016876	108.05560629	0.00925449	29.19324948	0.03425449	53
54	3.79392491	0.26357928	111.75699645	0.00894799	29.45682876	0.03394799	54
55	3.88877303	0.25715052	115.55092136	0.00865419	29.71397928	0.03365419	55
56	3.98599236	0.25087855	119.43969440	0.00837243	29.96485784	0.03337243	56
57	4.08564217	0.24475956	123.42568676	0.00810204	30.20961740	0.03310204	57
58	4.18778322	0.23878982	127.51132893	0.00784244	30.44840722	0.03284244	58
59	4.29247780	0.23296568	131.69911215	0.00759307	30.68137290	0.03259307	59
60	4.39978975	0.22728359	135.99158995	0.00735340	30.90865649	0.03235340	60
61	4.50978449	0.22174009	140.39137970	0.00712294	31.13039657	0.03212294	61
62	4.62252910	0.21633179	144.90116419	0.00690126	31.34672836	0.03190126	62
63	4.73809233	0.21105541	149.52369330	0.00668790	31.55778377	0.03168790	63
64	4.85654464	0.20590771	154.26178563	0.00648249	31.76369148	0.03148249	64
65	4.97795826	0.20088557	159.11833027	0.00628463	31.96457705	0.03128463	65
66	5.10240721	0.19598593	164.09628853	0.00609398	32.16056298	0.03109398	66
67	5.22996739	0.19120578	169.19869574	0.00591021	32.35176876	0.03091021	67
68	5.36071658	0.18654223	174.42866314	0.00573300	32.53831099	0.03073300	68
69	5.49473449	0.18199241	179.78937971	0.00556206	32.72030340	0.03056206	69
70	5.63210286	0.17755358	185.28411421	0.00539712	32.89785698	0.03039712	70
71	5.77290543	0.17322300	190.91621706	0.00523790	33.07107998	0.03023790	71
72	5.91722806	0.16899805	196.68912249	0.00508417	33.24007803	0.03008417	72
73	6.06515876	0.16487615	202.60635055	0.00493568	33.40495417	0.02993568	73
74	6.21678773	0.16085478	208.67150931	0.00479222	33.56580895	0.02979222	74
75	6.37220743	0.15693149	214.88829705	0.00465358	33.72274044	0.02965358	75
76	6.53151261	0.15310389	221.26050447	0.00451956	33.87584433	0.02951956	76
77	6.69480043	0.14936965	227.79201709	0.00438997	34.02521398	0.02938997	77
78	6.86217044	0.14572649	234.48681751	0.00426463	34.17094047	0.02926463	78
79	7.03372470	0.14217218	241.34898795	0.00414338	34.31311265	0.02914338	79
80	7.20956782	0.13870457	248.38271265	0.00402605	34.45181722	0.02902605	80

COMPOUND INTEREST FOR $1

$2\frac{1}{2}$%

PERIODS n	FUTURE AMOUNT $(1+i)^n$	PRESENT VALUE $(1+i)^{-n}$	AMOUNT OF ANNUITY $(S/p,i,n)$ $\frac{(1+i)^n - 1}{i}$	SINKING FUND $(p/S,i,n)$ $\frac{i}{(1+i)^n - 1}$	PRESENT VALUE OF ANNUITY $(V/p,i,n)$ $\frac{1-(1+i)^{-n}}{i}$	AMORTIZATION $(p/V,i,n)$ $\frac{i}{1-(1+i)^{-n}}$	PERIODS n
81	7.38980701	0.13532153	255.59228047	0.00391248	34.58713875	0.02891248	81
82	7.57455219	0.13202101	262.98208748	0.00380254	34.71915976	0.02880254	82
83	7.76391599	0.12880098	270.55663966	0.00369608	34.84796074	0.02869608	83
84	7.95801389	0.12565949	278.32055566	0.00359298	34.97362023	0.02859298	84
85	8.15696424	0.12259463	286.27856955	0.00349310	35.09621486	0.02849310	85
86	8.36088834	0.11960452	294.43553379	0.00339633	35.21581938	0.02839633	86
87	8.56991055	0.11668733	302.79642213	0.00330255	35.33250671	0.02830255	87
88	8.78415832	0.11384130	311.36633268	0.00321165	35.44634801	0.02821165	88
89	9.00376228	0.11106468	320.15049100	0.00312353	35.55741269	0.02812353	89
90	9.22885633	0.10835579	329.15425328	0.00303809	35.66576848	0.02803809	90
91	9.45957774	0.10571296	338.38310961	0.00295523	35.77148144	0.02795523	91
92	9.69606718	0.10313460	347.84268735	0.00287486	35.87461604	0.02787486	92
93	9.93846886	0.10061912	357.53875453	0.00279690	35.97523516	0.02779690	93
94	10.18693058	0.09816500	367.47722339	0.00272126	36.07340016	0.02772126	94
95	10.44160385	0.09577073	377.66415398	0.00264786	36.16917089	0.02764786	95
96	10.70264395	0.09343486	388.10575783	0.00257662	36.26260574	0.02757662	96
97	10.97021004	0.09115596	398.80840177	0.00250747	36.35376170	0.02750747	97
98	11.24446530	0.08893264	409.77861182	0.00244034	36.44269434	0.02744034	98
99	11.52557693	0.08676355	421.02307711	0.00237517	36.52945790	0.02737517	99
100	11.81371635	0.08464737	432.54865404	0.00231188	36.61410526	0.02731188	100
101	12.10905926	0.08258280	444.36237039	0.00225042	36.69668806	0.02725042	101
102	12.41178574	0.08056858	456.47142965	0.00219072	36.77725665	0.02719072	102
103	12.72208038	0.07860350	468.88321539	0.00213273	36.85586014	0.02713273	103
104	13.04013239	0.07668634	481.60529578	0.00207639	36.93254648	0.02707639	104
105	13.36613570	0.07481594	494.64542817	0.00202165	37.00736242	0.02702165	105
106	13.70028910	0.07299116	508.01156388	0.00196846	37.08035358	0.02696846	106
107	14.04279632	0.07121089	521.71185298	0.00191677	37.15156447	0.02691677	107
108	14.39386623	0.06947404	535.75464930	0.00186653	37.22103851	0.02686653	108
109	14.75371289	0.06777955	550.14851553	0.00181769	37.28881806	0.02681769	109
110	15.12255571	0.06612639	564.90222842	0.00177022	37.35494444	0.02677022	110
111	15.50061960	0.06451355	580.02478413	0.00172406	37.41945799	0.02672406	111
112	15.88813509	0.06294005	595.52540373	0.00167919	37.48239804	0.02667919	112
113	16.28533847	0.06140493	611.41353883	0.00163555	37.54380297	0.02663555	113
114	16.69247193	0.05990724	627.69887730	0.00159312	37.60371021	0.02659312	114
115	17.10978373	0.05844609	644.39134923	0.00155185	37.66215631	0.02655185	115
116	17.53752832	0.05702058	661.50113296	0.00151171	37.71917688	0.02651171	116
117	17.97596653	0.05562983	679.03866129	0.00147267	37.77480672	0.02647267	117
118	18.42536570	0.05427301	697.01462782	0.00143469	37.82907972	0.02643469	118
119	18.88599984	0.05294928	715.43999351	0.00139774	37.88202900	0.02639774	119
120	19.35814983	0.05165783	734.32599335	0.00136179	37.93368683	0.02636179	120

TABLE A-2

COMPOUND INTEREST FOR $1

3%

PERIODS n	FUTURE AMOUNT $(1+i)^n$	PRESENT VALUE $(1+i)^{-n}$	AMOUNT OF ANNUITY $(S/p,i,n)$ $\dfrac{(1+i)^n-1}{i}$	SINKING FUND $(p/S,i,n)$ $\dfrac{i}{(1+i)^n-1}$	PRESENT VALUE OF ANNUITY $(V/p,i,n)$ $\dfrac{1-(1+i)^{-n}}{i}$	AMORTIZATION $(p/V,i,n)$ $\dfrac{i}{1-(1+i)^{-n}}$	PERIODS n
1	1.03000000	0.97087379	1.00000000	1.00000000	0.97087379	1.03000000	1
2	1.06090000	0.94259591	2.03000000	0.49261084	1.91346970	0.52261084	2
3	1.09272700	0.91514166	3.09090000	0.32353036	2.82861135	0.35353036	3
4	1.12550881	0.88848705	4.18362700	0.23902705	3.71709840	0.26902705	4
5	1.15927407	0.86260878	5.30913581	0.18835457	4.57970719	0.21835457	5
6	1.19405230	0.83748426	6.46840988	0.15459750	5.41719144	0.18459750	6
7	1.22987387	0.81309151	7.66246218	0.13050635	6.23028296	0.16050635	7
8	1.26677008	0.78940923	8.89233605	0.11245639	7.01969219	0.14245639	8
9	1.30477318	0.76641673	10.15910613	0.09843386	7.78610892	0.12843386	9
10	1.34391638	0.74409391	11.46387931	0.08723051	8.53020284	0.11723051	10
11	1.38423387	0.72242128	12.80779569	0.07807745	9.25262411	0.10807745	11
12	1.42576089	0.70137988	14.19202956	0.07046209	9.95400399	0.10046209	12
13	1.46853371	0.68095134	15.61779045	0.06402954	10.63495533	0.09402954	13
14	1.51258972	0.66111781	17.08632416	0.05852634	11.29607314	0.08852634	14
15	1.55796742	0.64186195	18.59891389	0.05376658	11.93793509	0.08376658	15
16	1.60470644	0.62316694	20.15688130	0.04961085	12.56110203	0.07961085	16
17	1.65284763	0.60501645	21.76158774	0.04595253	13.16611847	0.07595253	17
18	1.70243306	0.58739461	23.41443537	0.04270870	13.75351308	0.07270870	18
19	1.75350605	0.57028603	25.11686844	0.03981388	14.32379911	0.06981388	19
20	1.80611123	0.55367575	26.87037449	0.03721571	14.87747486	0.06721571	20
21	1.86029457	0.53754928	28.67648572	0.03487178	15.41502414	0.06487178	21
22	1.91610341	0.52189250	30.53678030	0.03274739	15.93691664	0.06274739	22
23	1.97358651	0.50669175	32.45288370	0.03081390	16.44360839	0.06081390	23
24	2.03279411	0.49193374	34.42647022	0.02904742	16.93554212	0.05904742	24
25	2.09377793	0.47760557	36.45926432	0.02742787	17.41314769	0.05742787	25
26	2.15659127	0.46369473	38.55304225	0.02593829	17.87684242	0.05593829	26
27	2.22128901	0.45018906	40.70963352	0.02456421	18.32703147	0.05456421	27
28	2.28792768	0.43707675	42.93092252	0.02329323	18.76410823	0.05329323	28
29	2.35656551	0.42434636	45.21885020	0.02211467	19.18845459	0.05211467	29
30	2.42726247	0.41198676	47.57541571	0.02101926	19.60044135	0.05101926	30
31	2.50008035	0.39998715	50.00267818	0.01999893	20.00042849	0.04999893	31
32	2.57508276	0.38833703	52.50275852	0.01904662	20.38876553	0.04904662	32
33	2.65233524	0.37702625	55.07784128	0.01815612	20.76579178	0.04815612	33
34	2.73190530	0.36604490	57.73017652	0.01732196	21.13183668	0.04732196	34
35	2.81386245	0.35538340	60.46208181	0.01653929	21.48722007	0.04653929	35
36	2.89827833	0.34503243	63.27594427	0.01580379	21.83225250	0.04580379	36
37	2.98522668	0.33498294	66.17422259	0.01511162	22.16723544	0.04511162	37
38	3.07478348	0.32522615	69.15944927	0.01445934	22.49246159	0.04445934	38
39	3.16702698	0.31575355	72.23423275	0.01384385	22.80821513	0.04384385	39
40	3.26203779	0.30655684	75.40125973	0.01326238	23.11477197	0.04326238	40

TABLE A-2

COMPOUND INTEREST FOR $1

3%

PERIODS n	FUTURE AMOUNT $(1+i)^n$	PRESENT VALUE $(1+i)^{-n}$	AMOUNT OF ANNUITY $(S/p,i,n)$ $\dfrac{(1+i)^n-1}{i}$	SINKING FUND $(p/S,i,n)$ $\dfrac{i}{(1+i)^n-1}$	PRESENT VALUE OF ANNUITY $(V/p,i,n)$ $\dfrac{1-(1+i)^{-n}}{i}$	AMORTIZATION $(p/V,i,n)$ $\dfrac{i}{1-(1+i)^{-n}}$	PERIODS n
41	3.35989893	0.29762800	78.66329753	0.01271241	23.41239997	0.04271241	41
42	3.46069589	0.28895922	82.02319645	0.01219167	23.70135920	0.04219167	42
43	3.56451677	0.28054294	85.48389234	0.01169811	23.98190213	0.04169811	43
44	3.67145227	0.27237178	89.04840911	0.01122985	24.25427392	0.04122985	44
45	3.78159584	0.26443862	92.71986139	0.01078518	24.51871254	0.04078518	45
46	3.89504372	0.25673653	96.50145723	0.01036254	24.77544907	0.04036254	46
47	4.01189503	0.24925876	100.39650095	0.00996051	25.02470783	0.03996051	47
48	4.13225188	0.24199880	104.40839598	0.00957777	25.26670664	0.03957777	48
49	4.25621944	0.23495029	108.54064785	0.00921314	25.50165693	0.03921314	49
50	4.38390602	0.22810708	112.79686729	0.00886549	25.72976401	0.03886549	50
51	4.51542320	0.22146318	117.18077331	0.00853382	25.95122719	0.03853382	51
52	4.65088590	0.21501280	121.69619651	0.00821718	26.16623999	0.03821718	52
53	4.79041247	0.20875029	126.34708240	0.00791471	26.37499028	0.03791471	53
54	4.93412485	0.20267019	131.13749488	0.00762558	26.57766047	0.03762558	54
55	5.08214859	0.19676717	136.07161972	0.00734907	26.77442764	0.03734907	55
56	5.23461305	0.19103609	141.15376831	0.00708447	26.96546373	0.03708447	56
57	5.39165144	0.18547193	146.38838136	0.00683114	27.15093566	0.03683114	57
58	5.55340098	0.18006984	151.78003280	0.00658848	27.33100549	0.03658848	58
59	5.72000301	0.17482508	157.33343379	0.00635593	27.50583058	0.03635593	59
60	5.89160310	0.16973309	163.05343680	0.00613296	27.67556367	0.03613296	60
61	6.06835120	0.16478941	168.94503991	0.00591908	27.84035307	0.03591908	61
62	6.25040173	0.15998972	175.01339110	0.00571385	28.00034279	0.03571385	62
63	6.43791379	0.15532982	181.26379284	0.00551682	28.15567261	0.03551682	63
64	6.63105120	0.15080565	187.70170662	0.00532760	28.30647826	0.03532760	64
65	6.82998273	0.14641325	194.33275782	0.00514581	28.45289152	0.03514581	65
66	7.03488222	0.14214879	201.16274055	0.00497110	28.59504031	0.03497110	66
67	7.24592868	0.13800853	208.19762277	0.00480313	28.73304884	0.03480313	67
68	7.46330654	0.13398887	215.44355145	0.00464159	28.86703771	0.03464159	68
69	7.68720574	0.13008628	222.90685800	0.00448618	28.99712399	0.03448618	69
70	7.91782191	0.12629736	230.59406374	0.00433663	29.12342135	0.03433663	70
71	8.15535657	0.12261880	238.51188565	0.00419266	29.24604015	0.03419266	71
72	8.40001727	0.11904737	246.66724222	0.00405404	29.36508752	0.03405404	72
73	8.65201778	0.11557998	255.06725949	0.00392053	29.48066750	0.03392053	73
74	8.91157832	0.11221357	263.71927727	0.00379191	29.59288107	0.03379191	74
75	9.17892567	0.10894521	272.63085559	0.00366796	29.70182628	0.03366796	75
76	9.45429344	0.10577205	281.80978126	0.00354849	29.80759833	0.03354849	76
77	9.73792224	0.10269131	291.26407469	0.00343331	29.91028964	0.03343331	77
78	10.03005991	0.09970030	301.00199693	0.00332224	30.00998994	0.03332224	78
79	10.33096171	0.09679641	311.03205684	0.00321510	30.10678635	0.03321510	79
80	10.64089056	0.09397710	321.36301855	0.00311175	30.20076345	0.03311175	80

TABLE A-2

COMPOUND INTEREST FOR $1

3%

PERIODS n	FUTURE AMOUNT $(1+i)^n$	PRESENT VALUE $(1+i)^{-n}$	AMOUNT OF ANNUITY $(S/p,i,n)$ $\dfrac{(1+i)^n-1}{i}$	SINKING FUND $(p/S,i,n)$ $\dfrac{i}{(1+i)^n-1}$	PRESENT VALUE OF ANNUITY $(V/p,i,n)$ $\dfrac{1-(1+i)^{-n}}{i}$	AMORTIZATION $(p/V,i,n)$ $\dfrac{i}{1-(1+i)^{-n}}$	PERIODS n
81	10.96011727	0.09123990	332.00390910	0.00301201	30.29200335	0.03301201	81
82	11.28892079	0.08858243	342.96402638	0.00291576	30.38058577	0.03291576	82
83	11.62758842	0.08600236	354.25294717	0.00282284	30.46658813	0.03282284	83
84	11.97641607	0.08349743	365.88053558	0.00273313	30.55008556	0.03273313	84
85	12.33570855	0.08106547	377.85695165	0.00264650	30.63115103	0.03264650	85
86	12.70577981	0.07870434	390.19266020	0.00256284	30.70985537	0.03256284	86
87	13.08695320	0.07641198	402.89844001	0.00248202	30.78626735	0.03248202	87
88	13.47956180	0.07418639	415.98539321	0.00240393	30.86045374	0.03240393	88
89	13.88394865	0.07202562	429.46495500	0.00232848	30.93247936	0.03232848	89
90	14.30046711	0.06992779	443.34890365	0.00225556	31.00240714	0.03225556	90
91	14.72748112	0.06789105	457.64937076	0.00218508	31.07029820	0.03218508	91
92	15.17136556	0.06591364	472.37885189	0.00211694	31.13621184	0.03211694	92
93	15.62650652	0.06399383	487.55021744	0.00205107	31.20020567	0.03205107	93
94	16.09530172	0.06212993	503.17672397	0.00198737	31.26233560	0.03198737	94
95	16.57816077	0.06032032	519.27202568	0.00192577	31.32265592	0.03192577	95
96	17.07550559	0.05856342	535.85018645	0.00186619	31.38121934	0.03186619	96
97	17.58777076	0.05685769	552.92569205	0.00180856	31.43807703	0.03180856	97
98	18.11540388	0.05520164	570.51346281	0.00175281	31.49327867	0.03175281	98
99	18.65886600	0.05359383	588.62886669	0.00169886	31.54687250	0.03169886	99
100	19.21863198	0.05203284	607.28773270	0.00164667	31.59890534	0.03164667	100
101	19.79519094	0.05051732	626.50636468	0.00159615	31.64942266	0.03159615	101
102	20.38904667	0.04904594	646.30155562	0.00154727	31.69846860	0.03154727	102
103	21.00071807	0.04761742	666.69060228	0.00149995	31.74608602	0.03149995	103
104	21.63073961	0.04623050	687.69132035	0.00145414	31.79231652	0.03145414	104
105	22.27966180	0.04488398	709.32205996	0.00140980	31.83720051	0.03140980	105
106	22.94805165	0.04357668	731.60172176	0.00136686	31.88077719	0.03136686	106
107	23.63649320	0.04230746	754.54977342	0.00132529	31.92308465	0.03132529	107
108	24.34558800	0.04107520	778.18626662	0.00128504	31.96415986	0.03128504	108
109	25.07595564	0.03987884	802.53185462	0.00124606	32.00403870	0.03124606	109
110	25.82823431	0.03871732	827.60781026	0.00120830	32.04275602	0.03120830	110
111	26.60308134	0.03758963	853.43604456	0.00117173	32.08034565	0.03117173	111
112	27.40117378	0.03649479	880.03912590	0.00113631	32.11684043	0.03113631	112
113	28.22320899	0.03543183	907.44029968	0.00110200	32.15227227	0.03110200	113
114	29.06990526	0.03439984	935.66350867	0.00106876	32.18667210	0.03106876	114
115	29.94200242	0.03339790	964.73341393	0.00103656	32.22007000	0.03103656	115
116	30.84026249	0.03242515	994.67541634	0.00100535	32.25249515	0.03100535	116
117	31.76547037	0.03148072	1025.51567884	0.00097512	32.28397587	0.03097512	117
118	32.71843448	0.03056381	1057.28114920	0.00094582	32.31453968	0.03094582	118
119	33.69998751	0.02967360	1089.99958368	0.00091743	32.34421328	0.03091743	119
120	34.71098714	0.02880932	1123.69957119	0.00088992	32.37302261	0.03088992	120

TABLE A-2

COMPOUND INTEREST FOR $1

$3\frac{1}{2}\%$

PERIODS n	FUTURE AMOUNT $(1+i)^n$	PRESENT VALUE $(1+i)^{-n}$	AMOUNT OF ANNUITY $(S/p,i,n)$ $\dfrac{(1+i)^n-1}{i}$	SINKING FUND $(p/S,i,n)$ $\dfrac{i}{(1+i)^n-1}$	PRESENT VALUE OF ANNUITY $(V/p,i,n)$ $\dfrac{1-(1+i)^{-n}}{i}$	AMORTIZATION $(p/V,i,n)$ $\dfrac{i}{1-(1+i)^{-n}}$	PERIODS n
1	1.03500000	0.96618357	1.00000000	1.00000000	0.96618357	1.03500000	1
2	1.07122500	0.93351070	2.03500000	0.49140049	1.89969428	0.52640049	2
3	1.10871787	0.90194271	3.10622500	0.32193418	2.80163698	0.35693418	3
4	1.14752300	0.87144223	4.21494223	0.23725114	3.67307921	0.27225114	4
5	1.18768631	0.84197317	5.36246588	0.18648137	4.51505238	0.22148137	5
6	1.22925533	0.81350064	6.55015218	0.15266821	5.32855302	0.18766821	6
7	1.27227926	0.78599096	7.77940751	0.12854449	6.11454398	0.16354449	7
8	1.31680904	0.75941156	9.05168677	0.11047665	6.87395554	0.14547665	8
9	1.36289735	0.73373097	10.36849581	0.09644601	7.60768651	0.13144601	9
10	1.41059876	0.70891881	11.73139316	0.08524137	8.31660532	0.12024137	10
11	1.45996972	0.68494571	13.14199192	0.07609197	9.00155104	0.11109197	11
12	1.51106866	0.66178330	14.60196164	0.06848395	9.66333433	0.10348395	12
13	1.56395606	0.63940415	16.11303030	0.06206157	10.30273849	0.09706157	13
14	1.61869452	0.61778179	17.67698636	0.05657073	10.92052028	0.09157073	14
15	1.67534883	0.59689062	19.29568088	0.05182507	11.51741090	0.08682507	15
16	1.73398604	0.57670591	20.97102971	0.04768483	12.09411681	0.08268483	16
17	1.79467555	0.55720378	22.70501575	0.04404313	12.65132059	0.07904313	17
18	1.85748920	0.53836114	24.49969130	0.04081684	13.18968173	0.07581684	18
19	1.92250132	0.52015569	26.35718050	0.03794033	13.70983742	0.07294033	19
20	1.98978886	0.50256588	28.27968181	0.03536108	14.21240330	0.07036108	20
21	2.05943147	0.48557090	30.26947068	0.03303659	14.69797420	0.06803659	21
22	2.13151158	0.46915063	32.32890215	0.03093207	15.16712484	0.06593207	22
23	2.20611448	0.45328563	34.46041373	0.02901880	15.62041047	0.06401880	23
24	2.28332849	0.43795713	36.66652821	0.02727283	16.05836760	0.06227283	24
25	2.36324498	0.42314699	38.94985669	0.02567404	16.48151459	0.06067404	25
26	2.44595856	0.40883767	41.31310168	0.02420540	16.89035226	0.05920540	26
27	2.53156711	0.39501224	43.75906024	0.02285241	17.28536451	0.05785241	27
28	2.62017196	0.38165434	46.29062734	0.02160265	17.66701885	0.05660265	28
29	2.71187798	0.36874815	48.91079930	0.02044538	18.03576700	0.05544538	29
30	2.80679370	0.35627841	51.62267728	0.01937133	18.39204541	0.05437133	30
31	2.90503148	0.34423035	54.42947098	0.01837240	18.73627576	0.05337240	31
32	3.00670759	0.33258971	57.33450247	0.01744150	19.06886547	0.05244150	32
33	3.11194235	0.32134271	60.34121005	0.01657242	19.39020818	0.05157242	33
34	3.22086033	0.31047605	63.45315240	0.01575966	19.70068423	0.05075966	34
35	3.33359045	0.29997686	66.67401274	0.01499835	20.00066110	0.04999835	35
36	3.45026611	0.28983272	70.00760318	0.01428416	20.29049381	0.04928416	36
37	3.57102543	0.28003161	73.45786930	0.01361325	20.57052542	0.04861325	37
38	3.69601132	0.27056194	77.02889472	0.01298214	20.84108736	0.04798214	38
39	3.82537171	0.26141250	80.72490604	0.01238775	21.10249987	0.04738775	39
40	3.95925972	0.25257247	84.55027775	0.01182728	21.35507234	0.04682728	40

COMPOUND INTEREST FOR $1

$3\frac{1}{2}\%$

PERIODS	FUTURE AMOUNT	PRESENT VALUE	AMOUNT OF ANNUITY	SINKING FUND	PRESENT VALUE OF ANNUITY	AMORTIZATION	PERIODS
n	$(1+i)^n$	$(1+i)^{-n}$	$(S/p,i,n)$ $\dfrac{(1+i)^n-1}{i}$	$(p/S,i,n)$ $\dfrac{i}{(1+i)^n-1}$	$(V/p,i,n)$ $\dfrac{1-(1+i)^{-n}}{i}$	$(p/V,i,n)$ $\dfrac{i}{1-(1+i)^{-n}}$	n
41	4.09783381	0.24403137	88.50953747	0.01129822	21.59910371	0.04629822	41
42	4.24125799	0.23577910	92.60737128	0.01079828	21.83488281	0.04579828	42
43	4.38970202	0.22780590	96.84862928	0.01032539	22.06268870	0.04532539	43
44	4.54334160	0.22010231	101.23833130	0.00987768	22.28279102	0.04487768	44
45	4.70235855	0.21265924	105.78167290	0.00945343	22.49545026	0.04445343	45
46	4.86694110	0.20546787	110.48403145	0.00905108	22.70091813	0.04405108	46
47	5.03728404	0.19851968	115.35097255	0.00866919	22.89943780	0.04366919	47
48	5.21358898	0.19180645	120.38825659	0.00830646	23.09124425	0.04330646	48
49	5.39606459	0.18532024	125.60184557	0.00796167	23.27656450	0.04296167	49
50	5.58492686	0.17905337	130.99791016	0.00763371	23.45561787	0.04263371	50
51	5.78039930	0.17299843	136.58283702	0.00732156	23.62861630	0.04232156	51
52	5.98271327	0.16714824	142.36323631	0.00702429	23.79576454	0.04202429	52
53	6.19210824	0.16149589	148.34594958	0.00674100	23.95726043	0.04174100	53
54	6.40883202	0.15603467	154.53805782	0.00647090	24.11329510	0.04147090	54
55	6.63314114	0.15075814	160.94688984	0.00621323	24.26405323	0.04121323	55
56	6.86530108	0.14566004	167.58003099	0.00596730	24.40971327	0.04096730	56
57	7.10558662	0.14073433	174.44533207	0.00573245	24.55044760	0.04073245	57
58	7.35428215	0.13597520	181.55091869	0.00550810	24.68642281	0.04050810	58
59	7.61168203	0.13137701	188.90520085	0.00529366	24.81779981	0.04029366	59
60	7.87809090	0.12693431	196.51688288	0.00508862	24.94473412	0.04008862	60
61	8.15382408	0.12264184	204.39497378	0.00489249	25.06737596	0.03989249	61
62	8.43920793	0.11849453	212.54879786	0.00470480	25.18587049	0.03970480	62
63	8.73458020	0.11448747	220.98800579	0.00452513	25.30035796	0.03952513	63
64	9.04029051	0.11061591	229.72258599	0.00435308	25.41097388	0.03935308	64
65	9.35670068	0.10687528	238.76287650	0.00418826	25.51784916	0.03918826	65
66	9.68418520	0.10326114	248.11957718	0.00403031	25.62111030	0.03903031	66
67	10.02313168	0.09976922	257.80376238	0.00387892	25.72087951	0.03887892	67
68	10.37394129	0.09639538	267.82689406	0.00373375	25.81727489	0.03873375	68
69	10.73702924	0.09313563	278.20083535	0.00359453	25.91041052	0.03859453	69
70	11.11282526	0.08998612	288.93786459	0.00346095	26.00039664	0.03846095	70
71	11.50177414	0.08694311	300.05068985	0.00333277	26.08733975	0.03833277	71
72	11.90433624	0.08400300	311.55246400	0.00320973	26.17134275	0.03820973	72
73	12.32098801	0.08116232	323.45680024	0.00309160	26.25250508	0.03809160	73
74	12.75222259	0.07841770	335.77778824	0.00297816	26.33092278	0.03797816	74
75	13.19855038	0.07576590	348.53001083	0.00286919	26.40668868	0.03786919	75
76	13.66049964	0.07320376	361.72856121	0.00276450	26.47989244	0.03776450	76
77	14.13861713	0.07072827	375.38906085	0.00266390	26.55062072	0.03766390	77
78	14.63346873	0.06833650	389.52767798	0.00256721	26.61895721	0.03756721	78
79	15.14564013	0.06602560	404.16114671	0.00247426	26.68498281	0.03747426	79
80	15.67573754	0.06379285	419.30678685	0.00238489	26.74877567	0.03738489	80

TABLE A-2

COMPOUND INTEREST FOR $1

$3\frac{1}{2}\%$

PERIODS n	FUTURE AMOUNT $(1+i)^n$	PRESENT VALUE $(1+i)^{-n}$	AMOUNT OF ANNUITY (S/p,i,n) $\dfrac{(1+i)^n - 1}{i}$	SINKING FUND (p/S,i,n) $\dfrac{i}{(1+i)^n - 1}$	PRESENT VALUE OF ANNUITY (V/p,i,n) $\dfrac{1-(1+i)^{-n}}{i}$	AMORTIZATION (p/V,i,n) $\dfrac{i}{1-(1+i)^{-n}}$	PERIODS n
81	16.22438835	0.06163561	434.98252439	0.00229894	26.81041127	0.03729894	81
82	16.79224195	0.05955131	451.20691274	0.00221628	26.86996258	0.03721628	82
83	17.37997041	0.05753750	467.99915469	0.00213676	26.92750008	0.03713676	83
84	17.98826938	0.05559178	485.37912510	0.00206025	26.98309186	0.03706025	84
85	18.61785881	0.05371187	503.36739448	0.00198662	27.03680373	0.03698662	85
86	19.26948387	0.05189553	521.98525329	0.00191576	27.08869926	0.03691576	86
87	19.94391580	0.05014060	541.25473715	0.00184756	27.13883986	0.03684756	87
88	20.64195285	0.04844503	561.19865295	0.00178190	27.18728489	0.03678190	88
89	21.36442120	0.04680679	581.84060581	0.00171868	27.23409168	0.03671868	89
90	22.11217595	0.04522395	603.20502701	0.00165781	27.27931564	0.03665781	90
91	22.88610210	0.04369464	625.31720295	0.00159919	27.32301028	0.03659919	91
92	23.68711568	0.04221704	648.20330506	0.00154273	27.36522732	0.03654273	92
93	24.51616473	0.04078941	671.89042074	0.00148834	27.40601673	0.03648834	93
94	25.37423049	0.03941006	696.40658546	0.00143594	27.44542680	0.03643594	94
95	26.26232856	0.03807735	721.78081595	0.00138546	27.48350415	0.03638546	95
96	27.18151006	0.03678971	748.04314451	0.00133682	27.52029387	0.03633682	96
97	28.13286291	0.03554562	775.22465457	0.00128995	27.55583948	0.03628995	97
98	29.11751311	0.03434359	803.35751748	0.00124478	27.59018308	0.03624478	98
99	30.13662607	0.03318221	832.47503059	0.00120124	27.62336529	0.03620124	99
100	31.19140798	0.03206011	862.61165666	0.00115927	27.65542540	0.03615927	100
101	32.28310726	0.03097595	893.80306464	0.00111881	27.68640135	0.03611881	101
102	33.41301602	0.02992846	926.08617191	0.00107981	27.71632981	0.03607981	102
103	34.58247158	0.02891638	959.49918792	0.00104221	27.74524619	0.03604221	103
104	35.79285808	0.02793853	994.08165950	0.00100595	27.77318473	0.03600595	104
105	37.04560812	0.02699375	1029.87451758	0.00097099	27.80017848	0.03597099	105
106	38.34220440	0.02608092	1066.92012570	0.00093728	27.82625940	0.03593728	106
107	39.68418155	0.02519896	1105.26233010	0.00090476	27.85145836	0.03590476	107
108	41.07312791	0.02434682	1144.94651165	0.00087340	27.87580518	0.03587340	108
109	42.51068738	0.02352350	1186.01963956	0.00084316	27.89932868	0.03584316	109
110	43.99856144	0.02272802	1228.53032694	0.00081398	27.92205669	0.03581398	110
111	45.53851109	0.02195944	1272.52888839	0.00078584	27.94401613	0.03578584	111
112	47.13235898	0.02121685	1318.06739948	0.00075869	27.96523297	0.03575869	112
113	48.78199155	0.02049937	1365.19975846	0.00073249	27.98573234	0.03573249	113
114	50.48936125	0.01980615	1413.98175001	0.00070722	28.00553849	0.03570722	114
115	52.25648889	0.01913638	1464.47111126	0.00068284	28.02467487	0.03568284	115
116	54.08546601	0.01848926	1516.72760015	0.00065931	28.04316413	0.03565931	116
117	55.97845732	0.01786401	1570.81306616	0.00063661	28.06102814	0.03563661	117
118	57.93770332	0.01725992	1626.79152347	0.00061471	28.07828806	0.03561471	118
119	59.96552294	0.01667625	1684.72922679	0.00059357	28.09496431	0.03559357	119
120	62.06431624	0.01611232	1744.69474973	0.00057317	28.11107663	0.03557317	120

TABLE A-2

COMPOUND INTEREST FOR $1

4%

PERIODS n	FUTURE AMOUNT $(1+i)^n$	PRESENT VALUE $(1+i)^{-n}$	AMOUNT OF ANNUITY $(S/p,i,n)$ $\frac{(1+i)^n-1}{i}$	SINKING FUND $(p/S,i,n)$ $\frac{i}{(1+i)^n-1}$	PRESENT VALUE OF ANNUITY $(V/p,i,n)$ $\frac{1-(1+i)^{-n}}{i}$	AMORTIZATION $(p/V,i,n)$ $\frac{i}{1-(1+i)^{-n}}$	PERIODS n
1	1.04000000	0.96153846	1.00000000	1.00000000	0.96153846	1.04000000	1
2	1.08160000	0.92455621	2.04000000	0.49019608	1.88609467	0.53019608	2
3	1.12486400	0.88899636	3.12160000	0.32034854	2.77509103	0.36034854	3
4	1.16985856	0.85480419	4.24646400	0.23549005	3.62989522	0.27549005	4
5	1.21665290	0.82192711	5.41632256	0.18462711	4.45182233	0.22462711	5
6	1.26531902	0.79031453	6.63297546	0.15076190	5.24213686	0.19076190	6
7	1.31593178	0.75991781	7.89829448	0.12660961	6.00205467	0.16660961	7
8	1.36856905	0.73069021	9.21422626	0.10852783	6.73274487	0.14852783	8
9	1.42331181	0.70258674	10.58279531	0.09449299	7.43533161	0.13449299	9
10	1.48024428	0.67556417	12.00610712	0.08329094	8.11089578	0.12329094	10
11	1.53945406	0.64958093	13.48635141	0.07414904	8.76047671	0.11414904	11
12	1.60103222	0.62459705	15.02580546	0.06655217	9.38507376	0.10655217	12
13	1.66507351	0.60057409	16.62683768	0.06014373	9.98564785	0.10014373	13
14	1.73167645	0.57747508	18.29191119	0.05466897	10.56312293	0.09466897	14
15	1.80094351	0.55526450	20.02358764	0.04994110	11.11838743	0.08994110	15
16	1.87298125	0.53390818	21.82453114	0.04582000	11.65229561	0.08582000	16
17	1.94790050	0.51337325	23.69751239	0.04219852	12.16566885	0.08219852	17
18	2.02581652	0.49362812	25.64541288	0.03899333	12.65929697	0.07899333	18
19	2.10684918	0.47464242	27.67122940	0.03613862	13.13393940	0.07613862	19
20	2.19112314	0.45638695	29.77807858	0.03358175	13.59032634	0.07358175	20
21	2.27876807	0.43883360	31.96920172	0.03128011	14.02915995	0.07128011	21
22	2.36991879	0.42195539	34.24796979	0.02919881	14.45111533	0.06919881	22
23	2.46471554	0.40572633	36.61788858	0.02730906	14.85684167	0.06730906	23
24	2.56330416	0.39012147	39.08260412	0.02558683	15.24696314	0.06558683	24
25	2.66583633	0.37511680	41.64590829	0.02401196	15.62207994	0.06401196	25
26	2.77246978	0.36068923	44.31174462	0.02256738	15.98276918	0.06256738	26
27	2.88336858	0.34681657	47.08421440	0.02123854	16.32958575	0.06123854	27
28	2.99870332	0.33347747	49.96758298	0.02001298	16.66306322	0.06001298	28
29	3.11865145	0.32065141	52.96628630	0.01887993	16.98371463	0.05887993	29
30	3.24339751	0.30831867	56.08493775	0.01783010	17.29203330	0.05783010	30
31	3.37313341	0.29646026	59.32833526	0.01685535	17.58849356	0.05685535	31
32	3.50805875	0.28505794	62.70146867	0.01594859	17.87355150	0.05594859	32
33	3.64838110	0.27409417	66.20952742	0.01510357	18.14764567	0.05510357	33
34	3.79431634	0.26355209	69.85790851	0.01431477	18.41119776	0.05431477	34
35	3.94608899	0.25341547	73.65222486	0.01357732	18.66461323	0.05357732	35
36	4.10393255	0.24366872	77.59831385	0.01288688	18.90828195	0.05288688	36
37	4.26808986	0.23429685	81.70224640	0.01223957	19.14257880	0.05223957	37
38	4.43881345	0.22528543	85.97033626	0.01163192	19.36786423	0.05163192	38
39	4.61636599	0.21662061	90.40914971	0.01106083	19.58448484	0.05106083	39
40	4.80102063	0.20828904	95.02551570	0.01052349	19.79277388	0.05052349	40

COMPOUND INTEREST FOR $1

4%

PERIODS n	FUTURE AMOUNT $(1+i)^n$	PRESENT VALUE $(1+i)^{-n}$	AMOUNT OF ANNUITY $(S/p,i,n)$ $\dfrac{(1+i)^n - 1}{i}$	SINKING FUND $(p/S,i,n)$ $\dfrac{i}{(1+i)^n - 1}$	PRESENT VALUE OF ANNUITY $(V/p,i,n)$ $\dfrac{1-(1+i)^{-n}}{i}$	AMORTIZATION $(p/V,i,n)$ $\dfrac{i}{1-(1+i)^{-n}}$	PERIODS n
41	4.99306145	0.20027793	99.82653633	0.01001738	19.99305181	0.05001738	41
42	5.19278391	0.19257493	104.81959778	0.00954020	20.18562674	0.04954020	42
43	5.40049527	0.18516820	110.01238169	0.00908989	20.37079494	0.04908989	43
44	5.61651508	0.17804635	115.41287696	0.00866454	20.54884129	0.04866454	44
45	5.84117568	0.17119841	121.02939204	0.00826246	20.72003970	0.04826246	45
46	6.07482271	0.16461386	126.87056772	0.00788205	20.88465356	0.04788205	46
47	6.31781562	0.15828256	132.94539043	0.00752189	21.04293612	0.04752189	47
48	6.57052824	0.15219476	139.26320604	0.00718065	21.19513088	0.04718065	48
49	6.83334937	0.14634112	145.83373429	0.00685712	21.34147200	0.04685712	49
50	7.10668335	0.14071262	152.66708366	0.00655020	21.48218462	0.04655020	50
51	7.39095068	0.13530059	159.77376700	0.00625885	21.61748521	0.04625885	51
52	7.68658871	0.13009672	167.16471768	0.00598212	21.74758193	0.04598212	52
53	7.99405226	0.12509300	174.85130639	0.00571915	21.87267493	0.04571915	53
54	8.31381435	0.12028173	182.84535865	0.00546910	21.99295667	0.04546910	54
55	8.64636692	0.11565551	191.15917299	0.00523124	22.10861218	0.04523124	55
56	8.99222160	0.11120722	199.80553991	0.00500487	22.21981940	0.04500487	56
57	9.35191046	0.10693002	208.79776151	0.00478932	22.32674943	0.04478932	57
58	9.72598688	0.10281733	218.14967197	0.00458401	22.42956676	0.04458401	58
59	10.11502635	0.09886282	227.87565885	0.00438836	22.52842957	0.04438836	59
60	10.51962741	0.09506040	237.99068520	0.00420185	22.62348997	0.04420185	60
61	10.94041250	0.09140423	248.51031261	0.00402398	22.71489421	0.04402398	61
62	11.37802600	0.08788868	259.45072511	0.00385430	22.80278289	0.04385430	62
63	11.83315016	0.08450835	270.82875412	0.00369237	22.88729124	0.04369237	63
64	12.30647617	0.08125803	282.66190428	0.00353780	22.96854927	0.04353780	64
65	12.79873522	0.07813272	294.96838045	0.00339019	23.04668199	0.04339019	65
66	13.31068463	0.07512762	307.76711567	0.00324921	23.12180961	0.04324921	66
67	13.84311201	0.07223809	321.07780030	0.00311451	23.19404770	0.04311451	67
68	14.39683649	0.06945970	334.92091231	0.00298578	23.26350740	0.04298578	68
69	14.97270995	0.06678818	349.31774880	0.00286272	23.33029558	0.04286272	69
70	15.57161835	0.06421940	364.29045876	0.00274506	23.39451498	0.04274506	70
71	16.19448308	0.06174942	379.86207711	0.00263253	23.45626440	0.04263253	71
72	16.84226241	0.05937445	396.05656019	0.00252489	23.51563885	0.04252489	72
73	17.51595290	0.05709081	412.89882260	0.00242190	23.57272966	0.04242190	73
74	18.21659102	0.05489501	430.41477550	0.00232334	23.62762468	0.04232334	74
75	18.94525466	0.05278367	448.63136652	0.00222900	23.68040834	0.04222900	75
76	19.70306485	0.05075353	467.57662118	0.00213869	23.73116187	0.04213869	76
77	20.49118744	0.04880147	487.27968603	0.00205221	23.77996333	0.04205221	77
78	21.31083494	0.04692449	507.77087347	0.00196939	23.82688782	0.04196939	78
79	22.16326834	0.04511970	529.08170841	0.00189007	23.87200752	0.04189007	79
80	23.04979907	0.04338433	551.24497675	0.00181408	23.91539185	0.04181408	80

TABLE A-2

COMPOUND INTEREST FOR $1

4%

PERIODS n	FUTURE AMOUNT $(1+i)^n$	PRESENT VALUE $(1+i)^{-n}$	AMOUNT OF ANNUITY $(S/p,i,n)$ $\dfrac{(1+i)^n-1}{i}$	SINKING FUND $(p/S,i,n)$ $\dfrac{i}{(1+i)^n-1}$	PRESENT VALUE OF ANNUITY $(V/p,i,n)$ $\dfrac{1-(1+i)^{-n}}{i}$	AMORTIZATION $(p/V,i,n)$ $\dfrac{i}{1-(1+i)^{-n}}$	PERIODS n
81	23.97179103	0.04171570	574.29477582	0.00174127	23.95710755	0.04174127	81
82	24.93066267	0.04011125	598.26656685	0.00167150	23.99721879	0.04167150	82
83	25.92788918	0.03856851	623.19722952	0.00160463	24.03578730	0.04160463	83
84	26.96500475	0.03708510	649.12511870	0.00154054	24.07287241	0.04154054	84
85	28.04360494	0.03565875	676.09012345	0.00147909	24.10853116	0.04147909	85
86	29.16534914	0.03428726	704.13372839	0.00142018	24.14281842	0.04142018	86
87	30.33196310	0.03296852	733.29907753	0.00136370	24.17578694	0.04136370	87
88	31.54524163	0.03170050	763.63104063	0.00130953	24.20748745	0.04130953	88
89	32.80705129	0.03048125	795.17628225	0.00125758	24.23796870	0.04125758	89
90	34.11933334	0.02930890	827.98333354	0.00120775	24.26727759	0.04120775	90
91	35.48410668	0.02818163	862.10266688	0.00115995	24.29545923	0.04115995	91
92	36.90347094	0.02709772	897.58677356	0.00111410	24.32255695	0.04111410	92
93	38.37960978	0.02605550	934.49024450	0.00107010	24.34861245	0.04107010	93
94	39.91479417	0.02505337	972.86985428	0.00102789	24.37366582	0.04102789	94
95	41.51138594	0.02408978	1012.78464845	0.00098738	24.39775559	0.04098738	95
96	43.17184138	0.02316325	1054.29603439	0.00094850	24.42091884	0.04094850	96
97	44.89871503	0.02227235	1097.46787577	0.00091119	24.44319119	0.04091119	97
98	46.69466363	0.02141572	1142.36659080	0.00087538	24.46460692	0.04087538	98
99	48.56245018	0.02059204	1189.06125443	0.00084100	24.48519896	0.04084100	99
100	50.50494818	0.01980004	1237.62370461	0.00080800	24.50499900	0.04080800	100
101	52.52514611	0.01903850	1288.12865279	0.00077632	24.52403750	0.04077632	101
102	54.62615196	0.01830625	1340.65379890	0.00074590	24.54234375	0.04074590	102
103	56.81119803	0.01760216	1395.27995086	0.00071670	24.55994591	0.04071670	103
104	59.08364596	0.01692516	1452.09114889	0.00068866	24.57687107	0.04068866	104
105	61.44699179	0.01627419	1511.17479485	0.00066174	24.59314526	0.04066174	105
106	63.90487147	0.01564826	1572.62178664	0.00063588	24.60879352	0.04063588	106
107	66.46106632	0.01504640	1636.52665811	0.00061105	24.62383992	0.04061105	107
108	69.11950898	0.01446770	1702.98772443	0.00058720	24.63830762	0.04058720	108
109	71.88428934	0.01391125	1772.10723341	0.00056430	24.65221886	0.04056430	109
110	74.75966091	0.01337620	1843.99152275	0.00054230	24.66559506	0.04054230	110
111	77.75004735	0.01286173	1918.75118366	0.00052117	24.67845679	0.04052117	111
112	80.86004924	0.01236705	1996.50123100	0.00050088	24.69082383	0.04050088	112
113	84.09445121	0.01189139	2077.36128024	0.00048138	24.70271523	0.04048138	113
114	87.45822926	0.01143403	2161.45573145	0.00046265	24.71414925	0.04046265	114
115	90.95655843	0.01099426	2248.91396071	0.00044466	24.72514351	0.04044466	115
116	94.59482077	0.01057140	2339.87051914	0.00042737	24.73571492	0.04042737	116
117	98.37861360	0.01016481	2434.46533990	0.00041077	24.74587973	0.04041077	117
118	102.31375814	0.00977386	2532.84395350	0.00039481	24.75565359	0.04039481	118
119	106.40630847	0.00939794	2635.15771164	0.00037948	24.76505152	0.04037948	119
120	110.66256080	0.00903648	2741.56402011	0.00036476	24.77408800	0.04036476	120

TABLE A-2

COMPOUND INTEREST FOR $1

$4\frac{1}{2}\%$

PERIODS n	FUTURE AMOUNT $(1+i)^n$	PRESENT VALUE $(1+i)^{-n}$	AMOUNT OF ANNUITY $(S/p,i,n)$ $\dfrac{(1+i)^n-1}{i}$	SINKING FUND $(p/S,i,n)$ $\dfrac{i}{(1+i)^n-1}$	PRESENT VALUE OF ANNUITY $(V/p,i,n)$ $\dfrac{1-(1+i)^{-n}}{i}$	AMORTIZATION $(p/V,i,n)$ $\dfrac{i}{1-(1+i)^{-n}}$	PERIODS n
1	1.04500000	0.95693780	1.00000000	1.00000000	0.95693780	1.04500000	1
2	1.09202500	0.91572995	2.04500000	0.48899756	1.87266775	0.53399756	2
3	1.14116612	0.87629660	3.13702500	0.31877336	2.74896435	0.36377336	3
4	1.19251860	0.83856134	4.27819112	0.23374365	3.58752570	0.27874365	4
5	1.24618194	0.80245105	5.47070973	0.18279164	4.38997674	0.22779164	5
6	1.30226012	0.76789574	6.71689166	0.14887839	5.15787248	0.19387839	6
7	1.36086183	0.73482846	8.01915179	0.12470147	5.89270094	0.16970147	7
8	1.42210061	0.70318513	9.38001362	0.10660965	6.59588607	0.15160965	8
9	1.48609514	0.67290443	10.80211423	0.09257447	7.26879050	0.13757447	9
10	1.55296942	0.64392768	12.28820937	0.08137882	7.91271818	0.12637882	10
11	1.62285305	0.61619874	13.84117879	0.07224818	8.52891692	0.11724818	11
12	1.69588143	0.58966386	15.46403184	0.06466619	9.11858078	0.10966619	12
13	1.77219610	0.56427164	17.15991327	0.05827535	9.68285242	0.10327535	13
14	1.85194492	0.53997286	18.93210937	0.05282032	10.22282528	0.09782032	14
15	1.93528244	0.51672044	20.78405429	0.04811381	10.73954573	0.09311381	15
16	2.02237015	0.49446932	22.71933673	0.04401537	11.23401505	0.08901537	16
17	2.11337681	0.47317639	24.74170689	0.04041758	11.70719143	0.08541758	17
18	2.20847877	0.45280037	26.85508370	0.03723690	12.15999180	0.08223690	18
19	2.30786031	0.43330179	29.06356246	0.03440734	12.59329359	0.07940734	19
20	2.41171402	0.41464286	31.37142277	0.03187614	13.00793645	0.07687614	20
21	2.52024116	0.39678743	33.78313680	0.02960057	13.40472388	0.07460057	21
22	2.63365201	0.37970089	36.30337795	0.02754565	13.78442476	0.07254565	22
23	2.75216635	0.36335013	38.93702996	0.02568249	14.14777489	0.07068249	23
24	2.87601383	0.34770347	41.68919631	0.02398703	14.49547837	0.06898703	24
25	3.00543446	0.33273060	44.56521015	0.02243903	14.82820896	0.06743903	25
26	3.14067901	0.31840248	47.57064460	0.02102137	15.14661145	0.06602137	26
27	3.28200956	0.30469137	50.71132361	0.01971946	15.45130282	0.06471946	27
28	3.42969999	0.29157069	53.99333317	0.01852081	15.74287351	0.06352081	28
29	3.58403649	0.27901502	57.42303316	0.01741461	16.02188853	0.06241461	29
30	3.74531813	0.26700002	61.00706966	0.01639154	16.28888854	0.06139154	30
31	3.91385745	0.25550241	64.75238779	0.01544345	16.54439095	0.06044345	31
32	4.08998104	0.24449991	68.66624524	0.01456320	16.78889086	0.05956320	32
33	4.27403018	0.23397121	72.75622628	0.01374453	17.02286207	0.05874453	33
34	4.46636154	0.22389589	77.03025646	0.01298191	17.24675796	0.05798191	34
35	4.66734781	0.21425444	81.49661800	0.01227045	17.46101240	0.05727045	35
36	4.87737846	0.20502817	86.16396581	0.01160578	17.66604058	0.05660578	36
37	5.09686049	0.19619921	91.04134427	0.01098402	17.86223979	0.05598402	37
38	5.32621921	0.18775044	96.13820476	0.01040169	18.04999023	0.05540169	38
39	5.56589908	0.17966549	101.46442398	0.00985567	18.22965572	0.05485567	39
40	5.81636454	0.17192870	107.03032306	0.00934315	18.40158442	0.05434315	40

COMPOUND INTEREST FOR $1

$4\frac{1}{2}\%$

PERIODS n	FUTURE AMOUNT $(1+i)^n$	PRESENT VALUE $(1+i)^{-n}$	AMOUNT OF ANNUITY $(S/p,i,n)$ $\dfrac{(1+i)^n - 1}{i}$	SINKING FUND $(p/S,i,n)$ $\dfrac{i}{(1+i)^n - 1}$	PRESENT VALUE OF ANNUITY $(V/p,i,n)$ $\dfrac{1-(1+i)^{-n}}{i}$	AMORTIZATION $(p/V,i,n)$ $\dfrac{i}{1-(1+i)^{-n}}$	PERIODS n
41	6.07810094	0.16452507	112.84668760	0.00886158	18.56610949	0.05386158	41
42	6.35161548	0.15744026	118.92478854	0.00840868	18.72354975	0.05340868	42
43	6.63743818	0.15066054	125.27640402	0.00798235	18.87421029	0.05298235	43
44	6.93612290	0.14417276	131.91384220	0.00758071	19.01838305	0.05258071	44
45	7.24824843	0.13796437	138.84996510	0.00720202	19.15634742	0.05220202	45
46	7.57441961	0.13202332	146.09821353	0.00684471	19.28837074	0.05184471	46
47	7.91526849	0.12633810	153.67263314	0.00650734	19.41470884	0.05150734	47
48	8.27145557	0.12089771	161.58790163	0.00618858	19.53560654	0.05118858	48
49	8.64367107	0.11569158	169.85935720	0.00588722	19.65129813	0.05088722	49
50	9.03263627	0.11070965	178.50302828	0.00560215	19.76200778	0.05060215	50
51	9.43910490	0.10594225	187.53566455	0.00533232	19.86795003	0.05033232	51
52	9.86386463	0.10138014	196.97476946	0.00507679	19.96933017	0.05007679	52
53	10.30773853	0.09701449	206.83863408	0.00483469	20.06634466	0.04983469	53
54	10.77158677	0.09283683	217.14637262	0.00460519	20.15918149	0.04960519	54
55	11.25630817	0.08883907	227.91795938	0.00438754	20.24802057	0.04938754	55
56	11.76284204	0.08501347	239.17426756	0.00418105	20.33303404	0.04918105	56
57	12.29216993	0.08135260	250.93710960	0.00398506	20.41438664	0.04898506	57
58	12.84531758	0.07784938	263.22927953	0.00379897	20.49223602	0.04879897	58
59	13.42335687	0.07449701	276.07459711	0.00362221	20.56673303	0.04862221	59
60	14.02740793	0.07128901	289.49795398	0.00345426	20.63802204	0.04845426	60
61	14.65864129	0.06821915	303.52536190	0.00329462	20.70624118	0.04829462	61
62	15.31828014	0.06528148	318.18400319	0.00314284	20.77152266	0.04814284	62
63	16.00760275	0.06247032	333.50228333	0.00299848	20.83399298	0.04799848	63
64	16.72794487	0.05978021	349.50988608	0.00286115	20.89377319	0.04786115	64
65	17.48070239	0.05720594	366.23783096	0.00273047	20.95097913	0.04773047	65
66	18.26733400	0.05474253	383.71853335	0.00260608	21.00572165	0.04760608	66
67	19.08936403	0.05238519	401.98586735	0.00248765	21.05810684	0.04748765	67
68	19.94838541	0.05012937	421.07523138	0.00237487	21.10823621	0.04737487	68
69	20.84606276	0.04797069	441.02361679	0.00226745	21.15620690	0.04726745	69
70	21.78413558	0.04590497	461.86967955	0.00216511	21.20211187	0.04716511	70
71	22.76442168	0.04392820	483.65381513	0.00206759	21.24604007	0.04706759	71
72	23.78882066	0.04203655	506.41823681	0.00197465	21.28807662	0.04697465	72
73	24.85931759	0.04022637	530.20705747	0.00188606	21.32830298	0.04688606	73
74	25.97798688	0.03849413	555.06637505	0.00180159	21.36679711	0.04680159	74
75	27.14699629	0.03683649	581.04436193	0.00172104	21.40363360	0.04672104	75
76	28.36861112	0.03525023	608.19135822	0.00164422	21.43888383	0.04664422	76
77	29.64519862	0.03373228	636.55996934	0.00157094	21.47261611	0.04657094	77
78	30.97923256	0.03227969	666.20516796	0.00150104	21.50489579	0.04650104	78
79	32.37329802	0.03088965	697.18440052	0.00143434	21.53578545	0.04643434	79
80	33.83009643	0.02955948	729.55769854	0.00137069	21.56534493	0.04637069	80

TABLE A-2

COMPOUND INTEREST FOR $1

$4\frac{1}{2}\%$

PERIODS n	FUTURE AMOUNT $(1+i)^n$	PRESENT VALUE $(1+i)^{-n}$	AMOUNT OF ANNUITY (S/p,i,n) $\frac{(1+i)^n - 1}{i}$	SINKING FUND (p/S,i,n) $\frac{i}{(1+i)^n - 1}$	PRESENT VALUE OF ANNUITY (V/p,i,n) $\frac{1-(1+i)^{-n}}{i}$	AMORTIZATION (p/V,i,n) $\frac{i}{1-(1+i)^{-n}}$	PERIODS n
81	35.35245077	0.02828658	763.38779497	0.00130995	21.59363151	0.04630995	81
82	36.94331106	0.02706850	798.74024575	0.00125197	21.62070001	0.04625197	82
83	38.60576006	0.02590287	835.68355680	0.00119663	21.64660288	0.04619663	83
84	40.34301926	0.02478744	874.28931686	0.00114379	21.67139032	0.04614379	84
85	42.15845513	0.02372003	914.63233612	0.00109334	21.69511035	0.04609334	85
86	44.05558561	0.02269860	956.79079125	0.00104516	21.71780895	0.04604516	86
87	46.03808696	0.02172115	1000.84637685	0.00099915	21.73953009	0.04599915	87
88	48.10980087	0.02078579	1046.88446381	0.00095522	21.76031588	0.04595522	88
89	50.27474191	0.01989070	1094.99426468	0.00091325	21.78020658	0.04591325	89
90	52.53710530	0.01903417	1145.26900659	0.00087316	21.79924075	0.04587316	90
91	54.90127503	0.01821451	1197.80611189	0.00083486	21.81745526	0.04583486	91
92	57.37183241	0.01743016	1252.70738692	0.00079827	21.83488542	0.04579827	92
93	59.95356487	0.01667958	1310.07921933	0.00076331	21.85156499	0.04576331	93
94	62.65147529	0.01596132	1370.03278420	0.00072991	21.86752631	0.04572991	94
95	65.47079168	0.01527399	1432.68425949	0.00069799	21.88280030	0.04569799	95
96	68.41697730	0.01461626	1498.15505117	0.00066749	21.89741655	0.04566749	96
97	71.49574128	0.01398685	1566.57202847	0.00063834	21.91140340	0.04563834	97
98	74.71304964	0.01338454	1638.06776976	0.00061048	21.92478794	0.04561048	98
99	78.07513687	0.01280817	1712.78081939	0.00058385	21.93759612	0.04558385	99
100	81.58851803	0.01225663	1790.85595627	0.00055839	21.94985274	0.04555839	100
101	85.26000134	0.01172883	1872.44447430	0.00053406	21.96158157	0.04553406	101
102	89.09670140	0.01122376	1957.70447564	0.00051080	21.97280533	0.04551080	102
103	93.10605297	0.01074044	2046.80117705	0.00048857	21.98354577	0.04548857	103
104	97.29582535	0.01027793	2139.90723001	0.00046731	21.99382371	0.04546731	104
105	101.67413749	0.00983534	2237.20305536	0.00044699	22.00365905	0.04544699	105
106	106.24947368	0.00941181	2338.87719286	0.00042756	22.01307086	0.04542756	106
107	111.03069999	0.00900652	2445.12666653	0.00040898	22.02207738	0.04540898	107
108	116.02708149	0.00861868	2556.15736653	0.00039121	22.03069605	0.04539121	108
109	121.24830016	0.00824754	2672.18444802	0.00037423	22.03894359	0.04537423	109
110	126.70447367	0.00789238	2793.43274818	0.00035798	22.04683597	0.04535798	110
111	132.40617498	0.00755252	2920.13722185	0.00034245	22.05438849	0.04534245	111
112	138.36445286	0.00722729	3052.54339683	0.00032760	22.06161578	0.04532760	112
113	144.59085324	0.00691607	3190.90784969	0.00031339	22.06853185	0.04531339	113
114	151.09744163	0.00661825	3335.49870293	0.00029981	22.07515009	0.04529981	114
115	157.89682651	0.00633325	3486.59614456	0.00028681	22.08148334	0.04528681	115
116	165.00218370	0.00606053	3644.49297106	0.00027439	22.08754387	0.04527439	116
117	172.42728196	0.00579955	3809.49515476	0.00026250	22.09334342	0.04526250	117
118	180.18650965	0.00554981	3981.92243673	0.00025113	22.09889322	0.04525113	118
119	188.29490259	0.00531082	4162.10894638	0.00024026	22.10420404	0.04524026	119
120	196.76817320	0.00508212	4350.40384897	0.00022986	22.10928616	0.04522986	120

TABLE A-2

COMPOUND INTEREST FOR $1

5%

PERIODS n	FUTURE AMOUNT $(1+i)^n$	PRESENT VALUE $(1+i)^{-n}$	AMOUNT OF ANNUITY $(S/p,i,n)$ $\dfrac{(1+i)^n-1}{i}$	SINKING FUND $(p/S,i,n)$ $\dfrac{i}{(1+i)^n-1}$	PRESENT VALUE OF ANNUITY $(V/p,i,n)$ $\dfrac{1-(1+i)^{-n}}{i}$	AMORTIZATION $(p/V,i,n)$ $\dfrac{i}{1-(1+i)^{-n}}$	PERIODS n
1	1.05000000	0.95238095	1.00000000	1.00000000	0.95238095	1.05000000	1
2	1.10250000	0.90702948	2.05000000	0.48780488	1.85941043	0.53780488	2
3	1.15762500	0.86383760	3.15250000	0.31720856	2.72324803	0.36720856	3
4	1.21550625	0.82270247	4.31012500	0.23201183	3.54595050	0.28201183	4
5	1.27628156	0.78352617	5.52563125	0.18097480	4.32947667	0.23097480	5
6	1.34009564	0.74621540	6.80191281	0.14701747	5.07569207	0.19701747	6
7	1.40710042	0.71068133	8.14200845	0.12281982	5.78637340	0.17281982	7
8	1.47745544	0.67683936	9.54910888	0.10472181	6.46321276	0.15472181	8
9	1.55132822	0.64460892	11.02656432	0.09069008	7.10782168	0.14069008	9
10	1.62889463	0.61391325	12.57789254	0.07950457	7.72173493	0.12950457	10
11	1.71033936	0.58467929	14.20678716	0.07038889	8.30641422	0.12038889	11
12	1.79585633	0.55683742	15.91712652	0.06282541	8.86325164	0.11282541	12
13	1.88564914	0.53032135	17.71298285	0.05645577	9.39357299	0.10645577	13
14	1.97993160	0.50506795	19.59863199	0.05102397	9.89864094	0.10102397	14
15	2.07892818	0.48101710	21.57856359	0.04634229	10.37965804	0.09634229	15
16	2.18287459	0.45811152	23.65749177	0.04226991	10.83776956	0.09226991	16
17	2.29201832	0.43629669	25.84036636	0.03869914	11.27406625	0.08869914	17
18	2.40661923	0.41552065	28.13238467	0.03554622	11.68958690	0.08554622	18
19	2.52695020	0.39573396	30.53900391	0.03274501	12.08532086	0.08274501	19
20	2.65329771	0.37688948	33.06595410	0.03024259	12.46221034	0.08024259	20
21	2.78596259	0.35894236	35.71925181	0.02799611	12.82115271	0.07799611	21
22	2.92526072	0.34184987	38.50521440	0.02597051	13.16300258	0.07597051	22
23	3.07152376	0.32557131	41.43047512	0.02413682	13.48857388	0.07413682	23
24	3.22509994	0.31006791	44.50199887	0.02247090	13.79864179	0.07247090	24
25	3.38635494	0.29530277	47.72709882	0.02095246	14.09394457	0.07095246	25
26	3.55567269	0.28124073	51.11345376	0.01956432	14.37518530	0.06956432	26
27	3.73345632	0.26784832	54.66912645	0.01829186	14.64303362	0.06829186	27
28	3.92012914	0.25509364	58.40258277	0.01712253	14.89812726	0.06712253	28
29	4.11613560	0.24294632	62.32271191	0.01604551	15.14107358	0.06604551	29
30	4.32194238	0.23137745	66.43884750	0.01505144	15.37245103	0.06505144	30
31	4.53803949	0.22035947	70.76078988	0.01413212	15.59281050	0.06413212	31
32	4.76494147	0.20986617	75.29882937	0.01328042	15.80267667	0.06328042	32
33	5.00318854	0.19987254	80.06377084	0.01249004	16.00254921	0.06249004	33
34	5.25334797	0.19035480	85.06695938	0.01175545	16.19290401	0.06175545	34
35	5.51601537	0.18129029	90.32030735	0.01107171	16.37419429	0.06107171	35
36	5.79181614	0.17265741	95.83632272	0.01043446	16.54685171	0.06043446	36
37	6.08140694	0.16443563	101.62813886	0.00983979	16.71128734	0.05983979	37
38	6.38547729	0.15660536	107.70954580	0.00928423	16.86789271	0.05928423	38
39	6.70475115	0.14914797	114.09502309	0.00876462	17.01704067	0.05876462	39
40	7.03998871	0.14204568	120.79977424	0.00827816	17.15908635	0.05827816	40

TABLE A-2

COMPOUND INTEREST FOR $1

5%

PERIODS n	FUTURE AMOUNT $(1+i)^n$	PRESENT VALUE $(1+i)^{-n}$	AMOUNT OF ANNUITY $(S/p,i,n)$ $\dfrac{(1+i)^n-1}{i}$	SINKING FUND $(p/S,i,n)$ $\dfrac{i}{(1+i)^n-1}$	PRESENT VALUE OF ANNUITY $(V/p,i,n)$ $\dfrac{1-(1+i)^{-n}}{i}$	AMORTIZATION $(p/V,i,n)$ $\dfrac{i}{1-(1+i)^{-n}}$	PERIODS n
41	7.39198815	0.13528160	127.83976295	0.00782229	17.29436796	0.05782229	41
42	7.76158756	0.12883962	135.23175110	0.00739471	17.42320758	0.05739471	42
43	8.14966693	0.12270440	142.99333866	0.00699333	17.54591198	0.05699333	43
44	8.55715028	0.11686133	151.14300559	0.00661625	17.66277331	0.05661625	44
45	8.98500779	0.11129651	159.70015587	0.00626173	17.77406982	0.05626173	45
46	9.43425818	0.10599668	168.68516366	0.00592820	17.88006650	0.05592820	46
47	9.90597109	0.10094921	178.11942185	0.00561421	17.98101571	0.05561421	47
48	10.40126965	0.09614211	188.02539294	0.00531843	18.07715782	0.05531843	48
49	10.92133313	0.09156391	198.42666259	0.00503965	18.16872173	0.05503965	49
50	11.46739979	0.08720373	209.34799572	0.00477674	18.25592546	0.05477674	50
51	12.04076978	0.08305117	220.81539550	0.00452867	18.33897663	0.05452867	51
52	12.64280826	0.07909635	232.85616528	0.00429450	18.41807298	0.05429450	52
53	13.27494868	0.07532986	245.49897354	0.00407334	18.49340284	0.05407334	53
54	13.93869611	0.07174272	258.77392222	0.00386438	18.56514556	0.05386438	54
55	14.63563092	0.06832640	272.71261833	0.00366686	18.63347196	0.05366686	55
56	15.36741246	0.06507276	287.34824924	0.00348010	18.69854473	0.05348010	56
57	16.13578309	0.06197406	302.71566171	0.00330343	18.76051879	0.05330343	57
58	16.94257224	0.05902291	318.85144479	0.00313626	18.81954170	0.05313626	58
59	17.78970085	0.05621230	335.79401703	0.00297802	18.87575400	0.05297802	59
60	18.67918589	0.05353552	353.58371788	0.00282818	18.92928953	0.05282818	60
61	19.61314519	0.05098621	372.26290378	0.00268627	18.98027574	0.05268627	61
62	20.59380245	0.04855830	391.87604897	0.00255183	19.02883404	0.05255183	62
63	21.62349257	0.04624600	412.46985141	0.00242442	19.07508003	0.05242442	63
64	22.70466720	0.04404381	434.09334398	0.00230365	19.11912384	0.05230365	64
65	23.83990056	0.04194648	456.79801118	0.00218915	19.16107033	0.05218915	65
66	25.03189559	0.03994903	480.63791174	0.00208057	19.20101936	0.05208057	66
67	26.28349037	0.03804670	505.66980733	0.00197758	19.23906606	0.05197758	67
68	27.59766488	0.03623495	531.95329770	0.00187986	19.27530101	0.05187986	68
69	28.97754813	0.03450948	559.55096258	0.00178715	19.30981048	0.05178715	69
70	30.42642554	0.03286617	588.52851071	0.00169915	19.34267665	0.05169915	70
71	31.94774681	0.03130111	618.95493625	0.00161563	19.37397776	0.05161563	71
72	33.54513415	0.02981058	650.90268306	0.00153633	19.40378834	0.05153633	72
73	35.22239086	0.02839103	684.44781721	0.00146103	19.43217937	0.05146103	73
74	36.98351040	0.02703908	719.67020807	0.00138953	19.45921845	0.05138953	74
75	38.83268592	0.02575150	756.65371848	0.00132161	19.48496995	0.05132161	75
76	40.77432022	0.02452524	795.48640440	0.00125709	19.50949519	0.05125709	76
77	42.81303623	0.02335737	836.26072462	0.00119580	19.53285257	0.05119580	77
78	44.95368804	0.02224512	879.07376085	0.00113756	19.55509768	0.05113756	78
79	47.20137244	0.02118582	924.02744889	0.00108222	19.57628351	0.05108222	79
80	49.56144107	0.02017698	971.22882134	0.00102962	19.59646048	0.05102962	80

TABLE A-2

COMPOUND INTEREST FOR $1

5%

PERIODS n	FUTURE AMOUNT $(1+i)^n$	PRESENT VALUE $(1+i)^{-n}$	AMOUNT OF ANNUITY $(S/p,i,n)$ $\frac{(1+i)^n - 1}{i}$	SINKING FUND $(p/S,i,n)$ $\frac{i}{(1+i)^n - 1}$	PRESENT VALUE OF ANNUITY $(V/p,i,n)$ $\frac{1-(1+i)^{-n}}{i}$	AMORTIZATION $(p/V,i,n)$ $\frac{i}{1-(1+i)^{-n}}$	PERIODS n
81	52.03951312	0.01921617	1020.79026240	0.00097963	19.61567665	0.05097963	81
82	54.64148878	0.01830111	1072.82977552	0.00093211	19.63397776	0.05093211	82
83	57.37356322	0.01742963	1127.47126430	0.00088694	19.65140739	0.05088694	83
84	60.24224138	0.01659965	1184.84482752	0.00084399	19.66800704	0.05084399	84
85	63.25435344	0.01580919	1245.08706889	0.00080316	19.68381623	0.05080316	85
86	66.41707112	0.01505637	1308.34142234	0.00076433	19.69887260	0.05076433	86
87	69.73792467	0.01433940	1374.75849345	0.00072740	19.71321200	0.05072740	87
88	73.22482091	0.01365657	1444.49641812	0.00069228	19.72686857	0.05069228	88
89	76.88606195	0.01300626	1517.72123903	0.00065888	19.73987483	0.05065888	89
90	80.73036505	0.01238691	1594.60730098	0.00062711	19.75226174	0.05062711	90
91	84.76688330	0.01179706	1675.33766603	0.00059689	19.76405880	0.05059689	91
92	89.00522747	0.01123530	1760.10454933	0.00056815	19.77529410	0.05056815	92
93	93.45548884	0.01070028	1849.10977680	0.00054080	19.78599438	0.05054080	93
94	98.12826328	0.01019074	1942.56526564	0.00051478	19.79618512	0.05051478	94
95	103.03467645	0.00970547	2040.69352892	0.00049003	19.80589059	0.05049003	95
96	108.18641027	0.00924331	2143.72820537	0.00046648	19.81513390	0.05046648	96
97	113.59573078	0.00880315	2251.91461564	0.00044407	19.82393705	0.05044407	97
98	119.27551732	0.00838395	2365.51034642	0.00042274	19.83232100	0.05042274	98
99	125.23929319	0.00798471	2484.78586374	0.00040245	19.84030571	0.05040245	99
100	131.50125785	0.00760449	2610.02515693	0.00038314	19.84791020	0.05038314	100
101	138.07632074	0.00724237	2741.52641477	0.00036476	19.85515257	0.05036476	101
102	144.98013678	0.00689750	2879.60273551	0.00034727	19.86205007	0.05034727	102
103	152.22914361	0.00656904	3024.58287229	0.00033062	19.86861911	0.05033062	103
104	159.84060080	0.00625623	3176.81201590	0.00031478	19.87487535	0.05031478	104
105	167.83263083	0.00595832	3336.65261670	0.00029970	19.88083366	0.05029970	105
106	176.22426238	0.00567459	3504.48524753	0.00028535	19.88650825	0.05028535	106
107	185.03547550	0.00540437	3680.70950991	0.00027169	19.89191262	0.05027169	107
108	194.28724927	0.00514702	3865.74498540	0.00025868	19.89705964	0.05025868	108
109	204.00161173	0.00490192	4060.03223467	0.00024630	19.90196156	0.05024630	109
110	214.20169232	0.00466850	4264.03384641	0.00023452	19.90663006	0.05023452	110
111	224.91177694	0.00444619	4478.23553873	0.00022330	19.91107624	0.05022330	111
112	236.15736578	0.00423446	4703.14731566	0.00021262	19.91531071	0.05021262	112
113	247.96523407	0.00403282	4939.30468145	0.00020246	19.91934353	0.05020246	113
114	260.36349578	0.00384078	5187.26991552	0.00019278	19.92318432	0.05019278	114
115	273.38167056	0.00365789	5447.63341129	0.00018357	19.92684221	0.05018357	115
116	287.05075409	0.00348370	5721.01508186	0.00017479	19.93032591	0.05017479	116
117	301.40329180	0.00331781	6008.06583595	0.00016644	19.93364372	0.05016644	117
118	316.47345639	0.00315982	6309.46912775	0.00015849	19.93680355	0.05015849	118
119	332.29712921	0.00300935	6625.94258414	0.00015092	19.93981290	0.05015092	119
120	348.91198567	0.00286605	6958.23971334	0.00014371	19.94267895	0.05014371	120

TABLE A-2

COMPOUND INTEREST FOR $1

$5\frac{1}{2}\%$

PERIODS n	FUTURE AMOUNT $(1+i)^n$	PRESENT VALUE $(1+i)^{-n}$	AMOUNT OF ANNUITY $(S/p,i,n)$ $\dfrac{(1+i)^n-1}{i}$	SINKING FUND $(p/S,i,n)$ $\dfrac{i}{(1+i)^n-1}$	PRESENT VALUE OF ANNUITY $(V/p,i,n)$ $\dfrac{1-(1+i)^{-n}}{i}$	AMORTIZATION $(p/V,i,n)$ $\dfrac{i}{1-(1+i)^{-n}}$	PERIODS n
1	1.05500000	0.94786730	1.00000000	1.00000000	0.94786730	1.05500000	1
2	1.11302500	0.89845242	2.05500000	0.48661800	1.84631971	0.54161800	2
3	1.17424137	0.85161366	3.16802500	0.31565407	2.69793338	0.37065407	3
4	1.23882465	0.80721674	4.34226637	0.23029449	3.50515012	0.28529449	4
5	1.30696001	0.76513435	5.58109103	0.17917644	4.27028448	0.23417644	5
6	1.37884281	0.72524583	6.88805103	0.14517895	4.99553031	0.20017895	6
7	1.45467916	0.68743681	8.26689384	0.12096442	5.68296712	0.17596442	7
8	1.53468651	0.65159887	9.72157300	0.10286401	6.33456599	0.15786401	8
9	1.61909427	0.61762926	11.25625951	0.08883946	6.95219525	0.14383946	9
10	1.70814446	0.58543058	12.87535379	0.07766777	7.53762583	0.13266777	10
11	1.80209240	0.55491050	14.58349825	0.06857065	8.09253633	0.12357065	11
12	1.90120749	0.52598152	16.38559065	0.06102923	8.61851785	0.11602923	12
13	2.00577390	0.49856068	18.28679814	0.05468426	9.11707853	0.10968426	13
14	2.11609146	0.47256937	20.29257203	0.04927912	9.58964790	0.10427912	14
15	2.23247649	0.44793305	22.40866350	0.04462560	10.03758094	0.09962560	15
16	2.35526270	0.42458109	24.64113999	0.04058254	10.46216203	0.09558254	16
17	2.48480215	0.40244653	26.99640269	0.03704197	10.86460856	0.09204197	17
18	2.62146627	0.38146590	29.48120483	0.03391992	11.24607447	0.08891992	18
19	2.76564691	0.36157906	32.10267110	0.03115006	11.60765352	0.08615006	19
20	2.91775749	0.34272896	34.86831801	0.02867933	11.95038248	0.08367933	20
21	3.07823415	0.32486158	37.78607550	0.02646478	12.27524406	0.08146478	21
22	3.24753703	0.30792567	40.86430965	0.02447123	12.58316973	0.07947123	22
23	3.42615157	0.29187267	44.11184669	0.02266965	12.87504239	0.07766965	23
24	3.61458990	0.27665656	47.53799825	0.02103580	13.15169895	0.07603580	24
25	3.81339235	0.26223370	51.15258816	0.01954935	13.41393266	0.07454935	25
26	4.02312893	0.24856275	54.96598051	0.01819307	13.66249541	0.07319307	26
27	4.24440102	0.23560450	58.98910943	0.01695228	13.89809991	0.07195228	27
28	4.47784307	0.22332181	63.23351045	0.01581440	14.12142172	0.07081440	28
29	4.72412444	0.21167944	67.71135353	0.01476857	14.33310116	0.06976857	29
30	4.98395129	0.20064402	72.43547797	0.01380539	14.53374517	0.06880539	30
31	5.25806861	0.19018390	77.41942926	0.01291665	14.72392907	0.06791665	31
32	5.54726238	0.18026910	82.67749787	0.01209519	14.90419817	0.06709519	32
33	5.85236181	0.17087119	88.22476025	0.01133469	15.07506936	0.06633469	33
34	6.17424171	0.16196321	94.07712207	0.01062958	15.23703257	0.06562958	34
35	6.51382501	0.15351963	100.25136378	0.00997493	15.39055220	0.06497493	35
36	6.87208538	0.14551624	106.76518879	0.00936635	15.53606843	0.06436635	36
37	7.25005008	0.13793008	113.63727417	0.00879993	15.67399851	0.06379993	37
38	7.64880283	0.13073941	120.88732425	0.00827217	15.80473793	0.06327217	38
39	8.06948699	0.12392362	128.53612708	0.00777991	15.92866154	0.06277991	39
40	8.51330877	0.11746314	136.60561407	0.00732034	16.04612469	0.06232034	40

TABLE A-2

COMPOUND INTEREST FOR $1

$5\frac{1}{2}\%$

PERIODS n	FUTURE AMOUNT $(1+i)^n$	PRESENT VALUE $(1+i)^{-n}$	AMOUNT OF ANNUITY (S/p,i,n) $\dfrac{(1+i)^n-1}{i}$	SINKING FUND (p/S,i,n) $\dfrac{i}{(1+i)^n-1}$	PRESENT VALUE OF ANNUITY (V/p,i,n) $\dfrac{1-(1+i)^{-n}}{i}$	AMORTIZATION (p/V,i,n) $\dfrac{i}{1-(1+i)^{-n}}$	PERIODS n
41	8.98154076	0.11133947	145.11892285	0.00689090	16.15746416	0.06189090	41
42	9.47552550	0.10553504	154.10046360	0.00648927	16.26299920	0.06148927	42
43	9.99667940	0.10003322	163.57598910	0.00611337	16.36303242	0.06111337	43
44	10.54649677	0.09481822	173.57266850	0.00576128	16.45785063	0.06076128	44
45	11.12655409	0.08987509	184.17916527	0.00543127	16.54772572	0.06043127	45
46	11.73851456	0.08518965	195.24571936	0.00512175	16.63291537	0.06012175	46
47	12.38413287	0.08074849	206.98423392	0.00483129	16.71366386	0.05983129	47
48	13.06526017	0.07653885	219.36836679	0.00455854	16.79020271	0.05955854	48
49	13.78384948	0.07254867	232.43362696	0.00430230	16.86275139	0.05930230	49
50	14.54196120	0.06876652	246.21747645	0.00406145	16.93151790	0.05906145	50
51	15.34176907	0.06518153	260.75943765	0.00383495	16.99669943	0.05883495	51
52	16.18556637	0.06178344	276.10120672	0.00362186	17.05848287	0.05862186	52
53	17.07577252	0.05856250	292.28677309	0.00342130	17.11704538	0.05842130	53
54	18.01494001	0.05550948	309.36254561	0.00323245	17.17255486	0.05823245	54
55	19.00576171	0.05261562	327.37748562	0.00305458	17.22517048	0.05805458	55
56	20.05107860	0.04987263	346.38324733	0.00288698	17.27504311	0.05788698	56
57	21.15388793	0.04727263	366.43432593	0.00272900	17.32231575	0.05772900	57
58	22.31735176	0.04480818	387.58821386	0.00258006	17.36712393	0.05758006	58
59	23.54480611	0.04247221	409.90556562	0.00243959	17.40959614	0.05743959	59
60	24.83977045	0.04025802	433.45037173	0.00230707	17.44985416	0.05730707	60
61	26.20595782	0.03815926	458.29014217	0.00218202	17.48801343	0.05718202	61
62	27.64728550	0.03616992	484.49609994	0.00206400	17.52418334	0.05706400	62
63	29.16788620	0.03428428	512.14338549	0.00195258	17.55846762	0.05695258	63
64	30.77211994	0.03249695	541.31127170	0.00184737	17.59096457	0.05684737	64
65	32.46458654	0.03080279	572.08339164	0.00174800	17.62176737	0.05674800	65
66	34.25013880	0.02919696	604.54797818	0.00165413	17.65096433	0.05665413	66
67	36.13389643	0.02767485	638.79811698	0.00156544	17.67863917	0.05656544	67
68	38.12126074	0.02623208	674.93201341	0.00148163	17.70487125	0.05648163	68
69	40.21793008	0.02486453	713.05327415	0.00140242	17.72973579	0.05640242	69
70	42.42991623	0.02356828	753.27120423	0.00132754	17.75330406	0.05632754	70
71	44.76356163	0.02233960	795.70112046	0.00125675	17.77564366	0.05625675	71
72	47.22555751	0.02117498	840.46468209	0.00118982	17.79681864	0.05618982	72
73	49.82296318	0.02007107	887.69023960	0.00112652	17.81688970	0.05612652	73
74	52.56322615	0.01902471	937.51320278	0.00106665	17.83591441	0.05606665	74
75	55.45420359	0.01803290	990.07642893	0.00101002	17.85394731	0.05601002	75
76	58.50418479	0.01709279	1045.53063252	0.00095645	17.87104010	0.05595645	76
77	61.72191495	0.01620170	1104.03481731	0.00090577	17.88724180	0.05590577	77
78	65.11662027	0.01535706	1165.75673226	0.00085781	17.90259887	0.05585781	78
79	68.69803439	0.01455646	1230.87335254	0.00081243	17.91715532	0.05581243	79
80	72.47642628	0.01379759	1299.57138693	0.00076948	17.93095291	0.05576948	80

TABLE A-2

COMPOUND INTEREST FOR $1

6%

PERIODS n	FUTURE AMOUNT $(1+i)^n$	PRESENT VALUE $(1+i)^{-n}$	AMOUNT OF ANNUITY $(S/p,i,n)$ $\dfrac{(1+i)^n-1}{i}$	SINKING FUND $(p/S,i,n)$ $\dfrac{i}{(1+i)^n-1}$	PRESENT VALUE OF ANNUITY $(V/p,i,n)$ $\dfrac{1-(1+i)^{-n}}{i}$	AMORTIZATION $(p/V,i,n)$ $\dfrac{i}{1-(1+i)^{-n}}$	PERIODS n
1	1.06000000	0.94339623	1.00000000	1.00000000	0.94339623	1.06000000	1
2	1.12360000	0.88999644	2.06000000	0.48543689	1.83339267	0.54543689	2
3	1.19101600	0.83961928	3.18360000	0.31410981	2.67301195	0.37410981	3
4	1.26247696	0.79209366	4.37461600	0.22859149	3.46510561	0.28859149	4
5	1.33822558	0.74725817	5.63709296	0.17739640	4.21236379	0.23739640	5
6	1.41851911	0.70496054	6.97531854	0.14336263	4.91732433	0.20336263	6
7	1.50363026	0.66505711	8.39383765	0.11913502	5.58238144	0.17913502	7
8	1.59384807	0.62741237	9.89746791	0.10103594	6.20979381	0.16103594	8
9	1.68947896	0.59189846	11.49131598	0.08702224	6.80169227	0.14702224	9
10	1.79084770	0.55839478	13.18079494	0.07586796	7.36008705	0.13586796	10
11	1.89829856	0.52678753	14.97164264	0.06679294	7.88687458	0.12679294	11
12	2.01219647	0.49696936	16.86994120	0.05927703	8.38384394	0.11927703	12
13	2.13292826	0.46883902	18.88213767	0.05296011	8.85268296	0.11296011	13
14	2.26090396	0.44230096	21.01506593	0.04758491	9.29498393	0.10758491	14
15	2.39655819	0.41726506	23.27596988	0.04296276	9.71224899	0.10296276	15
16	2.54035168	0.39364628	25.67252808	0.03895214	10.10589527	0.09895214	16
17	2.69277279	0.37136442	28.21287976	0.03544480	10.47725969	0.09544480	17
18	2.85433915	0.35034379	30.90565255	0.03235654	10.82760348	0.09235654	18
19	3.02559950	0.33051301	33.75999170	0.02962086	11.15811649	0.08962086	19
20	3.20713547	0.31180473	36.78559120	0.02718456	11.46992122	0.08718456	20
21	3.39956360	0.29415540	39.99272668	0.02500455	11.76407662	0.08500455	21
22	3.60353742	0.27750510	43.39229028	0.02304557	12.04158172	0.08304557	22
23	3.81974966	0.26179726	46.99582769	0.02127848	12.30337898	0.08127848	23
24	4.04893464	0.24697855	50.81557735	0.01967900	12.55035753	0.07967900	24
25	4.29187072	0.23299863	54.86451200	0.01822672	12.78335616	0.07822672	25
26	4.54938296	0.21981003	59.15638272	0.01690435	13.00316619	0.07690435	26
27	4.82234594	0.20736795	63.70576568	0.01569717	13.21053414	0.07569717	27
28	5.11168670	0.19563014	68.52811162	0.01459255	13.40616428	0.07459255	28
29	5.41838790	0.18455674	73.63979832	0.01357961	13.59072102	0.07357961	29
30	5.74349117	0.17411013	79.05818622	0.01264891	13.76483115	0.07264891	30
31	6.08810064	0.16425484	84.80167739	0.01179222	13.92908599	0.07179222	31
32	6.45338668	0.15495740	90.88977803	0.01100234	14.08404339	0.07100234	32
33	6.84058988	0.14618622	97.34316471	0.01027293	14.23022961	0.07027293	33
34	7.25102528	0.13791153	104.18375460	0.00959843	14.36814114	0.06959843	34
35	7.68608679	0.13010522	111.43477987	0.00897386	14.49824636	0.06897386	35
36	8.14725200	0.12274077	119.12086666	0.00839483	14.62098713	0.06839483	36
37	8.63608712	0.11579318	127.26811866	0.00785743	14.73678031	0.06785743	37
38	9.15425235	0.10923885	135.90420578	0.00735812	14.84601916	0.06735812	38
39	9.70350749	0.10305552	145.05845813	0.00689377	14.94907468	0.06689377	39
40	10.28571794	0.09722219	154.76196562	0.00646154	15.04629687	0.06646154	40

TABLE A-2

COMPOUND INTEREST FOR $1

6%

PERIODS n	FUTURE AMOUNT $(1+i)^n$	PRESENT VALUE $(1+i)^{-n}$	AMOUNT OF ANNUITY $(S/p,i,n)$ $\dfrac{(1+i)^n - 1}{i}$	SINKING FUND $(p/S,i,n)$ $\dfrac{i}{(1+i)^n - 1}$	PRESENT VALUE OF ANNUITY $(V/p,i,n)$ $\dfrac{1-(1+i)^{-n}}{i}$	AMORTIZATION $(p/V,i,n)$ $\dfrac{i}{1-(1+i)^{-n}}$	PERIODS n
41	10.90286101	0.09171905	165.04768356	0.00605886	15.13801592	0.06605886	41
42	11.55703267	0.08652740	175.95054457	0.00568342	15.22454332	0.06568342	42
43	12.25045463	0.08162962	187.50757724	0.00533312	15.30617294	0.06533312	43
44	12.98548191	0.07700908	199.75803188	0.00500606	15.38318202	0.06500606	44
45	13.76461083	0.07265007	212.74351379	0.00470050	15.45583209	0.06470050	45
46	14.59048748	0.06853781	226.50812462	0.00441485	15.52436990	0.06441485	46
47	15.46591673	0.06465831	241.09861210	0.00414768	15.58902821	0.06414768	47
48	16.39387173	0.06099840	256.56452882	0.00389765	15.65002661	0.06389765	48
49	17.37750403	0.05754566	272.95840055	0.00366356	15.70757227	0.06366356	49
50	18.42015427	0.05428836	290.33590458	0.00344429	15.76186064	0.06344429	50
51	19.52536353	0.05121544	308.75605886	0.00323880	15.81307607	0.06323880	51
52	20.69688534	0.04831645	328.28142239	0.00304617	15.86139252	0.06304617	52
53	21.93869846	0.04558156	348.97830773	0.00286551	15.90697408	0.06286551	53
54	23.25502037	0.04300147	370.91700620	0.00269602	15.94997554	0.06269602	54
55	24.65032159	0.04056742	394.17202657	0.00253696	15.99054297	0.06253696	55
56	26.12934089	0.03827115	418.82234816	0.00238765	16.02881412	0.06238765	56
57	27.69710134	0.03610486	444.95168905	0.00224744	16.06491898	0.06224744	57
58	29.35892742	0.03406119	472.64879040	0.00211574	16.09898017	0.06211574	58
59	31.12046307	0.03213320	502.00771782	0.00199200	16.13111337	0.06199200	59
60	32.98769085	0.03031434	533.12818089	0.00187572	16.16142771	0.06187572	60
61	34.96695230	0.02859843	566.11587174	0.00176642	16.19002614	0.06176642	61
62	37.06496944	0.02697965	601.08282405	0.00166366	16.21700579	0.06166366	62
63	39.28886761	0.02545250	638.14779349	0.00156704	16.24245829	0.06156704	63
64	41.64619967	0.02401179	677.43666110	0.00147615	16.26647009	0.06147615	64
65	44.14497165	0.02265264	719.08286076	0.00139066	16.28912272	0.06139066	65
66	46.79366994	0.02137041	763.22783241	0.00131022	16.31049314	0.06131022	66
67	49.60129014	0.02016077	810.02150236	0.00123454	16.33065390	0.06123454	67
68	52.57736755	0.01901959	859.62279250	0.00116330	16.34967349	0.06116330	68
69	55.73200960	0.01794301	912.20016005	0.00109625	16.36761650	0.06109625	69
70	59.07593018	0.01692737	967.93216965	0.00103313	16.38454387	0.06103313	70
71	62.62048599	0.01596921	1027.00809983	0.00097370	16.40051308	0.06097370	71
72	66.37771515	0.01506530	1089.62858582	0.00091774	16.41557838	0.06091774	72
73	70.36037806	0.01421254	1156.00630097	0.00086505	16.42979093	0.06086505	73
74	74.58200074	0.01340806	1226.36667903	0.00081542	16.44319899	0.06081542	74
75	79.05692079	0.01264911	1300.94867977	0.00076867	16.45584810	0.06076867	75
76	83.80033603	0.01193313	1380.00560055	0.00072463	16.46778123	0.06072463	76
77	88.82835620	0.01125767	1463.80593659	0.00068315	16.47903889	0.06068315	77
78	94.15805757	0.01062044	1552.63429278	0.00064407	16.48965933	0.06064407	78
79	99.80754102	0.01001928	1646.79235035	0.00060724	16.49967862	0.06060724	79
80	105.79599348	0.00945215	1746.59989137	0.00057254	16.50913077	0.06057254	80

410

TABLE A-2

COMPOUND INTEREST FOR $1

$6\frac{1}{2}$ %

PERIODS n	FUTURE AMOUNT $(1+i)^n$	PRESENT VALUE $(1+i)^{-n}$	AMOUNT OF ANNUITY (S/p,i,n) $\dfrac{(1+i)^n-1}{i}$	SINKING FUND (p/S,i,n) $\dfrac{i}{(1+i)^n-1}$	PRESENT VALUE OF ANNUITY (V/p,i,n) $\dfrac{1-(1+i)^{-n}}{i}$	AMORTIZATION (p/V,i,n) $\dfrac{i}{1-(1+i)^{-n}}$	PERIODS n
1	1.06500000	0.93896714	1.00000000	1.00000000	0.93896714	1.06500000	1
2	1.13422500	0.88165928	2.06500000	0.48426150	1.82062642	0.54926150	2
3	1.20794962	0.82784909	3.19922500	0.31257570	2.64847551	0.37757570	3
4	1.28646635	0.77732309	4.40717462	0.22690274	3.42579860	0.29190274	4
5	1.37008666	0.72988084	5.69364098	0.17563454	4.15567944	0.24063454	5
6	1.45914230	0.68533412	7.06372764	0.14156831	4.84101356	0.20656831	6
7	1.55398655	0.64350621	8.52286994	0.11733137	5.48451977	0.18233137	7
8	1.65499567	0.60423119	10.07685648	0.09923730	6.08875096	0.16423730	8
9	1.76257039	0.56735323	11.73185215	0.08523803	6.65610419	0.15023803	9
10	1.87713747	0.53272604	13.49442254	0.07410469	7.18883022	0.13910469	10
11	1.99915140	0.50021224	15.37156001	0.06505521	7.68904246	0.13005521	11
12	2.12909624	0.46968285	17.37071141	0.05756817	8.15872532	0.12256817	12
13	2.26748750	0.44101676	19.49980765	0.05128256	8.59974208	0.11628256	13
14	2.41487418	0.41410025	21.76729515	0.04594048	9.01384233	0.11094048	14
15	2.57184101	0.38882652	24.18216933	0.04135278	9.40266885	0.10635278	15
16	2.73901067	0.36509533	26.75401034	0.03737757	9.76776418	0.10237757	16
17	2.91704637	0.34281251	29.49302101	0.03390633	10.11057670	0.09890633	17
18	3.10665438	0.32188969	32.41006738	0.03085461	10.43246638	0.09585461	18
19	3.30858691	0.30224384	35.51672176	0.02815575	10.73471022	0.09315575	19
20	3.52364506	0.28379703	38.82530867	0.02575640	11.01850725	0.09075640	20
21	3.75268199	0.26647608	42.34895373	0.02361333	11.28498333	0.08861333	21
22	3.99660632	0.25021228	46.10163573	0.02169120	11.53519562	0.08669120	22
23	4.25638573	0.23494111	50.09824205	0.01996078	11.77013673	0.08496078	23
24	4.53305081	0.22060198	54.35462778	0.01839770	11.99073871	0.08339770	24
25	4.82769911	0.20713801	58.88767859	0.01698148	12.19787673	0.08198148	25
26	5.14149955	0.19449579	63.71537769	0.01569480	12.39237251	0.08069480	26
27	5.47569702	0.18262515	68.85687725	0.01452288	12.57499766	0.07952288	27
28	5.83161733	0.17147902	74.33257427	0.01345305	12.74647668	0.07845305	28
29	6.21067245	0.16101316	80.16419159	0.01247440	12.90748984	0.07747440	29
30	6.61436616	0.15118607	86.37486405	0.01157744	13.05867591	0.07657744	30
31	7.04429996	0.14195875	92.98923021	0.01075393	13.20063465	0.07575393	31
32	7.50217946	0.13329460	100.03353017	0.00999665	13.33392925	0.07499665	32
33	7.98982113	0.12515925	107.53570963	0.00929924	13.45908850	0.07429924	33
34	8.50915950	0.11752042	115.52553076	0.00865610	13.57660892	0.07365610	34
35	9.06225487	0.11034781	124.03469026	0.00806226	13.68695673	0.07306226	35
36	9.65130143	0.10361297	133.09694513	0.00751332	13.79056970	0.07251332	36
37	10.27863603	0.09728917	142.74824656	0.00700534	13.88785887	0.07200534	37
38	10.94674737	0.09135134	153.02688259	0.00653480	13.97921021	0.07153480	38
39	11.65828595	0.08577590	163.97362996	0.00609854	14.06498611	0.07109854	39
40	12.41607453	0.08054075	175.63191590	0.00569373	14.14552687	0.07069373	40

TABLE A-2

COMPOUND INTEREST FOR $1

$6\frac{1}{2}\%$

PERIODS	FUTURE AMOUNT	PRESENT VALUE	AMOUNT OF ANNUITY	SINKING FUND	PRESENT VALUE OF ANNUITY	AMORTIZATION	PERIODS
n	$(1+i)^n$	$(1+i)^{-n}$	$(S/p,i,n)$ $\dfrac{(1+i)^n-1}{i}$	$(p/S,i,n)$ $\dfrac{i}{(1+i)^n-1}$	$(V/p,i,n)$ $\dfrac{1-(1+i)^{-n}}{i}$	$(p/V,i,n)$ $\dfrac{i}{1-(1+i)^{-n}}$	n
41	13.22311938	0.07562512	188.04799044	0.00531779	14.22115199	0.07031779	41
42	14.08262214	0.07100950	201.27110981	0.00496842	14.29216149	0.06996842	42
43	14.99799258	0.06667559	215.35373195	0.00464352	14.35883708	0.06964352	43
44	15.97286209	0.06260619	230.35172453	0.00434119	14.42144327	0.06934119	44
45	17.01109813	0.05878515	246.32458662	0.00405968	14.48022842	0.06905968	45
46	18.11681951	0.05519733	263.33568475	0.00379743	14.53542575	0.06879743	46
47	19.29441278	0.05182848	281.45250426	0.00355300	14.58725422	0.06855300	47
48	20.54854961	0.04866524	300.74691704	0.00332505	14.63591946	0.06832505	48
49	21.88420533	0.04569506	321.29546665	0.00311240	14.68161451	0.06811240	49
50	23.30667868	0.04290616	343.17967198	0.00291393	14.72452067	0.06791393	50
51	24.82161279	0.04028747	366.48635066	0.00272861	14.76480814	0.06772861	51
52	26.43501762	0.03782861	391.30796345	0.00255553	14.80263675	0.06755553	52
53	28.15329377	0.03551982	417.74298108	0.00239382	14.83815658	0.06739382	53
54	29.98325786	0.03335195	445.89627485	0.00224267	14.87150852	0.06724267	54
55	31.93216963	0.03131638	475.87953271	0.00210137	14.90282490	0.06710137	55
56	34.00776065	0.02940505	507.81170234	0.00196923	14.93222996	0.06696923	56
57	36.21826509	0.02761038	541.81946299	0.00184563	14.95984033	0.06684563	57
58	38.57245233	0.02592524	578.03772808	0.00172999	14.98576557	0.06672999	58
59	41.07966173	0.02434295	616.61018041	0.00162177	15.01010852	0.06662177	59
60	43.74983974	0.02285723	657.68984214	0.00152047	15.03296574	0.06652047	60
61	46.59357932	0.02146218	701.43968187	0.00142564	15.05442793	0.06642564	61
62	49.62216198	0.02015229	748.03326120	0.00133684	15.07458022	0.06633684	62
63	52.84760251	0.01892233	797.65542317	0.00125367	15.09350255	0.06625367	63
64	56.28269667	0.01776745	850.50302568	0.00117577	15.11127000	0.06617577	64
65	59.94107195	0.01668305	906.78572235	0.00110280	15.12795305	0.06610280	65
66	63.83724163	0.01566484	966.72679430	0.00103442	15.14361789	0.06603442	66
67	67.98666234	0.01470877	1030.56403593	0.00097034	15.15832666	0.06597034	67
68	72.40579539	0.01381105	1098.55069827	0.00091029	15.17213771	0.06591029	68
69	77.11217209	0.01296812	1170.95649365	0.00085400	15.18510583	0.06585400	69
70	82.12446327	0.01217664	1248.06866574	0.00080124	15.19728247	0.06580124	70
71	87.46255339	0.01143346	1330.19312901	0.00075177	15.20871593	0.06575177	71
72	93.14761936	0.01073565	1417.65568240	0.00070539	15.21945158	0.06570539	72
73	99.20221461	0.01008042	1510.80330176	0.00066190	15.22953200	0.06566190	73
74	105.65035856	0.00946518	1610.00551637	0.00062112	15.23899718	0.06562112	74
75	112.51763187	0.00888750	1715.65587493	0.00058287	15.24788468	0.06558287	75
76	119.83127794	0.00834507	1828.17350681	0.00054699	15.25622974	0.06554699	76
77	127.62031101	0.00783574	1948.00478475	0.00051335	15.26406549	0.06551335	77
78	135.91563122	0.00735751	2075.62509576	0.00048178	15.27142299	0.06548178	78
79	144.75014725	0.00690846	2211.54072698	0.00045217	15.27833145	0.06545217	79
80	154.15890683	0.00648681	2356.29087423	0.00042440	15.28481826	0.06542440	80

TABLE A-2

COMPOUND INTEREST FOR $1

7%

PERIODS n	FUTURE AMOUNT $(1+i)^n$	PRESENT VALUE $(1+i)^{-n}$	AMOUNT OF ANNUITY $(S/p,i,n)$ $\dfrac{(1+i)^n-1}{i}$	SINKING FUND $(p/S,i,n)$ $\dfrac{i}{(1+i)^n-1}$	PRESENT VALUE OF ANNUITY $(V/p,i,n)$ $\dfrac{1-(1+i)^{-n}}{i}$	AMORTIZATION $(p/V,i,n)$ $\dfrac{i}{1-(1+i)^{-n}}$	PERIODS n
1	1.07000000	0.93457944	1.00000000	1.00000000	0.93457944	1.07000000	1
2	1.14490000	0.87343873	2.07000000	0.48309179	1.80801817	0.55309179	2
3	1.22504300	0.81629788	3.21490000	0.31105167	2.62431604	0.38105167	3
4	1.31079601	0.76289521	4.43994300	0.22522812	3.38721126	0.29522812	4
5	1.40255173	0.71298618	5.75073901	0.17389069	4.10019744	0.24389069	5
6	1.50073035	0.66634222	7.15329074	0.13979580	4.76653966	0.20979580	6
7	1.60578148	0.62274974	8.65402109	0.11555322	5.38928940	0.18555322	7
8	1.71818618	0.58200910	10.25980257	0.09746776	5.97129851	0.16746776	8
9	1.83845921	0.54393374	11.97798875	0.08348647	6.51523225	0.15348647	9
10	1.96715136	0.50834929	13.81644796	0.07237750	7.02358154	0.14237750	10
11	2.10485195	0.47509280	15.78359932	0.06335690	7.49867434	0.13335690	11
12	2.25219159	0.44401196	17.88845127	0.05590199	7.94268630	0.12590199	12
13	2.40984500	0.41496445	20.14064286	0.04965085	8.35765074	0.11965085	13
14	2.57853415	0.38781724	22.55048786	0.04434494	8.74546799	0.11434494	14
15	2.75903154	0.36244602	25.12902201	0.03979462	9.10791401	0.10979462	15
16	2.95216375	0.33873460	27.88805355	0.03585765	9.44664860	0.10585765	16
17	3.15881521	0.31657439	30.84021730	0.03242519	9.76322299	0.10242519	17
18	3.37993228	0.29586392	33.99903251	0.02941260	10.05908691	0.09941260	18
19	3.61652754	0.27650833	37.37896479	0.02675301	10.33559524	0.09675301	19
20	3.86968446	0.25841900	40.99549232	0.02439293	10.59401425	0.09439293	20
21	4.14056237	0.24151309	44.86517678	0.02228900	10.83552733	0.09228900	21
22	4.43040174	0.22571317	49.00573916	0.02040577	11.06124050	0.09040577	22
23	4.74052986	0.21094688	53.43614090	0.01871393	11.27218738	0.08871393	23
24	5.07236695	0.19714662	58.17667076	0.01718902	11.46933400	0.08718902	24
25	5.42743264	0.18424918	63.24903772	0.01581052	11.65358318	0.08581052	25
26	5.80735292	0.17219549	68.67647036	0.01456103	11.82577867	0.08456103	26
27	6.21386763	0.16093037	74.48382328	0.01342573	11.98670904	0.08342573	27
28	6.64883836	0.15040221	80.69769091	0.01239193	12.13711125	0.08239193	28
29	7.11425705	0.14056282	87.34652927	0.01144865	12.27767407	0.08144865	29
30	7.61225504	0.13136712	94.46078632	0.01058640	12.40904118	0.08058640	30
31	8.14511290	0.12277301	102.07304137	0.00979691	12.53181419	0.07979691	31
32	8.71527080	0.11474113	110.21815426	0.00907292	12.64655532	0.07907292	32
33	9.32533975	0.10723470	118.93342506	0.00840807	12.75379002	0.07840807	33
34	9.97811354	0.10021934	128.25876481	0.00779674	12.85400936	0.07779674	34
35	10.67658148	0.09366294	138.23687835	0.00723396	12.94767230	0.07723396	35
36	11.42394219	0.08753546	148.91345984	0.00671531	13.03520776	0.07671531	36
37	12.22361814	0.08180884	160.33740202	0.00623685	13.11701660	0.07623685	37
38	13.07927141	0.07645686	172.56102017	0.00579505	13.19347345	0.07579505	38
39	13.99482041	0.07145501	185.64029158	0.00538676	13.26492846	0.07538676	39
40	14.97445784	0.06678038	199.63511199	0.00500914	13.33170884	0.07500914	40

TABLE A-2

COMPOUND INTEREST FOR $1

7%

PERIODS n	FUTURE AMOUNT $(1+i)^n$	PRESENT VALUE $(1+i)^{-n}$	AMOUNT OF ANNUITY $(S/p,i,n)$ $\dfrac{(1+i)^n-1}{i}$	SINKING FUND $(p/S,i,n)$ $\dfrac{i}{(1+i)^n-1}$	PRESENT VALUE OF ANNUITY $(V/p,i,n)$ $\dfrac{1-(1+i)^{-n}}{i}$	AMORTIZATION $(p/V,i,n)$ $\dfrac{i}{1-(1+i)^{-n}}$	PERIODS n
41	16.02266989	0.06241157	214.60956983	0.00465962	13.39412041	0.07465962	41
42	17.14425678	0.05832857	230.63229972	0.00433591	13.45244898	0.07433591	42
43	18.34435475	0.05451268	247.77649650	0.00403590	13.50696167	0.07403590	43
44	19.62845959	0.05094643	266.12085125	0.00375769	13.55790810	0.07375769	44
45	21.00245176	0.04761349	285.74931084	0.00349957	13.60552159	0.07349957	45
46	22.47262338	0.04449859	306.75176260	0.00325996	13.65002018	0.07325996	46
47	24.04570702	0.04158747	329.22438598	0.00303744	13.69160764	0.07303744	47
48	25.72890651	0.03886679	353.27009300	0.00283070	13.73047443	0.07283070	48
49	27.52992997	0.03632410	378.99899951	0.00263853	13.76679853	0.07263853	49
50	29.45702506	0.03394776	406.52892947	0.00245985	13.80074629	0.07245985	50
51	31.51901682	0.03172688	435.98595454	0.00229365	13.83247317	0.07229365	51
52	33.72534799	0.02965129	467.50497135	0.00213901	13.86212446	0.07213901	52
53	36.08612235	0.02771148	501.23031935	0.00199509	13.88983594	0.07199509	53
54	38.61215092	0.02589858	537.31644170	0.00186110	13.91573453	0.07186110	54
55	41.31500148	0.02420428	575.92859262	0.00173633	13.93993881	0.07173633	55
56	44.20705159	0.02262083	617.24359414	0.00162011	13.96255964	0.07162011	56
57	47.30154520	0.02114096	661.45064569	0.00151183	13.98370059	0.07151183	57
58	50.61265336	0.01975791	708.75219089	0.00141093	14.00345850	0.07141093	58
59	54.15553910	0.01846533	759.36484425	0.00131689	14.02192383	0.07131689	59
60	57.94642683	0.01725732	813.52038335	0.00122923	14.03918115	0.07122923	60
61	62.00267671	0.01612834	871.46681019	0.00114749	14.05530949	0.07114749	61
62	66.34286408	0.01507321	933.46948690	0.00107127	14.07038270	0.07107127	62
63	70.98686457	0.01408711	999.81235098	0.00100019	14.08446981	0.07100019	63
64	75.95594509	0.01316553	1070.79921555	0.00093388	14.09763534	0.07093388	64
65	81.27286124	0.01230423	1146.75516064	0.00087203	14.10993957	0.07087203	65
66	86.96196153	0.01149928	1228.02802188	0.00081431	14.12143885	0.07081431	66
67	93.04929884	0.01074699	1314.98998341	0.00076046	14.13218584	0.07076046	67
68	99.56274976	0.01004392	1408.03928225	0.00071021	14.14222976	0.07071021	68
69	106.53214224	0.00938684	1507.60203201	0.00066331	14.15161659	0.07066331	69
70	113.98939220	0.00877275	1614.13417425	0.00061953	14.16038934	0.07061953	70
71	121.96864965	0.00819883	1728.12356645	0.00057866	14.16858817	0.07057866	71
72	130.50645513	0.00766246	1850.09221610	0.00054051	14.17625063	0.07054051	72
73	139.64190699	0.00716117	1980.59867123	0.00050490	14.18341180	0.07050490	73
74	149.41684047	0.00669269	2120.24057821	0.00047164	14.19010449	0.07047164	74
75	159.87601931	0.00625485	2269.65741869	0.00044060	14.19635933	0.07044060	75
76	171.06734066	0.00584565	2429.53343800	0.00041160	14.20220498	0.07041160	76
77	183.04205451	0.00546323	2600.60077866	0.00038453	14.20766821	0.07038453	77
78	195.85499832	0.00510582	2783.64283316	0.00035924	14.21277403	0.07035924	78
79	209.56484820	0.00477179	2979.49783148	0.00033563	14.21754582	0.07033563	79
80	224.23438758	0.00445962	3189.06267969	0.00031357	14.22200544	0.07031357	80

TABLE A-2
COMPOUND INTEREST FOR $1

$7\frac{1}{2}$ %

PERIODS n	FUTURE AMOUNT $(1+i)^n$	PRESENT VALUE $(1+i)^{-n}$	AMOUNT OF ANNUITY $(S/p,i,n)$ $\dfrac{(1+i)^n-1}{i}$	SINKING FUND $(p/S,i,n)$ $\dfrac{i}{(1+i)^n-1}$	PRESENT VALUE OF ANNUITY $(V/p,i,n)$ $\dfrac{1-(1+i)^{-n}}{i}$	AMORTIZATION $(p/V,i,n)$ $\dfrac{i}{1-(1+i)^{-n}}$	PERIODS n
1	1.07500000	0.93023256	1.00000000	1.00000000	0.93023256	1.07500000	1
2	1.15562500	0.86533261	2.07500000	0.48192771	1.79556517	0.55692771	2
3	1.24229687	0.80496057	3.23062500	0.30953763	2.60052574	0.38453763	3
4	1.33546914	0.74880053	4.47292187	0.22356751	3.34932627	0.29856751	4
5	1.43562933	0.69655863	5.80839102	0.17216472	4.04588490	0.24716472	5
6	1.54330153	0.64796152	7.24402034	0.13804489	4.69384642	0.21304489	6
7	1.65904914	0.60275490	8.78732187	0.11380032	5.29660132	0.18880032	7
8	1.78347783	0.56070223	10.44637101	0.09572702	5.85730355	0.17072702	8
9	1.91723866	0.52158347	12.22984883	0.08176716	6.37888703	0.15676716	9
10	2.06103156	0.48519393	14.14708750	0.07068593	6.86408096	0.14568593	10
11	2.21560893	0.45134319	16.20811906	0.06169747	7.31542415	0.13669747	11
12	2.38177960	0.41985413	18.42372787	0.05427783	7.73527827	0.12927783	12
13	2.56041307	0.39056198	20.80550759	0.04806420	8.12584026	0.12306420	13
14	2.75244405	0.36331347	23.36592066	0.04279737	8.48915373	0.11779737	14
15	2.95887735	0.33796602	26.11836470	0.03828724	8.82711975	0.11328724	15
16	3.18079315	0.31438699	29.07724206	0.03439116	9.14150674	0.10939116	16
17	3.41935264	0.29245302	32.25803521	0.03100003	9.43395976	0.10600003	17
18	3.67580409	0.27204932	35.67738785	0.02802896	9.70600908	0.10302896	18
19	3.95148940	0.25306913	39.35319194	0.02541090	9.95907821	0.10041090	19
20	4.24785110	0.23541315	43.30468134	0.02309219	10.19449136	0.09809219	20
21	4.56643993	0.21898897	47.55253244	0.02102937	10.41348033	0.09602937	21
22	4.90892293	0.20371067	52.11897237	0.01918687	10.61719101	0.09418687	22
23	5.27709215	0.18949830	57.02789530	0.01753528	10.80668931	0.09253528	23
24	5.67287406	0.17627749	62.30498744	0.01605008	10.98296680	0.09105008	24
25	6.09833961	0.16397906	67.97786150	0.01471067	11.14694586	0.08971067	25
26	6.55571508	0.15253866	74.07620112	0.01349961	11.29948452	0.08849961	26
27	7.04739371	0.14189643	80.63191620	0.01240204	11.44138095	0.08740204	27
28	7.57594824	0.13199668	87.67930971	0.01140520	11.57337763	0.08640520	28
29	8.14414436	0.12278761	95.25525816	0.01049811	11.69616524	0.08549811	29
30	8.75495519	0.11422103	103.39940252	0.00967124	11.81038627	0.08467124	30
31	9.41157683	0.10625212	112.15435771	0.00891628	11.91663839	0.08391628	31
32	10.11744509	0.09883918	121.56593454	0.00822599	12.01547757	0.08322599	32
33	10.87625347	0.09194343	131.68337963	0.00759397	12.10742099	0.08259397	33
34	11.69197248	0.08552877	142.55963310	0.00701461	12.19294976	0.08201461	34
35	12.56887042	0.07956164	154.25160558	0.00648291	12.27251141	0.08148291	35
36	13.51153570	0.07401083	166.82047600	0.00599447	12.34652224	0.08099447	36
37	14.52490088	0.06884729	180.33201170	0.00554533	12.41536952	0.08054533	37
38	15.61426844	0.06404399	194.85691258	0.00513197	12.47941351	0.08013197	38
39	16.78533858	0.05957580	210.47118102	0.00475124	12.53898931	0.07975124	39
40	18.04423897	0.05541935	227.25651960	0.00440031	12.59440866	0.07940031	40

TABLE A-2

COMPOUND INTEREST FOR $1

$7\frac{1}{2}\%$

PERIODS n	FUTURE AMOUNT $(1+i)^n$	PRESENT VALUE $(1+i)^{-n}$	AMOUNT OF ANNUITY $(S/p,i,n)$ $\dfrac{(1+i)^n-1}{i}$	SINKING FUND $(p/S,i,n)$ $\dfrac{i}{(1+i)^n-1}$	PRESENT VALUE OF ANNUITY $(V/p,i,n)$ $\dfrac{1-(1+i)^{-n}}{i}$	AMORTIZATION $(p/V,i,n)$ $\dfrac{i}{1-(1+i)^{-n}}$	PERIODS n
41	19.39755689	0.05155288	245.30075857	0.00407663	12.64596155	0.07907663	41
42	20.85237366	0.04795617	264.69831546	0.00377789	12.69391772	0.07877789	42
43	22.41630168	0.04461039	285.55068912	0.00350201	12.73852811	0.07850201	43
44	24.09752431	0.04149804	307.96699080	0.00324710	12.78002615	0.07824710	44
45	25.90483863	0.03860283	332.06451511	0.00301146	12.81862898	0.07801146	45
46	27.84770153	0.03590961	357.96935375	0.00279354	12.85453858	0.07779354	46
47	29.93627915	0.03340428	385.81705528	0.00259190	12.88794287	0.07759190	47
48	32.18150008	0.03107375	415.75333442	0.00240527	12.91901662	0.07740527	48
49	34.59511259	0.02890582	447.93483451	0.00223247	12.94792244	0.07723247	49
50	37.18974603	0.02688913	482.52994709	0.00207241	12.97481157	0.07707241	50
51	39.97897698	0.02501315	519.71969313	0.00192411	12.99982472	0.07692411	51
52	42.97740026	0.02326804	559.69867011	0.00178668	13.02309276	0.07678668	52
53	46.20070528	0.02164469	602.67607037	0.00165927	13.04473745	0.07665927	53
54	49.66575817	0.02013460	648.87677565	0.00154112	13.06487205	0.07654112	54
55	53.39069004	0.01872986	698.54253382	0.00143155	13.08360190	0.07643155	55
56	57.39499179	0.01742312	751.93322386	0.00132991	13.10102503	0.07632991	56
57	61.69961617	0.01620756	809.32821564	0.00123559	13.11723258	0.07623559	57
58	66.32708739	0.01507680	871.02783182	0.00114807	13.13230938	0.07614807	58
59	71.30161894	0.01402493	937.35491920	0.00106683	13.14633431	0.07606683	59
60	76.64924036	0.01304644	1008.65653814	0.00099142	13.15938075	0.07599142	60
61	82.39793339	0.01213623	1085.30577851	0.00092140	13.17151698	0.07592140	61
62	88.57777829	0.01128951	1167.70371189	0.00085638	13.18280649	0.07585638	62
63	95.22111177	0.01050187	1256.28149029	0.00079600	13.19330836	0.07579600	63
64	102.36269515	0.00976918	1351.50260206	0.00073992	13.20307755	0.07573992	64
65	110.03989729	0.00908761	1453.86529721	0.00068782	13.21216516	0.07568782	65
66	118.29288959	0.00845359	1563.90519450	0.00063942	13.22061875	0.07563942	66
67	127.16485631	0.00786381	1682.19808409	0.00059446	13.22848256	0.07559446	67
68	136.70222053	0.00731517	1809.36294040	0.00055268	13.23579773	0.07555268	68
69	146.95488707	0.00680481	1946.06516093	0.00051386	13.24260254	0.07551386	69
70	157.97650360	0.00633006	2093.02004800	0.00047778	13.24893260	0.07547778	70
71	169.82474137	0.00588842	2250.99655160	0.00044425	13.25482102	0.07544425	71
72	182.56159697	0.00547760	2420.82129296	0.00041308	13.26029862	0.07541308	72
73	196.25371675	0.00509544	2603.38288994	0.00038412	13.26539407	0.07538412	73
74	210.97274550	0.00473995	2799.63660668	0.00035719	13.27013402	0.07535719	74
75	226.79570141	0.00440925	3010.60935218	0.00033216	13.27454327	0.07533216	75
76	243.80537902	0.00410163	3237.40505360	0.00030889	13.27864490	0.07530889	76
77	262.09078245	0.00381547	3481.21043262	0.00028726	13.28246038	0.07528726	77
78	281.74759113	0.00354928	3743.30121506	0.00026714	13.28600965	0.07526714	78
79	302.87866046	0.00330165	4025.04880619	0.00024844	13.28931130	0.07524844	79
80	325.59456000	0.00307130	4327.92746666	0.00023106	13.29238261	0.07523106	80

TABLE A-2

COMPOUND INTEREST FOR $1

8%

PERIODS n	FUTURE AMOUNT $(1+i)^n$	PRESENT VALUE $(1+i)^{-n}$	AMOUNT OF ANNUITY $(S/p,i,n)$ $\dfrac{(1+i)^n-1}{i}$	SINKING FUND $(p/S,i,n)$ $\dfrac{i}{(1+i)^n-1}$	PRESENT VALUE OF ANNUITY $(V/p,i,n)$ $\dfrac{1-(1+i)^{-n}}{i}$	AMORTIZATION $(p/V,i,n)$ $\dfrac{i}{1-(1+i)^{-n}}$	PERIODS n
1	1.08000000	0.92592593	1.00000000	1.00000000	0.92592593	1.08000000	1
2	1.16640000	0.85733882	2.08000000	0.48076923	1.78326475	0.56076923	2
3	1.25971200	0.79383224	3.24640000	0.30803351	2.57709699	0.38803351	3
4	1.36048896	0.73502985	4.50611200	0.22192080	3.31212684	0.30192080	4
5	1.46932808	0.68058320	5.86660096	0.17045645	3.99271004	0.25045645	5
6	1.58687432	0.63016963	7.33592904	0.13631539	4.62287966	0.21631539	6
7	1.71382427	0.58349040	8.92280336	0.11207240	5.20637006	0.19207240	7
8	1.85093021	0.54026888	10.63662763	0.09401476	5.74663894	0.17401476	8
9	1.99900463	0.50024897	12.48755784	0.08007971	6.24688791	0.16007971	9
10	2.15892500	0.46319349	14.48656247	0.06902949	6.71008140	0.14902949	10
11	2.33163900	0.42888286	16.64548746	0.06007634	7.13896426	0.14007634	11
12	2.51817012	0.39711376	18.97712646	0.05269502	7.53607802	0.13269502	12
13	2.71962373	0.36769792	21.49529658	0.04652181	7.90377594	0.12652181	13
14	2.93719362	0.34046104	24.21492030	0.04129685	8.24423698	0.12129685	14
15	3.17216911	0.31524170	27.15211393	0.03682954	8.55947869	0.11682954	15
16	3.42594264	0.29189047	30.32428304	0.03297687	8.85136916	0.11297687	16
17	3.70001805	0.27026895	33.75022569	0.02962943	9.12163811	0.10962943	17
18	3.99601950	0.25024903	37.45024374	0.02670210	9.37188714	0.10670210	18
19	4.31570106	0.23171206	41.44626324	0.02412763	9.60359920	0.10412763	19
20	4.66095714	0.21454821	45.76196430	0.02185221	9.81814741	0.10185221	20
21	5.03383372	0.19865575	50.42292144	0.01983225	10.01680316	0.09983225	21
22	5.43654041	0.18394051	55.45675516	0.01803207	10.20074366	0.09803207	22
23	5.87146365	0.17031528	60.89329557	0.01642217	10.37105895	0.09642217	23
24	6.34118074	0.15769934	66.76475922	0.01497796	10.52875828	0.09497796	24
25	6.84847520	0.14601790	73.10593995	0.01367878	10.67477619	0.09367878	25
26	7.39635321	0.13520176	79.95441515	0.01250713	10.80997795	0.09250713	26
27	7.98806147	0.12518682	87.35076836	0.01144810	10.93516477	0.09144810	27
28	8.62710639	0.11591372	95.33882983	0.01048891	11.05107849	0.09048891	28
29	9.31727490	0.10732752	103.96593622	0.00961854	11.15840601	0.08961854	29
30	10.06265689	0.09937733	113.28321111	0.00882743	11.25778334	0.08882743	30
31	10.86766944	0.09201605	123.34586800	0.00810728	11.34979939	0.08810728	31
32	11.73708300	0.08520005	134.21353744	0.00745081	11.43499944	0.08745081	32
33	12.67604964	0.07888893	145.95062044	0.00685163	11.51388837	0.08685163	33
34	13.69013361	0.07304531	158.62667007	0.00630411	11.58693367	0.08630411	34
35	14.78534429	0.06763454	172.31680368	0.00580326	11.65456822	0.08580326	35
36	15.96817184	0.06262458	187.10214797	0.00534467	11.71719279	0.08534467	36
37	17.24562558	0.05798572	203.07031981	0.00492440	11.77517851	0.08492440	37
38	18.62527563	0.05369048	220.31594540	0.00453894	11.82886899	0.08453894	38
39	20.11529768	0.04971341	238.94122103	0.00418513	11.87858240	0.08418513	39
40	21.72452150	0.04603093	259.05651871	0.00386016	11.92461333	0.08386016	40

TABLE A-2

COMPOUND INTEREST FOR $1

8%

PERIODS n	FUTURE AMOUNT $(1+i)^n$	PRESENT VALUE $(1+i)^{-n}$	AMOUNT OF ANNUITY $(S/p,i,n)$ $\dfrac{(1+i)^n-1}{i}$	SINKING FUND $(p/S,i,n)$ $\dfrac{i}{(1+i)^n-1}$	PRESENT VALUE OF ANNUITY $(V/p,i,n)$ $\dfrac{1-(1+i)^{-n}}{i}$	AMORTIZATION $(p/V,i,n)$ $\dfrac{i}{1-(1+i)^{-n}}$	PERIODS n
41	23.46248322	0.04262123	280.78104021	0.00356149	11.96723457	0.08356149	41
42	25.33948187	0.03946411	304.24352342	0.00328684	12.00669867	0.08328684	42
43	27.36664042	0.03654084	329.58300530	0.00303414	12.04323951	0.08303414	43
44	29.55597166	0.03383411	356.94964572	0.00280152	12.07707362	0.08280152	44
45	31.92044939	0.03132788	386.50561738	0.00258728	12.10840150	0.08258728	45
46	34.47408534	0.02900730	418.42606677	0.00238991	12.13740880	0.08238991	46
47	37.23201217	0.02685861	452.90015211	0.00220799	12.16426741	0.08220799	47
48	40.21057314	0.02486908	490.13216428	0.00204027	12.18913649	0.08204027	48
49	43.42741899	0.02302693	530.34273742	0.00188557	12.21216341	0.08188557	49
50	46.90161251	0.02132123	573.77015642	0.00174286	12.23348464	0.08174286	50
51	50.65374151	0.01974188	620.67176893	0.00161116	12.25322652	0.08161116	51
52	54.70604084	0.01827952	671.32551044	0.00148959	12.27150604	0.08148959	52
53	59.08252410	0.01692548	726.03155128	0.00137735	12.28843152	0.08137735	53
54	63.80912603	0.01567174	785.11407538	0.00127370	12.30410326	0.08127370	54
55	68.91385611	0.01451087	848.92320141	0.00117796	12.31861413	0.08117796	55
56	74.42696460	0.01343599	917.83705752	0.00108952	12.33205012	0.08108952	56
57	80.38112177	0.01244073	992.26402213	0.00100780	12.34449085	0.08100780	57
58	86.81161151	0.01151920	1072.64514390	0.00093227	12.35601005	0.08093227	58
59	93.75654043	0.01066592	1159.45675541	0.00086247	12.36667597	0.08086247	59
60	101.25706367	0.00987585	1253.21329584	0.00079795	12.37655182	0.08079795	60
61	109.35762876	0.00914431	1354.47035951	0.00073830	12.38569613	0.08073830	61
62	118.10623906	0.00846695	1463.82798827	0.00068314	12.39416308	0.08068314	62
63	127.55473819	0.00783977	1581.93422733	0.00063214	12.40200286	0.08063214	63
64	137.75911724	0.00725905	1709.48896552	0.00058497	12.40926190	0.08058497	64
65	148.77984662	0.00672134	1847.24808276	0.00054135	12.41598324	0.08054135	65
66	160.68223435	0.00622346	1996.02792938	0.00050099	12.42220671	0.08050099	66
67	173.53681310	0.00576247	2156.71016373	0.00046367	12.42796917	0.08046367	67
68	187.41975815	0.00533562	2330.24697683	0.00042914	12.43330479	0.08042914	68
69	202.41333880	0.00494039	2517.66673497	0.00039719	12.43824518	0.08039719	69
70	218.60640590	0.00457443	2720.08007377	0.00036764	12.44281961	0.08036764	70
71	236.09491837	0.00423558	2938.68647967	0.00034029	12.44705519	0.08034029	71
72	254.98251184	0.00392184	3174.78139805	0.00031498	12.45097703	0.08031498	72
73	275.38111279	0.00363133	3429.76390989	0.00029157	12.45460836	0.08029157	73
74	297.41160181	0.00336234	3705.14502268	0.00026989	12.45797070	0.08026989	74
75	321.20452996	0.00311328	4002.55662449	0.00024984	12.46108399	0.08024984	75
76	346.90089236	0.00288267	4323.76115445	0.00023128	12.46396665	0.08023128	76
77	374.65296374	0.00266914	4670.66204681	0.00021410	12.46663579	0.08021410	77
78	404.62520084	0.00247142	5045.31501056	0.00019820	12.46910721	0.08019820	78
79	436.99521691	0.00228835	5449.94021140	0.00018349	12.47139557	0.08018349	79
80	471.95483426	0.00211885	5886.93542831	0.00016987	12.47351441	0.08016987	80

TABLE A-2

COMPOUND INTEREST FOR $1

$8\frac{1}{2}\%$

PERIODS n	FUTURE AMOUNT $(1+i)^n$	PRESENT VALUE $(1+i)^{-n}$	AMOUNT OF ANNUITY $(S/p,i,n)$ $\dfrac{(1+i)^n-1}{i}$	SINKING FUND $(p/S,i,n)$ $\dfrac{i}{(1+i)^n-1}$	PRESENT VALUE OF ANNUITY $(V/p,i,n)$ $\dfrac{1-(1+i)^{-n}}{i}$	AMORTIZATION $(p/V,i,n)$ $\dfrac{i}{1-(1+i)^{-n}}$	PERIODS n
1	1.08500000	0.92165899	1.00000000	1.00000000	0.92165899	1.08500000	1
2	1.17722500	0.84945529	2.08500000	0.47961631	1.77111427	0.56461631	2
3	1.27728912	0.78290810	3.26222500	0.30653925	2.55402237	0.39153925	3
4	1.38585870	0.72157428	4.53951412	0.22028789	3.27559666	0.30528789	4
5	1.50365669	0.66504542	5.92537283	0.16876575	3.94064208	0.25376575	5
6	1.63146751	0.61294509	7.42902952	0.13460708	4.55358717	0.21960708	6
7	1.77014225	0.56492635	9.06049702	0.11036922	5.11851352	0.19536922	7
8	1.92060434	0.52066945	10.83063927	0.09233065	5.63918297	0.17733065	8
9	2.08385571	0.47987968	12.75124361	0.07842372	6.11906264	0.16342372	9
10	2.26098344	0.44228542	14.83509932	0.06740771	6.56134806	0.15240771	10
11	2.45316703	0.40763633	17.09608276	0.05849293	6.96898439	0.14349293	11
12	2.66168623	0.37570168	19.54924979	0.05115286	7.34468607	0.13615286	12
13	2.88792956	0.34626883	22.21093603	0.04502287	7.69095490	0.13002287	13
14	3.13340357	0.31914178	25.09886559	0.03984244	8.01009668	0.12484244	14
15	3.39974288	0.29413989	28.23226916	0.03542046	8.30423658	0.12042046	15
16	3.68872102	0.27109667	31.63201204	0.03161354	8.57533325	0.11661354	16
17	4.00226231	0.24985869	35.32073306	0.02831198	8.82519194	0.11331198	17
18	4.34245461	0.23028450	39.32299538	0.02543041	9.05547644	0.11043041	18
19	4.71156325	0.21224378	43.66544998	0.02290140	9.26772022	0.10790140	19
20	5.11204612	0.19561639	48.37701323	0.02067097	9.46333661	0.10567097	20
21	5.54657005	0.18029160	53.48905936	0.01869541	9.64362821	0.10369541	21
22	6.01802850	0.16616738	59.03562940	0.01693892	9.80979559	0.10193892	22
23	6.52956092	0.15314965	65.05365790	0.01537193	9.96294524	0.10037193	23
24	7.08457360	0.14115176	71.58321882	0.01396975	10.10409700	0.09896975	24
25	7.68676236	0.13009378	78.66779242	0.01271168	10.23419078	0.09771168	25
26	8.34013716	0.11990210	86.35455478	0.01158017	10.35409288	0.09658017	26
27	9.04904881	0.11050885	94.69469193	0.01056025	10.46460174	0.09556025	27
28	9.81821796	0.10185148	103.74374075	0.00963914	10.56645321	0.09463914	28
29	10.65276649	0.09387233	113.56195871	0.00880577	10.66032554	0.09380577	29
30	11.55825164	0.08651828	124.21472520	0.00805058	10.74684382	0.09305058	30
31	12.54070303	0.07974035	135.77297684	0.00736524	10.82658416	0.09236524	31
32	13.60666279	0.07349341	148.31367987	0.00674247	10.90007757	0.09174247	32
33	14.76322913	0.06773586	161.92034266	0.00617588	10.96781343	0.09117588	33
34	16.01810360	0.06242936	176.68357179	0.00565984	11.03024279	0.09065984	34
35	17.37964241	0.05753858	192.70167539	0.00518937	11.08778137	0.09018937	35
36	18.85691201	0.05303095	210.08131780	0.00476006	11.14081233	0.08976006	36
37	20.45974953	0.04887645	228.93822981	0.00436799	11.18968878	0.08936799	37
38	22.19882824	0.04504742	249.39797935	0.00400966	11.23473620	0.08900966	38
39	24.08572865	0.04151836	271.59680759	0.00368193	11.27625457	0.08868193	39
40	26.13301558	0.03826577	295.68253624	0.00338201	11.31452034	0.08838201	40

TABLE A-2

COMPOUND INTEREST FOR $1

$8\frac{1}{2}\%$

PERIODS n	FUTURE AMOUNT $(1+i)^n$	PRESENT VALUE $(1+i)^{-n}$	AMOUNT OF ANNUITY $(S/p,i,n)$ $\frac{(1+i)^n-1}{i}$	SINKING FUND $(p/S,i,n)$ $\frac{i}{(1+i)^n-1}$	PRESENT VALUE OF ANNUITY $(V/p,i,n)$ $\frac{1-(1+i)^{-n}}{i}$	AMORTIZATION $(p/V,i,n)$ $\frac{i}{1-(1+i)^{-n}}$	PERIODS n
41	28.35432190	0.03526799	321.81551182	0.00310737	11.34978833	0.08810737	41
42	30.76443927	0.03250506	350.16987372	0.00285576	11.38229339	0.08785576	42
43	33.37941660	0.02995858	380.93431299	0.00262512	11.41225197	0.08762512	43
44	36.21666702	0.02761160	414.31372959	0.00241363	11.43986357	0.08741363	44
45	39.29508371	0.02544848	450.53039661	0.00221961	11.46531205	0.08721961	45
46	42.63516583	0.02345482	489.82548032	0.00204154	11.48876686	0.08704154	46
47	46.25915492	0.02161734	532.46064615	0.00187807	11.51038420	0.08687807	47
48	50.19118309	0.01992382	578.71980107	0.00172795	11.53030802	0.08672795	48
49	54.45743365	0.01836297	628.91098416	0.00159005	11.54867099	0.08659005	49
50	59.08631551	0.01692439	683.36841782	0.00146334	11.56559538	0.08646334	50
51	64.10865233	0.01559852	742.45473333	0.00134688	11.58119390	0.08634688	51
52	69.55788778	0.01437651	806.56338566	0.00123983	11.59557041	0.08623983	52
53	75.47030824	0.01325024	876.12127345	0.00114139	11.60882066	0.08614139	53
54	81.88528444	0.01221221	951.59158169	0.00105087	11.62103287	0.08605087	54
55	88.84553362	0.01125549	1033.47686613	0.00096761	11.63228835	0.08596761	55
56	96.39740398	0.01037372	1122.32239975	0.00089101	11.64266208	0.08589101	56
57	104.59118332	0.00956104	1218.71980373	0.00082053	11.65222311	0.08582053	57
58	113.48143390	0.00881201	1323.31098705	0.00075568	11.66103513	0.08575568	58
59	123.12735578	0.00812167	1436.79242095	0.00069599	11.66915680	0.08569599	59
60	133.59318102	0.00748541	1559.91977673	0.00064106	11.67664221	0.08564106	60
61	144.94860141	0.00689900	1693.51295775	0.00059049	11.68354121	0.08559049	61
62	157.26923253	0.00635852	1838.46155916	0.00054393	11.68989973	0.08554393	62
63	170.63711729	0.00586039	1995.73079169	0.00050107	11.69576012	0.08550107	63
64	185.14127226	0.00540128	2166.36790898	0.00046160	11.70116140	0.08546160	64
65	200.87828041	0.00497814	2351.50918125	0.00042526	11.70613954	0.08542526	65
66	217.95293424	0.00458815	2552.38746165	0.00039179	11.71072769	0.08539179	66
67	236.47893365	0.00422871	2770.34039589	0.00036097	11.71495639	0.08536097	67
68	256.57964301	0.00389743	3006.81932954	0.00033258	11.71885382	0.08533258	68
69	278.38891267	0.00359210	3263.39897255	0.00030643	11.72244592	0.08530643	69
70	302.05197024	0.00331069	3541.78788522	0.00028234	11.72575661	0.08528234	70
71	327.72638771	0.00305133	3843.83985546	0.00026016	11.72880793	0.08526016	71
72	355.58313067	0.00281228	4171.56624318	0.00023972	11.73162021	0.08523972	72
73	385.80769678	0.00259196	4527.14937385	0.00022089	11.73421218	0.08522089	73
74	418.60135100	0.00238891	4912.95707063	0.00020354	11.73660109	0.08520354	74
75	454.18246584	0.00220176	5331.55842163	0.00018756	11.73880284	0.08518756	75
76	492.78797543	0.00202927	5785.74088747	0.00017284	11.74083211	0.08517284	76
77	534.67495335	0.00187030	6278.52886290	0.00015927	11.74270241	0.08515927	77
78	580.12232438	0.00172377	6813.20381625	0.00014677	11.74442618	0.08514677	78
79	629.43272195	0.00158873	7393.32614063	0.00013526	11.74601492	0.08513526	79
80	682.93450332	0.00146427	8022.75886259	0.00012465	11.74747919	0.08512465	80

TABLE A-2

COMPOUND INTEREST FOR $1

9%

PERIODS n	FUTURE AMOUNT $(1+i)^n$	PRESENT VALUE $(1+i)^{-n}$	AMOUNT OF ANNUITY (S/p,i,n) $\dfrac{(1+i)^n - 1}{i}$	SINKING FUND (p/S,i,n) $\dfrac{i}{(1+i)^n - 1}$	PRESENT VALUE OF ANNUITY (V/p,i,n) $\dfrac{1-(1+i)^{-n}}{i}$	AMORTIZATION (p/V,i,n) $\dfrac{i}{1-(1+i)^{-n}}$	PERIODS n
1	1.09000000	0.91743119	1.00000000	1.00000000	0.91743119	1.09000000	1
2	1.18810000	0.84167999	2.09000000	0.47846890	1.75911119	0.56846890	2
3	1.29502900	0.77218348	3.27810000	0.30505476	2.53129467	0.39505476	3
4	1.41158161	0.70842521	4.57312900	0.21866866	3.23971988	0.30866866	4
5	1.53862395	0.64993139	5.98471061	0.16709246	3.88965126	0.25709246	5
6	1.67710011	0.59626733	7.52333456	0.13291978	4.48591859	0.22291978	6
7	1.82803912	0.54703424	9.20043468	0.10869052	5.03295284	0.19869052	7
8	1.99256264	0.50186628	11.02847380	0.09067438	5.53481911	0.18067438	8
9	2.17189328	0.46042778	13.02103644	0.07679880	5.99524689	0.16679880	9
10	2.36736367	0.42241081	15.19292972	0.06582009	6.41765770	0.15582009	10
11	2.58042641	0.38753285	17.56029339	0.05694666	6.80519055	0.14694666	11
12	2.81266478	0.35553473	20.14071980	0.04965066	7.16072528	0.13965066	12
13	3.06580461	0.32617865	22.95338458	0.04356656	7.48690392	0.13356656	13
14	3.34172703	0.29924647	26.01918919	0.03843317	7.78615039	0.12843317	14
15	3.64248246	0.27453804	29.36091622	0.03405888	8.06068843	0.12405888	15
16	3.97030588	0.25186976	33.00339868	0.03029991	8.31255819	0.12029991	16
17	4.32763341	0.23107318	36.97370456	0.02704625	8.54363137	0.11704625	17
18	4.71712042	0.21199374	41.30133797	0.02421229	8.75562511	0.11421229	18
19	5.14166125	0.19448967	46.01845839	0.02173041	8.95011478	0.11173041	19
20	5.60441077	0.17843089	51.16011964	0.01954648	9.12854567	0.10954648	20
21	6.10880774	0.16369806	56.76453041	0.01761663	9.29224373	0.10761663	21
22	6.65860043	0.15018171	62.87333815	0.01590499	9.44242544	0.10590499	22
23	7.25787447	0.13778139	69.53193858	0.01438188	9.58020683	0.10438188	23
24	7.91108317	0.12640494	76.78981305	0.01302256	9.70661177	0.10302256	24
25	8.62308066	0.11596784	84.70089623	0.01180625	9.82257960	0.10180625	25
26	9.39915792	0.10639251	93.32397689	0.01071536	9.92897211	0.10071536	26
27	10.24508213	0.09760781	102.72313481	0.00973491	10.02657992	0.09973491	27
28	11.16713952	0.08954845	112.96821694	0.00885205	10.11612837	0.09885205	28
29	12.17218208	0.08215454	124.13535646	0.00805572	10.19828291	0.09805572	29
30	13.26767847	0.07537114	136.30753855	0.00733635	10.27365404	0.09733635	30
31	14.46176953	0.06914783	149.57521702	0.00668560	10.34280187	0.09668560	31
32	15.76332879	0.06343838	164.03698655	0.00609619	10.40624025	0.09609619	32
33	17.18202838	0.05820035	179.80031534	0.00556173	10.46444060	0.09556173	33
34	18.72841093	0.05339481	196.98234372	0.00507660	10.51783541	0.09507660	34
35	20.41396792	0.04898607	215.71075465	0.00463584	10.56682148	0.09463584	35
36	22.25122503	0.04494135	236.12472257	0.00423505	10.61176282	0.09423505	36
37	24.25383528	0.04123059	258.37594760	0.00387033	10.65299342	0.09387033	37
38	26.43668046	0.03782623	282.62978288	0.00353820	10.69081965	0.09353820	38
39	28.81598170	0.03470296	309.06646334	0.00323555	10.72552261	0.09323555	39
40	31.40942005	0.03183758	337.88244504	0.00295961	10.75736020	0.09295961	40

TABLE A-2

COMPOUND INTEREST FOR $1

$9\frac{1}{2}\%$

PERIODS	FUTURE AMOUNT	PRESENT VALUE	AMOUNT OF ANNUITY	SINKING FUND	PRESENT VALUE OF ANNUITY	AMORTIZATION	PERIODS
n	$(1+i)^n$	$(1+i)^{-n}$	$(S/p,i,n)$ $\dfrac{(1+i)^n-1}{i}$	$(p/S,i,n)$ $\dfrac{i}{(1+i)^n-1}$	$(V/p,i,n)$ $\dfrac{1-(1+i)^{-n}}{i}$	$(p/V,i,n)$ $\dfrac{i}{1-(1+i)^{-n}}$	n
1	1.09500000	0.91324201	1.00000000	1.00000000	0.91324201	1.09500000	1
2	1.19902500	0.83401097	2.09500000	0.47732697	1.74725298	0.57232697	2
3	1.31293237	0.76165385	3.29402500	0.30357997	2.50890683	0.39857997	3
4	1.43766095	0.69557429	4.60695737	0.21706300	3.20448112	0.31206300	4
5	1.57423874	0.63522767	6.04461833	0.16543642	3.83970879	0.26043642	5
6	1.72379142	0.58011659	7.61885707	0.13125328	4.41982538	0.22625328	6
7	1.88755161	0.52978684	9.34264849	0.10703603	4.94961222	0.20203603	7
8	2.06686901	0.48382360	11.23020009	0.08904561	5.43343581	0.18404561	8
9	2.26322156	0.44184803	13.29706910	0.07520454	5.87528385	0.17020454	9
10	2.47822761	0.40351419	15.56029067	0.06426615	6.27879803	0.15926615	10
11	2.71365924	0.36850611	18.03851828	0.05543693	6.64730414	0.15043693	11
12	2.97145686	0.33653526	20.75217752	0.04818771	6.98383940	0.14318771	12
13	3.25374527	0.30733813	23.72363438	0.04215206	7.29117753	0.13715206	13
14	3.56285107	0.28067410	26.97737965	0.03706809	7.57185163	0.13206809	14
15	3.90132192	0.25632337	30.54023072	0.03274370	7.82817500	0.12774370	15
16	4.27194750	0.23408527	34.44155263	0.02903470	8.06226028	0.12403470	16
17	4.67778251	0.21377651	38.71350013	0.02583078	8.27603678	0.12083078	17
18	5.12217185	0.19522969	43.39128265	0.02304610	8.47126647	0.11804610	18
19	5.60877818	0.17829195	48.51345450	0.02061284	8.64955842	0.11561284	19
20	6.14161210	0.16282370	54.12223267	0.01847670	8.81238212	0.11347670	20
21	6.72506525	0.14869744	60.26384478	0.01659370	8.96107956	0.11159370	21
22	7.36394645	0.13579675	66.98891003	0.01492784	9.09687631	0.10992784	22
23	8.06352137	0.12401530	74.35285649	0.01344938	9.22089161	0.10844938	23
24	8.82955590	0.11325598	82.41637785	0.01213351	9.33414759	0.10713351	24
25	9.66836371	0.10343012	91.24593375	0.01095939	9.43757770	0.10595939	25
26	10.58685826	0.09445673	100.91429745	0.00990940	9.53203443	0.10490940	26
27	11.59260979	0.08626185	111.50115571	0.00896852	9.61829629	0.10396852	27
28	12.69390772	0.07877795	123.09376551	0.00812389	9.69707423	0.10312389	28
29	13.89982896	0.07194333	135.78767323	0.00736444	9.76901756	0.10236444	29
30	15.22031271	0.06570167	149.68750218	0.00668058	9.83471924	0.10168058	30
31	16.66624241	0.06000153	164.90781489	0.00606399	9.89472076	0.10106399	31
32	18.24953544	0.05479592	181.57405731	0.00550739	9.94951668	0.10050739	32
33	19.98324131	0.05004193	199.82359275	0.00500441	9.99955861	0.10000441	33
34	21.88164924	0.04570039	219.80683406	0.00454945	10.04525901	0.09954945	34
35	23.96040591	0.04173552	241.68848330	0.00413756	10.08699453	0.09913756	35
36	26.23664448	0.03811463	265.64888921	0.00376437	10.12510916	0.09876437	36
37	28.72912570	0.03480788	291.88553369	0.00342600	10.15991704	0.09842600	37
38	31.45839264	0.03178802	320.61465939	0.00311901	10.19170506	0.09811901	38
39	34.44693994	0.02903015	352.07305203	0.00284032	10.22073521	0.09784032	39
40	37.71939924	0.02651156	386.51999197	0.00258719	10.24724677	0.09758719	40

TABLE A-2

COMPOUND INTEREST FOR $1

10%

PERIODS n	FUTURE AMOUNT $(1+i)^n$	PRESENT VALUE $(1+i)^{-n}$	AMOUNT OF ANNUITY (S/p,i,n) $\dfrac{(1+i)^n-1}{i}$	SINKING FUND (p/S,i,n) $\dfrac{i}{(1+i)^n-1}$	PRESENT VALUE OF ANNUITY (V/p,i,n) $\dfrac{1-(1+i)^{-n}}{i}$	AMORTIZATION (p/V,i,n) $\dfrac{i}{1-(1+i)^{-n}}$	PERIODS n
1	1.10000000	0.90909091	1.00000000	1.00000000	0.90909091	1.10000000	1
2	1.21000000	0.82644628	2.10000000	0.47619048	1.73553719	0.57619048	2
3	1.33100000	0.75131480	3.31000000	0.30211480	2.48685199	0.40211480	3
4	1.46410000	0.68301346	4.64100000	0.21547080	3.16986545	0.31547080	4
5	1.61051000	0.62092132	6.10510000	0.16379748	3.79078677	0.26379748	5
6	1.77156100	0.56447393	7.71561000	0.12960738	4.35526070	0.22960738	6
7	1.94871710	0.51315812	9.48717100	0.10540550	4.86841882	0.20540550	7
8	2.14358881	0.46650738	11.43588810	0.08744402	5.33492620	0.18744402	8
9	2.35794769	0.42409762	13.57947691	0.07364054	5.75902382	0.17364054	9
10	2.59374246	0.38554329	15.93742460	0.06274539	6.14456711	0.16274539	10
11	2.85311671	0.35049390	18.53116706	0.05396314	6.49506101	0.15396314	11
12	3.13842838	0.31863082	21.38428377	0.04676332	6.81369182	0.14676332	12
13	3.45227121	0.28966438	24.52271214	0.04077852	7.10335620	0.14077852	13
14	3.79749834	0.26333125	27.97498336	0.03574622	7.36668746	0.13574622	14
15	4.17724817	0.23939205	31.77248169	0.03147378	7.60607951	0.13147378	15
16	4.59497299	0.21762914	35.94972986	0.02781662	7.82370864	0.12781662	16
17	5.05447028	0.19784467	40.54470285	0.02466413	8.02155331	0.12466413	17
18	5.55991731	0.17985879	45.59917313	0.02193022	8.20141210	0.12193022	18
19	6.11590904	0.16350799	51.15909045	0.01954687	8.36492009	0.11954687	19
20	6.72749995	0.14864363	57.27499949	0.01745962	8.51356372	0.11745962	20
21	7.40024994	0.13513057	64.00249944	0.01562439	8.64869429	0.11562439	21
22	8.14027494	0.12284597	71.40274939	0.01400506	8.77154026	0.11400506	22
23	8.95430243	0.11167816	79.54302433	0.01257181	8.88321842	0.11257181	23
24	9.84973268	0.10152560	88.49732676	0.01129978	8.98474402	0.11129978	24
25	10.83470594	0.09229600	98.34705943	0.01016807	9.07704002	0.11016807	25
26	11.91817654	0.08390545	109.18176538	0.00915904	9.16094547	0.10915904	26
27	13.10999419	0.07627768	121.09994191	0.00825764	9.23722316	0.10825764	27
28	14.42099361	0.06934335	134.20993611	0.00745101	9.30656651	0.10745101	28
29	15.86309297	0.06303941	148.63092972	0.00672807	9.36960591	0.10672807	29
30	17.44940227	0.05730855	164.49402269	0.00607925	9.42691447	0.10607925	30
31	19.19434250	0.05209868	181.94342496	0.00549621	9.47901315	0.10549621	31
32	21.11377675	0.04736244	201.13776745	0.00497172	9.52637559	0.10497172	32
33	23.22515442	0.04305676	222.25154420	0.00449941	9.56943236	0.10449941	33
34	25.54766986	0.03914251	245.47669862	0.00407371	9.60857487	0.10407371	34
35	28.10243685	0.03558410	271.02436848	0.00368971	9.64415897	0.10368971	35
36	30.91268053	0.03234918	299.12680533	0.00334306	9.67650816	0.10334306	36
37	34.00394859	0.02940835	330.03948586	0.00302994	9.70591651	0.10302994	37
38	37.40434344	0.02673486	364.04343445	0.00274692	9.73265137	0.10274692	38
39	41.14477779	0.02430442	401.44777789	0.00249098	9.75695579	0.10249098	39
40	45.25925557	0.02209493	442.59255568	0.00225941	9.77905072	0.10225941	40

TABLE A-2

COMPOUND INTEREST FOR $1

$10\frac{1}{2}\%$

PERIODS n	FUTURE AMOUNT $(1+i)^n$	PRESENT VALUE $(1+i)^{-n}$	AMOUNT OF ANNUITY $(S/p,i,n)$ $\dfrac{(1+i)^n-1}{i}$	SINKING FUND $(p/S,i,n)$ $\dfrac{i}{(1+i)^n-1}$	PRESENT VALUE OF ANNUITY $(V/p,i,n)$ $\dfrac{1-(1+i)^{-n}}{i}$	AMORTIZATION $(p/V,i,n)$ $\dfrac{i}{1-(1+i)^{-n}}$	PERIODS n
1	1.10500000	0.90497738	1.00000000	1.00000000	0.90497738	1.10500000	1
2	1.22102500	0.81898405	2.10500000	0.47505938	1.72396143	0.58005938	2
3	1.34923262	0.74116204	3.32602500	0.30065920	2.46512346	0.40565920	3
4	1.49090205	0.67073487	4.67525762	0.21389196	3.13585834	0.31889196	4
5	1.64744677	0.60699989	6.16615968	0.16217550	3.74285822	0.26717550	5
6	1.82042868	0.54932116	7.81360644	0.12798187	4.29217939	0.23298187	6
7	2.01157369	0.49712323	9.63403512	0.10379867	4.78930261	0.20879867	7
8	2.22278892	0.44988527	11.64560881	0.08586928	5.23918789	0.19086928	8
9	2.45618176	0.40713599	13.86839773	0.07210638	5.64632388	0.17710638	9
10	2.71408085	0.36844886	16.32457949	0.06125732	6.01477274	0.16625732	10
11	2.99905934	0.33343788	19.03866034	0.05252470	6.34821062	0.15752470	11
12	3.31396057	0.30175374	22.03771967	0.04537675	6.64996437	0.15037675	12
13	3.66192643	0.27308031	25.35168024	0.03944512	6.92304468	0.14444512	13
14	4.04642870	0.24713150	29.01360666	0.03446659	7.17017618	0.13946659	14
15	4.47130371	0.22364842	33.06003536	0.03024800	7.39382459	0.13524800	15
16	4.94079060	0.20239676	37.53133908	0.02664440	7.59622135	0.13164440	16
17	5.45957362	0.18316449	42.47212968	0.02354485	7.77938584	0.12854485	17
18	6.03282885	0.16575972	47.93170330	0.02086302	7.94514556	0.12586302	18
19	6.66627588	0.15000879	53.96453214	0.01853069	8.09515435	0.12353069	19
20	7.36623484	0.13575456	60.63080802	0.01649327	8.23090891	0.12149327	20
21	8.13968950	0.12285481	67.99704286	0.01470652	8.35376372	0.11970652	21
22	8.99435690	0.11118082	76.13673236	0.01313426	8.46494455	0.11813426	22
23	9.93876437	0.10061613	85.13108926	0.01174659	8.56556067	0.11674659	23
24	10.98233463	0.09105532	95.06985363	0.01051858	8.65661599	0.11551858	24
25	12.13547977	0.08240301	106.05218826	0.00942932	8.73901900	0.11442932	25
26	13.40970514	0.07457286	118.18766803	0.00846112	8.81359186	0.11346112	26
27	14.81772418	0.06748675	131.59737317	0.00759894	8.88107860	0.11259894	27
28	16.37358522	0.06107398	146.41509736	0.00682990	8.94215258	0.11182990	28
29	18.09281167	0.05527057	162.78868258	0.00614293	8.99742315	0.11114293	29
30	19.99255690	0.05001861	180.88149425	0.00552848	9.04744176	0.11052848	30
31	22.09177537	0.04526571	200.87405114	0.00497824	9.09270748	0.10997824	31
32	24.41141178	0.04096445	222.96582651	0.00448499	9.13367193	0.10948499	32
33	26.97461002	0.03707190	247.37723830	0.00404241	9.17074383	0.10904241	33
34	29.80694407	0.03354923	274.35184832	0.00364495	9.20429305	0.10864495	34
35	32.93667320	0.03036129	304.15879239	0.00328776	9.23465435	0.10828776	35
36	36.39502389	0.02747628	337.09546560	0.00296652	9.26213063	0.10796652	36
37	40.21650140	0.02486542	373.49048948	0.00267744	9.28699605	0.10767744	37
38	44.43923404	0.02250264	413.70699088	0.00241717	9.30949868	0.10741717	38
39	49.10535362	0.02036438	458.14622492	0.00218271	9.32986306	0.10718271	39
40	54.26141575	0.01842930	507.25157854	0.00197141	9.34829237	0.10697141	40

PERIODS n	FUTURE AMOUNT $(1+i)^n$	PRESENT VALUE $(1+i)^{-n}$	AMOUNT OF ANNUITY (S/p,i,n) $\frac{(1+i)^n-1}{i}$	SINKING FUND (p/S,i,n) $\frac{i}{(1+i)^n-1}$	PRESENT VALUE OF ANNUITY (V/p,i,n) $\frac{1-(1+i)^{-n}}{i}$	AMORTIZATION (p/V,i,n) $\frac{i}{1-(1+i)^{-n}}$	PERIODS n
1	1.11000000	0.90090090	1.00000000	1.00000000	0.90090090	1.11000000	1
2	1.23210000	0.81162243	2.11000000	0.47393365	1.71252333	0.58393365	2
3	1.36763100	0.73119138	3.34210000	0.29921307	2.44371472	0.40921307	3
4	1.51807041	0.65873097	4.70973100	0.21232635	3.10244569	0.32232635	4
5	1.68505816	0.59345133	6.22780141	0.16057031	3.69589702	0.27057031	5
6	1.87041455	0.53464084	7.91285957	0.12637656	4.23053785	0.23637656	6
7	2.07616015	0.48165841	9.78327412	0.10221527	4.71219626	0.21221527	7
8	2.30453777	0.43392650	11.85943427	0.08432105	5.14612276	0.19432105	8
9	2.55803692	0.39092477	14.16397204	0.07060166	5.53704753	0.18060166	9
10	2.83942099	0.35218448	16.72200896	0.05980143	5.88923201	0.16980143	10
11	3.15175729	0.31728331	19.56142995	0.05112101	6.20651533	0.16112101	11
12	3.49845060	0.28584082	22.71318724	0.04402729	6.49235615	0.15402729	12
13	3.88328016	0.25751426	26.21163784	0.03815099	6.74987040	0.14815099	13
14	4.31044098	0.23199482	30.09491800	0.03322820	6.98186523	0.14322820	14
15	4.78458949	0.20900435	34.40535898	0.02906524	7.19086958	0.13906524	15
16	5.31089433	0.18829220	39.18994847	0.02551675	7.37916178	0.13551675	16
17	5.89509271	0.16963262	44.50084281	0.02247148	7.54879440	0.13247148	17
18	6.54355291	0.15282218	50.39593551	0.01984287	7.70161657	0.12984287	18
19	7.26334373	0.13767764	56.93948842	0.01756250	7.83929421	0.12756250	19
20	8.06231154	0.12403391	64.20283215	0.01557564	7.96332812	0.12557564	20
21	8.94916581	0.11174226	72.26514368	0.01383793	8.07507038	0.12383793	21
22	9.93357404	0.10066870	81.21430949	0.01231310	8.17573908	0.12231310	22
23	11.02626719	0.09069252	91.14788353	0.01097118	8.26643160	0.12097118	23
24	12.23915658	0.08170498	102.17415072	0.00978721	8.34813658	0.11978721	24
25	13.58546380	0.07360809	114.41330730	0.00874024	8.42174466	0.11874024	25
26	15.07986482	0.06631359	127.99877110	0.00781258	8.48805826	0.11781258	26
27	16.73864995	0.05974197	143.07863592	0.00698916	8.54780023	0.11698916	27
28	18.57990145	0.05382160	159.81728587	0.00625715	8.60162183	0.11625715	28
29	20.62369061	0.04848793	178.39718732	0.00560547	8.65010976	0.11560547	29
30	22.89229657	0.04368282	199.02087793	0.00502460	8.69379257	0.11502460	30
31	25.41044919	0.03935389	221.91317450	0.00450627	8.73314646	0.11450627	31
32	28.20559861	0.03545395	247.32362369	0.00404329	8.76860042	0.11404329	32
33	31.30821445	0.03194050	275.52922230	0.00362938	8.80054092	0.11362938	33
34	34.75211804	0.02877522	306.83743675	0.00325905	8.82931614	0.11325905	34
35	38.57485103	0.02592363	341.58955480	0.00292749	8.85523977	0.11292749	35
36	42.81808464	0.02335462	380.16440582	0.00263044	8.87859438	0.11263044	36
37	47.52807395	0.02104020	422.98249046	0.00236416	8.89963458	0.11236416	37
38	52.75616209	0.01895513	470.51056441	0.00212535	8.91858971	0.11212535	38
39	58.55939991	0.01707670	523.26672650	0.00191107	8.93566641	0.11191107	39
40	65.00086731	0.01538441	581.82606641	0.00171873	8.95105082	0.11171873	40

TABLE A-2

COMPOUND INTEREST FOR $1

$11\frac{1}{2}\%$

PERIODS n	FUTURE AMOUNT $(1+i)^n$	PRESENT VALUE $(1+i)^{-n}$	AMOUNT OF ANNUITY $(S/p,i,n)$ $\dfrac{(1+i)^n-1}{i}$	SINKING FUND $(p/S,i,n)$ $\dfrac{i}{(1+i)^n-1}$	PRESENT VALUE OF ANNUITY $(V/p,i,n)$ $\dfrac{1-(1+i)^{-n}}{i}$	AMORTIZATION $(p/V,i,n)$ $\dfrac{i}{1-(1+i)^{-n}}$	PERIODS n
1	1.15000000	0.89686099	1.00000000	1.00000000	0.89686099	1.11500000	1
2	1.24322500	0.80435963	2.11500000	0.47281324	1.70122062	0.58781324	2
3	1.38619587	0.72139877	3.35822500	0.29777636	2.42261939	0.41277636	3
4	1.54560840	0.64699441	4.74442087	0.21077388	3.06961380	0.32577388	4
5	1.72335337	0.58026405	6.29002928	0.15898177	3.64987785	0.27398177	5
6	1.92153900	0.52041619	8.01338264	0.12479125	4.17029403	0.23979125	6
7	2.14251599	0.46674097	9.93492165	0.10065505	4.63703501	0.21565505	7
8	2.38890533	0.41860177	12.07743764	0.08279902	5.05563678	0.19779902	8
9	2.66362944	0.37542760	14.46634296	0.06912597	5.43106437	0.18412597	9
10	2.96994683	0.33670636	17.12997240	0.05837721	5.76777074	0.17337721	10
11	3.31149071	0.30197880	20.09991923	0.04975144	6.06974954	0.16475144	11
12	3.69231214	0.27083301	23.41140994	0.04271422	6.34058255	0.15771422	12
13	4.11692804	0.24289956	27.10372209	0.03689530	6.58348211	0.15189530	13
14	4.59037476	0.21784714	31.22065013	0.03203008	6.80132924	0.14703008	14
15	5.11826786	0.19537860	35.81102489	0.02792436	6.99670784	0.14292436	15
16	5.70686867	0.17522744	40.92929275	0.02443238	7.17193528	0.13943238	16
17	6.36315856	0.15715466	46.63616142	0.02144259	7.32908994	0.13644259	17
18	7.09492180	0.14094588	52.99931998	0.01886817	7.47003582	0.13386817	18
19	7.91083780	0.12640886	60.09424178	0.01664053	7.59644468	0.13164053	19
20	8.82058415	0.11337118	68.00507958	0.01470478	7.70981586	0.12970478	20
21	9.83495133	0.10167818	76.82566374	0.01301648	7.81149404	0.12801648	21
22	10.96597073	0.09119120	86.66061507	0.01153927	7.90268524	0.12653927	22
23	12.22705737	0.08178583	97.62658580	0.01024311	7.98447107	0.12524311	23
24	13.63316896	0.07335052	109.85364317	0.00910302	8.05782159	0.12410302	24
25	15.20098340	0.06578522	123.48681213	0.00809803	8.12360680	0.12309803	25
26	16.94909649	0.05900020	138.68779553	0.00721044	8.18260700	0.12221044	26
27	18.89824258	0.05291497	155.63689201	0.00642521	8.23552197	0.12142521	27
28	21.07154048	0.04745738	174.53513459	0.00572951	8.28297935	0.12072951	28
29	23.49476763	0.04256267	195.60667507	0.00511230	8.32554202	0.12011230	29
30	26.19666591	0.03817280	219.10144270	0.00456410	8.36371481	0.11956410	30
31	29.20928249	0.03423569	245.29810861	0.00407667	8.39795050	0.11907667	31
32	32.56834998	0.03070466	274.50739111	0.00364289	8.42865516	0.11864289	32
33	36.31371022	0.02753781	307.07574108	0.00325653	8.45619297	0.11825653	33
34	40.48978690	0.02469759	343.38945131	0.00291215	8.48089056	0.11791215	34
35	45.14611239	0.02215030	383.87923821	0.00260499	8.50304086	0.11760499	35
36	50.33791532	0.01986574	429.02535060	0.00233086	8.52290660	0.11733086	36
37	56.12677558	0.01781681	479.36326592	0.00208610	8.54072341	0.11708610	37
38	62.58135477	0.01597920	535.49004150	0.00186745	8.55670261	0.11686745	38
39	69.77821057	0.01433112	598.07139627	0.00167204	8.57103373	0.11667204	39
40	77.80270479	0.01285302	667.84960685	0.00149734	8.58388675	0.11649734	40

COMPOUND INTEREST FOR $1

12%

PERIODS n	FUTURE AMOUNT $(1+i)^n$	PRESENT VALUE $(1+i)^{-n}$	AMOUNT OF ANNUITY $(S/p,i,n)$ $\dfrac{(1+i)^n - 1}{i}$	SINKING FUND $(p/S,i,n)$ $\dfrac{i}{(1+i)^n - 1}$	PRESENT VALUE OF ANNUITY $(V/p,i,n)$ $\dfrac{1-(1+i)^{-n}}{i}$	AMORTIZATION $(p/V,i,n)$ $\dfrac{i}{1-(1+i)^{-n}}$	PERIODS n
1	1.12000000	0.89285714	1.00000000	1.00000000	0.89285714	1.12000000	1
2	1.25440000	0.79719388	2.12000000	0.47169811	1.69005102	0.59169811	2
3	1.40492800	0.71178025	3.37440000	0.29634898	2.40183127	0.41634898	3
4	1.57351936	0.63551808	4.77932800	0.20923444	3.03734935	0.32923444	4
5	1.76234168	0.56742686	6.35284736	0.15740973	3.60477620	0.27740973	5
6	1.97382269	0.50663112	8.11518904	0.12322572	4.11140732	0.24322572	6
7	2.21068141	0.45234922	10.08901173	0.09911774	4.56375654	0.21911774	7
8	2.47596318	0.40388323	12.29969314	0.08130284	4.96763977	0.20130284	8
9	2.77307876	0.36061002	14.77565631	0.06767889	5.32824979	0.18767889	9
10	3.10584821	0.32197324	17.54873507	0.05698416	5.65022303	0.17698416	10
11	3.47854999	0.28747610	20.65458328	0.04841540	5.93769913	0.16841540	11
12	3.89597599	0.25667509	24.13313327	0.04143681	6.19437423	0.16143681	12
13	4.36349311	0.22917419	28.02910926	0.03567720	6.42354842	0.15567720	13
14	4.88711229	0.20461981	32.39260238	0.03087125	6.62816823	0.15087125	14
15	5.47356576	0.18269626	37.27971464	0.02682424	6.81086449	0.14682424	15
16	6.13039365	0.16312166	42.75328042	0.02339002	6.97398615	0.14339002	16
17	6.86604089	0.14564434	48.88367407	0.02045673	7.11963049	0.14045673	17
18	7.68996580	0.13003959	55.74971496	0.01793731	7.24967008	0.13793731	18
19	8.61276169	0.11610678	63.43968075	0.01576300	7.36577686	0.13576300	19
20	9.64629309	0.10366677	72.05244244	0.01388878	7.46944362	0.13388878	20
21	10.80384826	0.09255961	81.69873554	0.01224009	7.56200324	0.13224009	21
22	12.10031006	0.08264251	92.50258380	0.01081051	7.64464575	0.13081051	22
23	13.55234726	0.07378796	104.60289386	0.00955996	7.71843370	0.12955996	23
24	15.17862893	0.06588210	118.15524112	0.00846344	7.78431581	0.12846344	24
25	17.00006441	0.05882331	133.33387006	0.00749997	7.84313911	0.12749997	25
26	19.04007214	0.05252081	150.33393446	0.00665186	7.89565992	0.12665186	26
27	21.32488079	0.04689358	169.37400660	0.00590409	7.94255350	0.12590409	27
28	23.88386649	0.04186927	190.69888739	0.00524387	7.98442277	0.12524387	28
29	26.74993047	0.03738327	214.58275388	0.00466021	8.02180604	0.12466021	29
30	29.95992212	0.03337792	241.33268434	0.00414366	8.05518397	0.12414366	30
31	33.55511278	0.02980172	271.29260646	0.00368606	8.08498569	0.12368606	31
32	37.58172631	0.02660868	304.84771924	0.00328033	8.11159436	0.12328033	32
33	42.09153347	0.02375775	342.42944555	0.00292031	8.13535211	0.12292031	33
34	47.14251748	0.02121227	384.52097901	0.00260064	8.15656438	0.12260064	34
35	52.79961958	0.01893953	431.66349649	0.00231662	8.17550391	0.12231662	35
36	59.13557393	0.01691029	484.46311607	0.00206414	8.19241421	0.12206414	36
37	66.23184280	0.01509848	543.59869000	0.00183959	8.20751269	0.12183959	37
38	74.17966394	0.01348078	609.83053280	0.00163980	8.22099347	0.12163980	38
39	83.08122361	0.01203641	684.01019674	0.00146197	8.23302988	0.12146197	39
40	93.05097044	0.01074680	767.09142034	0.00130363	8.24377668	0.12130363	40

TABLE A-2

COMPOUND INTEREST FOR $1

$12\frac{1}{2}\%$

PERIODS n	FUTURE AMOUNT $(1+i)^n$	PRESENT VALUE $(1+i)^{-n}$	AMOUNT OF ANNUITY $(S/p,i,n)$ $\dfrac{(1+i)^n-1}{i}$	SINKING FUND $(p/S,i,n)$ $\dfrac{i}{(1+i)^n-1}$	PRESENT VALUE OF ANNUITY $(V/p,i,n)$ $\dfrac{1-(1+i)^{-n}}{i}$	AMORTIZATION $(p/V,i,n)$ $\dfrac{i}{1-(1+i)^{-n}}$	PERIODS n
1	1.12500000	0.88888889	1.00000000	1.00000000	0.88888889	1.12500000	1
2	1.26562500	0.79012346	2.12500000	0.47058824	1.67901235	0.59558824	2
3	1.42382812	0.70233196	3.39062500	0.29493088	2.38134431	0.41993088	3
4	1.60180664	0.62429508	4.81445312	0.20770791	3.00563938	0.33270791	4
5	1.80203247	0.55492896	6.41625977	0.15585404	3.56056834	0.28085404	5
6	2.02728653	0.49327018	8.21829224	0.12167978	4.05383853	0.24667978	6
7	2.28069735	0.43846239	10.24557877	0.09760308	4.49230091	0.22260308	7
8	2.56578451	0.38974434	12.52627611	0.07983219	4.88204525	0.20483219	8
9	2.88650758	0.34643942	15.09206063	0.06626000	5.22848467	0.19126000	9
10	3.24732103	0.30794615	17.97856820	0.05562178	5.53643082	0.18062178	10
11	3.65323615	0.27372991	21.22588923	0.04711228	5.81016073	0.17211228	11
12	4.10989067	0.24331547	24.87912538	0.04019434	6.05347620	0.16519434	12
13	4.62362701	0.21628042	28.98901606	0.03449582	6.26975662	0.15949582	13
14	5.20158038	0.19224926	33.61264306	0.02975071	6.46200589	0.15475071	14
15	5.85177793	0.17088823	38.81422345	0.02576375	6.63289412	0.15076375	15
16	6.58325017	0.15190065	44.66600138	0.02238839	6.78479478	0.14738839	16
17	7.40615644	0.13502280	51.24925155	0.01951248	6.91981758	0.14451248	17
18	8.33192600	0.12002027	58.65540799	0.01704873	7.03983785	0.14204873	18
19	9.37341675	0.10668468	66.98733399	0.01492820	7.14652253	0.13992820	19
20	10.54509384	0.09483083	76.36075074	0.01309573	7.24135336	0.13809573	20
21	11.86323057	0.08429407	86.90584458	0.01150671	7.32564743	0.13650671	21
22	13.34613439	0.07492806	98.76907515	0.01012463	7.40057550	0.13512463	22
23	15.01440119	0.06660272	112.11520955	0.00891940	7.46717822	0.13391940	23
24	16.89120134	0.05920242	127.12961074	0.00786599	7.52638064	0.13286599	24
25	19.00260151	0.05262437	144.02081209	0.00694344	7.57900501	0.13194344	25
26	21.37792670	0.04677722	163.02341360	0.00613409	7.62578223	0.13113409	26
27	24.05016754	0.04157975	184.40134030	0.00542295	7.66736198	0.13042295	27
28	27.05643848	0.03695978	208.45150783	0.00479728	7.70432176	0.12979728	28
29	30.43849329	0.03285314	235.50794631	0.00424614	7.73717490	0.12924614	29
30	34.24330495	0.02920279	265.94643960	0.00376016	7.76637769	0.12876016	30
31	38.52371807	0.02595803	300.18974455	0.00333123	7.79233572	0.12833123	31
32	43.33918283	0.02307381	338.71346262	0.00295235	7.81540953	0.12795235	32
33	48.75658068	0.02051005	382.05264545	0.00261744	7.83591958	0.12761744	33
34	54.85115327	0.01823116	430.80922613	0.00232121	7.85415074	0.12732121	34
35	61.70754742	0.01620547	485.66037939	0.00205905	7.87035622	0.12705905	35
36	69.42099085	0.01440486	547.36792682	0.00182692	7.88476108	0.12682692	36
37	78.09861471	0.01280432	616.78891767	0.00162130	7.89756540	0.12662130	37
38	87.86094155	0.01138162	694.88753238	0.00143908	7.90894703	0.12643908	38
39	98.84355924	0.01011700	782.74847393	0.00127755	7.91906402	0.12627755	39
40	111.19900415	0.00899289	881.59203317	0.00113431	7.92805691	0.12613431	40

TABLE A-2

COMPOUND INTEREST FOR $1

13%

PERIODS n	FUTURE AMOUNT $(1+i)^n$	PRESENT VALUE $(1+i)^{-n}$	AMOUNT OF ANNUITY (S/p,i,n) $\dfrac{(1+i)^n-1}{i}$	SINKING FUND (p/S,i,n) $\dfrac{i}{(1+i)^n-1}$	PRESENT VALUE OF ANNUITY (V/p,i,n) $\dfrac{1-(1+i)^{-n}}{i}$	AMORTIZATION (p/V,i,n) $\dfrac{i}{1-(1+i)^{-n}}$	PERIODS n
1	1.13000000	0.88495575	1.00000000	1.00000000	0.88495575	1.13000000	1
2	1.27690000	0.78314668	2.13000000	0.46948357	1.66810244	0.59948357	2
3	1.44289700	0.69305016	3.40690000	0.29352197	2.36115260	0.42352197	3
4	1.63047361	0.61331873	4.84979700	0.20619420	2.97447133	0.33619420	4
5	1.84243518	0.54275994	6.48027061	0.15431454	3.51723126	0.28431454	5
6	2.08195175	0.48031853	8.32270579	0.12015323	3.99754979	0.25015323	6
7	2.35260548	0.42506064	10.40465754	0.09611080	4.42261043	0.22611080	7
8	2.65844419	0.37615986	12.75726302	0.07838672	4.79877029	0.20838672	8
9	3.00404194	0.33288483	15.41570722	0.06486890	5.13165513	0.19486890	9
10	3.39456739	0.29458835	18.41974915	0.05428956	5.42624348	0.18428956	10
11	3.83586115	0.26069765	21.81431654	0.04584145	5.68694113	0.17584145	11
12	4.33452310	0.23070589	25.65017769	0.03898608	5.91764702	0.16898608	12
13	4.89801110	0.20416450	29.98470079	0.03335034	6.12181152	0.16335034	13
14	5.53475255	0.18067655	34.88271190	0.02866750	6.30248807	0.15866750	14
15	6.25427038	0.15989075	40.41746444	0.02474178	6.46237882	0.15474178	15
16	7.06732553	0.14149624	46.67173482	0.02142624	6.60387506	0.15142624	16
17	7.98607785	0.12521791	53.73906035	0.01860844	6.72909298	0.14860844	17
18	9.02426797	0.11081231	61.72513819	0.01620085	6.83990529	0.14620085	18
19	10.19742280	0.09806399	70.74940616	0.01413439	6.93796928	0.14413439	19
20	11.52308776	0.08678229	80.94682896	0.01235379	7.02475158	0.14235379	20
21	13.02108917	0.07679849	92.46991672	0.01081433	7.10155007	0.14081433	21
22	14.71383077	0.06796327	105.49100590	0.00947948	7.16951334	0.13947948	22
23	16.62662877	0.06014448	120.20483667	0.00831913	7.22965782	0.13831913	23
24	18.78809051	0.05322521	136.83146543	0.00730826	7.28288303	0.13730826	24
25	21.23054227	0.04710195	155.61955594	0.00642593	7.32998498	0.13642593	25
26	23.99051277	0.04168314	176.85009821	0.00565451	7.37166812	0.13565451	26
27	27.10927943	0.03688774	200.84061098	0.00497907	7.40855586	0.13497907	27
28	30.63348575	0.03264402	227.94989040	0.00438693	7.44119988	0.13438693	28
29	34.61583890	0.02888851	258.58337616	0.00386722	7.47008839	0.13386722	29
30	39.11589796	0.02556505	293.19921506	0.00341065	7.49565344	0.13341065	30
31	44.20096469	0.02262394	332.31511301	0.00300919	7.51827738	0.13300919	31
32	49.94709010	0.02002119	376.51607771	0.00265593	7.53829857	0.13265593	32
33	56.44021181	0.01771786	426.46316781	0.00234487	7.55601643	0.13234487	33
34	63.77743935	0.01567953	482.90337962	0.00207081	7.57169596	0.13207081	34
35	72.06850647	0.01387569	546.68081897	0.00182922	7.58557164	0.13182922	35
36	81.43741231	0.01227937	618.74932544	0.00161616	7.59785101	0.13161616	36
37	92.02427591	0.01086670	700.18673775	0.00142819	7.60871771	0.13142819	37
38	103.98743178	0.00961655	792.21101365	0.00126229	7.61833426	0.13126229	38
39	117.50579791	0.00851022	896.19844543	0.00111582	7.62684447	0.13111582	39
40	132.78155163	0.00753117	1013.70424333	0.00098648	7.63437564	0.13098648	40

429

TABLE A-2

COMPOUND INTEREST FOR $1

$13\frac{1}{2}\%$

PERIODS n	FUTURE AMOUNT $(1+i)^n$	PRESENT VALUE $(1+i)^{-n}$	AMOUNT OF ANNUITY $(S/p,i,n)$ $\dfrac{(1+i)^n-1}{i}$	SINKING FUND $(p/S,i,n)$ $\dfrac{i}{(1+i)^n-1}$	PRESENT VALUE OF ANNUITY $(V/p,i,n)$ $\dfrac{1-(1+i)^{-n}}{i}$	AMORTIZATION $(p/V,i,n)$ $\dfrac{i}{1-(1+i)^{-n}}$	PERIODS n
1	1.13500000	0.88105727	1.00000000	1.00000000	0.88105727	1.13500000	1
2	1.28822500	0.77626191	2.13500000	0.46838407	1.65731918	0.60338407	2
3	1.46213537	0.68393120	3.42322500	0.29212219	2.34125038	0.42712219	3
4	1.65952365	0.60258255	4.88536037	0.20469319	2.94383293	0.33969319	4
5	1.88355934	0.53090974	6.54488403	0.15279110	3.47474267	0.28779110	5
6	2.13783985	0.46776188	8.42844337	0.11864587	3.94250456	0.25364587	6
7	2.42644824	0.41212501	10.56628322	0.09464066	4.35462957	0.22964066	7
8	2.75401875	0.36310573	12.99273146	0.07696611	4.71773530	0.21196611	8
9	3.12581128	0.31991695	15.74675021	0.06350517	5.03765225	0.19850517	9
10	3.54779580	0.28186515	18.87256148	0.05298698	5.31951740	0.18798698	10
11	4.02674823	0.24833934	22.42035728	0.04460232	5.56785674	0.17960232	11
12	4.57035924	0.21880118	26.44710552	0.03781132	5.78665792	0.17281132	12
13	5.18735774	0.19277637	31.01746476	0.03223990	5.97943429	0.16723990	13
14	5.88765104	0.16984702	36.20482251	0.02762063	6.14928131	0.16262063	14
15	6.68248393	0.14964495	42.09247354	0.02375722	6.29892627	0.15875722	15
16	7.58461926	0.13184577	48.77495749	0.02050232	6.43077204	0.15550232	16
17	8.60854286	0.11616368	56.35957673	0.01774321	6.54693572	0.15274321	17
18	9.77069614	0.10234685	64.96811959	0.01539216	6.64928257	0.15039216	18
19	11.08974012	0.09017344	74.73881573	0.01337993	6.73945601	0.14837993	19
20	12.58685504	0.07944796	85.82855586	0.01165113	6.81890397	0.14665113	20
21	14.28608047	0.06999821	98.41541090	0.01016101	6.88890218	0.14516101	21
22	16.21470137	0.06167243	112.70149137	0.00887300	6.95057461	0.14387300	22
23	18.40368602	0.05433694	128.91619271	0.00775698	7.00491155	0.14275698	23
24	20.88818363	0.04787396	147.31987872	0.00678795	7.05278551	0.14178795	24
25	23.70808842	0.04217970	168.20806235	0.00594502	7.09496520	0.14094502	25
26	26.90868035	0.03716273	191.91615077	0.00521061	7.13212793	0.14021061	26
27	30.54135220	0.03274249	218.82483112	0.00456987	7.16487042	0.13956987	27
28	34.66443475	0.02884801	249.36618332	0.00401017	7.19371844	0.13901017	28
29	39.34413344	0.02541675	284.03061807	0.00352075	7.21913519	0.13852075	29
30	44.65559145	0.02239361	323.37475151	0.00309239	7.24152880	0.13809239	30
31	50.68409630	0.01973005	368.03034296	0.00271717	7.26125885	0.13771717	31
32	57.52644930	0.01738331	418.71443926	0.00238826	7.27864216	0.13738826	32
33	65.29251996	0.01531569	476.24088856	0.00209978	7.29395785	0.13709978	33
34	74.10701015	0.01349400	541.53340851	0.00184661	7.30745185	0.13684661	34
35	84.11145652	0.01188899	615.64041866	0.00162432	7.31934084	0.13662432	35
36	95.46650315	0.01047488	699.75187518	0.00142908	7.32981572	0.13642908	36
37	108.35448108	0.00922897	795.21837833	0.00125752	7.33904468	0.13625752	37
38	122.98233602	0.00813125	903.57285941	0.00110672	7.34717593	0.13610672	38
39	139.58495138	0.00716410	1026.55519543	0.00097413	7.35434003	0.13597413	39
40	158.42891982	0.00631198	1166.14014681	0.00085753	7.36065201	0.13585753	40

TABLE A-2

COMPOUND INTEREST FOR $1

14%

PERIODS n	FUTURE AMOUNT $(1+i)^n$	PRESENT VALUE $(1+i)^{-n}$	AMOUNT OF ANNUITY $(S/p,i,n)$ $\frac{(1+i)^n - 1}{i}$	SINKING FUND $(p/S,i,n)$ $\frac{i}{(1+i)^n - 1}$	PRESENT VALUE OF ANNUITY $(V/p,i,n)$ $\frac{1-(1+i)^{-n}}{i}$	AMORTIZATION $(p/V,i,n)$ $\frac{i}{1-(1+i)^{-n}}$	PERIODS n
1	1.14000000	0.87719298	1.00000000	1.00000000	0.87719298	1.14000000	1
2	1.29960000	0.76946753	2.14000000	0.46728972	1.64666051	0.60728972	2
3	1.48154400	0.67497152	3.43960000	0.29073148	2.32163203	0.43073148	3
4	1.68896016	0.59208028	4.92114400	0.20320478	2.91371230	0.34320478	4
5	1.92541458	0.51936866	6.61010416	0.15128355	3.43308097	0.29128355	5
6	2.19497262	0.45558655	8.53551874	0.11715750	3.88866752	0.25715750	6
7	2.50226879	0.39963732	10.73049137	0.09319238	4.28830484	0.23319238	7
8	2.85258642	0.35055905	13.23276016	0.07557002	4.63886389	0.21557002	8
9	3.25194852	0.30750794	16.08534658	0.06216838	4.94637184	0.20216838	9
10	3.70722131	0.26974381	19.33729510	0.05171354	5.21611565	0.19171354	10
11	4.22623230	0.23661738	23.04451641	0.04339427	5.45273302	0.18339427	11
12	4.81790482	0.20755910	27.27074871	0.03666933	5.66029213	0.17666933	12
13	5.49241149	0.18206939	32.08865353	0.03116366	5.84236151	0.17116366	13
14	6.26134910	0.15970999	37.58106503	0.02660914	6.00207150	0.16660914	14
15	7.13793798	0.14009648	43.84241413	0.02280896	6.14216799	0.16280896	15
16	8.13724930	0.12289165	50.98035211	0.01961540	6.26505964	0.15961540	16
17	9.27646420	0.10779969	59.11760141	0.01691544	6.37285933	0.15691544	17
18	10.57516918	0.09456113	68.39406560	0.01462115	6.46742046	0.15462115	18
19	12.05569287	0.08294836	78.96923479	0.01266316	6.55036883	0.15266316	19
20	13.74348987	0.07276172	91.02492766	0.01098600	6.62313055	0.15098600	20
21	15.66757845	0.06382607	104.76841753	0.00954486	6.68695662	0.14954486	21
22	17.86103944	0.05598778	120.43599598	0.00830317	6.74294441	0.14830317	22
23	20.36158496	0.04911209	138.29703542	0.00723081	6.79205650	0.14723081	23
24	23.21220685	0.04308078	158.65862038	0.00630284	6.83513728	0.14630284	24
25	26.46191581	0.03779016	181.87082723	0.00549841	6.87292744	0.14549841	25
26	30.16658403	0.03314926	208.33274304	0.00480001	6.90607670	0.14480001	26
27	34.38990579	0.02907830	238.49932707	0.00419288	6.93515500	0.14419288	27
28	39.20449260	0.02550728	272.88923286	0.00366449	6.96066228	0.14366449	28
29	44.69312156	0.02237481	312.09372546	0.00320417	6.98303709	0.14320417	29
30	50.95015858	0.01962702	356.78684702	0.00280279	7.00266411	0.14280279	30
31	58.08318078	0.01721669	407.73700561	0.00245256	7.01988080	0.14245256	31
32	66.21482609	0.01510236	465.82018639	0.00214675	7.03498316	0.14214675	32
33	75.48490175	0.01324768	532.03501249	0.00187958	7.04823084	0.14187958	33
34	86.05278799	0.01162077	607.51991423	0.00164604	7.05985161	0.14164604	34
35	98.10017831	0.01019366	693.57270223	0.00144181	7.07004528	0.14144181	35
36	111.83420328	0.00894181	791.67288054	0.00126315	7.07898708	0.14126315	36
37	127.49099173	0.00784369	903.50708382	0.00110680	7.08683078	0.14110680	37
38	145.33973058	0.00688043	1030.99807555	0.00096993	7.09371121	0.14096993	38
39	165.68729286	0.00603547	1176.33780613	0.00085010	7.09974667	0.14085010	39
40	188.88351386	0.00529427	1342.02509898	0.00074514	7.10504094	0.14074514	40

TABLE A-2

COMPOUND INTEREST FOR $1

$14\frac{1}{2}\%$

PERIODS n	FUTURE AMOUNT $(1+i)^n$	PRESENT VALUE $(1+i)^{-n}$	AMOUNT OF ANNUITY $(S/p,i,n)$ $\dfrac{(1+i)^n - 1}{i}$	SINKING FUND $(p/S,i,n)$ $\dfrac{i}{(1+i)^n - 1}$	PRESENT VALUE OF ANNUITY $(V/p,i,n)$ $\dfrac{1-(1+i)^{-n}}{i}$	AMORTIZATION $(p/V,i,n)$ $\dfrac{i}{1-(1+i)^{-n}}$	PERIODS n
1	1.14500000	0.87336245	1.00000000	1.00000000	0.87336245	1.14500000	1
2	1.31102500	0.76276196	2.14500000	0.46620047	1.63612441	0.61120047	2
3	1.50112362	0.66616765	3.45602500	0.28934976	2.30229206	0.43434976	3
4	1.71878655	0.58180581	4.95714862	0.20172887	2.88409787	0.34672887	4
5	1.96801060	0.50812734	6.67593518	0.14979175	3.39222521	0.29479175	5
6	2.25337214	0.44377934	8.64394578	0.11568791	3.83600455	0.26068791	6
7	2.58011110	0.38758021	10.89731791	0.09176570	4.22358476	0.23676570	7
8	2.95422721	0.33849800	13.47742901	0.07419813	4.56208276	0.21919813	8
9	3.38259015	0.29563144	16.43165622	0.06085814	4.85771420	0.20585814	9
10	3.87306572	0.25819340	19.81424637	0.05046874	5.11590760	0.19546874	10
11	4.43466025	0.22549642	23.68731209	0.04221669	5.34140402	0.18721669	11
12	5.07768599	0.19694010	28.12197235	0.03555938	5.53834412	0.18055938	12
13	5.81395046	0.17200009	33.19965834	0.03012079	5.71034421	0.17512079	13
14	6.65697328	0.15021842	39.01360880	0.02563208	5.86056263	0.17063208	14
15	7.62223440	0.13119513	45.67058207	0.02189593	5.99175775	0.16689593	15
16	8.72745839	0.11458090	53.29281647	0.01876426	6.10633865	0.16376426	16
17	9.99293985	0.10007065	62.02027486	0.01612376	6.20640930	0.16112376	17
18	11.44191613	0.08739795	72.01321471	0.01388634	6.29380725	0.15888634	18
19	13.10099397	0.07633009	83.45513085	0.01198249	6.37013734	0.15698249	19
20	15.00063810	0.06666383	96.55612482	0.01035667	6.43680117	0.15535667	20
21	17.17573062	0.05822169	111.55676292	0.00896405	6.49502285	0.15396405	21
22	19.66621156	0.05084863	128.73249354	0.00776805	6.54587149	0.15276805	22
23	22.51781224	0.04440929	148.39870511	0.00673860	6.59028078	0.15173860	23
24	25.78289502	0.03878540	170.91651735	0.00585081	6.62906618	0.15085081	24
25	29.52141479	0.03387372	196.69941236	0.00508390	6.66293989	0.15008390	25
26	33.80201994	0.02958403	226.22082715	0.00442046	6.69252393	0.14942046	26
27	38.70331283	0.02583758	260.02284709	0.00384582	6.71836151	0.14884582	27
28	44.31529319	0.02256557	298.72615992	0.00334755	6.74092708	0.14834755	28
29	50.74101070	0.01970792	343.04145311	0.00291510	6.76063500	0.14791510	29
30	58.09845725	0.01721216	393.78246381	0.00253947	6.77784717	0.14753947	30
31	66.52273355	0.01503246	451.88092106	0.00221297	6.79287962	0.14721297	31
32	76.16852992	0.01312878	518.40365461	0.00192900	6.80600840	0.14692900	32
33	87.21296676	0.01146618	594.57218453	0.00168188	6.81747459	0.14668188	33
34	99.85884694	0.01001414	681.78515129	0.00146674	6.82748872	0.14646674	34
35	114.33837974	0.00874597	781.64399823	0.00127935	6.83623469	0.14627935	35
36	130.91744481	0.00763840	895.98237797	0.00111609	6.84387309	0.14611609	36
37	149.90047430	0.00667109	1026.89982278	0.00097380	6.85054419	0.14597380	37
38	171.63604308	0.00582628	1176.80029708	0.00084976	6.85637047	0.14584976	38
39	196.52326932	0.00508846	1348.43634015	0.00074160	6.86145892	0.14574160	39
40	225.01914337	0.00444407	1544.95960948	0.00064727	6.86590299	0.14564727	40

TABLE A-2

COMPOUND INTEREST FOR $1

15%

PERIODS n	FUTURE AMOUNT $(1+i)^n$	PRESENT VALUE $(1+i)^{-n}$	AMOUNT OF ANNUITY (S/p,i,n) $\dfrac{(1+i)^n-1}{i}$	SINKING FUND (p/S,i,n) $\dfrac{i}{(1+i)^n-1}$	PRESENT VALUE OF ANNUITY (V/p,i,n) $\dfrac{1-(1+i)^{-n}}{i}$	AMORTIZATION (p/V,i,n) $\dfrac{i}{1-(1+i)^{-n}}$	PERIODS n
1	1.15000000	0.86956522	1.00000000	1.00000000	0.86956522	1.15000000	1
2	1.32250000	0.75614367	2.15000000	0.46511628	1.62570888	0.61511628	2
3	1.52087500	0.65751623	3.47250000	0.28797696	2.28322512	0.43797696	3
4	1.74900625	0.57175325	4.99337500	0.20026535	2.85497836	0.35026535	4
5	2.01135719	0.49717674	6.74238125	0.14831555	3.35215510	0.29831555	5
6	2.31306077	0.43232760	8.75373844	0.11423691	3.78448269	0.26423691	6
7	2.66001988	0.37593704	11.06679920	0.09036036	4.16041973	0.24036036	7
8	3.05902286	0.32690177	13.72681908	0.07285009	4.48732151	0.22285009	8
9	3.51787629	0.28426241	16.58584195	0.05957402	4.77158392	0.20957402	9
10	4.04555774	0.24718471	20.30371824	0.04925206	5.01876863	0.19925206	10
11	4.65239140	0.21494322	24.34927597	0.04106898	5.23371185	0.19106898	11
12	5.35025011	0.18690715	29.00166737	0.03448078	5.42061900	0.18448078	12
13	6.15278762	0.16252796	34.35191748	0.02911046	5.58314696	0.17911046	13
14	7.07570576	0.14132866	40.50470510	0.02468849	5.72447561	0.17468849	14
15	8.13706163	0.12289449	47.58041086	0.02101705	5.84737010	0.17101705	15
16	9.35762087	0.10686477	55.71747249	0.01794769	5.95423487	0.16794769	16
17	10.76126400	0.09292589	65.07509336	0.01536686	6.04716076	0.16536686	17
18	12.37545361	0.08080512	75.83635737	0.01318629	6.12796587	0.16318629	18
19	14.23177165	0.07026532	88.21181097	0.01133635	6.19823119	0.16133635	19
20	16.36653739	0.06110028	102.44358262	0.00976147	6.25933147	0.15976147	20
21	18.82151800	0.05313068	118.81012001	0.00841679	6.31246215	0.15841679	21
22	21.64474570	0.04620059	137.63163801	0.00726577	6.35866274	0.15726577	22
23	24.89145756	0.04017443	159.27638372	0.00627839	6.39883717	0.15627839	23
24	28.62517619	0.03493428	184.16784127	0.00542983	6.43377145	0.15542983	24
25	32.91895262	0.03037764	212.79301747	0.00469940	6.46414909	0.15469940	25
26	37.85679551	0.02641534	245.71197009	0.00406981	6.49056442	0.15406981	26
27	43.53531484	0.02296986	283.56876560	0.00352648	6.51353428	0.15352648	27
28	50.06561207	0.01997379	327.10408044	0.00305713	6.53350807	0.15305713	28
29	57.57545388	0.01736851	377.16969250	0.00265133	6.55087658	0.15265133	29
30	66.21177196	0.01510305	434.74514638	0.00230020	6.56597964	0.15230020	30
31	76.14353775	0.01313309	500.95691834	0.00199618	6.57911273	0.15199618	31
32	87.56506841	0.01142008	577.10045609	0.00173280	6.59053281	0.15173280	32
33	100.69982867	0.00993050	664.66552450	0.00150452	6.60046331	0.15150452	33
34	115.80480298	0.00863522	765.36535317	0.00130657	6.60909853	0.15130657	34
35	133.17552342	0.00750889	881.17015615	0.00113485	6.61660742	0.15113485	35
36	153.15185194	0.00652947	1014.34567957	0.00098586	6.62313689	0.15098586	36
37	176.12462973	0.00567780	1167.49753151	0.00085653	6.62881468	0.15085653	37
38	202.54332419	0.00493722	1343.62216123	0.00074426	6.63375190	0.15074426	38
39	232.92482281	0.00429323	1546.16540542	0.00064676	6.63804513	0.15064676	39
40	267.86354623	0.00373324	1779.09030823	0.00056209	6.64177837	0.15056209	40

TABLE A-2

COMPOUND INTEREST FOR $1

$15\frac{1}{2}\%$

PERIODS n	FUTURE AMOUNT $(1+i)^n$	PRESENT VALUE $(1+i)^{-n}$	AMOUNT OF ANNUITY $(S/p,i,n)$ $\dfrac{(1+i)^n-1}{i}$	SINKING FUND $(p/S,i,n)$ $\dfrac{i}{(1+i)^n-1}$	PRESENT VALUE OF ANNUITY $(V/p,i,n)$ $\dfrac{1-(1+i)^{-n}}{i}$	AMORTIZATION $(p/V,i,n)$ $\dfrac{i}{1-(1+i)^{-n}}$	PERIODS n
1	1.15500000	0.86580087	1.00000000	1.00000000	0.86580087	1.15500000	1
2	1.33402500	0.74961114	2.15500000	0.46403712	1.61541201	0.61903712	2
3	1.54079887	0.64901397	3.48902500	0.28661302	2.26442598	0.44161302	3
4	1.77962270	0.56191686	5.02982387	0.19881412	2.82634284	0.35381412	4
5	2.05546422	0.48650810	6.80944658	0.14685481	3.31285094	0.30185481	5
6	2.37406117	0.42121914	8.86491079	0.11280429	3.73407008	0.26780429	6
7	2.74204066	0.36469189	11.23897197	0.08897611	4.09876197	0.24397611	7
8	3.16705696	0.31575056	13.98101262	0.07152558	4.41451253	0.22652558	8
9	3.65795078	0.27337711	17.14806958	0.05831560	4.68788964	0.21331560	9
10	4.22493316	0.23669014	20.80602036	0.04806301	4.92457977	0.20306301	10
11	4.87979780	0.20492652	25.03095352	0.03995054	5.12950630	0.19495054	11
12	5.63616645	0.17742556	29.91075132	0.03343279	5.30693186	0.18843279	12
13	6.50977225	0.15361521	35.54691777	0.02813183	5.46054706	0.18313183	13
14	7.51878695	0.13300018	42.05669003	0.02377743	5.59354724	0.17877743	14
15	8.68419893	0.11515167	49.57547698	0.02017126	5.70869891	0.17517126	15
16	10.03024977	0.09969841	58.25967591	0.01716453	5.80839732	0.17216453	16
17	11.58493848	0.08631897	68.28992568	0.01464345	5.89471630	0.16964345	17
18	13.38060394	0.07473504	79.87486416	0.01251958	5.96945134	0.16751958	18
19	15.45459756	0.06470566	93.25546810	0.01072323	6.03415701	0.16572323	19
20	17.85006018	0.05602222	108.71006566	0.00919878	6.09017923	0.16419878	20
21	20.61681950	0.04850409	126.56012583	0.00790138	6.13868331	0.16290138	21
22	23.81242653	0.04199488	147.17694534	0.00679454	6.18067819	0.16179454	22
23	27.50335264	0.03635920	170.98937187	0.00584832	6.21703740	0.16084832	23
24	31.76637230	0.03147983	198.49272451	0.00503797	6.24851723	0.16003797	24
25	36.69016000	0.02725526	230.25909680	0.00434293	6.27577249	0.15934293	25
26	42.37713481	0.02359763	266.94925681	0.00374603	6.29937012	0.15874603	26
27	48.94559070	0.02043085	309.32639161	0.00323283	6.31980097	0.15823283	27
28	56.53215726	0.01768905	358.27198231	0.00279118	6.33749002	0.15779118	28
29	65.29464163	0.01531519	414.80413957	0.00241078	6.35280521	0.15741078	29
30	75.41531109	0.01325991	480.09878121	0.00208290	6.36606512	0.15708290	30
31	87.10468431	0.01148044	555.51409229	0.00180013	6.37754556	0.15680013	31
32	100.60591037	0.00993977	642.61877660	0.00155613	6.38748533	0.15655613	32
33	116.19982648	0.00860586	743.22468697	0.00134549	6.39609119	0.15634549	33
34	134.21079959	0.00745097	859.42451345	0.00116357	6.40354216	0.15616357	34
35	155.01347352	0.00645105	993.63531304	0.00100641	6.40999321	0.15600641	35
36	179.04056192	0.00558533	1148.64878656	0.00087059	6.41557854	0.15587059	36
37	206.79184901	0.00483578	1327.68934847	0.00075319	6.42041432	0.15575319	37
38	238.84458561	0.00418682	1534.48119749	0.00065169	6.42460114	0.15565169	38
39	275.86549638	0.00362495	1773.32578310	0.00056391	6.42822610	0.15556391	39
40	318.62464832	0.00313849	2049.19127948	0.00048800	6.43136459	0.15548800	40

TABLE A-2

COMPOUND INTEREST FOR $1

16%

PERIODS n	FUTURE AMOUNT $(1+i)^n$	PRESENT VALUE $(1+i)^{-n}$	AMOUNT OF ANNUITY $(S/p,i,n)$ $\dfrac{(1+i)^n - 1}{i}$	SINKING FUND $(p/S,i,n)$ $\dfrac{i}{(1+i)^n - 1}$	PRESENT VALUE OF ANNUITY $(V/p,i,n)$ $\dfrac{1-(1+i)^{-n}}{i}$	AMORTIZATION $(p/V,i,n)$ $\dfrac{i}{1-(1+i)^{-n}}$	PERIODS n
1	1.16000000	0.86206897	1.00000000	1.00000000	0.86206897	1.16000000	1
2	1.34560000	0.74316290	2.16000000	0.46296296	1.60523187	0.62296296	2
3	1.56089600	0.64065767	3.50560000	0.28525787	2.24588954	0.44525787	3
4	1.81063936	0.55229110	5.06649600	0.19737507	2.79818064	0.35737507	4
5	2.10034166	0.47611302	6.87713536	0.14540938	3.27429365	0.30540938	5
6	2.43639632	0.41044225	8.97747702	0.11138987	3.68473591	0.27138987	6
7	2.82621973	0.35382953	11.41387334	0.08761268	4.03856544	0.24761268	7
8	3.27841489	0.30502546	14.24009307	0.07022426	4.34359090	0.23022426	8
9	3.80296127	0.26295298	17.51850797	0.05708249	4.60654388	0.21708249	9
10	4.41143508	0.22668360	21.32146924	0.04690108	4.83322748	0.20690108	10
11	5.11726469	0.19541690	25.73290432	0.03886075	5.02864438	0.19886075	11
12	5.93602704	0.16846284	30.85016901	0.03241473	5.19710722	0.19241473	12
13	6.88579137	0.14522659	36.78619605	0.02718411	5.34233381	0.18718411	13
14	7.98751799	0.12519534	43.67198742	0.02289797	5.46752915	0.18289797	14
15	9.26552087	0.10792701	51.65950541	0.01935752	5.57545616	0.17935752	15
16	10.74800420	0.09304053	60.92502627	0.01641362	5.66849669	0.17641362	16
17	12.46768488	0.08020735	71.67303048	0.01395225	5.74870404	0.17395225	17
18	14.46251446	0.06914427	84.14071536	0.01188485	5.81784831	0.17188485	18
19	16.77651677	0.05960713	98.60322981	0.01014166	5.87745544	0.17014166	19
20	19.46075945	0.05138546	115.37974658	0.00866703	5.92884090	0.16866703	20
21	22.57448097	0.04429781	134.84050604	0.00741617	5.97313871	0.16741617	21
22	26.18639792	0.03818776	157.41498700	0.00635264	6.01132647	0.16635264	22
23	30.37622159	0.03292049	183.60138492	0.00544658	6.04424696	0.16544658	23
24	35.23641704	0.02837973	213.97760651	0.00467339	6.07262669	0.16467339	24
25	40.87424377	0.02446528	249.21402355	0.00401262	6.09709197	0.16401262	25
26	47.41412277	0.02109076	290.08826732	0.00344723	6.11818273	0.16344723	26
27	55.00038241	0.01818169	337.50239009	0.00296294	6.13636443	0.16296294	27
28	63.80044360	0.01567387	392.50277250	0.00254775	6.15203830	0.16254775	28
29	74.00851458	0.01351196	456.30321610	0.00219153	6.16555026	0.16219153	29
30	85.84987691	0.01164824	530.31173068	0.00188568	6.17719850	0.16188568	30
31	99.58585721	0.01004159	616.16160759	0.00162295	6.18724008	0.16162295	31
32	115.51959437	0.00865654	715.74746480	0.00139714	6.19589662	0.16139714	32
33	134.00272947	0.00746253	831.26705917	0.00120298	6.20335916	0.16120298	33
34	155.44316618	0.00643322	965.26978864	0.00103598	6.20979238	0.16103598	34
35	180.31407277	0.00554588	1120.71295482	0.00089229	6.21533826	0.16089229	35
36	209.16432441	0.00478093	1301.02702759	0.00076862	6.22011919	0.16076862	36
37	242.63061632	0.00412149	1510.19135201	0.00066217	6.22424068	0.16066217	37
38	281.45151493	0.00355301	1752.82196833	0.00057051	6.22779369	0.16057051	38
39	326.48375732	0.00306294	2034.27348326	0.00049158	6.23085663	0.16049158	39
40	378.72115849	0.00264047	2360.75724058	0.00042359	6.23349709	0.16042359	40

TABLE A-2

COMPOUND INTEREST FOR $1

$16\frac{1}{2}\%$

PERIODS n	FUTURE AMOUNT $(1+i)^n$	PRESENT VALUE $(1+i)^{-n}$	AMOUNT OF ANNUITY $(S/p,i,n)$ $\dfrac{(1+i)^n - 1}{i}$	SINKING FUND $(p/S,i,n)$ $\dfrac{i}{(1+i)^n - 1}$	PRESENT VALUE OF ANNUITY $(V/p,i,n)$ $\dfrac{1-(1+i)^{-n}}{i}$	AMORTIZATION $(p/V,i,n)$ $\dfrac{i}{1-(1+i)^{-n}}$	PERIODS n
1	1.16500000	0.85836910	1.00000000	1.00000000	0.85836910	1.16500000	1
2	1.35722500	0.73679751	2.16500000	0.46189376	1.59516661	0.62689376	2
3	1.58116712	0.63244421	3.52222500	0.28391145	2.22761082	0.44891145	3
4	1.84205970	0.54287057	5.10339212	0.19594810	2.77048139	0.36094810	4
5	2.14599955	0.46598332	6.94545183	0.14397911	3.23646471	0.30897911	5
6	2.50008948	0.39998568	9.09145138	0.10999344	3.63645040	0.27499344	6
7	2.91260424	0.34333535	11.59154085	0.08626981	3.97978575	0.25126981	7
8	3.39318394	0.29470846	14.50414509	0.06894581	4.27449421	0.23394581	8
9	3.95305929	0.25296863	17.89732904	0.05587426	4.52746284	0.22087426	9
10	4.60531407	0.21714046	21.85038833	0.04576578	4.74460329	0.21076578	10
11	5.36519090	0.18638666	26.45570240	0.03779903	4.93098995	0.20279903	11
12	6.25044739	0.15998855	31.82089330	0.03142589	5.09097850	0.19642589	12
13	7.28177121	0.13732923	38.07134069	0.02626648	5.22830773	0.19126648	13
14	8.48326346	0.11787916	45.35311190	0.02204920	5.34618689	0.18704920	14
15	9.88300194	0.10118383	53.83637537	0.01857480	5.44737072	0.18357480	15
16	11.51369726	0.08685307	63.71937730	0.01569381	5.53422379	0.18069381	16
17	13.41345730	0.07455199	75.23307456	0.01329203	5.60877579	0.17829203	17
18	15.62667776	0.06399313	88.64653186	0.01128076	5.67276892	0.17628076	18
19	18.20507959	0.05492972	104.27320962	0.00959019	5.72769864	0.17459019	19
20	21.20891772	0.04714998	122.47828921	0.00816471	5.77484862	0.17316471	20
21	24.70838914	0.04047208	143.68720693	0.00695956	5.81532070	0.17195956	21
22	28.78527335	0.03473999	168.39559607	0.00593840	5.85006069	0.17093840	22
23	33.53484345	0.02981973	197.18086942	0.00507149	5.87988042	0.17007149	23
24	39.06809262	0.02559634	230.71571287	0.00433434	5.90547676	0.16933434	24
25	45.51432791	0.02197110	269.78380550	0.00370667	5.92744786	0.16870667	25
26	53.02419201	0.01885932	315.29813340	0.00317160	5.94630717	0.16817160	26
27	61.77318369	0.01618825	368.32232542	0.00271501	5.96249543	0.16771501	27
28	71.96575900	0.01389550	430.09550911	0.00232506	5.97639093	0.16732506	28
29	83.84010924	0.01192747	502.06126811	0.00199179	5.98831839	0.16699179	29
30	97.67372726	0.01023747	585.90137735	0.00170677	5.99855656	0.16670677	30
31	113.78989226	0.00878813	683.57510461	0.00146290	6.00734469	0.16646290	31
32	132.56522448	0.00754346	797.36499687	0.00125413	6.01488814	0.16625413	32
33	154.43848652	0.00647507	929.93022136	0.00107535	6.02136321	0.16607535	33
34	179.92083680	0.00555800	1084.36870788	0.00092220	6.02692121	0.16592220	34
35	209.60777487	0.00477082	1264.28954468	0.00079096	6.03169203	0.16579096	35
36	244.19305773	0.00409512	1473.89731956	0.00067847	6.03578715	0.16567847	36
37	284.48491225	0.00351512	1718.09037728	0.00058204	6.03930227	0.16558204	37
38	331.42492277	0.00301727	2002.57528954	0.00049936	6.04231955	0.16549936	38
39	386.11003503	0.00258994	2334.00021231	0.00042845	6.04490948	0.16542845	39
40	449.81819081	0.00222312	2720.11024734	0.00036763	6.04713260	0.16536763	40

TABLE A-2

COMPOUND INTEREST FOR $1

17%

PERIODS n	FUTURE AMOUNT $(1+i)^n$	PRESENT VALUE $(1+i)^{-n}$	AMOUNT OF ANNUITY $(S/p,i,n)$ $\dfrac{(1+i)^n-1}{i}$	SINKING FUND $(p/S,i,n)$ $\dfrac{i}{(1+i)^n-1}$	PRESENT VALUE OF ANNUITY $(V/p,i,n)$ $\dfrac{1-(1+i)^{-n}}{i}$	AMORTIZATION $(p/V,i,n)$ $\dfrac{i}{1-(1+i)^{-n}}$	PERIODS n
1	1.17000000	0.85470085	1.00000000	1.00000000	0.85470085	1.17000000	1
2	1.36890000	0.73051355	2.17000000	0.46082949	1.58521441	0.63082949	2
3	1.60161300	0.62437056	3.53890000	0.28257368	2.20958496	0.45257368	3
4	1.87388721	0.53365005	5.14051300	0.19453311	2.74323501	0.36453311	4
5	2.19244804	0.45611115	7.01440021	0.14256386	3.19934616	0.31256386	5
6	2.56516420	0.38983859	9.20684825	0.10861480	3.58918475	0.27861480	6
7	3.00124212	0.33319538	11.77201245	0.08494724	3.92238013	0.25494724	7
8	3.51145328	0.28478237	14.77325456	0.06768989	4.20716251	0.23768989	8
9	4.10840033	0.24340374	18.28470784	0.05469051	4.45056624	0.22469051	9
10	4.80682839	0.20803738	22.39310817	0.04465660	4.65860363	0.21465660	10
11	5.62398922	0.17780973	27.19993656	0.03676479	4.83641336	0.20676479	11
12	6.58006738	0.15197413	32.82392578	0.03046558	4.98838748	0.20046558	12
13	7.69867884	0.12989242	39.40399316	0.02537814	5.11827990	0.19537814	13
14	9.00745424	0.11101916	47.10267200	0.02123022	5.22929906	0.19123022	14
15	10.53872146	0.09488817	56.11012623	0.01782209	5.32418723	0.18782209	15
16	12.33030411	0.08110100	66.64884769	0.01500401	5.40528823	0.18500401	16
17	14.42645581	0.06931709	78.97915180	0.01266157	5.47460533	0.18266157	17
18	16.87895329	0.05924538	93.40560761	0.01070600	5.53385071	0.18070600	18
19	19.74837535	0.05063708	110.28456090	0.00906745	5.58448778	0.17906745	19
20	23.10559916	0.04327955	130.03293626	0.00769036	5.62776734	0.17769036	20
21	27.03355102	0.03699107	153.13853542	0.00653004	5.66475841	0.17653004	21
22	31.62925470	0.03161630	180.17208644	0.00555025	5.69637471	0.17555025	22
23	37.00622799	0.02702248	211.80134114	0.00472141	5.72339719	0.17472141	23
24	43.29728675	0.02309614	248.80756913	0.00401917	5.74649332	0.17401917	24
25	50.65782550	0.01974029	292.10485588	0.00342343	5.76623361	0.17342343	25
26	59.26965584	0.01687204	342.76268138	0.00291747	5.78310565	0.17291747	26
27	69.34549733	0.01442055	402.03233722	0.00248736	5.79752619	0.17248736	27
28	81.13423187	0.01232525	471.37783454	0.00212144	5.80985145	0.17212144	28
29	94.92705129	0.01053440	552.51206642	0.00180992	5.82038585	0.17180992	29
30	111.06465001	0.00900376	647.43911771	0.00154455	5.82938962	0.17154455	30
31	129.94564051	0.00769553	758.50376772	0.00131839	5.83708514	0.17131839	31
32	152.03639940	0.00657737	888.44940823	0.00112556	5.84366252	0.17112556	32
33	177.88258730	0.00562169	1040.48580763	0.00096109	5.84928420	0.17096109	33
34	208.12262714	0.00480486	1218.36839493	0.00082077	5.85408906	0.17082077	34
35	243.50347375	0.00410672	1426.49102206	0.00070102	5.85819578	0.17070102	35
36	284.89906429	0.00351002	1669.99449581	0.00059880	5.86170579	0.17059880	36
37	333.31905522	0.00300001	1954.89356010	0.00051154	5.86470581	0.17051154	37
38	389.99332910	0.00256411	2288.22546532	0.00043702	5.86726992	0.17043702	38
39	456.29804505	0.00219155	2678.22379443	0.00037338	5.86946147	0.17037338	39
40	533.86871271	0.00187312	3134.52183948	0.00031903	5.87133459	0.17031903	40

TABLE A-2

COMPOUND INTEREST FOR $1

$17\frac{1}{2}\%$

PERIODS n	FUTURE AMOUNT $(1+i)^n$	PRESENT VALUE $(1+i)^{-n}$	AMOUNT OF ANNUITY $(S/p,i,n)$ $\dfrac{(1+i)^n - 1}{i}$	SINKING FUND $(p/S,i,n)$ $\dfrac{i}{(1+i)^n - 1}$	PRESENT VALUE OF ANNUITY $(V/p,i,n)$ $\dfrac{1-(1+i)^{-n}}{i}$	AMORTIZATION $(p/V,i,n)$ $\dfrac{i}{1-(1+i)^{-n}}$	PERIODS n
1	1.17500000	0.85106383	1.00000000	1.00000000	0.85106383	1.17500000	1
2	1.38062500	0.72430964	2.17500000	0.45977011	1.57537347	0.63477011	2
3	1.62223437	0.61643374	3.55562500	0.28124451	2.19180721	0.45624451	3
4	1.90612539	0.52462446	5.17785937	0.19313000	2.71643167	0.36813000	4
5	2.23969733	0.44648890	7.08398477	0.14116349	3.16292057	0.31616349	5
6	2.63164437	0.37999055	9.32368210	0.10725376	3.54291112	0.28225376	6
7	3.09218213	0.32339622	11.95532647	0.08364473	3.86630734	0.25864473	7
8	3.63331400	0.27523082	15.04750860	0.06645618	4.14153816	0.24145618	8
9	4.26914396	0.23423900	18.68082260	0.05353083	4.37577716	0.22853083	9
10	5.01624415	0.19935234	22.94996656	0.04357305	4.57512950	0.21857305	10
11	5.89408687	0.16966156	27.96621071	0.03575744	4.74479106	0.21075744	11
12	6.92555208	0.14439282	33.86029758	0.02953311	4.88918388	0.20453311	12
13	8.13752369	0.12288751	40.78584966	0.02451831	5.01207139	0.19951831	13
14	9.56159034	0.10458511	48.92337335	0.02044013	5.11665650	0.19544013	14
15	11.23486864	0.08900861	58.48496368	0.01709841	5.20566511	0.19209841	15
16	13.20097066	0.07575201	69.71983233	0.01434312	5.28141711	0.18934312	16
17	15.51114052	0.06446979	82.92080299	0.01205970	5.34588690	0.18705970	17
18	18.22559011	0.05486791	98.43194351	0.01015930	5.40075481	0.18515930	18
19	21.41506838	0.04669609	116.65753362	0.00857210	5.44745090	0.18357210	19
20	25.16270535	0.03974135	138.07260201	0.00724257	5.48719226	0.18224257	20
21	29.56617879	0.03382243	163.23530736	0.00612613	5.52101469	0.18112613	21
22	34.74026008	0.02878505	192.80148614	0.00518668	5.54979973	0.18018668	22
23	40.81980559	0.02449791	227.54174622	0.00439480	5.57429765	0.17939480	23
24	47.96327157	0.02084929	268.36155181	0.00372632	5.59514693	0.17872632	24
25	56.35684409	0.01774407	316.32482337	0.00316131	5.61289101	0.17816131	25
26	66.21929181	0.01510134	372.68166746	0.00268326	5.62799235	0.17768326	26
27	77.80766787	0.01285220	438.90095927	0.00227842	5.64084455	0.17727842	27
28	91.42400975	0.01093805	516.70862714	0.00193533	5.65178260	0.17693533	28
29	107.42321146	0.00930898	608.13263689	0.00164438	5.66109157	0.17664438	29
30	126.22227346	0.00792253	715.55584835	0.00139751	5.66901410	0.17639751	30
31	148.31117132	0.00674258	841.77812181	0.00118796	5.67575668	0.17618796	31
32	174.26562630	0.00573837	990.08929312	0.00101001	5.68149505	0.17601001	32
33	204.76211090	0.00488372	1164.35491942	0.00085884	5.68637877	0.17585884	33
34	240.59548031	0.00415635	1369.11703032	0.00073040	5.69053512	0.17573040	34
35	282.69968936	0.00353732	1609.71251063	0.00062123	5.69407244	0.17562123	35
36	332.17213500	0.00301049	1892.41219998	0.00052843	5.69708293	0.17552843	36
37	390.30225862	0.00256212	2224.58433498	0.00044952	5.69964505	0.17544952	37
38	458.60515388	0.00218052	2614.88659360	0.00038243	5.70182557	0.17538243	38
39	538.86105581	0.00185577	3073.49174748	0.00032536	5.70368134	0.17532536	39
40	633.16174058	0.00157938	3612.35280329	0.00027683	5.70526071	0.17527683	40

TABLE A-2

COMPOUND INTEREST FOR $1

18%

PERIODS n	FUTURE AMOUNT $(1+i)^n$	PRESENT VALUE $(1+i)^{-n}$	AMOUNT OF ANNUITY $(S/p,i,n)$ $\dfrac{(1+i)^n-1}{i}$	SINKING FUND $(p/S,i,n)$ $\dfrac{i}{(1+i)^n-1}$	PRESENT VALUE OF ANNUITY $(V/p,i,n)$ $\dfrac{1-(1+i)^{-n}}{i}$	AMORTIZATION $(p/V,i,n)$ $\dfrac{i}{1-(1+i)^{-n}}$	PERIODS n
1	1.18000000	0.84745763	1.00000000	1.00000000	0.84745763	1.18000000	1
2	1.39240000	0.71818443	2.18000000	0.45871560	1.56564206	0.63871560	2
3	1.64303200	0.60863087	3.57240000	0.27992386	2.17427293	0.45992386	3
4	1.93877776	0.51578888	5.21543200	0.19173867	2.69006180	0.37173867	4
5	2.28775776	0.43710922	7.15420976	0.13977784	3.12717102	0.31977784	5
6	2.69955415	0.37043154	9.44196752	0.10591013	3.49760256	0.28591013	6
7	3.18547390	0.31392503	12.14152167	0.08236200	3.81152759	0.26236200	7
8	3.75885920	0.26603816	15.32699557	0.06524436	4.07756576	0.24524436	8
9	4.43545386	0.22545607	19.08585477	0.05239482	4.30302183	0.23239482	9
10	5.23383555	0.19106447	23.52130863	0.04251464	4.49408629	0.22251464	10
11	6.17592595	0.16191904	28.75514419	0.03477639	4.65600533	0.21477639	11
12	7.28759263	0.13721953	34.93107014	0.02862781	4.79322486	0.20862781	12
13	8.59935930	0.11628773	42.21866276	0.02368621	4.90951259	0.20368621	13
14	10.14724397	0.09854893	50.81802206	0.01967806	5.00806152	0.19967806	14
15	11.97374789	0.08351604	60.96526603	0.01640278	5.09157756	0.19640278	15
16	14.12902251	0.07077630	72.93901392	0.01371008	5.16235386	0.19371008	16
17	16.67224656	0.05997992	87.06803642	0.01148527	5.22233378	0.19148527	17
18	19.67325094	0.05083044	103.74028298	0.00963946	5.27316422	0.18963946	18
19	23.21443611	0.04307664	123.41353392	0.00810284	5.31624087	0.18810284	19
20	27.39303460	0.03650563	146.62797002	0.00681998	5.35274650	0.18681998	20
21	32.32378083	0.03093698	174.02100463	0.00574643	5.38368347	0.18574643	21
22	38.14206138	0.02621778	206.34478546	0.00484626	5.40990125	0.18484626	22
23	45.00763243	0.02221845	244.48684684	0.00409020	5.43211970	0.18409020	23
24	53.10900627	0.01882920	289.49447928	0.00345430	5.45094890	0.18345430	24
25	62.66862740	0.01595695	342.60348554	0.00291883	5.46690585	0.18291883	25
26	73.94898033	0.01352284	405.27211294	0.00246748	5.48042868	0.18246748	26
27	87.25979679	0.01146003	479.22109327	0.00208672	5.49188872	0.18208672	27
28	102.96656021	0.00971189	566.48089006	0.00176528	5.50160061	0.18176528	28
29	121.50054105	0.00823042	669.44745027	0.00149377	5.50983102	0.18149377	29
30	143.37063844	0.00697493	790.94799132	0.00126431	5.51680595	0.18126431	30
31	169.17735336	0.00591096	934.31862976	0.00107030	5.52271691	0.18107030	31
32	199.62927696	0.00500929	1103.49598312	0.00090621	5.52772619	0.18090621	32
33	235.56254681	0.00424516	1303.12526008	0.00076739	5.53197135	0.18076739	33
34	277.96380524	0.00359759	1538.68780689	0.00064990	5.53556894	0.18064990	34
35	327.99729018	0.00304881	1816.65161213	0.00055046	5.53861775	0.18055046	35
36	387.03680242	0.00258373	2144.64890232	0.00046628	5.54120148	0.18046628	36
37	456.70342685	0.00218960	2531.68570473	0.00039499	5.54339108	0.18039499	37
38	538.91004369	0.00185560	2988.38913158	0.00033463	5.54524668	0.18033463	38
39	635.91385155	0.00157254	3527.29917527	0.00028350	5.54681922	0.18028350	39
40	750.37834483	0.00133266	4163.21302682	0.00024020	5.54815188	0.18024020	40

TABLE A-2

COMPOUND INTEREST FOR $1

$18\frac{1}{2}\%$

PERIODS n	FUTURE AMOUNT $(1+i)^n$	PRESENT VALUE $(1+i)^{-n}$	AMOUNT OF ANNUITY $(S/p,i,n)$ $\frac{(1+i)^n-1}{i}$	SINKING FUND $(p/S,i,n)$ $\frac{i}{(1+i)^n-1}$	PRESENT VALUE OF ANNUITY $(V/p,n)$ $\frac{1-(1+i)^{-n}}{i}$	AMORTIZATION $(p/V,i,n)$ $\frac{i}{1-(1+i)^{-n}}$	PERIODS n
1	1.18500000	0.84388186	1.00000000	1.00000000	0.84388186	1.18500000	1
2	1.40422500	0.71213659	2.18500000	0.45766590	1.55601844	0.64266590	2
3	1.66400662	0.60095915	3.58922500	0.27861168	2.15697759	0.46361168	3
4	1.97184785	0.50713852	5.25323162	0.19035902	2.66411611	0.37535902	4
5	2.33663970	0.42796500	7.22507948	0.13840678	3.09208111	0.32340678	5
6	2.76891805	0.36151189	9.56171918	0.10458370	3.45323300	0.28958370	6
7	3.28116789	0.30476953	12.33063723	0.08109881	3.75800253	0.26609881	7
8	3.88818395	0.25718948	15.61180511	0.06405409	4.01519201	0.24905409	8
9	4.60749798	0.21703753	19.49998906	0.05128208	4.23222954	0.23628208	9
10	5.45988510	0.18315404	24.10748704	0.04148089	4.41538358	0.22648089	10
11	6.46996385	0.15456037	29.56737214	0.03382106	4.56994395	0.21882106	11
12	7.66690716	0.13043069	36.03733598	0.02774900	4.70037464	0.21274900	12
13	9.08528498	0.11006809	43.70424314	0.02288107	4.81044274	0.20788107	13
14	10.76606270	0.09288447	52.78952812	0.01894315	4.90332720	0.20394315	14
15	12.75778430	0.07838352	63.55559082	0.01573426	4.98171072	0.20073426	15
16	15.11797440	0.06614643	76.31337512	0.01310386	5.04785715	0.19810386	16
17	17.91479966	0.05581977	91.43134952	0.01093717	5.10367692	0.19593717	17
18	21.22903760	0.04710529	109.34614918	0.00914527	5.15078221	0.19414527	18
19	25.15640955	0.03975130	130.57518678	0.00765842	5.19053351	0.19265842	19
20	29.81034532	0.03354540	155.73159634	0.00642130	5.22407891	0.19142130	20
21	35.32525921	0.02830836	185.54194166	0.00538962	5.25238727	0.19038962	21
22	41.86043216	0.02388891	220.86720087	0.00452761	5.27627617	0.18952761	22
23	49.60461211	0.02015942	262.72763303	0.00380622	5.29643559	0.18880622	23
24	58.78146535	0.01701217	312.33224514	0.00320172	5.31344776	0.18820172	24
25	69.65603644	0.01435626	371.11371049	0.00269459	5.32780401	0.18769459	25
26	82.54240318	0.01211499	440.76974693	0.00226876	5.33991900	0.18726876	26
27	97.81274777	0.01022362	523.31215011	0.00191091	5.35014261	0.18691091	27
28	115.90810611	0.00862752	621.12489788	0.00160998	5.35877014	0.18660998	28
29	137.35110574	0.00728061	737.03300399	0.00135679	5.36605075	0.18635679	29
30	162.76106030	0.00614398	874.38410973	0.00114366	5.37219473	0.18614366	30
31	192.87185646	0.00518479	1037.14517003	0.00096419	5.37737952	0.18596419	31
32	228.55314990	0.00437535	1230.01702649	0.00081300	5.38175487	0.18581300	32
33	270.83548263	0.00369228	1458.57017639	0.00068560	5.38544714	0.18568560	33
34	320.94004692	0.00311585	1729.40565902	0.00057823	5.38856299	0.18557823	34
35	380.31395560	0.00262941	2050.34570594	0.00048772	5.39119240	0.18548772	35
36	450.67203738	0.00221891	2430.65966153	0.00041141	5.39341131	0.18541141	36
37	534.04636430	0.00187250	2881.33169892	0.00034706	5.39528380	0.18534706	37
38	632.84494170	0.00158017	3415.37806322	0.00029279	5.39686397	0.18529279	38
39	749.92125591	0.00133347	4048.22300491	0.00024702	5.39819744	0.18524702	39
40	888.65668825	0.00112529	4798.14426082	0.00020841	5.39932274	0.18520841	40

COMPOUND INTEREST FOR $1

19%

PERIODS n	FUTURE AMOUNT $(1+i)^n$	PRESENT VALUE $(1+i)^{-n}$	AMOUNT OF ANNUITY $(S/p,i,n)$ $\frac{(1+i)^n-1}{i}$	SINKING FUND $(p/S,i,n)$ $\frac{i}{(1+i)^n-1}$	PRESENT VALUE OF ANNUITY $(V/p,i,n)$ $\frac{1-(1+i)^{-n}}{i}$	AMORTIZATION $(p/V,i,n)$ $\frac{i}{1-(1+i)^{-n}}$	PERIODS n
1	1.19000000	0.84033613	1.00000000	1.00000000	0.84033613	1.19000000	1
2	1.41610000	0.70616482	2.19000000	0.45662100	1.54650095	0.64662100	2
3	1.68515900	0.59341581	3.60610000	0.27730789	2.13991677	0.46730789	3
4	2.00533921	0.49866875	5.29125900	0.18899094	2.63858552	0.37899094	4
5	2.38635366	0.41904937	7.29659821	0.13705017	3.05763489	0.32705017	5
6	2.83976086	0.35214233	9.68295187	0.10327429	3.40977722	0.29327429	6
7	3.37931542	0.29591792	12.52271273	0.07985490	3.70569514	0.26985490	7
8	4.02138535	0.24867052	15.90202814	0.06288506	3.95436567	0.25288506	8
9	4.78544856	0.20896683	19.92341349	0.05019220	4.16333249	0.24019220	9
10	5.69468379	0.17560238	24.70886205	0.04047131	4.33893487	0.23047131	10
11	6.77667371	0.14756502	30.40354584	0.03289090	4.48649989	0.22289090	11
12	8.06424172	0.12400422	37.18021955	0.02689602	4.61050411	0.21689602	12
13	9.59644764	0.10420523	45.24446127	0.02210215	4.71470933	0.21210215	13
14	11.41977269	0.08756742	54.84090891	0.01823456	4.80227675	0.20823456	14
15	13.58952950	0.07358606	66.26068160	0.01509191	4.87586282	0.20509191	15
16	16.17154011	0.06183703	79.85021111	0.01252345	4.93769985	0.20252345	16
17	19.24413273	0.05196389	96.02175122	0.01041431	4.98966374	0.20041431	17
18	22.90051795	0.04366713	115.26588395	0.00867559	5.03333087	0.19867559	18
19	27.25161636	0.03669507	138.16640190	0.00723765	5.07002594	0.19723765	19
20	32.42942347	0.03083619	165.41801826	0.00604529	5.10086214	0.19604529	20
21	38.59101393	0.02591277	197.84744173	0.00505440	5.12677490	0.19505440	21
22	45.92330658	0.02177544	236.43845566	0.00422943	5.14855034	0.19422943	22
23	54.64873482	0.01829869	282.36176223	0.00354156	5.16684902	0.19354156	23
24	65.03199444	0.01537705	337.01049706	0.00296727	5.18222607	0.19296727	24
25	77.38807338	0.01292189	402.04249150	0.00248730	5.19514796	0.19248730	25
26	92.09180733	0.01085873	479.43056488	0.00208581	5.20600669	0.19208581	26
27	109.58925072	0.00912498	571.52237221	0.00174971	5.21513167	0.19174971	27
28	130.41120836	0.00766805	681.11162293	0.00146819	5.22279972	0.19146819	28
29	155.18933794	0.00644374	811.52283129	0.00123225	5.22924347	0.19123225	29
30	184.67531215	0.00541491	966.71216923	0.00103443	5.23465837	0.19103443	30
31	219.76362146	0.00455034	1151.38748139	0.00086852	5.23920872	0.19086852	31
32	261.51870954	0.00382382	1371.15110285	0.00072931	5.24303254	0.19072931	32
33	311.20726435	0.00321329	1632.66981239	0.00061249	5.24624583	0.19061249	33
34	370.33664458	0.00270025	1943.87707675	0.00051444	5.24894607	0.19051444	34
35	440.70060705	0.00226911	2314.21372133	0.00043211	5.25121519	0.19043211	35
36	524.43372239	0.00190682	2754.91432838	0.00036299	5.25312201	0.19036299	36
37	624.07612965	0.00160237	3279.34805077	0.00030494	5.25472438	0.19030494	37
38	742.65059428	0.00134653	3903.42418042	0.00025619	5.25607090	0.19025619	38
39	883.75420719	0.00113154	4646.07477470	0.00021524	5.25720244	0.19021524	39
40	1051.66750656	0.00095087	5529.82898189	0.00018084	5.25815331	0.19018084	40

TABLE A-2

COMPOUND INTEREST FOR $1

$19\frac{1}{2}\%$

PERIODS n	FUTURE AMOUNT $(1+i)^n$	PRESENT VALUE $(1+i)^{-n}$	AMOUNT OF ANNUITY $(S/p,i,n)$ $\dfrac{(1+i)^n - 1}{i}$	SINKING FUND $(p/S,i,n)$ $\dfrac{i}{(1+i)^n - 1}$	PRESENT VALUE OF ANNUITY $(V/p,i,n)$ $\dfrac{1-(1+i)^{-n}}{i}$	AMORTIZATION $(p/V,i,n)$ $\dfrac{i}{1-(1+i)^{-n}}$	PERIODS n
1	1.19500000	0.83682008	1.00000000	1.00000000	0.83682008	1.19500000	1
2	1.42802500	0.70026785	2.19500000	0.45558087	1.53708794	0.65058087	2
3	1.70648987	0.58599820	3.62302500	0.27601245	2.12308614	0.47101245	3
4	2.03925540	0.49037507	5.32951487	0.18763434	2.61346120	0.38263434	4
5	2.43691020	0.41035570	7.36877028	0.13570785	3.02381691	0.33070785	5
6	2.91210769	0.34339389	9.80568048	0.10198170	3.36721080	0.29698170	6
7	3.47996869	0.28735891	12.71778817	0.07863002	3.65456971	0.27363002	7
8	4.15856259	0.24046770	16.19775687	0.06173694	3.89503741	0.25673694	8
9	4.96948229	0.20122820	20.35631946	0.04912479	4.09626562	0.24412479	9
10	5.93853134	0.16839180	25.32580175	0.03948542	4.26465742	0.23448542	10
11	7.09654495	0.14091364	31.26433309	0.03198533	4.40557106	0.22698533	11
12	8.48037122	0.11791937	38.36087804	0.02606822	4.52349043	0.22106822	12
13	10.13404361	0.09867729	46.84124926	0.02134870	4.62216772	0.21634870	13
14	12.11018211	0.08257514	56.97529287	0.01755147	4.70474286	0.21255147	14
15	14.47166762	0.06910054	69.08547498	0.01447482	4.77384340	0.20947482	15
16	17.29364281	0.05782472	83.55714260	0.01196786	4.83166812	0.20696786	16
17	20.66590315	0.04838888	100.85078540	0.00991564	4.88005700	0.20491564	17
18	24.69575427	0.04049279	121.51668856	0.00822932	4.92054979	0.20322932	18
19	29.51142635	0.03388518	146.21244283	0.00683936	4.95443497	0.20183936	19
20	35.26615449	0.02835580	175.72386918	0.00569075	4.98279077	0.20069075	20
21	42.14305461	0.02372870	210.99002367	0.00473956	5.00651948	0.19973956	21
22	50.36095026	0.01985665	253.13307828	0.00395049	5.02637613	0.19895049	22
23	60.18133557	0.01661645	303.49402855	0.00329496	5.04299258	0.19829496	23
24	71.91669600	0.01390498	363.67536411	0.00274971	5.05689755	0.19774971	24
25	85.94045172	0.01163596	435.59206012	0.00229573	5.06853352	0.19729573	25
26	102.69883981	0.00973721	521.53251184	0.00191743	5.07827073	0.19691743	26
27	122.72511357	0.00814829	624.23135165	0.00160197	5.08641902	0.19660197	27
28	146.65651072	0.00681865	746.95646522	0.00133877	5.09323767	0.19633877	28
29	175.25453031	0.00570599	893.61297593	0.00111905	5.09894366	0.19611905	29
30	209.42916372	0.00477488	1068.86750624	0.00093557	5.10371854	0.19593557	30
31	250.26785064	0.00399572	1278.29666996	0.00078229	5.10771426	0.19578229	31
32	299.07008152	0.00334370	1528.56452060	0.00065421	5.11105796	0.19565421	32
33	357.38874741	0.00279807	1827.63460212	0.00054716	5.11385603	0.19554716	33
34	427.07955316	0.00234148	2185.02334953	0.00045766	5.11619752	0.19545766	34
35	510.36006602	0.00195940	2612.10290269	0.00038283	5.11815692	0.19538283	35
36	609.88027890	0.00163967	3122.46296871	0.00032026	5.11979658	0.19532026	36
37	728.80693328	0.00137211	3732.34324761	0.00026793	5.12116869	0.19526793	37
38	870.92428527	0.00114821	4461.15018090	0.00022416	5.12231690	0.19522416	38
39	1040.75452090	0.00096084	5332.07446617	0.00018754	5.12327774	0.19518754	39
40	1243.70165248	0.00080405	6372.82898707	0.00015692	5.12408179	0.19515692	40

TABLE A-2

COMPOUND INTEREST FOR $1

20%

PERIODS n	FUTURE AMOUNT $(1+i)^n$	PRESENT VALUE $(1+i)^{-n}$	AMOUNT OF ANNUITY $(S/p,i,n)$ $\dfrac{(1+i)^n-1}{i}$	SINKING FUND $(p/S,i,n)$ $\dfrac{i}{(1+i)^n-1}$	PRESENT VALUE OF ANNUITY $(V/p,i,n)$ $\dfrac{1-(1+i)^{-n}}{i}$	AMORTIZATION $(p/V,i,n)$ $\dfrac{i}{1-(1+i)^{-n}}$	PERIODS n
1	1.20000000	0.83333333	1.00000000	1.00000000	0.83333333	1.20000000	1
2	1.44000000	0.69444444	2.20000000	0.45454545	1.52777778	0.65454545	2
3	1.72800000	0.57870370	3.64000000	0.27472527	2.10648148	0.47472527	3
4	2.07360000	0.48225309	5.36800000	0.18628912	2.58873457	0.38628912	4
5	2.48832000	0.40187757	7.44160000	0.13437970	2.99061214	0.33437970	5
6	2.98598400	0.33489798	9.92992000	0.10070575	3.32551012	0.30070575	6
7	3.58318080	0.27908165	12.91590400	0.07742393	3.60459176	0.27742393	7
8	4.29981696	0.23256804	16.49908480	0.06060942	3.83715980	0.26060942	8
9	5.15978035	0.19380670	20.79890176	0.04807946	4.03096650	0.24807946	9
10	6.19173642	0.16150558	25.95868211	0.03852276	4.19247209	0.23852276	10
11	7.43008371	0.13458799	32.15041853	0.03110379	4.32706007	0.23110379	11
12	8.91610045	0.11215665	39.58050224	0.02526496	4.43921673	0.22526496	12
13	10.69932054	0.09346388	48.49660269	0.02062000	4.53268061	0.22062000	13
14	12.83918465	0.07788657	59.19592323	0.01689306	4.61056717	0.21689306	14
15	15.40702157	0.06490547	72.03510787	0.01388212	4.67547264	0.21388212	15
16	18.48842589	0.05408789	87.44212945	0.01143614	4.72956054	0.21143614	16
17	22.18611107	0.04507324	105.93055534	0.00944015	4.77463378	0.20944015	17
18	26.62333328	0.03756104	128.11666640	0.00780539	4.81219482	0.20780539	18
19	31.94799994	0.03130086	154.73999969	0.00646245	4.84349568	0.20646245	19
20	38.33759992	0.02608405	186.68799962	0.00535653	4.86957973	0.20535653	20
21	46.00511991	0.02173671	225.02559955	0.00444394	4.89131644	0.20444394	21
22	55.20614389	0.01811393	271.03071946	0.00368962	4.90943037	0.20368962	22
23	66.24737267	0.01509494	326.23686335	0.00306526	4.92452531	0.20306526	23
24	79.49684720	0.01257912	392.48423602	0.00254787	4.93710442	0.20254787	24
25	95.39621664	0.01048260	471.98108322	0.00211873	4.94758702	0.20211873	25
26	114.47545997	0.00873550	567.37729986	0.00176250	4.95632252	0.20176250	26
27	137.37055197	0.00727958	681.85275984	0.00146659	4.96360210	0.20146659	27
28	164.84466236	0.00606632	819.22331180	0.00122067	4.96966841	0.20122067	28
29	197.81359483	0.00505526	984.06797417	0.00101619	4.97472368	0.20101619	29
30	237.37631380	0.00421272	1181.88156900	0.00084611	4.97893640	0.20084611	30
31	284.85157656	0.00351060	1419.25788280	0.00070459	4.98244700	0.20070459	31
32	341.82189187	0.00292550	1704.10945936	0.00058682	4.98537250	0.20058682	32
33	410.18627025	0.00243792	2045.93135123	0.00048877	4.98781042	0.20048877	33
34	492.22352430	0.00203160	2456.11762148	0.00040715	4.98984201	0.20040715	34
35	590.66822915	0.00169300	2948.34114577	0.00033917	4.99153501	0.20033917	35
36	708.80187499	0.00141083	3539.00937493	0.00028256	4.99294584	0.20028256	36
37	850.56224998	0.00117569	4247.81124991	0.00023542	4.99412154	0.20023542	37
38	1020.67469998	0.00097974	5098.37349989	0.00019614	4.99510128	0.20019614	38
39	1224.80963997	0.00081645	6119.04819987	0.00016342	4.99591773	0.20016342	39
40	1469.77156797	0.00068038	7343.85783985	0.00013617	4.99659811	0.20013617	40

TABLE A-2

COMPOUND INTEREST FOR $1

$20\frac{1}{2}$%

PERIODS n	FUTURE AMOUNT $(1+i)^n$	PRESENT VALUE $(1+i)^{-n}$	AMOUNT OF ANNUITY (S/p,i,n) $\dfrac{(1+i)^n - 1}{i}$	SINKING FUND (p/S,i,n) $\dfrac{i}{(1+i)^n - 1}$	PRESENT VALUE OF ANNUITY (V/p,i,n) $\dfrac{1-(1+i)^{-n}}{i}$	AMORTIZATION (p/V,i,n) $\dfrac{i}{1-(1+i)^{-n}}$	PERIODS n
1	1.20500000	0.82987552	1.00000000	1.00000000	0.82987552	1.20500000	1
2	1.45202500	0.68869338	2.20500000	0.45351474	1.51856890	0.65851474	2
3	1.74969012	0.57152977	3.65702500	0.27344631	2.09009867	0.47844631	3
4	2.10837660	0.47429857	5.40671512	0.18495519	2.56439724	0.38995519	4
5	2.54059380	0.39360877	7.51509173	0.13306557	2.95800600	0.33806557	5
6	3.06141553	0.32664628	10.05568553	0.09944623	3.28465229	0.30444623	6
7	3.68900572	0.27107575	13.11710106	0.07623636	3.55572804	0.28123636	7
8	4.44525189	0.22495913	16.80610678	0.05950218	3.78068717	0.26450218	8
9	5.35652853	0.18668808	21.25135867	0.04705581	3.96737524	0.25205581	9
10	6.45461688	0.15492786	26.60788720	0.03758284	4.12230311	0.24258284	10
11	7.77781334	0.12857084	33.06250407	0.03024574	4.25087395	0.23524574	11
12	9.37226507	0.10669779	40.84031741	0.02448561	4.35757174	0.22948561	12
13	11.29357941	0.08854589	50.21258248	0.01991533	4.44611763	0.22491533	13
14	13.60876319	0.07348206	61.50616189	0.01625853	4.51959969	0.22125853	14
15	16.39855964	0.06098097	75.11492507	0.01331293	4.58058066	0.21831293	15
16	19.76026437	0.05060661	91.51348471	0.01092735	4.63118727	0.21592735	16
17	23.81111856	0.04199719	111.27374908	0.00898685	4.67318445	0.21398685	17
18	28.69239787	0.03485244	135.08486764	0.00740275	4.70803689	0.21240275	18
19	34.57433943	0.02892318	163.77726551	0.00610585	4.73696008	0.21110585	19
20	41.66207901	0.02400264	198.35160493	0.00504155	4.76096272	0.21004155	20
21	50.20280521	0.01991921	240.01368395	0.00416643	4.78088192	0.20916643	21
22	60.49438028	0.01653046	290.21648916	0.00344570	4.79741238	0.20844570	22
23	72.89572823	0.01371822	350.71086943	0.00285135	4.81113061	0.20785135	23
24	87.83935252	0.01138442	423.60659767	0.00236068	4.82251503	0.20736068	24
25	105.84641979	0.00944765	511.44595019	0.00195524	4.83196268	0.20695524	25
26	127.54493585	0.00784037	617.29236998	0.00161998	4.83980305	0.20661998	26
27	153.69164769	0.00650653	744.83730582	0.00134258	4.84630959	0.20634258	27
28	185.19843547	0.00539961	898.52895351	0.00111293	4.85170920	0.20611293	28
29	223.16411474	0.00448101	1083.72738899	0.00092274	4.85619021	0.20592274	29
30	268.91275826	0.00371868	1306.89150373	0.00076517	4.85990889	0.20576517	30
31	324.03987371	0.00308604	1575.80426199	0.00063460	4.86299493	0.20563460	31
32	390.46804782	0.00256103	1899.84413570	0.00052636	4.86555596	0.20552636	32
33	470.51399762	0.00212534	2290.31218352	0.00043662	4.86768129	0.20543662	33
34	566.96936713	0.00176376	2760.82618114	0.00036221	4.86944506	0.20536221	34
35	683.19808740	0.00146370	3327.79554827	0.00030050	4.87090876	0.20530050	35
36	823.25369531	0.00121469	4010.99363567	0.00024931	4.87212345	0.20524931	36
37	992.02070285	0.00100804	4834.24733098	0.00020686	4.87313150	0.20520686	37
38	1195.38494694	0.00083655	5826.26803383	0.00017164	4.87396805	0.20517164	38
39	1440.43886106	0.00069423	7021.65298077	0.00014242	4.87466228	0.20514242	39
40	1735.72882757	0.00057613	8462.09184183	0.00011817	4.87523841	0.20511817	40

TABLE A-2

COMPOUND INTEREST FOR $1

21%

PERIODS n	FUTURE AMOUNT $(1+i)^n$	PRESENT VALUE $(1+i)^{-n}$	AMOUNT OF ANNUITY (S/p,i,n) $\frac{(1+i)^n-1}{i}$	SINKING FUND (p/S,i,n) $\frac{i}{(1+i)^n-1}$	PRESENT VALUE OF ANNUITY (V/p,i,n) $\frac{1-(1+i)^{-n}}{i}$	AMORTIZATION (p/V,i,n) $\frac{i}{1-(1+i)^{-n}}$	PERIODS n
1	1.21000000	0.82644628	1.00000000	1.00000000	0.82644628	1.21000000	1
2	1.46410000	0.68301346	2.21000000	0.45248869	1.50945974	0.66248869	2
3	1.77156100	0.56447393	3.67410000	0.27217550	2.07393367	0.48217550	3
4	2.14358881	0.46650738	5.44566100	0.18363244	2.54044105	0.39363244	4
5	2.59374246	0.38554329	7.58924981	0.13176533	2.92598434	0.34176533	5
6	3.13842838	0.31863082	10.18299227	0.09820296	3.24461515	0.30820296	6
7	3.79749834	0.26333125	13.32142065	0.07506707	3.50794641	0.28506707	7
8	4.59497299	0.21762914	17.11891898	0.05841490	3.72557554	0.26841490	8
9	5.55991731	0.17985879	21.71389197	0.04605347	3.90543433	0.25605347	9
10	6.72749995	0.14864363	27.27380928	0.03666521	4.05407796	0.24666521	10
11	8.14027494	0.12284597	34.00130923	0.02941063	4.17692394	0.23941063	11
12	9.84973268	0.10152560	42.14158417	0.02372953	4.27844953	0.23372953	12
13	11.91817654	0.08390545	51.99131685	0.01923398	4.36235499	0.22923398	13
14	14.42099361	0.06934335	63.90949338	0.01564713	4.43169834	0.22564713	14
15	17.44940227	0.05730855	78.33048699	0.01276642	4.48900689	0.22276642	15
16	21.11377675	0.04736244	95.77988926	0.01044061	4.53636933	0.22044061	16
17	25.54766986	0.03914251	116.79366601	0.00855478	4.57551184	0.21855478	17
18	30.91268053	0.03234918	142.44133587	0.00702043	4.60786103	0.21702043	18
19	37.40434344	0.02673486	173.35401640	0.00576854	4.63459589	0.21576854	19
20	45.25925557	0.02209493	210.75835985	0.00474477	4.65669082	0.21474477	20
21	54.76369924	0.01826027	256.01761542	0.00390598	4.67495109	0.21390598	21
22	66.26407608	0.01509113	310.78131465	0.00321770	4.69004222	0.21321770	22
23	80.17953205	0.01247201	377.04539073	0.00265220	4.70251423	0.21265220	23
24	97.01723378	0.01030745	457.22492279	0.00218711	4.71282168	0.21218711	24
25	117.39085288	0.00851855	554.24215657	0.00180427	4.72134023	0.21180427	25
26	142.04293198	0.00704013	671.63300945	0.00148891	4.72838036	0.21148891	26
27	171.87194770	0.00581829	813.67594143	0.00122899	4.73419864	0.21122899	27
28	207.96505672	0.00480850	985.54788914	0.00101466	4.73900714	0.21101466	28
29	251.63771863	0.00397397	1193.51294585	0.00083786	4.74298111	0.21083786	29
30	304.48163954	0.00328427	1445.15066448	0.00069197	4.74626538	0.21069197	30
31	368.42278385	0.00271427	1749.63230402	0.00057155	4.74897965	0.21057155	31
32	445.79156845	0.00224320	2118.05508787	0.00047213	4.75122285	0.21047213	32
33	539.40779783	0.00185388	2563.84665632	0.00039004	4.75307674	0.21039004	33
34	652.68343537	0.00153214	3103.25445415	0.00032224	4.75460887	0.21032224	34
35	789.74695680	0.00126623	3755.93788952	0.00026625	4.75587510	0.21026625	35
36	955.59381773	0.00104647	4545.68484632	0.00021999	4.75692157	0.21021999	36
37	1156.26851945	0.00086485	5501.27866405	0.00018178	4.75778642	0.21018178	37
38	1399.08490853	0.00071475	6657.54718350	0.00015021	4.75850118	0.21015021	38
39	1692.89273933	0.00059070	8056.63209203	0.00012412	4.75909188	0.21012412	39
40	2048.40021459	0.00048819	9749.52483136	0.00010257	4.75958007	0.21010257	40

TABLE A-2

COMPOUND INTEREST FOR $1

$2\frac{1}{2}\%$

PERIODS n	FUTURE AMOUNT $(1+i)^n$	PRESENT VALUE $(1+i)^{-n}$	AMOUNT OF ANNUITY $(S/p,i,n)$ $\dfrac{(1+i)^n-1}{i}$	SINKING FUND $(p/S,i,n)$ $\dfrac{i}{(1+i)^n-1}$	PRESENT VALUE OF ANNUITY $(V/p,i,n)$ $\dfrac{1-(1+i)^{-n}}{i}$	AMORTIZATION $(p/V,i,n)$ $\dfrac{i}{1-(1+i)^{-n}}$	PERIODS n
1	1.21500000	0.82304527	1.00000000	1.00000000	0.82304527	1.21500000	1
2	1.47622500	0.67740351	2.21500000	0.45146727	1.50044878	0.66646727	2
3	1.79361337	0.55753376	3.69122500	0.27091277	2.05798253	0.48591277	3
4	2.17924025	0.45887552	5.48483837	0.18232078	2.51685805	0.39732078	4
5	2.64777690	0.37767532	7.66407863	0.13047883	2.89453338	0.34547883	5
6	3.21704894	0.31084389	10.31185553	0.09697576	3.20537727	0.31197576	6
7	3.90871446	0.25583859	13.52890447	0.07391582	3.46121586	0.28891582	7
8	4.74908807	0.21056674	17.43761893	0.05734728	3.67178260	0.27234728	8
9	5.77014200	0.17330596	22.18670700	0.04507203	3.84508856	0.26007203	9
10	7.01072254	0.14263865	27.95684900	0.03576941	3.98772721	0.25076941	10
11	8.51802788	0.11739807	34.96757154	0.02859793	4.10512527	0.24359793	11
12	10.34940388	0.09662392	43.48559942	0.02299612	4.20174920	0.23799612	12
13	12.57452571	0.07952586	53.83500330	0.01857528	4.28127506	0.23357528	13
14	15.27804874	0.06545338	66.40952901	0.01505808	4.34672844	0.23005808	14
15	18.56282921	0.05387110	81.68757774	0.01224176	4.40059954	0.22724176	15
16	22.55383750	0.04433835	100.25040696	0.00997502	4.44493789	0.22497502	16
17	27.40291256	0.03649247	122.80424445	0.00814304	4.48143037	0.22314304	17
18	33.29453876	0.03003496	150.20715701	0.00665747	4.51146532	0.22165747	18
19	40.45286459	0.02472013	183.50169577	0.00544954	4.53618545	0.22044954	19
20	49.15023048	0.02034578	223.95456036	0.00446519	4.55653123	0.21946519	20
21	59.71753003	0.01674550	273.10479084	0.00366160	4.57327674	0.21866160	21
22	72.55679899	0.01378231	332.82232087	0.00300461	4.58705904	0.21800461	22
23	88.15651077	0.01134346	405.37911985	0.00246683	4.59840250	0.21746683	23
24	107.11016058	0.00933618	493.53563062	0.00202620	4.60773869	0.21702620	24
25	130.13884511	0.00768410	600.64579121	0.00166487	4.61542279	0.21666487	25
26	158.11869681	0.00632436	730.78463632	0.00136839	4.62174715	0.21636839	26
27	192.11421662	0.00520524	888.90333313	0.00112498	4.62695239	0.21612498	27
28	233.41877320	0.00428415	1081.01754975	0.00092505	4.63123653	0.21592505	28
29	283.60380943	0.00352605	1314.43632294	0.00076078	4.63476258	0.21576078	29
30	344.57862846	0.00290210	1598.04013238	0.00062577	4.63766467	0.21562577	30

446

TABLE A-2

COMPOUND INTEREST FOR $1

22%

PERIODS n	FUTURE AMOUNT $(1+i)^n$	PRESENT VALUE $(1+i)^{-n}$	AMOUNT OF ANNUITY (S/p,i,n) $\dfrac{(1+i)^n - 1}{i}$	SINKING FUND (p/S,i,n) $\dfrac{i}{(1+i)^n - 1}$	PRESENT VALUE OF ANNUITY (V/p,i,n) $\dfrac{1-(1+i)^{-n}}{i}$	AMORTIZATION (p/V,i,n) $\dfrac{i}{1-(1+i)^{-n}}$	PERIODS n
1	1.22000000	0.81967213	1.00000000	1.00000000	0.81967213	1.22000000	1
2	1.48840000	0.67186240	2.22000000	0.45045045	1.49153453	0.67045045	2
3	1.81584800	0.55070689	3.70840000	0.26965807	2.04224142	0.48965807	3
4	2.21533456	0.45139909	5.52424800	0.18102011	2.49364051	0.40102011	4
5	2.70270816	0.36999925	7.73958256	0.12920593	2.86363976	0.34920593	5
6	3.29730396	0.30327808	10.44229072	0.09576443	3.16691784	0.31576443	6
7	4.02271083	0.24858859	13.73959468	0.07278235	3.41550642	0.29278235	7
8	4.90770721	0.20376114	17.76230551	0.05629900	3.61926756	0.27629900	8
9	5.98740280	0.16701733	22.67001273	0.04411114	3.78628489	0.26411114	9
10	7.30463142	0.13689945	28.65741552	0.03489498	3.92318433	0.25489498	10
11	8.91165033	0.11221266	35.96204694	0.02780709	4.03539699	0.24780709	11
12	10.87221340	0.09197759	44.87369727	0.02228477	4.12737459	0.24228477	12
13	13.26410035	0.07539147	55.74591067	0.01793854	4.20276605	0.23793854	13
14	16.18220242	0.06179629	69.01001101	0.01449065	4.26456234	0.23449065	14
15	19.74228696	0.05065269	85.19221343	0.01173816	4.31521503	0.23173816	15
16	24.08559009	0.04151860	104.93450039	0.00952975	4.35673363	0.22952975	16
17	29.38441990	0.03403164	129.72009048	0.00775073	4.39076527	0.22775073	17
18	35.84899228	0.02789479	158.40451038	0.00631295	4.41866006	0.22631295	18
19	43.73577059	0.02286458	194.25350266	0.00514791	4.44152464	0.22514791	19
20	53.35764012	0.01874146	237.98927325	0.00420187	4.46026610	0.22420187	20
21	65.09632094	0.01536185	291.34691337	0.00343233	4.47562795	0.22343233	21
22	79.41751155	0.01259168	356.44323431	0.00280550	4.48821963	0.22280550	22
23	96.88936409	0.01032105	435.86074585	0.00229431	4.49854068	0.22229431	23
24	118.20502419	0.00845988	532.75010994	0.00187705	4.50700056	0.22187705	24
25	144.21012951	0.00693433	650.95513413	0.00153620	4.51393488	0.22153620	25
26	175.93635800	0.00568387	795.16526364	0.00125760	4.51961876	0.22125760	26
27	214.64235676	0.00465891	971.10162164	0.00102976	4.52427767	0.22102976	27
28	261.86367525	0.00381878	1185.74397840	0.00084335	4.52809645	0.22084335	28
29	319.47368380	0.00313015	1447.60765365	0.00069079	4.53122660	0.22069079	29
30	389.75789424	0.00256570	1767.08133745	0.00056590	4.53379229	0.22056590	30

TABLE A-2

COMPOUND INTEREST FOR $1

$22\frac{1}{2}\%$

PERIODS n	FUTURE AMOUNT $(1+i)^n$	PRESENT VALUE $(1+i)^{-n}$	AMOUNT OF ANNUITY $(S/p,i,n)$ $\dfrac{(1+i)^n-1}{i}$	SINKING FUND $(p/S,i,n)$ $\dfrac{i}{(1+i)^n-1}$	PRESENT VALUE OF ANNUITY $(V/p,i,n)$ $\dfrac{1-(1+i)^{-n}}{i}$	AMORTIZATION $(p/V,i,n)$ $\dfrac{i}{1-(1+i)^{-n}}$	PERIODS n
1	1.22500000	0.81632653	1.00000000	1.00000000	0.81632653	1.22500000	1
2	1.50062500	0.66638900	2.22500000	0.44943820	1.48271554	0.67443820	2
3	1.83826562	0.54399102	3.72562500	0.26841134	2.02670656	0.49341134	3
4	2.25187539	0.44407431	5.56389062	0.17973035	2.47078086	0.40473035	4
5	2.75854735	0.36250964	7.81576602	0.12794651	2.83329050	0.35294651	5
6	3.37922051	0.29592623	10.57431337	0.09456879	3.12921674	0.31956879	6
7	4.13954512	0.24157244	13.95353388	0.07166643	3.37078917	0.29666643	7
8	5.07094277	0.19720199	18.09307900	0.05526975	3.56799116	0.28026975	8
9	6.21190490	0.16098122	23.16402177	0.04317040	3.72897238	0.26817040	9
10	7.60958350	0.13141324	29.37592667	0.03404148	3.86038561	0.25904148	10
11	9.32173979	0.10727611	36.98551018	0.02703762	3.96766173	0.25203762	11
12	11.41913124	0.08757234	46.30724996	0.02159489	4.05523406	0.24659489	12
13	13.98843577	0.07148762	57.72638121	0.01732310	4.12672168	0.24232310	13
14	17.13583382	0.05835724	71.71481698	0.01394412	4.18507892	0.23894412	14
15	20.99139643	0.04763856	88.85065080	0.01125484	4.23271749	0.23625484	15
16	25.71446063	0.03888862	109.84204723	0.00910398	4.27160611	0.23410398	16
17	31.50021427	0.03174582	135.55650785	0.00737700	4.30335193	0.23237700	17
18	38.58776248	0.02591495	167.05672212	0.00598599	4.32926688	0.23098599	18
19	47.27000903	0.02115506	205.64448460	0.00486276	4.35042194	0.22986276	19
20	57.90576107	0.01726944	252.91449363	0.00395391	4.36769138	0.22895391	20
21	70.93455731	0.01409750	310.82025470	0.00321729	4.38178888	0.22821729	21
22	86.89483270	0.01150816	381.75481201	0.00261948	4.39329705	0.22761948	22
23	106.44617006	0.00939442	468.64964471	0.00213379	4.40269147	0.22713379	23
24	130.39655832	0.00766891	575.09581477	0.00173884	4.41036038	0.22673884	24
25	159.73578395	0.00626034	705.49237310	0.00141745	4.41662072	0.22641745	25
26	195.67633533	0.00511048	865.22815704	0.00115576	4.42173120	0.22615576	26
27	239.70351078	0.00417182	1060.90449238	0.00094259	4.42590302	0.22594259	27
28	293.63680071	0.00340557	1300.60800316	0.00076887	4.42930859	0.22576887	28
29	359.70508087	0.00278006	1594.24480387	0.00062726	4.43208864	0.22562726	29
30	440.63872407	0.00226943	1953.94988474	0.00051178	4.43435808	0.22551178	30

TABLE A-2

COMPOUND INTEREST FOR $1

23%

PERIODS	FUTURE AMOUNT	PRESENT VALUE	AMOUNT OF ANNUITY	SINKING FUND	PRESENT VALUE OF ANNUITY	AMORTIZATION	PERIODS
n	$(1+i)^n$	$(1+i)^{-n}$	$(S/p,i,n)$ $\dfrac{(1+i)^n-1}{i}$	$(p/S,i,n)$ $\dfrac{i}{(1+i)^n-1}$	$(V/p,i,n)$ $\dfrac{1-(1+i)^{-n}}{i}$	$(p/V,i,n)$ $\dfrac{i}{1-(1+i)^{-n}}$	n
1	1.23000000	0.81300813	1.00000000	1.00000000	0.81300813	1.23000000	1
2	1.51290000	0.66098222	2.23000000	0.44843049	1.47399035	0.67843049	2
3	1.86086700	0.53738392	3.74290000	0.26717251	2.01137427	0.49717251	3
4	2.28886641	0.43689749	5.60376700	0.17845139	2.44827176	0.40845139	4
5	2.81530568	0.35520122	7.89263341	0.12670042	2.80347298	0.35670042	5
6	3.46282599	0.28878148	10.70793909	0.09338865	3.09225445	0.32338865	6
7	4.25927597	0.23478169	14.17076509	0.07056782	3.32703614	0.30056782	7
8	5.23890944	0.19087942	18.43004106	0.05425924	3.51791556	0.28425924	8
9	6.44385861	0.15518652	23.66895050	0.04224944	3.67310208	0.27224944	9
10	7.92594610	0.12616790	30.11280911	0.03320846	3.79926999	0.26320846	10
11	9.74891370	0.10257553	38.03875521	0.02628898	3.90184552	0.25628898	11
12	11.991116385	0.08339474	47.78766891	0.02092590	3.98524026	0.25092590	12
13	14.74913153	0.06780060	59.77883276	0.01672833	4.05304086	0.24672833	13
14	18.14143179	0.05512244	74.52796429	0.01341778	4.10816330	0.24341778	14
15	22.31396110	0.04481499	92.66939608	0.01079105	4.15297829	0.24079105	15
16	27.44617215	0.03643495	114.98335717	0.00869691	4.18941325	0.23869691	16
17	33.75879174	0.02962191	142.42952932	0.00702102	4.21903516	0.23702102	17
18	41.52331385	0.02408286	176.18832107	0.00567575	4.24311802	0.23567575	18
19	51.07367603	0.01957956	217.71163492	0.00459323	4.26269757	0.23459323	19
20	62.82062152	0.01591834	268.78531095	0.00372044	4.27861591	0.23372044	20
21	77.26936447	0.01294174	331.60593246	0.00301563	4.29155765	0.23301563	21
22	95.04131829	0.01052174	408.87529693	0.00244573	4.30207939	0.23244573	22
23	116.90082150	0.00855426	503.91661522	0.00198446	4.31063365	0.23198446	23
24	143.78801045	0.00695468	620.81743673	0.00161078	4.31758834	0.23161078	24
25	176.85925285	0.00565421	764.60544717	0.00130786	4.32324255	0.23130786	25
26	217.53688100	0.00459692	941.46470002	0.00106217	4.32783947	0.23106217	26
27	267.57036364	0.00373733	1159.00158103	0.00086281	4.33157681	0.23086281	27
28	329.11154727	0.00303848	1426.57194466	0.00070098	4.33461529	0.23070098	28
29	404.80720314	0.00247031	1755.68349193	0.00056958	4.33708560	0.23056958	29
30	497.91285987	0.00200838	2160.49069508	0.00046286	4.33909398	0.23046286	30

TABLE A-2

COMPOUND INTEREST FOR $1

$23\frac{1}{2}\%$

PERIODS n	FUTURE AMOUNT $(1+i)^n$	PRESENT VALUE $(1+i)^{-n}$	AMOUNT OF ANNUITY (S/p,i,n) $\frac{(1+i)^n-1}{i}$	SINKING FUND (p/S,i,n) $\frac{i}{(1+i)^n-1}$	PRESENT VALUE OF ANNUITY (V/p,i,n) $\frac{1-(1+i)^{-n}}{i}$	AMORTIZATION (p/V,i,n) $\frac{i}{1-(1+i)^{-n}}$	PERIODS n
1	1.235000000	0.80971660	1.00000000	1.00000000	0.80971660	1.23500000	1
2	1.525225000	0.65564097	2.23500000	0.44742729	1.46535757	0.68242729	2
3	1.883365287	0.53088338	3.76022500	0.26594153	1.99624095	0.50094153	3
4	2.326631130	0.42986508	5.64387787	0.17718314	2.42610603	0.41218314	4
5	2.872994446	0.34806889	7.97018918	0.12546754	2.77417492	0.36046754	5
6	3.548148815	0.28183716	10.84318363	0.09222384	3.05601208	0.32722384	6
7	4.381196297	0.22820823	14.39133179	0.06948627	3.28422031	0.30448627	7
8	5.411172427	0.18478399	18.77329475	0.05326715	3.46900430	0.28826715	8
9	6.683479947	0.14962266	24.18501902	0.04134791	3.61862696	0.27634791	9
10	8.254097715	0.12115195	30.86849849	0.03239549	3.73977892	0.26739549	10
11	10.19380998	0.09809875	39.12259564	0.02556068	3.83787767	0.26056068	11
12	12.58935532	0.07943218	49.31640561	0.02027723	3.91730985	0.25527723	12
13	15.54785382	0.06431756	61.90576093	0.01615359	3.98162741	0.25115359	13
14	19.20159947	0.05207899	77.45361475	0.01291095	4.03370640	0.24791095	14
15	23.71397534	0.04216923	96.65521422	0.01034605	4.07587563	0.24534605	15
16	29.28675955	0.03414512	120.36918956	0.00830777	4.11002075	0.24330777	16
17	36.16914804	0.02764787	149.65594911	0.00668199	4.13766863	0.24168199	17
18	44.66889783	0.02238694	185.82509715	0.00538140	4.16005557	0.24038140	18
19	55.16608882	0.01812708	230.49399498	0.00433851	4.17818265	0.23933851	19
20	68.13011969	0.01467780	285.66008379	0.00350066	4.19286044	0.23850066	20
21	84.14069782	0.01188486	353.79020349	0.00282653	4.20474530	0.23782653	21
22	103.91376181	0.00962336	437.93090131	0.00228347	4.21436866	0.23728347	22
23	128.33349583	0.00779220	541.84466311	0.00184555	4.22216086	0.23684555	23
24	158.49186735	0.00630947	670.17815894	0.00149214	4.22847033	0.23649214	24
25	195.73745618	0.00510888	828.67002630	0.00120675	4.23357922	0.23620675	25
26	241.73575838	0.00413675	1024.40748248	0.00097617	4.23771596	0.23597617	26
27	298.54366160	0.00334959	1266.14324086	0.00078980	4.24106556	0.23578980	27
28	368.70142208	0.00271222	1564.68690246	0.00063911	4.24377778	0.23563911	28
29	455.34625627	0.00219613	1933.38832454	0.00051723	4.24597391	0.23551723	29
30	562.35262649	0.00177824	2388.73458080	0.00041863	4.24775215	0.23541863	30

TABLE A-2

COMPOUND INTEREST FOR $1

24%

PERIODS n	FUTURE AMOUNT $(1+i)^n$	PRESENT VALUE $(1+i)^{-n}$	AMOUNT OF ANNUITY (S/p,i,n) $\dfrac{(1+i)^n - 1}{i}$	SINKING FUND (p/S,i,n) $\dfrac{i}{(1+i)^n - 1}$	PRESENT VALUE OF ANNUITY (V/p,i,n) $\dfrac{1-(1+i)^{-n}}{i}$	AMORTIZATION (p/V,i,n) $\dfrac{i}{1-(1+i)^{-n}}$	PERIODS n
1	1.24000000	0.80645161	1.00000000	1.00000000	0.80645161	1.24000000	1
2	1.53760000	0.65036420	2.24000000	0.44642857	1.45681582	0.68642857	2
3	1.90662400	0.52448726	3.77760000	0.26471834	1.98130308	0.50471834	3
4	2.36421376	0.42297360	5.68422400	0.17592551	2.40427668	0.41592551	4
5	2.93162506	0.34110774	8.04843776	0.12424771	2.74538442	0.36424771	5
6	3.63521508	0.27508689	10.98006282	0.09107416	3.02047130	0.33107416	6
7	4.50766670	0.22184426	14.61527790	0.06842155	3.24231557	0.30842155	7
8	5.58950670	0.17890666	19.12294460	0.05229320	3.42122223	0.29229320	8
9	6.93098831	0.14427957	24.71245130	0.04046543	3.56550180	0.28046543	9
10	8.59442551	0.11635449	31.64343961	0.03160213	3.68185629	0.27160213	10
11	10.65708763	0.09383427	40.23786512	0.02485221	3.77569056	0.26485221	11
12	13.21478866	0.07567280	50.89495274	0.01964831	3.85136335	0.25964831	12
13	16.38633794	0.06102645	64.10974140	0.01559825	3.91238980	0.25559825	13
14	20.31905904	0.04921488	80.49607934	0.01242297	3.96160468	0.25242297	14
15	25.19563321	0.03968942	100.81513838	0.00991915	4.00129409	0.24991915	15
16	31.24258518	0.03200759	126.01077159	0.00793583	4.03330169	0.24793583	16
17	38.74080563	0.02581258	157.25335678	0.00635916	4.05911427	0.24635916	17
18	48.03859898	0.02081659	195.99416240	0.00510219	4.07993086	0.24510219	18
19	59.56786273	0.01678758	244.03276138	0.00409781	4.09671843	0.24409781	19
20	73.86414979	0.01353837	303.60062411	0.00329380	4.11025680	0.24329380	20
21	91.59154574	0.01091804	377.46477390	0.00264925	4.12117484	0.24264925	21
22	113.57351671	0.00880487	469.05631963	0.00213194	4.12997971	0.24213194	22
23	140.83116072	0.00710070	582.62983634	0.00171636	4.13708041	0.24171636	23
24	174.63063930	0.00572637	723.46099707	0.00138224	4.14280678	0.24138224	24
25	216.54199273	0.00461804	898.09163636	0.00111347	4.14742483	0.24111347	25
26	268.51207098	0.00372423	1114.63362909	0.00089716	4.15114905	0.24089716	26
27	332.95496802	0.00300341	1383.14570007	0.00072299	4.15415246	0.24072299	27
28	412.86416034	0.00242210	1716.10066809	0.00058272	4.15657457	0.24058272	28
29	511.95155882	0.00195331	2128.96482843	0.00046971	4.15852788	0.24046971	29
30	634.81993294	0.00157525	2640.91638726	0.00037866	4.16010313	0.24037866	30

TABLE A-3

COMPOUND INTEREST FOR $1
FRACTIONAL INTEREST PERIODS

$$(S/p,i,c) = \frac{(1+i)^c - 1}{i} \qquad (V/p,i,c) = \frac{1 - (1+i)^{-c}}{i}$$

Band 1 — rates 1/12 %, 1/6 %, 1/4 %, 1/3 %

c	1/12 % AMOUNT (S/p,i,c)	1/12 % PRESENT VALUE (V/p,i,c)	1/6 % AMOUNT (S/p,i,c)	1/6 % PRESENT VALUE (V/p,i,c)	1/4 % AMOUNT (S/p,i,c)	1/4 % PRESENT VALUE (V/p,i,c)	1/3 % AMOUNT (S/p,i,c)	1/3 % PRESENT VALUE (V/p,i,c)
1/2	0.49989588	0.49968772	0.49979184	0.49937587	0.49968789	0.49906445	0.49958403	0.49875346
1/3	0.33324078	0.33314827	0.33314832	0.33296344	0.33305594	0.33277886	0.33296365	0.33259451
1/4	0.24992191	0.24986987	0.24984390	0.24973991	0.24976597	0.24961011	0.24968811	0.24948047
1/6	0.16660883	0.16658570	0.16655104	0.16650482	0.16649332	0.16642405	0.16643566	0.16634337
1/12	0.08330152	0.08329574	0.08326974	0.08325819	0.08323800	0.08322068	0.08320629	0.08318322
1/13	0.07689351	0.07688351	0.07686397	0.07685412	0.07683446	0.07681971	0.07680499	0.07678533
1/26	0.03844614	0.03844491	0.03843075	0.03842829	0.03841539	0.03841170	0.03840004	0.03839512
1/52	0.01922291	0.01922261	0.01921507	0.01921445	0.01920723	0.01920631	0.01919940	0.01919817

Band 2 — rates 5/12 %, 1/2 %, 7/12 %, 2/3 %

c	5/12 % AMOUNT (S/p,i,c)	5/12 % PRESENT VALUE (V/p,i,c)	1/2 % AMOUNT (S/p,i,c)	1/2 % PRESENT VALUE (V/p,i,c)	7/12 % AMOUNT (S/p,i,c)	7/12 % PRESENT VALUE (V/p,i,c)	2/3 % AMOUNT (S/p,i,c)	2/3 % PRESENT VALUE (V/p,i,c)
1/2	0.49948025	0.49844291	0.49937656	0.49813278	0.49927295	0.49782308	0.49916943	0.49751381
1/3	0.33287144	0.33241040	0.33277932	0.33222653	0.33268728	0.33204289	0.33259532	0.33185949
1/4	0.24961032	0.24935099	0.24953261	0.24922167	0.24945498	0.24909251	0.24937742	0.24896351
1/6	0.16637805	0.16626279	0.16632050	0.16618230	0.16626301	0.16610192	0.16620558	0.16602162
1/12	0.08317461	0.08314580	0.08314297	0.08310842	0.08311136	0.08307109	0.08307978	0.08303379
1/13	0.07677554	0.07675099	0.07674613	0.07671669	0.07671675	0.07668243	0.07668740	0.07664821
1/26	0.03838470	0.03837856	0.03836938	0.03836202	0.03835408	0.03834550	0.03833880	0.03832900
1/52	0.01919158	0.01919005	0.01918377	0.01918193	0.01917597	0.01917382	0.01916817	0.01916573

Band 3 — rates 3/4 %, 5/6 %, 11/12 %, 1 %

c	3/4 % AMOUNT (S/p,i,c)	3/4 % PRESENT VALUE (V/p,i,c)	5/6 % AMOUNT (S/p,i,c)	5/6 % PRESENT VALUE (V/p,i,c)	11/12 % AMOUNT (S/p,i,c)	11/12 % PRESENT VALUE (V/p,i,c)	1 % AMOUNT (S/p,i,c)	1 % PRESENT VALUE (V/p,i,c)
1/2	0.49906600	0.49720496	0.49896265	0.49689654	0.49885939	0.49658855	0.49875621	0.49628098
1/3	0.33250345	0.33167633	0.33241167	0.33149340	0.33231997	0.33131071	0.33222835	0.33112825
1/4	0.24929994	0.24883468	0.24922253	0.24870600	0.24914519	0.24857748	0.24906793	0.24844912
1/6	0.16614821	0.16594143	0.16609089	0.16586133	0.16603364	0.16578132	0.16597644	0.16570141
1/12	0.08304824	0.08301094	0.08301673	0.08295934	0.08298525	0.08292218	0.08295381	0.08288506
1/13	0.07665808	0.07661403	0.07662879	0.07657989	0.07659953	0.07654579	0.07657031	0.07651172
1/26	0.03832353	0.03831252	0.03830828	0.03829605	0.03829305	0.03827961	0.03827783	0.03826318
1/52	0.01916039	0.01915764	0.01915261	0.01914956	0.01914484	0.01914148	0.01913708	0.01913342

Band 4 — rates 1 1/12 %, 1 1/6 %, 1 1/4 %, 1 1/3 %

c	1 1/12 % AMOUNT (S/p,i,c)	1 1/12 % PRESENT VALUE (V/p,i,c)	1 1/6 % AMOUNT (S/p,i,c)	1 1/6 % PRESENT VALUE (V/p,i,c)	1 1/4 % AMOUNT (S/p,i,c)	1 1/4 % PRESENT VALUE (V/p,i,c)	1 1/3 % AMOUNT (S/p,i,c)	1 1/3 % PRESENT VALUE (V/p,i,c)
1/2	0.49865312	0.49597383	0.49855011	0.49566711	0.49844719	0.49536080	0.49834435	0.49505492
1/3	0.33213682	0.33094603	0.33204537	0.33076404	0.33195401	0.33058228	0.33186273	0.33040076
1/4	0.24899075	0.24832092	0.24891363	0.24819288	0.24883660	0.24806500	0.24875963	0.24793728
1/6	0.16591929	0.16562160	0.16586221	0.16554188	0.16580518	0.16546225	0.16574821	0.16538272
1/12	0.08292240	0.08284798	0.08289102	0.08281094	0.08285968	0.08277395	0.08282837	0.08273700
1/13	0.07654111	0.07647770	0.07651195	0.07644371	0.07648281	0.07640976	0.07645371	0.07637585
1/26	0.03826263	0.03824677	0.03824744	0.03823038	0.03823227	0.03821401	0.03821712	0.03819765
1/52	0.01912933	0.01912537	0.01912159	0.01911732	0.01911385	0.01910929	0.01910613	0.01910126

TABLE A-3

COMPOUND INTEREST FOR $1
FRACTIONAL INTEREST PERIODS

$$(S/p,i,c) = \frac{(1+i)^c - 1}{i} \qquad\qquad (V/p,i,c) = \frac{1-(1+i)^{-c}}{i}$$

Columns: AMOUNT OF ANNUITY $(S/p,i,c)$ — PRESENT VALUE OF ANNUITY $(V/p,i,c)$

Table (rates 1 5/12%, 1½%, 1¾%, 1 5/6%, 2½%, 3%, 4½%, 5%)

c	1 5/12% S	1 5/12% V	1½% S	1½% V	1¾% S	1¾% V	1 5/6% S	1 5/6% V	2½% S	2½% V	3% S	3% V	4½% S	4½% V	5% S	5% V
1/2	.49824160	.49474945	.49813893	.49444440	.49783143	.49353176	.49772910	.49322838	.49691346	.49081613	.49630522	.49002406	.49449811	.48373386	.49390153	.48199854
1/3	.33177153	.33021947	.33168042	.33003841	.33140758	.32949662	.33131679	.32931648	.33059350	.32788360	.33005447	.32681843	.32845470	.32367070	.32792714	.32263706
1/4	.24868274	.24780971	.24860593	.24768230	.24837592	.24730101	.24829940	.24717423	.24768985	.24616554	.24723573	.24541546	.24588868	.24319770	.24544469	.24246905
1/6	.16569130	.16530329	.16563445	.16523395	.16546423	.16498649	.16540760	.16490752	.16495662	.16427915	.16462073	.16381173	.16362496	.16242897	.16329692	.16197442
1/12	.08279709	.08270009	.08276585	.08266322	.08267231	.08255287	.08264120	.08251618	.08239345	.08222408	.08220899	.08200674	.08162243	.08136344	.08148248	.08115185
1/13	.07642464	.07634198	.07639560	.07630815	.07630866	.07620689	.07627974	.07617321	.07604947	.07590516	.07587803	.07570570	.07537007	.07511530	.07520282	.07492111
1/26	.03820198	.03818132	.03818686	.03816500	.03814160	.03811616	.03812654	.03809991	.03800668	.03797060	.03791745	.03787437	.03765313	.03758944	.03756613	.03749570
1/52	.01909841	.01909324	.01909070	.01908523	.01906762	.01906126	.01905994	.01905328	.01899883	.01898981	.01895334	.01894257	.01881860	.01880268	.01877425	.01875665

Table (rates 1 7/12%, 1⅔%, 1 11/12%, 2%, 3½%, 4%, 5½%, 6%)

1 7/12% S	1 7/12% V	1⅔% S	1⅔% V	1 11/12% S	1 11/12% V	2% S	2% V	3½% S	3½% V	4% S	4% V	5½% S	5½% V	6% S	6% V	c
.49803635	.49413977	.49793385	.49383556	.49762686	.49292541	.49752469	.49262285	.49569993	.48724645	.49509757	.48548311	.49330780	.48027696	.49271690	.47856896	1/2
.33158939	.32985758	.33149844	.32967698	.33122609	.32913657	.33113548	.32895689	.32951834	.32576129	.32898510	.32471208	.32740237	.32161108	.32688037	.32059265	1/3
.24852910	.24755505	.24845252	.24742795	.24822295	.24704760	.24814658	.24692113	.24678417	.24467084	.24633516	.24393161	.24500317	.24174561	.24456410	.24102731	1/4
.16557765	.16514470	.16552091	.16506555	.16535103	.16482865	.16529452	.16474987	.16428684	.16334759	.16395492	.16288668	.16297080	.16152300	.16264657	.16107468	1/6
.08273464	.08262640	.08270346	.08258962	.08261011	.08247952	.08257907	.08244290	.08202568	.08179086	.08184349	.08157643	.08130362	.08094167	.08112584	.08073287	1/12
.07636659	.07627436	.07633761	.07624061	.07625085	.07613957	.07622199	.07610597	.07570766	.07550758	.07553834	.07531079	.07503661	.07472820	.07487140	.07453656	1/13
.03817176	.03814870	.03815667	.03813242	.03811150	.03808369	.03809648	.03806748	.03782879	.03777877	.03774068	.03768379	.03747967	.03740257	.03739375	.03731004	1/26
.01908300	.01907723	.01907530	.01906924	.01905227	.01904532	.01904461	.01903736	.01890814	.01889563	.01886322	.01884900	.01873019	.01871091	.01868640	.01866547	1/52

453

TABLE A-3

COMPOUND INTEREST FOR $1
FRACTIONAL INTEREST PERIODS

$$(S/p,i,c) = \frac{(1+i)^c - 1}{i} \qquad (V/p,i,c) = \frac{1-(1+i)^{-c}}{i}$$

Interest rates 6½%, 7%, 7½%, 8%

c	6½% (S/p,i,c)	6½% (V/p,i,c)	7% (S/p,i,c)	7% (V/p,i,c)	7½% (S/p,i,c)	7½% (V/p,i,c)	8% (S/p,i,c)	8% (V/p,i,c)
1/2	.49212880	.47687437	.49154348	.47519301	.49096090	.47352474	.49038106	.47186939
1/3	.32636112	.31958169	.32584460	.31857811	.32533076	.31758183	.32481960	.31659276
1/4	.24412746	.24031409	.24369321	.23960589	.24326135	.23890266	.24283184	.23820435
1/6	.16232422	.16062940	.16200372	.16018715	.16168505	.15974789	.16136821	.15931159
1/12	.08094914	.08052544	.08077351	.08031937	.08059892	.08011463	.08042538	.07991123
1/13	.07470719	.07434617	.07454398	.07415702	.07438174	.07396910	.07422048	.07378239
1/26	.03730836	.03721810	.03722349	.03712675	.03713915	.03703599	.03705532	.03694579
1/52	.01864288	.01862032	.01859964	.01857545	.01855666	.01853087	.01851395	.01848657

Interest rates 8½%, 9%, 9½%, 10%

c	8½% (S/p,i,c)	8½% (V/p,i,c)	9% (S/p,i,c)	9% (V/p,i,c)	9½% (S/p,i,c)	9½% (V/p,i,c)	10% (S/p,i,c)	10% (V/p,i,c)
1/2	.48980392	.47022681	.48922945	.46859683	.48865765	.46697931	.48808848	.46537411
1/3	.32431108	.31561081	.32380518	.31463592	.32330188	.31366799	.32280115	.31270694
1/4	.24240466	.23751089	.24197979	.23682223	.24155721	.23613832	.24113689	.23545910
1/6	.16105317	.15887820	.16073991	.15844771	.16042842	.15802008	.16011868	.15759528
1/12	.08025286	.07970913	.08008137	.07950833	.07991089	.07930881	.07974140	.07911057
1/13	.07406018	.07359688	.07390083	.07341255	.07374242	.07322941	.07358494	.07304742
1/26	.03697199	.03685617	.03688918	.03676711	.03680686	.03667861	.03672503	.03659065
1/52	.01847150	.01844254	.01842930	.01839879	.01838737	.01835531	.01834569	.01831209

Interest rates 10½%, 11%, 11½%, 12%

c	10½% (S/p,i,c)	10½% (V/p,i,c)	11% (S/p,i,c)	11% (V/p,i,c)	11½% (S/p,i,c)	11½% (V/p,i,c)	12% (S/p,i,c)	12% (V/p,i,c)
1/2	.48752192	.46378106	.48695796	.46220004	.48639656	.46063089	.48583770	.45907348
1/3	.32230298	.31175270	.32180732	.31080519	.32131417	.30986434	.32082350	.30893006
1/4	.24071882	.23478453	.24030297	.23411455	.23988933	.23344911	.23947787	.23278816
1/6	.15981067	.15717328	.15950437	.15675405	.15919977	.15633755	.15889686	.15592376
1/12	.07957291	.07891358	.07940540	.07871783	.07923886	.07852331	.07907327	.07833002
1/13	.07342838	.07286658	.07327274	.07268689	.07311801	.07250832	.07296417	.07233086
1/26	.03664370	.03650325	.03656285	.03641638	.03648247	.03633005	.03640257	.03624425
1/52	.01830426	.01826915	.01826308	.01822646	.01822214	.01818404	.01818145	.01814187

Interest rates 12½%, 13%, 13½%, 14%

c	12½% (S/p,i,c)	12½% (V/p,i,c)	13% (S/p,i,c)	13% (V/p,i,c)	13½% (S/p,i,c)	13½% (V/p,i,c)	14% (S/p,i,c)	14% (V/p,i,c)
1/2	.48528137	.45752767	.48472755	.45599332	.48417620	.45447030	.48362732	.45295849
1/3	.32033529	.30800229	.31984952	.30708096	.31936616	.30616599	.31888519	.30525731
1/4	.23906858	.23213165	.23866142	.23147954	.23825639	.23083178	.23785346	.23018831
1/6	.15859561	.15551266	.15829601	.15510420	.15797805	.15469837	.15770171	.15429514
1/12	.07890864	.07813792	.07874496	.07794703	.07858220	.07775731	.07842037	.07756876
1/13	.07281121	.07215451	.07265914	.07197924	.07250793	.07180506	.07235759	.07163195
1/26	.03632315	.03615897	.03624418	.03607421	.03616568	.03598996	.03608763	.03590622
1/52	.01814100	.01809996	.01810079	.01805830	.01806082	.01801689	.01802108	.01797573

TABLE A-3

COMPOUND INTEREST FOR $1
FRACTIONAL INTEREST PERIODS

$$(S/p,i,c) = \frac{(1+i)^{c}-1}{i} \qquad (V/p,i,c) = \frac{1-(1+i)^{-c}}{i}$$

C	AMOUNT OF ANNUITY (S/p,i,c)	PRESENT VALUE OF ANNUITY (V/p,i,c)	AMOUNT OF ANNUITY (S/p,i,c)	PRESENT VALUE OF ANNUITY (V/p,i,c)	AMOUNT OF ANNUITY (S/p,i,c)	PRESENT VALUE OF ANNUITY (V/p,i,c)	AMOUNT OF ANNUITY (S/p,i,c)	PRESENT VALUE OF ANNUITY (V/p,i,c)	C
	$14\frac{1}{2}$ %		15 %		$15\frac{1}{2}$ %		16 %		
1/2	.48308088	.45145774	.48253686	.44996795	.48199525	.44848897	.48145601	.44702068	1/2
1/3	.31840660	.30435485	.31793035	.30345855	.31745644	.30256834	.31698484	.30168415	1/3
1/4	.23745262	.22954910	.23705384	.22891410	.23665711	.22828326	.23626241	.22765654	1/4
1/6	.15740697	.15389448	.15711382	.15349636	.15682225	.15310076	.15653223	.15270765	1/6
1/12	.07825946	.07738136	.07809945	.07719511	.07794033	.07701000	.07778211	.07682600	1/12
1/13	.07220810	.07145990	.07205945	.07128889	.07191164	.07111893	.07176466	.07094999	1/13
1/26	.03601004	.03582299	.03593289	.03574025	.03585618	.03565800	.03577991	.03557625	1/26
1/52	.01798158	.01793481	.01794230	.01789414	.01790325	.01785371	.01786443	.01781351	1/52
	$16\frac{1}{2}$ %		17 %		$17\frac{1}{2}$ %		18 %		
1/2	.48091913	.44556297	.48038460	.44411572	.47985240	.44267881	.47932250	.44125212	1/2
1/3	.31651553	.30080592	.31604849	.29993358	.31558370	.29906708	.31512114	.29820634	1/3
1/4	.23586972	.22703390	.23547902	.22641529	.23509030	.22580068	.23470353	.22519001	1/4
1/6	.15624377	.15231700	.15595683	.15192879	.15567141	.15154300	.15538750	.15115960	1/6
1/12	.07762477	.07664312	.07746830	.07646133	.07731270	.07628064	.07715795	.07610102	1/12
1/13	.07161850	.07078206	.07147315	.07061514	.07132861	.07044922	.07118486	.07028429	1/13
1/26	.03570408	.03549497	.03562868	.03541418	.03555370	.03533385	.03547914	.03525400	1/26
1/52	.01782582	.01777355	.01778744	.01773382	.01774928	.01769432	.01771134	.01765505	1/52
	$18\frac{1}{2}$ %		19 %		$19\frac{1}{2}$ %		20 %		
1/2	.47879488	.43983554	.47826953	.43842896	.47774644	.43703227	.47722558	.43564535	1/2
1/3	.31466079	.29735131	.31420264	.29650192	.31374667	.29565812	.31329285	.29481986	1/3
1/4	.23431870	.22458325	.23393580	.22398037	.23355480	.22338131	.23317570	.22278604	1/4
1/6	.15510507	.15077856	.15482412	.15039987	.15454464	.15002350	.15426660	.14964942	1/6
1/12	.07700405	.07592247	.07685098	.07574498	.07669876	.07556853	.07654735	.07539312	1/12
1/13	.07104191	.07012033	.07089974	.06995735	.07075834	.06979532	.07061772	.06963423	1/13
1/26	.03540500	.03517461	.03533128	.03509569	.03525797	.03501721	.03518506	.03493919	1/26
1/52	.01767361	.01761601	.01763609	.01757719	.01759879	.01753860	.01756169	.01750022	1/52
	$20\frac{1}{2}$ %		21 %		$21\frac{1}{2}$ %		22 %		
1/2	.47670693	.43426811	.47619048	.43290043	.47567621	.43154222	.47516410	.43019336	1/2
1/3	.31284116	.29398706	.31239160	.29315967	.31194415	.29233765	.31149877	.29152092	1/3
1/4	.23279846	.22219452	.23242309	.22160672	.23204955	.22102259	.23167784	.22044210	1/4
1/6	.15399001	.14927762	.15371484	.14890807	.15344108	.14854074	.15316871	.14817562	1/6
1/12	.07639677	.07521874	.07624699	.07504537	.07609802	.07487301	.07594984	.07470165	1/12
1/13	.07047785	.06947409	.07033874	.06931488	.07020038	.06915659	.07006275	.06899921	1/13
1/26	.03511255	.03486162	.03504045	.03478449	.03496874	.03470779	.03489742	.03463153	1/26
1/52	.01752480	.01746206	.01748811	.01742412	.01745163	.01738639	.01741535	.01734888	1/52

TABLE A-3

COMPOUND INTEREST FOR $1
FRACTIONAL INTEREST PERIODS

$$(S/p,i,c) = \frac{(1+i)^c - 1}{i} \qquad (V/p,i,c) = \frac{1-(1+i)^{-c}}{i}$$

c	22½% AMOUNT OF ANNUITY (S/p,i,c)	22½% PRESENT VALUE OF ANNUITY (V/p,i,c)	23% AMOUNT OF ANNUITY (S/p,i,c)	23% PRESENT VALUE OF ANNUITY (V/p,i,c)	23½% AMOUNT OF ANNUITY (S/p,i,c)	23½% PRESENT VALUE OF ANNUITY (V/p,i,c)	24% AMOUNT OF ANNUITY (S/p,i,c)	24% PRESENT VALUE OF ANNUITY (V/p,i,c)	c
1/2	.47465414	.42885376	.47414631	.42752333	.47364059	.42620195	.47313697	.42488954	1/2
1/3	.31105547	.29070945	.31061422	.28990317	.31017500	.28910203	.30973780	.28830597	1/3
1/4	.23130794	.21986521	.23093983	.21929189	.23057351	.21872210	.23020895	.21815581	1/4
1/6	.15289774	.14781269	.15262814	.14745192	.15235991	.14709329	.15209302	.14673679	1/6
1/12	.07580244	.07453127	.07565583	.07436187	.07551000	.07419345	.07536493	.07402598	1/12
1/13	.06992587	.06884274	.06978970	.06868716	.06965427	.06853247	.06951954	.06837866	1/13
1/26	.03482648	.03455571	.03475594	.03448030	.03468577	.03440532	.03461598	.03433076	1/26
1/52	.01737926	.01731157	.01734338	.01727447	.01730769	.01723758	.01727219	.01720089	1/52

TABLE A-4

COMPOUND INTEREST FOR $1
FRACTIONAL INTEREST PERIODS

$$\text{FUTURE AMOUNT} = (1+i)^c$$
$$\text{PRESENT VALUE} = (1+i)^{-c}$$

Band 1

c	1/3 % FUTURE AMOUNT	1/3 % PRESENT VALUE	2/3 % FUTURE AMOUNT	2/3 % PRESENT VALUE	1 % FUTURE AMOUNT	1 % PRESENT VALUE	1 1/3 % FUTURE AMOUNT	1 1/3 % PRESENT VALUE
1/2	1.00166528	.99833749	1.00332780	.99668324	1.00498756	.99503719	1.00664459	.99339927
1/3	1.00110988	.99889135	1.00221730	.99778760	1.00332228	.99668872	1.00442484	.99559466
1/4	1.00083229	.99916840	1.00166252	.99834024	1.00249068	.99751551	1.00331680	.99669417
1/6	1.00055479	.99944552	1.00110804	.99889319	1.00165976	.99834299	1.00220998	.99779490
1/12	1.00027735	.99972272	1.00055387	.99944644	1.00082954	.99917115	1.00110438	.99889684
1/13	1.00025602	.99974405	1.00051125	.99948901	1.00076570	.99923488	1.00101938	.99898166
1/26	1.00012800	.99987202	1.00025559	.99974447	1.00038278	.99961737	1.00050956	.99949070
1/52	1.00006400	.99993601	1.00012779	.99987223	1.00019137	.99980867	1.00025475	.99974532

Band 2

c	1/4 % FUTURE AMOUNT	1/4 % PRESENT VALUE	7/12 % FUTURE AMOUNT	7/12 % PRESENT VALUE	11/12 % FUTURE AMOUNT	11/12 % PRESENT VALUE	1 1/4 % FUTURE AMOUNT	1 1/4 % PRESENT VALUE
1/2	1.00124922	.99875234	1.00291243	.99709603	1.00457288	.99544794	1.00623059	.99380799
1/3	1.00083264	.99916805	1.00194068	.99806308	1.00304627	.99696299	1.00414943	.99586772
1/4	1.00062441	.99937597	1.00145515	.99854696	1.00228383	.99772137	1.00311046	.99689919
1/6	1.00041623	.99958394	1.00096987	.99903107	1.00152197	.99848034	1.00207256	.99793172
1/12	1.00020809	.99979195	1.00048482	.99951542	1.00076070	.99923988	1.00103575	.99896533
1/13	1.00019209	.99980795	1.00044751	.99955269	1.00070216	.99929833	1.00095604	.99904488
1/26	1.00009604	.99990397	1.00022373	.99977632	1.00035102	.99964910	1.00047790	.99952232
1/52	1.00004802	.99995198	1.00011186	.99988815	1.00017549	.99982454	1.00023892	.99976113

Band 3

c	1/6 % FUTURE AMOUNT	1/6 % PRESENT VALUE	1/2 % FUTURE AMOUNT	1/2 % PRESENT VALUE	5/6 % FUTURE AMOUNT	5/6 % PRESENT VALUE	1 1/6 % FUTURE AMOUNT	1 1/6 % PRESENT VALUE
1/2	1.00083299	.99916771	1.00249688	.99750934	1.00415802	.99585920	1.00581642	.99421722
1/3	1.00055525	.99944506	1.00166390	.99833887	1.00277010	.99723755	1.00387386	.99614109
1/4	1.00041641	.99958377	1.00124766	.99875389	1.00207685	.99792745	1.00290399	.99710442
1/6	1.00027759	.99972249	1.00083160	.99916909	1.00138409	.99861782	1.00193506	.99806868
1/12	1.00013878	.99986124	1.00041571	.99958446	1.00069181	.99930867	1.00096706	.99903387
1/13	1.00012811	.99987191	1.00038373	.99961642	1.00063857	.99936183	1.00089264	.99910816
1/26	1.00006405	.99993595	1.00019185	.99980819	1.00031924	.99968087	1.00044622	.99955398
1/52	1.00003203	.99996798	1.00009592	.99990409	1.00015961	.99984042	1.00022309	.99977696

Band 4

c	1/12 % FUTURE AMOUNT	1/12 % PRESENT VALUE	5/12 % FUTURE AMOUNT	5/12 % PRESENT VALUE	3/4 % FUTURE AMOUNT	3/4 % PRESENT VALUE	1 1/12 % FUTURE AMOUNT	1 1/12 % PRESENT VALUE
1/2	1.00041658	.99958359	1.00208117	.99792315	1.00374299	.99627096	1.00540208	.99462695
1/3	1.00027770	.99972238	1.00138696	.99861496	1.00249378	.99751243	1.00359815	.99641475
1/4	1.00020827	.99979178	1.00104004	.99896104	1.00186975	.99813374	1.00269740	.99730986
1/6	1.00013884	.99986118	1.00069324	.99930724	1.00124611	.99875544	1.00179746	.99820577
1/12	1.00006942	.99993059	1.00034656	.99965356	1.00062286	.99937753	1.00089833	.99910248
1/13	1.00006408	.99993593	1.00031990	.99968020	1.00057494	.99942425	1.00082920	.99917149
1/26	1.00003204	.99996796	1.00015994	.99984009	1.00028743	.99971266	1.00041451	.99958566
1/52	1.00001602	.99998398	1.00007996	.99992004	1.00014370	.99985632	1.00020723	.99979281

TABLE A-4

COMPOUND INTEREST FOR $1
FRACTIONAL INTEREST PERIODS

$$\text{FUTURE AMOUNT} = (1+i)^{c}$$
$$\text{PRESENT VALUE} = (1+i)^{-c}$$

Section 1

c	1 2/3% PV	1 2/3% FA	1 7/12% PV	1 7/12% FA	1 11/12% PV	1 11/12% FA	2% PV	2% FA	3½% PV	3½% FA	4% PV	4% FA	5½% PV	5½% FA	6% PV	6% FA
1/2	.99176941	1.00829890	.99217612	1.00788558	.99055226	1.00953785	.99014754	1.00995049	.98294637	1.01734950	.98058068	1.01980390	.97358477	1.02713193	.97128586	1.02956301
1/3	.99450538	1.00552497	.99477725	1.00525017	.99369155	1.00634850	.99342086	1.00662271	.98859835	1.01153314	.98701152	1.01315940	.98231139	1.01800713	.98076444	1.01961282
1/4	.99587620	1.00414088	.99608038	1.00393505	.99526492	1.00475761	.99506158	1.00496293	.99143652	1.00863745	.99024274	1.00985341	.98670399	1.01347517	.98553836	1.01467385
1/6	.99724891	1.00275868	.99738521	1.00262165	.99684078	1.00316923	.99670500	1.00330589	.99428283	1.00575004	.99348453	1.00655820	.99111623	1.00896339	.99033552	1.00975879
1/12	.99862351	1.00137839	.99869175	1.00130997	.99841914	1.00158336	.99835114	1.00165158	.99713732	1.00287090	.99673694	1.00327374	.99554821	1.00447170	.99515603	1.00486755
1/13	.99872932	1.00127229	.99879232	1.00120914	.99854066	1.00146147	.99847788	1.00152444	.99735723	1.00264977	.99698757	1.00302153	.99588995	1.00412701	.99552781	1.00449228
1/26	.99936446	1.00063594	.99939598	1.00060439	.99927006	1.00073047	.99923865	1.00076193	.99867774	1.00132401	.99849265	1.00150963	.99794286	1.00206138	.99776140	1.00224363
1/52	.99968218	1.00031792	.99969794	1.00030215	.99963496	1.00036517	.99961925	1.00038089	.99933865	1.00066178	.99924604	1.00075453	.99897090	1.00103016	.99888007	1.00112118

Section 2

c	1 5/12% FA	1 5/12% PV	1½% FA	1½% PV	1¾% FA	1¾% PV	1 5/6% FA	1 5/6% PV	2½% FA	2½% PV	3% FA	3% PV	4½% FA	4½% PV	5% FA	5% PV
1/2	1.00705842	.99299105	1.00747208	.99258333	1.00871205	.99136319	1.00912503	.99095748	1.01242284	.98772960	1.01488916	.98532928	1.02225242	.97823198	1.02469508	.97590007
1/3	1.00470010	.99532189	1.00497521	.99504942	1.00579963	.99423381	1.00607414	.99396253	1.00826484	.99180291	1.00990163	.99019545	1.01478046	.98543482	1.01639636	.98386815
1/4	1.00352301	.99649936	1.00372909	.99628477	1.00434658	.99567223	1.00455216	.99546847	1.00619225	.99384586	1.00741707	.99263754	1.01106499	.98905610	1.01227223	.98787655
1/6	1.00234729	.99765820	1.00248452	.99752164	1.00289562	.99711274	1.00303247	.99697670	1.00412392	.99589302	1.00493862	.99508565	1.00736312	.99269070	1.00816485	.99190128
1/12	1.00117296	.99882842	1.00124149	.99876005	1.00144677	.99855532	1.00151509	.99848720	1.00205984	.99794440	1.00246627	.99753980	1.00367481	.99633865	1.00407412	.99594241
1/13	1.00108268	.99891849	1.00114593	.99885538	1.00133540	.99866846	1.00139846	.99860349	1.00190124	.99810237	1.00227634	.99772883	1.00339165	.99661981	1.00376014	.99625394
1/26	1.00054119	.99945910	1.00057280	.99942752	1.00066748	.99933297	1.00069899	.99930150	1.00095017	.99905073	1.00113752	.99886377	1.00169439	.99830848	1.00187831	.99812521
1/52	1.00027056	.99972951	1.00028636	.99971372	1.00033368	.99966643	1.00034943	.99965069	1.00047497	.99952525	1.00056860	.99943172	1.00084684	.99915388	1.00093871	.99906217

TABLE A-4

COMPOUND INTEREST FOR $1
FRACTIONAL INTEREST PERIODS

FUTURE AMOUNT $= (1+i)^c$
PRESENT VALUE $= (1+i)^{-c}$

c	6½% FUTURE AMOUNT	6½% PRESENT VALUE	7% FUTURE AMOUNT	7% PRESENT VALUE	7½% FUTURE AMOUNT	7½% PRESENT VALUE	8% FUTURE AMOUNT	8% PRESENT VALUE
1/2	1.03198837	.96900317	1.03440804	.96673649	1.03682207	.96448564	1.03923048	.96225045
1/3	1.02121347	.97922719	1.02280912	.97769953	1.02439981	.97618136	1.02598557	.97467258
1/4	1.01586828	.98437958	1.01705853	.98322759	1.01824460	.98208230	1.01942655	.98094365
1/6	1.01055107	.98955909	1.01134026	.98878690	1.01212638	.98801891	1.01290946	.98725507
1/12	1.00526169	.99476585	1.00565415	.99437764	1.00604492	.99399140	1.00643403	.99360710
1/13	1.00485597	.99516750	1.00521808	.99480901	1.00557863	.99445232	1.00593764	.99409741
1/26	1.00242504	.99758082	1.00260564	.99740113	1.00278544	.99722230	1.00296443	.99704434
1/52	1.00121179	.99878968	1.00130197	.99869972	1.00139175	.99861018	1.00148112	.99852107

c	8½% FUTURE AMOUNT	8½% PRESENT VALUE	9% FUTURE AMOUNT	9% PRESENT VALUE	9½% FUTURE AMOUNT	9½% PRESENT VALUE	10% FUTURE AMOUNT	10% PRESENT VALUE
1/2	1.04163333	.96030072	1.04403065	.95782629	1.04642248	.95563697	1.04880885	.95346259
1/3	1.02756644	.97317308	1.02914247	.97168277	1.03071368	.97020154	1.03228012	.96872931
1/4	1.02060440	.97981157	1.02177818	.97868600	1.02294793	.97756686	1.02411369	.97645409
1/6	1.01368952	.98649535	1.01446659	.98573971	1.01524070	.98498809	1.01601187	.98424047
1/12	1.00682149	.99322472	1.00720732	.99284425	1.00759153	.99246566	1.00797414	.99208894
1/13	1.00629512	.99374427	1.00665107	.99339287	1.00700553	.99304321	1.00735849	.99269526
1/26	1.00314262	.99686723	1.00332003	.99669096	1.00349665	.99651553	1.00367250	.99634093
1/52	1.00157008	.99843238	1.00165864	.99834411	1.00174680	.99825625	1.00183457	.99816879

c	10½% FUTURE AMOUNT	10½% PRESENT VALUE	11% FUTURE AMOUNT	11% PRESENT VALUE	11½% FUTURE AMOUNT	11½% PRESENT VALUE	12% FUTURE AMOUNT	12% PRESENT VALUE
1/2	1.05118980	.95130299	1.05356538	.94915800	1.05593560	.94702745	1.05830052	.94491118
1/3	1.03384181	.96726597	1.03539881	.96581143	1.03695113	.96436560	1.03849882	.96292839
1/4	1.02527548	.97534762	1.02643333	.97424740	1.02758727	.97315335	1.02873734	.97206542
1/6	1.01678012	.98349681	1.01754548	.98275705	1.01830797	.98202118	1.01906762	.98128915
1/12	1.00835516	.99171407	1.00873459	.99134104	1.00911247	.99096982	1.00948879	.99060040
1/13	1.00770998	.99234901	1.00806000	.99200444	1.00840857	.99166154	1.00875570	.99132030
1/26	1.00384759	.99616716	1.00402191	.99599420	1.00419548	.99582204	1.00436831	.99565069
1/52	1.00192195	.99808174	1.00200894	.99799509	1.00209555	.99790884	1.00218177	.99782298

c	12½% FUTURE AMOUNT	12½% PRESENT VALUE	13% FUTURE AMOUNT	13% PRESENT VALUE	13½% FUTURE AMOUNT	13½% PRESENT VALUE	14% FUTURE AMOUNT	14% PRESENT VALUE
1/2	1.06066017	.94280904	1.06301458	.94072087	1.06536379	.93864651	1.06770783	.93658581
1/3	1.04004191	.96149971	1.04158044	.96007948	1.04311443	.95866759	1.04464393	.95726398
1/4	1.02988357	.97098354	1.03102598	.96990766	1.03216461	.96883771	1.03329948	.96777364
1/6	1.01982445	.98056092	1.02057848	.97983645	1.02132974	.97911572	1.02207824	.97839868
1/12	1.00986358	.99023276	1.01023684	.98986689	1.01060860	.98950276	1.01097885	.98914037
1/13	1.00910140	.99098069	1.00944569	.99064270	1.00978857	.99030632	1.01013006	.98997153
1/26	1.00454039	.99548013	1.00471174	.99531035	1.00488237	.99514136	1.00505227	.99497313
1/52	1.00226763	.99773750	1.00235310	.99765242	1.00243821	.99756772	1.00252295	.99748340

TABLE A-4

COMPOUND INTEREST FOR $1
FRACTIONAL INTEREST PERIODS

$$\text{FUTURE AMOUNT} = (1+i)^c$$
$$\text{PRESENT VALUE} = (1+i)^{-c}$$

c	14½% Future Amount	14½% Present Value	15% Future Amount	15% Present Value	15½% Future Amount	15½% Present Value	16% Future Amount	16% Present Value
1/2	1.07004673	.93453863	1.07238053	.93250481	1.07470926	.93048421	1.07703296	.92847669
1/3	1.04616896	.95586855	1.04768955	.95448122	1.04920575	.95310191	1.05071757	.95173054
1/4	1.03443063	.96671538	1.03555808	.96566289	1.03668185	.96461609	1.03780199	.96357495
1/6	1.02282401	.97768530	1.02356707	.97697555	1.02430745	.97626938	1.02504516	.97556678
1/12	1.01134762	.98877970	1.01171492	.98842073	1.01208075	.98806345	1.01244514	.98770784
1/13	1.01047017	.98963831	1.01080892	.98930667	1.01114630	.98897657	1.01148235	.98864800
1/26	1.00522146	.99480567	1.00538993	.99463896	1.00555771	.99447301	1.00572479	.99430780
1/52	1.00260733	.99739945	1.00269134	.99731588	1.00277500	.99723268	1.00285831	.99714984

c	16½% Future Amount	16½% Present Value	17% Future Amount	17% Present Value	17½% Future Amount	17½% Present Value	18% Future Amount	18% Present Value
1/2	1.07935166	.92648211	1.08166538	.92450033	1.08397417	.92253121	1.08627805	.92057462
1/3	1.05222506	.95036702	1.05372824	.94901129	1.05522715	.94766326	1.05672181	.94632286
1/4	1.03891850	.96253941	1.04003143	.96150940	1.04114080	.96048488	1.04224664	.95945580
1/6	1.02578022	.97486770	1.02651266	.97417211	1.02724250	.97347997	1.02796975	.97279127
1/12	1.01280809	.98735389	1.01316961	.98700157	1.01352972	.98665089	1.01388843	.98630182
1/13	1.01181705	.98832096	1.01215044	.98799543	1.01248251	.98767139	1.01281328	.98734883
1/26	1.00589117	.99414333	1.00605687	.99397959	1.00622190	.99381658	1.00638625	.99365428
1/52	1.00294126	.99706736	1.00302387	.99698525	1.00310612	.99690349	1.00318804	.99682209

c	18½% Future Amount	18½% Present Value	19% Future Amount	19% Present Value	19½% Future Amount	19½% Present Value	20% Future Amount	20% Present Value
1/2	1.08857705	.91863042	1.09087121	.91669850	1.09316056	.91477871	1.09544512	.91287093
1/3	1.05821225	.94499001	1.05969850	.94366463	1.06118060	.94234667	1.06265857	.94103603
1/4	1.04334896	.95845210	1.04444780	.95744373	1.04554319	.95644065	1.04663514	.95544279
1/6	1.02869444	.97210597	1.02941658	.97142402	1.03013620	.97074542	1.03085332	.97007012
1/12	1.01424575	.98595434	1.01460169	.98560845	1.01495626	.98526414	1.01530947	.98492138
1/13	1.01314275	.98702774	1.01347095	.98670810	1.01379788	.98638991	1.01412354	.98607315
1/26	1.00654993	.99349270	1.00671294	.99333182	1.00687530	.99317164	1.00703701	.99301216
1/52	1.00326962	.99674104	1.00335086	.99666033	1.00343176	.99657997	1.00351234	.99649996

c	20½% Future Amount	20½% Present Value	21% Future Amount	21% Present Value	21½% Future Amount	21½% Present Value	22% Future Amount	22% Present Value
1/2	1.09772492	.91097504	1.10000000	.90909091	1.10227038	.90721842	1.10453610	.90535746
1/3	1.06413244	.93973265	1.06560224	.93843647	1.06706799	.93714741	1.06852973	.93586540
1/4	1.04772368	.95445012	1.04880885	.95346259	1.04989065	.95248014	1.05096913	.95150274
1/6	1.03156795	.96939809	1.03228012	.96872931	1.03298983	.96806374	1.03369712	.96740136
1/12	1.01566134	.98458016	1.01601187	.98424047	1.01636107	.98390230	1.01670896	.98356564
1/13	1.01444796	.98575781	1.01477114	.98544388	1.01509308	.98513133	1.01541381	.98482010
1/26	1.00719807	.99285337	1.00735849	.99269526	1.00751828	.99253782	1.00767743	.99238106
1/52	1.00359258	.99642028	1.00367250	.99634093	1.00375210	.99626193	1.00383138	.99618325

TABLE A-4

COMPOUND INTEREST FOR $1
FRACTIONAL INTEREST PERIODS

FUTURE AMOUNT = $(1+i)^c$
PRESENT VALUE = $(1+i)^{-c}$

C	22½% FUTURE AMOUNT	22½% PRESENT VALUE	23% FUTURE AMOUNT	23% PRESENT VALUE	23½% FUTURE AMOUNT	23½% PRESENT VALUE	24% FUTURE AMOUNT	24% PRESENT VALUE	C
1/2	1.10679718	.90350790	1.10905365	.90166963	1.11130554	.89984254	1.11355287	.89802651	1/2
1/3	1.06998748	.93459037	1.07144127	.93332227	1.07289112	.93206102	1.07433707	.93080657	1/3
1/4	1.05204429	.95053033	1.05311616	.94956287	1.05418477	.94860031	1.05525015	.94764261	1/4
1/6	1.03440199	.96674214	1.03510447	.96608606	1.03580458	.96543308	1.03650233	.96478317	1/6
1/12	1.01705555	.98323046	1.01740084	.98289677	1.01774485	.98256454	1.01808758	.98223377	1/12
1/13	1.01573332	.98451038	1.01605163	.98420195	1.01636875	.98389487	1.01668469	.98358912	1/13
1/26	1.00783596	.99222497	1.00799387	.99206953	1.00815116	.99191475	1.00830783	.99176062	1/26
1/52	1.00391033	.99610490	1.00398898	.99602687	1.00406731	.99594917	1.00414533	.99587179	1/52

TABLE A-5

EXPONENTIALS

$e^{(365/360)RT}$

RT	0.000	0.001	0.002	0.003	0.004	0.005	0.006	0.007	0.008	0.009	RT
0.00	1.00000000	1.00101440	1.00202984	1.00304630	1.00406379	1.00508232	1.00610187	1.00712247	1.00814410	1.00916676	0.00
0.01	1.01019046	1.01121520	1.01224098	1.01326780	1.01429566	1.01532457	1.01635452	1.01738551	1.01841755	1.01945063	0.01
0.02	1.02048477	1.02151995	1.02255618	1.02359347	1.02463180	1.02567119	1.02671164	1.02775314	1.02879569	1.02983931	0.02
0.03	1.03088398	1.03192971	1.03297650	1.03402436	1.03507328	1.03612326	1.03717430	1.03822642	1.03927960	1.04033385	0.03
0.04	1.04138916	1.04244555	1.04350301	1.04456154	1.04562115	1.04668183	1.04774359	1.04880642	1.04987034	1.05093533	0.04
0.05	1.05200140	1.05306855	1.05413679	1.05520611	1.05627651	1.05734800	1.05842058	1.05949424	1.06056900	1.06164484	0.05
0.06	1.06272178	1.06379981	1.06487893	1.06595915	1.06704046	1.06812287	1.06920637	1.07029098	1.07137669	1.07246349	0.06
0.07	1.07355140	1.07464042	1.07573054	1.07682176	1.07791409	1.07900753	1.08010208	1.08119774	1.08229451	1.08339239	0.07
0.08	1.08449139	1.08559150	1.08669273	1.08779507	1.08889853	1.09000312	1.09110882	1.09221564	1.09332359	1.09443266	0.08
0.09	1.09554286	1.09665418	1.09776663	1.09888021	1.09999491	1.10111075	1.10222772	1.10334582	1.10446506	1.10558543	0.09
0.10	1.10670694	1.10782959	1.10895338	1.11007830	1.11120437	1.11233158	1.11345993	1.11458943	1.11572007	1.11685186	0.10
0.11	1.11798480	1.11911889	1.12025412	1.12139051	1.12252805	1.12366673	1.12480660	1.12594761	1.12708977	1.12823310	0.11
0.12	1.12937758	1.13052322	1.13167003	1.13281800	1.13396713	1.13511743	1.13626890	1.13742153	1.13857534	1.13973031	0.12
0.13	1.14088646	1.14204378	1.14320227	1.14436194	1.14552278	1.14668480	1.14784800	1.14901239	1.15017795	1.15134469	0.13
0.14	1.15251262	1.15368173	1.15485203	1.15602351	1.15719619	1.15837005	1.15954511	1.16072135	1.16189879	1.16307742	0.14
0.15	1.16425725	1.16543828	1.16662050	1.16780393	1.16898855	1.17017438	1.17136141	1.17254964	1.17373908	1.17492972	0.15
0.16	1.17612157	1.17731463	1.17850891	1.17970439	1.18090108	1.18209899	1.18329812	1.18449846	1.18570002	1.18690280	0.16
0.17	1.18810679	1.18931201	1.19051846	1.19172612	1.19293501	1.19414513	1.19535647	1.19656905	1.19778285	1.19899788	0.17
0.18	1.20021415	1.20143165	1.20265039	1.20387036	1.20509157	1.20631402	1.20753771	1.20876264	1.20998881	1.21121623	0.18
0.19	1.21244489	1.21367479	1.21490595	1.21613835	1.21737201	1.21860691	1.21984307	1.22108049	1.22231915	1.22355908	0.19
0.20	1.22480026	1.22604270	1.22728640	1.22853137	1.22977759	1.23102508	1.23227384	1.23352386	1.23477515	1.23602771	0.20
0.21	1.23728154	1.23853664	1.23979302	1.24105067	1.24230959	1.24356980	1.24483128	1.24609404	1.24735808	1.24862340	0.21
0.22	1.24989001	1.25115790	1.25242708	1.25369755	1.25496930	1.25624235	1.25751668	1.25879231	1.26006923	1.26134745	0.22
0.23	1.26262697	1.26390778	1.26518989	1.26647330	1.26775802	1.26904404	1.27033136	1.27161999	1.27290992	1.27420116	0.23
0.24	1.27549372	1.27678758	1.27808276	1.27937925	1.28067706	1.28197618	1.28327662	1.28457838	1.28588146	1.28718586	0.24
0.25	1.28849159	1.28979864	1.29110701	1.29241672	1.29372775	1.29504011	1.29635380	1.29766883	1.29898519	1.30030288	0.25
0.26	1.30162191	1.30294228	1.30426399	1.30558704	1.30691143	1.30823717	1.30956424	1.31089267	1.31222244	1.31355357	0.26
0.27	1.31488604	1.31621986	1.31755504	1.31889157	1.32022946	1.32156871	1.32290931	1.32425127	1.32559460	1.32693928	0.27
0.28	1.32828534	1.32963275	1.33098154	1.33233169	1.33368321	1.33503610	1.33639037	1.33774600	1.33910302	1.34046141	0.28
0.29	1.34182118	1.34318232	1.34454485	1.34590876	1.34727406	1.34864073	1.35000880	1.35137825	1.35274910	1.35412133	0.29
0.30	1.35549495	1.35686997	1.35824638	1.35962419	1.36100340	1.36238401	1.36376601	1.36514942	1.36653423	1.36792045	0.30
0.31	1.36930807	1.37069710	1.37208754	1.37347939	1.37487265	1.37626733	1.37766342	1.37906092	1.38045985	1.38186019	0.31
0.32	1.38326195	1.38466514	1.38606975	1.38747578	1.38888324	1.39029213	1.39170244	1.39311419	1.39452737	1.39594198	0.32
0.33	1.39735803	1.39877552	1.40019444	1.40161480	1.40303660	1.40445985	1.40588453	1.40731067	1.40873825	1.41016728	0.33
0.34	1.41159775	1.41302968	1.41446307	1.41589790	1.41733419	1.41877194	1.42021115	1.42165181	1.42309394	1.42453753	0.34
0.35	1.42598259	1.42742911	1.42887710	1.43032655	1.43177748	1.43322988	1.43468375	1.43613910	1.43759593	1.43905423	0.35
0.36	1.44051401	1.44197527	1.44343801	1.44490224	1.44636796	1.44783516	1.44930384	1.45077402	1.45224569	1.45371885	0.36
0.37	1.45519351	1.45666966	1.45814731	1.45962646	1.46110711	1.46258926	1.46407292	1.46555808	1.46704475	1.46853292	0.37
0.38	1.47002260	1.47151380	1.47300651	1.47450073	1.47599647	1.47749372	1.47899250	1.48049279	1.48199461	1.48349795	0.38
0.39	1.48500281	1.48650920	1.48801712	1.48952657	1.49103755	1.49255007	1.49406411	1.49557970	1.49709682	1.49861548	0.39
0.40	1.50013568	1.50165742	1.50318071	1.50470554	1.50623191	1.50775984	1.50928932	1.51082034	1.51235293	1.51388706	0.40
0.41	1.51542275	1.51696000	1.51849881	1.52003918	1.52158111	1.52312461	1.52466967	1.52621630	1.52776450	1.52931427	0.41
0.42	1.53086561	1.53241852	1.53397301	1.53552908	1.53708673	1.53864595	1.54020676	1.54176915	1.54333313	1.54489869	0.42
0.43	1.54646584	1.54803458	1.54960491	1.55117683	1.55275035	1.55432546	1.55590218	1.55748049	1.55906040	1.56064192	0.43
0.44	1.56222504	1.56380976	1.56539610	1.56698404	1.56857359	1.57016476	1.57175754	1.57335193	1.57494795	1.57654558	0.44
0.45	1.57814483	1.57974571	1.58134821	1.58295233	1.58455808	1.58616546	1.58777447	1.58938512	1.59099739	1.59261131	0.45
0.46	1.59422686	1.59584405	1.59746287	1.59908334	1.60070546	1.60232922	1.60395463	1.60558168	1.60721039	1.60884075	0.46
0.47	1.61047276	1.61210643	1.61374176	1.61537874	1.61701739	1.61865769	1.62029967	1.62194330	1.62358861	1.62523558	0.47
0.48	1.62688422	1.62853454	1.63018653	1.63184020	1.63349554	1.63515256	1.63681127	1.63847165	1.64013372	1.64179748	0.48
0.49	1.64346293	1.64513006	1.64679888	1.64846940	1.65014161	1.65181552	1.65349113	1.65516844	1.65684744	1.65852816	0.49

EXPONENTIALS

$e^{(365/360)RT}$

RT	0.000	0.001	0.002	0.003	0.004	0.005	0.006	0.007	0.008	0.009	RT
0.50	1.66021057	1.66189469	1.66358052	1.66526807	1.66695732	1.66864829	1.67034097	1.67203537	1.67373148	1.67542932	0.50
0.51	1.67712888	1.67883017	1.68053318	1.68223792	1.68394438	1.68565258	1.68736251	1.68907418	1.69078758	1.69250272	0.51
0.52	1.69421960	1.69593822	1.69765859	1.69938070	1.70110455	1.70283016	1.70455752	1.70628662	1.70801749	1.70975010	0.52
0.53	1.71148448	1.71322062	1.71495851	1.71669817	1.71843959	1.72018279	1.72192774	1.72367447	1.72542297	1.72717325	0.53
0.54	1.72892530	1.73067912	1.73243473	1.73419212	1.73595129	1.73771224	1.73947498	1.74123951	1.74300583	1.74477394	0.54
0.55	1.74654384	1.74831554	1.75008904	1.75186434	1.75364143	1.75542033	1.75720104	1.75898355	1.76076786	1.76255399	0.55
0.56	1.76434193	1.76613169	1.76792326	1.76971664	1.77151185	1.77330887	1.77510772	1.77690840	1.77871090	1.78051523	0.56
0.57	1.78232139	1.78412938	1.78593921	1.78775087	1.78956437	1.79137971	1.79319689	1.79501592	1.79683679	1.79865950	0.57
0.58	1.80048407	1.80231048	1.80413875	1.80596888	1.80780086	1.80963470	1.81147040	1.81330796	1.81514738	1.81698867	0.58
0.59	1.81883183	1.82067686	1.82252376	1.82437253	1.82622318	1.82807571	1.82993012	1.83178640	1.83364457	1.83550463	0.59
0.60	1.83736657	1.83923040	1.84109612	1.84296373	1.84483324	1.84670465	1.84857795	1.85045315	1.85233026	1.85420927	0.60
0.61	1.85609018	1.85797300	1.85985774	1.86174438	1.86363294	1.86552342	1.86741581	1.86931012	1.87120636	1.87310451	0.61
0.62	1.87500460	1.87690661	1.87881055	1.88071642	1.88262422	1.88453396	1.88644564	1.88835926	1.89027481	1.89219231	0.62
0.63	1.89411176	1.89603315	1.89795649	1.89988179	1.90180903	1.90373823	1.90566939	1.90760251	1.90953759	1.91147463	0.63
0.64	1.91341363	1.91535460	1.91729755	1.91924246	1.92118934	1.92313820	1.92508904	1.92704186	1.92899666	1.93095344	0.64
0.65	1.93291220	1.93487295	1.93683569	1.93880043	1.94076715	1.94273587	1.94470659	1.94667930	1.94865402	1.95063074	0.65
0.66	1.95260947	1.95459020	1.95657294	1.95855770	1.96054446	1.96253325	1.96452405	1.96651686	1.96851171	1.97050857	0.66
0.67	1.97250746	1.97450838	1.97651132	1.97851630	1.98052332	1.98253237	1.98454345	1.98655658	1.98857175	1.99058896	0.67
0.68	1.99260822	1.99462953	1.99665289	1.99867830	2.00070576	2.00273529	2.00476687	2.00680051	2.00883621	2.01087398	0.68
0.69	2.01291382	2.01495572	2.01699970	2.01904575	2.02109388	2.02314408	2.02519637	2.02725073	2.02930718	2.03136572	0.69
0.70	2.03342634	2.03548905	2.03755386	2.03962076	2.04168976	2.04376085	2.04583405	2.04790935	2.04998676	2.05206627	0.70
0.71	2.05414789	2.05623163	2.05831747	2.06040544	2.06249552	2.06458772	2.06668204	2.06877849	2.07087707	2.07297777	0.71
0.72	2.07508061	2.07718558	2.07929268	2.08140192	2.08351330	2.08562682	2.08774249	2.08986030	2.09198026	2.09410237	0.72
0.73	2.09622664	2.09835306	2.10048163	2.10261237	2.10474526	2.10688032	2.10901755	2.11115694	2.11329851	2.11544224	0.73
0.74	2.11758815	2.11973624	2.12188651	2.12403896	2.12619359	2.12835041	2.13050941	2.13267061	2.13483399	2.13699958	0.74
0.75	2.13916735	2.14133733	2.14350951	2.14568389	2.14786048	2.15003928	2.15222029	2.15440350	2.15658894	2.15877659	0.75
0.76	2.16096646	2.16315855	2.16535286	2.16754940	2.16974817	2.17194917	2.17415240	2.17635787	2.17856557	2.18077552	0.76
0.77	2.18298770	2.18520213	2.18741881	2.18963773	2.19185891	2.19408234	2.19630802	2.19853596	2.20076616	2.20299863	0.77
0.78	2.20523336	2.20747035	2.20970962	2.21195115	2.21419496	2.21644105	2.21868941	2.22094006	2.22319299	2.22544820	0.78
0.79	2.22770570	2.22996549	2.23222758	2.23449195	2.23675863	2.23902760	2.24129888	2.24357246	2.24584835	2.24812654	0.79
0.80	2.25040705	2.25268987	2.25497501	2.25726246	2.25955223	2.26184433	2.26413875	2.26643550	2.26873458	2.27103599	0.80
0.81	2.27333974	2.27564582	2.27795424	2.28026501	2.28257811	2.28489357	2.28721137	2.28953152	2.29185403	2.29417890	0.81
0.82	2.29650612	2.29883570	2.30116765	2.30350196	2.30583864	2.30817769	2.31051911	2.31286291	2.31520908	2.31755764	0.82
0.83	2.31990858	2.32226190	2.32461761	2.32697571	2.32933620	2.33169908	2.33406437	2.33643205	2.33880213	2.34117462	0.83
0.84	2.34354951	2.34592682	2.34830653	2.35068866	2.35307321	2.35546017	2.35784956	2.36024137	2.36263561	2.36503227	0.84
0.85	2.36743137	2.36983290	2.37223686	2.37464327	2.37705211	2.37946340	2.38187713	2.38429332	2.38671195	2.38913304	0.85
0.86	2.39155658	2.39398259	2.39641105	2.39884198	2.40127537	2.40371123	2.40614956	2.40859037	2.41103365	2.41347941	0.86
0.87	2.41592765	2.41837837	2.42083158	2.42328728	2.42574547	2.42820616	2.43066934	2.43313502	2.43560319	2.43807388	0.87
0.88	2.44054707	2.44302277	2.44550098	2.44798170	2.45046494	2.45295070	2.45543898	2.45792978	2.46042312	2.46291898	0.88
0.89	2.46541737	2.46791830	2.47042176	2.47292776	2.47543631	2.47794740	2.48046104	2.48297722	2.48549596	2.48801726	0.89
0.90	2.49054111	2.49306752	2.49559650	2.49812804	2.50066215	2.50319883	2.50573808	2.50827991	2.51082431	2.51337130	0.90
0.91	2.51592087	2.51847303	2.52102778	2.52358512	2.52614505	2.52870758	2.53127271	2.53384044	2.53641077	2.53898372	0.91
0.92	2.54155927	2.54413743	2.54671821	2.54930161	2.55188763	2.55447628	2.55706754	2.55966144	2.56225797	2.56485713	0.92
0.93	2.56745893	2.57006337	2.57267045	2.57528017	2.57789255	2.58050757	2.58312524	2.58574557	2.58836856	2.59099421	0.93
0.94	2.59362252	2.59625350	2.59888715	2.60152347	2.60416246	2.60680413	2.60944848	2.61209551	2.61474523	2.61739764	0.94
0.95	2.62005273	2.62271052	2.62537101	2.62803419	2.63070008	2.63336867	2.63603997	2.63871397	2.64139069	2.64407013	0.95
0.96	2.64675228	2.64943715	2.65212475	2.65481507	2.65750813	2.66020391	2.66290243	2.66560369	2.66830768	2.67101442	0.96
0.97	2.67372391	2.67643614	2.67915113	2.68186886	2.68458936	2.68731262	2.69003864	2.69276742	2.69549897	2.69823329	0.97
0.98	2.70097039	2.70371026	2.70645291	2.70919835	2.71194656	2.71469757	2.71745137	2.72020796	2.72296735	2.72572953	0.98
0.99	2.72849452	2.73126232	2.73403292	2.73680633	2.73958255	2.74236159	2.74514345	2.74792813	2.75071564	2.75350598	0.99

TABLE A-5

EXPONENTIALS

e(365/360)RT

RT	0.09	0.08	0.07	0.06	0.05	0.04	0.03	0.02	0.01	0.00	RT
1.0	3.019644	2.989183	2.959029	2.929179	2.899631	2.870380	2.841425	2.812761	2.784387	2.756299	1.0
1.1	3.341861	3.308149	3.274778	3.241743	3.209041	3.176670	3.144624	3.112902	3.081501	3.050415	1.1
1.2	3.698461	3.661152	3.624219	3.587659	3.551468	3.515642	3.480178	3.445071	3.410318	3.375916	1.2
1.3	4.093112	4.051822	4.010949	3.970488	3.930435	3.890786	3.851537	3.812684	3.774223	3.736150	1.3
1.4	4.529875	4.484180	4.438945	4.394166	4.349839	4.305960	4.262522	4.219524	4.176958	4.134823	1.4
1.5	5.013245	4.962673	4.912611	4.863054	4.813997	4.765435	4.717363	4.669776	4.622669	4.576037	1.5
1.6	5.548193	5.492224	5.436821	5.381976	5.327684	5.273940	5.220739	5.168074	5.115940	5.064332	1.6
1.7	6.140223	6.078283	6.016967	5.956270	5.896185	5.836706	5.777828	5.719543	5.661846	5.604731	1.7
1.8	6.795428	6.726878	6.659019	6.591845	6.525349	6.459524	6.394362	6.329858	6.266004	6.202795	1.8
1.9	7.520547	7.444682	7.369583	7.295241	7.221649	7.148800	7.076685	7.005298	6.934631	6.864676	1.9
2.0	8.323042	8.239082	8.155969	8.073694	7.992249	7.911626	7.831816	7.752812	7.674604	7.597185	2.0
2.1	9.211168	9.118249	9.026267	8.935213	8.845078	8.755852	8.667525	8.580090	8.493537	8.407857	2.1
2.2	10.194064	10.091229	9.989432	9.888662	9.788909	9.690162	9.592411	9.495646	9.399857	9.305034	2.2
2.3	11.281841	11.168034	11.055374	10.943851	10.833453	10.724169	10.615987	10.508897	10.402887	10.297946	2.3
2.4	12.485692	12.359740	12.235059	12.111636	11.989458	11.868513	11.748787	11.630269	11.512947	11.396808	2.4
2.5	13.818002	13.678610	13.540625	13.404032	13.268817	13.134965	13.002464	12.871300	12.741458	12.612927	2.5
2.6	15.292479	15.138213	14.985504	14.834335	14.684691	14.536557	14.389917	14.244757	14.101060	13.958814	2.6
2.7	16.924292	16.753566	16.584561	16.417262	16.251650	16.087709	15.925421	15.764771	15.605741	15.448316	2.7
2.8	18.730232	18.541287	18.354249	18.169098	17.985814	17.804379	17.624775	17.446982	17.270982	17.096759	2.8
2.9	20.728878	20.519772	20.312775	20.107867	19.905025	19.704230	19.505460	19.308696	19.113916	18.921101	2.9
3.0	22.940793	22.709374	22.480289	22.253516	22.029030	21.806808	21.586828	21.369068	21.153504	20.940114	3.0
3.1	25.388735	25.132622	24.879092	24.628120	24.379680	24.133746	23.890293	23.649296	23.410730	23.174570	3.1
3.2	28.097889	27.814447	27.533864	27.256112	26.981161	26.708984	26.439553	26.172840	25.908817	25.647458	3.2
3.3	31.076129	30.782441	30.471919	30.164528	29.860238	29.559018	29.260837	28.965663	28.673468	28.384219	3.3
3.4	34.414302	34.067142	33.723484	33.383293	33.046533	32.713171	32.383171	32.056501	31.733126	31.413013	3.4
3.5	38.086547	37.702342	37.322014	36.945522	36.572828	36.203893	35.838681	35.477152	35.119271	34.764999	3.5
3.6	42.150646	41.725444	41.304532	40.887866	40.475403	40.067100	39.662917	39.262811	38.866741	38.474666	3.6
3.7	46.648412	46.177839	45.712012	45.250885	44.794409	44.342538	43.895225	43.452425	43.014092	42.580180	3.7
3.8	51.626122	51.105335	50.589801	50.079468	49.574284	49.074195	48.579151	48.089101	47.603994	47.123781	3.8
3.9	57.134987	56.558629	55.988084	55.423295	54.864204	54.310752	53.762884	53.220542	52.683671	52.152216	3.9
4.0	63.231687	62.593827	61.962402	61.337346	60.718595	60.106087	59.499757	58.899543	58.305384	57.717219	4.0
4.1	69.978947	69.273023	68.574220	67.882467	67.197691	66.519823	65.848794	65.184533	64.526974	63.876047	4.1
4.2	77.446187	76.664936	75.891566	75.125997	74.368151	73.617951	72.875317	72.140176	71.412450	70.692065	4.2
4.3	85.710233	84.845617	83.989723	83.142463	82.303750	81.473497	80.651620	79.838033	79.032654	78.235399	4.3
4.4	94.856110	93.899233	92.952010	92.014341	91.086131	90.167285	89.257708	88.357306	87.465987	86.583660	4.4
4.5	104.977916	103.918934	102.870634	101.832910	100.805654	99.788760	98.782125	97.785644	96.799215	95.822737	4.5
4.6	116.179788	115.007806	113.847645	112.699189	111.562317	110.436914	109.322864	108.220051	107.128364	106.047690	4.6
4.7	128.576978	127.279937	125.995980	124.724975	123.466791	122.221300	120.988372	119.767882	118.559704	117.363714	4.7
4.8	142.297035	140.861590	139.440626	138.033996	136.641555	135.263161	133.898672	132.547903	131.210848	129.887237	4.8
4.9	157.481116	155.892500	154.319909	152.763181	151.222158	149.696680	148.186590	146.691733	145.211957	143.747107	4.9
5.0	174.285445	172.527312	170.786915	169.064074	167.358612	165.670355	163.999128	162.344760	160.707081	159.085922	5.0
5.1	192.882912	190.937174	189.011064	187.104384	185.216938	183.348532	181.498974	179.668073	177.855642	176.061494	5.1
5.2	213.464859	211.311497	209.179858	207.069722	204.980872	202.913094	200.866175	198.834074	196.834074	194.848478	5.2
5.3	236.243041	233.859901	231.500801	229.165499	226.853754	224.565330	222.299990	220.057503	217.837637	215.640164	5.3
5.4	261.451814	258.814376	256.203544	253.619049	251.060625	248.528010	246.020943	243.539147	241.082425	238.650467	5.4
5.5	289.350538	286.431668	283.542241	280.681962	277.850537	275.047674	272.273086	269.526487	266.807594	264.116129	5.5
5.6	320.226250	316.995915	313.798167	310.632677	307.499119	304.397171	301.326515	298.286835	295.277817	292.299154	5.6
5.7	354.396615	350.821581	347.282611	343.779341	340.311410	336.878463	333.480147	330.116111	326.786011	323.489503	5.7
5.8	392.213195	388.256680	384.340077	380.462984	376.625001	372.825735	369.064794	365.341793	361.656347	358.008080	5.8
5.9	434.065066	429.686364	425.351832	421.061026	416.813504	412.608829	408.446570	404.326299	400.247591	396.210028	5.9

TABLE A-6

EXPONENTIALS

$$e^{-(365/360)RT}$$

RT	0.000	0.001	0.002	0.003	0.004	0.005	0.006	0.007	0.008	0.009	RT
0.00	1.00000000	0.99898662	0.99797428	0.99696295	0.99595266	0.99494338	0.99393513	0.99292790	0.99192170	0.99091651	0.00
0.01	0.98991234	0.98890918	0.98790705	0.98690593	0.98590582	0.98490673	0.98390865	0.98291158	0.98191552	0.98092047	0.01
0.02	0.97992643	0.97893340	0.97794137	0.97695035	0.97596034	0.97497132	0.97398331	0.97299630	0.97201029	0.97102528	0.02
0.03	0.97004127	0.96905825	0.96807623	0.96709521	0.96611518	0.96513614	0.96415809	0.96318104	0.96220498	0.96122990	0.03
0.04	0.96025582	0.95928272	0.95831060	0.95733947	0.95636933	0.95540017	0.95443199	0.95346479	0.95249858	0.95153334	0.04
0.05	0.95056908	0.94960579	0.94864349	0.94768216	0.94672180	0.94576241	0.94480400	0.94384656	0.94289009	0.94193459	0.05
0.06	0.94098006	0.94002649	0.93907389	0.93812226	0.93717159	0.93622188	0.93527314	0.93432536	0.93337853	0.93243267	0.06
0.07	0.93148777	0.93054382	0.92960083	0.92865880	0.92771772	0.92677759	0.92583842	0.92490020	0.92396292	0.92302660	0.07
0.08	0.92209123	0.92115681	0.92022333	0.91929080	0.91835921	0.91742857	0.91649887	0.91557011	0.91464230	0.91371542	0.08
0.09	0.91278949	0.91186449	0.91094043	0.91001730	0.90909511	0.90817386	0.90725354	0.90633415	0.90541569	0.90449817	0.09
0.10	0.90358157	0.90266590	0.90175117	0.90083735	0.89992447	0.89901251	0.89810147	0.89719136	0.89628216	0.89537389	0.10
0.11	0.89446654	0.89356011	0.89265460	0.89175001	0.89084643	0.88994357	0.88904172	0.88814079	0.88724077	0.88634166	0.11
0.12	0.88544347	0.88454618	0.88364980	0.88275434	0.88185977	0.88096612	0.88007337	0.87918153	0.87829058	0.87740055	0.12
0.13	0.87651141	0.87562318	0.87473584	0.87384061	0.87296387	0.87207923	0.87119549	0.87031264	0.86943068	0.86854963	0.13
0.14	0.86766946	0.86679018	0.86591180	0.86503431	0.86415770	0.86328199	0.86240716	0.86153322	0.86066016	0.85978799	0.14
0.15	0.85891670	0.85804630	0.85717677	0.85630813	0.85544037	0.85457349	0.85370749	0.85284236	0.85197811	0.85111474	0.15
0.16	0.85025224	0.84939061	0.84852986	0.84766998	0.84681098	0.84595284	0.84509557	0.84423917	0.84338364	0.84252898	0.16
0.17	0.84167518	0.84082225	0.83997018	0.83911897	0.83826863	0.83741915	0.83657053	0.83572277	0.83487587	0.83402983	0.17
0.18	0.83318464	0.83234032	0.83149684	0.83065422	0.82981246	0.82897155	0.82813149	0.82729228	0.82645367	0.82561642	0.18
0.19	0.82477976	0.82394395	0.82310898	0.82227486	0.82144159	0.82060916	0.81977758	0.81894684	0.81811694	0.81728788	0.19
0.20	0.81645966	0.81563228	0.81480898	0.81398003	0.81315516	0.81233113	0.81150794	0.81068558	0.80986405	0.80904335	0.20
0.21	0.80822349	0.80740445	0.80658625	0.80576887	0.80495233	0.80413661	0.80332172	0.80250765	0.80169441	0.80088199	0.21
0.22	0.80007040	0.79925963	0.79844968	0.79764055	0.79683224	0.79602475	0.79521808	0.79441222	0.79360719	0.79280297	0.22
0.23	0.79199956	0.79119697	0.79039519	0.78959422	0.78879406	0.78799472	0.78719619	0.78639846	0.78560154	0.78480544	0.23
0.24	0.78401013	0.78321564	0.78242195	0.78162906	0.78083698	0.78004569	0.77925522	0.77846554	0.77767666	0.77688858	0.24
0.25	0.77610130	0.77531482	0.77452914	0.77374425	0.77296015	0.77217686	0.77139435	0.77061264	0.76983172	0.76905159	0.25
0.26	0.76827225	0.76749371	0.76671595	0.76593898	0.76516279	0.76438740	0.76361278	0.76283896	0.76206592	0.76129366	0.26
0.27	0.76052218	0.75975149	0.75898157	0.75821244	0.75744409	0.75667651	0.75590972	0.75514370	0.75437845	0.75361398	0.27
0.28	0.75285029	0.75208737	0.75132522	0.75056385	0.74980325	0.74904341	0.74828435	0.74752606	0.74676854	0.74601178	0.28
0.29	0.74525579	0.74450057	0.74374611	0.74299241	0.74223948	0.74148732	0.74073591	0.73998527	0.73923539	0.73848626	0.29
0.30	0.73773790	0.73699029	0.73624345	0.73549736	0.73475202	0.73400744	0.73326362	0.73252055	0.73177823	0.73103666	0.30
0.31	0.73029585	0.72955578	0.72881641	0.72807791	0.72734045	0.72660302	0.72586670	0.72513113	0.72439630	0.72366221	0.31
0.32	0.72292887	0.72219627	0.72146442	0.72073330	0.72000293	0.71927330	0.71854440	0.71781625	0.71708883	0.71636215	0.32
0.33	0.71563621	0.71491100	0.71418653	0.71346279	0.71273978	0.71201751	0.71129597	0.71057516	0.70985508	0.70913573	0.33
0.34	0.70841711	0.70769922	0.70698205	0.70626561	0.70554990	0.70483492	0.70412065	0.70340711	0.70269430	0.70198221	0.34
0.35	0.70127084	0.70056018	0.69985025	0.69914104	0.69843255	0.69772478	0.69701772	0.69631138	0.69560576	0.69490085	0.35
0.36	0.69419665	0.69349317	0.69279040	0.69208834	0.69138700	0.69068636	0.68998644	0.68928723	0.68858872	0.68789092	0.36
0.37	0.68719383	0.68649744	0.68580176	0.68510679	0.68441252	0.68371895	0.68302609	0.68233393	0.68164247	0.68095171	0.37
0.38	0.68026165	0.67957229	0.67888363	0.67819566	0.67750840	0.67682183	0.67613595	0.67545077	0.67476629	0.67408250	0.38
0.39	0.67339940	0.67271699	0.67203528	0.67135425	0.67067392	0.66999428	0.66931532	0.66863705	0.66795947	0.66728258	0.39
0.40	0.66660637	0.66593085	0.66525601	0.66458186	0.66390839	0.66323560	0.66256349	0.66189207	0.66122132	0.66055126	0.40
0.41	0.65988187	0.65921316	0.65854513	0.65787778	0.65721110	0.65654510	0.65587977	0.65521512	0.65455112	0.65388784	0.41
0.42	0.65322520	0.65256324	0.65190195	0.65124133	0.65058138	0.64992209	0.64926348	0.64860553	0.64794825	0.64729164	0.42
0.43	0.64663695	0.64598040	0.64532578	0.64467183	0.64401853	0.64336590	0.64271393	0.64206262	0.64141197	0.64076198	0.43
0.44	0.64011264	0.63946397	0.63881595	0.63816859	0.63752189	0.63687584	0.63623045	0.63558571	0.63494162	0.63429819	0.44
0.45	0.63365540	0.63301327	0.63237179	0.63173096	0.63109078	0.63045125	0.62981237	0.62917413	0.62853654	0.62789960	0.45
0.46	0.62726330	0.62662765	0.62599264	0.62535827	0.62472455	0.62409147	0.62345903	0.62282723	0.62219608	0.62156556	0.46
0.47	0.62093568	0.62030644	0.61967684	0.61904987	0.61842254	0.61779585	0.61716979	0.61654436	0.61591957	0.61529541	0.47
0.48	0.61467189	0.61404900	0.61342673	0.61280510	0.61218410	0.61156373	0.61094399	0.61032487	0.60970638	0.60908852	0.48
0.49	0.60847129	0.60785468	0.60723869	0.60662333	0.60600859	0.60539448	0.60478099	0.60416812	0.60355587	0.60294424	0.49

TABLE A-6

EXPONENTIALS

$e^{-(365/360)RT}$

RT	0.000	0.001	0.002	0.003	0.004	0.005	0.006	0.007	0.008	0.009	RT
0.50	0.60233323	0.60172284	0.60111307	0.60050392	0.59989538	0.59928746	0.59868016	0.59807347	0.59746740	0.59686194	0.50
0.51	0.59625710	0.59565287	0.59504925	0.59444624	0.59384384	0.59324205	0.59264088	0.59204031	0.59144035	0.59084100	0.51
0.52	0.59024226	0.58964412	0.58904659	0.58844966	0.58785334	0.58725763	0.58666252	0.58606801	0.58547410	0.58488079	0.52
0.53	0.58428809	0.58369599	0.58310449	0.58251358	0.58192328	0.58133357	0.58074446	0.58015595	0.57956803	0.57898071	0.53
0.54	0.57839399	0.57780786	0.57722232	0.57663738	0.57605303	0.57546927	0.57488611	0.57430353	0.57372155	0.57314015	0.54
0.55	0.57255935	0.57197913	0.57139950	0.57082046	0.57024200	0.56966413	0.56908685	0.56851015	0.56793404	0.56735851	0.55
0.56	0.56678356	0.56620919	0.56563541	0.56506221	0.56448959	0.56391755	0.56334609	0.56277521	0.56220491	0.56163518	0.56
0.57	0.56106604	0.56049747	0.55992907	0.55936205	0.55879521	0.55822894	0.55766325	0.55709812	0.55653357	0.55596960	0.57
0.58	0.55540619	0.55484336	0.55428109	0.55371940	0.55315827	0.55259772	0.55203773	0.55147831	0.55091945	0.55036116	0.58
0.59	0.54980344	0.54924628	0.54868969	0.54813366	0.54757820	0.54702330	0.54646896	0.54591518	0.54536196	0.54480931	0.59
0.60	0.54425721	0.54370567	0.54315469	0.54260428	0.54205441	0.54150511	0.54095636	0.54040817	0.53986053	0.53931345	0.60
0.61	0.53876693	0.53822095	0.53767553	0.53713067	0.53658635	0.53604259	0.53549938	0.53495671	0.53441460	0.53387304	0.61
0.62	0.53333203	0.53279156	0.53225164	0.53171227	0.53117345	0.53063517	0.53009744	0.52956025	0.52902361	0.52848751	0.62
0.63	0.52795195	0.52741694	0.52688247	0.52634854	0.52581515	0.52528230	0.52474999	0.52421822	0.52368699	0.52315630	0.63
0.64	0.52262615	0.52209653	0.52156745	0.52103891	0.52051090	0.51998343	0.51945649	0.51893530	0.51840422	0.51787888	0.64
0.65	0.51735407	0.51682980	0.51630606	0.51578285	0.51526016	0.51473801	0.51421639	0.51369530	0.51317473	0.51265469	0.65
0.66	0.51213518	0.51161619	0.51109774	0.51057980	0.51006239	0.50954551	0.50902915	0.50851331	0.50799800	0.50748320	0.66
0.67	0.50696893	0.50645518	0.50594195	0.50542924	0.50491705	0.50440538	0.50389423	0.50338360	0.50287348	0.50236388	0.67
0.68	0.50185480	0.50134623	0.50083818	0.50033064	0.49982362	0.49931711	0.49881112	0.49830563	0.49780066	0.49729621	0.68
0.69	0.49679226	0.49628882	0.49578589	0.49528348	0.49478157	0.49428017	0.49377928	0.49327889	0.49277902	0.49227965	0.69
0.70	0.49178078	0.49128243	0.49078457	0.49028722	0.48979038	0.48929404	0.48879820	0.48830286	0.48780803	0.48731370	0.70
0.71	0.48681987	0.48632653	0.48583370	0.48534137	0.48484954	0.48435820	0.48386737	0.48337703	0.48288719	0.48239784	0.71
0.72	0.48190899	0.48142064	0.48093278	0.48044541	0.47995854	0.47947216	0.47898628	0.47850088	0.47801598	0.47753157	0.72
0.73	0.47704765	0.47656423	0.47608129	0.47559884	0.47511688	0.47463541	0.47415442	0.47367393	0.47319392	0.47271440	0.73
0.74	0.47223536	0.47175681	0.47127874	0.47080116	0.47032406	0.46984744	0.46937131	0.46889566	0.46842050	0.46794581	0.74
0.75	0.46747161	0.46699788	0.46652464	0.46605187	0.46557959	0.46510778	0.46463645	0.46416560	0.46369523	0.46322533	0.75
0.76	0.46275591	0.46228696	0.46181849	0.46135050	0.46088298	0.46041593	0.45994936	0.45948326	0.45901763	0.45855247	0.76
0.77	0.45808778	0.45762357	0.45715983	0.45669655	0.45623375	0.45577141	0.45530954	0.45484814	0.45438721	0.45392675	0.77
0.78	0.45346675	0.45300722	0.45254815	0.45208955	0.45163141	0.45117374	0.45071653	0.45025979	0.44980351	0.44934769	0.78
0.79	0.44889233	0.44843743	0.44798300	0.44752902	0.44707551	0.44662245	0.44616986	0.44571772	0.44526604	0.44481482	0.79
0.80	0.44436405	0.44391375	0.44346390	0.44301450	0.44256556	0.44211708	0.44166904	0.44122147	0.44077435	0.44032768	0.80
0.81	0.43988146	0.43943569	0.43899038	0.43854552	0.43810117	0.43765515	0.43721364	0.43677057	0.43632796	0.43588580	0.81
0.82	0.43544408	0.43500281	0.43456199	0.43412162	0.43368169	0.43324221	0.43280317	0.43236458	0.43192643	0.43148873	0.82
0.83	0.43105147	0.43061465	0.43017828	0.42974235	0.42930686	0.42887181	0.42843720	0.42800303	0.42756930	0.42713602	0.83
0.84	0.42670317	0.42627076	0.42583878	0.42540725	0.42497615	0.42454549	0.42411527	0.42368548	0.42325613	0.42282721	0.84
0.85	0.42239873	0.42197068	0.42154307	0.42111588	0.42068914	0.42026282	0.41983694	0.41941148	0.41898646	0.41856187	0.85
0.86	0.41813771	0.41771398	0.41729068	0.41686781	0.41644537	0.41602335	0.41560176	0.41518060	0.41475987	0.41433956	0.86
0.87	0.41391968	0.41350022	0.41308119	0.41266259	0.41224441	0.41182665	0.41140731	0.41099240	0.41057591	0.41015984	0.87
0.88	0.40974420	0.40932897	0.40891417	0.40849979	0.40808582	0.40767228	0.40725915	0.40684645	0.40643416	0.40602229	0.88
0.89	0.40561084	0.40519980	0.40478918	0.40437898	0.40396919	0.40355982	0.40315086	0.40274232	0.40233419	0.40192647	0.89
0.90	0.40151917	0.40111228	0.40070580	0.40029974	0.39989408	0.39948884	0.39908401	0.39867959	0.39827558	0.39787197	0.90
0.91	0.39746878	0.39706600	0.39666362	0.39626165	0.39586009	0.39545893	0.39505818	0.39465784	0.39425791	0.39385837	0.91
0.92	0.39345925	0.39306053	0.39266221	0.39226429	0.39186968	0.39146968	0.39107297	0.39067667	0.39028076	0.38988526	0.92
0.93	0.38949016	0.38909546	0.38870116	0.38830726	0.38791376	0.38752066	0.38712796	0.38673565	0.38634374	0.38595223	0.93
0.94	0.38556112	0.38517040	0.38478008	0.38439015	0.38400062	0.38361148	0.38322274	0.38283439	0.38244644	0.38205888	0.94
0.95	0.38167171	0.38128493	0.38089855	0.38051255	0.38012695	0.37974174	0.37935692	0.37897249	0.37858845	0.37820479	0.95
0.96	0.37782153	0.37743866	0.37705617	0.37667407	0.37629236	0.37591103	0.37553009	0.37514954	0.37476937	0.37438959	0.96
0.97	0.37401020	0.37363118	0.37325255	0.37287431	0.37249645	0.37211897	0.37174187	0.37136516	0.37098883	0.37061288	0.97
0.98	0.37023731	0.36986212	0.36948731	0.36911288	0.36873883	0.36836516	0.36799187	0.36761895	0.36724642	0.36687426	0.98
0.99	0.36650248	0.36613107	0.36576004	0.36538939	0.36501912	0.36464921	0.36427969	0.36391054	0.36354176	0.36317335	0.99

TABLE A-6

EXPONENTIALS

$e^{-(365/360)RT}$

RT	0.00	0.01	0.02	0.03	0.04	0.05	0.06	0.07	0.08	0.09	RT
1.0	0.362805	0.359145	0.355523	0.351936	0.348386	0.344872	0.341393	0.337949	0.334540	0.331165	1.0
1.1	0.327824	0.324517	0.321244	0.318003	0.314795	0.311620	0.308476	0.305364	0.302284	0.299234	1.1
1.2	0.296216	0.293228	0.290270	0.287342	0.284443	0.281574	0.278733	0.275921	0.273138	0.270383	1.2
1.3	0.267655	0.264955	0.262282	0.259637	0.257017	0.254425	0.251858	0.249318	0.246803	0.244313	1.3
1.4	0.241848	0.239409	0.236994	0.234603	0.232236	0.229894	0.227574	0.225279	0.223006	0.220757	1.4
1.5	0.218530	0.216325	0.214143	0.211983	0.209844	0.207728	0.205632	0.203558	0.201504	0.199472	1.5
1.6	0.197459	0.195468	0.193496	0.191544	0.189612	0.187699	0.185805	0.183931	0.182076	0.180239	1.6
1.7	0.178421	0.176621	0.174839	0.173075	0.171330	0.169601	0.167890	0.166197	0.164520	0.162861	1.7
1.8	0.161218	0.159591	0.157981	0.156388	0.154810	0.153249	0.151703	0.150172	0.148657	0.147158	1.8
1.9	0.145673	0.144204	0.142749	0.141309	0.139884	0.138473	0.137076	0.135693	0.134324	0.132969	1.9
2.0	0.131628	0.130300	0.128985	0.127684	0.126396	0.125121	0.123859	0.122610	0.121373	0.120148	2.0
2.1	0.118936	0.117737	0.116549	0.115373	0.114209	0.113057	0.111917	0.110788	0.109670	0.108564	2.1
2.2	0.107469	0.106385	0.105311	0.104249	0.103197	0.102156	0.101126	0.100106	0.099096	0.098096	2.2
2.3	0.097107	0.096127	0.095157	0.094198	0.093247	0.092307	0.091376	0.090454	0.089541	0.088638	2.3
2.4	0.087744	0.086859	0.085983	0.085115	0.084257	0.083407	0.082565	0.081732	0.080908	0.080092	2.4
2.5	0.079284	0.078484	0.077692	0.076908	0.076133	0.075365	0.074604	0.073852	0.073107	0.072369	2.5
2.6	0.071639	0.070917	0.070201	0.069493	0.068792	0.068098	0.067411	0.066731	0.066058	0.065392	2.6
2.7	0.064732	0.064079	0.063433	0.062793	0.062159	0.061532	0.060911	0.060297	0.059689	0.059087	2.7
2.8	0.058491	0.057901	0.057317	0.056738	0.056166	0.055599	0.055039	0.054483	0.053934	0.053390	2.8
2.9	0.052851	0.052318	0.051790	0.051268	0.050751	0.050239	0.049732	0.049230	0.048733	0.048242	2.9
3.0	0.047755	0.047273	0.046797	0.046325	0.045857	0.045395	0.044937	0.044483	0.044035	0.043590	3.0
3.1	0.043151	0.042715	0.042285	0.041858	0.041436	0.041018	0.040604	0.040194	0.039789	0.039388	3.1
3.2	0.038990	0.038597	0.038208	0.037822	0.037441	0.037063	0.036689	0.036319	0.035953	0.035590	3.2
3.3	0.035231	0.034875	0.034524	0.034175	0.033831	0.033489	0.033152	0.032817	0.032486	0.032158	3.3
3.4	0.031834	0.031513	0.031195	0.030880	0.030569	0.030260	0.029955	0.029653	0.029354	0.029058	3.4
3.5	0.028765	0.028474	0.028187	0.027903	0.027621	0.027343	0.027067	0.026794	0.026524	0.026256	3.5
3.6	0.025991	0.025729	0.025469	0.025212	0.024958	0.024706	0.024457	0.024210	0.023966	0.023724	3.6
3.7	0.023485	0.023248	0.023014	0.022782	0.022552	0.022324	0.022099	0.021876	0.021655	0.021437	3.7
3.8	0.021221	0.021007	0.020795	0.020585	0.020377	0.020172	0.019968	0.019767	0.019567	0.019370	3.8
3.9	0.019175	0.018981	0.018790	0.018600	0.018413	0.018227	0.018043	0.017861	0.017681	0.017502	3.9
4.0	0.017326	0.017151	0.016978	0.016807	0.016637	0.016469	0.016303	0.016139	0.015976	0.015815	4.0
4.1	0.015655	0.015497	0.015341	0.015186	0.015033	0.014881	0.014731	0.014583	0.014436	0.014290	4.1
4.2	0.014146	0.014003	0.013862	0.013722	0.013584	0.013447	0.013311	0.013177	0.013044	0.012912	4.2
4.3	0.012782	0.012653	0.012525	0.012399	0.012274	0.012150	0.012028	0.011906	0.011786	0.011667	4.3
4.4	0.011550	0.011433	0.011318	0.011204	0.011090	0.010979	0.010868	0.010758	0.010650	0.010542	4.4
4.5	0.010436	0.010331	0.010226	0.010123	0.010021	0.009920	0.009820	0.009721	0.009623	0.009526	4.5
4.6	0.009430	0.009335	0.009240	0.009147	0.009055	0.008964	0.008873	0.008784	0.008695	0.008607	4.6
4.7	0.008521	0.008435	0.008349	0.008265	0.008182	0.008099	0.008018	0.007937	0.007857	0.007777	4.7
4.8	0.007699	0.007621	0.007544	0.007468	0.007393	0.007318	0.007245	0.007172	0.007099	0.007028	4.8
4.9	0.006957	0.006886	0.006817	0.006748	0.006680	0.006613	0.006546	0.006480	0.006415	0.006350	4.9
5.0	0.006286	0.006223	0.006160	0.006098	0.006036	0.005975	0.005915	0.005855	0.005796	0.005738	5.0
5.1	0.005680	0.005623	0.005566	0.005510	0.005454	0.005399	0.005345	0.005291	0.005237	0.005184	5.1
5.2	0.005132	0.005080	0.005029	0.004978	0.004928	0.004879	0.004829	0.004781	0.004732	0.004685	5.2
5.3	0.004637	0.004591	0.004544	0.004498	0.004453	0.004408	0.004364	0.004320	0.004276	0.004233	5.3
5.4	0.004190	0.004148	0.004106	0.004065	0.004024	0.003983	0.003943	0.003903	0.003864	0.003825	5.4
5.5	0.003786	0.003748	0.003710	0.003673	0.003636	0.003599	0.003563	0.003527	0.003491	0.003456	5.5
5.6	0.003421	0.003387	0.003352	0.003319	0.003285	0.003252	0.003219	0.003187	0.003155	0.003123	5.6
5.7	0.003091	0.003060	0.003029	0.002999	0.002968	0.002938	0.002909	0.002879	0.002850	0.002822	5.7
5.8	0.002793	0.002765	0.002737	0.002710	0.002682	0.002655	0.002628	0.002602	0.002576	0.002550	5.8
5.9	0.002524	0.002498	0.002473	0.002448	0.002424	0.002399	0.002375	0.002351	0.002327	0.002304	5.9

TABLE A-7

EXPONENTIALS

$$e^{RT}$$

RT	0.000	0.001	0.002	0.003	0.004	0.005	0.006	0.007	0.008	0.009	RT
0.00	1.00000000	1.00100050	1.00200200	1.00300450	1.00400801	1.00501252	1.00601804	1.00702456	1.00803209	1.00904062	0.00
0.01	1.01005017	1.01106072	1.01207229	1.01308487	1.01409846	1.01511306	1.01612869	1.01714532	1.01816298	1.01918165	0.01
0.02	1.02020134	1.02122205	1.02224378	1.02326654	1.02429032	1.02531512	1.02634095	1.02736780	1.02839568	1.02942459	0.02
0.03	1.03045453	1.03148550	1.03251751	1.03355054	1.03458461	1.03561971	1.03665585	1.03769302	1.03873123	1.03977048	0.03
0.04	1.04081077	1.04185211	1.04289448	1.04393789	1.04498235	1.04602786	1.04707441	1.04812201	1.04917066	1.05022035	0.04
0.05	1.05127110	1.05232289	1.05337574	1.05442965	1.05548460	1.05654061	1.05759768	1.05865581	1.05971500	1.06077524	0.05
0.06	1.06183655	1.06289891	1.06396234	1.06502684	1.06609240	1.06715902	1.06822672	1.06929548	1.07036531	1.07143621	0.06
0.07	1.07250818	1.07358123	1.07465534	1.07573054	1.07680681	1.07788415	1.07896257	1.08004208	1.08112266	1.08220432	0.07
0.08	1.08328707	1.08437090	1.08545581	1.08654181	1.08762889	1.08871707	1.08980633	1.09089668	1.09198812	1.09308066	0.08
0.09	1.09417428	1.09526901	1.09636482	1.09746174	1.09855975	1.09965886	1.10075906	1.10186037	1.10296279	1.10406630	0.09
0.10	1.10517092	1.10627664	1.10738347	1.10849141	1.10960045	1.11071061	1.11182188	1.11293425	1.11404775	1.11516235	0.10
0.11	1.11627807	1.11739491	1.11851286	1.11963193	1.12075212	1.12187344	1.12299587	1.12411943	1.12524411	1.12636992	0.11
0.12	1.12749685	1.12862491	1.12975410	1.13088442	1.13201587	1.13314845	1.13428217	1.13541702	1.13655300	1.13769012	0.12
0.13	1.13882838	1.13996778	1.14110832	1.14225000	1.14339282	1.14453678	1.14568189	1.14682815	1.14797555	1.14912410	0.13
0.14	1.15027380	1.15142465	1.15257665	1.15372980	1.15488411	1.15603957	1.15719619	1.15835396	1.15951290	1.16067299	0.14
0.15	1.16183424	1.16299666	1.16416024	1.16532498	1.16649089	1.16765796	1.16882620	1.16999561	1.17116619	1.17233795	0.15
0.16	1.17351087	1.17468497	1.17586024	1.17703669	1.17821432	1.17939312	1.18057310	1.18175427	1.18293661	1.18412014	0.16
0.17	1.18530485	1.18649075	1.18767783	1.18886611	1.19005557	1.19124622	1.19243806	1.19363109	1.19482532	1.19602074	0.17
0.18	1.19721736	1.19841518	1.19961419	1.20081441	1.20201582	1.20321844	1.20442226	1.20562729	1.20683352	1.20804095	0.18
0.19	1.20924960	1.21045945	1.21167052	1.21288279	1.21409628	1.21531099	1.21652691	1.21774404	1.21896239	1.22018197	0.19
0.20	1.22140276	1.22262477	1.22384801	1.22507247	1.22629815	1.22752506	1.22875320	1.22998257	1.23121317	1.23244500	0.20
0.21	1.23367806	1.23491236	1.23614789	1.23738465	1.23862265	1.23986190	1.24110238	1.24234410	1.24358707	1.24483128	0.21
0.22	1.24607673	1.24732343	1.24857138	1.24982057	1.25107102	1.25232272	1.25357567	1.25482987	1.25608533	1.25734204	0.22
0.23	1.25860001	1.25985924	1.26111973	1.26238148	1.26364449	1.26490877	1.26617431	1.26744112	1.26870919	1.26997854	0.23
0.24	1.27124915	1.27252104	1.27379419	1.27506862	1.27634433	1.27762131	1.27889957	1.28017911	1.28145993	1.28274203	0.24
0.25	1.28402542	1.28531008	1.28659604	1.28788328	1.28917180	1.29046162	1.29175273	1.29304513	1.29433882	1.29563380	0.25
0.26	1.29693009	1.29822767	1.29952654	1.30082672	1.30212820	1.30343098	1.30473506	1.30604045	1.30734714	1.30865514	0.26
0.27	1.30996445	1.31127507	1.31258700	1.31390024	1.31521480	1.31653067	1.31784786	1.31916637	1.32048620	1.32180734	0.27
0.28	1.32312981	1.32445360	1.32577872	1.32710516	1.32843293	1.32976203	1.33109246	1.33242421	1.33375730	1.33509173	0.28
0.29	1.33642749	1.33776458	1.33910302	1.34044279	1.34178390	1.34312636	1.34447016	1.34581530	1.34716179	1.34850962	0.29
0.30	1.34985881	1.35120934	1.35256123	1.35391446	1.35526906	1.35662500	1.35798231	1.35934097	1.36070148	1.36206237	0.30
0.31	1.36342511	1.36478922	1.36615469	1.36752153	1.36888974	1.37025931	1.37163026	1.37300257	1.37437626	1.37575132	0.31
0.32	1.37712776	1.37850558	1.37988478	1.38126535	1.38264731	1.38403065	1.38541537	1.38680148	1.38818897	1.38957786	0.32
0.33	1.39096813	1.39235979	1.39375285	1.39514730	1.39654314	1.39794039	1.39933902	1.40073906	1.40214050	1.40354335	0.33
0.34	1.40494759	1.40635324	1.40776030	1.40916876	1.41057864	1.41198992	1.41340262	1.41481673	1.41623225	1.41764919	0.34
0.35	1.41906755	1.42048733	1.42190852	1.42333114	1.42475519	1.42618065	1.42760755	1.42903587	1.43046562	1.43189680	0.35
0.36	1.43332941	1.43476346	1.43619894	1.43763586	1.43907421	1.44051401	1.44195524	1.44339792	1.44484204	1.44628760	0.36
0.37	1.44773461	1.44918307	1.45063298	1.45208434	1.45353715	1.45499141	1.45644713	1.45790431	1.45936294	1.46082304	0.37
0.38	1.46228459	1.46374761	1.46521209	1.46667803	1.46814544	1.46961432	1.47108467	1.47255649	1.47402978	1.47550455	0.38
0.39	1.47698079	1.47845851	1.47993771	1.48141839	1.48290055	1.48438419	1.48586932	1.48735593	1.48884403	1.49033362	0.39
0.40	1.49182470	1.49331727	1.49481133	1.49630689	1.49780395	1.49930250	1.50080255	1.50230411	1.50380716	1.50531172	0.40
0.41	1.50681779	1.50832536	1.50983444	1.51134503	1.51285713	1.51437074	1.51588587	1.51740251	1.51892067	1.52044035	0.41
0.42	1.52196156	1.52348428	1.52500852	1.52653430	1.52806159	1.52959042	1.53112078	1.53265266	1.53418608	1.53572103	0.42
0.43	1.53725752	1.53879555	1.54033512	1.54187622	1.54341887	1.54496306	1.54650879	1.54805608	1.54960491	1.55115529	0.43
0.44	1.55270722	1.55426070	1.55581574	1.55737233	1.55893049	1.56049020	1.56205147	1.56361430	1.56517870	1.56674466	0.44
0.45	1.56831219	1.56988128	1.57145195	1.57302419	1.57459800	1.57617338	1.57775034	1.57932888	1.58090900	1.58249070	0.45
0.46	1.58407398	1.58565885	1.58724530	1.58883334	1.59042297	1.59201419	1.59360700	1.59520140	1.59679740	1.59839500	0.46
0.47	1.59999419	1.60159499	1.60319738	1.60480138	1.60640699	1.60801420	1.60962302	1.61123344	1.61284548	1.61445914	0.47
0.48	1.61607440	1.61769128	1.61930979	1.62092991	1.62255165	1.62417501	1.62580000	1.62742661	1.62905485	1.63068472	0.48
0.49	1.63231622	1.63394935	1.63558412	1.63722052	1.63885856	1.64049824	1.64213956	1.64378252	1.64542712	1.64707337	0.49

TABLE A-7

EXPONENTIALS

$$e^{RT}$$

RT	0.000	0.001	0.002	0.003	0.004	0.005	0.006	0.007	0.008	0.009	RT
0.50	1.64872127	1.65037082	1.65202201	1.65367486	1.65532936	1.65698552	1.65864333	1.66030281	1.66196394	1.66362674	0.50
0.51	1.66529119	1.66695732	1.66862511	1.67029457	1.67196570	1.67363850	1.67531298	1.67698913	1.67866696	1.68034646	0.51
0.52	1.68202765	1.68371052	1.68539507	1.68708131	1.68876923	1.69045885	1.69215015	1.69384315	1.69553784	1.69723423	0.52
0.53	1.69893231	1.70063209	1.70233357	1.70403676	1.70574165	1.70744824	1.70915654	1.71086656	1.71257828	1.71429171	0.53
0.54	1.71600686	1.71772373	1.71944231	1.72116261	1.72288464	1.72460838	1.72633385	1.72806105	1.72978998	1.73152063	0.54
0.55	1.73325302	1.73498714	1.73672299	1.73846058	1.74019991	1.74194098	1.74368380	1.74542835	1.74717465	1.74892270	0.55
0.56	1.75067250	1.75242405	1.75417735	1.75593240	1.75768921	1.75944778	1.76120811	1.76297020	1.76473405	1.76649967	0.56
0.57	1.76826705	1.77003620	1.77180712	1.77357982	1.77535428	1.77713053	1.77890855	1.78068834	1.78246992	1.78425329	0.57
0.58	1.78603843	1.78782536	1.78961408	1.79140459	1.79319689	1.79499099	1.79678687	1.79858456	1.80038404	1.80218533	0.58
0.59	1.80398842	1.80579331	1.80760000	1.80940851	1.81121882	1.81303094	1.81484488	1.81666064	1.81847820	1.82029759	0.59
0.60	1.82211880	1.82394183	1.82576668	1.82759336	1.82942187	1.83125221	1.83308438	1.83491838	1.83675421	1.83859189	0.60
0.61	1.84043140	1.84227275	1.84411594	1.84596098	1.84780787	1.84965660	1.85150718	1.85335961	1.85521390	1.85707004	0.61
0.62	1.85892804	1.86078790	1.86264962	1.86451320	1.86637865	1.86824596	1.87011514	1.87198619	1.87385911	1.87573391	0.62
0.63	1.87761058	1.87948913	1.88136956	1.88325187	1.88513606	1.88702214	1.88891011	1.89079996	1.89269171	1.89458535	0.63
0.64	1.89648088	1.89837831	1.90027764	1.90217886	1.90408199	1.90598703	1.90789397	1.90980282	1.91171358	1.91362625	0.64
0.65	1.91554083	1.91745733	1.91937769	1.92129608	1.92321834	1.92514252	1.92706862	1.92899703	1.93092662	1.93285851	0.65
0.66	1.93479233	1.93672809	1.93866579	1.94060543	1.94254700	1.94449052	1.94643598	1.94838339	1.95033275	1.95228406	0.66
0.67	1.95423732	1.95619254	1.95814971	1.96010884	1.96206992	1.96403298	1.96599799	1.96796497	1.96993392	1.97190484	0.67
0.68	1.97387773	1.97585260	1.97782944	1.97980826	1.98178906	1.98377184	1.98575660	1.98774335	1.98973209	1.99172281	0.68
0.69	1.99371553	1.99571025	1.99770695	1.99970566	2.00170637	2.00370907	2.00571379	2.00772050	2.00972923	2.01173996	0.69
0.70	2.01375271	2.01576747	2.01778424	2.01980304	2.02182385	2.02384668	2.02587154	2.02789843	2.02992734	2.03195828	0.70
0.71	2.03399126	2.03602627	2.03806331	2.04010239	2.04214352	2.04418668	2.04623189	2.04827915	2.05032845	2.05237980	0.71
0.72	2.05443321	2.05648867	2.05854619	2.06060574	2.06266740	2.06473110	2.06679686	2.06886469	2.07093459	2.07300656	0.72
0.73	2.07508061	2.07715673	2.07923492	2.08131520	2.08339755	2.08548199	2.08756852	2.08965713	2.09174783	2.09384063	0.73
0.74	2.09593551	2.09803250	2.10013158	2.10223276	2.10433605	2.10644143	2.10854893	2.11065853	2.11277025	2.11488407	0.74
0.75	2.11700002	2.11911808	2.12123825	2.12336055	2.12548498	2.12761152	2.12974020	2.13187100	2.13400394	2.13613901	0.75
0.76	2.13827622	2.14041557	2.14255705	2.14470068	2.14684645	2.14899437	2.15114444	2.15329666	2.15545104	2.15760757	0.76
0.77	2.15976625	2.16192710	2.16409011	2.16625528	2.16842262	2.17059213	2.17276380	2.17493766	2.17711368	2.17929188	0.77
0.78	2.18147227	2.18365483	2.18583958	2.18802651	2.19021563	2.19240694	2.19460044	2.19679614	2.19899404	2.20119413	0.78
0.79	2.20339643	2.20560092	2.20780763	2.21001654	2.21222766	2.21444100	2.21665655	2.21887431	2.22109429	2.22331650	0.79
0.80	2.22554093	2.22776758	2.22999646	2.23222758	2.23446092	2.23669650	2.23893431	2.24117437	2.24341666	2.24566120	0.80
0.81	2.24790799	2.25015702	2.25240830	2.25466184	2.25691763	2.25917567	2.26143598	2.26369855	2.26596338	2.26823047	0.81
0.82	2.27049984	2.27277147	2.27504538	2.27732156	2.27960003	2.28188077	2.28416379	2.28644959	2.28873669	2.29102657	0.82
0.83	2.29331874	2.29561321	2.29790997	2.30020903	2.30250903	2.30481405	2.30712002	2.30942829	2.31173887	2.31405177	0.83
0.84	2.31636698	2.31868450	2.32100435	2.32332651	2.32565100	2.32797781	2.33030696	2.33263843	2.33497223	2.33730837	0.84
0.85	2.33964685	2.34198767	2.34433083	2.34667633	2.34902418	2.35137438	2.35372693	2.35608184	2.35843910	2.36079871	0.85
0.86	2.36316069	2.36552504	2.36789174	2.37026082	2.37263227	2.37500609	2.37738228	2.37976085	2.38214180	2.38452514	0.86
0.87	2.38691085	2.38929896	2.39168945	2.39408234	2.39647762	2.39887529	2.40127537	2.40367785	2.40608273	2.40849001	0.87
0.88	2.41089971	2.41331181	2.41572653	2.41814327	2.42056262	2.42298439	2.42540662	2.42783521	2.43026426	2.43269574	0.88
0.89	2.43512965	2.43756600	2.44000478	2.44244601	2.44488968	2.44733579	2.44978435	2.45223536	2.45468882	2.45714474	0.89
0.90	2.45960311	2.46206394	2.46452724	2.46699300	2.46946123	2.47193192	2.47440509	2.47688073	2.47935885	2.48183945	0.90
0.91	2.48432253	2.48680810	2.48929615	2.49178669	2.49427972	2.49677525	2.49927328	2.50177380	2.50427682	2.50678235	0.91
0.92	2.50929039	2.51180094	2.51431399	2.51682956	2.51934765	2.52186826	2.52439139	2.52691704	2.52944522	2.53197594	0.92
0.93	2.53450918	2.53704495	2.53958327	2.54212412	2.54466752	2.54721346	2.54976195	2.55231298	2.55486657	2.55742272	0.93
0.94	2.55998142	2.56254268	2.56510650	2.56767289	2.57024185	2.57281338	2.57538748	2.57796415	2.58054341	2.58312524	0.94
0.95	2.58570966	2.58829666	2.59088625	2.59347844	2.59607321	2.59867058	2.60127055	2.60387312	2.60647830	2.60908608	0.95
0.96	2.61169647	2.61430948	2.61692509	2.61954333	2.62216418	2.62478766	2.62741376	2.63004248	2.63267384	2.63530783	0.96
0.97	2.63794446	2.64058372	2.64322563	2.64587018	2.64851737	2.65116721	2.65381970	2.65647485	2.65913265	2.66179312	0.97
0.98	2.66445624	2.66712203	2.66979049	2.67246161	2.67513541	2.67781188	2.68049104	2.68317287	2.68585738	2.68854458	0.98
0.99	2.69123447	2.69392705	2.69662233	2.69932030	2.70202097	2.70472434	2.70743042	2.71013920	2.71285070	2.71556491	0.99

TABLE A-7

EXPONENTIALS

e^{RT}

RT	0.00	0.01	0.02	0.03	0.04	0.05	0.06	0.07	0.08	0.09
1.0	2.718282	2.745601	2.773195	2.801066	2.829217	2.857651	2.886371	2.915379	2.944680	2.974274
1.1	3.004166	3.034358	3.064854	3.095657	3.126768	3.158193	3.189933	3.221993	3.254374	3.287081
1.2	3.320117	3.353485	3.387188	3.421230	3.455613	3.490343	3.525421	3.560853	3.596640	3.632787
1.3	3.669297	3.706174	3.743421	3.781043	3.819044	3.857426	3.896193	3.935351	3.974902	4.014850
1.4	4.055200	4.095955	4.137120	4.178699	4.220696	4.263115	4.305960	4.349235	4.392946	4.437096
1.5	4.481689	4.526731	4.572225	4.618177	4.664590	4.711470	4.758821	4.806648	4.854956	4.903749
1.6	4.953032	5.002811	5.053090	5.103875	5.155170	5.206980	5.259311	5.312168	5.365556	5.419481
1.7	5.473947	5.528961	5.584528	5.640654	5.697343	5.754603	5.812437	5.870853	5.929856	5.989452
1.8	6.049647	6.110447	6.171858	6.233887	6.296538	6.359820	6.423737	6.488296	6.553505	6.619369
1.9	6.685894	6.753089	6.820958	6.889510	6.958751	7.028688	7.099327	7.170676	7.242743	7.315534
2.0	7.389056	7.463317	7.538325	7.614086	7.690609	7.767901	7.845970	7.924823	8.004469	8.084915
2.1	8.166170	8.248241	8.331137	8.414867	8.499438	8.584858	8.671138	8.758284	8.846306	8.935213
2.2	9.025013	9.115716	9.207331	9.299866	9.393331	9.487736	9.583089	9.679401	9.776680	9.874938
2.3	9.974182	10.074425	10.175674	10.277942	10.381237	10.485570	10.590951	10.697392	10.804903	10.913494
2.4	11.023176	11.133961	11.245859	11.358882	11.473041	11.588347	11.704812	11.822447	11.941264	12.061276
2.5	12.182494	12.304930	12.428597	12.553506	12.679671	12.807104	12.935817	13.065824	13.197138	13.329772
2.6	13.463738	13.599051	13.735724	13.873709	14.013004	14.154039	14.296289	14.439969	14.585093	14.781676
2.7	14.879732	15.029276	15.180322	15.332887	15.486985	15.642632	15.799843	15.958634	16.119021	16.281020
2.8	16.444647	16.609918	16.776851	16.945461	17.115766	17.287782	17.461527	17.637018	17.814273	17.993310
2.9	18.174145	18.356799	18.541287	18.727630	18.915846	19.105954	19.297972	19.491920	19.687817	19.885682
3.0	20.085537	20.287400	20.491292	20.697233	20.905243	21.115344	21.327557	21.541903	21.758402	21.977078
3.1	22.197951	22.421044	22.646380	22.873980	23.103867	23.336065	23.570596	23.807484	24.046754	24.288427
3.2	24.532530	24.779086	25.028120	25.279657	25.533722	25.790340	26.049537	26.311339	26.575773	26.842864
3.3	27.112639	27.385125	27.660351	27.938342	28.219127	28.502734	28.789191	29.078527	29.370771	29.665952
3.4	29.964100	30.265244	30.569415	30.876643	31.186958	31.500392	31.816977	32.136742	32.459722	32.785948
3.5	33.115452	33.448268	33.784428	34.123968	34.466919	34.813317	35.163197	35.516593	35.873541	36.234076
3.6	36.598234	36.966053	37.337568	37.712817	38.091837	38.474666	38.861343	39.251906	39.646394	40.044847
3.7	40.447304	40.853807	41.264394	41.679108	42.097990	42.521082	42.946426	43.380065	43.816042	44.256400
3.8	44.701184	45.150439	45.604208	46.062538	46.525474	46.993063	47.465351	47.942386	48.424215	48.910887
3.9	49.402449	49.898952	50.400445	50.906978	51.418601	51.935367	52.457326	52.984531	53.517034	54.054889
4.0	54.598150	55.146871	55.701106	56.260911	56.826343	57.397457	57.974311	58.556963	59.145470	59.739892
4.1	60.340288	60.946718	61.559242	62.177923	62.802821	63.434000	64.071523	64.715452	65.365853	66.022791
4.2	66.686331	67.356540	68.033484	68.717232	69.407852	70.105412	70.809983	71.521636	72.240440	72.966468
4.3	73.699794	74.440489	75.188628	75.944287	76.707539	77.478463	78.257134	79.043632	79.838033	80.640419
4.4	81.450869	82.269464	83.096285	83.931417	84.774942	85.626944	86.487509	87.356723	88.234673	89.121446
4.5	90.017131	90.921819	91.835598	92.758561	93.690800	94.632408	95.583480	96.544110	97.514394	98.494430
4.6	99.484316	100.484150	101.494032	102.514064	103.544348	104.584986	105.636082	106.697742	107.770073	108.853180
4.7	109.947172	111.052160	112.168253	113.295562	114.434202	115.584285	116.745926	117.919242	119.104350	120.301369
4.8	121.510418	122.731618	123.965091	125.210961	126.469352	127.740390	129.024202	130.309917	131.630664	132.953574
4.9	134.289780	135.639414	137.002613	138.379512	139.770250	141.174964	142.593796	144.026887	145.474382	146.936423
5.0	148.413159	149.904736	151.411304	152.933013	154.470015	156.022464	157.590516	159.174327	160.774056	162.389862
5.1	164.021907	165.670355	167.335370	169.017118	170.715768	172.431490	174.164456	175.914837	177.682811	179.468553
5.2	181.272242	183.094058	184.934184	186.792804	188.670102	190.566268	192.481491	194.415962	196.369875	198.343425
5.3	200.336810	202.350228	204.383882	206.437974	208.512710	210.608298	212.724946	214.862868	217.022275	219.203386
5.4	221.406416	223.631588	225.879123	228.149245	230.442183	232.758166	235.097424	237.460193	239.846707	242.257207
5.5	244.691932	247.151127	249.635037	252.143911	254.677999	257.237556	259.822836	262.434099	265.071606	267.735620
5.6	270.426407	273.144238	275.889383	278.662118	281.462718	284.291466	287.148643	290.034534	292.949430	295.893621
5.7	298.867401	301.871068	304.904923	307.969268	311.064411	314.190660	317.348329	320.537733	323.759190	327.013024
5.8	330.299560	333.619126	336.972054	340.358679	343.779341	347.234380	350.724144	354.248980	357.809242	361.405284
5.9	365.037468	368.706155	372.411714	376.154514	379.934930	383.753339	387.610124	391.505671	395.440368	399.414610

TABLE A-8

EXPONENTIALS

$$e^{-RT}$$

RT	0.009	0.008	0.007	0.006	0.005	0.004	0.003	0.002	0.001	0.000	RT
0.00	0.99104038	0.99203191	0.99302444	0.99401796	0.99501248	0.99600799	0.99700450	0.99800200	0.99900050	1.00000000	0.00
0.01	0.98117936	0.98216103	0.98314368	0.98412732	0.98511194	0.98609754	0.98708414	0.98807171	0.98906028	0.99004983	0.01
0.02	0.97141646	0.97238837	0.97336124	0.97433509	0.97530991	0.97628571	0.97726248	0.97824024	0.97921896	0.98019867	0.02
0.03	0.96175071	0.96271294	0.96367614	0.96464029	0.96560542	0.96657150	0.96753856	0.96850658	0.96947557	0.97044553	0.03
0.04	0.95218113	0.95313379	0.95408740	0.95504196	0.95599748	0.95695396	0.95791139	0.95886978	0.95982913	0.96078944	0.04
0.05	0.94270677	0.94364995	0.94459407	0.94553914	0.94648515	0.94743211	0.94838001	0.94932887	0.95027867	0.95122942	0.05
0.06	0.93332668	0.93426047	0.93519520	0.93613086	0.93706746	0.93800500	0.93894347	0.93988289	0.94082324	0.94176453	0.06
0.07	0.92403992	0.92496443	0.92588985	0.92681621	0.92774349	0.92867169	0.92960083	0.93053090	0.93146189	0.93239382	0.07
0.08	0.91484557	0.91576088	0.91667710	0.91759423	0.91851228	0.91943126	0.92035115	0.92127196	0.92219369	0.92311635	0.08
0.09	0.90574271	0.90664890	0.90755601	0.90846402	0.90937293	0.91028276	0.91119350	0.91210515	0.91301771	0.91393119	0.09
0.10	0.89673042	0.89762760	0.89852567	0.89942465	0.90032452	0.90122530	0.90212697	0.90302955	0.90393303	0.90483742	0.10
0.11	0.88780780	0.88869605	0.88958519	0.89047522	0.89136614	0.89225796	0.89315068	0.89404428	0.89493875	0.89583414	0.11
0.12	0.87897397	0.87985338	0.88073367	0.88161485	0.88249690	0.88337984	0.88426366	0.88514837	0.88603396	0.88692044	0.12
0.13	0.87022803	0.87109869	0.87197023	0.87284263	0.87371591	0.87459006	0.87546509	0.87634100	0.87721777	0.87809543	0.13
0.14	0.86156911	0.86243111	0.86329398	0.86415770	0.86502229	0.86588775	0.86675407	0.86762126	0.86848931	0.86935824	0.14
0.15	0.85299636	0.85384978	0.85470406	0.85555919	0.85641518	0.85727202	0.85812972	0.85898828	0.85984770	0.86070798	0.15
0.16	0.84450890	0.84535383	0.84619761	0.84704406	0.84789370	0.84874202	0.84959119	0.85044120	0.85129207	0.85214379	0.16
0.17	0.83610590	0.83694242	0.83777978	0.83861798	0.83945702	0.84029690	0.84113761	0.84197917	0.84282157	0.84366482	0.17
0.18	0.82778651	0.82861471	0.82944374	0.83027359	0.83110428	0.83193580	0.83276816	0.83360134	0.83443536	0.83527021	0.18
0.19	0.81954989	0.82036985	0.82119063	0.82201223	0.82283466	0.82365790	0.82448197	0.82530687	0.82613259	0.82695913	0.19
0.20	0.81139524	0.81220704	0.81301965	0.81383308	0.81464732	0.81546237	0.81627824	0.81709493	0.81791243	0.81873075	0.20
0.21	0.80332172	0.80412544	0.80492997	0.80573530	0.80654144	0.80734839	0.80815614	0.80896470	0.80977407	0.81058425	0.21
0.22	0.79532853	0.79612426	0.79692078	0.79771810	0.79851622	0.79931513	0.80011485	0.80091536	0.80171668	0.80251880	0.22
0.23	0.78741488	0.78820269	0.78899129	0.78978067	0.79057085	0.79136182	0.79215357	0.79294612	0.79373947	0.79453360	0.23
0.24	0.77957997	0.78035994	0.78114069	0.78192222	0.78270454	0.78348763	0.78427151	0.78505618	0.78584163	0.78662786	0.24
0.25	0.77182302	0.77259523	0.77336821	0.77414197	0.77491650	0.77569180	0.77646788	0.77724474	0.77802237	0.77880078	0.25
0.26	0.76414326	0.76490778	0.76567307	0.76643913	0.76720595	0.76797354	0.76874190	0.76951102	0.77028092	0.77105159	0.26
0.27	0.75653990	0.75729682	0.75805450	0.75881293	0.75957212	0.76033208	0.76109279	0.76185426	0.76261650	0.76337949	0.27
0.28	0.74901221	0.74976159	0.75051173	0.75126262	0.75201425	0.75276664	0.75351979	0.75427368	0.75502834	0.75578374	0.28
0.29	0.74155941	0.74230134	0.74304401	0.74378743	0.74453159	0.74527649	0.74602214	0.74676854	0.74751568	0.74826357	0.29
0.30	0.73418077	0.73491532	0.73565060	0.73638662	0.73712337	0.73786087	0.73859910	0.73933806	0.74007777	0.74081822	0.30
0.31	0.72687555	0.72760279	0.72833076	0.72905945	0.72978887	0.73051903	0.73124991	0.73198153	0.73271388	0.73344696	0.31
0.32	0.71964302	0.72036302	0.72108374	0.72180519	0.72252735	0.72325024	0.72397385	0.72469819	0.72542325	0.72614904	0.32
0.33	0.71248245	0.71319529	0.71390828	0.71462311	0.71533809	0.71605378	0.71677019	0.71748732	0.71820591	0.71892373	0.33
0.34	0.70539313	0.70609588	0.70680533	0.70751249	0.70822035	0.70892893	0.70963821	0.71034889	0.71105891	0.71177032	0.34
0.35	0.69837435	0.69907308	0.69977250	0.70047262	0.70117344	0.70187497	0.70257719	0.70328012	0.70398375	0.70468809	0.35
0.36	0.69142541	0.69211718	0.69280965	0.69350280	0.69419665	0.69489119	0.69558643	0.69628237	0.69697900	0.69767633	0.36
0.37	0.68454561	0.68523050	0.68591607	0.68660233	0.68728928	0.68797691	0.68866523	0.68935424	0.69004394	0.69073433	0.37
0.38	0.67773427	0.67841234	0.67909109	0.67977053	0.68045064	0.68113143	0.68181290	0.68249505	0.68317789	0.68386141	0.38
0.39	0.67099070	0.67166203	0.67233403	0.67300670	0.67368004	0.67435406	0.67502875	0.67570411	0.67638016	0.67705687	0.39
0.40	0.66431423	0.66497888	0.66564419	0.66631017	0.66697681	0.66764412	0.66831210	0.66898075	0.66965006	0.67032005	0.40
0.41	0.65770420	0.65836223	0.65902092	0.65968027	0.66034028	0.66100095	0.66166228	0.66232428	0.66298693	0.66365025	0.41
0.42	0.65115993	0.65181141	0.65246355	0.65311634	0.65376979	0.65442388	0.65507863	0.65573404	0.65639010	0.65704682	0.42
0.43	0.64468078	0.64532578	0.64597143	0.64661773	0.64726467	0.64791226	0.64856049	0.64920938	0.64985891	0.65050909	0.43
0.44	0.63826610	0.63890468	0.63954391	0.64018377	0.64082428	0.64146542	0.64210721	0.64274964	0.64339271	0.64403642	0.44
0.45	0.63191524	0.63254748	0.63318034	0.63381384	0.63444797	0.63508273	0.63571813	0.63635417	0.63699084	0.63762815	0.45
0.46	0.62562758	0.62625352	0.62688009	0.62750728	0.62813511	0.62876355	0.62939263	0.63002234	0.63065268	0.63128365	0.46
0.47	0.61940248	0.62002220	0.62064253	0.62126348	0.62188506	0.62250725	0.62313007	0.62375351	0.62437758	0.62500227	0.47
0.48	0.61323933	0.61385287	0.61446703	0.61508181	0.61569720	0.61631320	0.61692982	0.61754706	0.61816492	0.61878339	0.48
0.49	0.60713749	0.60774493	0.60835298	0.60896164	0.60957091	0.61018078	0.61079127	0.61140237	0.61201407	0.61262639	0.49

TABLE A-8

EXPONENTIALS

e^{-RT}

RT	0.000	0.001	0.002	0.003	0.004	0.005	0.006	0.007	0.008	0.009
0.50	0.60653066	0.60592443	0.60531881	0.60471379	0.60410938	0.60350558	0.60290237	0.60229977	0.60169777	0.60109637
0.51	0.60049558	0.59989538	0.59929579	0.59869679	0.59809839	0.59750059	0.59690339	0.59630679	0.59571078	0.59511537
0.52	0.59452055	0.59392632	0.59333270	0.59273966	0.59214722	0.59155536	0.59096410	0.59037344	0.58978336	0.58919387
0.53	0.58860497	0.58801666	0.58742894	0.58684180	0.58625525	0.58566929	0.58508391	0.58449912	0.58391492	0.58333129
0.54	0.58274825	0.58216580	0.58158392	0.58100263	0.58042192	0.57984178	0.57926223	0.57868326	0.57810486	0.57752705
0.55	0.57694981	0.57637315	0.57579706	0.57522155	0.57464662	0.57407226	0.57349848	0.57292526	0.57235263	0.57178056
0.56	0.57120906	0.57063814	0.57006779	0.56949800	0.56892879	0.56836015	0.56779207	0.56722456	0.56665762	0.56609125
0.57	0.56552544	0.56496020	0.56439552	0.56383140	0.56326786	0.56270487	0.56214245	0.56158058	0.56101928	0.56045854
0.58	0.55989837	0.55933875	0.55877969	0.55822119	0.55766325	0.55710586	0.55654903	0.55599276	0.55543705	0.55488189
0.59	0.55432728	0.55377323	0.55321974	0.55266679	0.55211440	0.55156257	0.55101128	0.55046054	0.54991036	0.54936072
0.60	0.54881164	0.54826310	0.54771511	0.54716767	0.54662077	0.54607443	0.54552863	0.54498337	0.54443866	0.54389450
0.61	0.54335087	0.54280779	0.54226525	0.54172326	0.54118181	0.54064090	0.54010052	0.53956069	0.53902140	0.53848265
0.62	0.53794444	0.53740676	0.53686962	0.53633302	0.53579696	0.53526143	0.53472643	0.53419198	0.53365805	0.53312466
0.63	0.53259180	0.53205948	0.53152768	0.53099642	0.53046569	0.52993549	0.52940582	0.52887668	0.52834806	0.52781998
0.64	0.52729242	0.52676540	0.52623889	0.52571292	0.52518747	0.52466254	0.52413814	0.52361427	0.52309091	0.52256808
0.65	0.52204578	0.52152399	0.52100273	0.52048199	0.51996177	0.51944206	0.51892288	0.51840422	0.51788607	0.51736844
0.66	0.51685133	0.51633474	0.51581866	0.51530310	0.51478806	0.51427353	0.51375951	0.51324601	0.51273602	0.51222054
0.67	0.51170858	0.51119712	0.51068618	0.51017575	0.50966583	0.50915642	0.50864752	0.50813913	0.50763124	0.50712386
0.68	0.50661699	0.50611063	0.50560477	0.50509942	0.50459457	0.50409023	0.50358639	0.50308306	0.50258023	0.50207790
0.69	0.50157607	0.50107474	0.50057392	0.50007360	0.49957377	0.49907445	0.49857562	0.49807730	0.49757947	0.49708214
0.70	0.49658530	0.49608897	0.49559313	0.49509778	0.49460293	0.49410857	0.49361471	0.49312134	0.49262847	0.49213609
0.71	0.49164420	0.49115280	0.49066189	0.49017148	0.48968155	0.48919211	0.48870316	0.48821471	0.48772673	0.48723925
0.72	0.48675226	0.48626575	0.48577972	0.48529419	0.48480914	0.48432457	0.48384049	0.48335689	0.48287377	0.48239114
0.73	0.48190899	0.48142732	0.48094614	0.48046543	0.47998520	0.47950546	0.47902619	0.47854741	0.47806910	0.47759127
0.74	0.47711392	0.47663704	0.47616064	0.47568472	0.47520927	0.47473430	0.47425980	0.47378578	0.47331223	0.47283916
0.75	0.47236655	0.47189442	0.47142276	0.47095158	0.47048086	0.47001061	0.46954084	0.46907153	0.46860270	0.46813433
0.76	0.46766643	0.46719899	0.46673203	0.46626553	0.46579950	0.46533393	0.46486883	0.46440419	0.46394002	0.46347631
0.77	0.46301307	0.46255029	0.46208797	0.46162611	0.46116472	0.46070378	0.46024331	0.45978329	0.45932374	0.45886465
0.78	0.45840601	0.45794783	0.45749012	0.45703285	0.45657605	0.45611970	0.45566381	0.45520837	0.45475339	0.45429887
0.79	0.45384480	0.45339118	0.45293801	0.45248530	0.45203304	0.45158123	0.45112988	0.45067898	0.45022852	0.44977852
0.80	0.44932896	0.44887986	0.44843120	0.44798300	0.44753524	0.44708793	0.44664106	0.44619464	0.44574867	0.44530315
0.81	0.44485807	0.44441343	0.44396924	0.44352549	0.44308219	0.44263933	0.44219691	0.44175493	0.44131340	0.44087231
0.82	0.44043165	0.43999144	0.43955167	0.43911234	0.43867345	0.43823499	0.43779698	0.43735940	0.43692226	0.43648555
0.83	0.43604929	0.43561345	0.43517806	0.43474310	0.43430857	0.43387448	0.43344082	0.43300760	0.43257481	0.43214245
0.84	0.43171052	0.43127903	0.43084797	0.43041733	0.42998713	0.42955736	0.42912802	0.42869915	0.42827062	0.42784256
0.85	0.42741493	0.42698773	0.42656096	0.42613461	0.42570869	0.42528319	0.42485812	0.42443347	0.42400925	0.42358546
0.86	0.42316208	0.42273913	0.42231660	0.42189450	0.42147281	0.42105155	0.42063071	0.42021029	0.41979029	0.41937071
0.87	0.41895155	0.41853281	0.41811448	0.41769658	0.41727909	0.41686202	0.41644537	0.41602913	0.41561331	0.41519790
0.88	0.41478291	0.41436834	0.41395417	0.41354043	0.41312709	0.41271417	0.41230167	0.41188957	0.41147789	0.41106661
0.89	0.41065575	0.41024530	0.40983526	0.40942563	0.40901641	0.40860760	0.40819920	0.40779120	0.40738361	0.40697643
0.90	0.40656966	0.40616329	0.40575733	0.40535178	0.40494663	0.40454189	0.40413755	0.40373361	0.40333008	0.40292695
0.91	0.40252422	0.40212190	0.40171998	0.40131846	0.40091734	0.40051663	0.40011631	0.39971639	0.39931688	0.39891776
0.92	0.39851904	0.39812072	0.39772280	0.39732528	0.39692815	0.39653142	0.39613509	0.39573915	0.39534361	0.39494846
0.93	0.39455371	0.39415935	0.39376539	0.39337182	0.39297865	0.39258587	0.39219348	0.39180148	0.39140987	0.39101866
0.94	0.39062784	0.39023740	0.38984736	0.38945771	0.38906844	0.38867957	0.38829109	0.38790299	0.38751528	0.38712796
0.95	0.38674102	0.38635448	0.38596831	0.38558254	0.38519715	0.38481214	0.38442752	0.38404329	0.38365944	0.38327597
0.96	0.38289289	0.38251018	0.38212787	0.38174593	0.38136437	0.38098320	0.38060241	0.38022199	0.37984196	0.37946231
0.97	0.37908304	0.37870414	0.37832563	0.37794749	0.37756973	0.37719235	0.37681535	0.37643872	0.37606247	0.37568660
0.98	0.37531110	0.37493598	0.37456123	0.37418685	0.37381285	0.37343923	0.37306597	0.37269309	0.37232059	0.37194845
0.99	0.37157669	0.37120530	0.37083428	0.37046363	0.37009335	0.36972344	0.36935391	0.36898474	0.36861594	0.36824750

TABLE A-8

EXPONENTIALS

e^{-RT}

RT	0.00	0.01	0.02	0.03	0.04	0.05	0.06	0.07	0.08	0.09
1.0	0.367879	0.364219	0.360595	0.357007	0.353455	0.349938	0.346456	0.343009	0.339596	0.336216
1.1	0.332871	0.329559	0.326280	0.323033	0.319819	0.316637	0.313486	0.310367	0.307279	0.304221
1.2	0.301194	0.298197	0.295230	0.292293	0.289384	0.286505	0.283654	0.280832	0.278037	0.275271
1.3	0.272532	0.269820	0.267135	0.264477	0.261846	0.259240	0.256661	0.254107	0.251579	0.249075
1.4	0.246597	0.244143	0.241714	0.239309	0.236928	0.234570	0.232236	0.229925	0.227638	0.225373
1.5	0.223130	0.220910	0.218712	0.216536	0.214381	0.212248	0.210136	0.208045	0.205975	0.203926
1.6	0.201897	0.199888	0.197899	0.195930	0.193980	0.192050	0.190139	0.188247	0.186374	0.184520
1.7	0.182684	0.180866	0.179066	0.177284	0.175520	0.173774	0.172045	0.170333	0.168638	0.166960
1.8	0.165299	0.163654	0.162026	0.160414	0.158817	0.157237	0.155673	0.154124	0.152590	0.151072
1.9	0.149569	0.148080	0.146607	0.145148	0.143704	0.142274	0.140858	0.139457	0.138069	0.136695
2.0	0.135335	0.133989	0.132655	0.131336	0.130029	0.128735	0.127454	0.126186	0.124930	0.123687
2.1	0.122456	0.121238	0.120032	0.118837	0.117655	0.116484	0.115325	0.114178	0.113042	0.111917
2.2	0.110803	0.109701	0.108609	0.107528	0.106459	0.105399	0.104350	0.103312	0.102284	0.101266
2.3	0.100259	0.099261	0.098274	0.097296	0.096328	0.095369	0.094420	0.093481	0.092551	0.091630
2.4	0.090718	0.089815	0.088922	0.088037	0.087161	0.086294	0.085435	0.084585	0.083743	0.082910
2.5	0.082085	0.081268	0.080460	0.079659	0.078866	0.078082	0.077305	0.076536	0.075774	0.075020
2.6	0.074274	0.073535	0.072803	0.072078	0.071361	0.070651	0.069948	0.069252	0.068563	0.067881
2.7	0.067206	0.066537	0.065875	0.065219	0.064570	0.063928	0.063292	0.062662	0.062039	0.061421
2.8	0.060810	0.060205	0.059606	0.059013	0.058426	0.057844	0.057269	0.056699	0.056135	0.055576
2.9	0.055023	0.054476	0.053934	0.053397	0.052866	0.052340	0.051819	0.051303	0.050793	0.050287
3.0	0.049787	0.049292	0.048801	0.048316	0.047835	0.047359	0.046888	0.046421	0.045959	0.045502
3.1	0.045049	0.044601	0.044157	0.043718	0.043283	0.042852	0.042426	0.042004	0.041586	0.041172
3.2	0.040762	0.040357	0.039955	0.039557	0.039164	0.038774	0.038388	0.038006	0.037628	0.037254
3.3	0.036883	0.036516	0.036153	0.035793	0.035437	0.035084	0.034735	0.034390	0.034047	0.033709
3.4	0.033373	0.033041	0.032712	0.032387	0.032065	0.031746	0.031430	0.031117	0.030807	0.030501
3.5	0.030197	0.029897	0.029599	0.029305	0.029013	0.028725	0.028439	0.028156	0.027876	0.027598
3.6	0.027324	0.027052	0.026783	0.026516	0.026252	0.025991	0.025733	0.025476	0.025223	0.024972
3.7	0.024724	0.024478	0.024234	0.023993	0.023754	0.023518	0.023284	0.023052	0.022823	0.022596
3.8	0.022371	0.022148	0.021928	0.021710	0.021494	0.021280	0.021068	0.020858	0.020651	0.020445
3.9	0.020242	0.020041	0.019841	0.019644	0.019448	0.019255	0.019063	0.018873	0.018686	0.018500
4.0	0.018316	0.018133	0.017953	0.017774	0.017597	0.017422	0.017249	0.017077	0.016907	0.016739
4.1	0.016573	0.016408	0.016245	0.016083	0.015923	0.015764	0.015608	0.015452	0.015299	0.015146
4.2	0.014996	0.014846	0.014699	0.014552	0.014408	0.014264	0.014122	0.013982	0.013843	0.013705
4.3	0.013569	0.013434	0.013300	0.013168	0.013037	0.012907	0.012778	0.012651	0.012525	0.012401
4.4	0.012277	0.012155	0.012034	0.011914	0.011796	0.011679	0.011562	0.011447	0.011333	0.011221
4.5	0.011109	0.010998	0.010889	0.010781	0.010673	0.010567	0.010462	0.010358	0.010255	0.010153
4.6	0.010052	0.009952	0.009853	0.009755	0.009658	0.009562	0.009466	0.009372	0.009279	0.009187
4.7	0.009095	0.009005	0.008915	0.008826	0.008739	0.008652	0.008566	0.008480	0.008396	0.008312
4.8	0.008230	0.008148	0.008067	0.007987	0.007907	0.007828	0.007750	0.007673	0.007597	0.007521
4.9	0.007447	0.007372	0.007299	0.007227	0.007155	0.007083	0.007013	0.006943	0.006874	0.006806
5.0	0.006738	0.006671	0.006605	0.006539	0.006474	0.006409	0.006346	0.006282	0.006220	0.006158
5.1	0.006097	0.006036	0.005976	0.005917	0.005858	0.005799	0.005742	0.005685	0.005628	0.005572
5.2	0.005517	0.005462	0.005407	0.005354	0.005300	0.005248	0.005195	0.005144	0.005092	0.005042
5.3	0.004992	0.004942	0.004893	0.004844	0.004796	0.004748	0.004701	0.004654	0.004608	0.004562
5.4	0.004517	0.004472	0.004427	0.004383	0.004339	0.004296	0.004254	0.004211	0.004169	0.004128
5.5	0.004087	0.004046	0.004006	0.003966	0.003927	0.003887	0.003849	0.003810	0.003773	0.003735
5.6	0.003698	0.003661	0.003625	0.003589	0.003553	0.003518	0.003483	0.003448	0.003414	0.003380
5.7	0.003346	0.003313	0.003280	0.003247	0.003215	0.003183	0.003151	0.003120	0.003089	0.003058
5.8	0.003028	0.002997	0.002968	0.002938	0.002909	0.002880	0.002851	0.002823	0.002795	0.002767
5.9	0.002739	0.002712	0.002685	0.002658	0.002632	0.002606	0.002580	0.002554	0.002529	0.002504

COMMON LOGARITHMS

N	0.00	0.01	0.02	0.03	0.04	0.05	0.06	0.07	0.08	0.09	N
6.0	0.77815125	0.77887447	0.77959649	0.78031731	0.78103694	0.78175537	0.78247262	0.78318869	0.78390358	0.78461729	6.0
6.1	0.78532984	0.78604121	0.78675142	0.78746047	0.78816837	0.78887512	0.78958071	0.79028516	0.79098848	0.79169065	6.1
6.2	0.79239169	0.79309160	0.79379038	0.79448805	0.79518459	0.79588002	0.79657433	0.79726754	0.79795964	0.79865065	6.2
6.3	0.79934055	0.80002936	0.80071708	0.80140371	0.80208926	0.80277373	0.80345712	0.80413943	0.80482068	0.80550086	6.3
6.4	0.80617997	0.80685803	0.80753503	0.80821097	0.80888587	0.80955971	0.81023252	0.81090428	0.81157501	0.81224470	6.4
6.5	0.81291336	0.81358099	0.81424760	0.81491318	0.81557775	0.81624130	0.81690384	0.81756537	0.81822589	0.81888541	6.5
6.6	0.81954394	0.82020146	0.82085799	0.82151353	0.82216808	0.82282165	0.82347423	0.82412583	0.82477646	0.82542612	6.6
6.7	0.82607480	0.82672252	0.82736927	0.82801506	0.82865990	0.82930377	0.82994670	0.83058867	0.83122969	0.83186977	6.7
6.8	0.83250891	0.83314711	0.83378437	0.83442070	0.83505610	0.83569057	0.83632412	0.83695674	0.83758844	0.83821922	6.8
6.9	0.83884909	0.83947805	0.84010609	0.84073323	0.84135947	0.84198480	0.84260924	0.84323278	0.84385542	0.84447718	6.9
7.0	0.84509804	0.84571802	0.84633711	0.84695533	0.84757266	0.84818912	0.84880470	0.84941941*	0.85003326	0.85064624	7.0
7.1	0.85125835	0.85186960	0.85247999	0.85308953	0.85369821	0.85430604	0.85491302	0.85551916	0.85612444	0.85672889	7.1
7.2	0.85733250	0.85793526	0.85853720	0.85913830	0.85973837	0.86033801	0.86093662	0.86153441	0.86213138	0.86272753	7.2
7.3	0.86332286	0.86391738	0.86451108	0.86510397	0.86569606	0.86628734	0.86687781	0.86746749	0.86805636	0.86864444	7.3
7.4	0.86923172	0.86981821	0.87040391	0.87098881	0.87157294	0.87215627	0.87273883	0.87332060	0.87390160	0.87448182	7.4
7.5	0.87506126	0.87563994	0.87621784	0.87679498	0.87737135	0.87794695	0.87852180	0.87909588	0.87966921	0.88024178	7.5
7.6	0.88081359	0.88138466	0.88195497	0.88252454	0.88309336	0.88366144	0.88422877	0.88479536	0.88536122	0.88592634	7.6
7.7	0.88649073	0.88705438	0.88761730	0.88817949	0.88874096	0.88930170	0.88986172	0.89042102	0.89097960	0.89153746	7.7
7.8	0.89209460	0.89265103	0.89320675	0.89376176	0.89431606	0.89486966	0.89542255	0.89597473	0.89652622	0.89707700	7.8
7.9	0.89762709	0.89817648	0.89872518	0.89927319	0.89982050	0.90036713	0.90091307	0.90145832	0.90200289	0.90254678	7.9
8.0	0.90308999	0.90363252	0.90417437	0.90471555	0.90525605	0.90579588	0.90633504	0.90687353	0.90741136	0.90794852	8.0
8.1	0.90848502	0.90902085	0.90955603	0.91009055	0.91062440	0.91115761	0.91169016	0.91222206	0.91275330	0.91328390	8.1
8.2	0.91381385	0.91434316	0.91487182	0.91539984	0.91592721	0.91645395	0.91698005	0.91750551	0.91803034	0.91855453	8.2
8.3	0.91907809	0.91960102	0.92012333	0.92064500	0.92116605	0.92168648	0.92220628	0.92272546	0.92324402	0.92376196	8.3
8.4	0.92427929	0.92479600	0.92531209	0.92582757	0.92634245	0.92685671	0.92737036	0.92788341	0.92839585	0.92890769	8.4
8.5	0.92941893	0.92992956	0.93043959	0.93094903	0.93145787	0.93196611	0.93247376	0.93298082	0.93348729	0.93399316	8.5
8.6	0.93449845	0.93500315	0.93550727	0.93601080	0.93651374	0.93701611	0.93751789	0.93801910	0.93851973	0.93901978	8.6
8.7	0.93951925	0.94001816	0.94051648	0.94101424	0.94151143	0.94200805	0.94250411	0.94299959	0.94349452	0.94398888	8.7
8.8	0.94448267	0.94497591	0.94546859	0.94596070	0.94645227	0.94694327	0.94743372	0.94792362	0.94841297	0.94890176	8.8
8.9	0.94939001	0.94987770	0.95036485	0.95085146	0.95133752	0.95182304	0.95230801	0.95279244	0.95327634	0.95375969	8.9
9.0	0.95424251	0.95472479	0.95520654	0.95568775	0.95616843	0.95664858	0.95712820	0.95760729	0.95808585	0.95856388	9.0
9.1	0.95904139	0.95951838	0.95999484	0.96047078	0.96094620	0.96142109	0.96189547	0.96236934	0.96284268	0.96331551	9.1
9.2	0.96378783	0.96425963	0.96473092	0.96520170	0.96567197	0.96614173	0.96661099	0.96707973	0.96754798	0.96801571	9.2
9.3	0.96848295	0.96894968	0.96941591	0.96988164	0.97034688	0.97081161	0.97127585	0.97173959	0.97220284	0.97266559	9.3
9.4	0.97312785	0.97358962	0.97405090	0.97451169	0.97497499	0.97543181	0.97589114	0.97634998	0.97680834	0.97726621	9.4
9.5	0.97772361	0.97818052	0.97863695	0.97909290	0.97954837	0.98000337	0.98045789	0.98091194	0.98136551	0.98181861	9.5
9.6	0.98227123	0.98272339	0.98317507	0.98362629	0.98407703	0.98452731	0.98497713	0.98542647	0.98587536	0.98632378	9.6
9.7	0.98677173	0.98721923	0.98766626	0.98811284	0.98855896	0.98900462	0.98944982	0.98989456	0.99033885	0.99078269	9.7
9.8	0.99122608	0.99166901	0.99211149	0.99255352	0.99299510	0.99343623	0.99387691	0.99431715	0.99475694	0.99519629	9.8
9.9	0.99563519	0.99607365	0.99651167	0.99694925	0.99738638	0.99782308	0.99825934	0.99869516	0.99913054	0.99956549	9.9

TABLE A-9

COMMON LOGARITHMS

N	0.00	0.01	0.02	0.03	0.04	0.05	0.06	0.07	0.08	0.09
1.0	0.00000000	0.00432137	0.00860017	0.01283722	0.01703334	0.02118930	0.02530587	0.02938378	0.03342376	0.03742650
1.1	0.04139269	0.04532298	0.04921802	0.05307844	0.05690485	0.06069784	0.06445799	0.06818586	0.07188201	0.07554696
1.2	0.07918125	0.08278537	0.08635983	0.08990511	0.09342169	0.09691001	0.10037055	0.10380372	0.10720997	0.11058971
1.3	0.11394335	0.11727130	0.12057393	0.12385164	0.12710480	0.13033377	0.13353891	0.13672057	0.13987909	0.14301480
1.4	0.14612804	0.14921911	0.15228834	0.15533604	0.15836249	0.16136800	0.16435286	0.16731733	0.17026172	0.17318627
1.5	0.17609126	0.17897695	0.18184359	0.18469143	0.18752072	0.19033170	0.19312460	0.19589965	0.19865709	0.20139712
1.6	0.20411998	0.20682588	0.20951501	0.21218760	0.21484385	0.21748394	0.22010809	0.22271647	0.22530928	0.22788670
1.7	0.23044892	0.23299611	0.23552845	0.23804610	0.24054925	0.24303805	0.24551267	0.24797327	0.25042000	0.25285303
1.8	0.25527251	0.25767857	0.26007139	0.26245109	0.26481782	0.26717173	0.26951294	0.27184161	0.27415785	0.27646180
1.9	0.27875360	0.28103337	0.28330123	0.28555731	0.28780173	0.29003461	0.29225607	0.29446623	0.29666519	0.29885308
2.0	0.30103000	0.30319606	0.30535137	0.30749604	0.30963017	0.31175386	0.31386722	0.31597035	0.31806333	0.32014629
2.1	0.32221929	0.32428246	0.32633586	0.32837960	0.33041377	0.33243846	0.33445375	0.33645973	0.33845649	0.34044411
2.2	0.34242268	0.34439227	0.34635297	0.34830486	0.35024802	0.35218252	0.35410844	0.35602586	0.35793485	0.35983548
2.3	0.36172784	0.36361198	0.36548798	0.36735592	0.36921586	0.37106786	0.37291200	0.37474835	0.37657696	0.37839790
2.4	0.38021124	0.38201704	0.38381537	0.38560627	0.38738983	0.38916608	0.39093511	0.39269695	0.39445168	0.39619935
2.5	0.39794001	0.39967372	0.40140054	0.40312052	0.40483372	0.40654018	0.40823997	0.40993312	0.41161971	0.41329976
2.6	0.41497335	0.41664051	0.41830129	0.41995575	0.42160393	0.42324587	0.42488164	0.42651126	0.42813479	0.42975228
2.7	0.43136376	0.43296929	0.43456890	0.43616265	0.43775056	0.43933269	0.44090908	0.44247977	0.44404480	0.44560420
2.8	0.44715803	0.44870632	0.45024911	0.45178644	0.45331834	0.45484486	0.45636603	0.45788190	0.45939249	0.46089784
2.9	0.46239800	0.46389299	0.46538285	0.46686762	0.46834733	0.46982202	0.47129171	0.47275645	0.47421626	0.47567119
3.0	0.47712125	0.47856650	0.48000694	0.48144263	0.48287358	0.48429984	0.48572143	0.48713838	0.48855072	0.48995848
3.1	0.49136169	0.49276039	0.49415459	0.49554434	0.49692965	0.49831055	0.49968708	0.50105926	0.50242712	0.50379068
3.2	0.50514998	0.50650503	0.50785587	0.50920252	0.51054501	0.51188336	0.51321760	0.51454775	0.51587384	0.51719590
3.3	0.51851394	0.51982799	0.52113808	0.52244423	0.52374647	0.52504481	0.52633928	0.52762990	0.52891670	0.53019970
3.4	0.53147892	0.53275438	0.53402611	0.53529412	0.53655844	0.53781910	0.53907610	0.54032947	0.54157924	0.54282543
3.5	0.54406804	0.54530712	0.54654266	0.54777471	0.54900326	0.55022835	0.55145000	0.55266822	0.55388303	0.55509445
3.6	0.55630250	0.55750720	0.55870857	0.55990663	0.56110138	0.56229286	0.56348109	0.56466606	0.56584782	0.56702637
3.7	0.56820172	0.56937391	0.57054294	0.57170883	0.57287160	0.57403127	0.57518784	0.57634135	0.57749180	0.57863921
3.8	0.57978360	0.58092498	0.58206336	0.58319877	0.58433122	0.58546073	0.58658730	0.58771097	0.58883173	0.58994960
3.9	0.59106461	0.59217676	0.59328607	0.59439255	0.59549622	0.59659710	0.59769519	0.59879051	0.59988307	0.60097290
4.0	0.60205999	0.60314437	0.60422605	0.60530505	0.60638137	0.60745502	0.60852603	0.60959441	0.61066016	0.61172331
4.1	0.61278386	0.61384182	0.61489722	0.61595005	0.61700034	0.61804810	0.61909333	0.62013605	0.62117628	0.62221402
4.2	0.62324929	0.62428210	0.62531245	0.62634037	0.62736586	0.62838893	0.62940959	0.63042788	0.63144377	0.63245729
4.3	0.63346846	0.63447727	0.63548375	0.63648790	0.63748973	0.63848926	0.63948649	0.64048144	0.64147411	0.64246452
4.4	0.64345268	0.64443859	0.64542227	0.64640373	0.64738297	0.64836001	0.64933486	0.65030752	0.65127801	0.65224634
4.5	0.65321251	0.65417654	0.65513843	0.65609820	0.65705585	0.65801140	0.65896484	0.65991620	0.66086548	0.66181269
4.6	0.66275783	0.66370093	0.66464198	0.66558099	0.66651798	0.66745295	0.66838592	0.66931688	0.67024585	0.67117284
4.7	0.67209786	0.67302091	0.67394200	0.67486114	0.67577834	0.67669361	0.67760695	0.67851838	0.67942790	0.68033551
4.8	0.68124124	0.68214508	0.68304704	0.68394713	0.68484536	0.68574174	0.68663627	0.68752896	0.68841982	0.68930886
4.9	0.69019608	0.69108149	0.69196510	0.69284692	0.69372695	0.69460520	0.69548168	0.69635639	0.69722934	0.69810055
5.0	0.69897000	0.69983773	0.70070372	0.70156799	0.70243054	0.70329138	0.70415052	0.70500796	0.70586371	0.70671778
5.1	0.70757018	0.70842090	0.70926996	0.71011737	0.71096312	0.71180723	0.71264970	0.71349054	0.71432976	0.71516736
5.2	0.71600334	0.71683772	0.71767050	0.71850169	0.71933129	0.72015930	0.72098574	0.72181062	0.72263392	0.72345567
5.3	0.72427587	0.72509452	0.72591163	0.72672721	0.72754126	0.72835378	0.72916479	0.72997429	0.73078228	0.73158877
5.4	0.73239376	0.73319727	0.73399929	0.73479983	0.73559890	0.73639650	0.73719264	0.73798733	0.73878056	0.73957234
5.5	0.74036269	0.74115160	0.74193908	0.74272513	0.74350976	0.74429298	0.74507479	0.74585520	0.74663420	0.74741181
5.6	0.74818803	0.74896286	0.74973632	0.75050839	0.75127910	0.75204845	0.75281643	0.75358306	0.75434834	0.75511227
5.7	0.75587486	0.75663611	0.75739603	0.75815462	0.75891189	0.75966784	0.76042248	0.76117581	0.76192784	0.76267856
5.8	0.76342799	0.76417613	0.76492298	0.76566855	0.76641285	0.76715587	0.76789762	0.76863810	0.76937733	0.77011529
5.9	0.77085201	0.77158748	0.77232171	0.77305469	0.77378644	0.77451697	0.77524626	0.77597433	0.77670118	0.77742682

TABLE A-10

NATURAL LOGARITHMS

N	0.00	0.01	0.02	0.03	0.04	0.05	0.06	0.07	0.08	0.09
1.0	0.00000000	0.00995033	0.01980263	0.02955880	0.03922071	0.04879016	0.05826891	0.06765865	0.07696104	0.08617770
1.1	0.09531018	0.10436002	0.11332869	0.12221763	0.13102826	0.13976194	0.14842001	0.15700375	0.16551444	0.17395331
1.2	0.18232156	0.19062036	0.19885086	0.20701417	0.21511138	0.22314355	0.23111172	0.23901690	0.24686008	0.25464222
1.3	0.26236426	0.27002714	0.27763174	0.28517894	0.29266961	0.30010459	0.30748470	0.31481074	0.32208350	0.32930375
1.4	0.33647224	0.34358970	0.35065687	0.35767444	0.36464311	0.37156356	0.37843644	0.38526240	0.39204209	0.39877612
1.5	0.40546511	0.41210965	0.41871033	0.42526774	0.43178242	0.43825493	0.44468582	0.45107562	0.45742485	0.46373402
1.6	0.47000363	0.47623418	0.48242615	0.48858001	0.49469624	0.50077529	0.50681760	0.51282363	0.51879379	0.52472853
1.7	0.53062825	0.53649337	0.54232429	0.54812141	0.55388511	0.55961579	0.56531381	0.57097955	0.57661336	0.58221562
1.8	0.58778666	0.59332685	0.59883650	0.60431597	0.60976557	0.61518564	0.62057649	0.62593843	0.63127178	0.63657683
1.9	0.64185389	0.64710324	0.65232519	0.65752000	0.66268797	0.66782937	0.67294447	0.67803354	0.68309684	0.68813464
2.0	0.69314718	0.69813472	0.70309751	0.70803579	0.71294981	0.71783979	0.72270598	0.72754861	0.73236789	0.73716407
2.1	0.74193734	0.74668795	0.75141609	0.75612198	0.76080583	0.76546784	0.77010822	0.77472717	0.77932488	0.78390154
2.2	0.78845736	0.79299252	0.79750720	0.80200159	0.80647587	0.81093022	0.81536481	0.81977983	0.82417544	0.82855182
2.3	0.83290912	0.83724752	0.84156719	0.84586827	0.85015093	0.85441533	0.85866162	0.86288996	0.86710049	0.87129337
2.4	0.87546874	0.87962675	0.88376754	0.88789126	0.89199804	0.89608802	0.90016135	0.90421815	0.90825856	0.91228271
2.5	0.91629073	0.92028275	0.92425930	0.92821930	0.93216408	0.93609336	0.94000726	0.94390590	0.94778940	0.95165788
2.6	0.95551145	0.95935022	0.96317432	0.96698385	0.97077892	0.97455964	0.97832612	0.98207847	0.98581679	0.98954119
2.7	0.99325177	0.99694863	1.00063188	1.00430161	1.00795792	1.01160091	1.01523068	1.01884732	1.02245093	1.02604160
2.8	1.02961942	1.03318448	1.03673688	1.04027671	1.04380405	1.04731899	1.05082162	1.05431203	1.05779029	1.06125650
2.9	1.06471074	1.06815308	1.07158362	1.07500242	1.07840958	1.08180517	1.08518927	1.08856195	1.09192330	1.09527339
3.0	1.09861229	1.10194008	1.10525683	1.10856262	1.11185752	1.11514159	1.11841492	1.12167756	1.12492960	1.12817109
3.1	1.13140211	1.13462273	1.13783300	1.14103300	1.14422280	1.14740245	1.15057203	1.15373159	1.15688120	1.16002092
3.2	1.16315081	1.16627094	1.16938136	1.17248214	1.17557333	1.17865500	1.18172720	1.18478998	1.18784342	1.19088756
3.3	1.19392247	1.19694819	1.19996478	1.20297230	1.20597081	1.20896035	1.21194097	1.21491274	1.21787571	1.22082992
3.4	1.22377543	1.22671229	1.22964055	1.23256026	1.23547147	1.23837423	1.24126859	1.24415459	1.24703229	1.24990174
3.5	1.25276297	1.25561604	1.25846099	1.26129787	1.26412673	1.26694760	1.26976054	1.27256560	1.27536280	1.27815220
3.6	1.28093385	1.28370777	1.28647403	1.28923265	1.29198368	1.29472717	1.29746315	1.30019166	1.30291275	1.30562646
3.7	1.30833282	1.31103188	1.31372367	1.31640823	1.31908561	1.32175584	1.32441896	1.32707500	1.32972401	1.33236602
3.8	1.33500107	1.33762919	1.34025042	1.34286480	1.34547237	1.34807315	1.35066718	1.35325451	1.35583515	1.35840916
3.9	1.36097655	1.36353737	1.36609165	1.36863943	1.37118072	1.37371558	1.37624403	1.37876609	1.38128182	1.38379123
4.0	1.38629436	1.38879124	1.39128190	1.39376638	1.39624469	1.39871688	1.40118297	1.40364300	1.40609699	1.40854497
4.1	1.41098697	1.41342303	1.41585316	1.41827741	1.42069579	1.42310833	1.42551507	1.42791604	1.43031125	1.43270073
4.2	1.43508453	1.43746265	1.43983513	1.44220199	1.44456327	1.44691898	1.44926916	1.45161383	1.45395301	1.45628673
4.3	1.45861502	1.46093790	1.46325540	1.46556754	1.46787435	1.47017585	1.47247206	1.47476301	1.47704872	1.47932923
4.4	1.48160454	1.48387469	1.48613970	1.48839958	1.49065438	1.49290410	1.49514877	1.49738841	1.49962305	1.50185270
4.5	1.50407740	1.50629715	1.50851199	1.51072194	1.51292701	1.51512723	1.51732262	1.51951320	1.52169900	1.52388000
4.6	1.52605630	1.52822786	1.53039471	1.53255687	1.53471437	1.53686722	1.53901545	1.54115907	1.54329811	1.54543258
4.7	1.54756251	1.54968791	1.55180880	1.55392520	1.55603714	1.55814462	1.56024767	1.56234630	1.56444055	1.56653041
4.8	1.56861592	1.57069708	1.57277393	1.57484647	1.57691472	1.57897870	1.58103844	1.58309394	1.58514522	1.58719230
4.9	1.58923521	1.59127394	1.59330853	1.59533899	1.59736533	1.59938758	1.60140574	1.60341984	1.60542989	1.60743591
5.0	1.60943791	1.61143592	1.61342993	1.61541998	1.61740608	1.61938824	1.62136648	1.62334082	1.62531126	1.62727783
5.1	1.62924054	1.63119940	1.63315444	1.63510566	1.63705308	1.63899671	1.64093658	1.64287269	1.64480506	1.64673370
5.2	1.64865863	1.65057986	1.65249740	1.65441128	1.65632150	1.65822808	1.66013103	1.66203036	1.66392610	1.66581825
5.3	1.66770682	1.66959184	1.67147330	1.67335124	1.67522565	1.67709656	1.67896398	1.68082791	1.68268837	1.68454538
5.4	1.68639895	1.68824909	1.69009582	1.69193913	1.69377906	1.69561561	1.69744879	1.69927862	1.70110510	1.70292826
5.5	1.70474809	1.70656462	1.70837786	1.71018782	1.71199450	1.71379793	1.71559811	1.71739505	1.71918878	1.72097929
5.6	1.72276660	1.72455072	1.72633166	1.72810944	1.72988407	1.73165555	1.73342389	1.73518912	1.73695123	1.73871025
5.7	1.74046617	1.74221902	1.74396881	1.74571553	1.74745921	1.74919985	1.75093747	1.75267208	1.75440368	1.75613229
5.8	1.75785792	1.75958057	1.76130026	1.76301700	1.76473080	1.76644166	1.76814960	1.76985463	1.77155676	1.77325600
5.9	1.77495235	1.77664583	1.77833645	1.78002421	1.78170913	1.78339122	1.78507048	1.78674693	1.78842057	1.79009141

TABLE A-10

NATURAL LOGARITHMS

N	0.00	0.01	0.02	0.03	0.04	0.05	0.06	0.07	0.08	0.09
6.0	1.79175947	1.79342475	1.79508726	1.79674701	1.79840401	1.80005827	1.80170980	1.80335861	1.80500470	1.80664808
6.1	1.80828877	1.80992677	1.81156210	1.81319475	1.81482474	1.81645208	1.81807678	1.81969884	1.82131827	1.82293509
6.2	1.82454929	1.82616090	1.82776991	1.82937633	1.83098018	1.83258146	1.83418019	1.83577635	1.83736998	1.83896107
6.3	1.84054963	1.84213568	1.84371921	1.84530024	1.84687877	1.84845481	1.85002838	1.85159947	1.85316810	1.85473427
6.4	1.85629799	1.85785927	1.85941812	1.86097454	1.86252854	1.86408013	1.86562932	1.86717611	1.86872051	1.87026253
6.5	1.87180218	1.87333946	1.87487438	1.87640694	1.87793717	1.87946505	1.88099060	1.88251383	1.88403475	1.88555335
6.6	1.88706965	1.88858365	1.89009537	1.89160480	1.89311196	1.89461685	1.89611948	1.89761986	1.89911799	1.90061387
6.7	1.90210753	1.90359895	1.90508815	1.90657514	1.90805992	1.90954250	1.91102289	1.91250109	1.91397710	1.91545094
6.8	1.91692261	1.91839212	1.91985947	1.92132467	1.92278773	1.92424865	1.92570744	1.92716411	1.92861865	1.93007109
6.9	1.93152141	1.93296964	1.93441577	1.93585981	1.93730177	1.93874166	1.94017947	1.94161522	1.94304892	1.94448056
7.0	1.94591015	1.94733770	1.94876322	1.95018671	1.95160817	1.95302762	1.95444505	1.95586048	1.95727391	1.95868534
7.1	1.96009478	1.96150224	1.96290773	1.96431123	1.96571278	1.96711236	1.96850998	1.96990565	1.97129938	1.97269117
7.2	1.97408103	1.97546895	1.97685495	1.97823904	1.97962121	1.98100147	1.98237983	1.98375629	1.98513086	1.98650355
7.3	1.98787435	1.98924327	1.99061033	1.99197552	1.99333884	1.99470031	1.99605993	1.99741771	1.99877364	2.00012773
7.4	2.00148000	2.00283044	2.00417906	2.00552586	2.00687085	2.00821403	2.00955541	2.01089500	2.01223279	2.01356880
7.5	2.01490302	2.01623547	2.01756614	2.01889504	2.02022218	2.02154756	2.02287119	2.02419307	2.02551320	2.02683159
7.6	2.02814825	2.02946317	2.03077637	2.03208785	2.03339760	2.03470565	2.03601198	2.03731662	2.03861955	2.03992078
7.7	2.04122033	2.04251819	2.04381436	2.04510886	2.04640169	2.04769284	2.04898233	2.05027016	2.05155634	2.05284086
7.8	2.05412373	2.05540496	2.05668455	2.05796251	2.05923883	2.06051353	2.06178661	2.06305806	2.06432790	2.06559613
7.9	2.06686276	2.06812778	2.06939121	2.07065304	2.07191328	2.07317193	2.07442900	2.07568449	2.07693841	2.07819076
8.0	2.07944154	2.08069076	2.08193842	2.08318453	2.08442908	2.08567209	2.08691356	2.08815348	2.08939187	2.09062873
8.1	2.09186406	2.09309787	2.09433015	2.09556092	2.09679018	2.09801793	2.09924417	2.10046891	2.10169215	2.10291390
8.2	2.10413415	2.10535292	2.10657021	2.10778601	2.10900034	2.11021320	2.11142459	2.11263451	2.11384297	2.11504997
8.3	2.11625551	2.11745961	2.11866225	2.11986346	2.12106322	2.12226154	2.12345843	2.12465388	2.12584791	2.12704052
8.4	2.12823171	2.12942147	2.13060983	2.13179677	2.13298231	2.13416644	2.13534917	2.13653051	2.13771045	2.13888900
8.5	2.14006616	2.14124194	2.14241634	2.14358936	2.14476101	2.14593128	2.14710019	2.14826773	2.14943391	2.15059874
8.6	2.15176220	2.15292432	2.15408508	2.15524451	2.15640258	2.15755932	2.15871472	2.15986879	2.16102153	2.16217294
8.7	2.16332303	2.16447179	2.16561924	2.16676537	2.16791019	2.16905370	2.17019590	2.17133681	2.17247641	2.17361471
8.8	2.17475172	2.17588744	2.17702187	2.17815501	2.17928688	2.18041746	2.18154676	2.18267480	2.18380156	2.18492705
8.9	2.18605128	2.18717424	2.18829595	2.18941639	2.19053559	2.19165353	2.19277023	2.19388568	2.19499988	2.19611285
9.0	2.19722458	2.19833507	2.19944433	2.20055237	2.20165917	2.20276476	2.20386912	2.20497226	2.20607419	2.20717491
9.1	2.20827441	2.20937271	2.21046980	2.21156569	2.21266039	2.21375388	2.21484618	2.21593729	2.21702720	2.21811594
9.2	2.21920348	2.22028985	2.22137504	2.22245905	2.22354189	2.22462355	2.22570405	2.22678338	2.22786155	2.22893855
9.3	2.23001440	2.23108909	2.23216263	2.23323501	2.23430625	2.23537634	2.23644529	2.23751310	2.23857976	2.23964529
9.4	2.24070969	2.24177295	2.24283509	2.24389610	2.24495598	2.24601474	2.24707238	2.24812891	2.24918432	2.25023861
9.5	2.25129180	2.25234388	2.25339485	2.25444472	2.25549349	2.25654115	2.25758773	2.25863321	2.25967759	2.26072089
9.6	2.26176310	2.26280422	2.26384426	2.26488323	2.26592111	2.26695792	2.26799365	2.26902831	2.27006190	2.27109443
9.7	2.27212589	2.27315628	2.27418562	2.27521390	2.27624112	2.27726729	2.27829240	2.27931647	2.28033948	2.28136146
9.8	2.28238239	2.28340227	2.28442112	2.28543893	2.28645571	2.28747146	2.28848617	2.28949985	2.29051251	2.29152415
9.9	2.29253476	2.29354435	2.29455292	2.29556048	2.29656702	2.29757255	2.29857707	2.29958058	2.30058309	2.30158459

INDEX

INDEX